# CONSERVATIVE PARTY POLITICS

Edited by
## Zig Layton-Henry
*Lecturer in Politics*
*University of Warwick*

Foreword by
## Sir Ian Gilmour, M.P.

*066138*

*First published 1980 by*
THE MACMILLAN PRESS LTD
*London and Basingstoke*
*Associated companies in Delhi*
*Dublin Hong Kong Johannesburg Lagos*
*Melbourne New York Singapore Tokyo*

*Printed in Great Britain by*
*Billing and Sons Ltd,*
*Guildford, Worcester and London*

British Library Cataloguing in Publication Data

Conservative Party politics
 1. Conservative and Unionist Party
 I. Layton-Henry, Zig
 329.9′41    JN1129.C7

ISBN 0-333-26601-3
ISBN 0-333-26602-1 (Paper)

For Barbara

# Contents

# Foreword

The British Conservative Party is a very peculiar institution, and British Conservatism is scarcely less distinctive.

In the sense of gaining votes from all sections of the community, the Tories were, even in October 1974, still the most representative of the parties.[1] Except in views, however, the Conservative party in Parliament, as David Butler and Michael Pinto-Duschinsky emphasise, is unrepresentative of Conservative voters in the country. That is, of course, to some extent true of all parliamentary parties. Labour MPs are now more likely to be polytechnic lecturers than anything else. Parliamentary parties abroad are in occupation and class also unrepresentative of their voters. Lawyers are very thick on the parliamentary ground in practically every democratic country, especially in the United States. The only so-called parliament that provides a mirror image of the electorate is the East German, which is not in other respects the model of a democratic assembly.

Nevertheless, the British Conservative party is even more unrepresentative socially than most other democratic parliamentary parties, though this is at least partly explained by the tying of the trade union movement to the Labour party. Furthermore, it has a larger mass organisation than most do, and it gives greater power to its leader. In addition, it has been more successful electorally, at least until recent times, than its nearest equivalent elsewhere. Finally, it has had no consistent body of doctrine and its policies have widely varied from time to time.

For reasons connected with all this, British Conservatism is very different from any other conservatism. Indeed the word Conservative has a different meaning in Europe from what it has here. Yet French, German and British Conservatism all had a

1. *Financial Times*, 25 October 1974 (Harris poll reproduced and commented upon by David Watt).

common origin in reaction to the French Revolution.

French Conservatism soon got mixed up with the ideal of a united Christendom under a united Church. French Conservatives believed that spiritual unity was the basis of political order, and that that unity must be complete. Hence, there was no room for moderation or for the sometimes messy compromises of democracy or liberty. Plainly unity in that sense is either there or it is not; there can be no partial unity. And equally plainly, democracy and liberty necessarily lead to a breaking up of that unity. Therefore, liberty and democracy are incompatible with the French Conservative ideal. In consequence, French Conservatism ended up, paradoxically, far closer to Rousseau than to Burke. And its version of harmony and unity made it Utopian, which to the eyes of British Conservatives is the very opposite of Conservatism.

German Conservatism got into even bigger trouble. It soon became associated with a very high view of the State. According to German Conservatives, the State was more real and more rational than its individual members. Only the organic state was fully rational, and it was more real than the individual in the same way that the whole is more real than its parts. And we all know where that idea ended up.[2]

British Conservatism also dates from the French Revolution, but it avoided the excesses of French and German Conservatism for a variety of reasons. Firstly, there was no revolution or foreign conquest. It is very difficult to be Conservative in the British sense after a revolution. Secondly, the British State was just about the oldest and best established in Europe. Thirdly, Britain had a settled if continually changing constitution and a living and unbroken political tradition.

British Conservatism thus never sought to restore something that had been lost or to return to a previous allegedly golden age, or to move into a new idyllic condition of things. In contrast, the French Conservatives wanted to restore something that had not existed under the *Ancien Régime* — a united Christendom — and the Germans wanted to establish something they had never possessed — a single powerful state, governing all the German peoples. Had they ever possessed such a State, they would not have taken such an exalted view of it.

2. For my remarks on French and German Conservatism I am indebted to Noël O'Sullivan's *Conservatism*.

As a result, neither the ideas of the French Revolution, nor the ideas of the reaction to the French Revolution, had as much impact here as they had elsewhere. There were breakwaters in Britain against the waves of new ideas which did not exist in other countries. Thus the younger Pitt, who was, after all, running the country at the time, said of Burke's writings on the French Revolution that he saw in them much to admire and nothing to agree with. Burke himself took a high view of the State, — 'the State is a partnership in all perfection' — but he did not hold the organic theory of the State. The State, he believed, was in some ways like an organism, but it was not one. And while he was highly religious, he did not believe that spiritual or ecclesiastical unity could or should be enforced.

Because of its origins, because Conservatism did not in England fall on virgin ground but in an established political tradition, and because Burke was a very much wiser man than any of his continental equivalents, English Conservatism has always been very different from any other version and the Conservative party different from other parties. Burke did not seek to erect a complete philosophical system. Indeed he eloquently denounced the French Revolutionaries as ideologues, and he was unalterably opposed to metaphysical speculation in politics. Like Halifax and Hume before him, he stressed the overriding importance of 'circumstances'. No rational man, he pointed out, governed himself 'by abstractions and universals'.

Hence, political ideas should be judged not by their speculative attractiveness, but by their 'practical consequences'. Political problems, Burke said, do not 'primarily concern truth or falsehood. They relate to good or evil. What in the result is likely to produce evil is politically false, that which is productive of good, politically true'. Thus for Burke, 'expediency' is not in opposition to 'right'. What is expedient is right. 'Expedience is that which is good for the community and good for every individual in it. . . . ' The test is a practical one. Does it work?

'Prudence', Burke thought, was 'not only the first in rank of the virtues, political and moral, but she is the director, the regulator, the standard of them all'. He combined this 'prudence' with a strong defence of property and liberty. But it was 'liberty connected with order'. Not even liberty, then, can be pursued as an end in itself.

Burke reflected the long-standing practice of British politics, and by his moderate theory or theories he helped to perpetuate them. The fact that British Conservatism has never been a system or an ideology has had profound consequences. In Britain, on the Right but not on the Left, there has been little tension between theory and practice. And since British Conservatism is not a system, balance and moderation have been an important element in it. If you have a system, you do not need balance and moderation. Your system is, by definition, right and you do not want to modify it, since that would make it imperfect.

But British Conservatism is admittedly imperfect; it accepts diversity and imperfection. If you do not have a system, you have to be empirical and you have to take circumstances into account. You have no 'crib', to use Oakeshott's word, to help you steer through every conceivable difficulty. You have, therefore, to judge issues on their merits and not by doctrine. This means, too, or it should mean, that means are distinguished from ends and are not erected into ends. Thus, while patriotism and a belief in the national identity have always been at the heart of Conservatism, they did not stop the Conservative party, in response to a change of circumstances, from being strongly in favour of joining Europe.

Two other important features of the Conservative party stem from Disraeli. They are that the party must be a national party and that 'the condition of the people' must be its abiding concern. These themes were present before Disraeli — Peel in rather a different fashion understood and used them — but they are with reason particularly associated with Disraeli. And since his day, with only occasional backsliding, the Tory party has always been a national party, appealing to all classes, and nowadays to be so is a condition of survival.

Yet, as the editor points out in his introduction, in March 1979 the Conservatives had lost four out of five successive elections. Admittedly Labour's first two victories gave the party less than six years of power, and its second two only a little more than five. The virtual monopoly of power by the Tories in the inter-war years is not something they could expect often to repeat, and by 1979 the major parties had since the end of the wartime coalition been in office for roughly equal periods. Even so, the Conservatives' recent electoral record has been dispiriting.

Certainly the Tories are as avid for office as any other party[3]. But it is less their electoral failure than the observed results of Labour rule that has caused Tory disquiet. After all there was a not

3. This foreword was written before the recent general election.

dissimilar Conservative unease in the early years of this century—under a Conservative Government. Had the consequences of Labour dominance for eleven out of the last fourteen years been a thriving economy and social peace, the Conservative attitude would have been at worst tolerance and at best admiration. But Anthony Crosland was frank enough to admit the failure of the first Wilson Government of 1964–70, and a similarly harsh verdict on 1974–9 seems inescapable.

So the Conservative malaise has far deeper causes than mere electoral disappointment. These are in essence: Britain's economic decline in comparison with our friends and neighbours; and the threat to the constitution presented by Labour's flouting of the constitutional and political conventions during the seventies. (Conservative anxiety on these matters does not presuppose that the Tory party is itself entirely blameless.) Both the economic sickness and the constitutional threat posed a challenge to traditional Conservatism.

Britain's economic decay suggested that we could not long go on as we were, and Labour's breaking of the post-war consensus after 1970 revealed that the British constitution based as it is largely on convention and containing few legal curbs on the activities of a temporary majority of the House of Commons, even one elected by only a small minority of the electorate, was something of a hangover from more scrupulous days and less dogmatic politics. Yet the Tory emphasis on the virtue of gradual change and on the national advantage to be gained from each party generally accepting the work in government of its opponents assumes that the country will be reasonably well governed whichever party is in power and that there will be no massive deterioration in the economic or social fabric. If on the contrary the other party has not observed the constitutional conventions and unmistakeable damage has been done to the economy, mere passive acceptance of such a legacy is clearly not a particularly seductive option for an incoming Conservative government. For the Tory party to be the guardian of national continuity is one thing; for it to be the guardian of national failure is quite another.

Although Disraeli put the maintenance of the country's institutions on the same level of importance as the economic well-being of the people, the party's response to the economic problem has been very different from its response to the constitutional one. During the last few years, there has been intense discussion of the economy within the party and a reasonable measure of agreement on a change of course though not a violent one. But there has been relatively little discussion of the constitution and no agreement. Our institutions are in palpable disrepair, and Britain is less well protected than any other democratic country against the arbitrary actions of a temporary parliamentary majority. Yet, although Nevil Johnson is no doubt right in saying that piecemeal reform of the constitution is now difficult, it is surely remarkable that there is within the party no consensus even on one measure of piecemeal reform. There is not even a consensus on the reform that seems the most obvious and the easiest: to make the House of Lords an elected instead of an hereditary and an appointed Chamber.

Thus the Tory party has dealt with the economic problem in a fairly traditional manner, and it has shirked dealing with the constitutional problem also in a fairly traditional manner. Or to put it in another way, while the economic policies of the next Conservative government have been largely decided, constitutional reforms to prevent the next Labour government, with little popular support, wrecking those policies and much else besides have been neglected. This suggests either a touching Tory confidence in uninterrupted Conservative rule or an equally touching faith in the Labour party's capacity for repentance and redemption.

Like all political parties, the Conservative party has many defects, as these essays make clear. Yet by being a truly national party, which means amongst other things being concerned to represent the British people's hopes and aspirations and to preserve the unity and continuity of the country, rather than being concerned to execute a set of doctrinaire schemes and theories, the Conservative party has been the most successful right of centre party in the world. It has achieved that success because it has almost never been reactionary.

Zig Layton-Henry is much to be congratulated both on the distinguished contributors he has collected and on the quality of their contributions. These essays will not make the Conservative party seem any less peculiar; they will certainly make it more understandable.

*Ian Gilmour*

# Acknowledgements

This volume is based on a conference which was sponsored by the Social Science Research Council and was held at Nuffield College, Oxford, in July 1978. The development of the book has been assisted by generous help and encouragement from colleagues and friends, especially David Butler, Jack Lively, Lewis Minkin, and Willie Paterson. I also wish to thank Daniel Lawrence and Bob Miles for their helpful comments on Chapter 3, and Wyn Grant and Jim Bulpitt for sharing their ideas and enthusiasm. I am indebted to Ann Clark and Iris Host for their efficient secretarial assistance.

Z. L.-H.

# Notes on the Contributors

NIGEL ASHFORD is a graduate student at the University of Warwick, carrying out research on the Conservative party and European unity. He was Secretary-General of European Democrat Students for two years.

VERNON BOGDANOR is Fellow and Tutor in Politics at Brasenose College, Oxford. He is author of *Devolution*, editor and contributor to *The Age of Affluence 1951–64*, and editor of Disraeli's *Lothair*.

MARTIN BURCH studied at the Universities of Hull and Glasgow and at the latter completed his doctorate on Conservative party politics in the 1960s. Since 1974 he has been a Lecturer in the Department of Government at the University of Manchester, where he specialises in policy analysis.

DAVID BUTLER is Fellow of Nuffield College, Oxford. He is author of numerous books on electoral politics, including the Nuffield studies of British General Elections. He is co-author of *Political Change in Britain* and his more recent publications include *The Canberra Model* and *Coalitions in British Politics*.

IVOR CREWE is Director of the SSRC Survey Archive and Co-Director of the British Election Study, both at the University of Essex. He is currently editor of the *British Journal of Political Science*. His publications include numerous articles on electoral behaviour and public opinion in Britain and the co-editorship of *Party Identification and Beyond*.

ANDREW GAMBLE is lecturer in modern British political economy at the University of Sheffield. He is author of *The Conservative Nation* and co-author of *Capitalism in Crisis*.

NEVIL JOHNSON has been Nuffield Reader in the Comparative Study of Institutions at Oxford since 1969 and is a Fellow of Nuffield College. He is the author of *Parliament and Administration: The Estimates Committee 1945–65* (1966), *Government in the Federal Republic of Germany* (1974) and *In Search of the Constitution* (1977). He has been honorary editor of the journal *Public Administration* since 1967.

ZIG LAYTON-HENRY is Lecturer in Politics at the University of Warwick, and author of numerous articles on political youth movements, the Conservative party, and the politics of race in Britain.

CHRIS PATTEN was the Director of the Conservative Research Department and is now M.P. for Bath.

MICHAEL PINTO-DUSCHINSKY is Lecturer in Government at Brunel University and Secretary to the International Political Science Association's Study Group on Political Finance and Corruption. He is author of *The Political Thought of Lord Salisbury 1854–68*, co-author of *The British General Election of 1970*, and author of a forthcoming book on *British Political Finance*.

ANDREW ROWE was a Lecturer at Edinburgh University before becoming Director of the Department of Community Affairs at Conservative Central Office. His responsibilities include the Conservative Trade Unionist Organisation. He is author of *Democracy Renewed*.

BO SÄRLVIK is Professor of Government at the University of Essex and author of Opinionsbildningen vid folkomröstningen (1957, 1959), and also of numerous articles on electoral behaviour.

PATRICK SEYD is Lecturer in Modern British Politics at the University of Sheffield. His main research interest is the British party system and he has published numerous articles on aspects of party politics.

# Introduction

The decisive victory in the general election of 3 May 1979 has ended a period of considerable frustration and uncertainty for members of the Conservative party. The euphoria of victory and the practical problems of government have caused a reassertion of party unity behind Mrs Thatcher's leadership and her new administration. It has also caused a revival of confidence in the success of the party and in hopes for the future. This new mood of optimism is in marked contrast to the doubts and uncertainties which assailed many Conservatives only a few months ago, and which may do so again if the new administration is unable to arrest Britain's economic decline and realise the expectations of economic expansion and growth that Conservative leaders have promised the electorate.

The post-war period has witnessed considerable fluctuations in the fortunes of the major political parties. For those who are able to remember the Conservative ascendancy before the Second World War and witnessed the Conservative recovery from post-war defeat, the Labour government of 1945–51 must have appeared as an interlude of opposition for the 'natural' party of government. It was an interlude from which the Conservative party emerged refreshed and revitalised, having reformed its policies, overhauled its organisation and refurbished its image. In contrast the more recent period from October 1964 to May 1979 has been one of Labour party ascendancy during which the Conservative government of 1970–4 appears as a short, traumatic interlude. During this period the Labour party won four out of five general elections in the sense that it emerged as the largest party and formed the government. Labour held office for eleven of these fifteen years.

The Conservative party has been deeply influenced by this long period in opposition. Many leading Conservatives have become increasingly dissatisfied with economic and social trends in society and were frustrated by their inability to influence events. They became less and less satisfied with policies that merely sought to conserve and increasingly wished to roll back and dismantle parts of the social democratic, welfare state which had been created and extended by both Conservative and Labour governments since the war. The Heath government of 1970–4 was influenced by a similar mood and came to office committed to a wide range of new initiatives and reforms. Some of these reforms, like the taxation proposals, were associated with the commitment to join the EEC, while others reflected a 'non-conservative' determination to reform inefficient and outdated institutions and practices such as the commitments to reform industrial relations and local government. The failures of the Heath government to achieve the economic investment and expansion it hoped for and its failure to reform industrial relations led to a serious debate in the party between those who wished to restore the foundations of a free market economy and those who accepted the necessity for widespread government intervention. Gamble argues that the supporters of a social market economy are only a minority among the Conservative leadership and that the first priority for the new government will be to promote economic growth. Free market policies are likely to be applied selectively to encourage changes in attitudes and behaviour favourable to a more efficient economy but there will be enormous pressures on the government to adopt a cautious approach. These constraints will be imposed partly by the difficulties of managing the economy in a period of world economic uncertainty and recession and partly by the pressures from a large public sector and a powerful trade union movement. Also many industrialists, especially those managing large companies, favour certain forms of government intervention and help for industry, and would not support a sharp move towards a free market economy.

This debate over economic policy is reflected in debates in other areas of policy in the Conservative party. In opposition a party is inevitably deeply involved in re-examining its policies as part of its strategy to regain office. Patten shows how in opposition recent party leaders have involved wide sections of the party in policy discussions and challenges the view that the Conservative party leader has a high degree of autonomy in determining party policy. He argues that the shadow cabinet is the collective policy-making body in opposition and that to some extent the party manifesto and other policy statements can be regarded as treaties between different groups in the party. The debates over economic policy in the party and the compromise documents that have emerged like

*The Right Approach* and *The Right Approach to the Economy* are good illustrations of this process. This is not to say that the leader cannot take major policy initiatives but to be successful they do need substantial support in the party. Ashford argues, for example, that Macmillan's initiative to apply for membership of the EEC was not as radical as it appeared because many groups in the party and interests associated with Conservatism were already in favour of membership of the EEC. It was, therefore, not difficult to mobilise a substantial majority in the party behind his initiative. On de-volution in Scotland, the party has been much less certain, and Heath's initiative in supporting a devolved Scottish assembly at Perth in 1968 did not rouse strong feelings for or against in the party. Gradually opinion among English back-bench Tories has hardened against devolution during a period when Scottish Conservatism has been in rapid decline. Scottish Conservatives are seriously divided on the issue and the prospects for a firmly-based Conservative revival in Scotland look bleak, in spite of the recent gains from the Scottish Nationalists. Bogdanor feels that the weakness of the Conservative party in Scotland may lessen the ability of a Conservative government to manage Scottish affairs. The decline of Scottish Conservatism and the break with the Ulster Unionists has also weakened Conservative claims to be the party of the United Kingdom as it has become more dependent on its suburban and rural strength in southern and central England.

The analysis of Conservative policy on immigration illustrates how the failure of party leaders to take early action can reduce their autonomy in determining party policy. If members of the cabinet in the early 1950s had foreseen the reaction to coloured immigration they might have initiated policies that would have aided the integration of members of the new ethnic minorities. Instead immigration was ignored until the campaign for immigration control was well advanced. Party leaders were then panicked into hurried measures by a combination of pressures within and without the party demanding control and also by a large increase in immigration which itself was partly a response to the campaign for control. Since 1962 immigration policy has been determined largely by calculations of electoral advantage, and paradoxically the growing electoral importance of Asian and West Indian voters may push a reluctant Conservative party towards more positive policies in the areas of race relations and racial discrimination.

Nevil Johnson discusses the dilemma facing Conservatives who are no longer confident that 'whichever party is in office, the Conservatives are always in power'. Should Conservatives support constitutional reform in order to preserve the constitution? The growing support in the Conservative party for a Bill of Rights and for electoral reform reflects a fear that a future Labour government, elected on a minority vote but with a majority in the Commons, might introduce radical constitutional reforms which the opposition would be powerless to resist, because of the sovereignty of the Commons. The crisis in Ulster, the question of devolution for Scotland and Wales, the demands for reform of the House of Lords and entry into the EEC have made constitutional issues of central importance once again even though these issues tend to be pushed aside by the more immediate importance of economic problems.

Crewe suggests that when a major party goes into opposition a battle frequently commences between those fundamentalists who wish to return to the first principles of the party, and those with experience of office who wish to maintain a pragmatic approach. Burch makes a similar distinction when he compares the critical approach to opposition with the alternative government approach. As he regards Heath as the exemplar of the credible alternative government approach, perhaps it is not surprising that Mrs Thatcher should have emphasised party principles and followed the path of leading a critical opposition rather more than her predecessor. This style of leadership in opposition is certainly more suited to a politician of conviction. As leader of the Conservative party before 1970 Mr Heath cultivated an alternative government approach to opposition and ran the Conservative party as an alternative prime minister insisting, for example, on collective responsibility for members of the shadow cabinet. This style of leadership continued after 1970 and Heath's premiership has been described as a paradigm of 'prime ministerial government'. Mr Heath received much of the credit for the unexpected Conservative victory in 1970 but his style of leadership antagonised many back-bench MPs who became increasingly ready to dissent in the division lobbies and who were only too ready to blame him for the electoral defeats of 1974. The bitterness of the ensuing leadership struggle is only gradually subsiding and is not yet fully healed as Mr Heath's exclusion from the cabinet shows. Mrs Thatcher has been more careful to keep in close touch with back-bench opinion and to involve backbenchers in policy-making. This is partly a natural consequence of opposition when defeat is often attributed to the failure of party leaders to remain in contact with grass roots opinion in the party but it is also due to the manner of Mrs Thatcher's election to the leadership which was the result of a back-bench revolt. It is also on the back benches that many of her strongest supporters are to be found. As Prime Minister, Mrs Thatcher is likely to be much more attentive to back-bench opinion than her predecessor. Seyd is also concerned with the growing incidence of conflict and factionalism in the party and argues that this is largely due to the lengthy period of opposition the Tories have experienced since 1964. He argues that the achievement of office is likely to reduce the incidence of factionalism as party members concentrate on the 'realities of government'. However, the level of Conservative dissent in parliament was substantial during the Heath government and its level is likely to depend as much on the success of Mrs Thatcher's policies as on her ability to manage back-bench opinion.

The problems of electoral strategy facing the Conservative party are considered by a number of contributors. Crewe analyses the most rational electoral strategy for the Conservatives in relation to socioeconomic and popular authoritarian issues. He suggests that a fundamentalist electoral strategy appears more promising on matters of law and order and traditional morality than it does on issues of race where, while the electorate supports strong immigration controls, it is divided and moderate. Crewe argues that the Conservative party may be tempted to exploit popular authoritarian issues in a situation where it may not be able to offer the electorate substantial hopes of economic improvement or more competent leadership. Butler and Pinto-Duschinsky examine the composition of the Conservative elite in parliament and in the constituency parties and suggest reasons why the restricted social composition of the party elites may make it less attractive electorally, and may weaken its ability to develop an understanding with the trade union movement. The ability of the new Conservative administration to work with the trade unions and gain their acceptance of, or acquiescence to, Conservative policies, especially those concerned to reform trade union law, will be a major test facing the government. The electoral importance of the trade unions appeared to have changed considerably after the election of February 1974. Before that election, the links between the Labour party and the trade unions were widely regarded as an electoral disadvantage for the Labour party. After the election this seemed less certain and it appeared that the Conservative party's difficulties in working with the trade unions might be a source of electoral weakness. The strikes of last winter and the failure of Mr Healey's 5 per cent incomes policy showed that neither party had a monopoly of trade union goodwill. Nevertheless it was surprising that Mrs Thatcher did not make more public efforts to conciliate trade union leaders before the general election. The chapter by Rowe shows that party leaders and officials are well aware of the need to come to terms with the growth in trade union membership and influence, and to educate party members about trade union values, assumptions and practices. The revival of the Conservative trade union organisation has been dramatic and they held a well-publicised rally during the general election campaign. However, Rowe's ideas about the role of Conservative trade unionists and their long term objectives may well cause the established Labour leaders of the trade unions to feel that organised Conservative trade unionists would be a Trojan Horse in their midst.

This book is largely, though not exclusively, concerned with the Conservative party as a party in opposition, which has been their role for most of the last fifteen years. The impact of opposition can be seen in the internal divisions over policy, the conflict over the leadership and the growth in factional activity. The achievement of office with a substantial majority has, however, endorsed Mrs Thatcher's leadership with the imprimatur of success and has reduced many of the reasons for dissent and dissatisfaction. It has also provided her with the opportunity to show whether the politics of conviction can be as successful as the politics of compromise. Mrs Thatcher and her colleagues will be judged on their ability to return to an economy of free enterprise and profitability, to restrict the excesses of trade union power, to make a success of Britain's membership of the EEC and to manage the other major issues that confront them such as Rhodesia and Ulster. The success with which the new government tackles these problems will determine whether the party returns to opposition after another interlude in office or whether the victory of 3 May is the beginning of another period of Conservative ascendancy in British politics.

# PART ONE

# POLICY MAKING

# 1 Policy Making in Opposition[1]

## Chris Patten

## I INTRODUCTION

The study of the way in which the Conservative party makes policy, and of the pressures which help to determine what that policy should be, is clearly of the greatest importance. No-one, for example, could properly consider the history of the Conservative government from 1970–4 without examining how and why it came to office with the particular commitments on industrial relations, tax, housing finance and so on, which helped both to shape its life and precipitate its death.

Yet the literature on this subject is not as extensive as one might expect. J. D. Hoffman[2] and R. M. Punnett[3] admittedly look at policy making in some detail, and there is a scattering of references in general works on politics (like the Nuffield Election Studies[4]) and a good essay by Anthony King in *New Society*.[5] But otherwise the student of politics has to rely on references of a more or less anecdotal nature in politicians' biographies (of which the most useful is Lord Butler's[6]) and journalists' gleanings, based on the indiscretions of politicians and the more discreet guidance of officials.[7]

The main reason why there is not more published work on policy-making may lie in the natural reluctance of officials and even, perhaps more surprisingly, of front-bench politicians to disclose exactly what happens. The caution of these first-hand sources is understandable. Some of the pressures which produce a particular policy response may not look very attractive to the electorate and the occasional flimsiness of the research behind a new policy initiative could be equally embarrassing. Politicians are not unique in wishing to appear more rational, high-minded and well-organised than circumstances or personalities often allow any of us to be. In addition, those from outside the political arena who play a part in policy-making may wish to draw a veil over their political activities, and those most closely involved as officials have usually taken a lead from the party's most distinguished post-war civil servant, Lord Fraser of Kilmorack,[8] who once observed that the correct place for backroom boys is in the back room. But in fact the process of policy making is on the whole—as I shall attempt to show—much more thorough, respectable and responsible, and much less conspiratorial, partisan and superficial, than this political reticence might make some observers suppose.

An examination of the business of making policy inevitably concentrates on periods when the Conservative party is in opposition. In government the parliamentary party, the party organisation, and the party conference naturally make some contribution to policy, and the machinery for sounding opinion, mobilising arguments and producing documents still operates. But most policy work during these periods is done by ministers and officials; it emerges very largely from reactions to events, from tackling the problems of governing the country.

In or out of office, as Hoffman has argued, 'the party constitution accords what appear to be very close to dictatorial powers to the leader of the party in the matter of policy-making'.[9] In practice, the leader carries out this work in consultation with his or her chosen close colleagues in the cabinet or the shadow cabinet, and with members of the parliamentary party. The leader must also take account of the views of the party outside parliament, as expressed, for example, at the party conference, though this body does not have the same quasi-democratic binding role as the Labour party conference in determining policy. The leader is assisted by two bodies specifically established for the purpose.

The first is the Advisory Committee on Policy. This committee was one of the fruits of the Maxwell-Fyfe Committee on the Party Organisation, whose report was passed by the Central Council on 15 July 1949. It replaced the Advisory Committee on Policy and Political Education—set up in 1945 as part of the party's post-war reconstruction—but the change was greater than the modification of the committee's name would suggest since henceforth the Advisory Committee on Policy was to be directly responsible to the leader, who was to appoint the chairman and vice-chairman, and not to the National Union.

The current composition of the Advisory Committee on Policy under its chairman, Sir Keith Joseph, is:

| | |
|---|---|
| Parliamentary Party: | two from the House of Lords and five (appointed by the 1922 Committee) from the House of Commons; |
| National Union: | eight, of whom four are ex-officio, including, invariably, the chairman of the Young Conservatives, and four elected; |
| Five ex-officio members: | the chairman and deputy chairmen of the party, the director of the Research Department, and the director of the Conservative Political Centre; |
| Up to six co-opted members | who include, by tradition, the chairman of the Federation of Conservative Students |
| The secretary of the Advisory Committee on Policy, | who has always been a member of the Conservative Research Department |

The Advisory Committee on Policy meets about once a month when parliament is sitting and discusses some aspects of policy often prepared by one of the party's policy groups. It also considers the reports of Conservative Political Centre discussion groups and, when in office, trends in departmental policies. The discussion is usually introduced by a shadow minister (or minister). In addition, the committee discusses, and may suggest amendments to, the party's manifestos and other policy documents. It acts as a sounding-board on policy for the party leadership. Anthony King has noted that 'Unlike Labour's NEC, the Advisory Committee on Policy has no formal policy-making status; but it does have a traditional claim to be consulted, to advise, and to warn'.[10]

The second body, which has a central role in policy work, is the Conservative Research Department.[11] This was set up, independent of the Central Office, in 1929 or 1930 by Neville Chamberlain or Viscount Davidson (the adjudication on year of birth and paternity must await John Ramsden's further researches). The department is physically separate from the party headquarters with offices in Old Queen Street near Parliament Square. It is usually chaired by a senior politician, at present Mr Angus Maude, who is also deputy chairman of the party. It has four principal roles. It provides a secretariat for the shadow cabinet with individual members acting as research assistants to front-bench spokesmen. Its director and senior officials also attend and service the meetings of the shadow cabinet, preparing papers and arranging the agenda. (In government, the relationship with ministers is obviously looser, but members still provide help with party political tasks.) The second role is to provide the official 'civil service' support for policy work—for example, servicing the Advisory Committee on Policy, and individual policy groups. The department's desk officers act, in Richard Rose's words, as 'not so much innovators as brokers between MPs concerned with day-to-day parliamentary problems and experts outside Westminster, whether in the universities, business and industry, professions, or trade unions'.[12] Thirdly, the Research Department briefs the parliamentary party as a whole, with officials acting as secretaries of the back-bench subject committees. Fourthly, it produces a series of information publications for the whole party and a wider audience, most notably its regular fortnightly journal *Politics Today* and the *Campaign Guides*, a series of unique reference books prepared before general election campaigns.

The Research Department usually employs up to 35 graduates in opposition (the number falls in government when the burdens are lighter). There is a supporting staff of about 30. Many members go on to a career in the House of Commons. There are today 21 ex-Research Department officers there.


## II POLICY MAKING 1945–51

Under Lord Butler's chairmanship after the war, the department was the boiler-room in the work of restating policy for the 1950 and 1951 elections. There was initially some resistance to doing this at all. The leader of the party, Winston Churchill, never disguised his doubts about the wisdom of the party trying to make policy while in opposition. 'When an opposition spells out its policy in detail . . . having failed to win the sweets of Office, it fails equally to enjoy the benefits of being out of Office.'[13] However, as Lord Butler, who quotes this statement, goes on, 'The 1946 Party Conference at Blackpool had overwhelmingly demanded some re-formulation of our policy and Churchill moved to meet this demand soon after'.[14] Lord Woolton, the party chairman from 1946 to 1955, gave the main reason for this demand in his *Memoirs*: 'It is always dangerous in politics to be committed to detail in any programme. But I concluded it was at least as dangerous to be so vague that the nation would think that the Conservatism that we were expounding would be no different from the Conservatism of the thirties. We therefore decided to take the risk of defining in terms the policies we would encourage the nation to undertake.'[15]

The main policy statements of that period were *The Industrial Charter* (1947), *The Agricultural Charter* (1948), *The Conservative Policy for Wales and Monmouthshire, Imperial Policy, Scottish Control of Scottish Affairs*, and a synoptic policy document, *The Right Road for Britain* (all published in 1949). The party's manifestos in 1950 and 1951 drew heavily on these documents.

While the leader was closely consulted about these statements and left his unmistakeable imprint on some of them, they were usually the product of small committees of his senior colleagues aided by a few backbenchers and the staff of the Research Department. Each of the charters was presented to, and approved by, the annual party conference.

The differences with the policy exercise of 1964–70 are quite extensive. First, the total scope of the exercise was much more limited. There was a handful of wide-ranging committees or groups instead of some 30 or more dealing with fairly specific detailed questions.

Secondly, even on the subjects covered, the policy recommendations in the earlier period were much less detailed, or as Lord Butler puts it, 'more impressionistic'.[16] Contrary to some reports, the policy work of 1964–70 was never developed to the point where draft legislation was prepared. Nevertheless, in many fields (notably industrial relations, housing finance, tax reform and the structure of central government) very detailed reports were produced which were made available to ministers when the party took office. These could serve as blueprints for legislation or administrative arrangements. After 1951, civil servants would have had little more than a general impression of the attitude that the new government would adopt to the problems confronting it.

Thirdly, although back-bench MPs were associated with the work in the earlier period, 'for the most part', as Punnett points out, 'the members of the Shadow Cabinet were the dominant figures of the committees'.[17] Equally important, the very small number of committees enabled each one to include a fairly wide range of front-benchers. It could act as a genuine sub-committee of the shadow cabinet with additions from the back benches; in 1964–70, most committees were made up of a single shadow minister with back-bench and non-parliamentary members.

Fourthly, there does not seem to have been a very organised or systematic arrangement for tapping expert opinion. The Research Department officers who serviced the committees would certainly draw on their contacts in the academic, business and professional worlds for expert advice when required, and distinguished outsiders would have been consulted by members of the committee. But from 1964–70 non-parliamentary members contributed more directly to the work.

It seems probable that after the war there was, in fact, a fairly wide technical consensus, at least among 'informed opinion'. The main lines, or at least general direction, of policy over a large area— education, full employment, social services, the health service, etc.—had been developed in the closing years of the war in a largely bipartisan spirit by a variety of Royal Commissions, inter-departmental committees and the like. Butler himself seems to have regarded the party's Advisory Committee on Policy as an extension into conditions of opposition of the previous Conservative 'caretaker' government's Post-War Problems Committee, which itself had its origins under the wartime coalition. In effect, the job of party policy formation was to draw on this body of 'sound' economic and administrative principles, weaving together a programme that would conform to Conservative philosophy and would be accepted—or could be rendered acceptable—to the party.

A good deal of emphasis throughout this period seems to have been placed on 'political education',[18] meaning the education of the party itself into the ideas of a post-Beveridge, post-Keynes epoch. The work was successful and proved highly effective politically because the party realised, in a way the Labour party failed to do, the potential of these new ideas. Labour certainly accepted the Keynesian analysis, but the Conservatives saw that the shift to macro-economics opened the way for a return to the liberal economic values that had been in eclipse since the early years of the century, and rendered unnecessary the detailed micro-economic controls that the Labour government were reluctant to abandon and which had been by and large the orthodoxy for some years. By offering an alternative cure to the scourge of unemployment, Conservatives were able responsibly to claim that in government they could 'Set the People Free'.

## III POLICY MAKING 1964–70

In 1964–70 there was not the same need for a fundamental shift in the attitudes of the party. But after thirteen years of office, it had grown stale. It had exhausted the intellectual capital with which it arrived in government in 1951, and become captured by the negative attitude of the Whitehall machine, which is usually more conscious of the difficulties of any departure from the existing way of doing things than of the benefits of new ideas. Unlike the situation in 1945, there were no powerful voices raised to oppose the idea of detailed policy work. On the contrary, fairly soon after the 1964 defeat, Sir Alec Douglas-Home asked Mr Heath, as chairman of the Advisory Committee on Policy, to set in motion a review of policy in all the main fields.

The instrument chosen for this review was a series of policy study groups that at one stage numbered more than 30. The chairman (normally the appropriate shadow minister) and each member of a policy group was personally appointed from the start by the chairman of the Advisory Committee on Policy 'with the agreement of the leader of the party' before he himself became leader. The typical policy group consisted of a chairman, half a dozen backbench MPs, and an equivalent number of experts from outside the parliamentary party, including representatives from the National Union. The back-bench parliamentary MPs were chosen from those who had been most actively interested in the subject and in such a way as to cover, as far as possible, the spectrum of views inside the parliamentary party. Each policy group was serviced by the appropriate Research Department officer, who also remained responsible for parliamentary briefing on the subject and for looking after the relevant back-bench parliamentary committee. So there was very close correspondence between the short-term parliamentary work and the longer-term policy work. Thus the pledge to abolish SET came first, and what this meant in terms of a complete restructuring of indirect taxation developed from that decision.

The main policy documents during this period were the synoptic *Putting Britain Ahead* (1965) on which the 1966 manifesto was based, *Fair Deal at Work* (1968) which set out the party's proposals on industrial relations reform, and *Make Life Better* (1968) which was presented to the party conference as a general statement of policy. As with any large-scale voluntary effort, the results of all this policy work were uneven. Some groups had relatively little to show for their efforts. Others produced reforms like the restructuring of the taxation system, which was by any standards a considerable achievement. The beginning of the concept of the Tax Credit Scheme can also be traced to work at this time on what was then called Negative Income Tax. Other projects—like the reforms of industrial relations and housing finance—seemed equally impressive at the time. The subsequent political difficulties to which they led may be blamed on ill-judged implementation, on the strength of the forces which they were trying to reform, on the irresponsibility of Labour in opposition, or on sheer bad luck, but it cannot be said that they were caused by inadequate preparation.

Some observers find it impossible to be equally charitable about other areas of policy. Whatever else can be said in its favour, the re-organisation of local government does not appear to have been successfully thought through and argued out within the party before 1970. Other more serious criticisms have been made about concentration on institutional reform at the expense of hammering out a coherent and detailed approach to economic policy. An unnamed critic, quoted by Butler and Pinto-Duschinsky, argued in 1970, for instance, 'I have been saying for years that we have been making too much policy. We have come out with a glorious set of platitudes and have avoided having a detailed set of economic policies.'[19] In later years, others were to echo this view. But the most serious criticism that is made about the policy work of 1964–70 is of the eclecticism which was probably fostered to some extent by the emphasis placed on problem-solving and by the structure of distinct, separate policy groups. The principle of collective shadow cabinet responsibility was maintained and policies were not accepted until they had been discussed and agreed by the whole shadow cabinet. This, however,—according to the critics—may have been more a matter of arguing a case for specific policy recommendations than agreeing a general approach to policy.

Even the very full and lengthy discussions that took place over a whole weekend at the Selsdon Park Hotel in 1970 did not, as popular mythology would have us believe, result in the formulation of some general concept which could be termed 'Selsdon Man'. This conference remained a series of discussions—often in very considerable detail—on a collection of specific policies listed for inclusion in the draft manifesto. The 'general concept' which achieved notoriety was the result of Sir Harold Wilson's fertile political mind.

This acceptance of the principle of collective shadow cabinet responsibility, which can be argued to be something of a constitutional innovation, did not prevent the persistence of some underlying divisions of opinion, at least of a technical nature. Of these, the most important—recognised to a limited extent at the time, but more obvious in the light of subsequent events—was the difference of emphasis about the relative importance of monetary and competition policy on the one hand and some, not necessarily statutory, form of incomes policy on the other.

## IV POLICY MAKING 1974–9

Policy work in the immediate aftermath of the defeat in February 1974 was largely governed by the circumstances of that election and the imminence of another campaign. The main problem was not to show that the Conservative party had built up a new stock of ideas for governing the country, but in the wake of the miners' strike and the 'Who Governs?' campaign that it was capable of running the country at all. In addition, it was believed that the electorate had been offered too harsh a choice by Conservatives in February. Though the economic consequences of the four-fold increase in the price of oil limited the number of attractive policies which could be included responsibly in the manifesto for protecting or raising the standard of living of particular groups, it was felt that it should contain more than the prospect of 'blood, sweat and tears'.

One other factor helped to determine the outcome of the policy work. Even before the February election, there had been some criticism within the party about the economic policies pursued by the Conservative government. It was argued that it had paid too little attention to monetary policy, had become too dirigiste, and in particular had got entangled in the statutory control of prices and incomes at a considerable economic and political cost. This criticism became more open and widespread after the election defeat. It initiated a debate about the whole balance of the party's economic policy between those who wanted a more market-orientated approach and those who thought that the previous government's intervention in the economy was inevitable and justified. The argument was pursued with great vigour and differences were often exaggerated by the enthusiasm for controversy of the protagonists. The manifesto in October obviously had to be broadly acceptable to both sides, and to that extent may be thought to represent—like later documents—a treaty between those with different points of view.

Between February and the October election, there was no time for the sort of broad, elaborate and detailed policy-making that had taken place in earlier periods. But it is not true, as the *Economist* has argued,[20] that there were no formal policy groups. A small number (like those on housing and local government finance) was in fact set up on much the same model as 1964–70 and serviced by the Research Department. The manifesto, published in September, was based on the work of those groups and on some of the policy speeches made by shadow ministers, particularly the then shadow chancellor, Mr Robert Carr.

The next stage of policy work followed the October defeat and the election of Mrs Thatcher as the new party leader in 1975. She appointed Sir Keith Joseph as chairman of the Advisory Committee on Policy with overall responsibility for policy work. Sir Ian Gilmour left his post as chairman of the Research Department and was replaced by Mr Angus Maude. Mrs Thatcher's election and Sir Keith Joseph's appointment were seen as shifts towards the market wing of the party.

Many of the principal features of the organisation of policy work in this period were similar to those of 1964–70. Most policy groups were chaired by a shadow minister, or by a backbencher nominated by him. Membership of groups was drawn from the parliamentary party and from a number of outside experts. The shadow cabinet was the focus of the policy work and decided collectively which recommendations of policy groups could be accepted as party policy. The chairman of the Advisory Committee on Policy and the chairman of the Research Department determined the direction of the work and its coordination and the whole exercise was serviced by the Research Department. The Advisory Committee on Policy acted as a sounding board; an early draft of the party's 1976 review of policy, *The Right Approach*, was, for example, considered in detail by this committee at about the same time as it was discussed by the shadow cabinet.

There were, however, some differences. First, since 1975 the party was more concerned with its philosophy and its general approach than it was in the 1960s. This owes something to the change in the style of leadership. It is also partly the result of scepticism about the 'problem-solving' attitude to policy work, a deep awareness of the constraints within which any British government today has to operate, a caution about promising too much or attempting too many changes in government too rapidly, and a growing opposition to the notion that a detailed manifesto should be regarded by the nation as holy writ for a five-year parliament. These attitudes were not solely or mainly a reaction to the party's record in the decade 1965–75. They stemmed much more from a view of Britain's problems and of the role of government in trying to solve them.

Another major difference is that the policy work was less tightly controlled than in 1964–70. All policy work had to be funnelled eventually through the Research Department, the Advisory Committee on Policy, the shadow cabinet, and the 'inner' shadow cabinet—known as the Steering Committee and made up of the leader's most senior colleagues—before it received official endorsement. But there were more policy groups, running on an initially lighter rein, than before. Again, this owed something to the change. More backbenchers wanted to be involved in policy work and the shadow cabinet was wisely disposed to let a hundred flowers bloom. In order to ensure that they could be picked without placing too large a burden on the shadow cabinet itself, which must necessarily spend quite a lot of its time determining parliamentary tactics week by week, a policy sub-committee under Sir Keith Joseph's chairmanship was established to vet policy proposals before their submission to the shadow cabinet. This sub-committee, all of whose members were in the shadow cabinet, met from time to time over lunch in the Research Department.

The principal documents produced during this period have been *The Right Approach* and *The Right Approach to the Economy* (1977). A Scottish policy document, *Onward to Victory*, was published for the Scottish party conference in 1978. *The Right Approach* was based on an exhaustive and exhausting shadow cabinet review of the first year's policy work. It showed the party's concern for setting out coherent general principles of action rather than a detailed blueprint for office. It is significant that it was always referred to initially as a *strategy* rather than a *policy* document. Publication of *The Right Approach* brought the first phase of work to a conclusion, so that many policy groups finished the main part of their work at the same time. A rather tighter grip was subsequently imposed on policy work. *The Right Approach to the Economy* brought together the main policy work undertaken in the fields of public expenditure, taxation, industrial policy and industrial relations. It set out once more the party's general approach, but also presented an intellectually rigorous argument on the problems of economic reform. The fact that the document was signed by Sir Keith Joseph, Sir Geoffrey Howe and Mr James Prior—who had been associated from time to time with different shades of the economic argument—led some commentators to see it as another example of the policy document as treaty. The manifesto for the next election was based on these documents, just as the 1950 and 1951 manifestos were based on the *Charters*.

It was intended that policy work after the publication of *The Right Approach to the Economy* should be completed by the late summer of 1978 before the election campaign widely expected in the autumn. A manifesto was actually completed and approved by the shadow cabinet, and discussed by the Advisory Committee on Policy, before the Prime Minister's announcement that he intended to carry on into the winter and perhaps beyond. This work was not wasted, however. It brought to attention a few areas where more work needed to be done, and the last stage of policy work in the parliament was directed towards them.

Policy making throughout this period consciously drew on the experiences of 1945–51 and 1964–70. Before work began, the Research Department undertook a review of the earlier periods and some of the findings of this review are included in this chapter. As things have turned out, the exercise this time clearly reflects some of the different strengths of the earlier periods. Much detailed work of a technically proficient nature was done, but the party was more concerned to convey a broad approach rather than to scatter public commitments over a wide area. *The Right Approach*, for example, owes much of its style and sweep to the *Charters*. Whether the work since 1975 also repeats earlier mistakes, or has managed to produce new ones, will be for others in time to argue.

## V CONCLUSION

Four rather obvious questions emerge from any study of policy-making. First, does all the policy work matter? As King points out,[21] a party today cannot campaign on 'men not measures', and when it is out of power, policy making gives its MPs and leading party activists 'a sense of purpose and something to do'. It may be fair to question whether all this work, however skilfully planned and efficiently carried out, actually makes much difference to voting behaviour. King seems to be arguing that even the Conservative party conceded this in 1970 when, though its policy-making exercise may have been sophisticated, 'its electoral appeal was pretty primitive'.[22]

But showing that it is prepared for government is an important, if small, weapon in an opposition's armoury. Of all the factors that affect voting, the performance of the government of the day is one of the most significant. In a real sense a general election is an opportunity for the electorate to give or withhold a vote of confidence in the government and to that extent it is true that governments do lose elections rather than oppositions winning them. This is not, however, the whole truth. The opposition has to be a credible alternative government in order to pick up support, and because policy making contributes to or detracts from its credibility it can be very important indeed.

The second question is how detailed policy has to be. I have already quoted Churchill's reply to this and, as Punnett notes, he was only repeating what others (including Disraeli) had said before. But in the event, Churchill went along, albeit reluctantly, with the policy-making work master-minded by Lord Butler. This work succeeded in the vote-maximising task of balancing credibility as an alternative government against the political embarrassment of taking too many commitments publicly on board.

There are four main potential embarrassments. First, there is always a danger that opponents will steal some of the more attractive policies produced. This is sometimes seen by com-mentators as an attempt in the run-up to an election to capture the middle ground of politics. A wise party does not allow itself to be provoked, as a result, into changing its policies to ones that are less attractive—and appear less moderate—just in order to look different. Imitation is flattering, and not unhelpful, in politics as in the rest of life.

Secondly, an opposition may incur electoral unpopularity by setting out policies which appeal more to its activists, who had a say in producing them, than to anyone else. Labour does this periodically with proposals for enlarging the public sector, raising taxation and extending socialism in ways which may enthuse the constituency workers but not its private pollsters.

Thirdly, it may be only too obvious when a policy is scrutinised by the experts that it cannot easily be implemented.

Fourthly, circumstances can change so much as to make commitments undertaken sometime previously look impractical or harmful as time passes.

A party in opposition has to surmount these difficulties as well as it can, and it may not always have a totally free hand in determining where to place the balance between the general and the particular. In 1964, as we noted, the Conservative party was obliged by the public mood to demonstrate intellectual vigour across the whole field. In 1974–5, there was a greater demand to know what the party stood for in general before specific policy questions were tackled. A party's own supporters in parliament and in the country can shift the balance, and the same can be true of its political leaders' inclinations. They may well conclude that turning out the vote by a lowest common denominator approach should not be their main preoccupation, that they know what is good for the country, and that they will not be able to do what they want unless they are fully prepared for office and have worked out their policies in sufficient detail to answer the questions that civil servants will raise. Even if this work can be done behind the scenes, there is always the danger of leaks, with work that was never meant for public consumption appearing indigestibly with the daily papers on everyone's breakfast table. Preoccupation with detailed policy work can also obscure the main message that a party is trying to communicate; it may finish up with a lot of cleverly conceived items of policy but no comprehensible message at all.

A successful opposition will seek to strike a balance which ensures that its general message is clear and is presented with sufficient supporting evidence to be credible. The quantity of the evidence which is necessary has probably increased with the growth in sophistication of political commentary and interrogation. Mr Heath has put this point: 'There is probably a place for both the main themes and for detailed policies. The argument for detail is this: people today are so cynical and sceptical about the whole machinery of government that detail is needed to convince them that you really intend to carry out your promises.'[23]

Political craft will always be needed in opposition policy making to counter the 'heads I win, tails you lose' attack that every government will make on its opponents—claiming both that they have no policies and are therefore unfit to govern, and that they do have policies which would lead to instant disaster if they were ever given the chance to carry them out.

The third question, which was referred to earlier, is who makes policy in the Conservative party? The theoretical model that the leader alone is responsible for policy, and the 'presidential model' school of political scientists, both underestimate the extent to which decisions are collective.

Since the Conservative party does not suffer from the 'general will' notion of political authority which afflicts the Labour party, the role of the party conference is not so decisive in policy making, though its influence is not negligible and no party leadership could afford to ride roughshod year after year over its fixed and prevailing opinions. The celebrated '300,000 houses' amendment at Blackpool in 1950 illustrates what a Conservative party conference can achieve if it gets the bit between its teeth. Furthermore, as the textbooks have all pointed out since R. T. McKenzie's classic study *British Political Parties* first published in 1955, though the party is authoritarian in theory, its whole structure in practice provides for a constant process of consultation and two-way flow of ideas within its rank and file. The process ensures that in the measures they advocate, leaders and MPs have the views of their rank and file well to the fore of their minds. The Conservative party is a mass party.

But the really effective policy-making college is the shadow cabinet, and within that body the views of those who have been irreverently called 'the big beasts in the jungle'—the senior political figures—obviously matter most. The leader can and should point the direction in which policies will develop. She (or he) can make the running on policy both publicly and privately to an extent and with an authority denied to colleagues. The leader can decide which colleagues are in the most influential positions to shape policy and indeed (within certain obvious constraints) who should have a seat in the college of cardinals. Yet there is no papal throne. The shadow cabinet is in effect the collective policy-making body in opposition, and because of the additional strength which this gives to any policy statement, no sensible leader would have it otherwise.

The last question—and most important—is how good are the policies that emerge? Performance is both uneven, as I suggested earlier, and more untidy than this sort of review might suggest. This is inevitable in any exercise which depends on voluntary effort by busy and sometimes temperamental people. The absence of the resources of government also affects quality of work, and its relevance can be limited by the fact that planning in opposition tends to concentrate on policies that touch on more or less permanent features of government. Responding to transient features is bound to be less planned, and yet dealing with the passing scene is what government is about for much of the time.

Even allowing for all that, a fair-minded critic of, say, the policies produced in the 1964–70 period would surely conclude that technically many of them would have done credit to a Brookings Institute or some other school of public policy. Major reforms of structures that had been left untouched for decades were carried out in ingenious and sometimes administratively elegant ways.

Nevertheless, the resources for policy work in Britain are decidedly meagre and the technical loads placed on a party in opposition are immense. More work on policy by long-term policy units attached to the political parties as in Germany, by schools of public policy, and by strengthened select committees, would help to eliminate those policy options which are unlikely to work in practice and to ensure more careful study of the practical operation and effect of those options which have more to recommend them.

This should also have the advantage of raising the level of informed political debate. Policy-making in opposition is not just a matter of finding sophisticated solutions to the problems that are faced by governments; it is also a question of mobilising consent for those policies. Most of the Conservative party's failures of the recent past can be found in this area of political persuasion and education. Conservative politicians in the last fifteen years have failed more as persuaders than as policy innovators. The result has not been conspicuously good for the country.

NOTES

1. In writing this paper, I have drawn extensively on the unpublished work of my predecessor as director of the Conservative Research Department, Mr James Douglas, and have been assisted on the history of the Conservative party and the Research Department by my colleague Mr Geoffrey Block.

2. J. D. Hoffman, *The Conservative Party in Opposition 1945–51* (London: MacGibbon and Kee, 1964).

3. R. M. Punnett, *Front-Bench Opposition* (London: Heinemann, 1973).

4. Studies of British general elections since 1945 carried out by David Butler and associates, e.g. D. Butler and D. Kavanagh, *The British General Election of October 1974* (London: Macmillan, 1975).

5. A. King, 'How the Conservatives Evolve Policies', *New Society*, 20 July 1972, pp. 122–4.
   There are also a number of unpublished monographs on various aspects of policy in the form of higher degree theses deposited at British and American universities, and which deserve more attention than they perhaps get.

6. Lord Butler, *The Art of the Possible* (London: Hamish Hamilton, 1971), especially Chapter 7.

7. John Ramsden's history of the Conservative Research Department, commissioned to mark its 50th birthday in 1979–80, should do much to fill this gap.

8. Lord Fraser was director of the Conservative Research Department from 1951–64, and chairman of the Department from 1970–74. He was deputy chairman of the Conservative party from 1964–75.

9. J. D. Hoffman, op. cit.

10. A. King, op. cit.

11. There is one full-length study of the Research Department in the form of a PhD thesis: Arnold Beichman, *The Conservative Research Department: how an elite subsystem within the British Conservative Party participates in the policy-making process* (Colombia University Thesis, 1973), obtainable from Xerox University Microfilms.

12. R. Rose, *The Problem of Party Government* (London: Macmillan, 1974), p. 186.

13. Lord Butler, op. cit., p. 135.

14. Ibid.

15. Lord Woolton, *Memoirs* (London: Cassell, 1959), p. 347.

16. Lord Butler, op. cit.

17. R. M. Punnett, op. cit., p. 264.

18. Political education involved local study-groups, political education officers in every area, a 'two-way movement of ideas' on pre-determined themes, area and national seminars, and Swinton college courses. All these built up the education movement in the late forties and fifties and did much to transform opinion in the country.

19. D. Butler and M. Pinto-Duschinsky, *The British General Election of 1970* (London: Macmillan, 1971), p. 89.

20. *The Economist*, 15th April 1978, pp. 37–42.

21. A. King, op. cit.

22. Ibid.

23. Quoted in D. Butler and M. Pinto-Duschinsky, op. cit., p. 66.

# 2 Economic Policy

## Andrew Gamble

We were returned to office to change the course of history of this nation—nothing less. It is this course—the new course—which the Government—your Government—is now shaping.

Edward Heath, Conservative Party Conference 1970

We believe that Government knows less about business than businessmen, less about investment than investors, and less about pay bargaining than trade union negotiators and employers. We think we understand the limitations on what a government alone can do. This is surely the beginning of wisdom and common sense.

*The Right Approach to the Economy* (1977) p. 53

## I INTRODUCTION

In framing their economic policy since the war, Conservative leaders have stressed individual responsibility and freedom, opposing the disciplines of the market to the interference of the state, urging reductions in taxation and public expenditure, and fighting the extension of state ownership and state intervention. The most recent expression of these ideas has been the doctrine of the social market economy,[1] pioneered initially by Enoch Powell and the Institute for Economic Affairs, and promulgated since 1974 by the Centre for Policy Studies (founded by Sir Keith Joseph and Margaret Thatcher), the Selsdon Group, and the National Association for Freedom, as well as the leader writers of the *Daily Telegraph* and *The Times*, and economic commentators such as Samuel Brittan and Peter Jay.

The chief impulse behind the spread of social market thinking has been the reaction against the policy of Keynesian demand management[2] and the associated policies of high public expenditure and intervention in the markets for labour and products, which have been pursued by all governments since the war, and with extra effort since 1960. This reaction in turn reflects the growing problems that have beset economic policy-making in Britain in the 1970s; among them, the acceleration of inflation, the rise in unemployment, the commodity price boom, the undermining of the stability of the international monetary system and the difficulty of financing public expenditure. Underlying those symptoms of disorder has been a crisis of profitability which led to the first major recession in the world economy since the war in 1974–5, ending a period of unprecedented expansion. The very Keynesian techniques which, at the height of the boom, had been praised as the means whereby the performance of capitalist economies had been so much improved were now seen to be frail instruments indeed, unable to cope with many of the new problems, particularly inflation. Social market thinking went one stage further, however, in arguing that Keynesian and interventionist policies were not just disarmed in the face of the new slump but were the chief reasons for it.

Four main strands in social market thinking mark it out from the orthodoxy that has ruled economic policy since the war:

(i) Economic management: monetarist ideas replace Keynesian; the control of the money supply becomes the most important target for policy in place of full employment and economic growth. Intervention to fix or control either prices or incomes is ruled out.
(ii) Taxation and public expenditure: levels of both are considered far too high and drastic changes in policy are proposed to permit a reduction to around 25 per cent of GNP in order to create real personal incentives and restore individual responsibility.
(iii) Industrial policies: all forms of intervention in industry—national and regional subsidies, public ownership, price control, support for bankrupt and declining concerns—would be phased out on the grounds that the market is distorted by such policies and that the state is a much less efficient entrepreneur than private firms, and a much less efficient allocator of credit than the City of London.
(iv) Trade unions: the union problem would be dealt with partly by legislation, to withdraw many legal privileges the unions currently enjoy, partly by administrative means to reduce the

effectiveness of strikes. In addition, government avoidance of pay policies and return to responsible free collective bargaining would end the 'politicisation' of industrial relations and restore the disciplines of the market in pay determination.

At first glance the doctrine of the social market economy might seem to be only a more radical version of the programmes for government developed by the Conservative party during their last two spells in opposition—the call in 1951 to 'set the people free' and the plans in 1970 for a 'quiet revolution' to 'change the course of history of this nation'. It seems surprising, therefore, that the social market doctrine has created a deep division on economic policy within the leadership, a division which is more than just a matter of emphasis or personal rivalry and can be seen in retrospect to have been developing since 1960.[3] Within the common ideology of the free market there is now a much sharper ideological divide than ever before over the question of how far the party should go in framing its policies in accordance with those beliefs when it is in office. The dispute is not simply over techniques for controlling inflation or restraining the growth of public expenditure; it is about whether the Conservatives can and should govern within the institutional constraints of social democracy, or whether it should seek to alter those constraints by changing the balance of forces on which they ultimately rest. The dispute thus concerns the fundamental question of the role of the Conservative party in British politics and its relation to the state. The 'Tory' wing of the leadership, which is opposed to social market doctrine, argues that the Conservatives have always governed according to circumstances rather than according to principles;[4] they have conceived their political task to be directing the affairs of the state by being flexible and making concessions when circumstances suggested they were necessary or desirable. This Tory view of government is explicitly countered by 'social market' Conservatives who are convinced that such a policy leads to a steady retreat before the advance of collectivism and that what is required is not pragmatism in government but a set of clearly defined principles which can help Conservative ministers resist the short-term pressures they will face in government and reverse the 'ratchet' of socialism.[5]

To understand the forces that shape Conservative economic policy in office and in opposition it is first necessary to grasp why it is that the doctrine of the social market economy, although intellectually highly fashionable, espoused by the party leader and some of her principal lieutenants, and promulgated by numerous groups and institutes, and so much in tune with one of the fundamental strands of the party's ideology, has yet occasioned so much hostility within the party and was resisted by a majority of the shadow cabinet. The question might be put another way. What is there in the experience of government that persistently separates the outlook of the majority of the party leaders from that of many of their supporters and gives the Tory perspective within the party such resilience whatever may be its shortcomings in intellectual coherence? This chapter intends to explore these questions by looking firstly at the context of policy making in government, and secondly at how Conservative economic policy has evolved since 1960.

## II THE POLITICAL ECONOMY OF SOCIAL DEMOCRACY

In matters of economic policy the Conservative party was traditionally the party of the national economy and the party of protection, opposed to the doctrines of free trade and economic liberalism.[6] Its leaders were strong defenders of the rights of property but not of the idea of the free market. The party of the land and of the institutions of the state proved itself at times a vigorous champion of particular business interests but its political and ideological links with industry, and particularly finance, remained weak until the 1920s, when it became the umbrella party for the protection of all property in the face of the apparent threat of confiscation posed by the Labour movement. The party's ideological rhetoric at this time became noticeably more liberal in economic terms and the party's financial policy more orthodox, but it did not rule out policies in the 1930s that protected the national economy by reinforcing economic ties with the Empire and restricting domestic competition by encouraging cartels and price agreements.

Conservative economic policy has developed since the war within the limits set by the external relations of the British economy and the organisation of the social democratic state. For more than one hundred years Britain has been dependent upon its political and trading relationships with other territories in the world economy for the food and raw materials necessary to support its specialised industries and urban population. Britain's industrial and commercial superiority permitted the development of an international financial centre in the City of London as well as great export industries. The international perspectives and activities of these interests, now reinforced by the largest group of multinationals outside the United States, have exerted enormous direct and indirect pressures on British governments to maintain and, where they can, increase the openness of the British economy to the free flow of goods and capital. Relinquishing the Empire meant relinquishing also the prospect of any viable alternative to linking British prosperity to the prosperity of the world economy and accepting the severe disciplines of the world market and world division of labour which make cost competitiveness and comparative advantage the criteria for determining the survival of economic activities. The economic rationale for more ambitious protectionist policies which the existence of the Empire provided, as well as the limited protection it gave to British trade and living standards, has been removed. This made the balance of payments a much more direct concern of policy and led to the major policy initiative undertaken by the Conservatives since the war—the application to join the EEC.

Since 1940 the establishment of a social democratic state by the wartime Coalition and the succeeding Labour administration created a significantly different context for internal economic policy. The main changes were firstly the considerable enlargement of the public sector in terms of employment and expenditure and the financial implications of this for levels of taxation; and secondly the acceptance by government of a much greater responsibility for economic outcomes, particularly in four areas: prices, employment, the balance of payments and living standards. The techniques for governments' new role were supplied by Keynesian economics, and the rationale by the size of the existing public sector, but the pressure for it came largely from the long-standing demands of the Labour movement for policies that promoted social justice and economic welfare, demands whose legitimacy were recognised in the New Conservatism that arose under Mr Butler's careful cultivation after 1945.

The social democratic state brought with it a new political economy, in the sense of a new set of constraints, techniques and principles for economic policy, and established an important degree of consensus between the parties on how the economy should be handled, based on the acceptance of a 'mixed economy', the idea of an economy that remained capitalist in ownership and organisation but which contained a large public sector enabling public agencies to oversee and influence its development and realise wider social purposes. Such economic management has been guided by three main objectives. Governments have sought to use Keynesian monetary and fiscal measures to 'fine tune' the level of aggregate demand, so as to minimise fluctuations in output and maintain full employment without inflation, by making investment and expansion profitable. Secondly, governments have accepted an obligation to promote investment in the infrastructure of the economy—particularly in energy and transport and in high technology sectors such as aircraft, and to bear many other costs, such as research and education. Thirdly, governments have accepted the desirability of high levels of government spending to provide welfare for and promote equality between all members of the community and all regions of the economy.

Certain political trends have developed as a result. The state itself has had to be funded increasingly by taxation levied on the great majority of the population (the overall balance of the tax system is slightly regressive,[7] and as the tax has risen so public expenditure has appeared to be directly financed out of wage packets); unions and employers have become involved more and more in the formulation and implementation of economic policy; and the leaderships of the two main parties have become used to competing for the prize of taking office and directing the great administrative apparatus, through a process of competitive bidding for votes and the raising of expectations about government performance that has helped to make the state of the economy the single most important issue in determining how people vote.[8]

These three aspects of the political economy of the social democratic state reflect and are limited by the balance of forces in the major political and economic markets. These forces include the powerful financial sector, independent of the state and industry; an industrial sector split between internationally-oriented, capital-intensive firms and declining heavy and basic industries; a highly efficient capital-intensive agriculture; a unified Labour movement, containing approximately 50 per cent of the labour force, and organised both industrially and politically; and an electoral market lacking major regional, religious, or racial divisions and in which manual workers predominate.

The constraints on economic policy-making may therefore be

summarised in terms of the four main markets that policy makers
have to reckon with and which supply the short-term pressures
which are generally much more powerful than the most pressing of
pressure groups in concentrating the minds of ministers.

|  | Supply | major conditions for supply | failure to maintain conditions | main sanction |
|---|---|---|---|---|
| Financial Markets | credit, foreign exchange | stable money values | sterling crisis; public expenditure crisis | withholding of credit |
| Product Markets | consumer & capital goods | profit- ability | unemploy- ment crisis | cutbacks in output and investment |
| Labour Markets | labour power | real wages | pay crisis | strikes |
| Political Markets | votes | standard of living | electoral defeats | withdrawal of support |

An economic policy that fails to maintain the confidence and
consent of the agents in each of these markets can swiftly multiply
the pressures for a change of policy. Economic management
becomes a matter of navigating between these rival perils, and
accounts for many of the dramatic conversions and 'U-turns' of
policy which recent British political history displays. The constraints are tight and have grown tighter as external economic
relations have worsened, so that managing to keep the confidence of
all four markets and avoiding a crisis in any one of them is an art no
government since 1960 can claim to have mastered, and explains
the frequency of the attempts to intervene directly in one or more of
these markets so as to smother their pressures and create greater
freedom for the implementation of government policy. In opposition, however, parties are subjected to direct pressures only from
the political market. The tendency has been for each set of leaders to
condemn the form of intervention practised by their opponents, and
promise greater 'freedom'. The serpentine trails left by the

economic policies of the two main parties owe much to the adversary style of British politics and the frequent changes of government.[9]


## III MANAGING SOCIAL DEMOCRACY

.Ever since the end of the war the British economy has suffered from stop go . . . I knew there was only one way to create the prosperity which our people rightly demanded . . . That was a faster rate of expansion. So I determined that whatever the immediate problems which inevitably beset a government from time to time during any Parliament, I would not be deflected from that strategy.

Anthony Barber, Conservative Conference, 1973

Once returned to office in 1951 the Conservatives were anxious to demonstrate that setting the people free stopped short of dismantling the social democratic state and that they could govern successfully within its constraints. The government continued the relaxation of controls, reduced public expenditure and taxation by modest amounts, and revived monetary policy as a major instrument of economic management. It was fortunate enough to preside over the surge of prosperity in the 1950s which was part of the great expansion in the world economy, and won two further elections by being identified with it. It was in this period that electoral and trade union expectations about steadily improving living standards were created and the state of the economy became the decisive factor in the electoral popularity of governments.

Conservative priorities in the 1950s were to maintain the strength of sterling by aiming for a balance of payments surplus; to maintain full employment by manipulating aggregate demand; and to satisfy expectations about living standards by adopting a conciliatory approach to pay negotiations. In this way pressures were warded off, the most difficult proving to be keeping the confidence of the financial markets. Though there was a trading surplus on the balance of payments it was frequently insufficient to support the scale of overseas military spending and capital export that was desired by British military, diplomatic, and financial interests, and maintain the position of sterling as an international currency given its weak reserve position.[10] To maintain financial confidence in sterling the government was forced to deflate the economy periodically to reduce imports and create a temporary balance of payments surplus at considerable cost to industrial investment and economic growth. These checks to the growth of output and productivity made the containment of costs more difficult and produced the first clashes on pay. They also helped ensure that although the rise in living standards in the 1950s was faster than at any time since 1870, it was much slower than the average for Western Europe.

This awareness of relative economic decline and its long-term implications caused mounting impatience with the policy of deflation to protect the balance of payments and the exchange rate, and produced a marked change of emphasis in the party's economic policy after their third election victory in 1959, and their third sterling crisis in 1961. The Conservatives now became the party of Europe and the party of growth. To remedy the evident shortcomings of British industrial performance, indicative planning measures were introduced, institutionalised in bodies like the NEDC, and aimed at securing agreement between industry, labour, and government on a strategy for the growth of production and incomes and the containment of costs. The government also launched major new public spending plans to modernise the transport system, hospitals and education, and in 1963 embarked on a reflation of the economy which was planned to be self-sustaining and which the government pledged would not be cut short by deflationary measures to ward off a sterling crisis. Making growth the priority instead of the balance of payments was made possible firstly by the political decision to complete the withdrawal from Empire and seek entry to the EEC, which recognised Britain's reduced status as a world power and so brought into question the wisdom and feasibility of maintaining sterling as a reserve currency; and secondly by the growing pressures that the policy of 'stop-go' was creating in other markets.[11]

Maudling's belief that Britain could break out of the 'stop-go' cycle and enjoy its own belated 'economic miracle' was based on a plan to borrow overseas to cover the temporary deficit which was expected on the balance of payments and so maintain the expansion of demand.[12] Whether the policy could have prevented a further crisis in the financial markets, and how the Conservatives would have reacted, was never tested because Labour won the election in 1964, inherited the deficit, precipitated the crisis, and were soon busy sacrificing their own plans for growth to protect the exchange rate.

Though the Conservatives in opposition criticised Labour's interventionist policies which for the most part were continuations of Conservative initiatives, the building of a strong, expanding national economy able to compete within the EEC remained the central priority of their economic policy. But in reaction to Labour's failures to build such an economy, despite the battery of interventionist measures employed, the Conservatives began to stress the need for greater market disciplines, lower public expenditure, more incentives and trade union reform, and launched a detailed policy-making exercise based on their 1965 policy document *Putting Britain Right Ahead*. As a result, the preparation for government between 1964 and 1970 was the most thorough ever undertaken by an opposition in Britain. The 'competition' policy that emerged was certainly liberal in inspiration and devoted to shaking up the British economy by injecting more dynamism, speeding change, and enforcing greater efficiency, particularly through the reform of tax and industrial relations. Heath has sometimes been accused of not being a Conservative at all, and it is true that economic liberalism is a radical rather than a conservative doctrine in its implications for the pace and desirability of social change. But Heath was never an economic liberal like Powell or the later social market Conservatives. His conception of government remained Tory and the purpose behind the competition policy was to find a better set of instruments for forcing unwelcome change on the British economy in the belief that only industrial strength would allow Britain to play a leading political role in the EEC.[13]

Against the background, however, of the tensions, frustrations and failures of the Labour government's policies and the industrial and social turmoil of the late-1960s, the Conservative leadership was subjected to intense pressure from its own supporters and from the increasing number of economic liberals in the party to promise a major change of direction in economic policy that would overturn many of the policies that had not been challenged since the war. This process reached a climax at the Selsdon Park Conference[14] at the beginning of 1970, which was planned to co-ordinate the work of the various policy committees and finalise the details of the competition policy ready for the election. But with the assistance of the Conservative press, and Harold Wilson, the conference was publicised as committing the party to radical policies aimed at restoring order, discipline and individual responsibility in both economy and society by introducing tough new laws against strikers, demonstrators and prospective immigrants, and allowing the free play of market forces in welfare, housing and the distribution of income.

This impression was confirmed by the first two years of the new government which saw so many of the policies discussed in opposition put into practice with a determination that marked a significant rupture with the established policies of the welfare consensus and made the Heath government the only radical government in actions as well as rhetoric since the war-time Coalition. But it is important to grasp the nature of this radicalism in order to understand the reason for the several 'U-turns' in policy in 1972 that were so criticised in the party, particularly after the election defeats in 1974. Such criticisms are often based on the mistaken notion that the Heath government was attempting to establish a social market economy in its first two years of office— reducing public expenditure and taxation, abolishing the agencies and instruments of government intervention in the economy, reforming trade union law, allowing market forces to determine pay and prices—an attempt which was then recklessly abandoned in 1972 because the government 'panicked' in the face of industrial militancy, the steep rise in unemployment, and the fear that inflation would accelerate following the successful miners' strike.[15]

In many respects, however, the government's new course fell far short of a coherent social market strategy, one bent not just on giving a different emphasis to economic policy but on changing the framework that determines which economic policies are politically possible. The purpose of the competition policy, including its Selsdon version, was to give the highest priority to economic growth (despite the manifesto commitment to halting inflation), because it was held that only a rapidly expanding economy could reverse Britain's relative economic decline, overcome the economic failures of the 1960s and defuse the social tensions they were creating. Free market policies were the favoured instrument but were applied selectively to force changes in the attitudes and behaviour which were thought to be obstacles to creating a dynamic and efficient economy. Such economic shock treatment made the quiet revolution a very noisy one, as subsidies were withdrawn from lame ducks, some trade unions were fined, a few trade unionists were jailed and charges imposed on many public services from school milk to museum admissions. Whilst such policies and the manner of their introduction stirred up considerable political and industrial conflict (five states of emergency had to be declared between 1970 and 1974), they did not represent an adherence to social market principles by the Conservative leadership. The priority remained improving the relatively slow rate of growth of the British economy rather than restoring the conditions for a free market economy as the economic liberals conceived them, and implied a particular strategy for handling the pressures from the economic markets.

Like its Conservative predecessor in 1963–4, the Heath government was determined not to permit the balance of payments to obstruct economic growth, although it, too, was inconsistently committed at first to fixed exchange rates. The large balance of payments surplus inherited from Labour, however, defused any immediate pressure from the financial markets. By the time the Conservatives began reflating the economy they had also been forced to float the pound, which removed (briefly) a fundamental obstacle to an expansionist policy.

The government attempted to cope with labour market pressures by reforming trade union law and renouncing a formal incomes policy as it had pledged itself to do in the 1970 manifesto, hoping that the new laws and market pressures would contain wage costs. The Industrial Relations Act,[16] however, was not a credible social market measure and reflected the ambiguity in Conservative party attitudes to trade unions that had existed since the war, the problem of whether Conservative policy should aim at increasing or reducing union power: creating strong, centralised industrial unions which have control over their members and can bargain 'responsibly', trading higher productivity for higher wages; or weak, decentralised unions that are incapable of resisting supply and demand pressures in the labour market, mounting effective strikes and 'coercing' private employers, that is, interfering with managers' freedom to direct production. The 1971 Act contained some clauses, such as outlawing the closed shop, that favoured the latter, but more, such as increasing the power of union officials over shop stewards, which favoured the former. Containing both, the Act helped to unite most sections of the Labour movement against it, failing to achieve its main objectives, increasing industrial conflict in the process, and damaging the prospects for co-operation with the Labour movement when the government actively began to seek it in

1972 for its counter-inflation policy. Governing with rather than against the trade unions had been a fundamental axiom of policy since the war, expressed most clearly in the commitment to full employment. Relaxing the constraint of the trade unions on policy would have required a much more far-reaching measure than the Industrial Relations Act. By February 1974 the Act had been effectively crippled and the Conservative manifesto was promising substantial amendments.

On pay the Conservatives abolished all Labour's incomes policy machinery and professed to rely on market forces and free collective bargaining to control inflation, but quickly encountered the problem of pay determination in the public sector. The attempt to set an example to the private sector and gradually lower pay settlements in the public sector, the 'N minus 1' policy, led to a series of strikes and courts of enquiry which resulted in some victories and some defeats for the government. The explanation, however, of the government's sudden abandonment of this policy and conversion to the need for a statutory incomes policy was not only due to the fear of accelerating inflation following the 1972 miners' strike, [17] but also because ministers had become convinced that, given the priority of raising the rate of growth, the best means of containing rising costs in the labour markets was a formal prices and incomes policy.

In the product markets, government policy was aimed, firstly, at reducing public expenditure so as to permit large tax reductions that would restore the incentives for risk-taking and effort; secondly, at withdrawing most subsidies and other forms of government interference to force industry to solve its own problems and become more efficient and competitive (and more eager to resist excessive pay claims). The overriding aim was to restore profitability, boost investment and so pave the way for a rapid expansion of output and productivity. The outcome in both cases, however, fell short of a social market policy, and both were reversed in the face of the pressures they generated.

Barber's package of measures in October 1970 followed a familiar Conservative logic by reducing the planned *rate* of growth of public expenditure (though by less than 1 per cent), and cutting direct taxes. In subsequent years direct taxes were reduced further, particularly on high incomes, and major tax reforms were introduced, (like VAT) or foreshadowed (like the tax credit scheme). After 1971, however, public expenditure was expanded again to play its part in the growth strategy. At no time were changes in policy contemplated of the kind advocated by Enoch Powell before the election in his 'Morecambe budget',[18] which alone could have provided the scope for really substantial cuts in direct taxation. The tax incentives that were provided after 1971 were not financed by cuts in public expenditure but by an increase in the budget deficit designed to help expand the economy, and more effort went into reforming taxes than into reducing them. In the face of the sluggish response of industry to the quiet revolution, the government came to consider that boosting the demand for the products of industry by maintaining and increasing public expenditure was more important in encouraging growth than boosting individual incentives by cutting public expenditure further.

A similar pattern was evident in industrial policy. The policy of withdrawing subsidies from 'lame ducks' was selective and ambiguous from the start, as was apparent when John Davies tried to explain it at the 1970 Conference:

> I believe that simply to abandon great sectors of our productive community at their moment of maximum weakness would be folly indeed . . . But I will not bolster up or bail out companies where I can see no end to the process of propping them up.[19]

The government made no move to end the public funding of major technological projects in aerospace and heavy engineering like Concorde, nor did it try to sell off or break up those industries already publicly owned, apart from hiving off profitable subsidiaries which made little difference to the monopoly status of these industries or the constraint they placed on government policy in the fields of pay and finance. Apart from the well-publicised decisions like the refusal of further aid to Upper Clyde Shipbuilders in 1971, the new policy made little progress in raising investment to the levels required for the growth strategy, so when the government decided to meet what it took to be a rising trend of unemployment in 1971–2 by reflating the economy, it also revised its industrial policies and began providing large sums for firms in difficulties and for firms that would expand in regions where unemployment was high. These policies seemed more sure of success than the ones they replaced, and the 1972 Industry Act, whilst not re-establishing the Industrial Reorganisation Corporation, gave new and far-reaching powers of intervention to the Secretary of State for Industry, powers which were to prove sufficient for most of the subsequent interventionist forays undertaken by Labour. The Conservatives had decided that a close partnership between state and industry was necessary to raise the rate of growth, and except in the field of finance, they did not shrink from equipping the state with the powers of intervention they thought necessary.

Pressures from the economic markets thus prevented the new government from wandering too far from social democratic orthodoxy and prompted in 1972 the adoption of a more familiar set of policies for achieving growth. The apparent 'U-turns'—the reversal of the industrial policy, the increases in public spending, the counter-inflation policy—were dictated by the change of emphasis in the growth strategy, and have been criticised as betrayals of the 1970 Manifesto, but the aspect of policy which attracted least criticism (at the time, although most since), was the handling of the money supply.

It is a curious feature of post-war economic policy that the Conservatives have generally proved far more financially irresponsible than Labour, which may reflect the greater political necessity for the Conservatives to preside over an expanding economy, and the greater fear Labour ministers have of the financial markets. Social market Conservatives now argue that the acceleration of inflation to 26 per cent in 1974/5 was directly caused by the monetary expansion of 1972/3. The government and most observers were only dimly aware of the scale of this monetary growth,[20] and Keynesian theory held in any case that the growth in the money supply was less important than the growth in the economy it might stimulate. The Barber boom was in many respects a re-run of the Maudling plan of 1963/4. Heath had inherited Macmillan's political perspective that Britain's full participation in the EEC was necessary and desirable, that the shortcomings in British economic performance had to be remedied to make this possible, and that the Conservative party could not afford to be identified electorally with a negative deflationary policy but must actively encourage faster rates of economic growth, if necessary by using state agencies to prod private capital into more efficient and ambitious levels of production. In 1972/3 the Heath government showed it was prepared to risk inflation in order to achieve growth, but it believed in any case that the upward spiral of costs and prices could be controlled in the short term by the counter-inflation policy and that if the policy of reflation succeeded in raising profitability, investment and output, the increase in demand would not prove inflationary in the long run.[21]

This belief was never tested because although a 5 per cent growth rate was achieved in 1973 and the counter-inflation policy proved very successful in its first two stages, the whole policy suffered spectacular shipwreck at the end of 1973 with the quadrupling of oil prices (the final phase of the great commodity price boom) with its implications for the balance of payments, already in severe deficit, and by the eruption of a pay crisis caused by the miners' refusal to settle within the Stage Three guidelines which led to the dramatic decision to put industry on a three-day week and the holding of an early general election. This failure and the subsequent onset of recession in the world economy was greatly to discredit Keynesian demand management as a means for maintaining prosperity and speeding growth, and led to inflation becoming for the first time since the war the major priority of government policy. But it is also important to remember that the monetary boom and the subsequent inflation would have been much smaller if the increase in public spending and the reduction of interest rates to stimulate industrial investment had not sparked off an explosion of bank lending, the proliferation of secondary banks and an unprecedented boom in property values and other non-industrial investment—which was made possible by the adoption in 1971 of *Competition and Credit Control*—a new freedom for the banking system much applauded by economic liberals and monetarists at the time. This was one aspect of the new course which could well have done with a 'U-turn', but none was forthcoming.[22]

IV THE SEARCH FOR THE RIGHT APPROACH

The highest national interest, overtopping all others in the economic sphere, is honest money—money that holds its value. Growth, full employment, expanding public services—all these are worth nothing unless that first and great condition is fulfilled.
Enoch Powell, Conservative Party Conference, 1973.

After 1974 the Conservatives found themselves once more in opposition facing a serious task of rebuilding their electoral support and restoring the confidence of their party rank and file, encumbered by a record in government which had certainly not enhanced the party's reputation as the party that could best handle national affairs. A major debate began on economic policy and the party's aims since the war and, following the change of the leadership in 1975 and the removal of some of Heath's closest supporters from the shadow cabinet,[23] the impression was given that a major break with previous Conservative policy was contemplated and that a future Conservative government would be committed to the establishment of a social market economy. But although the social market Conservatives filled the major economic ministries after the election, and Mrs Thatcher's speeches in opposition gave the party's economic policy a more thorough-going liberal image, social market doctrine has remained a minority viewpoint in the leadership as a whole. The 'Tory' majority in the leadership has fought back with such success that if an election had been held in October 1978 the Conservatives would have fought it on a programme less radical in several important respects than its programme in 1970.

The two main policy documents, *The Right Approach* and *The Right Approach to the Economy*, are fairly vague, consensual documents which commit the party to extremely little in detail and keep all policy options open. It is a technique known in the party as 'positive ambiguity'.[24] The main change that can be observed is that the party leadership as a whole has become very much less ambitious. In the new world economic climate managing the economy means managing the recession and, like the government, the Conservative party has made the control of inflation its central priority. As *The Right Approach to the Economy* puts it: 'If the management of money is handled wrongly everything goes wrong'.[25] The document lists a number of guidelines for policy, among them:

a. The provision of 'a more stable economic climate';
b. strict control of the rate of growth of money supply;
c. 'firm management' of government expenditure, (the idea being that it should drop as a percentage of GNP each year);
d. lower taxes (a number of specific proposals are made, involving a further switch from the principle of pay as you earn to pay as you spend);
e. the removal of 'unnecessary restrictions' on business expansion;
f. the encouragement of 'better methods of collective bargaining' (but legislation explicitly ruled out) and

g. the education of the public about the 'inescapable financial constraints'.[26]

Amidst these vague and hardly radical proposals the main sign of the influence of social market doctrine is the attempt to signal a phased withdrawal of government from the responsibility it hitherto accepted for economic outcomes. The monetarist ideal of the neutral policy stance is a restatement of pre-war financial orthodoxy. The government's job is envisaged once again as enforcing the laws on property and contract and maintaining the value of the currency, creating a framework in which whether the economy grows or not depends on decisions of individual workers, consumers, savers and employers, and whether unemployment is high or not depends on the real wage trade unions insist on.

Relinquishing responsibility for what happens in the economy, however, does not immediately bring relief from the pressures which the economic and political markets continually generate. Monetary restraint and monetarist logic can easily produce a spiral of deflation and industrial unrest of the kind experienced by the French government in 1979. The Tory wing of the leadership seems well aware of this, and on the evidence of the policy statements issued in 1976 and 1977 it seems unlikely that a future Conservative government will go through a phase of refusing to bail out companies on the grounds of social market principles, or suddenly to cease support for the large number of companies, including British Leyland, [27] that are currently receiving state aid. The result will be less than a social market economy, though it may well produce a stagnant market economy, since the commitment on inflation will rule out a major new expansionist policy.

Such cautious policies may well offer the best hope of holding the party together in government. The social market faction would be satisfied that the government was not pursuing interventionist policies, imposing statutory controls on incomes and prices, or increasing public expenditure. The Tory faction would welcome both the pragmatic response to specific problems faced by firms and regions, and also the maintenance of high levels of public spending and public involvement. Whether it will prove viable in a wider political sense is more doubtful. The policy of monetary targets will reassure the City of London and keep sterling strong; the CBI will welcome a reduction in some kinds of government intervention. But the central question which has dominated British economic policy since 1960—how to reverse the relative decline—will not be resolved. Since it is the inability of successive British governments to improve the poor performance of the national economy that caused the substantial loss of support for the two main parties in 1974 and the increasing readiness of voters to change their party, any party that returns to government without an effective policy for national revival is likely to find its support hard to maintain.[28]

Within the social market group in the leadership two views on decline may be seen. There are those like John Biffen who support social market policies on libertarian grounds and who advocate them whether or not they assist a revival of British national economic fortunes and Conservative political fortunes (though they believe they can do both).[29] But there are many others like Keith Joseph who believe social market policies to be the only means for national economic recovery. They see the social market policy as far more than just a déflationary, defensive policy, imposed by the economic failures of recent governments and the unfavourable world economy. It is rather an ambitious attempt to change the balance of political forces, preventing governments from using the public sector to manage the economy, in order to restore the foundations for expansion and prosperity.

The key policy associated with the social market group is monetarism, but as the Labour government showed between 1976 and 1979, monetarism as a technique can be employed to reassure the financial markets without making any fundamental changes or abandoning budget deficits, incomes policies, or industrial strategies. The social market persuasion in the party has, to some extent, been sheltering behind monetarism in the past few years, often giving the impression that monetarism offers a painless way of managing the economy and avoiding the kind of crisis in the labour markets over pay which incomes policies have regularly provoked in their later stages. Until the events of the winter of 1978/79 the Conservatives were strong supporters of 'responsible' collective bargaining.[30] The only reason offered as to why it should be responsible was contained in the proposal for a national economic forum which would spread 'understanding' about the economic facts of life.

Monetary guidelines can indeed only be the beginning for a social market policy. What would also be needed are policies that reduce the pressures governments face in their management of the economy—in the markets for products, for labour, and for votes.[31]

One priority would therefore be a major and irreversible dismantling of the public sector—the phasing out of all subsidies and interventionist agencies including the NEB and BNOC (both reprieved in the party's latest plans), the repeal of the 1972 Industry Act, a commitment to denationalisation and major changes in the financing of major services like road construction and health to shift them out of the public sector altogether. Only in this way can the mixed economy be unmixed and the size of public sector employment and expenditure, and hence the resulting pressure for the government to intervene to control pay and prices and to promote economic growth, be significantly reduced, and the opportunity for tax changes created on a scale that would make a noticeable difference to net incomes.

In isolation, however, a policy that dismantled the institutional reasons for government intervention might only intensify the slump that monetary policies were already creating. So the second priority would be to reduce trade union 'monopoly' power in the labour markets so as to restore the opportunity for profitable investment throughout industry to compensate for losing the cushioning of profits by government subsidies and the management of demand. Any social market policy that did not attempt to transform the labour market would merely be inviting deflation and stagnation, not a promising platform for Conservatives on which to appeal for support, however adept at it Labour governments may have become. From the social market perspective the problem of union power was set out very clearly by Enoch Powell in the 1960s when he argued[32] that the 'private coercion' of the trade unions rested on three legal privileges: the freedom to intimidate (peaceful picketing), the freedom to impose costs on others with impunity and the immunity of trade unions from action of tort. These legal privileges, he claimed, were enhanced by the closed shop but not caused by it. From this viewpoint trade unions have no economic merits and impose severe economic costs on a capitalist economy—overmanning, restrictions on productivity and the distortion of pay relativities. To redress the balance, measures to curb the ability to strike have been canvassed.[33] As Sir Keith Joseph has declared on many occasions, 'Monetarism is not enough', and where it most obviously is not enough is in its ability to reduce the power of organised labour.

V CONCLUSION

The theme of this chapter has been that all Conservatives since the war have drawn on the liberal ideology of individual responsibility and the free market to differentiate their economic policy from that of their opponents by identifying themselves as the party of lower taxes, reduced public expenditure and less government intervention. Nevertheless they have accepted the political economy of post-war social democracy—Keynesian demand management, to promote full employment and rising living standards, and high public spending on welfare. Such a stance has guaranteed the party regular spells in office, but it has failed to produce policies that could stem the accumulation of problems arising from the relatively poor performance of the British economy. Two distinct responses have emerged in the party in the last twenty years to this dilemma. The party under Macmillan, Home and Heath committed itself to the EEC and a strategy of growth and a readiness to use the spending, administrative and legal powers of the state as levers to create the right framework for expansion, when market policies appeared to be failing. This policy meant trying to solve the problems of the social democratic state within the institutional constraints of that state—that is, without challenging fundamentally the size of the public sector, the bargaining strength of the unions, or the expectations of the electorate. The social market approach of Powell and Joseph by contrast seeks to restore the foundations of a market economy—a 'flexible' labour market, the rule of law, minimal government (with a consequent reduction in electoral expectations), monetary disciplines, low taxes and low public expenditure. The best chance of achieving such an economy was in the 1950s when internal and external conditions were most propitious, but the government at that time was preoccupied with protecting sterling and Britain's world role, showing it could avoid conflict with the unions and maintain high levels of public spending. Social market medicine may now seem too harsh for the patient, but the social market case is that no other medicine will effect a cure.

Both positions lay claim to the Conservative tradition of One Nation and the Middle Way because both are seeking a viable political strategy for the party, an economic policy that will win support for the defence of capitalist institutions. Any such policy must in a representative democratic state seek co-operation between capital and labour, but whereas Tories believe this is best secured through the state, using public agencies where necessary to remedy deficiencies and injustices in the private sector, social market Conservatives believe it can only be achieved through the market by winning popular support for its operation. The progress of the dispute is to some extent obscured because under Margaret Thatcher the party has often identified itself with populist responses to economic issues—the burden of taxation, the inefficiency of bureaucracy and nationalised industries, the abuses of welfare, the injustices of pay policy and, in 1979, the power of the unions, and may in the process have raised expectations about what a Conservative government can achieve that the party will find difficult to fulfil with its stated policies, particularly as it inherited a sizeable budget deficit (unlike 1970) and is pledged to increase defence spending (unlike 1951). Amidst the smoke and turmoil of its early days, it will be surprising if, in the end, the new administration does not become another exercise in Tory government which will disappoint many of the hopes that have been raised, shorn as it will be of the ambitious programme of national revival proposed by either Peter Walker[34], or Keith Joseph. But the reality of relative economic decline remains, ameliorated but not averted by income from oil in the North Sea and overseas investments, and it is by its ability or good fortune in halting it that the economic policy of the Conservative government will be judged, and on which the political future of the Conservative party may come to rest.

NOTES

1. Social market thinking may be sampled by looking at the publications of the Institute for Economic Affairs and the Centre for Policy Studies; especially, *Why Britain needs a Social Market Economy* (London: CPS, 1975); S. Brittan, *Government and the Market Economy* (London: IEA, 1971); Sir Keith Joseph, *Reversing the Trend* (London: CPS, 1975); Sir Keith Joseph, *Stranded on the Middle Ground* (London: CPS, 1976); J. E. Powell, *Freedom and Reality* (London: Batsford, 1969). The theoretical underpinnings for the doctrine can be found in the writings of F. A. Hayek and Milton Friedman.
2. The theoretical principles and practical consequences of Keynesian demand management can be found in the following: A. Shonfield, *Modern Capitalism* (London: Oxford University Press, 1965); M. Stewart, *Keynes and After* (London: Penguin Books, 1972); and S. Brittan, *Steering the Economy* (London: Penguin Books, 1971).
3. For recent accounts of this split see T. Russel, *The Tory Party* (London: Penguin Books, 1978) and T. E. Utley, 'The Significance of Mrs Thatcher' in M. Cowling (ed.) *Conservative Essays* (London: Cassell, 1978).
4. I. Gilmour, *Inside Right* (London: Hutchinson, 1977).

5. *Inter alia*, Sir Keith Joseph, *Reversing the Trend*, and R. Boyson, *Centre Forward* (London: Temple Smith, 1978).

6. The best account of protectionism in the Conservative party before 1914 is contained in B. Semmel, *Imperialism and Social Reform* (London: Allen & Unwin, 1960).

7. F. Field *et al.*, *To Him Who Hath* (London: Penguin, 1977).

8. D. Butler & D. Stokes, *Political Change in Britain* (London: Macmillan, 1974) ch. 18.

9. M. Stewart, *The Jekyll and Hyde Years* (London: Dent, 1977).

10. S. Strange, *Sterling and British Policy* (London: Oxford University Press, 1971).

11. Particularly the rising unemployment which peaked at 878,000 in February 1963, and the battles over the government's Pay Pause.

12. For Maudling's own account as well as some interesting memoranda by him on incomes policy see his *Memoirs* (London: Sidwick & Jackson, 1978).

13. See the important account of the formulation of the new policies and their implementation by B. Sewill, the former head of the Conservative Research Dept., 'In Place of Strikes' in R. Harris (ed.) *British economic policy 1970–74* (London: IEA, 1975).

14. D. Butler & M. Pinto-Duschinsky, *The British General Election of 1970* (London: Macmillan, 1971) ch. 6.

15. A point of view presented by R. Harris 'A Self-Confessed Monetarist . . . ?' in Harris, op. cit. For an assessment of the meagre size of the tax cuts see P. Hutber, *The Decline and Fall of the Middle Classes* (London: Penguin Books, 1977) ch. 5.

16. The provisions and the passage of the Act are described by M. Moran, *The Politics of Industrial Relations* (London: Macmillan, 1977). See also C. Crouch, *Class conflict and the Industrial Relations Crisis* (London: Heinemann, 1977).

17. S. Brittan, *The Economic Consequences of Democracy* (London: Temple Smith, 1977) ch. 7.

18. E. Powell, *Income Tax at 4/3 in the £* (London: Stacey, 1970).

19. J. Davies, quoted in *Notes on Current Politics*, no. 15, Conservative Research Dept. (1970) p. 334.

20. Indeed, Anthony Barber claimed at the party conference in 1973 that the M1 measure of money supply was under tight control. For a discussion of both sides of the question see Harris, op. cit. In 1972 M1 rose 14 per cent and M3 28 per cent; in 1973 M1 rose 7 per cent and M3 29 per cent.

21. See Barber's speech at the party conference, October 1973. The scale and structure of the boom can be seen from the following figures cited in M. Stewart (1977) op. cit.

    1971–3 (constant prices)

    | | |
    |---|---|
    | consumers expenditure | +11 per cent |
    | public consumption | + 8 per cent |
    | GDP | + 7 per cent |
    | investment | + 5 per cent |
    | imports | +27 per cent |
    | exports | +14 per cent |

22. Until the secondary bank collapse in 1974 after the Conservatives had left office. Bank lending to the private sector rose by 48 per cent in 1972 and 43 per cent in 1973.

23. See the account by R. Behrens, *The Conservative Party in Opposition 1974–1977*, Department of Applied Social Studies, Lanchester Polytechnic, Coventry (1977).

24. Peter Jay began his review of *The Right Approach* in the *Times*, headed 'All Things to all Tories', as follows: 'The spectacle of a political party coming down resoundingly on both sides of an issue, more particularly when a sharp fence divides the rival points of view, can be distressing or hilarious according to one's sensibilities' (7 October 1976).

25. *The Right Approach to the Economy* (London: Conservative Central Office, 1977) p. 14.

26. Ibid., p. 7.

27. Although 50 Conservative MPs voted against the granting of further subsidies to British Leyland in 1975. In an unpublished paper 'The Price for Conservatism: the Conservative party and the economy since 1974', delivered to the PSA Contemporary British Politics Workshop in January 1978, Michael Moran concludes that there are few differences of substance between the policies the Conservatives followed in government and the policies they have become committed to in opposition.

28. In 1970 the Conservatives lost popularity faster than any government since the war, and the parliament saw major shifts of electoral opinion to third parties.

29. See J. Biffen, *Political Office or Political Power?* (London: CPS, 1977).

30. See the two policy documents and the Conference debates on industrial relations and economic policy in 1976 and 1977.

31. Despite the hostility of the social market wing to electoral reform it may prove that only after the adversary two-party system has been reformed will a sustained, long-term experiment with social market policies become possible.

32. E. Powell, *Freedom and Reality*, op. cit., ch. 10.

33. The general problems which the public sector and union power create for a social market strategy have been recognised by Sir Keith Joseph in two important speeches. *Monetarism is Not Enough* (London: CPS, 1976), and *Solving the Union Problem is The Key to Britain's Recovery* (London: CPS, 1979). During the winter of 1978/79 the Conservative party moved towards a new commitment to introduce legislation on industrial relations, concentrating on picketing, the closed shop and welfare benefits for strikers. But any proposals seemed likely to fall far short of the concentrated assault on the right and the ability to strike thought necessary by many economic liberals.

34. Peter Walker's views are contained in *The Ascent of Britain* (London: Sidgwick & Jackson, 1977). He is a modern representative of the Chamberlain tradition within the party.

# 3 Immigration

## Zig Layton-Henry

## I INTRODUCTION

At the end of the Second World War the Conservative party still regarded the Empire and the Commonwealth as the supreme achievement of the British people and as the most successful experiment in international relations that the world has ever known.[1] Many Conservatives felt that Britain's role in the world as a great power depended in large measure upon the Empire which was still an institution worth preserving, and both the Empire and Commonwealth had contributed mightily to the war effort. One of the major factors maintaining the unity of Empire and Commonwealth, and especially the links with Britain, was the common citizenship and allegiance that all British subjects owed to the Crown. While many of the King's subjects were also British by birth or descent, the vast majority were neither born in Britain nor did they have any family ties with the mother country, but they were all British subjects.

In 1948 the Labour government introduced a British Nationality Bill. This was partly in response to the Canadian Citizenship Act of 1946 and partly in anticipation of similar legislation being enacted in newly independent Commonwealth countries, notably India. The Nationality Act divided British citizens into two classes: citizens of independent Commonwealth countries, and the remainder who were classified as citizens of the United Kingdom and Colonies. The bill was opposed by the Conservative opposition who felt it was unnecessary and that by giving primacy to local citizenship the derivative British nationality would gradually decline in importance and eventually lapse altogether thus weakening the unity of the Commonwealth.

Sir David Maxwell-Fyfe, who led Conservative opposition to the bill, was also concerned lest its provisions might be used to discriminate against Commonwealth citizens. He argued that there would be no point in these new categories unless to drop the idea of the common status and our proud boast of the open door. 'We are proud,' he stated, 'that we impose no colour bar restrictions making it difficult for them when they come here'.[2] The opposition was so concerned with the implications of the bill that they reserved the right to revert to the old common citizenship if this should be the wish of the other Dominions and member states of the Commonwealth.

It was a considerable source of pride among many Conservatives that a British subject from any part of the Empire (and Commonwealth), no matter what his colour or creed, could come to the mother country, serve in the armed forces or public service, stand for parliament, and enjoy the same rights and obligations as any other British citizen. *Civis Britannicus sum* was not an empty phrase but a statement of considerable substance, part of the ideology which legitimised British rule in the Empire. 'In a world in which restrictions on personal movement and immigration have increased we still take pride in the fact that a man can say *civis Britannicus sum* whatever his colour may be, and we take pride in the fact that he wants and can come to the Mother Country.'[3]

It is worth emphasising the importance of Britain's imperial past not only because it was the legacy of common citizenship which facilitated migration from the West Indies and South Asia to Britain but also because it contributed substantially to the reluctance of Conservative governments to initiate immigration controls before 1962. Many Conservative ministers, members of parliament and leading party officers had served in the Empire or had relatives who had done so, for example as governors, administrators or soldiers. Many more had relatives who had emigrated to the Old Dominions or parts of Africa. These Conservatives were reluctant to allow any weakening of imperial ties, including both the granting of independence to the colonies and the weakening of the obligations of the mother country.

The Conservative party was therefore committed to common citizenship for all British subjects in the Empire and Commonwealth, and to complete freedom of migration between Britain and the Empire. 'There must be freedom of movement among its members within the British Empire and Commonwealth. New opportunities will present themselves not only in the countries overseas but in the Mother Country and must be open to all citizens.'[4] It was assumed that the movement of population was likely to continue to be an outflow from Britain to the older Dominions and to the climatically suitable parts of Africa but it was emphasised that a welcome should be extended to all those who came from the Dominions and colonies to live and work in Britain.

After the war, the government found that the economy was being seriously held back by an acute shortage of labour. A number of schemes were initiated by the government to resolve the problem, such as the Polish Resettlement Act and the European Voluntary Workers Scheme, but these did little to meet the crisis. When traditional migration to the Old Dominions resumed, the government became seriously concerned. This was the situation facing the Conservatives who assumed office in 1951. However, by then the migration from the West Indies had begun, encouraged both by the availability of work in Britain and, after 1952, by the blocking of traditional West Indian migration to the United States due to the passing by Congress of the McCarran-Walter Immigration Act. At this time there were no readily available sources of labour in Europe, apart from Eire, as the expanding European economies were absorbing millions of workers from eastern Europe and southern Italy.

The practical implications of migration from the West Indies were raised in the House of Commons at the very start of the migration by a Labour member, James Harrison. He was concerned at the problems of accommodation and integration that the new immigrants on the SS Windrush, which docked in June 1948, would face. He even raised the possibility of the need to control such immigration. However, his concern went unheeded and almost unnoticed. Gradually immigration from the West Indies grew as the early migrants quickly found employment in the expanding British economy. It was shortly followed by immigration from India and Pakistan.

The reaction to the immigration of black and brown Commonwealth citizens was initially subdued. Certain industries welcomed them eagerly due to the serious problems of obtaining skilled and unskilled labour. In 1956 the London Transport Executive established liaison with the Barbados Immigrant Service so that migrants would have a job waiting as soon as they arrived. The most serious initial problems of helping the immigrants fell on the local authorities and few additional resources were made

TABLE 3.1    Estimated net immigration from the New Commonwealth 1953–62[5]

|  | West Indies | India | Pakistan | Others | Total |
|---|---|---|---|---|---|
| 1953 | 2,000 | – | – | – | 2,000 |
| 1954 | 11,000 | – | – | – | 11,000 |
| 1955 | 27,500 | 5,800 | 1,850 | 7,500 | 42,650 |
| 1956 | 29,800 | 5,600 | 2,050 | 9,350 | 46,800 |
| 1957 | 23,000 | 6,600 | 5,200 | 7,600 | 42,400 |
| 1958 | 15,000 | 6,200 | 4,700 | 3,950 | 29,850 |
| 1959 | 16,400 | 2,950 | 850 | 1,400 | 21,600 |
| 1960 | 49,650 | 5,900 | 2,500 | −350 | 57,700 |
| 1961 | 66,300 | 23,750 | 25,100 | 21,250 | 136,400 |
| 1962 (First 6 months) | 31,800 | 19,050 | 25,080 | 18,970 | 94,900 |

available to those local authorities with special problems caused by
the concentration of immigrant settlement in particular areas.


II  THE CAMPAIGN AGAINST IMMIGRATION

A campaign against coloured immigration from the new
Commonwealth was initiated early in the period of migration by
Cyril Osborne, Conservative MP for Louth. His campaign was
conducted largely in the House of Commons and the press. In the
period 1952–7 Osborne's campaign had little success. His questions
in the House on disease and crime among immigrants received little
consideration from Sir Anthony Eden, Harold Macmillan and the
other ministers who had to deal with them.[6] Frequently, in reply,
ministers paid tribute to the contribution of West Indian nurses to
the hospital service and other West Indians to public transport. The
cabinet gave every appearance of being determined not to interfere
with the free movement of Commonwealth citizens.

The ministers in charge of Commonwealth relations and the
colonies tended to be strongly opposed to control and there were
important reasons for this. The progress of the West Indian colonies
towards independence was proving difficult as the British government attempted to create and sustain the ill-fated Federation of the
West Indies. There were also the complicated negotiations which
preceded the granting of independence to the colonies in east and
central Africa. The imposition of immigration controls, it was felt,

would make relations with Commonwealth countries and colonial governments much more difficult and jeopardise the transition from Empire to Commonwealth.

Surprisingly, Harold Macmillan reveals in his memoirs that the problem of coloured immigration was brought to the attention of the cabinet in 1954 and that early in 1955, after some rather desultory discussions, it was agreed that a bill should be tentatively drafted. 'I remember,' he writes, 'that Churchill, rather maliciously, observed that perhaps the cry of "Keep Britain White" might be a good slogan for the election which we should soon have to fight without the benefit of his leadership'.[7] Macmillan notes that the matter was shelved and no action was taken until the racial disturbances in Nottingham and Notting Hill brought the issue forcibly to public attention. However, this incident suggests that many members of the cabinet shared popular concern about coloured immigration and were not in principle opposed to the introduction of controls. It was not, however, a high priority.

Pressures on the cabinet continued to increase. Some local authorities were lobbying the government for help in housing, educating and integrating the immigrants. After 1955 Cyril Osborne was joined in his campaign by Norman Pannell (Kirkdale) and Martin Lindsey (Solihull), and the number of questions and adjournment motions demanding control increased. Opposition to coloured immigration was also gaining support among the Conservative rank and file. In 1955 the Central Council passed a resolution, by a small majority, proposing that the laws against aliens should be applied against Commonwealth citizens and at the party conference in October there were five resolutions demanding health checks on immigrants. Gradually resolutions on immigration favouring control appeared on the agendas of annual party conferences.[8]

The campaign for control gained considerable impetus in the latter half of 1958. The racial attacks in Nottingham and Notting Hill in August and September dramatically publicised the problems of integration and growing public hostility to continuing coloured immigration. In October Sir Alec Douglas Home, Minister of State for Commonwealth Relations, speaking in Vancouver, said that 'curbs will have to be put on the unrestricted flow of immigrants from the West Indies'.[9] Later that same month the Conservative party conference, despite Butler's opposition, passed a resolution favouring immigration control.

Cyril Osborne immediately stepped up his campaign, raising the issue in the debate on the Queen's speech and again in a private member's motion on 5 December, but David Renton, replying for the government, stated that this country was proud to be the centre of an inter-racial Commonwealth, and denied that there was any need for control.[10] However, the *Economist* reported that in many government departments the view was that controls could not be long postponed.[11]

Immigration was not an issue in the general election of 1959, except in one or two local contests like North Kensington where Sir Oswald Mosley stood as the candidate of his own Union Movement. Mosley came bottom of the poll and lost his deposit despite a well-publicised campaign. However, the general election had greatly strengthened the position of those favouring control in the House of Commons, as a strong contingent of Birmingham MPs who favoured immigration control was returned.[12]

Despite the growth in pressure for control, the government remained reluctant to take action. Most ministers still regarded the Commonwealth as a major asset to British standing and diplomacy in the world although doubts as to the value to Britain of the new Commonwealth members had grown after India's strong condemnation of British action over Suez in 1956. The civil service was also divided as the treasury could see strong economic reasons for supporting free entry while other home departments favoured control. In the cabinet Boyle and Macleod were the leading opponents of control and the cabinet appeared unwilling to override their opposition. In July 1960 Butler told the House that 'It is very unlikely that this country will turn away from her traditional policy of free entry'.[13]

In October no provision was made for a debate on immigration at the annual party conference, although there were seven resolutions sent in from constituency associations. On 13 October the Birmingham Immigration Control Association was established and this strengthened the position of those Birmingham MPs who were pressing for control. In December and again in January Harold Gurden organised a series of meetings of backbench MPs to discuss control and lobby the Home Secretary. In February Butler told Gurden he was prepared to consider controls but there was still no agreement in cabinet on the need for positive action and David Renton, again replying to a private member's bill introduced by Cyril Osborne, told the House that the government refused to contemplate legislation which might restrict the historic right of every British subject regardless of race or colour, freely to enter and stay in the United Kingdom.[14]

However, by the summer it was clear that the numbers of immigrants entering Britain had risen dramatically, partly in response to the growing campaign in Britain to restrict entry, and popular concern was reflected in the lobbying of MPs, the resolutions to the Conservative annual conference, and in the opinion polls. In May 1961 the Gallup Poll found 73 per cent in favour of control (6 per cent wanted a total ban on all immigration) and 21 per cent in favour of free entry, with 6 per cent undecided.[15] There were 39 resolutions at the annual conference demanding control, and while Butler made no positive commitment to introduce a bill in reply to the debate, the strength of feeling at the conference and the dramatic rise in numbers convinced the cabinet that action was urgently needed. A bill was hurriedly prepared, the decision to legislate was announced in the Queen's speech on 31 October and the bill was published the following day.

Since control had been considered by the cabinet as early as 1954 and as the Home Office had been asked to prepare legislation in 1955, it is remarkable that the bill presented in 1962 was so rushed and poorly prepared. The government felt the legislation would command general support and were amazed by the opposition the bill received from the Labour and Liberal parties and in the press. Macmillan and Butler were shocked by Gaitskell's furious onslaught on the bill and found it difficult to counter his arguments. Gaitskell argued that immigration was self-regulating and that the substantial increase in immigration had been caused by the wholly artificial conditions created by the growing campaign to introduce controls. Gaitskell also exploited the ambiguities in the bill and the mishandling of the Irish provisions by Macmillan. Despite this opposition to the bill there is no doubt that it commanded widespread support among the electorate.

The conversion of the Conservative party from free entry for all Commonwealth citizens thus coincided with the decline of Britain from a great power with world-wide territories and commitments to a European power which was making more and more insistent attempts to join the EEC, of which full membership was finally achieved on 1 January 1973. Some Conservatives who still believed in the importance of the Empire and of its successor, the Commonwealth, were reluctant to see any weakening of

Commonwealth unity which might result from legislation against Commonwealth citizens. Lady Huggins, the wife of a former governor of Jamaica, gave expression to this view when she said, 'The increase in West Indian immigration in recent years has created domestic difficulties in this country. But what is the Commonwealth worth? Is domestic difficulty here an adequate reason for abandoning the whole concept of the Commonwealth? If we are not prepared to pay that price we shall imperil our whole colonial policy and our whole Commonwealth ideal.'[16] The commitment to the Commonwealth made many of these Conservatives opposed to moves to join the EEC. However, during the 1960s these Conservatives had become increasingly disillusioned with the Commonwealth as the new Commonwealth members refused to show the loyalty and support which Britain had received in the past from the Old Dominions. The Suez crisis in 1956, when Britain was strongly condemned by India in the United Nations for the invasion, and the withdrawal of South Africa from the Commonwealth in 1961 were two important factors contributing to this disillusionment.

Conservatives on the progressive wing of the party had also opposed immigration controls but for rather different reasons from those who wished to maintain imperial traditions. They favoured the transformation of the Empire into the Commonwealth and hoped that a multi-racial Commonwealth would be an important influence in the world and give Britain greater moral authority in world councils. They were opposed to controls because they suggested racial discrimination and colour prejudice. Those Conservatives who most strongly supported controls appeared to be the self-made Conservatives, small businessmen and working-class Conservatives with popular authoritarian views, who belonged to the 'radical right' of the party. These Conservatives were stronger in the constituencies and the electorate than in parliament or the executive committee of the National Union. In parliament their views were supported by MPs usually representing constituencies with substantial numbers of working-class Conservatives, often in areas 'threatened' by an influx of immigrants. The newly-elected MPs for Birmingham could be said to represent this section of the party.

The major factors contributing to the change in Conservative policy were firstly the growing feeling among many ministers that increasing racial tension could only be avoided if controls were introduced. The substantial increase in coloured immigration after

1959 raised more acutely the problems facing local authorities but it was the possible reaction of the indigenous population against coloured immigration, if immigration remained uncontrolled, which concerned members of the government. Secondly, the pressure for control was building up strongly in the National Union to such an extent that party leaders felt concessions had to be made. Thirdly, it also appeared that electorally such legislation would be very popular and although the party leadership was reluctant to make much of this it clearly was an important consideration.

The Commonwealth Immigration Act of 1962 does not seem to have allayed public concern for long. In September 1963 the Southall Residents Association was formed to protest against the increasing numbers of Indians settling in the borough and the growing proportion of immigrant children in Southall schools. In the 1964 general election campaign, immigration control was not an issue in the national campaigns of the parties, although Sir Alec Douglas Home, one of the early converts to control in the cabinet, raised the issue in speeches at Bradford and Birmingham, claiming credit for excluding a million coloured immigrants who would have come to Britain but for the Act.[17] The dramatic importance of the election was, of course, the impact of Peter Griffiths' victory at Smethwick after an anti-immigrant campaign. Griffiths captured the seat with a 7.5 per cent swing to the Conservatives in the face of a national swing of 3.2 per cent to Labour. The Labour party's cautious move away from Gaitskell's total opposition to controls was accelerated by the Smethwick result and completed by Gordon Walker's further defeat at Leyton, where race was thought to be an unspoken issue.[18] The Labour party's about-turn on this issue was dramatic. In less than three years the Labour party had moved from furious opposition to any controls, to acceptance of controls and by 1965 to proposing even tougher controls. Moreover, the Conservatives were criticised for introducing weak and ineffective controls and some Labour candidates were reported to be blaming them for allowing coloured immigration to occur at all![19]

The explanation for Labour's change was largely the fear of electoral disaster. Crossman has argued in his Diaries that 'ever since the Smethwick election it has been quite clear that immigration can be the greatest potential vote loser for the Labour party' and 'We felt we had to out-trump the Tories by doing what they would have done and so transforming their policy into a bipartisan policy'.[20] The smallness of Labour's majority and the likelihood of an early election made Labour leaders determined to remove race as an issue dividing the parties. Labour MPs were also coming under increasing pressure from their own constituents and party members to support immigration control.

There were also signs that the Conservative party, having accepted the need for control, would propose tougher and more effective measures. This was the implication of Sir Alec's speech in Hampstead on 3 February and also of his replacement of Edward Boyle by Peter Thorneycroft as party spokesman on race and immigration, later in the month. Edward Boyle no longer represented party opinion on immigration control and his replacement was probably precipitated by Cyril Osborne's success in the ballot for private members bills—the second consecutive time! Osborne, continuing his campaign as vigorously as ever, announced yet another bill to control immigration, proposing to ban all immigrants except those whose parents or grandparents were born in the United Kingdom. Such a bill would have been anathema to Edward Boyle. Thorneycroft persuaded Osborne to modify the provisions of his bill which was then supported by Sir Alec and many members of the shadow cabinet. On 6 March, shortly after his bill had been defeated by 99 votes, the Central Council passed a resolution in support of further legislation to control immigration. The motion had the support of the shadow cabinet.[21] Cyril Osborne must have felt that his long campaign had finally triumphed in the party!

Since 1962 the Conservative party has adopted a dual approach to the problems of immigration and race relations. The first part of this approach has been an emphasis on firm controls to limit the entry of new immigrants and the conditions under which they were allowed to enter. The second part of the policy was a commitment to positive steps to 'fit into our country those immigrants already here who wish to remain'. 'We are determined', said Sir Alec, 'that every immigrant who comes here is treated like any other British citizen'.[22] However, the Conservative party has given most priority to the first part of the dual policy and tended to ignore the second. The pressures within the party and policy preferences of the electorate have contributed to this bias. Perhaps a prime reason has been the continuing campaign of those opposed to coloured immigration which has increased rather than subsided as tougher controls have been introduced and has also found an oratorical champion in the person of Enoch Powell.

III THE RE-ESTABLISHMENT OF CONSENSUS

This dual approach to immigration and race relations was also adopted by the Labour party. However, Labour appeared to place more emphasis on both sides of the policy equation. The Labour government came to office committed to a Race Relations Bill to outlaw racial discrimination and this was published in April 1965. However, this more even-handed approach went together with a determination not to be outbid by Conservative calls for tougher controls on immigration and a bipartisan policy on immigration and race relations appears to have been established by the end of March. The Commons debate on race and immigration, which was held on 25 March, saw a great deal of unanimity in the speeches on both sides of the House and much self-congratulation on the bipartisanship shown in the debate. The government reaffirmed its commitment to effective control of immigration.

Labour's commitment to the bipartisan approach was endorsed by the white paper entitled 'Immigration from the Commonwealth' published in August, which reduced the quotas of vouchers in a period of acute labour shortage, and strengthened deportation provisions.[23] It confirmed that further substantial immigration from the new Commonwealth was over. Further evidence of the government's determination to remove immigration and race relations as an issue dividing the parties occurred in the autumn when the Race Relations Bill was passed after the government had accepted Conservative proposals to substitute conciliation for criminal sanctions. It was clear that the Labour government was more concerned to impress public opinion with its tough policies on immigration control than it was to outlaw racial discrimination and support those bodies it had created to promote good race relations, like the National Council for Commonwealth Immigrants and the Race Relations Board.

The success of Labour's policy can be seen in the general election of 1966 when Conservative claims that the Labour party had adopted their policies were endorsed by the electorate, at least to the extent that 61 per cent could see no appreciable difference between the parties on the issue.[24] The fact that immigration played such a small part in the general election was also due to Mr Heath's insistence that the issue should not be exploited by Conservative parliamentary candidates. The recapture of Smethwick and other seats where racism was thought to have played a role in the previous general election caused considerable relief and a widespread feeling that the exploitation of race had been eliminated as an election-winning issue.

## IV ENOCH POWELL'S CAMPAIGN

Before the general election of 1964 Enoch Powell does not appear to have been active in attacking Commonwealth immigration. As a minister he defended government policy and when Cyril Osborne approached him in 1958 to support his campaign he refused.[25] After rejoining the government in 1960 he became a firm advocate of control within the cabinet but he did not break collective cabinet responsibility and campaign publicly. In the House of Commons, as Minister of Health, he paid tribute to the work of overseas doctors in British hospitals. It was not until the series of anonymous articles in *The Times* in April 1964 that Powell was to state categorically his disenchantment with the Commonwealth and his opposition to coloured immigration.[26] From 1964 Powell gradually developed his campaign which was to become a major challenge to the party leadership.

The bipartisan approach continued after the election although some Conservatives were concerned at the Home Secretary's plans to extend the Race Relations Act and introduce further anti-discrimination legislation. However, by 1968 immigration and race relations had once again become central issues in British politics. In February, after a campaign by Duncan Sandys and Enoch Powell, the government rushed through legislation restricting the entry of British Asians from Kenya. Although the opposition did not formally oppose the bill, many Conservatives were outraged at the betrayal of promises made by a previous Conservative adminis-tration and every previous Colonial Office minister in both Houses, except Sandys, opposed the legislation.[27] Iain Macleod strongly attacked Sandys' campaign as it was Sandys himself who had been instrumental in providing the loophole for non-African Kenyans to retain British citizenship; although the main aim of the arrange-ment was to safeguard the position of white settlers who might not wish to remain under an African government, it was realised and accepted that the commitment extended to the Asian community as well.[28]

The Conservative opposition was also deeply divided on how to react to the Race Relations Bill which was published by the government at the beginning of April. The bill had enthusiastic supporters on the progressive wing of the party, including some support in the shadow cabinet, but the bulk of party opinion on the back benches and in the constituencies was opposed to the bill. The compromise which was agreed—a reasoned amendment approving the principles of the bill but deploring the measures themselves— was a victory for the anti-immigration Conservatives and a defeat for the liberal progressives, one of whom resigned from the party in protest.[29]

It was in the middle of these deep emotional divisions within the party that Powell made his apocalyptical speech on immigration and race relations which so outraged his colleagues in the shadow cabinet. Heath's immediate dismissal of Powell prevented the disintegration of the shadow cabinet but the enormous publicity that Powell's speech obtained and the widespread popular support it evoked made Powell a major political figure overnight and even a threat to the leader. The popular support for Powell could be measured in the polls, the deluge of letters he received, and the public demonstrations of support. It was clear that Powell's views and Powell himself commanded much wider support in the constituency associations and among the electorate than they did on the Conservative benches in the House of Commons. He had become a factor that the party leader could not ignore. Powell's speech tapped the widespread popular frustration with the bipartisan approach to immigration and race relations which had existed since 1965. There was dissatisfaction with the anti-discrimination legislation which many people did not understand or support. Some felt it gave coloured immigrants a privileged position. Moreover, the growing support for the Monday Club suggested there might be an organised section within the Conservative party which could turn to Powell for leadership.

There was substantial evidence to suggest that Powell's views had considerable support within the party and this was confirmed by the agenda for the annual party conference which included 80 resolutions on immigration and race relations, most of which demanded further controls. In September Mr Heath announced that Commonwealth immigrants should only enter Britain under the same conditions as aliens and that dependants would also be subject to controls. Even this was not enough for Powell who argued at the conference that immigration control was not enough, and he had considerable support, as the official Conservative policy was only narrowly endorsed. He spelt out his views in more detail at Eastbourne in November when he emphasised the importance of re-emigration or repatriation. In January 1969 Mr Heath called for legislation to prevent further settlement by Commonwealth immigrants so that new immigrants would not automatically have the right to bring their dependants with them. This speech anticipated the Conservative government's immigration bill of 1971 and represented the complete abandonment of the ideal of Commonwealth citizenship. Henceforth the citizens of independent Commonwealth countries, unless they were patrials, would be treated as aliens. This was a far cry from the common citizenship which the party had supported twenty years earlier.

The pressures within the party, which had forced the leadership to abandon Commonwealth citizenship and impose tighter and tighter controls, had been considerable. Nevertheless the policies which Mr Heath proposed in 1969 appeared to contradict the fundamental beliefs of many prominent Conservatives, like Lord Hailsham. Every compromise was not enough to satisfy the 'radical right' of the party who felt they had widespread support both within the party and among the electorate. The reasoned amendment to the 1968 Race Relations Bill, which had been adopted to appease the right wing, was not sufficient to prevent 45 Conservative MPs voting against the bill on the third reading. The support for Powell and his views among constituency associations was so substantial that the shadow cabinet made concessions again and again.[30]

## V THE GENERAL ELECTION OF 1970

The party leaders did not exploit the race issue in the general election despite the fact that opinion polls suggested that the Conservative move towards tougher controls was preferred by most electors and that the issue was considered to be the fourth most important in the campaign. Only 26 per cent of Conservative candidates mentioned immigration in their election addresses and only 2 per cent of Labour candidates.[31] The reticence on the Conservative side was largely due to central disapproval of using the issue. Crossman even suggested there was a tacit understanding by the party leaders not to raise the issue in the campaign.[32] The

Conservative manifesto reflected Mr Heath's more recent policy statements. It reaffirmed the commitment to existing Commonwealth immigrants that they could bring in their wives and young children but confirmed Conservative intentions to end further large-scale immigration by ensuring that work permits in the future would not carry the right of permanent settlement for the holder or his dependants and that they would normally only be issued for twelve months.

The most extraordinary feature of the 1970 election campaign was the role of Mr Powell who, though a Conservative candidate, acted as though he were a political force in his own right. His election address, issued early in the campaign, was treated by the press as a manifesto and on the issues of immigration and the Common Market was a direct challenge to the party leadership. It was widely believed that if the Tories lost the election Mr Powell would attempt to gain the leadership for himself. Powell's impact was increased by the virulent attack on him by Wedgwood Benn and in the closing stages of the campaign by Mr Powell's dramatic accusations that there were traitors in the civil service who were concealing from a worried public the true extent of coloured immigration. Mr Heath refused to disown Powell as a Conservative candidate and contented himself with saying that 'I will never use words or support actions which exploit or intensify divisions within our society'.[33] The violence of the language used by Mr Benn against Powell distracted attention from the Conservative leader's embarrassment with his maverick colleague. Powell realised that he would have no chance of serving in a Conservative administration if Mr Heath won the election, but perhaps hoping to succeed the Conservative leader after the likely defeat, he called on his supporters to vote Conservative.

The unexpected Conservative victory enormously strengthened Mr Heath's position in the party and led to Powell's increasing isolation and finally his departure to the Ulster Unionists. However, his role and impact on the result of the election remains difficult to assess. Initial analyses concentrated on Powell's role in mobilising the immigrant vote for Labour and contributing to their substantially higher turnout than in previous general elections.[34] However, the very high swings to the Conservative party in parts of the West Midlands suggested that Mr Powell's campaign had an important local effect in Birmingham and parts of the Black Country. In constituencies in Birmingham with substantial numbers of immigrant voters the effect was beneficial to the Labour party but in other constituencies there were some dramatic swings to the Conservatives, although not consistently in seats where Mr Powell's supporters were candidates.[35] It is extremely difficult to assess the national impact of Mr Powell's campaign. Certainly after his 'rivers of blood' speech in April 1968 the opinion polls showed that the public perceived the Conservative party as being much more restrictive in their immigration policies than the Labour party and these policies were preferred by most of the electorate. One recent analysis of the 1970 election suggests that the national impact of the immigration issue was very substantial and made a considerable contribution to the Conservative victory, but the author admits there may have been other factors contributing to this result.[36]

## VI THE CONSERVATIVE GOVERNMENT 1970–4

The new Conservative administration proceeded to fulfil its policy commitments by introducing the Immigration Act of 1971, which came into force on 1 January 1973. The main provisions of the bill were that employment vouchers would be replaced by work permits which would not carry the right of permanent residence or the right of entry for dependants; secondly, that patrials, that is, people with close connections with the United Kingdom through birth or descent, would be free from all controls. There were also provisions to strengthen the powers to prevent illegal immigration and finally voluntary repatriation was to receive some financial assistance. This legislation appeared to fulfil the Conservative manifesto promise that 'there will be no further large-scale permanent immigration'.

The hope that this legislation would defuse the race issue was brutally shattered on 4 August when General Amin, the President of Uganda, announced the expulsion of Asians from his country. The Ugandan Asian crisis, which received considerable publicity in the press, was a boon to the anti-immigrant organisations within the Conservative party and on the far right. The Monday Club, which had a growing membership and was very hostile to many of Mr Heath's policies, started a 'Halt Immigration Now' campaign and the National Front, exploiting the issue for all it was worth, began a period of growth and electoral advance that continued until 1976. There was considerable lobbying of Conservative MPs by their associations and constituents but the government remained firm and insisted that British commitments should be honoured. The majority of the Ugandan Asians were admitted to Britain although substantial numbers were accepted by India, Canada and other countries.

At the annual party conference in October immigration was not chosen for debate but a resolution on this issue from Hackney South and Shoreditch was placed on the agenda by ballot; it was to be moved by the president of the association, Mr Enoch Powell. Fortunately for the party leaders, the Young Conservatives and Conservative students—who are allowed generous representation at party conferences—determined to mobilise the progressives in the party to defend the government's actions. David Hunt, chairman of the Young Conservatives, moved an amendment to Powell's motion 'congratulating the government on its swift action to accept responsibility for the Asian refugees from Uganda'. The amended motion was carried by a substantial majority.[37] It was a rare victory for progressive Conservatism. However, the defeat infuriated some Conservatives who felt that the Young Conservatives had fixed the result.[38]

Meanwhile there appeared to be increasing cooperation between members of the Monday Club and the National Front, and it appeared that in some cases this was due to National Front infiltration of Club branches. At the Monday Club rally on 16 September in the Central Hall, Westminster, there was ample evidence of National Front participation. At the Uxbridge by-election in December the West Middlesex branch of the Monday Club was dissolved for endorsing the National Front candidate. There also appeared to be support by members of the Club for the anti-Common Market candidate at the Sutton and Cheam by-election.[39] These activities discredited the Monday Club as an influential group within the Conservative party and most of its prominent members quickly resigned. The Club then became increasingly involved in an internal struggle over the leadership which was to leave it a spent force by 1974.

VII DEVELOPMENTS SINCE 1974

Immigration and race relations were overwhelmed by other issues in the general elections of 1974. In February the constitutional crisis between the government and the miners, the three-day week and the defection of Enoch Powell focused public attention on constitutional and economic issues. However, in the analyses of the results the growing importance of Asian and West Indian voters became apparent to both the major parties and this led to a reappraisal of party policy towards these minorities. There had already been requests from constituency associations with significant numbers of immigrant voters for help from Central Office and suggestions from prominent immigrants for the Conservative party to make more positive efforts to appeal to and recruit Asians and West Indians. These factors led to the establishment of an ethnic minorities unit in Central Office. The establishment of the Anglo-Asian and Anglo-West Indian Conservative Societies were early initiatives of the new unit. The Conservative party thus appeared to be moving towards a more positive approach. There were now too many Asian and West Indian voters for the party to ignore and leave to Labour by default.

However, in February 1976 the arrival of Asians from Malawi raised the salience of the immigration issue once more and inspired many of the 140 resolutions on the issue which appeared on the agenda of the annual party conference. Both Mr Whitelaw's speech to the conference and the section on immigration in *The Right Approach* suggested a further hardening of Conservative party policy in order to reduce immigration which had 'increased by a very substantial amount under this government'.[40] Mr Whitelaw did go out of his way to emphasise the commitment of the party to equality of treatment for all immigrants now settled here but argued that a harmonious and multi-racial society could only be promoted if a policy were followed, which was clearly designed to work towards an end of immigration as we have seen it in the post-war years.[41]

In the autumn the Conservative party's policies on immigration and race relations became increasingly confused. On immigration control the party was committed to even tougher policies than those envisaged in the 1971 Act and also to a tighter definition of UK citizenship. On race relations, which had before 1976 been a matter of empty rhetoric, the party appeared to be moving in a positive direction. The decision by the shadow cabinet not to oppose the Race Relations Act (1976), which greatly strengthened previous legislation, suggested that the party leadership wished to support efforts to encourage harmonious race relations and oppose incitement to racial hatred. Mr Whitelaw also gave strong support to the

Federation of Conservative Students' campaign against racialism which was launched in November 1977. However, the efforts to involve the Conservative party in the Joint Committee Against Racialism led to confusion and embarrassment for the party, especially the unprecedented decision by the executive committee of the National Union to overrule Mrs Thatcher and participate against her wishes. It suggested that there was a serious division within the party on the extent to which it should be identified with public campaigns against racialism in cooperation with other political groups.

The controversy over the leaks concerning the Speed proposals and Mrs Thatcher's subsequent statements on immigration have emphasised the divisions within the party and the problems facing party leaders in developing a coherent policy. Mrs Thatcher was clearly under pressure from members of the shadow cabinet, backbenchers and constituency associations who wished her to commit the party to end coloured immigration as quickly as possible and also to exploit the issue for electoral advantage. She was clearly tempted to follow this strategy. However, there were others in the shadow cabinet, in Central Office, and in parliament, who would have preferred priority to be given to solving the problems of racial integration and especially unemployment among coloured youth which they saw as major future sources of division and conflict within society.[42] Many Conservative MPs would welcome a more positive approach as they are aware of the growing numbers of their constituents who are of Asian or West Indian ethnic origin. It is uncertain, at the present time, how these conflicting pressures will be resolved.

## VIII CONCLUSION

The contention by some observers that public hostility to immigration has been created by party politicians in order to achieve electoral advantage is hard to sustain.[43] Certainly some politicians were opposed to coloured immigration almost from its beginning and attempted to mobilise support against it. However, these politicians carried little weight in the highest councils of the Conservative party and had little support among the general body of MPs. Their efforts to influence party policy were unsuccessful for a number of years. The government was more concerned with maintaining a strong economy at home, which would have been held back by an acute shortage of labour without immigration; and it was also determined to create a multi-racial Commonwealth to ease the process of decolonialisation and mitigate the effects of imperial decline.

The government was supported in this policy by two currents of opinion in the Conservative party. Many Conservatives on the right of the party still felt, in the 1950s, that the Empire was an important expression of Britain's greatness and believed, paternalistically, that the mother country had the duty to protect and support, as well as exploit, the various parts of the Empire. While many Conservatives in this tradition were reluctant to accept the 'wind of change' and independence for the colonies, some of them saw the Commonwealth as a continuation of the Empire through which British influence could be maintained. Part of their belief was the ideal of common citizenship throughout the Empire (and Commonwealth)—*civis Britannicus sum*—and to many of these Conservatives the obligations of the mother country outweighed the problems created in Britain by the arrival of relatively small numbers of Commonwealth immigrants. This view was also held by the ministers in charge of the colonies and Commonwealth relations. If the Commonwealth were to be a success, Britain should be seen to take the lead in maintaining Commonwealth ties and obligations. During the early period of migration the immigrants were from colonies in the West Indies and not from independent Commonwealth countries, so legislation barring them from entry would have been unthinkable.

It was only during the 1960s that it became clear that the relationship between Britain and the Old Dominions could not be sustained with the new Commonwealth countries. The Suez crisis, the withdrawal of South Africa from the Commonwealth and the collapse of the Central African Federation showed that the vision of maintaining a dominant role for Britain through the Commonwealth could not be maintained as new Commonwealth countries became the largest group in the Commonwealth. It became clear that many new Commonwealth countries felt they had more in common with the newly independent countries of the Third World than with their old imperial power, and in fact were anxious to prove their independence by criticising British policy. By the middle-sixties many imperial Conservatives were reconciling themselves to a Britain which was increasingly a European power and not a world power. They increasingly came to favour strict immigration controls.

The second body of opinion in the party which opposed immigration controls can be described as liberal progressive. The Conservatives associated with this tradition had a different vision of the Commonwealth from those influenced by the imperial tradition. They supported independence for the colonies as progressive and inevitable and felt that the colonies would only become responsible nations if they were given responsibility. This was also the best way for Britain to maintain good relations with her former colonies. They saw the Commonwealth as a multi-racial forum in a world in danger of serious divisions between rich, white nations and poor, black or brown nations. They were therefore opposed to immigration controls which they saw as racialist and as a danger to their ideal of a multi-racial Commonwealth. Many of them also realised the valuable contribution immigration was making to the British economy and standard of living.

Those Conservatives who campaigned for immigration controls and who were eventually successful in determining party policy belonged to a tradition that was narrowly chauvinistic, and which saw immigration as an invasion of foreigners entering the country and taking the jobs, housing and welfare benefits which belonged to British citizens. They were in the same tradition as those who had opposed Jewish immigration at the turn of the century. They would agree with Powell in his view that 'The West Indian or Asian does not, by being born in England, become an Englishman. In law he is a United Kingdom citizen by birth; in fact he is a West Indian or Asian still'.[44] Cyril Osborne, Norman Pannel and Peter Griffiths represented this view in the Conservative party.

The campaign by Osborne and Pannel initially had very little support in parliament where their efforts to obtain immigration controls met with constant rebuffs. Macmillan's revelations show, however, that their views had more support in the cabinet than was publicly admitted. It was the racial clashes in 1958 which gave considerable impetus to the campaign for control and this campaign stimulated immigration, which added fuel to the campaign. After 1959 the small group of MPs promoting the campaign in parliament were supported by considerable numbers of activists in local Conservative parties and growing support in the opinion polls. The growing campaign in the party and the rise in immigration figures caused the party leaders to introduce the first bill to control

Commonwealth immigration in 1961. Since then the level of immigration control and its administration have become political issues of some electoral importance and the Conservative party has led the way towards accepting populist demands to end coloured immigration as far as possible. The Conservative party has justified the policy of strict controls on the grounds that these are needed to preserve racial harmony and to encourage integration within Britain. But the party has not developed a positive strategy to foster integration or eliminated the discrimination from which the members of the new ethnic minorities suffer. The one advantage Commonwealth immigrants have compared with immigrants from the EEC or southern Europe is that they are British citizens and their growing electoral importance may encourage the Conservative party to develop a more positive approach to the problems facing Britons belonging to the new ethnic minorities.

NOTES

1. *Imperial Policy* (Conservative and Unionist Central Office [CUCO], June 1949) p. 1.
2. *Hansard*, 453, col. 405 (7 July 1948). N. Deakin, 'The British Nationality Act of 1948', *Race* (July 1969) p. 81.
3. Henry Hopkinson, Minister of State for the Colonies, *Hansard*, 532, col. 827 (5 November 1954).
4. *The Right Road for Britain* (CUCO, July 1949) p. 58.
5. House of Commons Library Research Paper no. 56, *Commonwealth Immigration into the UK from the 1950s to 1975—a survey of statistical sources.*
6. e.g. *Hansard*, 563, col. 392 (24 January 1957).
7. H. Macmillan, *At the End of the Day* (Macmillan, 1973) p. 73.
8. The number of resolutions demanding immigration control 1957–61 were:

| | | | |
|---|---|---|---|
| 1957 | 3 | 1960 | 7 |
| 1958 | 6 | 1961 | 39 |

*Agendas and Reports of Conservative Party Conferences 1957–61* (CUCO).
9. P. Foot, *Immigration and Race in Britain Politics* (Harmondsworth: Penguin Books, 1965) pp. 154–5.
10. *Hansard*, 596, col. 1579–80 (5 December 1958). Also cited in Ira Katznelson, *Black Men, White Cities* (Oxford, 1973) p. 127.
11. The *Economist* (29 November 1958).
12. Among newly-elected members who supported control were Leonard Seymour (Yardley), Leslie Cleaver (Sparkbrook), John Hollingsworth (All Saints). Other MPs who supported control were Harold Gurden (Selly Oak), Geoffrey Lloyd (Sutton Coldfield), Martin Lindsey (Solihull), Edith Pitt

(Edgbaston). Two Birmingham MPs strongly opposed to controls were Sir Edward Boyle (Handsworth), Aubrey Jones (Hall Green).

13. *Hansard*, 626, col. 689 (7 July 1960).
14. *Hansard*, 634, col. 2009–19 (17 February 1961).
15. H. Macmillan, op. cit., p. 73.
16. Lady Molly Huggins, 28 April 1959, cited in P. Foot, *The Rise of Enoch Powell* (Cornmarket, 1969) p. 155.
17. D. Butler and A. King, *The British General Election of 1964* (London: Macmillan, 1965) p. 363.
18. L. A. Teear, *Colour and Immigration in British Politics*, M.A. Thesis (unpublished), University of Sussex (1966).
19. P. Foot, *Immigration and Race*, op. cit., pp. 180–1.
20. R. Crossman, *Diaries of a Cabinet Minister* (Hamish Hamilton and Jonathan Cape, 1975) p. 149.
21. P. Foot, *Immigration and Race*, op. cit., pp. 150–2.
22. *The Campaign Guide 1966* (CUCO, 1966) p. 245.
23. *Immigration from the Commonwealth*, Cmnd. 2739 (HMSO 1965).
24. D. Studlar, 'Policy Voting in Britain: The Coloured Immigration Issue in the 1964, 1966 and 1970 General Elections', *American Political Science Review*, 72 (1978) pp. 46–64.
25. P. Foot, *Enoch Powell*, op. cit., p. 35.
26. *The Times*, 1, 2, 3 April. There appears to be wide agreement that the author was Powell. See Foot, *Enoch Powell*, op. cit., p. 29.
27. N. Fisher, *Iain Macleod* (Andre Deutsch, 1973) p. 296.
28. Iain Macleod, 'A Shameful and Unnecessary Act', *Spectator*, 1 March 1963.
29. R. R. James, *Ambitions and Realities, British Politics 1964–70* (Weidenfeld and Nicolson, 1972), part III, p. 180. H. Berkeley, *Crossing the Floor* (London: Allen & Unwin, 1972) pp. 36–7.
30. M. Walker, *The National Front* (Glasgow: Fontana, 1977) p. 111. In December 1968 the Conservative Political Centre conducted a survey to establish the views of their 412 constituency groups. 327 wanted all immigration stopped indefinitely and a further 55 wanted strictly limited quotas of dependants combined with a five-year halt on immigration.
31. D. Butler, M. Pinto-Duschinsky, *The British General Election of 1970* (Macmillan, 1971), pp. 439–40.
32. N. Deakin, J. Bourne, 'Powell, the Minorities and the 1970 Election', *Political Quarterly*, 41 (1970) pp. 399–415.
33. D. Butler, M. Pinto-Duschinsky, op. cit., p. 163.
34. Ibid.
35. Z. Layton-Henry, 'Race, Electoral Strategy and the Major Parties', *Parliamentary Affairs*, XXXI, 3, (1978) pp. 268–81.
36. D. Studlar, op. cit.
37. Conservative Party Conference Report 1972.
38. Interview with Anthony Reed-Herbert, who resigned from the Conservative party after this conference and joined the National Front.
39. M. Walker, op. cit., Ch. 5. D. Humphrey and M. Ward, *Passports and Politics* (Harmondsworth: Penguin Books, 1974), pp. 129–31.
40. *The Right Approach* (CUCO, 1976), pp. 47–8.
41. Conservative Party Conference Report (1976) pp. 40–7.

42. e.g. P. Walker, 'Race the Real Divide', *Guardian*, 4 February 1978; 'The Road of the Crowd', *Spectator*, 15 April 1978.
43. P. Foot, *Immigration and Race*, op. cit., pp. 233–4.
44. Speech to the London Rotary Club, Eastbourne, 16 November 1968.

# Appendixes

1   Net immigration to UK from the New Commonwealth and Pakistan 1962–77[a]

| 1962 (2nd half) | 16,453 | 1970 | 37,893 |
|---|---|---|---|
| 1963 | 56,071 | 1971 | 44,261 |
| 1964 | 52,840 | 1972 | 68,519 |
| 1965 | 53,887 | 1973 | 32,247 |
| 1966 | 48,104 | 1974 | 42,531 |
| 1967 | 60,633 | 1975 | 53,265 |
| 1968 | 60,620 | 1976 | 55,013 |
| 1969 | 44,503 | 1977 | 44,155 |

NOTE
[a] Control of Immigration statistics 1977, Cmnd. 7160 (HMSO 1978).

2   Resolutions to the Conservative Party Conference on immigration and race relations

| 1957 | 3 | 1968 | 80 |
|---|---|---|---|
| 1958 | 6 | 1969 | 31 |
| 1959 | a | 1970 | 19 |
| 1960 | 7 | 1971 | 30 |
| 1961 | 40 | 1972 | 30 |
| 1962 | 1 | 1973 | 54 |
| 1963 | 2 | 1974 | a |
| 1964 | a | 1975 | 17 |
| 1965 | 31 | 1976 | 140 |
| 1966 | 5 | 1977 | 60 |
| 1967 | 0 | 1978 | 31 |

[a] This indicates no conference.

# 4 Devolution

## Vernon Bogdanor

Never have the servants of the state looked at the whole of your complicated interests in one connected view. They have taken things by bits and scraps, some at one time and one pretence, and some at another, just as they pressed, without any sort of regard to their relations or dependencies.

(Burke: Speech on American Taxation)

## I INTRODUCTION—TORY ATTITUDES

The Conservative party is once again the Unionist party in Scotland. Yet its defence of the Scottish Union has not been marked by that unswerving consistency which characterised the struggle against Irish Home Rule before the First World War. In 1950, Winston Churchill flirted with the Scottish nationalists; and in 1968, Edward Heath promised devolution in opposition only to ignore it in office. It took the Conservatives fully ten years from the time of the SNP challenge to become unambiguous Scottish Unionists. This uncertainty of touch can be traced back not only to a basic lack of awareness of Scottish conditions by a predominantly English leadership, but also to the failure to articulate clearly a principle of dispersal of power which ought to be fundamental to Conservatives.

For devolution poses two fundamental questions: the first is whether national unity is best secured by centralised government, or by distributing power between the centre and the component parts of a country; and the second is whether the recognition of a sense of nationality in one of the component parts of a country is compatible with the maintenance of the state itself. These questions, however, are not to be answered by *a priori* reasoning but through a consideration of the circumstances surrounding particular claims.

The Conservative party became Unionist not to defend the 1707 settlement with Scotland which was, after all, a triumph of Whig statesmanship, and therefore not an object of Tory veneration, but to defend Pitt's Union with Ireland. The difference between Tory attitudes to the Union with Scotland and the Union with Ireland can be ascribed surely to factors of national psychology, to the attraction or dislike which the English feel for the other component nations of the United Kingdom. For political attitudes towards these nations have always been indelibly coloured by cultural images; and the Conservative party has always been better disposed to the claims of Scotland than to the demands of Parnell or De Valera. In this, Conservatives were doing no more than reflecting wider English cultural attitudes, for what killed Irish Home Rule in the nineteenth century was less the force of constitutional argument than anti-Irish and anti-Roman Catholic prejudice—'the Anglo-Saxon stereotype of the Irish Celt'[1]—who has always occupied a peculiarly disreputable position in the catalogue of English demonology.

About the Irish Nationalist movement, Conservatives had no doubts—Irish Home Rule was 'repulsive to them because they regard it as the triumph of a movement deeply tainted with Jacobinism'.[2] They could not, therefore, accept Gladstone's contention that Home Rule was itself a policy of conservative character, based upon securing a community of interest between an Irish upper class led by Parnell and the rulers of the Empire. For Conservatives, the Parnellites were men motivated by a deep-rooted antagonism to England, and that antagonism could be assuaged only by separation.

But Scottish nationalism could not be disposed of so easily. For the Scots were not as hostile to the English connection as the Irish seemed to be, and after the failure of the '45, most Scots were willing to accept the Union. But this acceptance was conditional upon the preservation of Scottish institutions, and Scottish Tories, in particular, saw themselves as guardians of the sense of Scottish identity which these institutions sustained. In Scotland it was the Tories who were the nationalists:

For the Tory noble houses and the landed gentry, with their memories of the role their ancestors had played on the stage of history when Scotland was a Stewart Kingdom, it was a matter of

family pride to exalt the past, to cling to tradition, to seek to save
what remained of Scottish ways of life and speech from the
insidious pressure of English influence. It was the Whigs the
Hanoverians, the party led by the professional middle class who
were the anglicisers, the assimilationists in Scotland.[3]

If the Union was an accomplished fact, a solid part of the
established order, and therefore sanctified for the Conservative by
history, how much older were the national traditions of Scotland
which could at any time be endangered by the insensitivity of
London politicians. Contemplating the Union, Sir Walter Scott,
'the outstanding example of what Scottish nationalism meant both
in its depth of feeling and in its practical good sense',[4] found welling
up within him a 'mixture of feelings which I do not attempt to
describe'.[5] In 1808, after a debate in which he had fiercely opposed
alterations in the procedure of the Scottish judicial system, his
companions began to joke about it:

> 'No, no' cried Scott, ' 'tis no laughing matter; little by little,
> whatever your wishes may be, you will destroy and undermine
> until nothing of what makes Scotland Scotland shall remain'.
> And so saying, he turned round to conceal his agitation—but not
> until Mr Jeffrey saw tears gushing down his cheek.[6]

Conservatives then could respect the feelings which animated
Scottish nationalism, and they were therefore able to support
reforms designed to decentralise administration in Scotland. The
creation of the office of Secretary for Scotland in 1885 resulted from
a bipartisan policy; the first holder of the post, the Duke of
Richmond, was a Conservative; and under Conservative administrations, the holder of the office was made a Secretary of State in
1926 and the Scottish Office was moved to Edinburgh in 1939.

But clearly the Conservative party could not support a policy of
Home Rule for Scotland at a time when the *raison d'être* of the
Unionist coalition created in 1886 was opposition to Irish Home
Rule; and so until the Second World War, Scottish nationalism
appeared to be a left-wing cause. The first secretary of the Scottish
Home Rule Association established in May 1886—the date is
significant in relation to Gladstone's espousal of Irish Home Rule—
was Ramsay MacDonald, and its president was Dr G. P. Clark, the
member for Caithness, and the crofters' champion. Later in the

1920s, Scottish nationalism was associated with red Clydeside, with near-Communists such as John Maclean; and Conservative newspapers of the 1920s attempted to discredit nationalism by associating it with 'Bolshevism' and 'Papists'.

## II SCOTTISH NATIONALISM AND ANTI-SOCIALISM

Nevertheless, during all these years, the bulk of the nationalist movement remained moderate, and contented itself with demanding devolution rather than separation. After 1945, the main vehicle for Scottish nationalism came to be the Scottish Convention, an all-party movement for devolution led by John MacCormick. For a brief period, Conservatives and Nationalists became allies in their complaints against the depredations of 'London government'. The Attlee administration adopted an unimaginative attitude towards Scottish claims, and its nationalisation programmes transformed industries hitherto managed in Scotland into branches of London-based public corporations. 'For Scotland', claimed Walter Elliot, a former Secretary of State, 'nationalisation means de-nationalisation'.[7]

Scottish nationalism could thus be harnessed to the anti-socialist chariot. When MacCormick stood in the Paisley by-election in February 1948, he found himself supported not only by Walter Elliot, but by such unlikely figures as Peter Thorneycroft, Reginald Manningham-Buller (later Lord Dilhorne), and Lady Grant (later Lady Tweedsmuir). And, in the election campaign of 1950, Winston Churchill, speaking in Edinburgh, explicitly bid for the nationalist vote.

If England became an absolute Socialist state, owning all the means of production, distribution and exchange, ruled only by politicians and their officials in the London offices, I personally cannot feel that Scotland would be bound to accept such a dispensation. I do not therefore wonder that the question of Scottish home rule and all this movement of Scottish nationalism has gained in strength with the growth of Socialist authority and ambitions in England. I would never adopt the view that Scotland should be forced into the serfdom of Socialism as the result of a vote in the House of Commons. It is an alteration so fundamental in our way of life that it would require a searching review of our historical relations.

But here I speak to the Scottish Nationalists in words, as diplomatic language puts it, of great truth and respect, and I say this position has not yet been reached. If we act together with our united strength it may never arise.

Scotsmen would make a wrong decision if they tried to separate their fortunes from ours at a moment when together we may lift them all to a higher plane of freedom and security. It would indeed be foolish to cast splitting votes or support splitting candidates, the result of which might be to bring about that evil Whitehall tyranny and centralisation, when by one broad heave of the British national shoulders the whole gimcrack structure of Socialist jargon and malice may be cast in splinters to the ground.[8]

Churchill was not in favour of legislative devolution; but he appointed his close friend, James Stuart, as Secretary of State, and Lord Home as Minister of State at the Scottish Office was given instructions to 'quell those turbulent Scots'.[9] A Royal Commission was set up to consider the structure of government in Scotland. Its terms of reference precluded it from advocating devolution, but it recommended further administrative decentralisation to Edinburgh, and this was accepted by the Churchill government.

III   THE COMMITMENT TO DEVOLUTION AND ITS ABANDONMENT

The Conservatives reached their post-war peak in Scotland in 1955 when they secured both a majority of the Scottish seats and a majority of the Scottish vote—the only time that this has been achieved by any party since 1945. By 1966, however, the Scottish Conservatives were in sharp decline, and they had lost within eleven years sixteen seats and 12.4 per cent of their vote in Scotland. At a time when Scotland's economic problems seemed more serious than those of England, the traditionalist attitudes of Scottish Conservatives seemed to have little to offer that was specifically Scottish. Christopher Harvie has suggested that during the period of the Macmillan government, the appearance of the Prime Minister north of the Border 'suggested that the Tories still viewed Scotland as a huge sporting estate, and were only doing their best to keep it that way. Their perception of English politics seemed to be that of the custodians of the picturesque political museum whose exhibits—Clydeside reds and Grousemoor lairds alike—were to be cherished rather than challenged.'[10]

The response of the Scottish Conservatives was to set up a committee under the chairmanship of Sir William McEwan Younger to consider how governmental arrangements in Scotland could be improved. At the same time, a parallel investigation into Scottish government was being carried out by a new Conservative 'ginger group' called the Thistle Group and founded in the summer of 1967. The stated purpose of the Thistle Group was to reintroduce into the Conservative party an element of Scottish awareness which seemed to be lacking, and it issued its first publication a few days after the Hamilton by-election, in which Winifred Ewing succeeded in capturing one of Labour's safest strongholds for the SNP. It received, therefore, a degree of publicity which surprised even its most optimistic members. This pamphlet took the form of a general critique of the Conservative party in Scotland and emphasised the need for a greater awareness of Scottish political identity both in the Conservative party and in British politics generally. Although the pamphlet did not specifically mention devolution, the group came to be regarded as a pressure group for devolution, and just before the Scottish Conservatives' conference at Perth in 1968, the group issued a second pamphlet which contained an article arguing for a Scottish parliament.

It should be emphasised that both the McEwan Younger committee and the Thistle Group began their work well before the Hamilton by-election, and were motivated by a concern for the structure of Scottish government and the fortunes of the Conservative party in Scotland, rather than by the rise of the SNP. Although there were no direct consultations between the two groups, they came to strikingly similar conclusions. They both claimed that the existing structure of government in Scotland was inefficient, because the range of functions for which the Scottish Office was responsible was too wide to be scrutinised properly either by parliament or by ministers, and the system therefore allowed too much power to rest in the hands of civil servants. The Conservative case for devolution, then, was based not upon 'exploitation' of Scotland by England, as claimed by the nationalists, but upon the unsatisfactory nature of governmental arrangements in Scotland.

The party leadership could, of course, have ignored these grass-roots attitudes, especially since there was still considerable hostility to devolution in the Scottish party. But Mr Heath was himself deeply worried by the decline of the Conservative party in Scotland and he told Richard Crossman a week before the Hamilton by-election that 'nationalism is the biggest single factor in our politics today'.[11] If the Conservatives were to regain lost ground, they badly needed a distinctive policy to differentiate themselves from the centralising Socialists and the separatist SNP. In the 'Declaration of Perth' made to the Scottish Conservative conference in 1968, therefore, Mr Heath committed the Conservative party to the principle of a directly elected assembly in Scotland. But this declaration seems to have been made after only perfunctory consultation with the shadow cabinet, and none at all with the parliamentary party. This was to cause serious difficulties later, when English members came to appreciate the nature and extent of the commitment.

Mr Heath's speech at the Perth conference was remarkable in that, coming from a leader thought at that time to be stolid and unimaginative, it contained many of the themes which were to animate British politics in the 1970s. It displayed a far-sightedness which, if circumstances had been more fortunate, could have gone a long way towards dealing with the new issues posed by the nationalists.

Mr Heath began by contrasting the Conservative party's stand for diversity with the pressures in 'a world of mass industrialisation, mass communications and increasingly complex organisation' towards 'uniformity and centralisation'. He instanced the United States where power was seeping away from the states towards the federal government; and Europe, where countries were being asked to merge their sovereignty into a larger unit.

But large institutions caused political alienation, a feeling on the part of many individuals that they were losing control over the shaping of their lives: this led to frustration and resentment towards government. Members of the Labour party, according to Heath, were natural centralisers, and unable to understand the nature of this discontent; the SNP understood it, but proposed an unrealistic remedy which involved sacrificing the gains of centralised economic management together with the losses. 'The art of government', however, was 'to reconcile these divergent needs: the need to modernise our institutions so as to cope with our complex changing society; and the need to give each citizen a greater opportunity to participate in the decisions that affect him, his family, and the community in which he lives'.

If these needs were to be reconciled, a balance had to be found between two fundamental principles. The first was the unity of the United Kingdom which the very name of the Scottish Conservatives—Unionists—showed that they existed to defend; but the second was 'our belief in the devolution of power'. And Mr Heath concluded his analysis by quoting from Quintin Hogg's *Case for Conservatism*:[12] 'Political liberty is nothing else but the diffusion of power. If power is not to be abused, it must be spread as widely as possible throughout the community'.

Mr Heath then proposed that a small constitutional committee be established—'not a Royal Commission, which is too large, too slow, and too cumbersome'—to consider whether an elected Scottish assembly was constitutionally viable, and what form it should take.

When the Labour government rejected this suggestion, Mr Heath himself set up a committee under the chairmanship of Sir Alec Douglas-Home with an impressive membership including Sir David Milne, the vice-chairman, a former permanent under-secretary of state at the Scottish Office; Sir Arthur Goodhart, formerly Professor of Jurisprudence at Oxford; J. D. B. Mitchell, Professor of Law at Edinburgh; and Sir Charles Wilson, Principal of Glasgow University. The two constitutional advisers to the committee were Sir Robert Menzies, the former Prime Minister of Australia, and Sir Kenneth Wheare, then Rector of Exeter College, Oxford, and a leading authority on federal government.

The committee's terms of reference were not, however, wholly clear: was it to consider the case for devolution, or to consider how devolution might be implemented? Mr Heath's declaration would seem to indicate that the latter was the purpose which he had in mind; yet two members of the committee, Professor Mitchell and Sir Charles Wilson, were hostile to the principle of devolution, and unable to accept the committee's report, published in March 1970.

The committee asked itself whether it were possible, while preserving 'the essential principle of the sovereignty of parliament'[13] to meet the 'very reasonable desire of the majority of the people of Scotland to have a greater say in the conduct of their own affairs'.[14] These considerations could, it appeared, be reconciled, but only if the proposed Scottish assembly were 'to be a natural evolution and extension of parliamentary practice as we know it'.[15] It should therefore be a part of the Westminster machinery—the equivalent of a third chamber of parliament dealing with the second reading, committee and report stages of Scottish bills, thus taking over much of the work done by the Scottish standing committees and the Scottish Grand Committee. Parliamentary sovereignty would, according to the committee, be preserved, since the third reading of Scottish bills and the legislative stages in the Lords would still remain at Westminster.

If the proposed assembly, or convention, were to yield a genuine improvement in the machinery of government in Scotland, and act as a focus for Scottish opinion, it had to be directly elected. Otherwise it would be dominated by the local authorities and, according to Sir William McEwan Younger, the reorganisation of local government in Scotland would not itself lead to decentralisation. 'The effect could, in practice, very well be the opposite. If no other body is interposed, these much larger units could easily become an instrument of greater, even of much greater, centralisation'.[16]

The central advantage of the proposed reform was that it did not make too great a breach with existing constitutional practice. The unitary system of government could continue unchallenged, and there would be no case for reducing Scotland's representation in the Commons. A critic, however, might complain that the proposed remedy was hardly proportionate to the serious weaknesses in the government of Scotland which the committee itself had diagnosed. For example, the committee showed itself anxious that decision-making on Scottish industrial matters should be speeded up. 'Long delays in deciding on matters which seriously affect the level of Scottish employment and generally influence the Scottish standard of living cannot be tolerated.' And the committee found itself 'particularly impressed by evidence of the operations of the Northern Ireland Ministry of Commerce—and especially by the speed of its decision-making'.[17] Yet what was proposed fell far short of the Stormont model. The Scottish convention would have little power to prevent delays in decision-making; for it would be a purely legislative body without any executive powers. It is not indeed wholly clear from the arguments presented by the committee why it did not proceed to recommend full-scale legislative devolution.

It could also be argued that the committee placed rather too much emphasis upon legislative activity as an influence upon government; for parliamentary activity is a far less important vehicle of political influence than the gaining of a share in the formation of public policy. By the time a bill is presented before parliament, its main outlines have usually been agreed after consultations between government departments and the relevant interest groups, and governments will generally be unwilling to re-open the package at the request of parliament. Yet the Scottish convention proposal did not offer Scotland an improved role in the process of policy formation, since Scotland's executive would remain responsible to parliament and not to the convention. Moreover, any legislative proposals made by the convention could be overturned at Westminster, and this might exacerbate conflict and cause yet further disillusionment with London governments.

The viability of the proposal depended upon a presumption of goodwill and consensus in Scotland. 'Our proposal', the committee stated, 'does involve an act of faith in the commonsense, objectivity, and tolerance of Scottish people'.[18] But would such 'commonsense, objectivity, and tolerance' be able to sustain a directly-elected convention whose majority was different from that at Westminster, especially when it was in the interest of one of the parties which would be represented at the convention—the SNP—so to exacerbate conflict as to secure political pressure for separation?

The committee, however, argued that conflict would be lessened, because Scottish legislation 'in the main consists of legislation which is not unduly controversial'.[19] But this meant that the Scottish convention would not be given the powers to deal with the issues that really worried Scots voters and had tempted them to turn to the SNP; for such issues were, almost by definition, controversial in their nature. If the convention was to be restricted to bills of a merely technical kind, it would hardly be likely to attract the interest of the general public, or to assuage Scottish discontent. It would, therefore, either be revealed as a talking-shop, or it would intensify bitterness in Scotland.

Nevertheless, these objections to the scheme need not have been fatal. For the establishing of the convention would itself be in the nature of a symbolic act, signalling to the Scottish electorate that Westminster would take more notice of the Scottish point of view. Once the principle of a directly-elected assembly was accepted, perhaps the particular kind of assembly that was actually established was an issue of smaller importance; and perhaps the setting up of an assembly might have succeeded in pre-empting the rise of the SNP.

It is difficult to estimate the extent of the support amongst Scottish Conservatives for the Douglas-Home proposals. They certainly secured some surprising adherents: Mr Alex Fletcher, later a fervent anti-devolutionist, had come out in favour of an elected assembly as early as November 1968, and Mr Teddy Taylor welcomed the Douglas-Home committee's report as offering 'an exciting new prospect for the nation's administration and economic future'.[20] But many observers believed that grass-roots opinion was hostile. Mr Charles Graham, the chief leader writer of the *Scottish Daily Express*, complained that the Scottish Tories 'even reject, in large numbers, Ted Heath's very moderate plan for a Scottish assembly'[21]; and Mr Robert Black, at the time prospective parliamentary candidate for North Lanark, complained: 'It is a comment on Scottish Conservatives' political awareness that they have been offered something of a political gift horse and can't even recognise it as such'.[22] Nevertheless, the Conservative election manifesto of 1970 promised that the Douglas-Home report, including the 'Scottish convention sitting in Edinburgh, will form a basis for the proposals we will place before parliament, taking account of the impending re-organisation of local government', and the Queen's Speech in July 1970 promised that plans would be produced 'for giving the Scottish people a greater say in their own affairs'.

But the Conservative government of 1970–4 made no move to establish the Scottish assembly, since it felt itself compelled to wait for the report of the Royal Commission on the Constitution set up by the Wilson government in 1969; for, if the Conservatives had proceeded with legislation on devolution, the Commission intended to resign, and this would have caused the government considerable embarrassment. In 1970, the Commission's report was expected to appear within the year. In the event, it was delayed until October 1973, by which time Britain was in the grip of the rise in oil prices following the Yom Kippur war, and governments had other things to think about.

Instead of devolution, the Conservatives decided to proceed with local government reform in Scotland along lines advocated by the Wheatley committee which reported in 1969. Local government reform in itself need not have precluded devolution, but the particular reform proposed by Wheatley involved a two-tier system of local government in Scotland, the upper tier consisting of regions, the largest of which, Strathclyde, would contain nearly half of the population of Scotland. Such a local government structure would almost certainly not have been adopted if local government reform had been seen in the context of devolution. Indeed, on 13 October

1975 Mr Malcolm Rifkind, then a front-bench spokesman, claimed: 'We find it inconceivable that Strathclyde could long survive the assembly. It cannot be desirable that the assembly should operate alongside a local authority that covers a massive geographical area and over half the population of Scotland.[23]

As we have seen, the Conservative commitment had been to establish a Scottish assembly, *'taking account of the impending reorganisation of local government'* and, since Wheatley reported in 1969, it cannot be said that local government reform was a new issue, or one that confronted the Conservative government unexpectedly. Indeed, the committee chaired by Sir William McEwan Younger had written to Sir Alec Douglas-Home when the constitutional committee was established, saying:

> We feel most strongly that whilst any proposals for the reform of the central government mechanism must be seen in the context of a reformed local government structure, they must not be subordinated to it. The mechanism of government in Scotland must be settled first, and the local government structure must then be designed as a coordinated component of that mechanism.[24]

For the most natural way to reform Scottish local government, if devolution were seriously intended, would be to allow a Scottish assembly, as the representative body of Scotland, to put forward and discuss its own proposals, rather than presenting it with a *fait accompli*.

Mr Geoffrey Smith has argued that the failure of the Heath government to implement its promise of a directly-elected assembly was due 'like so much else in that government's record, to three factors: an imperfectly considered promise, bad timing, and bad luck'.[25] The probability is that at no time during the government's period of office did devolution seem an urgent priority. The SNP had failed to make gains in the general election of 1970; and until late 1973, it did not seem a serious threat in Scotland. Perhaps if the Secretary of State for Scotland had been a strong political personality, the issue would have been pressed in cabinet, but Mr Gordon Campbell, who held the office, lacked the weight, and also the political backing, as the representative of a minority party in Scotland, to press such proposals, and his permanent under-secretary of state, Sir Douglas Haddow, was widely thought to favour local government reform as an alternative to devolution. Moreover, Conservative opinion in Scotland was becoming markedly hostile to devolution, and in 1973 the Scottish Conservative conference turned down by a large majority a proposal to establish a directly-elected assembly.

In the February 1974 general election, the Scottish Conservatives lost four seats to the SNP, and Mr Campbell himself was defeated by Mrs Winifred Ewing. The Conservative share of the vote in Scotland slumped from 38 per cent to 32.9 per cent, and was lower than it had been even in 1966. The new shadow secretary of state for Scotland, Mr Alick Buchanan-Smith, was, however, a confirmed devolutionist, and he proceeded to set up a devolution committee to rethink the party's commitment. But the 1974 Scottish Conservative conference at Ayr marked a further retreat in that the party now committed itself only to an indirectly elected assembly, and in the Conservative party's Scottish manifesto for the October election, it was stated that 'Initially the assembly's membership will be drawn from the elected members of the new local authorities though direct elections could evolve in the future'.

The October election, however, marked a further decline in the fortunes of the Scottish Conservatives. They lost five more seats in Scotland, four more to the SNP and one to Labour and now held only 16 of the 71 Scottish seats. The Conservative percentage of the vote in Scotland fell by a further 8.2 per cent to 24.7 per cent, nearly 6 per cent behind the support for the SNP. After this election Mr Buchanan-Smith immediately proposed a directly-elected assembly for Scotland although, in contrast to the Labour proposals, the assembly would lack a separate executive, and it would approximate to the local government style of organisation. Yet another committee, chaired by Malcolm Rifkind, MP for Edinburgh Pentlands, was set up to work out precise proposals. But Conservative plans were again put in the melting pot when, in February 1975, Mrs Thatcher became leader of the party.

It is generally assumed that Mrs Thatcher's succession to the leadership was the crucial factor leading to the abandonment of the Conservative commitment to devolution. But that is only a partial explanation. For both the change of leadership and the abandoning of the commitment were themselves consequences of back-bench dissatisfaction with the personality and style of leadership offered by Mr Heath. Not only had he lost two elections in rapid succession, but in the later phase of his administration he had, in the view of many back-benchers, strayed far from the tenets of traditional Conservatism.

It is obviously impossible to know whether, if Mr Heath had retained the leadership, the commitment to devolution would also have been retained. It had always sat lightly upon the shoulders of Conservative MPs; it had 'never really entered the party's bloodstream. It did not become part of the essential being of a Conservative.'[26]

On 19 January 1976 Mr Whitelaw, then the party's spokesman on devolution, argued that English Conservatives, who comprised 253 out of the 277 Conservative MPs, 'have only now started to give their minds to the problem. It is as if English members—and certainly our constituents—have awoken to the cold realities of a morning which many find extremely unwelcome. This is irritating the Scottish and Welsh members, who have been living with the problem for many years.'[37]

Mr Heath had done little to prepare English Conservatives for devolution, and this was partly because, until he lost the leadership, he was offering only devolution of a very limited kind; but it was a result also of his high-handed methods with back-benchers. Ronald Bell was surely speaking for many when he said of Mr Heath, 'He thinks that if something is discussed in the policy committee of the Conservative party, which is a very small body, it is somehow percolated and permeated through the whole party, and we all know about it. That is a lot of rubbish.'[28]

A major difficulty—perhaps *the* major difficulty—in securing a satisfactory constitutional settlement in Scotland has always been the difference in time-scale between Scotland and England. A reform which then seemed to many Scots to be one of some urgency was seen by English members as calling for leisurely and prolonged consideration before action could be taken. When English members came to be aware of the implications of devolution they were almost unanimously hostile, as were the Welsh Conservatives. Even the sixteen Scottish Conservative MPs were deeply divided on the issue, and little love was lost between the factions.

It could, however, be argued that skilful leadership might have helped persuade English and Welsh MPs not to oppose Scottish devolution but to allow a free vote on the issue. But under Mrs Thatcher's leadership the opposition of English MPs to devolution hardened, because of her known attitude, to hostility. Nevertheless Mrs Thatcher was very loth during the early months of her leadership to overthrow any of Mr Heath's commitments. Realising that many of the senior members of the party had been opposed to her campaign for the leadership, she was determined to tread cautiously, even though her basic instincts were hostile to devolution. At the Scottish Conservative conference in 1976, both she and Mr Whitelaw, the deputy leader of the party, reaffirmed their support for a directly-elected Scottish assembly; and consequently the pro-devolutionists were able to beat off a strong challenge from a 'Scotland is British' committee set up by Mr Iain Sproat, the member for South Aberdeen, Mr Michael Clark Hutchison, the member for Edinburgh South, and Miss Betty Harvie Anderson, the member for East Renfrewshire and a respected senior backbencher.

In December 1976, however, the shadow cabinet had to determine its attitude to the Labour government's Scotland and Wales bill. After a very long argument, the shadow cabinet decided to issue a three-line whip opposing the bill, although it was prepared to conciliate Mr Buchanan-Smith by first putting forward a reasoned amendment to it. For it sought desperately to preserve unity in the party by reaffirming its general commitment to devolution, while rejecting the Labour government's proposals.

This attempt at compromise did not work, however, since Mr Buchanan-Smith refused to vote against the Scotland and Wales bill on second reading on the grounds that, however defective the bill itself might be, a second reading vote was a vote on the principle of devolution, and therefore a vote against would be interpreted in Scotland as a vote against devolution. He resigned from the shadow cabinet, and was replaced by Mr Teddy Taylor, now a fervent unionist, and representing a know-nothing populist version of Conservatism whose connection with any of the historic tenets of the party remains obscure. After the defeat of the guillotine motion on the Scotland and Wales bill, abortive all-party talks on devolution were begun, and in May 1977 Mr Pym announced that the Conservative commitment to devolution was now 'inoperative' although he also indicated that the party would be prepared to examine various other forms of devolution, varying from a mild tinkering with the Grand Committee system to a full-scale federal structure. Mr Pym called for all-party talks to examine the various options and, in December 1978, in a pamphlet published shortly before the beginning of the referendum campaign, he insisted that

. . . the people of Scotland should be aware that the Scotland Act is not the only possible form of devolution . . . Other viable schemes are available, and if the Scotland Act is rejected the Conservative party will ensure that these are considered and that the changes that are made as a result will actually overcome existing defects in the government of Scotland without creating a whole new range of problems for its relationship with the rest of the UK.[29]

During the referendum campaign, Lord Home, the Conservative who, in the eyes of many, had done the most to educate the party to the need for devolution in Scotland, advised rejection of the Scotland Act, on the grounds that it did not secure proportional representation in the elections to the proposed Assembly, and that it did not give the Assembly revenue-raising powers. It would be better, in his view, for the proposals to be returned to parliament for further consideration rather than endorse legislation so fundamentally flawed as the Scotland Act. Mrs Thatcher also opted for this approach, and ensured Scottish electors that a 'No' majority in the referendum would not be interpreted to mean a rejection of devolution.

The result of the referendum—a narrow 'Yes' majority, 32.85 per cent compared with a 'No' vote of 30.78 per cent, and falling far short of the 40 per cent requirement laid down by parliament—would seem to indicate that most Conservatives followed Mrs Thatcher's advice. For there were 'Yes'· majorities only in the central belt of Labour–controlled regional authorities, and in the Highlands and the Western Isles. The issue of devolution had become intertwined with the survival of the Labour government, and the collapse of Labour popularity in Scotland following a winter of industrial disruption put paid to chances of implementing the Scotland Act. There was, moreover, a deep public scepticism as to the value of further institutional change, and a yearning for stability and the retention of familiar landmarks. Mrs Thatcher shared this feeling, and identified herself with it, sensing accurately the public mood of disenchantment. To that extent, the referendum result confirmed her political judgment that the Scotland Act could be defeated and Mr Callaghan's government humiliated, through determined Conservative opposition.

Yet the verdict of the electorate in Scotland can be seen as a Unionist triumph only in a very superficial sense. The Conservative

Party may find itself embarrassed by its commitment to consider alternative forms of devolution following the repeal of the Scotland Act, since many Conservatives remain opposed to devolution in any shape or form. Moreover, Parliament may be unwilling to give detailed consideration to further devolution legislation, having already spent two years on the subject; nor can there be any guarantee that an improved version of devolution can be found, eliminating the flaws of the Scotland Act while still capable of securing a majority in the Commons.

More fundamentally, the Conservative government has to confront a situation in which a Scottish majority, however narrow, has voted for devolution while Westminster is unprepared to grant it. Such a polarisation of opinion between England and Scotland might well benefit the SNP, rather than the Conservative party, and the Conservatives may find it difficult to govern a Scotland in which they continue to hold only a minority of seats— 22 out of 71 in the general election of 1979. It cannot be said, therefore, that the repeal of the Scotland Act offers a final settlement of the constitutional issue raised by devolution.

## IV THE ROLE OF THE LEADER

The course of events just described well illustrates McKenzie's dictum that in the Conservative party, 'when appointed, the leader leads and the party follows, except when the party decides not to follow—then the leader ceases to be leader'.[30] The leader of the Conservative party is given what amounts to very nearly a *carte blanche* to make policy, so long as his authority is accepted. In 1968, Mr Heath was perfectly at liberty to decide whether he would or would not respond to the pressures for devolution in Scotland. In deciding to do so, there is no evidence that he was in any way influenced by back-benchers, by the party machinery, or by outside pressures. Yet always in the background of Conservative politics there lies the implicit threat of veto on the part of back-benchers when the leader's electoral prowess is seen to be failing, or when the traditional sentiments of Conservatives are outraged. The switch in the party's policy in 1976–7 owes just as much to the force of English back-bench opinion as to the change of leadership, and if Mrs Thatcher's instincts had not been in tune with that opinion, she would have found it a difficult task to win the support of English

MPs for devolution. The back-bench power of veto is something that generally lies dormant in the Conservative party, a reason why it often goes unnoticed by political commentators—but a wise Conservative leader will take good care to ensure that it is never exercised.

After losing the leadership, Mr Heath showed a more powerful commitment to devolution than many had suspected; he has committed himself to a federal solution for Scotland, and argued in favour of an assembly for Wales, although in 1969 he had forbidden Mr Gibson-Watt, then shadow Welsh secretary, from giving evidence to the Royal Commission on the Constitution, something which the Labour party has continually cited to support its claim that the Conservatives do not care about government in Wales.

Thus the issue of devolution became entangled in the dispute over the leadership, and it could be argued that Mr Heath's support for devolution has been a mixed blessing to other Conservative devolutionists. In these events, one can perhaps see a new pattern in Conservative politics, a pattern hitherto confined to the Labour party, whereby personal differences become transmuted into ideological disputes through a process which makes compromise and the recovery of party unity exceedingly difficult to attain.


## V DEVOLUTION AND CONSTITUTIONAL CHANGE

Much of the literature on devolution has been concerned with the shortcomings of the Scotland and Wales Acts, and the process of political expediency through which the Labour party became the party of devolution, although its instincts told it that the success of social democracy rested upon centralisation; since only a powerful central government could ensure that the distribution of economic resources between different regions of the United Kingdom was based upon considerations of need, rather than upon regional political pressures.

Yet if the Labour party's record is a chequered one, it is doubtful if many Conservatives are proud of their own party's record on devolution. For the Conservative party seems to have been unable to pursue any consistent policy for very long; and the basic principles which should animate Conservative policy toward Scotland and Wales have never been clearly defined. The Conservatives might have adopted either of two alternative strategies: they could have offered a full-blooded defence of the Union, stressing the benefits to be obtained from a revival of British patriotism; or they might have welcomed devolution as an aid to the dispersal of power which, by removing decisions on matters such as pay beds and comprehensive schools away from central government entirely, would prevent the imposition of socialist policies at national level. But the party preferred to adopt a policy of ambiguity, supporting devolution in theory while opposing it in practice. It has been unwilling to lay before the electorate any constructive picture of the kind of society it seeks to create. Instead of grappling with the complex problems raised by the advance of the SNP, and the need to combat over-centralised government, the Conservative party preferred to adopt a policy which, by clouding the issue, could secure the support both of devolutionists and anti-devolutionists. The success of such a tactic must depend upon the future course of events in Scotland. If the SNP disappears, it will be said that the party kept its head, while all around them panicked; but if Scottish devolution returns to haunt British politics as Irish Home Rule tormented an earlier generation, then the Conservatives will stand exposed to the accusation drawn up two hundred years ago by Edmund Burke against a Tory government unwilling to devolve power to the American colonies, the accusation 'of not having large and liberal ideas in the management of great affairs'.[31]

NOTES

1. L. P. Curtis Jnr, *Anglo-Saxons and Celts* (Bridgeport, Conn., 1964) p. 103.
2. Lord Hugh Cecil, *Conservatism* (London: Williams and Norgate, 1912) p. 241.
3. Sir Reginald Coupland, *Welsh and Scottish Nationalism* (London: Collins, 1954) p. 246.
4. Ibid.
5. Scott's phrase in the introduction to his *Minstrelsy of the Scottish Border*, (London: Harrap, 1971) p. 70.
6. J. G. Lockhart, *Life of Sir Walter Scott*, vol. i (Paris: C. A. & W. Galignani & Co., 1838) p. 299.
7. Quoted in William Ferguson, *Scotland: 1689 to the Present*, (London: Oliver and Boyd, 1968) p. 388.
8. R. Rhodes James (ed.), *Winston S. Churchill: His Complete Speeches, 1897–1963*, vol. viii, 1950–63 (New York: Chelsea House, 1974) pp. 7937–8, Election Address, February 14, 1950.
9. Lord Home, *The Way the Wind Blows*, (London: Collins, 1976) p. 103.
10. C. Harvie, *Scotland and Nationalism*, (London: Allen & Unwin, 1977) pp. 182, 184.

11. R. Crossman, *Diaries of a Cabinet Minister*, vol. ii (London: Hamish Hamilton and Jonathan Cape) pp. 550–1.
12. Quintin Hogg, *The Case for Conservatism*, (London: Penguin Books, 1947, rev. ed. 1959).
13. *Scotland's Government*: The Report of the Scottish Constitutional. Committee, (Edinburgh, 1970) p. 62.
14. Sir William McEwan Younger, in *New Scotland*, no. 15, (Summer 1970).
15. *Scotland's Government*, preface, p. v.
16. *New Scotland*, op. cit.
17. *Scotland's Government*, op. cit., p. 41.
18. Ibid., p. vi.
19. Ibid., p. 65.
20. Quoted in *New Scotland*, op. cit., no. 15 (Summer 1970).
21. Ibid., no. 8 (April 1969).
22. Ibid., no. 11 (July 1969).
23. Press release by the Scottish Conservative party.
24. Quoted in G. Smith, 'Devolution and not saying what you mean', *Spectator* (26 February 1977).
25. Ibid.
26. G. Smith, 'The Conservative Commitment to Devolution', *Spectator* (19 February 1977).
27. *Hansard*, vol. 1046 (House of Commons) col. 903.
28. Ibid., vol. 903, col. 623, 15 January 1976.
29. Francis Pym, MP, and Leon Brittan, MP, *The Conservative Party and Devolution*, (Scottish Conservative Party December 1978) pp. 1–2.
30. R. T. McKenzie, *British Political Parties*, (London: Mercury Books, 1970) p. 145.
31. E. Burke, *Speeches and Letters on American Affairs*, (London: Everyman, 1961) p. 8, Speech on American Taxation.

# 5 The European Economic Community

## Nigel Ashford

I CONSERVATIVES AND EUROPE 1945–75

*'With Europe but not of Europe' 1945–61*

In the immediate post-war period the Conservatives were seen on the Continent as the great hope for the idea of European unity in Great Britain. The Labour government of Attlee appeared ignorant, uninterested and sometimes even hostile to the European movement. In contrast, Winston Churchill gave the movement great impetus with his Zurich speech of September 1946, when he called for the creation of 'a kind of United States of Europe'.[1] The United Europe Movement was launched in 1947, largely at the instigation of Conservatives, especially Duncan Sandys, Churchill's son-in-law, who persuaded him to become chairman. A strong Conservative delegation attended the Congress of the Hague in 1948, which launched the Council of Europe. At the Council's Parliamentary Assembly, the Conservatives played an active role, nicknamed 'the Tory Strasbourgers'. In 1948 a motion in favour of federalism was signed by 60 Conservative MPs. When the Schuman Plan was launched for the European Coal and Steel Community, the Conservatives urged participation in the discussions, and attacked the Labour government for their hostility.

Many Europeans, both in Britain and abroad, were thus very disappointed when the new Conservative government, elected in 1951, failed to participate in the European initiatives. Churchill's attitudes had been widely misunderstood. In his Zurich speech he had talked of Britain as one of 'the friends and sponsors' of a united Europe, not as a member. His participation in European affairs had been at the encouragement of others, such as Sandys, although he soon appreciated that this was an arena where he could act as an international statesman. His attitude was clearly expressed in 1953 when he told the House of Commons that Britain was with Europe but not of Europe. Conservative policy was based on the concept of Britain at the centre of three interlocking circles: the USA, the Commonwealth and Europe. For Conservatives Europe was one of the circles, with a certain degree of importance, in contrast to the attitude of the Labour party, and there was an active body of Conservative MPs including Sir David Maxwell-Fyfe and Harold Macmillan in the Cabinet who sought to place greater emphasis on the European circle. However, both Churchill and his Foreign Secretary, Anthony Eden, who together dominated Conservative foreign policy for most of the 1950s, viewed Britain as still a great world power. Eden, in particular, was very unsympathetic to the idea of European unity, failing to participate in the United Europe Movement and coming out against a European Army.

Conservative policy until 1961 was to support European co-operation at an intergovernmental level, while resisting any moves towards supranational structures. The 1950s were marked by a series of Conservative attempts to prevent a divided Europe, as federalist forces on the Continent gained strength. In 1954 Eden proposed that the Coal and Steel Community should be within the auspices of the Council of Europe; in 1956 the Grand Design proposed that the institution of the Six should be incorporated with the intergovernmental institutions such as the Council of Europe and the Western European Union; in 1956 the government wanted a free trade area (FTA) for the whole of Western Europe, to avoid the more far-reaching integration of the Treaty of Rome; and the European Free Trade Area (EFTA) was created as a block to build a bridge with the EEC. Many Conservative MPs, through their participation in the Council of Europe and the Western European Union, came to understand and share the impulses for European unity, but Eden failed to understand these forces and continued to look warily on European developments.

## The First Application 1961–63

The decision for Britain to join the European Economic Community was the personal decision of Harold Macmillan. This is not the appropriate place to discuss the reasons for his decision but they included the decline of Britain as a world power; the declining value, both politically and economically, of the Commonwealth; the weak economic situation marked by 'stop-go'; the unexpected success of the EEC; and the shift of opinion in informed circles of Whitehall, business and the media. Another element in the decision was the need to provide new inspiration and energy to the Conservative government, and give the party an exciting and progressive policy to win votes, especially of the young, in the next election.

The problem was to win the support of all sections of the Conservative party for the new policy of membership. For years the Conservative leaders had argued that British vital interests conflicted with full participation in European integration. The major difficulties hindering membership were four: EFTA, the Commonwealth, agriculture and sovereignty. None of these difficulties were as great as they seemed: some members of EFTA would join the EEC if Britain joined, and agreements could be made to protect the interests of others; the Commonwealth was no longer so dependent on trade with Britain and special conditions could be achieved for the developing nations as existed for the former French colonies; a common agricultural policy had not yet been adopted by the EEC although the principle to have a common policy had been accepted; and the EEC had been less supranational in practice than British governments had feared. The problem was that this was not the situation that the party leadership had been presenting to the party membership. Macmillan decided on a strategy of 'softly, softly', or as Neustadt aptly puts it, he acted 'by disguising his strategic choice as a commercial deal'.[2] The decision to apply was sold in stages, firstly just as discussions about whether to begin negotiations, then negotiations just to discover the conditions, and then discussions on improving the conditions, and only then would a decision to apply actually be made. Of course, Macmillan knew that the credibility of the government would become dependent on the success of the application, and thus the pressures for acceptance by the cabinet would be very great.

The second element of his strategy was to lay down certain conditions of membership, based on the four problem areas. Macmillan knew that the spirit of these conditions was in contradiction to membership of the Community. Gradually these conditions became weaker and less specific, until they became little more than a request for confidence. Thus Macmillan was able to

obtain the acquiescence of the Commonwealth and the National
Farmers' Union, even if not their support. Edward Heath, the
negotiator in Brussels, was able to demonstrate a genuine attempt to
protect their interests.

The third element was to ensure that no major figure in the party
would publicly oppose his policy. A cabinet reshuffle in July 1960
had placed pro-Europeans in certain key positions: Lord Home as
Foreign Secretary, Edward Heath, Lord Privy Seal, as Minister for
Europe, Duncan Sandys as Commonwealth Secretary, Christopher
Soames as Minister for Agriculture and Peter Thorneycroft as
Minister of Aviation. There were three potential sources of
opposition within the cabinet. Rab Butler was unsympathetic to
Europe (his autobiography does not even mention the European
Community), so Macmillan appointed him chairman of the
committee to oversee the negotiations where he was able to express
his concern about the situation of his agricultural and horticultural
constituents in Saffron Walden. By co-opting Butler into the
negotiations, Macmillan added to Butler's natural sense of the
importance of unity in the party together, perhaps, with his natural
ambition to follow Macmillan as party leader. Butler gradually
became committed to the policy. Lord Hailsham, Lord Chancellor,
was the second possible source of opposition, but he was attracted to
European unity as the defence of Western Christian values, even if
uncomfortable with the technicalities of economic cooperation.
Perhaps a simple lack of interest in the question prevented him from
playing any role, either for or against. The third possible source was
Reginald Maudling, who favoured the free trade area, but as he
doubted that the negotiations would succeed he concentrated on his
portfolio as Colonial Secretary. So no major cabinet figure strongly
opposed the step-by-step decisions, even though several were
markedly unenthusiastic. The consequence was that no member of
the government, not even a parliamentary private secretary,
resigned over the final decision to apply for membership.

The final element of Macmillan's strategy was an active
campaign to convert the party activists, through a series of
publications and meetings. The 1961 party conference in Brighton,
which immediately followed the start of the negotiations in Brussels,
endorsed the policy as a question of confidence in the government.
The real campaign was concentrated on ensuring overwhelming
support at the 1962 conference in Llandudno. Exceptionally,
Macmillan published a pamphlet, called *Britain, the Commonwealth*

*and Europe*,[3] designed to influence the conference vote (as the party leader traditionally spoke only at the end). An excellent speech by Butler attacking Labour led to an overwhelming vote in favour of Britain's membership, with only 50 delegates voting against. Thus Macmillan obtained the endorsement of the party that he wanted.

The traditional interpretation of the change of policy in favour of Community membership by the Conservative party is that it was a demonstration of the tremendous power of the Conservative leader to determine his party's policy. This interpretation, however, ignores important factors. Firstly the existence of a strong European lobby within the party has not been given the importance that it deserves. In the cabinet there was a group of ministers who were far more enthusiastic Europeans than either Macmillan or Heath. Duncan Sandys, Lord Kilmuir, Christopher Soames and Peter Thorneycroft had long been publicly committed Europeans. In the parliamentary party there was an active group of Europeans, many of whom had been on parliamentary delegations to the Council of Europe or Western European Union, and throughout the fifties there had been motions and amendments from Conservative MPs urging greater participation in Europe. Three prominent Europeans in the parliamentary party were Geoffrey Rippon, Peter Kirk and Maurice Macmillan. There was thus already a substantial body of support in the parliamentary party.

The second factor favouring membership of the EEC was the changing mood of the business community. This was due to the EEC becoming the major growth area for exports, the desire for competitive stimulus and the advantages of economies of scale. Large firms had become firmly in favour, together with leading industrial spokesmen such as Lord Chandos, head of the Institute of Directors. The Federation of British Industries, due to its consensual nature, failed actively to promote membership, but the major industrial leaders made their position clear.

The third factor was the declaration of support for membership of most of the Conservative-oriented press. The *Observer*, the *Economist* and the *Financial Times* came out in favour of membership in 1960, followed in early 1961 by the *Sunday Times*, *Daily Telegraph*, *Daily Mail* and *The Times*. The only Tory newspaper in opposition, and in violent opposition, was the *Daily Express*. Macmillan thus had the support, even before his announcement, of most of the Conservative press.

Fourthly, the depth of attachment to the Commonwealth in the party was exaggerated. The Commonwealth was no longer the Empire. South Africa had been excluded, Imperial Preference had increasingly worked against British products, the increasingly poor image of the Commonwealth served to undermine feelings of kinship, and the younger generation lacked the emotional attachment toward the former Empire. These factors, together with the behaviour of some Commonwealth leaders towards Britain, served to undermine possible opposition based on the Commonwealth. There was probably one Commonwealth figure with enough respect in the Conservative party to have had a substantial impact—Sir Robert Menzies, Prime Minister of Australia—but he kept his substantial fears largely to himself, and placed his confidence in the Macmillan government.

Another substantial body normally viewed as in opposition was the agricultural interest in the Conservative party. However, the political importance of the farmers' vote has been exaggerated.[4] More significantly, agriculture was by no means united in its opposition. There were expected real benefits for certain sections of British agriculture as a result of membership, and those sections, particularly among large farmers, favoured membership. One survey in the East Midlands showed 42 per cent of the farmers interviewed in favour.[5] Lord Netherthorpe, NFU President 1946–60, favoured membership, together with many agricultural economists. Much of the agricultural debate was not in terms of opposition to entry, but in terms of obtaining entry on the best possible conditions for British agriculture.

The main focus of criticism by the parliamentary anti-marketeers was the question of sovereignty. Why did this issue not gain more attention? The situation can better be understood when it is remembered that the Conservative party had already accepted the surrender of sovereignty in the field of defence in its support for NATO. For many Conservatives, British membership was part of the increasing need for Western democratic nations to combine together against the Soviet threat. The 1961 party conference was held after the building of the Berlin Wall and the failure of Macmillan's attempts at détente. Macmillan appealed to this sense of threat in his speech. 'We must now accept the fact that the bleak ideological struggle may last for another generation, perhaps even longer. We cannot retire from this contest, but we cannot wage it alone. It is with this in mind that we have approached the question of Europe and of the Common Market.'[6] While the question of the

EEC entering the field of defence was never raised, the need for European cooperation against the Communist threat established a good reason for the supposed loss of sovereignty. The effect of economic weakness on defence was established with the cancellation of the Blue Streak missiles. Thus sovereignty failed to establish itself as a major issue.

The weakness of the Conservative anti-marketeers was not only due to the appeal for loyalty. They failed to win the support of any leading Conservative. Lord Avon was much courted by Beaverbrook, who offered finance and publicity if he would lead the opposition, but his health was too poor. They were led by men of moderate stature, former ministers such as Derek Walker-Smith and Robin Turton, but they were elderly men out of touch with the younger members of the parliamentary party. The Anti-Common Market League was founded in August 1961 to rally anti-market Conservatives but it never established substantial support. An expected source of support, among the Suez diehards, proved to be disappointing, with one of its leading figures, Julian Amery, a fervent European. The anti-marketeers were vocal but never secured a strong base in the party.

In fact, British membership was popular with some segments of the party. The 1962 conference showed a degree of enthusiasm that conflicts with the image of a party being dragged into membership only out of loyalty to its leadership. The Young Conservatives, who account for up to one quarter of the conference representatives, enthusiastically wore 'Yes' buttons, together with many other representatives. Many Conservatives felt that this was an issue which was an election-winner.

Labour opposition had been expected, indeed perhaps hoped for, by Macmillan. When it came with a speech by Hugh Gaitskell accusing the Government of turning their backs on 'a thousand years of history' just before the 1962 Conservative conference the issue became a partisan one, and this enabled partisan rhetoric to be used in favour of membership, as it was, effectively, by Rab Butler when he said, 'For the Labour party a thousand years of history. For us, the future.' The issue gave the Conservatives a progressive and internationalist image, which contrasted with a reactionary and inward-looking image of the Labour party over this issue.

A major element in the Conservative conversion to the EEC was the belief that Europe would win the party the next election. The government had appeared tired and lacking in ideas. The EEC gave the government new inspiration, as Macmillan had intended. Macleod, the party chairman, and Conservative Central Office believed that Europe should be the main platform in the election campaign, where it should be presented 'with trumpets'. The young and opinion-formers were the key to success and they were strongly pro-European. One Central Office worker described Europe as the 'deus ex machina'[7] of the Conservative election campaign. Opinion polls showed that more people favoured membership than favoured the Conservatives, and these were a potential source of support. Above all, Europe gave the Conservatives a new image as a forward-looking party that could compete for the new technocratic middle class votes.

Macmillan's personal decision, and the appeal to party loyalty, obviously played an important role in the decision to apply for membership, but Macmillan would never have taken that decision unless there had existed a substantial body of party opinion in favour of membership. Macmillan took a risk but not as large as it has usually been portrayed.

## From Disillusion to Renewed Support 1963–70

De Gaulle's veto stunned the party, and the country, and the ability of the party to recover as much as it did in the 1964 election was astounding. Everyone accepted that British membership was not a realistic possibility. The 1964 election manifesto called for a strong Atlantic partnership and for the closest cooperation with the Six. However, an important decision with regard to the Conservative party and Europe was made with the election of Edward Heath as leader against Reginald Maudling in 1965. While Heath was not as committed a European as some other Conservatives before the decision to apply in 1961, he had developed a strong commitment during the negotiations. He established, in the 1966 manifesto, the policy of working energetically for entry at the first favourable opportunity. It is noticeable that there was no mention of protecting the Commonwealth's interests as a condition of entry.

The most important new development in European policy under Heath was that new policies were designed with British membership in mind, such as the reform of agriculture towards levies, and the introduction of value added tax. These policies were presented as valid in themselves but they were clearly meant to ease British membership.

At the 1966 conference a ballot was held on British membership, with 1452 votes in favour and 475 against. This was a large increase in opposition, due to disillusion over the de Gaulle veto, the fact that the Labour government had decided to seek entry, and that the party leadership usually has less influence in opposition.

Europe did not play a major role in the Conservative party in opposition. The party loyally supported attempts at entry by the Labour government, despite criticism that the opposition should oppose, and their own commitment remained firm. However, by 1969 there were a number of disturbing trends. Firstly, Europe was unpopular in the opinion polls. Secondly, the Conservative anti-marketeers had found a leader in Enoch Powell, who had already established strong support over his immigration policies. Thirdly, there was a danger that the Labour government would obtain entry and thus 'dish the Tories'. Finally, there was strong criticism of a certain inflexibility by Heath in the face of party criticism. These factors led to the decision not to emphasise Europe at the party conference in 1969. Home, speaking on Europe, 'deliberately drained his speech of all emotion',[8] emphasising that a final decision could only be taken after negotiations. The vote in favour of membership was only two to one.

Thus Europe did not play a primary role in the election campaign. The manifesto emphasised that 'Obviously there is a price we would not be prepared to pay', that only after negotiations could the price be known, and that 'Our sole commitment is to negotiate; no more, no less'. Only 3 per cent of Heath's speeches during the campaign were on Europe, and there was little mention in the candidates' election addresses.

## Campaign for Entry 1970-3

However, after the surprise election victory in June 1970, Heath established membership as a major priority of the new government, beginning negotiations only twelve days after the election, and appointing his close friend, Anthony Barber, to be in charge of the negotiations. Heath seemed confident that, having established a good relationship with President Pompidou, the negotiations would be successful. The major problem was to ensure that entry would achieve the support of a Conservative majority in the Commons, without reliance on other parties. This was necessary, firstly, to relieve the pressure on Labour marketeers to vote against in order to bring down the government; secondly, to maintain the credibility of the government that one of its major policies did not depend upon opposition votes; and thirdly, to establish Heath's mastery over the party.

The problem in the party was greater than with the first application. Firstly, the party no longer saw Europe as an election winner, and it was widely perceived as an election liability. Secondly, the anti-marketeers now had an articulate and well-known leader in Enoch Powell, who had belonged to the Macmillan government which applied for entry but who now felt that the political arguments against membership were too strong. Powell was strong enough to create real divisions in the party, far deeper than just on the question of Europe, which could leave deep wounds. Thirdly, some MPs felt that their local Conservative associations were uncertain on the EEC, and they were reluctant to offend them. Central Office judged the feeling in the constituencies to be pro-market, but there was concern over specific questions, such as sovereignty and the Common Agricultural Policy, and the party workers felt that they were not well-informed, and that they had not been adequately consulted.

Thus the strategy was to create strong enthusiasm and support for British entry, which would both enable the more insecure MPs to vote in favour and place the maximum pressure on those liable to vote against. The main thrust of the campaign was to deal with the fears expressed, to calm fears rather than make converts; special pamphlets were produced dealing with sovereignty, food prices, the regions and industry.

There followed the largest internal education campaign that has ever been undertaken inside the Conservative party. The party machine supported the government through a massive campaign of leaflets, pamphlets, discussion groups, speakers, conferences and meetings. An advisory service to answer questions from MPs was set up, and special briefs were written by the Conservative Research Department for MPs. After a year's campaign, a large meeting of up to 3000 leading Conservative activists (officially called the Central Council) met at Central Hall, Westminster, on 14 July 1971 to listen to Heath and ask questions. The massive support there demonstrated that the party activists were now firmly in favour.

Inside the parliamentary party, the Conservative Group for Europe, an unofficial party pressure group associated with the

European Movement, with membership of over half the parliamentary party, appointed Norman St John Stevas as an unofficial whip. It also provided parliamentary questions sympathetic to Europe to balance those of the anti-marketeers, organised parliamentary delegations to Brussels, held briefing sessions in the House, sustained marketeers under pressure from their local parties, exercised informal 'family-type' pressure on doubters and provided a useful and amazingly accurate estimate of feeling inside the party.

The anti-marketeers organised themselves into the '1970 Group', more popularly known as 'Derek's Diner', as they regularly met for dinner under the auspices of Sir Derek Walker-Smith. They cooperated on party and parliamentary committees, asked hostile questions and cooperated with anti-marketeers in the country. The anti-marketeers were clearly identifiable at an early stage. They were the traditional opposition from the first application: Walker-Smith, Turton, Marten and Fell, five Ulster Unionists who had now broken off relations with the Conservatives, ten of the new MPs, some fishing MPs and Powell and his close supporter, John Biffen. The Anti-Common Market League reorganised itself, although it never became as strong as in 1961–3. The doubters in parliament were Du Cann, Goodhart, some MPs from the Celtic fringe and a few with specific interests such as horticulture or New Zealand.

Heath's original timetable was for a parliamentary vote in July 1971, but he was strongly advised against this, because MPs wanted to be sure that support in their local parties was solid, they did not wish to appear to be in haste so soon after the publication of the terms, and they wanted to demonstrate that they had fully discussed and consulted with their local parties. Heath reluctantly agreed to postpone the decision until October. The party conference was held on 13–16 October, just before the parliamentary vote. Everything demonstrated party support. 69 motions had been received in favour, 25 in favour with reservations, and 4 against. The Conservative Political Centre announced that their two-way contact exercise, whereby the party was able to judge feeling in the constituencies, had shown overwhelming support. The Young Conservatives demonstrated their enthusiastic support—they had always been an important base of European feeling inside the party—and it was a YC motion welcoming entry which was presented to conference. The debate emphasised sovereignty and the political opportunities of membership. The motion was passed by an overwhelming majority, but unprecedentedly Heath demanded a card vote which revealed 2474 votes for and 324 votes against, a vote of about eight to one. The vote was received with wild enthusiasm and a parade of YC 'Eurodollies' reminiscent of an American convention. Thus the pressure was for a maximum Conservative vote in parliament.

Heath insisted on a three-line whip, stating that as entry was a major plank in the government's policy it had the right to insist on the votes of its supporters. However, this policy was widely criticised inside the party, and not only by anti-marketeers. The issue was perceived by many as an issue of such importance that it was an issue of 'conscience', which demanded a free vote. Only after considerable debate with the 1922 Committee, evidence that a free vote would increase the Conservative anti-Europeans by a maximum of only twelve votes, reports that the question of a three-line whip was causing considerable resentment and the persuasive arguments of Francis Pym, did Heath agree to a free vote.

The first parliamentary vote on Britain's membership was held on 28 October 1971, when 282 Conservative MPs voted in favour, with only 39 against and two abstentions. The leading anti-marketeers continued their opposition throughout the complicated process of legislation, but most of the Tory opposition accepted the defeat and did nothing to prevent the passing of the bill. Thus Britain became a member of the European Community on 1 January 1973.

Explanations of the victory of the Europeans within the Conservative party from 1970–2 have been based on the three following factors: the power of the Conservative party leader, the appeal to party loyalty and the strong formal and informal whipping of MPs. These factors were of course important but there were also other neglected factors.

First, the party activists were not 'converted' to Europe between 1970 and 1971. The evidence was that the party members were pro-European, but felt ill-informed about certain specific problems. The internal campaign was conducted not to convert, but to provide information, to create the feeling of consultation, and to deal with the arguments about which the party members felt unsure. The aim of the campaign, and its success, was to change this soft support into hard, firm and sometimes enthusiastic commitment.

Secondly, public opinion shifted in favour of Britain's entry, particularly among Conservatives. The British government, for the first time, attempted to explain the implications of membership to the mass electorate. The rise in public support weakened fears in the party that Europe would be an electoral liability.

Thirdly, the Labour party came out increasingly against membership on 'Tory terms', which aroused partisan feelings among party activists and MPs. One of the most popular party publications on Europe was a Research Department pamphlet called *Words to Remember*, which quoted Conservative and Labour politicians on the EEC. Quotations from it were widely used by Conservative speakers to attack Labour leaders, and it acquired a degree of notoriety with Harold Wilson.

Fourthly, the anti-marketeers proved in fact much weaker than everyone expected. Powell did not emerge as their leader, partly because he was too much of a lone wolf successfully to lead, and partly because the old anti-market leaders did not want to appear as if they were launching an attack on Heath's leadership by following Powell. The anti-market cause had become associated with the Labour party, and especially its left wing. Above all, the anti-marketeers were surprised at how little support they received in the local parties. They had interpreted the expression of doubts and fears as evidence of opposition, which proved not to be the case. As far as the party in the country was concerned, the campaign was conducted with few long-term divisive consequences.

Finally, and perhaps most surprisingly, many MPs were reluctant to vote in favour of entry if it was in total opposition to the position of their local party. After re-election, Conservative MPs are generally considered to act very independently of their local party, even if not of the parliamentary party. Considerable emphasis was placed on full consultation between the MP and his local party, and this was the major factor in the decision to delay the parliamentary vote until October. There seems to be little evidence that these MPs felt their re-selection to be threatened (except perhaps in the case of a few anti-marketeers). No adequate explanation can be put forward here, but an explanation may be sought in the personal relationships and friendships that MPs establish with the leading members of their association. MPs did not want to see these threatened by a divisive political issue. Therefore MPs spent a considerable amount of time and effort explaining their own position, and encouraging the local party to go along with it. This factor is perhaps one that has been neglected in past analysis of the relationship between the MP and his Conservative association.

Thus the internal debate on Europe within the Conservative party in 1970–1 should be seen not as a demonstration of the power of the party leader to lead the party wherever he wishes to go, but as a period of consolidation of support for Europe, and as evidence of sensitivity to local party feeling by MPs and ultimately the party leadership.

## The Referendum

The period between entry and the referendum in June 1975 was marked by a number of important events unrelated to Europe. The Conservative government lost office in February 1974, was further defeated in October 1974, and Edward Heath lost the leadership of the party to Margaret Thatcher in February 1975. One significant event was the call of Enoch Powell to vote Labour in February 1974 over the Common Market issue, and he claimed some influence over the defeat of the Conservatives. Within the Labour party opposition to entry grew stronger, even after the election of a Labour government. Eventually Harold Wilson decided to resolve the internal conflict inside the party by renegotiating the terms of entry and holding a referendum.

The Conservatives were placed in a difficult position. The final attitude of the Labour government was not yet clear, and there was the danger that the government would succeed in creating the impression that the Conservatives had entered the Community on poor terms. However, official Labour government support was important to win the referendum, so criticism of the government had to be delicately handled. The second problem was the need to help protect the Labour pro-marketeers. Informal contact with them had been established through the European Movement, and the Conservatives were fully aware of their difficulties. Partisan attacks on the government would make their own position weaker. Thirdly, there was the problem of the growing unpopularity of the EEC among the electorate. Too close an identification with the Conservatives could be electorally damaging.

The decision was taken that the full Conservative campaign should be submerged into the all-party Britain-in-Europe campaign. Britain-in-Europe was highly dependent on the Conservatives for personnel, expertise, and the existence of a national organisation. As the pro-marketeers recognised, 'the Conservative party had the only effective machinery for putting on a nationwide campaign'.[9] Conservatives provided the backbone for very many, if not most local Britain-in-Europe groups, and worked hard for all-party cooperation. The huge pro-European campaign effort would have been impossible without the full support of the Conservative party.

Conservative efforts were directed mainly through Britain-in-Europe, therefore there was little of a distinctly party role to be played. William Whitelaw, Deputy Leader, became the Conservative representative in BIE. Lord Fraser returned to Central Office to supervise the party's contribution to the campaign. A series of leaflets were produced, and twelve regional seminars were held, mainly to revive enthusiasm. Central Office provided much of the professional work, printing and distribution of referendum materials. Generally the party did not seek to play a prominent role in the campaign.

This cannot be said to be primarily due to the strength of anti-market feeling in the party. In only 30 Conservative associations was even one of the three key figures (chairman, agent and candidate) anti-market; only two Conservative associations came out officially against; Neil Marten was the leading Conservative anti-marketeer, and Conservatives Against the Treaty of Rome (CATOR) was created, but played very little role either in the party or in the general anti-market campaign. The fears that the referendum would reopen old wounds were not substantiated.

One issue that did arise during the campaign was the role of Mrs Thatcher. As party leader she did not play an active role in the campaign, in direct contrast to the vigorous campaigning of Edward Heath. Doubts about her own commitment were raised. These doubts were based on little evidence. Mrs Thatcher was a firm supporter of British membership, primarily for political rather than economic reasons. She gave her full support, although usually quietly, to the Conservative involvement in the campaign. The decision on her role was a tactical one, based on two factors: firstly, she did not want to create competition within the campaign between herself and Heath (she asked Heath to lead the Conservative campaign but he refused), and secondly, her advisers suggested that Europe was not a popular issue to be identified with by the electorate.

The referendum on 5 June 1975 gave an overwhelming 'yes' vote of 67.2 per cent. The verdict was interpreted as an overwhelming defeat for the left wing of the Labour party. The Conservatives, despite their major contribution, appear to have benefited little from the campaign. They were simply glad that the campaign had concluded without major internal problems, that Powell had not re-emerged as a major threat and that the issue of British membership had at last been settled.

## II CONSERVATIVE RESPONSE TO MEMBERSHIP

### Attitudes to Future Development

Debate within the Conservative party about the European Community is no longer primarily concerned with the question of membership, but revolves around the question of the future direction and development of the Community. Attitudes can roughly be divided into four groups: federalists, confederalists, sympathisers and anti-marketeers.

The federalists believe that the European Community is part of the process of the creation of a united Europe, with a European government with limited functions but real powers, exercised in the interests of Europe as a whole. The federalists demand increased powers for the European parliament, the more frequent use of majority voting in the Council of Ministers, and generally a more 'communitaire' policy. Conservative federalists can generally be found in three groups: a number of old, respected Conservatives who became committed federalists in the immediate post-war period, such as Duncan Sandys; business and professional people who feel at home in Europe, many of whom can be found in the Conservative Group for Europe, a pressure group within the Conservative party; and the youth organisations — the Young Conservatives and the Federation of Conservative Students — who have long been enthusiastic Europeans and are both committed to federalism. The federalists are not a numerically strong group and they do not occupy major influential positions, but their primary commitment to the European cause—they are often described as Eurofanatics—has given them a certain degree of influence.

Most Conservative Europeans are confederalists, viewing the Community as essentially an institution for co-operation between nation-states. Mrs Thatcher told the *Times*, 'I believe that we should continue to have a partnership of nation-states each retaining the right to protect its vital interests but developing more effectively than at present the habit of working together'.[10]

The confederalists favour three major areas of cooperation: firstly, foreign policy, with Mrs Thatcher stating 'It is precisely because we want to see Britain making a lively and energetic contribution to the world, as befits her character, that we are working for the success of our European partnership';[11] secondly, defence, primarily to create a greater consciousness of the need for a greater Western European role in its own defence against the Soviet threat; and thirdly economic policy, recognising the British economic dependence on international trade, and the Community's major role in international trade. The confederalists believe that British interests, especially internationally, can best be promoted through the Community, and therefore support further development of the Community. Party policy can currently be described as confederalist.

The bulk of the Conservative party, both members of parliament and party activists, can be described as sympathetic but unenthusiastic towards Europe. Europe has been on the issue-agenda of British politics for so long that most Conservatives seek a rest from it and a return to more traditional Conservative themes. The massive effort in previous years by the party leadership has left a basically positive attitude towards Europe—what has been described as 'common-sense Europeanism'—among party members, combined with a degree of boredom and irritation with the results of certain Community policies, such as the CAP mountains and excessive harmonisation.

Most anti-marketeers have accepted the results of the referendum. They concern themselves with other issues, hope that the Community does not grow stronger, and even welcome elections to the European parliament as a means of demonstrating the limited commitment of the British people. A few anti-marketeers still strongly oppose any new developments in the Community and believe that British withdrawal or Community collapse is only a matter of time. Neil Marten told the House of Commons in April 1976 that Britain has no reason 'to get further enmeshed in a common market which was beginning to break up' and feared 'an immense and decisive shift of power and control from the British parliament to the European parliament'.[12] The anti-marketeers are no longer an influential force, although they are sometimes used as a balance against the federalists.

The position within the Conservative party can be summed up as generally positive, with the anti-marketeers virtually irrelevant, a small but vocal group of federalists, and with party policy in the hands of confederalists. The party leadership is faced with the problem of ensuring that the debate on European developments between federalists and confederalists, inevitable with direct elections, does not cause serious divisions within the party.

*Community Policy*

European policy has not been a major priority for the Conservative party since the referendum. There are five reasons for this. First, as mentioned previously, the party faithful are somewhat tired of Europe and favour a rest. Secondly, the party is unclear about what its policy should be. Much of their argument for membership has been based on 'spontaneous' benefits, such as increased trade, rather than as a means of new policy initiatives. Thirdly, Mrs Thatcher is certainly a European, but she lacks both the emotional commitment and the intellectual interest towards Europe of the former leader, Edward Heath. Fourthly, party spokesmen on foreign affairs have been disappointing. Reginald Maudling, always known as a reluctant European, was very widely criticised for his inactivity, especially in European affairs. This was noticeable in the reception to his reply to the European debate at the party conference in 1975. His successor, John Davies, while a convinced European, proved to be a well-informed but uninspiring shadow foreign secretary. The appointment of Douglas Hurd as European spokesman in January 1976, however, was widely welcomed in European circles. Fifthly, many Conservatives, including some advisers to Mrs Thatcher, consider that Europe is an electoral liability, with a strongly held public image of the Community as a bureaucratic threat to British interests and values. Thus Europe has not been a major Conservative theme since the 1975 referendum.

Conservative European strategy has been based on four themes: criticism of the Labour government for its anti-Community position, the restatement that the Conservative party is *the* European party in Britain, suspicion of institutional innovations and a set of policies based on reformism rather than new initiatives.

The Labour government is strongly attacked for its lack of European spirit, and Conservative spokesmen have emphasised the continued influence of anti-marketeers like John Silkin, the departure of social democrat marketeers like Roy Jenkins, and the negative attitude towards direct elections of the Labour party conference and National Executive Committee. Douglas Hurd attacked the Labour government in March 1976 'which in its dealings with the Community slithers unhappily between bluster and back-sliding'.[13]

'We are the European Party in the British Parliament and among the British people and we want to cooperate wholeheartedly with our partners in this joint venture' (Mrs Thatcher).[14] Conservative spokesmen, led by Mrs Thatcher, have emphasised that the Conservatives are the only major European party in Britain, and that without the Conservatives Britain would not now be a member of the Community. The targets for these pronouncements appear to be first those Europeans within the Conservative party who may have doubts about the commitment of the present leadership, and secondly to impress on potential European allies that the Conservatives are their only viable partner in Britain.

Party pronouncements seem to favour the present method of decision-making in the Community. Mrs Thatcher told the Conservative Group for Europe, 'It is a Community of nation-states with the Council of Ministers as the chief decision-making body. I believe that this will be true for many years and that national government and national parliaments will continue to have a determining role.'[15] The party has no proposals for institutional reforms, states that 'the European Parliament could not take fresh powers by its own decision' (Hurd),[16] favours closer scrutiny of Community legislation in the House of Commons, and appears to be opposed to decision making by majority vote in the Council of Ministers. Their approach is therefore embedded in a confederalist conception of the Community.

The Conservative delegation to the European parliament, known as the European Conservative Group (ECG), was faced with responding to issues in the parliament where the group was expected to take a position and yet lacked any clear direction from London. Attempts by the group to develop their own policies led to concern that conflict would develop between the policies of the European Conservative Group and the Westminster parliamentary party. The group therefore pursued a low-profile, low-initiative role, which frustrated its ability for coalition-building inside the parliament. The closest the group came to policy-making was the publication, *Our Common Cause*, which identified areas of Conservative interest without giving any clear policy direction.[17] The real impetus for policy formation came from the possibility that as early as May 1978 the party could be faced with European elections. An informal Group on Europe was set up which invited high-ranking Conservatives interested in Europe to present their views on a European policy. In January 1977 a European Policy Committee, chaired by John Davies, was formed to draw up a manifesto for the elections. After the postponement of the elections, the role of the committee was widened to consider European policy and coordinate policy between Westminster and Strasbourg, in effect acting as a sub-committee of the shadow cabinet. By May 1977 a draft campaign guide and a draft manifesto was ready for the elections, and was updated by the end of 1978.

The main themes of the Party's European policies can already be identified: A stronger *foreign policy role* for the Community will be proposed towards the rest of the world, especially the developing countries. One idea being floated is for a foreign policy secretariat to co-ordinate national foreign policies and perhaps even reach a common foreign policy, even though foreign policy is beyond the terms of the Treaty of Rome. This was the major theme of an important speech by Mrs Thatcher in Brussels.

The Conservatives will attack *bureaucratisation* in the Community emphasising attempts at excessive harmonisation, which provoked a highly critical motion at the party conference in 1976 and, exceptionally, an amendment was accepted to the pro-European motion at the conference in 1978 which said that the party should not be afraid to criticise the Community. Mrs Thatcher said in Brussels, 'the cause of European unity is surely not advanced by hundreds of petty internal regulations, such as on the content of ice cream, or the activities of door-step salesmen'.[18]

A major theme will be reform of the *Common Agricultural Policy*, which continues to dominate British discussion of the Community, but not the wholesale replacement of the CAP with a new policy. A number of reforms will be proposed, but the basic structure will be retained.[19]

The view that British *economic* problems can only be solved in concert with our European partners will be given, with emphasis on a Community energy policy.

The Conservative party has developed the institutional mechanism for European policy-making and shows the ability to adapt to the new environment. It is thus far ahead of the Labour party. Future areas of interest will be whether conflict develops between party policies for European and Westminster elections, to what extent the ECG will be inflexibly tied to party policy in their activities in the parliament, and how the party can balance between its general support for the Community and criticism of certain policies.

## Direct elections to the European Parliament

The Treaty of Rome provided for the eventual direct election of the European parliament and after considerable pressure from the parliament, the European Council of Heads of State agreed in December 1975 to the principle of direct elections.[20] Conservative spokesmen in the referendum stated party support for direct elections; this was reaffirmed at the party conference in 1975 when Reginald Maudling said, 'We are committed by the Treaty of Rome to the principle of direct elections. There is no going back',[21] and the conference overwhelmingly passed a European motion which included, 'This conference also encourages the Conservative party to work continually for direct elections to the European parliament'.[22]

The Conservatives were thus firmly committed to the principle of direct elections, in marked contrast to the Labour party whose conference in October 1976 rejected the principle of direct elections; not until 26 April 1978 did the National Executive Committee agree to begin the process of preparation.

The European parliament, endorsed by the European Council, had proposed May or June 1978 for the first set of European elections. The Conservatives set up a committee under Sir Anthony Royle, MP, to consider policy towards the detailed aspects of direct elections legislation. The Labour government was very slow to present legislation because of internal differences within the cabinet and the fear that the proposals would reopen the old wounds between Labour pro- and anti-marketeers. The government finally presented the European Assemblies Bill on 24 June 1976.

The bill, however, presented the Conservatives with an awkward dilemma. The Labour government, as part of its compact with the Liberals, presented in the bill two alternative electoral systems. The first was a form of the regional list system, criticised even by supporters of proportional representation for its anomalies, but at least a proportional system acceptable to the Liberals. Most

Conservatives, and especially Mrs Thatcher, are strongly opposed to proportional representation and, therefore, could be expected to oppose the regional list. However, the other alternative, the traditional British first-past-the-post system, required an elaborate process of presentation and appeals for constituency boundaries, which would be unlikely to be completed in time for elections to be held in May 1978 unless the traditional appeal system were abandoned. The Conservatives feared that by voting against the regional list system, the party would be blamed for delaying the elections, which would damage their European image, especially with other centre-right parties. In response to this, influential Conservatives favoured supporting the regional list, or some compromise formula. Indeed, the *Economist* reported that a majority of the shadow cabinet favoured that course.[23] Douglas Hurd argued that it would be a mistake to have a new electoral system for the first election, when a common Community system will be introduced in 1984 which would require yet another change. This argument, together with strong hostility inside the parliamentary party to proportional representation in principle, led to a Conservative free vote but an unofficial whip against it, and an eventual majority for first-past-the-post.

During the passage of legislation, the Conservatives criticised the delay in introducing legislation and expressed fears that the elections would be delayed throughout the Community by the British government's indifference. The debate provided an opportunity for Tory anti-marketeers to repeat their attacks on the Community, but generally there was strong Conservative front-bench and back-bench support for the bill.

The bill, however, faced the opposition with another dilemma. The government presented their guillotine motion for the bill on 26 January 1978. It is, of course, traditional for the opposition to oppose the guillotine motion. However, with strong Labour opposition to the elections, there was a serious danger that the guillotine motion would be defeated, and that the legislation would fail to reach its passage by the end of the parliamentary session. The Conservatives once again wished to avoid the blame for delaying the elections, and therefore for the first time ever the opposition, led by Mrs Thatcher, supported the government's guillotine which enabled the bill to be passed on 16 February 1978. This, however, was too late for a June 1978 election, so the election was postponed until 7 June 1979.

*Election Preparations*

The party responded to European elections with a new organisational structure, an information and educational campaign and a new selection procedure for European candidates. If the national election had been held, as they expected, in October 1978, then the party would have given top priority to the European elections. The possibility of a general election at any time up to and including the European elections reduced the emphasis that could be placed on the European elections.

The National Union, the voluntary side of the party, responded to the prospect of European elections by setting up high level National and Area Steering Committees on European Elections, with broad party representation, to co-ordinate activity, to brief candidates and activists, and to submit ideas on policy and organisation. The National Union proposed the formation of European Constituency Councils (ECCs), with the six top officers of the (usually eight) Westminster constituencies within the European constituency. The ECC would have responsibility for the selection of the candidate, the appointment of a 'Euroagent' from amongst the Westminster agents, and the organisation for the election. Formation of the ECCs awaited the results of the Boundary Commission recommendations, but intense consultations within probable Euroconstituencies began earlier. One source of friction was that each Westminster constituency was given equal representation on the bodies of the ECC, while contributions to the ECC, in terms of personnel, work and time were likely to be unequal.

The need to educate, inform and stimulate preparations for the elections among party workers was recognised as an important priority, especially considering the positive but unenthusiastic attitude generally prevalent, the widespread feeling that the local parties were not well-informed on developments, and the fact that the elections would be the first for an institution largely unknown to the public, in a constituency different from normal, requiring the establishment of close relations between different constituencies. On 4 August 1977 the Advisory Committee on Direct Elections, chaired by Douglas Hurd, was set up to co-ordinate activities in the field of information and in January 1978 a full-time European Elections Officer, Roger Boaden, was appointed. The main information activities were the distribution of literature produced by the European Elections Office, the European Conservative Group, the

European parliament, the Commission and the Conservative Group for Europe; the organisation of the visits to the Commission and the parliament for party activists and organisers, including everyone expected to play a leading role in the ECCs; and twelve regional conferences with sessions on the parliament, policy and organisation, involving 300 to 400 people at each meeting. Finance for informational activities was available from the European parliament, via the European Conservative Group. A major problem in the ECCs was the problem of raising finance for European elections, along with the other financial commitments.

A Standing Advisory Committee on European Candidates (Euro-SAC) was formed to draw up the candidates list for the elections. In form, it is similar to the system of selecting Westminster candidates. The applicant for the list met first with the vice-chairman of the party responsible for candidates (then Marcus Fox, MP), and then met an interviewing panel with representatives of the National Union and the European Conservative Group. If accepted on the list, the candidate could apply for selection to the ECCs who were expected to form selection committees of two representatives from each Westminster constituency. The selection committee was to present at least five candidates to the ECC, which in turn would select three candidates for recommendation to a general meeting, consisting of a minimum of 25 members appointed from each UK constituency association, and it was recommended that the process of selection should involve as many members as possible.

The selection of European candidates was far more rigorous than for Westminster candidates. The Euro-SAC 'set itself definite objectives as far as the qualifications of candidates are concerned, in order to ensure a high standard and representation of diverse occupations and experience'.[24] The party received well over 2000 enquiries, and had hoped to establish a short list of approved candidates, but the number of applications forced a somewhat larger list than expected. Many applicants were discouraged even from filling in an application form, many highly qualified candidates were rejected, and even those accepted testified to the tough interview. The Euro-SAC was concerned to present a more highly qualified candidate than for the Westminster list, and may have attempted to exercise a greater degree of influence over local candidate selection. Candidate selection was expected to proceed quickly from the final decision of the constituency boundaries (probably November 1978) to the end of February 1979. The party strongly discouraged, but did not forbid, the holding of the dual mandate at both Westminster and Strasbourg.

The Conservative party thus proceeded very rapidly with their preparations for the European elections. At this stage the exact nature of the impact of the European elections on the party is unclear, but a number of interesting questions are raised. Will the structure for the European elections develop an independent and separate status from the Westminster structure? What will be the reaction of party activists to the elections, especially when there will be no obvious concrete result such as the election of a Conservative government? How will the party cope with the finances of the elections, especially at the local level? Will the size of the constituencies change the nature of local campaigning, perhaps towards a more media-oriented campaign? Will the European parliament create a new political career structure? Will the selection procedure lead to both greater control of the candidates by the centre at the early stage of selection, and a more open primary type selection at the end? The impact of European elections on the Conservative party organisation is uncertain, but it will clearly not emerge unchanged.

*Centre-Right Cooperation*

The Conservative party has no immediately natural allies inside the European Community. The only other Conservative party is the rather small Danish Conservative People's party with whom they form the ECG. The Conservatives strongly seek alliances with other centre-right parties, both to strengthen them during the election campaign and to be able to exert greater influence in the parliament. The party has extremely close relations with the Christian Democrat Union in the Federal Republic of Germany with frequent visits and exchanges at all levels of the parties, and a great deal of agreement on policy questions. The Conservatives therefore seek an alliance with the European Christian Democrats.

The Christian Democrat Parties, however, in Belgium, Netherlands and Italy are opposed to cooperation with the Conservative party. This is for four reasons. First, these parties take the word Christian in their names very seriously, and references to Christian values can be easily found in party pronouncements.

They are therefore suspicious of a secular Conservative party. Secondly, the word conservative translates into their languages as fascist or reactionary, and this view is reinforced by a generally bad press in these countries. Thirdly, these parties have strong left wings associated with Christian trade unions. Fourthly, they have all formed, at one time or other, government coalitions with the socialists. Thus the Conservative party has had to promote an active policy to improve its relations with these parties.

The only international 'organisation' (before the EDU) in which the Conservative party participated was the Inter-Party meeting, which was an annual meeting of centre-right parties to discuss particular policy areas. However, the meetings were only informal affairs, lacking any permanent structure, or decision-making procedure. Sections of the party have created very extensive inter-party links. The International Office of the party maintains extensive links with centre-right parties in Europe and throughout the world. The Women's National Advisory Committee is affiliated to the European Union of Women, with fourteen affiliates in fourteen countries. The Young Conservatives belong to the Democratic Youth Community of Europe, with fifteen affiliates in fourteen countries; and the Federation of Conservative Students belongs to European Democrat Students, with eighteen affiliates in sixteen countries.

At the 1975 party conference the delegates balloted for the motion on inter-party cooperation, and passed the motion overwhelmingly. The motion read:

> This Conference, recognising that Britain is now securely a member of the European Community, urges the Conservative Party to work more closely with our political allies in Europe towards the formation of a moderate centre-right alliance (a European Democrat Party) able effectively to oppose the Socialist grouping in the European Parliament and able to take positive initiatives in the development of Europe.

Mrs Thatcher has played an active role in the search for centre-right cooperation. At the annual conference of the CDU in Hanover on 25 May 1976, she gave a highly successful speech in which she said, 'I am convinced that the Christian Democratic, Conservative and Centre Parties in Europe should now join together in an effective working alliance. I believe that this is a task of historic importance, and one in which we should invest all our energies.'[25] In December 1976 Mrs Thatcher visited the Netherlands for talks with the Dutch Christian Democrats and in June 1977 she visited Rome to meet Christian Democrat leaders and gave a speech called 'Europe as I See It', directly aimed at the Italian Christian Democrat party. 'I would ask those who shy away from the word (Conservative) to concentrate on the common ground which exists between the British Conservative party, and the Christian Democrats and other centre-right parties in Europe.'[26] Thus the question of centre-right cooperation is a major one for the Conservative party, including the party leader.

With British entry to the Community, the Conservative delegation to the European parliament formed their own party group with the Danish Conservatives and did not join the Christian Democrat Group, much to the disappointment of the CDU. Initial problems of mutual misunderstandings, compounded by personal rivalries and ambitions, led to a bad relationship between the two groups. The *Economist* in August 1976 described the Tory-Christian Democrat alliance as being 'in bad shape'.[27] The election of two new group leaders in Sir Geoffrey Rippon and Egon Klepsch led to a much improved relationship. The Christian Democrats and Conservatives invited each other to observe their 'Study Days', and even to give presentations at each other's group meetings. There is considerable contact between the groups in the search for common positions. Group relations, however, have not permeated far beyond the parliament.

The problem of Christian Democrat–Conservative cooperation arose again with the creation of the European People's Party (EPP) in April 1976 as the European Christian Democrat party for the elections. Opposition from some Christian Democrats led to the creation of the EPP without a British member. There were long and intense debates led by the CDU to create the EPP with the possibility of future Conservative membership. The statutes were ambiguous but appeared to allow membership to all who 'share its fundamental concepts and subscribe to its political programme',[28] but there was no possibility that the Conservatives could join the EPP before the first European elections in June 1979.

The search for a European centre-right alliance began in earnest in 1972 when the student and youth sections of nine parties proclaimed a 'Charter' for the European Democrat party in London. The word 'European Democrat' was proposed as the most acceptable to Christian Democrat, Conservative, right-wing Liberal and centrist parties.

In September 1975 there was a party leaders' meeting in Klesheim, Austria, under the auspices of the Inter-Party meeting, which took the principle decision to create a European Democratic Union. After long and difficult negotiations, during which the CDU tried to get other Christian Democrat parties to join, the EDU was eventually formed on 24 April 1978. EDU members at its formation were:

| EEC | Full | Permanent Observer | ad hoc Observer |
|---|---|---|---|
| UK | Conservative | | |
| Germany | CDU | | |
| | CSU | | |
| France | RPR (Gaullists) | | Republicans (Giscardiens) |
| Denmark | Conservative | | |
| Italy | | South Tirol People's Party Trentino People's Party | |
| *Non-EEC* | | | |
| Austria | People's Party | | |
| Finland | National Coalition | Swedish People's Party | |
| Greece | | | New Democracy |
| Malta | | Nationalist | |
| Norway | Conservative | | |
| Portugal | Centre Social Democrats | | |
| Spain | | | Centre Democrats |
| Sweden | Moderate | | |
| Switzerland | | Christian Democratic Party | |

The EDU set up four working commissions on European policy, Eurocommunism, energy policy and unemployment; it created an executive committee under the chairmanship of Dr Josef Taus, the leader of the Austrian People's party, and planned a formal congress. However, the EDU created problems of its own. The majority of EDU members were not within the European Community. Of those who were Community members, the CDU/ CSU were committed to campaign for the EPP, and the Gaullists would campaign on a nationalist platform. Thus the Conservatives did not really find the alliance for the European elections that they sought. Some Conservatives never saw the EDU as primarily an electoral alliance at all but wanted it to develop as a centre-right International like the Socialist International, which could play a role in supporting centre-right parties in emerging democracies like Portugal and Spain. However, without the electoral value for European elections, the EDU may lack the impetus for development into a centre-right international role.

Although the EDU will not campaign in the European elections, the other Christian Democrat parties see it as a threat to the EPP. They were seriously upset at the EDU, and strongly urged the CDU to play down the EDU. Some Conservatives believed that the creation of the EDU should have been postponed until the majority of Christian Democrat parties within the Community could be persuaded to join. Others, however, were concerned that continual postponement would have killed the idea completely.

The Conservatives at last belong to an international grouping, the European Democratic Union. However, the problem of broad centre-right cooperation for the European elections, the method by which the Conservatives can conciliate the reluctant Christian Democrats, and the role of the EDU in the future, all remain unsolved.

CONCLUSION

The traditional view of the Conservative party has been a hierarchical one where the initiative lies with the leader and other members of the party follow his lead. With regard to the initiative to join the European Community, the decision has been presented as a personal one taken by the leader against traditional party principles and values. The success in getting the party to support Community membership has been attributed to the tremendous powers of the leader and their use by both Harold Macmillan and Edward Heath. Whilst not rejecting the importance of the role of the leader, it may be more useful to view the party as a collection of interest and attitude groups, which the leader seeks to unite into a coalition behind his policies. The support of all the various groups within the party cannot be assumed but must be sought and wooed, although there may exist a reserve of loyalty which the leader can draw upon.

A leader can successfully lead the party in new directions when he is certain that there is widespread support for his initiative. Macmillan was able to lead his party into support for EEC membership because many of the interests and groups in the party and associated with it were already pro-European. Such groups included the early 'Europeans', the Tory press, much of industry and agriculture, the defence lobby, intellectuals, professionals and young Conservatives. Those groups which opposed entry, such as the Commonwealth group, the 'imperialists' and part of the agriculturalist interest were by no means united in their opposition. Under Heath some Conservatives in parliament and outside objected to unnecessary haste in making decisions committing Britain to EEC membership and only supported membership when their doubts had been conciliated. By the time of the referendum many Conservatives at local and national level had become convinced Europeans and participated in the referendum campaign without the necessity of a strong lead from above. Thus the traditional hierarchical view of the Conservative party may need to be revised towards a more complex, group-based analysis.

Since Britain's entry into the Community, further factors have undermined the hierarchical view, with the development of semi-autonomous decision-making by the European Conservative Group, the creation of a new institutional structure for the European elections and the need to take account of potential centre-right allies in the European parliament. The growth of these new interests will inevitably make coalition-building in the Conservative party more difficult in the future.

NOTES

1. W. S. Churchill, *Europe Unites* (London: Hollis and Carter, 1949).
2. R. Neustadt, 'Whitehouse and Whitehall', in A. King: *British Prime Ministers* (London: Macmillan, 1969) p. 141.
3. H. Macmillan, *Britain, the Commonwealth and Europe* (Conservative Central Office, October 1962).
4. P. Self & H. Storing: *The State and the Farmers* (London: Allen & Unwin, 1962).

5. R. Lieber: *British Politics and European Unity* (Berkeley: University of California Press, 1970).
6. *Conservative Conference Verbatim Report, 1961* (Conservative Central Office, 1961).
7. D. Butler & A. King: *The General Election of 1964* (London: Macmillan, 1965) p. 79.
8. K. Young: *Sir Alec Douglas-Home* (London: Dent, 1970) p. 254.
9. D. Butler & U. Kitzinger: *The 1975 Referendum* (London: Macmillan, 1976) p. 78.
10. *The Times* (January 1977).
11. Mrs Thatcher, Foundation Meeting of the European Democratic Union, Klesheim, Austria, 24 April 1978.
12. Parliamentary Debates (Hansard) vol. 908 (1975–6) col. 969.
13. Douglas Hurd, MP, Norwich (20 March 1976).
14. Mrs Thatcher: *Europe As I See It* (European Conservative Group, August 1977) p. 6.
15. Mrs Thatcher, speech to the Conservative Group for Europe, 24 November 1976.
16. Douglas Hurd, Norwich, (20 March 1976.)
17. European Conservative Group, *Our Common Cause* (September 1974).
18. Mrs Thatcher, *The Sinews of Foreign Policy* (European Conservative Group, June 1978).
19. See publications of the European Conservative Group e.g. *Our Common Cause*, op. cit., 32–4. *Europe As I See It*, op. cit., 6–7. Jim Scott-Hopkins & John Corrie: *Towards a Community Rural Policy* (European Conservative Group, February 1978). Jim Scott-Hopkins: *Food for Thought* (European Conservative Group, April 1978).
20. See Nigel Ashford, *Direct Elections to the European Parliament*, (working paper no. 9 Department of Politics, University of Warwick, May 1976) for the background to the decision directly to elect the European Parliament.
21. *Conservative Party Conference Verbatim Report 1976* (Conservative Central Office, 1976).
22. Ibid.
23. The *Economist* (19 March 1977).
24. Letter by Sir Charles Johnstone, Chairman of the National Union, to the National Union (6 September 1976).
25. Mrs Thatcher, speech to the CDU Congress, Hanover (25 May 1976).
26. Mrs Thatcher: *Europe As I See It*, op. cit., p. 10.
27. The *Economist* (18 October 1976) p. 74.
28. Statutes, European People's Party.

# 6 Constitutional Reform: Some Dilemmas for a Conservative Philosophy

## Nevil Johnson

### I INTRODUCTION: THE NATURE OF THE DILEMMA

The Conservative party today finds itself in the somewhat unusual role of protagonist of constitutional reform. This is not to suggest that it speaks with one voice on the matter, nor even that it has entered into serious commitments to reform the constitution as soon as it has the power to do so. But what is beyond doubt is that many Conservatives are worried about the state of the constitution and that in public discussion of what kind of constitutional reforms might be needed, it is Conservatives who have made the running rather than their political opponents. As I shall seek to explain, this puts the party in an unusual stance and indeed presents a serious dilemma for Conservative philosophy.

It is worth beginning with an outline of the nature of this dilemma. Within the tradition of conservative political thinking it has been held that political institutions grow out of and are sustained by social habits and manners: to quote Burke, 'Politics ought to be adjusted not to human reasoning but to human nature'.[1] Political values themselves are rooted in social life and can be learnt only from growing up in a particular tradition of civility. It is a mistake to conceive of political behaviour narrowly as conduct appropriate only to transactions within the confines of political institutions and activity. On the contrary, such virtue as there may be in public life is but the manifestation of principles derived from experience in the family, the school, the club or private association, the practice of a profession, the place of work or business and so on.

Similarly, there is no sharp separation between the institutions of the political realm, the methods by which society is governed, and the infinitely complex network of social institutions and practices[2] through which people are held together in society and enabled to cooperate with each other for the satisfaction of their needs. The political institutions grow out of social arrangements and are sustained by them. It is accepted that political institutions have an important and indeed essential regulative purpose, but their form and *modus operandi* represent a distillation of the wisdom gained in social experience: their shape and character reflect the genius of a people rather than the inspiration of the philosopher or law-giver.

This last remark is important. It has been a persistent theme in British Conservative thought that political institutions should not be constructed on abstract principles. Indeed, more than that, it has frequently been asserted that they cannot be so constructed and that any attempt to do so is foredoomed to failure. The attack on abstract principles is a *leitmotiv* in Burke's writings and is echoed in a similar vein in Disraeli. We find it once more in Salisbury and again in the twentieth century in figures as different one from the other as Baldwin and Oakeshott. No doubt there is a certain plausibility in the view that it is foolish to attempt to shape the political institutions of a stable society by the application of general principles which take no account of time, place and circumstance, nor of the particularity of that society's historical experience. Moreover, the criticism of the appeal to abstract principles is consistent with the emphasis given in conservative thought to the dominant influence of social behaviour and relationships in the complex processes through which political institutions and practices evolve. Nevertheless, the rejection of abstract principles in the structuring of political life reveals an important deficiency in conservative thinking and underlines in an ironic way the dilemmas facing the contemporary Conservative who seeks constitutional reform.

What conservatism in its traditional guise lacks is an adequate explanation of deliberate change. It would be unreasonable to argue either that all change is bad or that all change, good or bad, merely occurs by chance. We have substantial historical experience of deliberate and contrived change, sometimes even contrived with the aid of force and violence, and we know that such change has on occasion been judged beneficial and necessary. We know, too, that people are capable of thinking intelligently about their affairs and in far less dramatic ways than through civil war or revolution have shown themselves capable of establishing new procedures for the regulation of various aspects of their social and political relations. For the Burkean conservative this is all something of a mystery: his postulates require him to decry abstract principles, yet the indulgence in abstract thought and the pursuit of its intimations into practical affairs is a persistent human experience. The difficulty arises, of course, because the conservative view of human nature and behaviour is lop-sided. Too much emphasis is placed on the unreflecting aspects of social life, on 'prejudice' in the sense given to that word by Burke,[3] and not enough on the rational faculties of human beings and their capacity to take thought and to exercise foresight. As a result, deliberate political action and the thinking which may precede and motivate it are seen as peculiarly disturbing irritants, threatening to disrupt the harmonious emergence from the interplay of social interests and habits of such political procedures and policy decisions as are compatible with the underlying preferences of society.

It will be obvious that this traditional suspicion of abstract principles in politics sharpens the dilemma facing the Conservative constitutional reformer. It is difficult to see how he can set about constitutional reform without first undertaking an examination of principles. And, as will be argued later, the condition of the British constitution is such that its reform invites far more than a cautious nibble at abstract principles here and there: on the contrary, it invites the wholesale application of principles for the very reason that it appears to have lost all definition as a body of easily identifiable practices justified by appeal to principles which they can be said to embody. Of course, the traditional Conservative who shares the dislike of theorising in politics might take refuge in Burke's famous remark about the necessary connection between conservation and reform, and recommend that we approach constitutional reform pragmatically, searching in the past for those clues which will unlock the gates to moderate and limited improvement. The difficulty here is that it has become harder to find guidance in the past. Many feel with de Tocqueville that 'as the past has ceased to throw its light upon the future, the mind of man wanders in obscurity'.[4] The rate of social and technical change has depreciated the value of the wisdom of our ancestors, perhaps rendered much of it irrelevant. And as will be argued more fully below, it is the sad fate of an unwritten constitution, resting largely on convention, to be more seriously eroded by a rapid rate of change in social values and habits than one which has greater formality and visibility. Thus, the appeal to the past for guidance in the matter of constitutional change often turns out to be mere romanticism, an appeal to conditions and experiences which have vanished for good. This kind of Conservative constitutional reformer finds himself struggling to put Humpty Dumpty together again and there is no evidence that this can be done.

Before bringing these introductory remarks to a close it is worth commenting on the motives impelling many Conservatives to contemplate various schemes of constitutional reform. It seems not unfair to conclude that what they seek in the first place is protection against radical social change facilitated by political practices and constitutional conventions which no longer impose much restraint on governments. It is not so much that traditional constitutional rules are sharply criticised or rejected, but rather that their inability to achieve the effects they are thought to have had in the past is deplored. Thus the intention expressed in Conservative constitutional argument is generally not radically to change or re-design the constitution, but to seek its restoration or re-invigoration. In this way Conservative constitutionalists tend to be clearly distinguishable, for example, from Utilitarian theorists of the early nineteenth century or a few of the socialist thinkers in the Fabian mould of recent times, all of whom were moved by a desire to re-construct the polity in different ways and to make it substantially better. In contrast the Conservative reformer sees himself as repairing the defences or plugging the dykes; he eschews any optimistic commitment to a better world and hopes to ward off present evils.

Two problems arise out of this defensive and protective approach to constitutional reform. One is that the reformer is liable to be attacked by his opponents as a fraud or special pleader. He will be told that his case for reform is but a smoke-screen for the preservation of vested interests. Fundamentally this is an incoherent and foolish line of attack, but that does not deprive it of weight in day-to-day political controversy. The second problem is more serious and consists in the fact that as the Conservative constitutional theorist seeks to identify what can be restored and how, he is driven to solutions (partial or more far-reaching) which in fact change the ground on which he stands. The would-be protector becomes the innovator, the Conservative risks finding himself playing the part of the radical reformer guided by abstract principles. The individual conservative thinker and even the individual politician preoccupied with day-to-day affairs might be prepared to accept this mutation in his position brought about by the logic of pursuing improvement in a constitution which has atrophied. But there still remains the task of persuading those in the party and those who support it to follow the path of reform. For there is reason to believe that their suspicion of contrived change and their attachment to Burkean 'prejudice' are sufficiently strong to repel most proposals for reform and, what is more, such attachment to prescription and habit extends far beyond the limits of Conservative support in the country. Thus, in a curious way the Conservative constitutional reformer finds himself confronted with the paradox inherent in the Burkean account of the relationship between social life and political institutions: it is social habits and manners which must and ought to determine the course of constitutional evolution. But how then do we explain change and, above all, how can we justify proposals for change to those who believe that it must emerge naturally and mysteriously from the intricate life of the whole society?

In this introduction I have tried to do two things. First, an effort has been made to identify some aspects of conservative political thought which bear most closely on the problem of constitutional rules and their adaptation to new demands or threatening dangers. Second, I have underlined what appears to me to be the difficulty or dilemma in which most contemporary Conservatives find themselves when they think seriously about constitutional problems and how to deal with them. They face the prospect of having to reappraise substantial elements in their own political philosophy should they have the tenacity to work through to a coherent justification of the reform proposals they contemplate. For if constitutional reform is to be serious, and not to remain at the level of pious declamation or unobtrusive tinkering, it must represent an attempt to structure institutions deliberately in the hope of thereby maintaining or establishing political values and practices seen to be desirable. It means recognising that Montesquieu or Hamilton, Madison and Jay—to quote but two famous sources of rational conservatism—are better guides to constitutional re-appraisal than the Burke of the Reflections on the Revolution in France.

II PHILOSOPHICAL    FOUNDATIONS    AND    CONSTITUTIONAL
CONSEQUENCES

I want to turn now to a number of the more specific characteristics
of conservative political philosophy which can then be linked
closely with the contemporary argument about the constitution as
well as with some of the ideas which have been put forward for
constitutional reform.

It is necessary to present these elements of the conservative
political tradition only in summary form since they are familiar and
have been discussed by many writers. They can be expressed as
follows:

(i) The rights and privileges which individuals and associations
enjoy are grounded in property.

(ii) Freedom requires equality before the law. This concept of
equality refers as much to the equal protection of unequal claims as
to the safeguarding of those rights which can be said to be equally
distributed or allocated.[5]

(iii) The successful government of a society depends upon the
presence of an elite conscious of its obligations towards the society.
Such an elite, no matter how composed, is more likely to enjoy trust
(a vital factor in constitutional government) if it has a secure social
status.

(iv) Trust in government is created and sustained by appropriate
behaviour on the part of officeholders. This is what generates the
habits and prescriptions on which constitutional norms defining
responsibility in government rest.

(v) Given the importance of the social foundations of politics and
the limited role that can be allowed to government, political or
constitutional change should be gradual and evolutionary.

(vi) Just as the health of society requires a diffusion of varied
interests and sentiments, so it is desirable to maintain a balance
amongst the political institutions in order to ensure that no one
interest can impose itself on all others.

It seems to me that these elements—or something like them—
together constitute the basis of a doctrine of constitutional and
limited government which seeks to maintain freedom under the law.
They contain no clear guidance as to the proper limits of
government action and perhaps for this reason have rendered

Conservatives too passive and perplexed in the face of the extension of the role of the state during the twentieth century. Nevertheless, they do imply that the role of government should at least be as limited as is compatible with allowing the maximum scope possible for individuals to regulate their lives and relations with each other autonomously. The underlying view of freedom is grounded in a recognition of necessary social differences and of variations in the importance which people will attach to particular rights in virtue of their own situations. The attitude to law expressed in these postulates is for the most part negative, and well within that Common Law tradition out of which much conservative thinking has sprung. Law is seen pre-eminently as codified social practice whether it is the law built up by judges in their decisions or the law laid down in statute by parliament.[6] There is little room, too, for an idea of law as an attempt to achieve a condition of justice or for the argument that positive law might itself be in need of justification by appeal to principles of right or justice. Precisely because so much emphasis is placed on the importance of trust as the cement which binds the polity together, there is a prejudice in favour of allowing to public authorities a wide discretion in the discharge of their functions. This has been held to be reasonable both on practical grounds—we cannot prescribe in detail for the unforeseeable circumstances of the future—and on account of the belief that trust between the rulers and the ruled can develop and survive only when there are present in society, and in the conduct transmitted from social life into politics, implicit restraints determining what it is proper to do. In other words, the conservative theory of limited government does not advocate the institutionalisation of suspicions and mistrust,[7] but instead proposes that those in power are restrained by their own sense of the limits to their authority, as well as by the pressures, moral and material, in society which they have to respect.

It hardly needs to be said that the world has changed since the epoch in which this view of how to maintain an acceptable political order took shape. It has become more and more difficult to ground rights in the ownership and use of property, partly because a more abstract view of rights has begun to exercise a powerful influence over our legislation, partly because the more obvious rights attaching to property have steadily been eroded. The use and enjoyment of property is restricted in innumerable ways; its acquisition and disposal are often rendered difficult; an increasingly large amount of property has passed into public ownership, a trend which has serious implications for the very understanding of the term 'property'. Perhaps the only form of property ownership which might be said to be wholly respectable is the private dwelling— provided it is not too large and is not a second holiday home. There is no space here to explore in detail the ramifications of the changes which have taken place over the past 75 years or so in the status and role of property in British social organisation. But it hardly appears to be an exaggeration to suggest that one of the load-bearing timbers on which the Conservative view of how rights are acquired and secured in society has been infected with dry-rot. And what has replaced it is the claim of the political authority to determine the content of rights abstractly and to alter these in accordance with its view of how best to maximise welfare. By this process the claims of the political authority are exalted and profound changes have taken place in the pattern of constraints on government which exists in society.[8]

In respect of the second point, equality before the law as a condition of freedom, the adequacy of the very principle has been challenged and the discussion of equality, its meanings and application, has become a central preoccupation in political and social analysis. This argument will not be pursued here, but two aspects of the changes affecting the idea of equality before the law which have taken place should be underlined. One is the manner in which the system of adjudication—the courts in more familiar terms—has been fragmented. It will be recollected that one of the terms on which Dicey defined the rule of law was the supremacy of the ordinary courts of the land. It can well be argued that Dicey exaggerated substantially the significance of this condition. Nevertheless, lying behind the argument was an important assumption, namely that the rule of law requires a certain unity and coherence in the law and that this has to be achieved through a system of adjudication which is itself coherent and ultimately subject to a single source of interpretation on appeal. This condition is nowadays fulfilled only in a formal and limited sense. This is because large areas of adjudication have been withdrawn from the ordinary courts of law or never even entrusted to them.[9] This happens, of course, predominantly in the wide field of social provision, in which tribunals of one kind and another abound. However their decisions may be evaluated, one thing is certain: they do not provide an easily accessible and public body of case law. Nor can it be said with confidence that they operate under consistent and equitable general guidelines; instead they apply conventions, statutory requirements and administrative preferences peculiar to their own particular jurisdictions. In such conditions the practical realisation of equality before the law is bound to be heavily qualified: we move steadily towards rule by exception.

The other aspect of this matter to be stressed is the impact of a different view of equality on the older notion of civil equality before the law. I refer to a theory of substantive equality according to which equality is defined in terms of the realisation of a continuing claim by all to an equal share of material benefits in society. Only on this basis, so it is argued, can the inequalities inherent in the idea of formal equality before the law and in the concept of equality of opportunity be mitigated or overcome. It is recognised that if the concept of substantive equality is expressed in radical terms like this, the number of those who take it seriously is far less than of those who merely find it convenient to pay lip-service to the notion. There are many, too, who firmly reject such a view. Nevertheless, it is apparent from the history of the past 30 years that substantive equality in various diluted forms has had a deep influence on many sectors of public policy and to some extent has constituted one of the watch-words in political debate in the country. The outcome has been a shift towards an egalitarian bias in many sectors of social provision, economic intervention by government, taxation policy, education etc., which Conservatives locally and nationally have not been able to check or reverse. Thus we have had the spectacle of Conservative governments pursuing policies they cannot really believe in, hesitating to contemplate changes which might fracture what is held to be a consensus, and encouraging developments which can hardly fail further to undermine confidence in the more narrowly defined idea of equality which has been dominant in the conservative tradition. It is clear that such a situation has implications, too, for the extent to which the party can retain the confidence of its supporters, many of whom see it as too prone to apply the policies of its political rivals, and for the very rationale of a competitive two-party system. Competition there may be, but its object may be simply office rather than the opportunity to pursue the policies that are publicly proclaimed.

There is no need to say much about the third factor. A clearly identifiable social elite has virtually disappeared and though status remains an ubiquitous (and inescapable) social phenomenon its expression in hierarchical relationships is greatly attenuated. The social basis of political careers and of political action has become amorphous and ill-defined, a situation which in different ways affects other political parties as much as the Conservatives. Similarly, it is much harder to talk of a political elite except perhaps in a narrow functional sense. Political scientists may choose to identify 635 or 1000 or perhaps even 2000 persons as constituting the political elite of this country. But to do so is merely to identify officeholders and a group of 'influentials' said to be close to them. This is a narrow concept of an elite, specifying next to nothing of the qualities in virtue of which its members establish a claim to respect and authority *qua elite*. Indeed, the problem which faces the conservative political theorist as well as the conservative politician is that there is no longer a ruling class, something which has nearly always been at one and the same time a social and political phenomenon. There are no longer 'natural rulers' and this does far more than disrupt the foundations of deference. It calls into question the terms on which trust develops in society and can be evoked by those who achieve political office. Yet another of the timbers in the Burkean structure seems unable to carry the weight imposed upon it by this feature of the conservative conception of how political authority can be sustained.

These remarks carry over in their application to the fourth element in a conservative theory of politics. That aspect of the problem of trust in government and responsibility on the part of officeholders that deserves to be stressed is the extent to which political institutions and officeholders are the victims of changes in attitudes and values in society. Even though it is held that trust in those holding office in government is sustained by their conduct, it has to be remembered that we are talking about two-way relationships. Whilst the ability of contemporary politicians to maintain an independent judgement of what is right and prudent to recommend may have been eroded by the gradual breakdown of a well-defined social elite sensitive to its political functions, equally they are exposed to pressures from a society in which the ties of habit have been loosened and agreement on what is appropriate conduct dissolved. The censure of public opinion remains, but it has become more capricious and is formed all too often by disappointment over the non-fulfilment of material expectations which it may not be within the power of the politician to satisfy. Correspondingly public opinion focuses less often on the manner in which politicians and officials have behaved and on the degree to which they have adhered to certain procedures and standards of conduct. The outcome of these trends is that at least part of the basis in society for the understanding of constitutional norms has been taken away; if the constitution is in danger it is as much because many people do not care about it as because politicians have misused it.

Then there is the preference for evolutionary change. No doubt many politicians (and not only in the Conservative party) would still express support for a policy of gradualism. However, it would be naïve to overlook a momentous transformation in the context in which decisions of policy are now taken. Whereas 50 or more years ago there was a widespread presumption that proposals for change had to be justified by those who put them forward, the burden of proof has now shifted to those who oppose change. There is a presumption that change is beneficent or inevitable or both, and if specific changes are under consideration, it is the critics who must make out a case against them. There could hardly be a better example of this than the history of local government reform 1966–74. A conviction took root amongst many of those concerned with local government that some kind of structural overhaul was imperative. Report followed report and finally· a Conservative government carried out a drastic territorial simplification in 1972. If there was an argument of substance in favour of the change, it was that it would promote efficiency and facilitate integrated policy-making in fields where administrative boundaries stood in, the way of a unified approach. Whether this argument was well-founded is still hotly contested and, at best, judgment on its validity must be reserved. What is certain is that there was no great popular demand for local government reform and many local authorities opposed their own disappearance or reincarnation. Nevertheless, once the belief in the inevitability of change took root, nobody seemed able to look critically at the case for change or to prevent it happening. And there were Conservative ministers who congratulated themselves on their ability to apply progressive managerialism more effectively than their opponents.[10]

This example illustrates how hard it has become for even a Conservative government to resist what look like well-founded calls for change. Once more the Conservative finds himself in an uncomfortable position *vis-à-vis* the tradition he inherits. He may discern that it counsels scepticism in relation to the benefits presumed to flow from reforming legislation and questions the wisdom of applying to complex social relationships the equalising and centralising remedies of statute law, unless it is clear beyond doubt that only in this way can legitimate grievances be removed or widely supported purposes be fulfilled. But the prejudices of the age are against him and he finds it hard to work against some of those prejudices without resort to more systematic counter-arguments that his tradition has provided.

We come now to the sixth element, the one most directly related to the institutions of government and therefore to the issues of constitutional reform. It is perhaps a fair summary of the whole conservative way of thinking about government from the early eighteenth century down to the present to suggest that the persistent theme has been that of mixed and therefore limited government. At different periods the theme has been expressed in terms appropriate to the existing social and political structures. If we turn to the early writings of Disraeli we find that the idea of popular representation is attacked through an appeal to the historical continuity of estates, each of which was represented in the political institutions of the country.[11] Later the emphasis switches to the balance in parliament between Lords and Commons, and in modern times the balance is sought in the competition of organised parties for popular support within the conventions laid down by the parliamentary system. But, of course, there are other balancing factors: the restraining influence of the monarchy, the independence of the courts, the legal autonomy of local municipal corporations, the freedoms of the professions, the diffusion of interests organised in society and so on. For Conservatives, as indeed for many of different political persuasions, the British appeared to have made a remarkable success of parliamentary government. They had made a peaceful transition to universal suffrage without disruption of the social basis of political life, they had virtually invented the modern political party as a means of mobilising support and enabling the electorate to choose a government or, what is more important, to reject one, they had sustained a sovereign parliament whose powers are in principle unlimited and illimitable, and they had preserved intact a capacity to regulate political life through the conventions of an unwritten and very flexible constitution. They had, in addition, permitted the sovereignty of parliament to be claimed effectively by the government of the day, which increasingly felt entitled to legislate for the extension of public powers in virtue of its popular mandate, and they had devised a bureaucracy for the exercise of these public powers which has been uniquely detached from party political commitment.

Such in outline has been the modern development of the constitution, and Conservatives did, until recently at any rate, approve of it. The achievement appeared to be a tribute to the political sagacity of the nation and to a capacity to work out that accommodation between social needs and attitudes on the one hand and appropriate modes of political action on the other which conservative philosophy recommended as the only prudent course of political development. That Conservative governments presided over much of this evolution no doubt accounts for part of the approval which it has enjoyed. But there was, too, a more substantial reason for satisfaction. The course of social reform as well as the pace of constitutional change was gradual; within and between institutions pressures were at work which maintained a balance, and in society at large there were many sources of obstruction to measures which would have disturbed existing interests too violently, and to procedures which would have short-circuited those laid down by custom and convention as well as by earlier statutory enactment. Within this framework two-party competition was held to be fruitful and itself a mechanism by which moderation was enforced and government subjected to the ultimate control of the electorate. Moreover, when there was clear evidence of deep-seated popular support for changes put through by a radical government, Conservatives were generally prepared to respect such changes and to treat them as part of a new *status quo*. Such, of course, was their attitude to most of the legislation of the Labour government 1945–50.

This satisfaction with the constitutional system and the manner in which it has worked has been replaced by a mood of doubt and anxiety. It is easy to dismiss this as nothing but an expression of the fears and frustrations of a party in opposition, unable to prevent the carrying-out of policies which it dislikes and which in several cases are gravely disadvantageous to interests which it supports (and which in turn tend to support the party). But this is too cynical a verdict on the reasons for Conservative anxiety about the constitution and the present interest in constitutional reform within the party. Some of the actions of the Labour party between 1967 and 1970 when in government, the behaviour of the Labour party in opposition after 1970, the events of 1973–4, the legislative record of the Wilson government 1974–6, and the disturbing developments in several Labour constituency parties during recent years have all conspired to make Conservatives doubt whether there is any longer the will to work the constitution in the accustomed way and to cast a question-mark over the validity of a number of its accepted conventions. Perhaps, too, there are more thoughtful Conservatives who wonder whether the government of Edward Heath with its obsessive pursuit of major legislative changes on the basis of a slender parliamentary majority and a minority of votes in the country did not also contribute to the undermining of confidence in the terms on which the country is governed.

Criticism of constitutional trends has focused on four issues, although there are several less crucial matters which have claimed attention. First, there is the realisation that parliamentary sovereignty can be seriously misused in the sense that it can be harnessed to the fulfilment of a programme for which there is neither a majority in the country nor even an overall majority of the ruling party in parliament. Moreover, there is nothing to stop the authority of parliament being used to push through measures demanded by vociferous interests outside parliament which are subject to little or no popular control at all. The discovery that parliamentary sovereignty is a double-edged sword tends to prompt either or both of two reactions. One is to ask whether there should be formal limits to its exercise, in other words should not some conditions be withdrawn from change at the whim of a transient simple majority in parliament? The other is to consider again the structure of parliament and to look to means of checking the *de facto* claim of the Commons to exercise parliamentary sovereignty alone. This leads, of course, to the question of reform of the House of Lords.

The second issue is linked with the first and concerns the majority principle. If a majority is to be entitled to get its way on virtually anything, should we not look seriously at what constitutes a majority and the terms on which one is produced? Should not the application of the majority principle be subject to certain conditions of reinsurance? Although the experience in terms of electoral statistics is by no means new, it has been demonstrated since 1974 in a remarkably vivid way that a relative majority in the House of Commons may rest on a minority position in the country. Government on these terms is tolerable if the party in power recognises that there are limits to what it is entitled to do. But if it claims that it has a mandate for its programme when in commonsense terms it is clear that it has not, then one of the restraining

conditions on which British parliamentary government has operated collapses. It becomes acceptable for minorities to impose their
will and the majority must put up with it. Faced with the
unpalatable consequences of the lack of congruence between the
parliamentary majority and the majority in the country, it is
impossible to avoid the conclusion that the electoral system has
something to do with it. Hence we find Conservatives considering
whether an electoral system sanctified by centuries of practice
should not be modified in order to provide some assurance that a
majority in parliament will be a genuine majority. Taken together
these two issues—the misuse of parliamentary sovereignty and the
risk of perversion of the majority principle—have been taken to add
up to the danger of elective dictatorship, a matter on which Lord
Hailsham has expended much eloquence.[12] Underlying them is
uneasiness at the manner in which the British competitive two-party
system has developed, increasingly undermining areas of consensus
and discouraging that degree of continuity in policy which is
necessary to good government.

The third issue which has seriously worried many Conservatives
is the way in which particular conventions governing institutional
roles and relationships have been eroded. Collective responsibility
of the Cabinet has occasionally been set aside, a Government has
inclined to condone the actions of those in public office who have
openly flouted the law, the House of Lords has been threatened and
pushed around, political patronage has been extended in the civil
service (and elsewhere for that matter too), adverse votes even on
major issues in the House of Commons appear to entail no
consequences for a government so long as a formal vote of no-
confidence is not passed, the device of the referendum has been
taken up despite its implications for the authority of parliament. No
doubt all these shifts in practice can be presented as justifiable
responses to difficult situations and in no way directed in a spirit of
hostility against existing constitutional conventions. On the whole,
however, this seems to be a rosy view of the matter. The conventions
governing institutional roles have weakened and lost something of
their compelling force: so far nothing much has been put in their
place.

Finally, there is the issue of the role of law in society and in
political life. Here I refer not to the popular law and order theme,
nor to the argument that the Labour party has been less than
wholehearted in its respect for measures passed by a Conservative

government and still on the statute book. It is rather whether the body of law has not become too complex, too uncertain in its effects, too malleable, and not infrequently oppressive. This is, of course, by no means exclusively a British problem and to a large extent it stems from the contemporary view of the role of the public authority in guaranteeing what is regarded as a desirable level of economic and social welfare. But it is not unreasonable to conclude that the more heavily law weighs on society, the greater is the risk that respect for it will decline. To this situation there are two responses, not necessarily mutually exclusive. One is to try to reduce the burden of legal regulation, the other is to try to develop within the legal system regulative principles which the citizen can invoke for his protection. Both these lines of thought find expression in Conservative thinking about constitutional reform.

In summary, Conservative anxieties about British constitutional development stem from the belief that limited and mixed government is in danger. It has been undermined by the vast expansion of state power which has taken place, by the wear and tear imposed by the competition of two disciplined political parties which has magnified the distance between them in respect of political and social values, by the arrogant application of the doctrine of parliamentary sovereignty, and by the erosion of those values and pressures in society which previously imposed constraints on what government felt entitled to undertake. Should present trends continue, many Conservatives would foresee the emergence of a form of populist party oligarchy: the country would be ruled by the dominant minority within a party with a nominal majority, and this minority would justify its position by claiming in some obscure manner to represent the real will of the people. The major political institutions would sink further into the status of dignified parts of the constitution, whilst some might even be candidates for the lumber-room. The effective institution would be the ruling party's central or. executive committee and that in turn might be some curious fusion of cabinet and extra-parliamentary party executive. Such a form of government is by no means unknown and it is often claimed to be democratic into the bargain. That such a constitutional outcome would be accompanied by more measures of social and economic regulation to which Conservatives are bitterly opposed would merely compound its disagreeable quality.

### III PROPOSALS FOR CONSTITUTIONAL REFORM: THEMES RATHER THAN COMMITMENTS?

The next stage is to examine the reaction of the party in the light of this appreciation of the present position and to assess the significance of the constitutional reform proposals which have been aired within the party.

The initial reaction has been defensive and protective, that is to say, to concentrate on possible ways of warding off the constitutional dangers which are perceived to exist. Proposals have come from various sources and there has been an unusual degree of intra-party discussion and recommendation, some of it officially sponsored by the leadership, some of it coming spontaneously from groups within the party. It must be accepted that so far, despite the intensity of argument and the proliferation of suggestions for reform, very little has been taken over into the party's official policy. This probably reflects more than just caution on the part of the leader and differences of opinion among leading Conservatives.[13] It expresses, too, the hesitations which many experienced Conservative politicians feel once they see where some of the reform proposals may be leading. The dilemma to which I referred at the outset becomes explicit and the result so far is a refusal to enter into policy commitments on constitutional reform. That there are problems is admitted, that they can and should be dealt with by deliberate measures of constitutional innovation and restoration is a conclusion from which many still recoil, sensing, too, that the average party activist would share a similar reluctance to appeal to what look suspiciously like abstract principles.

I propose to discuss briefly only five topics on the agenda of constitutional reform, and one of them, devolution, will be dealt with very briefly as it is a problem receiving separate consideration in this collection of essays.

Reform of the House of Lords is in some respects the easiest to begin with since the nature of the problem is clearly understood and familiar. The primary justification for House of Lords reform is to provide a more effective check on the legislative activities of the government and Commons through the opportunities for legislative revision which fall to the upper house. The present chamber may perform this role tolerably well given the limitations imposed by its composition and working methods. Yet, as we know, it exists on sufferance on account of its composition and is constantly exposed to threats of further attenuation of its powers, or abolition, from the Labour party. Thus it treads softly and recognises how narrow is its room for manoeuvre. Without question the Conservative party prefers to maintain a two-chamber parliament and would support more strongly now than in the fifties the argument that if there are to be institutional checks on the Commons, one at least must be a second chamber. Such a view renders a reform of the composition of the Lords inevitable and it is proposals to that end which an official party committee under Lord Home has recently presented.[14] Essentially these represent a compromise between traditionalists and root and branch reformers. The latter would have a wholly-elected second chamber, the former are very reluctant to see the continuity of the Lords destroyed and some of them would perhaps prefer to risk abolition rather than surrender the concept of a House based on rank and status in society. Thus it is a part-elected, part-nominated chamber which is recommended, though with the elected element preponderant after a transitional period. Only a modest strengthening of the powers through a return to the two-year delaying power is suggested.

In essentials these seem to be prudent and modest proposals, justified in terms of offering the prospect of a return to a more stable balance within a bicameral parliament. That the Labour party should oppose such proposals is not surprising. What, however, of their chances within the Conservative party? It is highly questionable whether they will be implemented, even should the party gain a substantial majority. There are several reasons for this. The Commons collectively (and this includes Conservatives) is very sensitive to any aggrandisement of the upper house. It has lived for three generations and longer in an atmosphere of rivalry and mistrust in its relations with the Lords and as a result will brook no competitor who might claim equal legitimacy in the passage of laws. Thus getting a reform measure through would almost certainly be difficult and perhaps impossible. Then there are the traditionalist sentiments in the party at large, feelings which are bound up with the history of the party and the role which the hereditary peerage has played in it. Those who cherish such sentiments cannot easily envisage their party transforming what is for them a venerable and somewhat romanticised institution. There are influential members of the party, too, who believe that now a Conservative majority has been returned, all will be well. The threat of single chamber government will recede and a balance will be restored naturally.

Finally, there are those who are both practical and sophisticated, discerning that to tackle the House of Lords problem seriously is to embark on a process of change which will have unforeseen consequences and may well entail a far more extensive overhaul of constitutional arrangements than they care to envisage. For they recognise that within the institutions of a country the different pieces are connected one with another; to redesign one is to run the risk that another and yet another will have to be re-fashioned. Inevitably at the end of the day you face the need for a completely revised constitution and on what can that be based if not on abstract principles?

Devolution, about the details of which I will say nothing, presents a marked contrast in intent at least to the approach to the House of Lords issue. The party was early in the field with modest proposals published in 1970[15] for an elected assembly to be associated in the passage of Scottish legislation at Westminster. But in office after 1970 nothing was done and the party's subsequent reaction to proposals advanced by the Labour government has been sometimes ambiguous and generally hostile. In a somewhat desultory way the party has had various internal consultative groups on devolution since 1975, but once the original Scotland and Wales Bill was introduced, the initiative in opposing it shifted to hostile English backbenchers and to those Scottish members who were against the scheme and feared that support for it would merely strengthen the Scottish National party. That some of the Scottish opponents might be described as Tory populists is not without significance. Fundamentally, a majority in the party is hostile to devolution, treating it as a peripheral aberration, a likely source of conflict and an additional burden on taxpayers throughout the United Kingdom.

It is a striking fact that the party of the Union continues to display little sympathy for the claims of the non-English parts of the UK to self-government, and relatively little interest in the question whether the demand for devolution stems from a deep-seated reaction against Whitehall dominance and, if so, whether it could be met in a manner compatible with the survival of the British state. There is another peculiarity of this disinterest in devolution and in the reasons why it has become a major issue which is that a stress on the importance of local self-governing communities as a counter-weight to an over-powerful central government was an important element in Conservative constitutional thinking in the first half of the last century. Not only has the Conservative party in recent years shown little appreciation of local government as an element in our constitutional balance, but it has also failed to see that devolution— assuming that there is a sustained demand for it—could also contribute to restraining the claims of the central authority to know best what policies should everywhere be pursued and how resources should be distributed. If the expansion of central governmental powers is to be checked, here may be an opportunity to make a start.

Yet the party's recent record on devolution is largely negative: the instinctive reactions rooted in the past predominate and no doubt the experience in handling the problems of Northern Ireland reinforced a certain dislike of devolution. However, underlying the critical reaction to the Scotland and Wales Bills is a continuing attachment to the unitary state and the place of parliament within it. More than that, there is the suspicion that to have a genuine scheme of devolution requires a more explicit step towards something like a federal arrangement than the Labour government has been prepared to recognise. However, federalism is associated with legalism, with formal constitutional provisions and with an increased authority for judges in the interpretation of powers. Dicey's polemic against Home Rule continues to echo down the years, even though there are doubtless few active in contemporary politics who have ever read it.[16] The outcome is that it is chiefly a handful of Scottish Conservatives of a liberal disposition and a few of their kinsmen sitting for English seats who actively advocate a devolutionary settlement for Scotland and would be prepared to contemplate a scheme less fussy, ambiguous and inequitable than that which laboured through parliament in 1977–8. For the rest the party remains obstinately attached to the unitary state, even though the price of that may be a minority position at Westminster.[17]

It has already been suggested that the experiences of 1974 strengthened the doubts which some Conservatives had about the simple majority principle and its application in a sovereign parliament. The upsurge in the Liberal vote brought home to the party the danger of being condemned to a permanent minority position should the Liberals decide to give their support to a Labour government. And perhaps the most decisive of all was the belief born of the activities of the Labour government in 1974 and 1975 that there was under the existing system of voting little or no protection against policies judged by many to be doctrinaire and sectarian. These circumstances helped to stimulate a re-appraisal of the electoral system. This, however, has been very much a free-enterprise activity within the party, carried on chiefly by the Conservative Action for Electoral Reform.

This body, which appears to have had generous backers, has not only produced an impressive range of pamphlets and articles, but has also brought over into the electoral reform camp a substantial number of senior figures in the party who have associated themselves publicly with the campaign. It is probable that roughly 80 members of the parliamentary party could in 1978 be counted as supporters or sympathisers.

The details of the reform schemes proposed need not be discussed here except in relation to one aspect of them. That is the strong preference expressed by CAER for the additional member system, i.e. an adaptation of the West German method of combining single-member constituencies with lists to ensure proportionality. The significance of this lies in the retention of single-member constituencies which it facilitates. There seems no doubt that there is a strong attachment in the party to the constituency as the basis of representation and were it ever to support electoral reform, it would certainly be on condition that constituencies of reasonably small size were maintained. Here we can detect a very strong streak of instinctive conservatism, the belief that members do and should represent pieces of territory as they have claimed to do since time immemorial. The fact that they are now mainly detached from their 'territory', people who have no ties of family, education and career with the constituency, is ignored. So, too, is the fact that it is parties which are supported rather than persons. Thus we find the party determined to maintain at least one element in a mode of representation which owes its characteristics to a totally different political context.

The official attitude of the party towards electoral reform remains, however, persistently hostile. The leadership dislikes the idea of coalition (an attitude equally widespread in the Labour party) and questions whether the Liberals would be reliable partners. Indeed it fears that electoral reform might even put the seal of permanence on the minority position to which the party was relegated in 1974. At a more opportunistic level the party's leaders clearly believe that it would be foolish to forego the chance of an overall majority which the British electoral system always has on offer. Thus it is questionable whether the party can be forced into a policy commitment to electoral reform without traumatic experiences. Such might be the case if it found itself again frustrated in office by trade union opposition or if there were a repetition of the 1974 voting pattern, with the party excluded then from office and powerless to prevent Labour policies supported by only a minority of voters from being put into effect. But the root objection to electoral reform remains dislike of a new and unfamiliar style of politics which it would be likely to impose. The politics of genuine as opposed to emergency coalition is not something that the Conservative party cares to contemplate. And it is worth noting that a move to proportionality would seriously affect the behaviour and structure of the House of Commons, perhaps making it impossible to maintain there that fusion of the functions of government with the leadership of the House which has been one of the most decisive characteristics of the British form of parliamentary government.

Finally it needs to be remembered that on this issue the party has officially been unbending in its opposition to proportional voting both for European assembly and for the Scottish and Welsh assemblies.[18] 'No experiments' has been the motto of the leadership and regularly the 'thin end of the wedge' objection has been wheeled out. Clearly there is a long way to go before the party is prepared to accept that if genuine majorities are desired and if competitive two-party warfare is to be moderated or replaced by something more like consensus politics, then electoral reform may well be the only measure capable of bringing about such changes.

Linked to some extent with the electoral reform question is the matter of the referendum. The initial reaction of Mrs Margaret Thatcher to the EEC referendum proposal was one of hostility and she criticised it on familiar constitutional grounds besides condemning it as a device for holding together the Labour party on the EEC issue.[19] More recently she expressed somewhat different views and let it be known that there may be circumstances in which a referendum would be positively desirable. It is probable that Mrs Thatcher is in a minority with her view and that most Conservative politicians still look with suspicion on direct appeals to the people, regarding such methods as subversive of the political responsibility of the government and of the authority of parliament. Nevertheless, it would appear that the party leader is moved by a serious consideration, even though the referendum may not be the appropriate way of dealing with the problem. What worries some Conservative leaders is the prospect of militant opposition outisde parliament to the decisions of a Conservative government, perhaps entailing results similar to those of February 1974. In such a situation the politician is tempted to think in terms of an appeal to the people on a specific issue, something which can rarely if ever be achieved through a general election. Should the appeal be successful, it can then be asserted that there is a definite majority in the country against the militant opponents of a particular policy.

Other elements enter into the referendum discussion. There is in the Conservative party a streak of populism which may be more likely to find expression now that the party in parliament emerges from a socially heterogeneous group. This populist strain sees the people (and quite rightly too) as a bastion against certain types of change and appreciates what kind of fears or resentment can be mobilised both against change and against unpopular or recalcitrant minorities. In addition there is widespread feeling (also probably justified) that government and parliament simply impose on the people nowadays measures, regulations and policies which they dislike and would certainly not agree to support if consulted directly. Thus there is a radical democratic element in the argument for the referendum, too, and it ties in closely with the hostility felt in the Conservative party for the apparently inexorable growth of public bureaucracy.

The difficulties and dangers in the referendum proposal are, however, very obvious. There is the risk of the mobilisation of prejudice; there is the prospect of encouraging irresponsibility in parliament; there is the almost insuperable difficulty of determining what kind of questions really could be put to a popular vote in the hope of mobilising support against the actions of recalcitrant minorities, e.g. a trade union striking for higher pay in defiance of government pay policy. And there are the dangers inherent in all plebiscitary devices when the results go against those who use them. But one obstacle above all stands in the way of the referendum in Britain in a form which would make sense constitutionally and limit the destabilising effects of the procedure. This consists in the impossibility as matters now stand of devising a rule or rules prescribing the conditions under which a referendum might be held. Under our present constitution a referendum can be no more than an expression of will—the will of a majority in parliament. Whether a referendum is decreed and on what issues is a matter of pure discretion and hence of political opportunism. There is no escape from this position without wholesale constitutional change.

Had Britain a written constitution, the amendment of that document itself could be made subject to popular vote. That would be one kind of rule and a perfectly respectable one. Within a formalised constitution provision could be made for a consultative referendum, perhaps related to impending legislation. Similarly within such a framework it would be possible to envisage a form of popular initiative leading to a referendum if certain conditions were met. But what remains a riddle is how to formulate principles to govern the use of referendums within the terms of our present conventional constitution, the only bedrock of which is the sovereignty of parliament. Once again the Conservative reformer finds himself (or herself) in an impasse.

A fifth area of constitutional discussion has been individual rights. In the light of the fairly influential part played by Common Law lawyers in the Conservative party, it is not surprising that there should have been much criticism of the manner in which individual rights have been hemmed in and restricted by the growth of public powers, and more recently by the actions of trade unions demanding compulsory membership, the closed shop. The case for affording a sharper definition of basic individual rights and more protection for them has been mixed up, too, with the fear in some parts of the Conservative party that obstructive groups in society have become more inclined to refuse obedience to the law and to press their claims in defiance of court decisions. So the argument on behalf of individual rights as against collective power, public and private, becomes also an argument about the extent to which the state should use its power to uphold such individual rights, even though to do so may provoke social conflict.

In the era of Mr Heath's leadership there were clear signs that the Conservative party was sympathetic to a more effective and creative use of law for the regulation of competing claims and the adjudication of rights than had been common in the 1950s and 1960s. The 1971 Industrial Relations Act stands as a frustrated monument to that line of thought and it is worth recalling that despite its repeal, much of the approach embodied in it has been followed in subsequent enactments. Nevertheless the experience of that Act has cast doubts over the advisability of using the law in sectors of social relationships where there is strong objection to the intrusion of formalised principles and enforceable adjudication by a court. Rather sadly, the prospects for a more creative use of law in many areas of social life where the public authority intervenes or confers special privileges on a private body corporate or association do not look good.

However, there has been another line of exploration which has attracted support and that is the notion of a Bill of Rights enforceable through the courts. It is probable that most lawyers bred in the Common Law tradition still remain hostile to the proposal, or at any rate find it hard to understand how it might operate in practice.[20] Similarly, most politicians are instinctively suspicious, believing themselves to possess a unique insight into how to resolve conflicts over claims and rights which is mysteriously denied to judges. Moreover, they sense, too, that the logic of a Bill of Rights is to enhance the judicial role (though the experience of Canada since 1960 suggests that such enhancement may be modest in scale) and they believe for reasons which remain obscure that this must be harmful to politicians. Thus there are only a few enthusiastic supporters of a Bill of Rights, amongst whom Lord Hailsham must now be numbered. What has, however, been achieved is some awareness in the party that the protection of individual rights in Britain is often made difficult by the narrowness of the terms of reference within which cases involving infringement of rights have to be decided by the courts. Cases often resemble lotteries, their outcome depending on the attitudes of the judges who are called upon to reach a decision and on the contingent statutory conditions out of which a case arises. What a Bill of Rights offers is at the least the prospect of more general principles being applied both to the settlement of cases and to the drafting of legislation. Such principles would be broadly comprehensible to laymen, and it would be possible to look forward to the development of a case-law in which legal *and* political considerations would play a part. It is, of course, precisely at the stage when he perceives such prospects that the Conservative advocate of the protection of rights draws back. For on the horizon he sees the possibility that parliament itself will be limited by the terms in which rights are laid down and interpreted.

## IV THE RADICALISM OF CONSTITUTIONAL REFORM AS THE SOURCE OF THE DILEMMA

I have considered only five aspects of constitutional change which have in different ways been discussed within the Conservative party and on which in two cases so far proposals have been made by official party committees.[21] Without doubt the discussion of these matters in the party has been beneficial: those involved have felt that serious and worthwhile issues are at stake and on the whole the quality of the arguments used in support of the different proposals made has been high. Yet the practical outcome is meagre: the party appears to believe that the constitution is in some danger and that something should be done. There remains, however, a marked reluctance to enter into firm commitments, and it is hard not to conclude that now the party has returned to power it will concentrate on day-to-day problems and on implementing some of its economic and social policies, leaving the constitutional issues for another day. For a while it will believe that the constitution is not in such a bad state after all and may return to its mood of doubt only if relegated again to opposition.

Why is this so? It seems to me that a purely opportunist explanation is not adequate. The irresolution with regard to the constitutional problems which undoubtedly face this country stems from some awareness of the dilemma with which I began. The social, moral and legal basis of the informal constitution in the shape it gradually acquired after 1832 has been seriously weakened. Political habits and manners have changed; expectations of government have changed; the purposes of government and of law have changed; the balance between state and society has tilted in favour of the former, though the latter increasingly asserts *its* sovereignty. Under the impact of such changes it is not surprising that political institutions cannot operate and relate to each other on the terms still regarded as 'normal' according to the description and justification of the constitution on which we have been nurtured. Most decisive of all, disciplined political parties have come to monopolise the constitution, to treat it as an elusive bit of property to an extent that qualifies substantially the claim so often made in the Conservative tradition that the constitution offers a guarantee of limited government.

I shall not pursue this argument further, if only because I have done so at length elsewhere.[22] The conclusion to which it points is that the constitutional system we have known, the unwritten tradition, is nearing the end of its useful life and that it would be prudent to set in train a radical overhaul. Many Conservatives are reluctant to accept such a conclusion, partly because they retain a streak of optimism, partly because it runs counter to the philosophy they have inherited and to which reference was made at the outset. The course of constitutional argument within the party during the last three or four years does, however, suggest that the very attempt to think pragmatically about this or that feature of our constitutional arrangements forces those engaged in it to recognise that piecemeal reform has become at best very difficult, at worst impossible. For despite the contempt generally shown in Conservative theorising on politics for 'abstract principles', a mature constitutional system reveals a certain coherence and has an internal logic of its own for those who care to reflect on its operation and on the justifications given for it. It is when we begin to contemplate particular reforms in the British constitution that we are struck by the extraordinary coherence which it has or, to be more accurate, which finds expression in the classic expositions of it. Indeed it might even be argued that the informal constitutional tradition has lasted so long and been so successful precisely because it embodied a higher degree of coherence in the understanding of compatible political practices than is usually attainable within a formalised tradition which, almost by definition, must legislate constitutionally for the arbitration of conflict and in this way takes out an insurance policy against the loss of coherence.

But it is possible that the contemporary Conservative reformer contemplates an idealised constitution. This helps to persuade him that the coherence which has been lost in reality can somehow be recovered without radical change, requiring perhaps only a return to patterns of behaviour which once sustained the pattern of limited government which he prefers. There is more than a touch of romanticism in such a conclusion. Yet it is understandable that the Conservative who perceives that the reform of one part of the constitution relentlessly leads on to a scrutiny of another part, should then draw back in doubt. For what then becomes clear to him is that he is engaged in an attempt to establish a new coherence in the structure of institutions and in the principles on which they rest. This is a radical undertaking for which his tradition gives him no taste. Moreover, it would be worse than useless to embark on it if society at large is not yet ready for such a work of reconstruction. This is why it is reasonable to ask what might be the political cost of such an attempt and whether there is indeed strong popular support for such an endeavour. It is perhaps at this point that the traditional Conservative view of political and constitutional evolution reasserts itself: a constitution consists of rules and conventions sanctified by understandings, values and practices in society; it is not an artificial or contrived product but the natural expression of the political skills of a people; and it is dangerous to uproot what you already have, not just because to do so is to risk instability, but because extensive reconstruction can proceed only through the clarification of principles and the definition of how they are to be applied. Here the circle closes itself: the Burkean Conservative is trapped by the postulates of his own argument.

Such seems to be the dilemma which inhibits an active commitment to constitutional reform by the Conservative party. Conservatism is a very English phenomenon, at any rate under that name. Yet there are other traditions of political thought which in their outcome are conservative and which in different ways have overcome the fear of abstract principles which has been such a prominent feature of English Conservatism. We owe to Montesquieu the principal elements of a powerful theory of limited government which is perhaps still the soundest basis for an alternative to the thoroughly Hobbesian theory of parliamentary sovereignty. And from the most penetrating of all conservative political thinkers, Hegel,[23] we can learn that it is possible (and indeed necessary) to distinguish between abstract principles and rational principles. But to pursue that distinction would require another paper.[24] Let it suffice to suggest that the British constitution in its present condition reveals a deficit of rational principles and that even a Conservative in the British tradition need not fear the reproach of inconsistency if he embarks on the pursuit of a more rational pattern of constitutional arrangements. For that means that he would through reform be seeking practical conclusions more consistent with his political values and better adapted to their maintenance and survival than is British constitutional practice today.

NOTES

1. E. Burke: *Observations on a Late State of the Nation* (London: J. Dodsley, 1769).
2. Social institutions include, of course, legal relationships established in England through the development of Common Law.
3. Burke quite rightly emphasised the crucial role of prejudice—acquired and unreflecting habits in social behaviour—in holding society together. He was probably right, too, to argue that we can find wisdom in prejudice. But to grant this much still does not justify neglect of man's reflective and critical capacities.

4. De Tocqueville, *Democracy in America* (London: Oxford University Press, 1961) p. 593.

5. It seems to me to be important to point out that inequalities of condition, position and prospects in life can be justified on Utilitarian grounds, e.g. in terms of the beneficial consequences of such a situation, but that such is *not* the primary justification in the conservative tradition. That tradition takes its stand on a view of the diversity of human nature and on the necessary quality of inequalities in social life: to deny inequality is equivalent to denying to human beings natural opportunities for self-development and for satisfying their desires. A precise and restricted view of equality is entailed by this.

6. It might be held that this understanding of law is now obsolescent and fails to take account of the extent to which much modern public law is a form of deliberate social engineering, resting on formalised norms and bureaucratic procedures for implementation.

7. It should be noted that the theory of the separation of powers in its various forms is directed to the institutionalisation of mistrust in the interest of liberty.

8. One of the more profound political consequences of policies of redistributive equalisation in society is precisely that many of the political obstacles to the increase in centralised governmental power are dissolved in the process. Tocqueville shows this more clearly than any other writer.

9. See, for example, on this point L. Scarman, *English Law: the New Dimension* (London: Stevens, 1974).

10. Local government reform is only one example of 'non-evolutionary' change and of the tendency to believe without conclusive evidence that some kind of changes must be made, e.g. also the reorganisation of the National Health Service and of the Water industry in 1973-4.

11. For example, in B. Disraeli, *Vindication of the English Constitution* (London: Leadenhall Press, 1835), Chapters XII to XVI.

12. Most recently, Lord Hailsham, *The Dilemma of Democracy* (London: Collins, 1978).

13. Whether caution stems from doubts about the value of constitutional reform proposals in terms of electoral advantage of disadvantage is a matter not discussed here. It seems doubtful whether any conclusive judgment is possible.

14. *The House of Lords*, Report of the Conservative Review Committee chaired by Lord Home, published by the Conservative Central Office, March 1978.

15. *Scotland's Government*, Report of the Scottish Constitutional Committee under the chairmanship of Sir Alec Douglas-Home, March 1970.

16. A. V. Dicey, *England's Case against Home Rule* (London: John Murray 1886). The most notable contemporary expositor of Dicey's denial of the possibility of reconciling Home Rule (= Devolution) with a unitary system of parliamentary government is Mr Enoch Powell. There is no doubt some irony in the fact that he now sits for a Northern Ireland constituency and that this is attributable in some degree to the destruction of the Unionist party political fabric which resulted from the abolition of Stormont in 1972 by a Conservative government.

17. There is almost certainly more support amongst Conservative MPs for some form of Scottish devolution than for Welsh devolution. But this reflects the widespread belief, confirmed by the referendum result, that the demand for

devolution is weaker in Wales and in addition the Conservative party is unlikely to lose support there through opposition to the scheme.

18. The disapproval of the leadership did not prevent some Conservative MPs from supporting a list system for elections to the European assembly and amendments to provide for proportional voting for the Scottish assembly. In the House of Lords amendments were in fact passed to ensure proportional representation in Scotland, but the Conservative party allowed a free vote in the Commons which effectively meant helping the government to override such amendments.

19. Parliamentary Debates (Hansard) vol. 888, 1974–5, cols. 304–17.

20. It is worth noting that the most persistent exponent of the codification of basic rights on the judicial bench (Lord Scarman) has to be described as a liberal and perhaps even as a libertarian too. The most recent discussion of the Bill of Rights proposal is to be found in the report of the House of Lords Select Committee on a Bill of Rights, H.L. 176, 1977–8.

21. A committee to examine the referendum was set up in April 1978 by the party leader. Its report, *The Referendum and the Constitution* was published in September 1978 as a Conservative Research Department Paper (no. 16). The other committee was, of course, the Home Committee on the House of Lords referred to previously.

22. Nevil Johnson, *In Search of the Constitution* (Oxford: Pergamon Press, 1977).

23. It is in some respects inaccurate to describe Hegel as conservative. Yet his great achievement was to encompass the fact of change and the experience of rational thought within a political theory which vindicated the claim that all serious reflection on the practice of politics must in its outcome be 'conservative' in respect of the political order it justifies. On this basis a thorough-going programme of constitutional reform can, in some circumstances, be justified as 'conservative'.

24. This is the appropriate point at which to note that I have in this paper deliberately avoided drawing comparisons between the dilemmas presented by the pursuit of constitutional reform, and those presented by the attempt to formulate a coherent view of the limits of state action in relation to the economy and the provision of social benefits by government. The effort to develop something like a social market economy philosophy to guide a Conservative government in the formulation of its economic and social policies has run into objections which, *mutatis mutandis*, are similar to those brought against the constitutional reformers on the Conservative side. It is somewhat surprising that Sir Keith Joseph and others who share his commitment to the redefinition of the economic and social aspects of Conservative philosophy appear to show little interest in the constitutional implications of their arguments: the impression is often conveyed that political institutions are rather secondary bits of organisation which a management consultant can re-jig according to need. In contrast the political and constitutional dimension was always central to the arguments of the German neo-liberal advocates of the *soziale Marktwirtschaft*. Once more, there is here a topic for another and far more extensive paper.

# PART TWO

# PARTY POLITICS

# 7 Approaches to Leadership in Opposition: Edward Heath and Margaret Thatcher[1]

Martin Burch

## I INTRODUCTION

The opposition context is relatively neglected in studies of major British political parties.[2] It is often assumed that the party as opposition and the party as government, while differing marginally, are broadly equivalent types of organisations. Though there are substantial and important elements of continuity, it is worth emphasising that when a major party enters or leaves office certain aspects of the structure and purpose of the party are radically altered. Indeed, it can be reasonably argued that in some areas of party activity, for example policy-making, the transformation is of such a degree that it makes more sense to speak of the system of party politics in the UK over the post-war period as being characteristically a four- rather than two-party one.[3]

As far as Conservative politics is concerned, this neglect of the opposition dimension is further compounded by a strongly held view amongst some observers that the Conservative party is the natural and proper party of government. It is the *natural* party of government because historically it has been in office for longer than any other party. About two-thirds of the period since the 1884 Reform Act has been dominated by Conservative or Conservative-led governments. It is the *proper* party of government because, it is alleged, Conservatives traditionally regard their party as being the best qualified and most suited to govern, so that any period out of office is seen as a temporary break in the usual ruling pattern and an opportunity to rest and regroup before the normal situation is resumed once more.[4]

The assumption that the Conservative party is pre-eminently a party of government is based on observations made in the 1950s and early 1960s. From the perspective of the late-1970s, however, this assumption no longer appears quite as tenable. In particular the Conservatives' experience of opposition can no longer be regarded as negligible and, therefore, abnormal. In the post-war period, for instance, during the almost unbroken thirty-three year span of the two-party parliamentary system, the Conservatives have actually been in opposition for nearly half that time. Moreover, since the 1964 election defeat, mindful perhaps of possible changes in the electoral base of the two-party system, many Conservatives seem to have lost much of their alleged confidence about their party's future and its central place in British politics. It seems, therefore, that if labels are to be given, then there is as much justification for describing the Conservative party as a party of opposition as there is for calling it a party of government.

The following involves a small attempt to remedy the neglect of the opposition perspective by considering the nature of Conservative leadership during two periods in opposition: from 1964 to 1970, and from 1975 to the present.[5] A central concern is with the approaches to opposition leadership adopted by Edward Heath and Margaret Thatcher. Initially, attention is given to the broad context in which leadership operates and to the tasks Conservative leaders may be expected to perform when their party is in opposition. Thereafter the examination moves to consider the approaches of both leaders to the problems of opposition leadership and to provide some contrast between them. Analysis is concentrated upon certain particular aspects of leadership activity including party organisation, policy production, and public relations. The conclusion examines some explanations of the difference in approach exhibited by these two leaders of the Conservative opposition. Readers might note that there will be no attempt to provide a searching analysis of the psychological and personality factors involved;[6] rather the discussion will stick to the staple diet of political science with an emphasis upon institutions, processes, and policies.

## II THE CONTEXT OF LEADERSHIP

A good prime minister does not always make a good leader of the opposition and vice-versa. Not surprisingly, the leadership skills required are different. In part this is because each context of party action (government or opposition) provides a different framework of constraints and potentialities within which leadership must operate and this framework serves to shape and guide the approach developed by each particular leader. To understand the context of leadership in the Conservative party as opposition it is necessary to consider at least two sets of factors. First, those which generally apply to opposition leadership in the UK two-party parliamentary system, and secondly, those which apply particularly to the Conservative party as opposition.

### Party Leadership in Opposition

An obvious but central distinction from which much else follows is that in opposition party leaders are ultimately concerned with *winning* power whereas in government, as prime ministers, they are generally concerned with *maintaining* it. These differences in purpose are important because they require the development of distinctive strategies of party action and organisation in line with the different resources available to the leader in government and opposition. The party as government, for instance, in attempting to maintain power, is primarily to be judged on the basis of its performance in office, so that the tried calibre of its personnel and its general competence in managing the country's affairs are liable to be of central importance and, therefore, of vital concern to the leader. In opposition, however, the leader is not concerned to oversee the development of a detailed legislative programme, and he or she[7] lacks the patronage available in government, and the initiative in establishing the issue and terms of debate. So in opposition the leader must find other means of achieving his party's return to office.

Broadly speaking, two models are available, and each involves a different perception of the proper strategy and organisation of the opposition party.[8] First, there is what might be termed a *critical* approach to opposition, whereby the leader chooses to concentrate resources upon criticising the governing party in order to exploit its weaknesses with the aim of undermining its support amongst the electorate and of maintaining the unity of the opposition party. This concept of opposition strategy has some connection with the extreme nineteenth century view that it is the duty of an opposition 'to oppose everything and propose nothing'.[9] In its modern form, however, the critical approach is not quite so negative, for the opposition may be expected to have some alternative proposals to put forward, if only in broad outline. The critical strategy is based on the assumption that it is principally governments which lose elections and not oppositions which win them, and closely related to this is a concept of party organisation in opposition which places great emphasis on the need to exploit the benefits to be had from being no longer responsible for the day to day administration of the country. In particular, the leader should avoid appointing a rigidly defined shadow administration and should allow his colleagues a degree of freedom in debate and argument[10] so that, as in the nineteenth century notion of 'men in opposition', a measure of flexibility is preserved and broad ideas can be considered and developed.

The second model might be labelled the *alternative government* approach. According to this view, the leader should concentrate resources upon presenting the opposition as a real, responsible and viable alternative to the existing administration with the aim of strengthening party support and morale and, in time, gaining victory at the polls. The alternative government strategy has developed in parallel with the party system and is, therefore, largely a twentieth-century phenomenon.[11] Its increased acceptance in recent years reflects in part the programmatic approach to party politics initiated by the Labour party and the demands of modern mass communications for instant, but informed alternative re-actions to government pronouncements.[12] It is based upon the concept that the opposition can win elections or, at the very least, cannot credibly criticise the government without having a well thought-out alternative to put over. As far as party organisation is concerned, it is the leader's task to develop an alternative team and alternative measures. Hence policy should be produced in some detail and leading members of the opposition should be given specific shadow ministerial duties to perform. Moreover, the opposition must act responsibly and avoid purely negative tactics if it is to appear credible as an alternative government.

In choosing whether to place primary emphasis upon the critical or the alternative government approach, a party leader needs to consider carefully the problems inherent in each. Too great an emphasis upon the critical viewpoint, for instance, may result in the party returning to office without being fully prepared, while over-negative, 'ding-dong parliamentary battles'[13] may undermine the party's credibility amongst the electorate and, at the same time, devalue the reputation of the parliamentary system. Additionally there is the problem of party management: too much flexibility and too deep a discussion of the fundamentals of party belief may lead to division and a lack of control from the centre.

The alternative government approach is no less problematic. A responsible approach to opposition may fail to satisfy party supporters, while the desire to project a real and distinct alternative to the existing administration may lead to the adoption of extreme positions impossible to maintain or to implement when returned to office. There are also problems involved in the production of an alternative programme: for instance, the difficulties of producing realistic policies without the information and assistance available in government, or the difficulties of producing proposals in the present to be implemented in a future situation, the exact circumstances of which cannot be foreseen.[14] Overall there is the danger of limiting the freedom of manoeuvre of a future administration by encumbering it with too many detailed policies, publicised and committed to in advance. A too closely organised shadow administration may also have its drawbacks. Some members may feel constrained by the lack of flexibility allowed them, and the opportunity to re-examine intelligently the fundamentals of party belief which opposition affords may be smothered in the detail of particular policy responsibilities.

## Conservative Party Leadership in Opposition

Although both the critical and alternative government models are applicable to the exercise of opposition leadership in either of the two major British political parties, there are at least two other considerations which are peculiar to the Conservative party and are especially relevant to an understanding of the context within which Edward Heath and Margaret Thatcher have developed their own distinctive approaches. First, there is the tradition of past practice bequeathed by previous leaders of the Conservative opposition in the post-war period. Secondly, there are certain important structural features of the Conservative party as opposition which, relative to the situation in government, serve to alter the resources available to the leader and the channels of communication and contact between him and his followers. These also may be expected to affect the nature and operation of leadership.

As far as past practice is concerned, the 1945-51 experience provides two influential precedents. More importantly, there is Churchill's example which conforms broadly with the critical concept of opposition leadership. Churchill was greatly concerned to avoid giving hostages to fortune by making commitments which could not be fulfilled in the future, and his main objective was to preserve flexibility. He therefore declined from establishing a system of sharply defined shadow ministries, preferring instead to command a front-bench with loosely determined responsibilities, and whenever possible he preferred to avoid making precise policy statements.[15] A slightly contrary approach was developed by R. A. Butler, to whom much of the responsibility for policy production was delegated. Butler veered towards the alternative government perception with a strong belief in the need to formulate a distinct alternative programme, although not in great detail.[16] The aim should be to give a general impression of intent rather than to set out a series of precise proposals.

As opposition leader, Douglas-Home showed a marked preference for Butler's viewpoint. He considered that an opposition could only make an impact if it suggested itself as a 'competent alternative' by acting constructively and responsibly and by presenting a substantial alternative programme. Furthermore, for Douglas-Home the opposition could only be 'effective' if it remained united, for nothing would harm potential support more than disunity.[17] Hence he placed great emphasis upon matters of party management, and introduced measures designed to increase the degree of coordination between the leader and the various subsections of the party. His concern to create a competent and effective alternative was reflected in his initiation of a wide-scale reassessment of party policy under Heath and the establishment of a shadow administration of 60 (including a 'shadow cabinet' of nineteen members) with clearly defined responsibilities.[18]

As well as being influenced by past performances, Conservative opposition leaders must learn to operate within the changed structure of the Conservative party as opposition. Most obviously, instead of presiding over a cabinet and ministerial team, the leader is in command of some kind of shadow administration organised around the leader's Consultative Committee or shadow cabinet. Although the size, organisation and membership of the opposition team are matters for the leader to decide,[19] relative to the situation in government, his status and prestige and his powers of appointment and patronage are greatly reduced and consequently his hold over his senior colleagues is somewhat weakened.

In opposition there are also important differences in the organisation of the parliamentary party which serve to extend the contacts between the leader and his front-bench colleagues on the one hand and their back-bench followers on the other. In particular, the party's back-bench subject committees are chaired by the relevant front-bench spokesman, whereas in government the chairman is elected by the back-benchers. In addition, since the 1945–51 period it has been customary to establish a Business Committee to liaise between the leadership and the back-benches. According to Punnett, the membership of this committee in the October 1964 to July 1965 period included all front-bench spokesmen not in the Consultative Committee together with the elected officers (vice-chairmen, secretaries and sometimes treasurers) of the back-bench committees. It met weekly at 6.15 on Wednesday after Consultative Committee meetings, when a senior member of the latter would report to the Business Committee on the decisions of the Consultative Committee regarding the following week's business in the House.[20]

Contacts between the leader, the front-bench and the party bureaucracy are also transformed, especially those involving Research Department personnel. For, in lieu of the advice and assistance of the permanent civil service, the leader and his colleagues fall back upon the services of the Research Department: the leader has first call on the resources of the Department, while each front-bench spokesman is able to call upon the assistance of the desk officer relevant to his subject area. The same desk officer also serves as minutes secretary to the relevant back-bench subject committee so that through the Department the network of relationships between front and back-benchers is further extended. In addition, Research Department officers are involved in servicing the various committees in which the leader and his colleagues are involved, such as the Steering Committee and the Consultative Committee. Of course, in government, party officers are usually excluded from cabinet and ministerial meetings and the contacts between the leadership and Research Department officers (with the possible exception of the director) are not as close nor as frequent as they are in opposition.[21]

In general, in opposition the structure of the Conservative party changes so that the network of contacts and the channels of communication and potential influence centring upon the leader are more closely located within the party than is the case in government. In particular, the contacts between the leader and his front-bench colleagues, and the back-benches and the Research Department are significantly extended and the leader is thus brought closer to party opinion than is the case in government. At the same time the formal relations with extra-party organisations (especially the civil service and major pressure groups), which the leader is subject to in office, are either severed or altered in terms of their nature and intensity.

It is within this broad context of the Conservative party as opposition that both Edward Heath and Margaret Thatcher have developed their own distinctive approaches to the party leadership. How did they set about the tasks in hand? What contrasting approaches to leadership have they exhibited?

## III EDWARD HEATH AS OPPOSITION LEADER 1965–70

Heath was elected to the leadership by the parliamentary party in July 1965. He had already been deeply involved in the development of the opposition under Douglas-Home when, following the party's October 1964 general election defeat, Heath was appointed chairman of the Advisory Committee on Policy (ACP) and was given charge of the party's policy review. He also, as opposition spokesman on economic affairs, led the Conservatives' effective examination and critique of the Labour government's 1965 Finance Bill. Heath thus promised to be a well-rounded leader of the opposition capable of providing effective criticism of the Labour government on the one hand and a thorough presentation of the Conservative alternative on the other. His distinctive approach to opposition leadership can be best exhibited in relation to certain key areas of activity, most especially, policy-making and the organisation and operation of his front-bench.

In the policy field, Heath was deeply concerned with both the machinery and content of policy-making. As chairman of the ACP prior to his election as leader Heath launched a systematic and organised re-examination of party policy and remained the driving force behind this policy exercise throughout the opposition period. He kept a close interest and involvement in the machinery of policy-making and its operation, even though formal responsibility was delegated to the subsequent chairmen of the ACP: Edward Boyle until late 1968 and Reginald Maudling thereafter. Heath's concern that the review should be extensive and intelligently organised is reflected in the machinery that he established which in terms of its nature and scale was an innovation in British opposition politics. The building blocks of the exercise were the various policy groups (23 before the 1966 election and 29 thereafter) which brought together Conservative parliamentarians and outside experts to develop detailed proposals in specific areas such as agriculture, housing and industrial relations.[22] In theory these groups reported to the ACP, though in practice their reports often went directly to the leader. Heath also actively encouraged the establishment and operation of two policy research projects: the Conservative Systems Research Centre and the Conservative Public Sector Research Unit.[23] These were directly responsible to the leader and they were concerned with, amongst other things, the compatability of different policies and the problems of implementing them once returned to power.

Heath's interest in the organisation of policy-making was further reflected in his concern with the forward planning and management of policy development. He was concerned that the exercise should be timetabled well in advance and, that as far as possible, schedules should be kept to. In the period prior to the 1966 general election, as an election was expected at any time, the exercise was planned around the production of a policy statement which could serve as an election manifesto if the need arose, but otherwise would be published in the autumn of 1965 as an indication of the party's altered policy direction. After the March 1966 election, with the prospect of a long spell in opposition, plans could be made with greater certainty and it was decided that from the autumn of 1966 to the early part of 1968 the policy group exercise would continue, but its work would not be publicised or emphasised. In the summer of 1968 the various policy group reports were to be drawn together in the form of a generalised mid-term manifesto to be published in the autumn. Thereafter, until the next general election, particular policies were to be refined in preparation for office. This plan was more or less adhered to throughout the post-1966 period of opposition.

The concern with the organisation and planning of the machinery of policy-making had consequences for policy content. In initiating the policy review in 1964 Heath was concerned to establish the broad outline of future Conservative policy at an early date so that the policy groups could take over the job of filling in the details. The first draft of this outline in part reflected Heath's analysis of the reasons for the party's 1964 election defeat, and it was later re-drafted by the director of the CPC, David Howell, into an 8000-word skeleton manifesto which was approved by Douglas-Home in January 1965. The approach developed in that document formed the basis of the autumn 1965 policy statement, 'Putting Britain Right Ahead', which contained most of the major policy themes (with the particular exception of machinery of government questions) that were further refined throughout the opposition period. In particular, two central objectives were emphasised: the encouragement of individual initiative and enterprise and the creation of 'a new dynamic within industry' by measures of increased competition. These objectives were related to certain elements of policy such as tax reductions and incentives, selectivity in the social services, trade union reform and entry to Europe.[24]

By establishing the broad framework of policy production at an early stage, Heath was able to keep a close hold on the policy exercise. In addition, he was able to limit discussion upon the fundamentals of party belief: the broad purposes had been determined, and thereafter it was a matter of refining and developing them. Partly for reasons of party management, Heath was anxious to avoid wide ranging debates about the nature of Conservatism. They seemed to him likely to create deep division within the party which in turn might serve to undermine the credibility of the opposition in the eyes of the electorate. He thus tended to limit or proscribe debates on certain key issues, especially in the economic sphere, such as incomes policy and economic planning. His attempts to avoid the discussion of contentious issues sometimes led to the adoption of ambiguous policy positions, for rather than risk splitting his front-bench, he tended to try to avoid decision and keep the options open.

The emphasis upon thorough policy work in opposition reflected a view that policy should be prepared in some detail in readiness for office. Considerable and fairly detailed proposals were prepared in some key areas, such as taxation, industrial relations and the reorganisation of the social services, but this did not mean that the details had to be made public beforehand. In fact, a good deal of detailed work, especially on taxation, was kept secret. Heath's emphasis upon the machinery of policy-making and the thoroughness of the policy exercise suggests a view that policy problems are capable of right solutions and that once the fundamental moral framework has been decided the 'best policy' can be formulated if the right information and expertise are united.

Like all party leaders, Heath was more interested in certain areas of policy than others. Entry into the EEC was a major interest and this helps to explain a good many of the policy proposals produced during the opposition period, such as those on taxation and agriculture.[25] Machinery of government questions were also matters of importance to Heath and he seemed as much concerned with the technology and efficient organisation of government as he was with questions of its purpose and control. Economic policy was a further, major concern and was regarded by him as the central key part of the party programme.

Heath's interest in organisation and party management is further evidenced in his approach to the nature and operation of his front-bench team. He rejected Macmillan's advice to 'do what Winston did' and preserve flexibility and, like his predecessor, he maintained a large shadow administration,[26] initially appointing 72 spokesmen each with clearly defined responsibilities, the only exceptions being Maudling as deputy leader (an innovation) and Hogg, who was without departmental responsibilities. Heath divided his front-bench into a number of specialist teams on each of the major subjects under a leading spokesman. This also was an innovation in opposition politics but it was abandoned after the 1966 election and the front-bench was cut down to 37, though each remained responsible for specific policy areas. Later the front-bench team was extended once more so that by 1970 it numbered 50.

To some degree, Heath attempted to operate his shadow administration in accordance with the proceedings of cabinet government. Consultative Committee meetings tended to be fairly brisk and were tied to a specific agenda; the idea was not to have broad debates as in Churchill's period, but to deal competently with the business in hand. He continued Douglas-Home's arrangement whereby meetings were held twice a week on Wednesdays, mainly to discuss parliamentary business, and on Mondays to discuss broader issues, usually questions of policy. Decision-making tended to be collective except in some areas, such as the decision to keep incomes policy off the agenda and the commitment to a Scottish assembly, where the leader exercised his right to make policy decisions in isolation. The doctrines of collective and ministerial responsibility were applied and front-benchers were expected to keep within the confines of their policy areas and to support the collective policy of the party in public. Some clearly felt constrained by the lack of freedom to debate and argue that this arrangement allowed, and both Maude and Powell, though the circumstances of each case were different, lost their position on the front-bench partly because of their failure to stick to the rules and keep within their allocated responsibilities.[27]

Under Heath, the contacts between the leader and certain sections of his party were extended and developed. He involved the back-benchers in the work of the party to a greater degree than had been the case in any previous period of opposition. Many were engaged in the detailed policy work being undertaken by the policy groups. For instance, in the 1965–6 period, 181 MPs and Peers were brought into the policy groups exercise and 191 in the years thereafter.[28] Heath also developed the practice, especially after the 1966 election, of bringing forward back-bench committee officers to speak on a temporary basis from the front-bench. In this way new talent could be spotted and back-benchers had an added opportunity to make their mark in the party. Heath continued the operation of the Business Committee and began the practice whereby the leader generally attended in person to report on the decisions of the Consultative Committee. However, the Business Committee was mainly used as a means by which the leader could inform his followers and not as a forum for policy debates or as a two-way channel of communication between front and back-benches.

As Heath was relatively unknown to Conservatives in the country when he became leader, one of his major tasks was to develop close contacts between himself and the mass party. According to his biographer, Heath travelled more extensively visiting local branches and attending party functions than any previous Conservative leader.[29] He was also the first leader to attend the annual party conference in full (this he did in 1965 and every year thereafter), he was a frequent visitor to Central Council meetings and he made a habit of speaking at some of the annual conferences of the various sub-sections of the NUCUA, such as the Young Conservatives and the Women's section.

In his concern with policy production, the operation of the front-bench and in developing contacts with the party in the country, Heath was greatly assisted by a relatively substantial personal machinery of leadership. His private office, in terms of its scale, was an innovation in British opposition politics and was modelled on the Prime Minister's office at No. 10. The office was headed by John MacGregor until early 1968 when Douglas Hurd took over and at its full complement in 1969 it had a staff of thirteen, including seven secretaries and Heath's two PPSs, Prior and Kershaw. As well as dealing with press and campaign arrangements, members of the private office carried out a number of executive functions on behalf of the leader. They deputised for Heath on various committees and organisations, they briefed him on current issues and policy proposals and they were often involved in the preparation of speeches, though this task was usually in the hands of Michael Wolff. In addition to his personal staff, Heath depended on a relatively small group of individuals for advice and assistance, though most were drawn from within the Conservative party, often from the front-bench and the Research Department. The machinery of leadership established by him enabled Heath to delegate a great deal of activity and work to a loyal and efficient team and thus, in the formal organisational sense, he was able to extend his leadership potential more considerably than any previous leader of the Conservative party in opposition.

Heath's emphasis upon policy production should not be taken to mean that he was unaware of the need to attack and criticise the Labour government. Though not averse to the cut and thrust of parliamentary opposition, he tended to adopt more 'critical' tactics mainly in response to demands from his followers for a more vigorous approach. This was particularly the case during the period from March 1966 to 1968, when policy-making was at a low key and the party was divided over defence, Rhodesia, immigration and incomes policy. But Heath never seemed happy with a substantially negative approach and tended to use the parliamentary tactic of a reasoned amendment, rather than outright rejection. While this may have served to preserve the unity and credibility of the opposition it did not always satisfy his parliamentary followers.

A further difficulty was Heath's approach to putting the party's message across to the electorate and his followers in the country. He was not easily persuaded to adapt to the requirements of good public relations, and unless the subject was Europe, he seldom seemed to inspire the party faithful. His major speeches were often rather dry catalogues of policy proposals and, according to his biographer, he was more comfortable and effective when briefing small, informal groups.[30] Heath perhaps lacked facility at one of the major skills required of the opposition leader, that of using words to inspire and persuade. He never seemed happy with many of his set speeches, continually re-drafting at a late stage. Overall he was more interested in concentrating on the business of policy production than on the development and delivery of speeches.

In general, Heath was a classic exponent of the alternative government approach to opposition leadership. This is reflected in his desire to create a real and viable alternative involving a well-tried team of men and a thoroughly considered, though not necessarily publicised, alternative programme. He never publicly advocated the adoption of an opposition for opposition's sake posture, preferring instead vigorous opposition conducted in a responsible and constructive manner. His major interest seems to have been concentrated on preparing for regaining power in the future, hence his concern with the details of policy and with issues relevant to the machinery of government and policy implementation. It could be said in criticism that Heath was too much interested in what was to be done once the party got back into power and did not give enough attention to how the party was to get there. He was poor at communicating the party's programme and potential, seemed frustrated by opposition and showed a lack of concern with the vital persuasive aspects of opposition politics. Heath also placed great emphasis upon the need to preserve the unity of the opposition. This concern with party management and control was reflected in his tight hold over the organisation and operation of his front-bench, his concern to limit discussion on party fundamentals, the development of a substantial personal machine and the establishment of closer lines of communication between the leader and, in particular, his parliamentary followers.

## IV MARGARET THATCHER AS OPPOSITION LEADER 1975-9

A major difficulty in analysing Margaret Thatcher's period as opposition leader is that it is not yet over and the events involved are too recent to be either easily accessible to outside observers or capable of supporting a rounded judgment. However, some generalisations can be made, if only tentatively. It is important to stress that there are substantial areas of continuity and significant similarities, especially in terms of policy content, with the 1964–70 period. In fact, Thatcher's leadership of the party as opposition has involved extensions in many of the initiatives introduced by her predecessor, though she has of course introduced her own distinctive approach—particularly in relation to policy presentation and contacts with the parliamentary party.

In comparison to Heath, Thatcher has shown relatively little interest in the organisation and machinery of policy-making. Although the policy review has been as extensive as in the 1964–70 period with over 60 policy groups operating at one time or another, the leader has not been intimately involved and she has delegated organisational and day to day responsibility to Sir Keith Joseph (chairman of the ACP) and Angus Maude (chairman of the Research Department). She tends to take part in the policy process at a relatively late stage, usually after a report has gone through Joseph's policy steering committee and before it proceeds to the policy sub-committee of the Consultative Committee which she chairs. She may on receipt of a report decide that it should not go further and send it back for reconsideration or re-drafting, though this is unusual. Equally, she has not concerned herself with the detailed forward planning of policy development. This has tended to be left to others especially the director and other key officers of the Research Department.

One significant change in the organisation of the policy review under Thatcher's leadership is the greater attention given to matters of party management. For example, back-benchers generally play a more central role in the policy groups and outside experts tend to be used on a consultancy basis. Moreover, the groups' membership tends to be selected, not only on the grounds of expertise and interest, but also to keep a balance of views between the various divisions within the shadow administration. Though questions of party management were also a concern of the Heath period, they were not as strongly emphasised, whereas under Thatcher it is not only a question of what is the best policy but also what is acceptable to the party.

As far as policy content is concerned, Thatcher is less involved in the details of policy than was Heath. She seems to dislike giving too much attention to specifics and is concerned to avoid making precise public commitments which may limit the flexibility of a future Conservative administration. Her approach is to develop the general philosophical outlines of policy, what some have termed a 'broad brush' approach which involves getting the general objectives right in readiness for office while providing some impression of the details.[31] The solutions to the problems of carrying through the party's purpose if returned to office are seen as depending more on developing and refining the right set of values which can then be applied to the particular situation, rather than on preparing detailed plans in the present. There is, however, one exception— economic policy—for it is on the success of this that all other policies are seen to rest. Hence, the leader has been greatly concerned with detailed policy development in this area, especially in relation to taxation and public expenditure control.[32]

Thatcher's apparent unease about the production and publication of detailed policy has not been wholly carried through in practice. Under her leadership about as much detailed policy has been produced as in the 1964–70 period and a substantial, though more selective, amount has been publicised.[33] The difference is in terms of presentation and the more cautious tone adopted. Policy statements tend to be couched in a language which stresses the qualifications involved in implementing the policy: that it may take a full parliament, that present plans can only be tentative, that much depends on getting the general economic framework right, etc. These types of preliminary cautions were trundled out during the 1964–70 period, but they were not so heavily underlined.

In relation to the organisation and operation of her shadow administration, Thatcher was initially faced with a major problem: she inherited the substantial membership of her front-bench from her predecessor and she may well, especially in the Consultative Committee, have found herself in a minority on some issues. Hence a central concern has been to find ways of managing and developing her front-bench team so as to by-pass or counteract the initial bias against her. She has gradually altered the composition of her shadow administration. Initially, six members of Heath's previous team were excluded and new members unconnected with the Heath leadership (such as Maude and Neave) were brought in. There have since been important changes in the nature of the team, and although the re-distribution has taken account of the need to balance the various tendencies within the parliamentary party, it is today more sympathetic to the leader's command and authority. Thatcher has continued Heath's practice of bringing forward backbench committee officers and, like Heath, she has maintained a large shadow administration numbering 45 initially (including a Consultative Committee of 21) which has now expanded to a total of 50, most with precisely defined responsibilities.

The pattern and proceedings of Consultative Committee meetings remain much the same. Decision-making still generally tends to be collective, though the leader has shown a tendency to make broad policy pronouncements in advance of committee discussions, as in the case of immigration, with the consequence that either the leader must back-track or her colleagues must go along with her. She has also, like Heath, taken the initiative on certain issues such as her proposal on the use of referenda in the case of major industrial troubles and her Glasgow speech rejecting the idea of a planned incomes policy.[34]

An added difficulty for Thatcher on becoming leader was that she was relatively unknown to members of the party generally in parliament, in the bureaucracy and in the country. Previously she had tended to be a specialist front-bencher and had not been greatly involved in party affairs. Additionally, a major point in her leadership election platform was that Heath had lost contact with the various sections of the party.[35] Thus a central feature of her approach to opposition leadership has been the development of contacts between the leader and her followers, and the closer co-ordination of the three major parts of the party.

As far as contacts with the parliamentary party are concerned the leader has made some important innovations. She has made a point of holding twice-yearly meetings with all front-bench spokesmen not in the Consultative Committee and she has held occasional meetings with all Conservative spokesmen in the House of Lords. She has attempted to involve the back-benchers in the policy process to a greater extent than was the case under Heath. Their increased role in the policy groups has already been noted. In addition, however, the back-bench subject committees have to some extent been brought into the formal process of policy-making by the introduction of the practice whereby each year the chairman of a particular policy group will report to the appropriate back-bench committee on current progress within the group and seek the comments of the assembled back-benchers, while the leader has sometimes encouraged front-bench spokesmen to check the attitudes of their back-bench committee before proceeding with an initiative.

Thatcher's concern with gauging back-bench opinion is further reflected in the changed status and operation of the Business Committee. This is treated far more respectfully and is used less as a means of providing back-benchers with information about front-bench thinking and more as a two-way channel of communication with greater opportunity for back-bench comment. Generally the whole of the Consultative Committee will attend the meetings unless there are other pressing engagements, and the leader will report to the committee collectively on behalf of her colleagues on the opposition's proposed approach to the parliamentary business, for the coming week. The leader tends to use the committee quite positively as a sounding board to take the temperature of the party and often asks for comments to be expressed and sometimes asks the relevant front-bench spokesman to reply. In one or two cases the strength of the views expressed by the back-benchers have led to the Consultative Committee reconsidering an issue and occasionally changes have been made in the original proposals. During the early months of Thatcher's leadership, before she had extended her influence over her front-bench, on certain items of business, the expression of back-bench opinion through the Business Committee occasionally served to strengthen the leader's position *vis-à-vis* a dominant and opposing view in the Consultative Committee.[36]

Thatcher has managed to build up a relatively close liaison with the Central Office and Research Department, though she does not depend upon the latter's assistance to the same degree as Heath did and has tended to delegate responsibility for the operation of the party bureaucracy to Thorneycroft, Joseph and Maude. She has, like Heath, attempted to develop contacts with the party in the country. For example, since becoming leader, Thatcher has visited more than 200 constituencies and has dropped the rule that the leader does not take part in parliamentary by-election campaigns: she has attended every one. She has also extended Heath's initiative by attending almost all the conferences of the major sub-sections of the mass party. Her concern with contact and co-ordination between the various elements of the party is reflected in the establishment of a new co-ordinating committee under her chairmanship. It usually meets once a fortnight, and has a membership of about eight, including the chairman of the 1922 Committee, the chairman of the National Union Executive Committee, the deputy leader, the chief whip and the chairman of the party. The committee may occasionally discuss strategy but is mainly used as a sounding board for opinions and as a channel of communication.

Like Heath, Thatcher runs a substantial private office: including her two PPPs (Stanley and Butler), the office has a staff of about fourteen and is under the overall control of Airey Neave, though the management of the office is in the hands of Richard Ryder. It differs from Heath's office in two principal ways.[37] First, the head of the office is a political figure, a close confidant and adviser of the leader, a front-bench spokesman and member of the Consultative Committee. Secondly, the remaining staff tend to fill more of a secretarial than an executive function: they are mainly concerned with briefing the leader, arranging schedules and campaign tours and handling correspondence. For information and advice Thatcher tends to rely on a more varied range of sources than was the case with Heath. As already noted, though relationships are necessarily close, she is less dependent on the party bureaucracy and tends to draw on sources outside her own front-bench and sometimes from outside the formal party structure. For example, speech writing involves the leader in drawing together many drafts which may be submitted by, in addition to party specialists (front-benchers and officials) and some back-benchers, others from outside the formal structure of the Conservative party including sympathetic journalists and academics and certain individuals closely connected with the party such as the director of the Centre for Policy Studies. Considerable press attention has been given to the leader's briefing sessions prior to Prime Minister's questions which usually involve certain back-benchers.[38] Overall, in comparison to Heath as opposition leader, Thatcher has tended to use sources of assistance and advice drawn from outside the traditional mainstream of the party.

Her approach to criticising the Labour government has not been noticeably more vigorous than Heath's, and during the early period of her leadership the lack of effectiveness of the opposition was much criticised. She has developed a distinct critique of her opponents around the label 'Socialism' and under her leadership the Conservatives have occasionally developed aggressive parliamentary tactics as in the case of the refusal of pairing arrangements, though this seems more likely to reflect the problems of minority government than to indicate a tendency to adopt a predominantly critical approach to opposition leadership.

In articulating the Conservative message to followers and the general public, Thatcher seems to have proved herself more capable than Heath in exploiting the persuasive aspect of politics. She is more amenable to the demands of public relations and on such matters she is closely advised by the party's publicity director, Gordon Reece. She has undertaken a number of extensive campaign tours with particular attention being given to Scotland and the 90 or so key seats which the Conservatives, in order to return to power, must hold or win in any future general election. For Thatcher, speech writing and delivery are clearly seen as important tasks for the opposition leader and she spends a great deal of time drawing together the various drafts submitted. She is often capable of inspiring a party audience, though sometimes her speeches seem too partisan to have a broader appeal. While clearly having a strong appreciation of the importance of words to the opposition politician, the major weakness tends to be in terms of presentation and style of delivery.

In general, compared with Heath, Thatcher's approach to opposition leadership places less emphasis upon the alternative government concept. In her attitude to policy-making, her concern to avoid precise commitments and her desire to develop the broad outline of Conservative purpose, Thatcher has more in common with the type of leadership developed in the 1945–51 period. In terms of her attitudes towards the organisation and development of the front-bench, however, there are marked similarities between Thatcher and Heath. Moreover, while she has developed a distinctive critique of the Labour government, she has not shown a marked preference for tactics of opposition for opposition's sake, seeming instead to regard opposition as an opportunity to consider and re-examine the fundamentals of party belief. This is a major contrast with Heath and his concern to avoid deep ideological debates. Thatcher seems more in the tradition of the 'men in opposition' concept, allowing for the discussion and development of ideas, but with the important proviso that the pace and direction of the discussion should be superintended and controlled from the centre.

Like Heath, she has also shown great concern about the problem of party unity, though this is to be achieved not through limiting discussion on fundamentals, but by increased measures of co-ordination and contact between the various sections of the party and particularly the leadership and the back-benchers. The consequence is, however, not simply to achieve agreement, but also to alter the balance of dominant attitudes and values within the party. In general a central feature of her approach to opposition has been a concern with party issues and party questions. A clear danger of such an approach is that it may prove too partisan to ensure either a return to power or, if returned, a successful period in office thereafter.

## V ACCOUNTING FOR DIFFERENCES IN APPROACH

The different approaches to opposition leadership exhibited by Heath and Thatcher are necessarily the product of a complex and varied set of factors and it would be foolish to argue that any one factor can be judged to be primary or dominant. However, there are certain issues which are clearly important and these concern both the changing political and party context and the personalities of the individuals involved.

Most obviously both leaders have had to come to terms with different political situations. The more certain parliamentary situation operating from 1966–70 with an overall Labour majority of 96, for instance, allowed for a more planned and systematic approach than has been possible during the post-1975 period, with an initial overall Labour majority of three subsequently reduced to a minority. Moreover, the electoral circumstances of the Conservative party have changed radically. In the 1964 general election, the Conservatives received 43.4 per cent of the votes cast; by October 1974 their share had declined to 36.5 per cent and was more substantially concentrated in suburban and rural areas in the south and west of England and amongst the more aged and middle-class sections of the community.[39] These alterations in the electoral base of the party have presumably had some consequences for policy presentation and public relations.

The intellectual climate within which policy-making takes place has also altered substantially. In the 1960s much political and academic debate was concerned with the efficient operation of economic and political institutions, and about how changes in the scale and organisation of the machinery of government might facilitate a more rational and intelligent use of resources.[40] Heath's concern with the organisation of policy-making, his problem solving approach to policy issues and his interest in machinery of government questions was very much in keeping with the managerial emphasis of current thinking in the 1960s. By contrast, the debate in the 1970s has been concerned not so much with the potentialities of government but more with its problems and limitations. Attention has been given to the difficulties of establishing clear criteria for the operation of public services and the problems of carrying through or implementing policies.[41] At the same time, broader and more traditional questions about the purpose and control of public agencies have once more become central issues of debate and argument. Thatcher's emphasis upon broad philosophical themes and her cautious approach to policy presentation and commitment is in line with a wider debate about the nature and capability of government.

Both leaders have learnt from past experience, but from a different vantage point. For Heath a prime example was the Labour party's period in opposition under Gaitskell and Wilson and the relatively substantial amount of policy work that was carried out under their leaderships. Thus Heath, by indulging in a detailed policy review, was simply further extending what had already become a major trend of British opposition politics. Equally, the Labour party's deep divisions over Clause IV and disarmament provided telling evidence of the dangers to party unity involved in allowing wide-ranging debates about party beliefs. Thatcher, on the other hand, has had the experience of the 1964-74 period to learn from. The development of detailed policy commitments in that earlier period of opposition and the failure to carry some of them through later in office has undoubtedly influenced her development of a broad brush approach, her wariness about policy details and her belief in the need to get the overall strategy right in readiness for office.

In addition to these broader considerations, the circumstances of Heath's and Thatcher's emergence as leaders of the Conservative party can help to explain both some of the similarities and some of the differences between them. Both have had to contend with the problem of exercising power in opposition and they share the unusual distinction of having become Conservative leaders during such a period.[42] The Conservative leader who emerges in opposition can hardly expect to command the same moral authority as one who emerges in government, for he is in a sense a leader on trial who has yet to prove his quality and potential by winning and holding office. This variation in leadership status may in part explain why, relative to earlier Conservative leaders, both Heath and Thatcher have been greatly concerned with developing closer liaison and contact with their followers.

Other aspects of the circumstances surrounding, and the nature of, their rise to power were, however, significantly different. Heath came to power as an insider drawn from the accepted and dominant group within the Conservative hierarchy. As chief whip and later as a senior minister in the Macmillan and Douglas-Home administrations, he had been at the centre of Conservative party affairs. His succession to the leadership meant a continuation of the mainstream in the Conservative power structure. Thatcher, by contrast, came to the leadership as a challenger and an outsider in opposition to the overwhelming majority of the existing leadership group and as a result of what amounted to a back-bench revolt.[43] She inherited a split party and a party machine still dominated by supporters of her predecessor. Hence, relative to Heath, she has shown a greater concern with matters of party management and co-ordination and has tended to call on advice and assistance from outside traditional party channels.

By virtue of being a challenger to the existing power structure within the party, the task of Thatcher as opposition leader has had an added dimension, namely the need to produce a dual alternative: to the Labour government on the one hand and to the policies of the previous Conservative government and leadership on the other. A central part of the policy approach enunciated by Thatcher has been a rejection of the 'conventional wisdom' of the 1960s and 1970s, so that to a large extent she has been reacting against sections in her own party at the same time as developing an alternative to the existing administration.[44]

The different approaches to leadership exhibited by Heath and Thatcher have developed in accord with the changing power structure of the Conservative party. One of the most important changes, strongly emphasised in this paper, has been the gradual extension of back-bench influence both under Heath and Thatcher. In addition to the points noted in earlier sections of this paper, this development is further reflected in the progressive expansion in the number of back-bench committees from less than 27 in 1964 to 36 in 1978, and in the important part played by back-bench groupings in influencing and shaping official policy, especially during the post-1975 period in relation to immigration and devolution.[45] This growth of back-bench influence may in part reflect a more frequent and prolonged experience of opposition for, as already noted, the formal opportunities for back-benchers to influence the policy and practices of their party are substantially greater in opposition than in government. However, the extended role of the back-bencher appears to be a cumulative development and is not simply or wholly to be explained as a product of the party's political circumstances. To some extent it is an inevitable outcome of the 1965 reforms in the leadership selection process, for once the facility to choose and, later, replace the leader was given to the back-benchers, the nature of the power balance within the party was significantly altered with certain important consequences for the practice and operation of leadership. Both Heath's and especially Thatcher's approaches to opposition leadership indicate a recognition of this change.

Finally, approaches to leadership must in part be regarded as a product of the different personalities involved and one or two brief, but relevant, points may be noted. Heath, with his background as an ex-civil servant, chief whip and effective and active minister, seems more concerned with getting things done rather than extensively exploring the principles and philosophy involved. An energetic organiser and administrator with an 'inborn taste for order, system, preparation, planning',[46] he takes a problem-solving approach to political matters and is said to be capable of an amazing grasp of details. By contrast, Thatcher, with her legal background, tends to deploy facts as part of a wider argument and tends to move from the general to the particular. Though very cautious and careful in making decisions, she seems both more romantic and more impulsive than Heath and more at home with ideas and general statements.

To conclude briefly, although this chapter has been concerned with the differences between Heath and Thatcher, some references have been made to the important continuities in approach especially in relation to the organisation of the front-bench, the development of a personal machinery of leadership and the concern to develop wider contacts within the party. Naturally as both have been subject to equivalent demands and limitations as leaders of the Conservative party as opposition their behaviour displays certain similarities. In particular, under their leaderships, the Conservative party as opposition has emerged as an institution in its own right with its own distinctive machinery and purposes. It is an interesting speculation as to whether, as a result of the more frequent and sustained experience of opposition, the values of an opposition party have increasingly begun to dominate the practices and operation of the Conservative party.

NOTES

1. This paper was written in June and marginally revised in September 1978. I should like to thank those Conservatives, both parliamentarians and officials, who kindly answered my questions on the subject matter of this paper.
2. An obvious exception is R. M. Punnett, *Front Bench Opposition* (London: Heinemann, 1973). See also, Saul Rose 'Policy Decision in Opposition', *Political Studies*, vol. IV, no. 2 (1956).
3. As long as it is specified which area of party activity is being considered.
4. See Andrew Gamble, *The Conservative Nation* (London: Routledge Kegan Paul, 1974) p. 9; S. H. Beer, *Modern British Politics* ( London: Faber, 1965) p. 299; Nigel Harris, *Competition and the Corporate Society* (London: Methuen, 1972) pp. 254–62.
5. I have left out the February 1974 to February 1975 period of opposition because (a) from February 1974 to October 1974 the party was more a government in exile and the strong coalition flavour of leadership-thinking suggested a change in their perception of the two-party parliamentary system; (b) from October 1974 to February 1975 the party was almost wholly taken up with the leadership question. Thus the 1964–70 and 1974 to present day periods are the most strictly comparable.
6. See, by contrast, J. H. Grainger, *Character and Style in English Politics* (London: Cambridge University Press, 1969) p. 3 ff; A. F. Davies, 'The Concept of Administrative Style', *The Australian Journal of Politics and History*, vol. XII (1966).
7. To be consistent, the third person singular will subsequently be in the male gender.
8. For an early outline see Bernard Crick, 'Two Theories of Opposition', *New Statesman* (18 June 1960).
9. Attributed to George Tierney, quoted in H. J. Hanham, 'Opposition Techniques in British Politics: 1867–1914', *Government and Opposition*, vol. 2 (1 January 1967).
10. Churchill's view, see Lord Butler, *The Art of the Possible* (London: Hamish Hamilton, 1971) p. 133.
11. See G. Ionescu and I. de Madariaga, *Opposition*, (London: Watts, 1968) pp. 102–21.
12. Alan Beattie, *English Party Politics* (London: Weidenfeld & Nicolson, 1970) p. 235ff.
13. Kenneth Young, *Sir Alec Douglas-Home* (London: Dent, 1970) p. 239.
14. See speech by Reginald Maudling *NUCUA 84th Annual Conference Report*, 1966, p. 126.
15. J. D. Hoffman, *The Conservative Party in Opposition 1945–1951* (London: McGibbon & Kee, 1964) pp. 135–6.
16. Butler, op. cit., p. 135.
17. Robert Rhodes James, *Ambitions and Realities* (London: Weidenfeld & Nicolson, 1972) p. 116.
18. Punnett, op. cit., Appendix D.
19. Subject, of course, to the usual considerations of party management etc; for a thorough examination see ibid, p. 234.
20. Ibid, p. 303. The senior member of the Consultative Committee who liaised

with the Business Committee in 1964–5 was Selwyn Lloyd.

21. There are no significant formal changes in the relations between the leader and the NUCUA when the party is in opposition, though of course, in the absence of the demands of government, the leader will have more time and opportunity to develop contacts with his followers in the country.

22. For a full list see D. Butler and M. Pinto-Duschinsky, *The British General Election of 1970* (London: Macmillan, 1971) p. 67, f. n.

23. The former was under Mervyn Pike and Michael Spicer and the latter involved Ernest Marples, David Howell and Mark Schreiber. It is difficult to ascertain precisely what contribution these organisations (as distinct from the individuals involved) made to Conservative policy-making. However, they do indicate Heath's concern with problems of policy production and the machinery of policy-making.

24. *Putting Britain Right Ahead* (CCO, 1965) pp. 7–8, 11, 13 and 20.

25. On Heath's European commitment, see Andrew Roth, *Heath and the Heathmen* (London: Routledge Kegan Paul, 1972) ch. 15.

26. George Hutchinson, *Edward Heath: A Personal and Political Biography* (London: Longmans, 1970) p. 172.

27. Punnett, op. cit., p. 302 suggests two junior spokesmen, Channon and Fisher, may also have fallen foul of the individual and collective responsibility rules.

28. Butler and Pinto-Duschinsky, op. cit.

29. Hutchinson, op. cit., p. 190 ff.

30. Ibid, p. 186.

31. Patrick Cosgrave, *Margaret Thatcher* (London: Hutchinson, 1978) p. 168ff.

32. Ibid.

33. Considerable detail has been published in relation to housing, education, social security, structure of industry, immigration and certain aspects of law and order. Also see the relatively detailed economic proposals contained in *The Right Approach to the Economy* (CCO, 1977).

34. See, 'The Making of Tory Policy: 1978', The *Economist* (15 April 1978).

35. For Thatcher's leadership election platform see George Gardiner, *Margaret Thatcher* (London: Kimber, 1975) Appendix C.

36. For some indication of these changes see, Geoffrey Smith, 'The hey-day of the party rebel', *The Times* (12 May 1978).

37. There is the additional difference that Airey Neave had been Thatcher's leadership campaign manager and that originally her two PPSs were Fergus Montgomery and William Shelton, both of whom, particularly the latter, were closely involved in initiating and organising her successful bid for the party leadership. Thus initially her private office mirrored very closely her election campaign organisation. In Heath's case there was less continuity between his campaign team and his private office.

38. Certain MPs are usually mentioned such as George Gardiner, Geoffrey Pattie and Norman Tebbit. Despite speculation to the contrary, there is nothing new about this practice; most opposition leaders have prepared for prime minister's questions, though they are not generally advised by back-benchers.

39. For detailed figures and analysis see D. E. Butler and Dennis Kavanagh, *The British General Election of October 1974* (London: Macmillan, 1975) p. 330ff.

40. This managerial emphasis was in part reflected in a large number of official reports and papers, including the Fulton Report on the Civil Service, the

Redcliffe-Maud Report on local government and the Seebohn Report on the social services.

41. See, for instance, Jeffrey L. Pressmen and Aaron B. Wildavsky, *Implementation* (University of California Press, 1973); Christopher Hood, *The Limits of Administration* (Wiley, 1976); A. J. Culyer, *Need and the National Health Service* (London: Martin Robertson, 1976); Anthony King, *et al.*, *Why is Britain Becoming Harder to Govern?* (London: BBC, 1976).

42. Heath was the first to become leader of the Conservative party during a period in opposition since Bonar Law in 1911; though this is arguable, there is the problem of Conservative leadership in the Lords and the case of J. Austen Chamberlain in 1921. However, the point is clear: it's a long time since a Conservative leader has emerged in opposition. Heath and Thatcher also share the distinction of being the first to be elected to the leadership by the parliamentary party.

43. For informed accounts of the 1975 leadership battle see Gardiner, op. cit., chs. 13, 14 and 15; Cosgrave, op. cit., ch. 2; 'The selling of Margaret Thatcher', *The Sunday Times* (9 February 1975).

44. Though it is worth noting that the policy change that has taken place under Thatcher's leadership, at least in economic affairs, is not altogether different from that which took place during the 1964 to 1970 period. There is the additional point, that it is a tendency of opposition parties to break away from policies previously pursued by them in office.

45. In the case of devolution and the dropping of the party's commitment to a directly-elected Scottish assembly, an important and influential role was played by the Union Flag Group—an ad hoc and unofficial back-bench group of about 70 members, which as well as influencing opinion within the Conservative parliamentary party also liaised with Labour and Ulster Unionist opponents of devolution in a successful attempt to impede the passage of the 1976 Devolution Bill.

46. Hutchinson, op. cit., p. 172.

# 8 The Conservative Elite, 1918–78: Does Unrepresentativeness Matter?

David Butler and Michael Pinto-Duschinsky

## I INTRODUCTION

Are measures more important than men? Do we judge our parties more by what they do than by who the people are who do them? The answers to such questions are complex and unclear. Yet a party's destiny, as well as its public image, certainly rests partly on its leaders. It is instructive to consider how the Conservative party in and out of parliament has changed or failed to change over recent generations.

When the Conservative strategists set about the task of re-establishing the party after its defeat in 1945, they did so in two ways: firstly by reformulating Conservative policy, and secondly by attempting to widen the social composition of the party. This two-pronged approach reflected a long-standing tenet that the party's electoral success demanded not only a popular programme but also the recruitment of men and women from differing backgrounds into the party leadership. Accordingly, two major documents were produced. *The Industrial Charter*[1] dealt with policy; *The Maxwell-Fyfe Report*[2] proposed far-reaching internal organisational reforms.

Looking back at these landmark reports 30 years later, there is a clear contrast between the importance of *The Industrial Charter* and the lack of impact of the changes proposed by Sir David Maxwell-Fyfe's committee. Firstly in terms of policy, the leftward move inaugurated by *The Industrial Charter* has proved more decisive than its authors could possibly have foreseen. Their acceptance of the Welfare State and a mixed economy has conditioned every subsequent Conservative manifesto. But, secondly, the party has altered slowly in its social composition. The absence of working-class representatives and dominance of the upper-middle-class in the senior Conservative ranks, both in parliament and in the constituencies, is nearly as marked today as it was in the late-1940s when the Maxwell-Fyfe proposals were introduced. Moreover, there have been few broad changes since the period after the First World War.

This chapter first outlines the main Maxwell-Fyfe reforms of 1948–9 and their aims; secondly, it charts the changes—or lack of them—in the composition of the Conservative hierarchy in the House of Commons and in the constituencies; and thirdly, it considers whether the unrepresentative pattern of Conservative leadership is a serious handicap to the party.


## II THE MAXWELL-FYFE REFORMS 1948–9

The desire to end the social elitism of the pre-war Conservative party was a major motive for many of the organisational innovations during the late-1940s, when Lord Woolton was party chairman. This aim lay behind several of the Maxwell-Fyfe proposals.

The Special Committee on Party Organisation, which met under the chairmanship of Sir David Maxwell-Fyfe (later Lord Kilmuir), was set up in June 1948. Its Interim and Final Reports were approved by the 1948 annual conference and by a special meeting of the Central Council in July 1949.

The main reform emerging from the Maxwell-Fyfe Committee was the removal of financial burdens from parliamentary candidates. Clauses 1, 5 and 6 of the new rules stipulated that:

1. The entire election expenses of Conservative candidates in every constituency shall be the responsibility of the constituency associations . . . and no subscription shall be made directly or indirectly by the candidate to the fund for statutory election expenses . . .
5. Candidates may, by arrangement with their constituency associations, make nominal subscriptions each year, but the

subscriptions must in no case exceed £25; the annual subscription of members of parliament to their associations shall in no case exceed £50.
6. In no circumstances shall the question of an annual subscription be mentioned by any constituency selection committee to any candidate before he has been selected.[3]

The objective of these regulations was to remove the financial barriers which had, it was thought, prevented working-class and ordinary middle-class Conservatives from standing for parliament before the Second World War. As Lord Woolton wrote in his *Memoirs*, 'it was no use saying that the Conservative party was not a "class" party if a working-man Conservative could not afford to stand as a candidate'.[4]

The pre-war situation—which the new rules aimed to alter—had been highlighted in a memorandum written in 1939 by Ian Harvey.[5] According to Harvey, a young Conservative who was later to become a Conservative MP, the Conservative constituency associations operated 'A plutocratic system'. He claimed that there were three categories of would-be candidates:

Class 'A': those willing to pay all their election expenses (£400–£1200) and to subscribe £500–£1000 a year to the local association;

Class 'B': those willing to pay half their election expenses and to subscribe £250–£450 per annum;

Class 'C': those unable to pay any election expenses or to contribute more than £100 per annum.

According to the memorandum:

‘ 'A' Class have always an excellent chance of being adopted . . . 'C' Class hardly any chances at all'.[6]

Harvey complained that the system resulted in bad, unrepresentative candidates and led to the defection of Conservative voters. This was an analysis which Lord Woolton and Sir David Maxwell-Fyfe apparently accepted in the late-1940s. According to Lord Woolton's *Memoirs*, the banning of local subscriptions by candidates:

was revolutionary and, in my view, did more than any single factor to save the Conservative party . . . the Conservative party had become at least as broad-based as the Socialist party . . . Here was Tory democracy in action. The way was clear for men and women of ability to seek election to Westminister.[7]

Besides this change in the financial arrangements of candidates, the Maxwell-Fyfe Committee sought to democratise the party in other ways. For example, a 'quota' scheme was introduced to encourage local associations to contribute to the funds of Conservative Central Office. (At the same time it was proposed to publish annual party accounts since, according to the committee, this was 'the only effective basis' from which to persuade the local parties to contribute to the central funds.[8] This latter proposal was, however, not implemented for another twenty years.)

The ban on financial payments by candidates and the quota scheme both imposed heavy extra burdens on the constituency associations and gave them the incentive to find new members. Before the Maxwell-Fyfe Committee was set up, and while it was sitting, vigorous recruitment campaigns were in progress. These were to raise membership levels to an all-time record.

The reforms of the late-1940s have had some lasting effects:

1. The ban on the 'selling of seats' to candidates by local associations appears to have been completely effective.

2. Widespread, small-scale fund-raising at the constituency level has replaced the common pre-war system of funding by a few rich supporters. The new methods have not only provided for the needs of the local parties but have also produced surpluses for 'quotas' to Central Office. Between 1966 and 1977, constituency quotas provided £3½ million. This was about a fifth of total central party income.

3. Although party membership has dropped considerably below the temporary peak of 2.8 million, which was recorded in 1953, it has remained high by pre-war standards and by comparison with other parties. According to the constituency survey carried out for the Houghton Committee, there were about 1½ million Conservative members in 1974—nearly five times the Labour total and eight times that of the Liberals.[9]

Yet, all these democratic developments have had relatively little effect on the social composition of the party, either within or outside the House of Commons. Lord Woolton's claim that the Conservative party has 'become at least as broad-based as the Socialist party' is without foundation.


III  THE MIDDLE-CLASS HIERARCHY

In post-war elections approximately half of all Conservative voters have been working-class (the percentage has varied between 52 per cent in 1950 and 44 per cent in October 1974). But the working-class Conservatives have remained almost completely passive adherents. Moreover, Conservatives from the lower middle-class (social group C/1) have made little impact upon the party hierarchy, though (unlike working-class Conservatives) they seem to have been active as party members. The only change of any significance is the gradual decline of aristocrats and of rich businessmen and their replacement by professionals and managers. This seems to have happened both within the parliamentary party and in the constituency associations. But it must be emphasised that this development has left the solidly upper and upper-middle-class nature of the party elite almost unchanged.

*Conservative MPs and Front-benchers*

'The country has been transformed but the Tory MP stays the same.' This assertion is patently untrue, in all sorts of ways. Yet it is easy to offer evidence for it. Consider Table 8.1:

TABLE 8.1   Conservative MPs 1923 and 1974

|  | Con. MPs. | Education | | | | Occupation | | |
| --- | --- | --- | --- | --- | --- | --- | --- | --- |
|  |  | Etonian % | Public School % | Oxbridge % | All Univ. % | Professional % | Manual % | Women % |
| 1923 | 258 | 25 | 79 | 40 | 50 | 52 | 4 | 1 |
| 1974 (Oct) | 277 | 17 | 75 | 56 | 69 | 46 | 1 | 3 |

NOTE
1923 was the interwar year with the fewest Conservative MPs. It is cited here because it comes nearer to matching the 277 Conservative MPs of 1974 than 1922 (345) or 1918 (358). But the comparison would be almost the same with other elections in the 1920s or 1930s as the Appendix on p. 207 shows.

The educational and occupational background of Conservative MPs appears to have altered little over 50 years. The most striking feature of the table is the absence of working-class Conservative MPs. In fact, the proportion with origins in manual labour, never substantial, has shrunk almost to nothing. In all the years since the Maxwell-Fyfe reforms, there have only been two working-class Tory MPs. At the other end of the social scale, the proportion of Etonians has gradually fallen—but this one school still provides nearly a fifth of the parliamentary party and the public school element has hardly diminished. The biggest change lies in the increase in MPs with a university education, but the Oxbridge dominance has not been challenged.

Of the 277 Conservatives elected in October 1974, 208 went to Headmasters Conference Schools and 159 of them went to Oxford or Cambridge. A further 23 went to Oxbridge from other schools. Thus, only 46 Conservative MPs (under 17 per cent) had neither of these elite labels 'Public School' or 'Oxbridge'. The proportion of women remains negligible. The picture of 1923 and 1974 alike is of a party that draws its representatives from male members of the upper-middle class.

The same is even more true of the party's leaders as Table 8.2 shows:

TABLE 8.2   Conservative Leadership 1924 and 1978

| | | Class | | | | Education | | | |
| | | | | | | All | | | |
| | | Aristo- | Middle- | Working- | | Public | Ox- | All | |
| | Total | crat | class | class | Eton | School | bridge | Univ. | Women |
|---|---|---|---|---|---|---|---|---|---|
| Cabinet 1924 | 21 | 9 | 12 | — | 7 | 21 | 16 | 16 | — |
| Shadow Cabinet 1978[1] | 20 | 3 | 17 | — | 6 | 18 | 15 | 16 | 2 |

See Appendix for definitions.

NOTES

In May 1978, of the front bench spokesmen outside the shadow cabinet and party whips—39 in all—33 were from public schools and 26 were from Oxbridge. This means that 84 per cent of front-benchers, inside and outside the shadow cabinet, were from public schools.

Mrs Thatcher now, like Mr Baldwin after the First World War, is surrounded by a public school, Oxbridge elite. They are less aristocratic than 50 years ago, but the shadow cabinet before the May 1979 election includes, besides Mrs Thatcher, only one who did not go to a Headmasters' Conference school.

Of course there have been changes in the body of MPs that Table 8.1 does not reveal. In 1924 there were 35 sons of hereditary peers on the Conservative benches. In 1974 there were only nine. In 1923 a significant proportion, perhaps a fifth of Conservative MPs could only be classed as of 'private means'. Now almost every MP can claim to have had a genuine occupation. There has been a significant move from the aristocracy to the professional classes. Yet one reservation must be made. There was only one heir to a peerage and eight other sons of hereditary peers among the 277 Conservative MPs elected in October 1974, yet of the first 26 selections made to replace Conservative MPs elected in October 1974, six went to sons of hereditary peers, four of them heirs to the title. Is the pendulum swinging back?

Twenty years ago one encountered Conservatives who lamented the Maxwell-Fyfe rules, which ended the purchase of seats, on the ground that free constituency choice meant uniform choice. The identikit candidate was replacing the diversity of aristocratic eccentrics, country squires, self-made men and successful QCs who brought their way into parliament. Working-class people, women, Jews and Catholics now found it hard to be selected.

In recent years the religious barriers have diminished. From one practising Jew in 1959 the number has jumped to twelve—a number comparable to pre-war. But there were only seven women out of 277 Conservative MPs in October 1974 (in 1964 there had been eleven out of 304), and the working class still had to be content with Ray Mawby and Sir Edward Brown as their only Conservative representatives.

One other change has come over Conservative MPs. They are not only more university educated: they are, by general consent, of a higher level of average ability than they used to be. The relatively dumb knight of the shire is said to be a dying breed, replaced by the thrusting city banker or advertising man. The Conservative benches are filled by competent and, usually, enlightened men: the number whom their colleagues have cause to blush for in terms of their intelligence or their prejudices is probably smaller than ever before. The job of an MP has changed even in the last ten years. It is incompatible with most occupations: certainly it is no place for the captains of industry or the wealthy idlers who were a recognisable element in pre-war parliaments. But there has been no compensating move towards a more diversified party.

The uniformity of Conservative MPs is not the fault of the party hierarchy. Constituency democracy is hard to control. Central Office has long since learnt how hard it is to place meritorious candidates. Constituency chairmen and their shortlisting groups, while agreeing that the party needs more women, or more working-class MPs, will always feel that their seat is not the one to make the sacrifice. And selection committees, composed in a fairly similar way across the country, seem to have fairly similar tastes when it comes to choosing a candidate.

This is not the place to argue the merits of alternative electoral systems. But it is relevant to point out that, all over the world, when parties have to put up a slate of several names rather than an individual candidate, they produce a balanced ticket, with some consideration for sex, class and race. It is, for example, not a matter of regional prejudice that there are more women councillors in the north than the south but merely a reflection of the fact that many more councils in the north have multi-member wards, selecting three candidates at a time instead of one.

## Constituency Leaders and Activists

Biographical information about party activists in the constituencies is much more difficult to obtain than for members of parliament. In particular, it is not possible to collect full data about the pre-war period and the 1940s and 1950s. An accurate time-series cannot, therefore, be constructed. However, material is available from a number of sources about the social composition in the 1960s of Conservatives at various levels of the party outside parliament.

This shows, as might be expected, that the higher the level of the party, the smaller the extent of working-class and lower-middle-class participation. The pattern, based on information collected between 1964 and 1969, is shown in Figure 8.1:

Since there were about fourteen million Conservative identifiers and about 300,000 Conservative activists during 1964, the statistics in Figure 8.1 indicate that roughly one out of 105 working-class Conservatives carried out some kind of activity on behalf of the party. Middle-class Conservatives were nearly four times as likely to be active in support of the party. The ratio of identifiers to activists

TABLE 8.3   Occupations of Conservative Constituency Chairmen, 1969, and Parliamentary Candidates, 1966

| | Constituency Chairmen % | Parliamentary Candidates % |
|---|---|---|
| *Professional* | | |
| Barrister | – | 16 |
| Solicitor | 7 | 8 |
| Chartered Secretary/Accountant | 7 | 5 |
| Civil Servant/Local Government | 1 | 5 |
| Armed Services | 3 | 6 |
| Teaching (university, adult and school) | 3 | 4 |
| Other | 3 | 3 |
| | 24 | 47 |
| *Business* | | |
| Large proprietors and directors | 17 | 13 |
| Medium proprietors and executives | 16 | 11 |
| Commerce, insurance, salesmen | 3 | 7 |
| Small proprietors, shopkeepers | 16 | 2 |
| Managers, clerks | 14 | 2 |
| | 66 | 35 |
| *Miscellaneous White-Collar* | | |
| Farmer, landowner | 9 | 7 |
| Other (journalist, private means etc.) | – | 10 |
| | 9 | 17 |
| *Manual workers* | 1 | 1 |
| *Total* | 100% | 100% |

SOURCE
As for Figure 8.1 for constituency chairmen and for candidates, D. Butler and A. King, *The British General Election of 1966* (1966) pp. 208–9.

NOTE
Former officers in the armed services are categorised under their existing occupations unless retired. Wives are categorised under their husbands' occupations. Apparent inconsistencies in the total result from rounding.

was one to 30 for lower-middle-class (C1) and one to 27 for upper-middle-class Conservatives.

Apart from the expected difference between middle-class and working-class participation, the notable aspect of the figures is the perhaps unexpected extent of lower-middle-class involvement in

Fig. 8.1   The social pyramid: working-class, lower-middle-class, and upper-middle-class participation in the extra-parliamentary Conservative party, 1964–9.

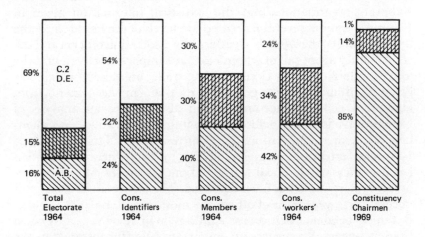

SOURCES

(a)  D. Butler and D. Stokes, 1964 survey for *Political Change in Britain* (cols. 1–3);
(b)  a private survey carried out for the Conservative Research Department by the British Market Research Bureau, *The Determination of Political Attitudes and Voting Behaviour: Party Workers*, (1966), (col. 4) and
(c)  interviews carried out by M. Pinto-Duschinsky with area agents in England and Wales in 1969, which produced information on 380 constituency chairmen (col. 5).

NOTE

The division between social groups A and B on the one hand and C1 on the other hand needs to be treated with caution for col. 5, as information on occupations given by area agents was sometimes not sufficiently precise to determine social group. For example, the social group of a shop-keeper is determined by the number of his shop-assistants—information which was not available. The C1 category of constituency chairmen consists of clerks, and a third of those identified as small business proprietors, shopkeepers, salesmen and managers.

party work. Conservatives in social grade C1 were nearly as likely to participate as those in grades A and B. However, the distinction between the lower and upper-middle-groups emerges very clearly further up the constituency hierarchy. The constituency leaders, especially in Conservative-held seats, are predominantly uppemiddle class. The ratio of constituency chairmen to ordinary party workers is about five times greater for upper than for lower-middle-class Conservatives. This is seen in the contrast between columns 4 and 5 of Figure 8.1. However, constituency associations are elaborate organisations and the statistical information given in Figure 8.1 ignores several intermediate levels of the hierarchy—the branch officers, the women's leaders, the association officers and the constituency agent (all of whom can have important roles), and the local organisations of Conservative trade unionists (which are generally small and insignificant despite encouragement from above). A complete account would also require an analysis of Conservative local councillors, of Young Conservatives and members of the area and national committees of the National Union.

Special attention is given below to constituency chairmen because they are the local leaders about whom the most comprehensive information has been collected. The chairman is, during his normal three-year term of office, the most important single officer. But the dependence of most associations on finances raised by ward branches generally ensures an important role (for instance in the selection of parliamentary candidates) for the branch chairmen. Their backgrounds seem, from case studies of particular constituencies, to be halfway between those of party activists and of chairmen. This conforms with the general 'filter' pattern whereby each higher level is more socially exclusive than the last.

A closer look at the constituency chairmen reveals broadly the same solidly middle-class, male pattern as for Conservative MPs, although constituency chairmen as a group are a notch lower on the social scale.

Apart from a few constituencies, most of them Labour-held, local associations generally have middle-class, male chairmen. Of local party chairmen in 1969, 94 per cent were male. Only 1 per cent of chairmen were skilled or unskilled manual workers (the same percentage as for MPs). Like MPs, the vast majority of chairmen were professionals or businessmen. But there was a marked difference in the balance. Whereas MPs and candidates were strongly professional, the majority of chairmen were businessmen, executives or small proprietors. This emerges from Table 8.3 which ~~ares the occupations of all Conservative candidates in 1966 ~69 chairmen in 1969.

~mination of their educational backgrounds shows that 95 ~chairmen in Conservative-held seats had been to public or grammar schools. The proportion of chairmen in all seats who had been to such schools was 84 per cent. However, the proportion with public school backgrounds was distinctly lower among chairmen than among parliamentary candidates or MPs. For example, 50 per cent of chairmen in Conservative-held seats in 1969 were from public schools as compared to 80 per cent of Conservative MPs.

TABLE 8.4    Educational Background of Conservative Constituency Chairmen, 1969

|  | Public Schooling % | Grammar Schooling % | Elementary Schooling % | % |
|---|---|---|---|---|
| Safe Conservative | 52 | 44 | 3 | 100 |
| Marginal Conservative | 44 | 47 | 9 | 100 |
| Marginal Labour | 25 | 56 | 19 | 100 |
| Safe Labour | 20 | 49 | 30 | 100 |
| All Constituencies | 36 | 49 | 16 | 100 |

NOTE

The definitions of 'grammar' and 'elementary' school used here are cruder than the classifications of MPs' schooling in the Nuffield election studies. This is because the table is based on information about local party chairmen supplied by area agents, often speaking without exact information. The table is therefore not strictly comparable to, or as reliable as, Table 8.1.

Have these social patterns changed over recent decades? Accounts of individual associations suggest that there have been significant developments both in urban and rural constituencies. In the rural areas, the influence and participation of leading local aristocrats and landowners seems to have declined gradually and steadily. In urban areas, the pre-war leadership of substantial businessmen has largely disappeared. In the 1920s and 1930s, and to a lesser extent after the war, large proprietors were frequently the financial mainstay of their local Conservative associations and, to all intents and purposes, employed the agent. The modern constituency leaders are expected to contribute their time rather than their money. They are normally well-established, respectable professionals and businessmen—solicitors, accountants, executives and proprietors of small or medium-sized companies. But they are a different breed from the landowners and business magnates who controlled many associations before the war.[10]

In summary, it appears that the pre-war influence of aristocrats and of very rich capitalists has given way both in the parliamentary party and in the constituencies to the dominance of the 'ordinary' upper-middle-classes. The hierarchy includes fewer sons of peers, millionaires and men of leisure. But this change has not opened the party to participation by members of the working class and the lower-middle class. Although these groups provide three-quarters of the party's voters and over a half of its constituency workers, they have continued to be almost completely excluded from the constituency and parliamentary leadership.

## IV DOES UNREPRESENTATIVENESS MATTER?

Ought the uniform social character of the party hierarchy to be a matter of concern to Conservative strategists? Are voters really influenced, either directly or indirectly, by the absence of working class voices on the Tory benches in the House of Commons and among the constituency leaders? Besides the possible electoral consequences, does Conservative unrepresentativeness harm the party in other ways? This concluding section will list some of the opposing arguments about these questions.

### Why a party's social composition is unimportant

Elections in Britain are being won and lost to an increasing extent on the basis of policy issues. It is by no means certain that the continued predominance of the upper-middle classes has led the Conservatives to advocate unpopular or unrepresentative stands. Etonians, though untypical in their backgrounds, are not necessarily so unrepresentative in their opinions. Some of the party's leading moderates have been drawn from the upper-classes (one example is Lord Boyle), whereas some of the most vocal right-wingers in the party have recently been those with relatively modest social origins. Defenders of the large group of Etonians in the present hierarchy have even gone so far as to suggest that their exit, if it ever occurred, would lead to a rightward lurch in policy and to a loss of popular support for the party. This claim is exaggerated. There have been right-wing aristocrats among Conservative MPs and ministers (the late Lord Salisbury and the Hon. Nicholas Ridley, for instance) as well as left-wingers with less elite backgrounds (such as Peter Walker). In reality, there is no clear connection between the class and the policy views of MPs. In any case, to the extent that issues determine votes, the socio-economic backgrounds of the senior Conservatives are irrelevant. Moreover, statistical demonstrations like those of Table 8.1 and 8.2 are limited to a comparison of readily measurable facts. Whether an MP hated his father may influence his politics far more than where he went to school. Whether he is a kind man may signify more than whether he had a manual occupation. It is at least possible that in many essential personal characteristics Conservative MPs are closer to being mirrors of the population than these tables suggest.

Insofar as personalities are significant, the party leader is the only person who really matters. The leader makes as great an impact on the voters as all his (or her) cabinet colleagues put together. Individual MPs, candidates and constituency chiefs are of even less account, as the uniformity of constituency swings in general elections demonstrates. This means that the social composition of the party's front-benchers, MPs and local leaders makes virtually no direct impact on votes.

Moreover, the popularity of party leaders seems to be determined by their personal qualities and only to a small extent on the basis of their class. This is seen in the case of Sir Alec Douglas-Home—one of the less popular and more aristocratic Conservative leaders of recent times. Survey evidence indicates that Sir Alec's unpopularity was not connected with his background. When asked to list what they liked and disliked about him, respondents included few mentions of his class (and a majority of them were positive); the unfavourable mentions were mostly about his personal defects:

*Some Favourable and Unfavourable References to Sir Alec Douglas-Home, 1964*[11]

|  | Class background | Personal qualities |
|---|---|---|
| *Favourable* | Upper class, well educated. | Strong, decisive, courageous, good PM. |
|  | 132 | 218 |
| *Unfavourable* | Educational background—snobbish. | Weak, indecisive, bad PM. |
|  | 25 | 546 |

Modern political campaigns concentrate on national propaganda. The image of the typical Conservative more often reaches the voter on television than via the old-style doorstep canvass. If the image-makers at Central Office wish to present a picture of a broadly based party they can use party political broadcasts to feature interviews with working-class supporters, regardless of whether they represent a large section of the constituency organisations or not.

The high social status of the Conservative hierarchy is a positive attraction to some electors who give their 'deferential' support to the party.

The arguments suggest that the social composition of the hierarchy is largely irrelevant to the party's electoral appeal and, insofar as it is relevant, it may lead to a gain rather than a loss of votes.

It can also be argued, in more general terms, that there is no reason why legislators should resemble their electors. Being an MP is a specialist job, requiring education and finesse. If we wanted parliament to be a microcosm of the nation we should choose its members by lot from the electoral rolls. But the qualities that make a man or woman want to be an MP and the qualities that make them a good MP are not distributed at random throughout the population. There is, on this argument, nothing wrong with MPs being an elite drawn from the more highly-qualified segments of society. Sociological indices that show how unrepresentative MPs are by their high status in education and occupation can indeed be turned into evidence of how well-fitted they are to their jobs.

## Why a Party's Social Composition is Important

General attitudes and beliefs about the parties are still more important than specific policy issues in determining voting choice. This holds true despite the fact that party alignments and class images have been diminishing in their hold over votes, despite the growing volatility of electoral behaviour, and despite the growing importance of issues and other short-term factors.

Surveys continue to indicate that, among these general images about the major parties, those relating to class are enormously important. The belief that parties represent class interests or class norms remains especially strong among working-class Labour supporters, over 90 per cent of whom express this view. Moreover, the majority of responses about the link between parties and class interests are favourable to Labour and unfavourable to the Conservatives. There can be no doubt that the Conservatives are damaged by being seen as a class party.

The association of the Conservative party with middle-class interests has been built up over a long period and in many ways. It is uncertain what part the social composition of the party's hierarchy has played in this process. However, it seems obvious that the exclusive image of the Conservatives held by most working-class Labour voters must have been reinforced by the style and accents of Tory spokesmen, which have inevitably reflected their Oxbridge, public school backgrounds.

In the post-war period the two major parties have reached very similar positions on many policy issues. Their electorate appeal has therefore concentrated in the claim that they will perform better than their opponents. Both sides acknowledge the need to reduce unemployment, inflation, and strikes, and to increase economic growth. Each attacks the record of the other and promises to do better. Since there are few differences in policy positions, the credibility of each party's message becomes all-important. This is particularly the case in the vital area of economic policy. There can be no serious doubt that the Conservative party is considerably handicapped in presenting their views on the economy by the failure to recruit any senior or well-known member of the working class into its ranks. It can hardly escape the notice of trade union members that, notwithstanding the efforts of Central Office, there is not a single trade union leader who publicly backs the Conservative party.

Although the appeal of the Conservative leader does not seem to be directly affected by his (or her) social class, it is indirectly affected by the social structure of the party. A British political party is a closed institution. The leader must choose the vast majority of his ministerial team from the ranks of his MPs. It is not possible for the British prime minister or leader of the opposition to follow the practice of US presidents in recruiting outsiders from a variety of backgrounds (and popular with a variety of electoral groups). When choosing the members of the cabinet or shadow cabinet a British leader is stuck with the talent already in parliament. Moreover, the MPs of a party must all pass the gauntlet of a constituency selection committee. There is no alternative pathway to the House of Commons such as that provided to would-be US congressmen by the primary system. It is this exclusive power of candidate selection that gives particular importance to the constituency leaders.

The Conservative party (like the Labour party) thus forms a world of its own. The party leader must spend a great amount of time in the party milieu and is likely to be influenced by these contacts. They are likely to affect his language and manner. Some of the leader's pronouncements must be directed not to the electorate but to the party faithful. But these party speeches are also monitored by the press and television. The leader's speech to the party conference is also seen by the electorate at large. Party demands prevent a leader from straying too far from the views and attitudes of the Conservative faithful. Thus, even if—as with Mr Heath and Mrs Thatcher—the party elects a leader who did not go to a public school, that leader is under pressure to adopt the upper middle-class accents and styles which dominate the party hierarchy.

It will be seen from these complex arguments that the absence of working-class representatives is not an automatic disadvantage to the party electorally. Where the Conservatives adopt popular policies and choose personable leaders, the narrow social composition of the hierarchy becomes irrelevant; and, insofar as the party appeals to deferential voters, it may even be a positive advantage. On the other hand, the lack of a broad social base is potentially a very serious handicap, because of three features of the British system: first, the importance of general class images, second, the importance of valence issues and third, the exclusive control of the constituency associations and the parliamentary party over access to cabinet office and the premiership (and consequently their influence over the style of party leadership).

The uniformity of the Tory hierarchy also damages the party in the ways that are unrelated to considerations of electoral advantage. It arguably limits the party's ability to formulate policy and to govern effectively. The problem is not that some social groups (particularly the working class) are under-represented in the upper ranks of the party. They are hardly represented at all. There is no compelling reason in democratic theory or in political practice for the senior office-holders of a party to reflect in their social composition that of the party supporters at large. The fact that half of all Conservative voters are working-class does not mean that precisely half the party's MPs should be working-class as well. The absurdities of this position were demonstrated at the 1972

Convention of US Democrats which tried to apply conditions of social representativeness to state delegations. However, it seems reasonable that a group that forms such an important section of the party's voters should at least have some voice in the top councils of the party. It is the virtually complete absence of working-class representation that is the core of the Conservative problem. The constituency associations have selected only two working-class MPs since the war and neither has gained cabinet rank.

There can be little doubt that recent Labour government have gained by having in their ranks a few members—like Mr Lever—whose experience of business has given them a rapport with the business community. No senior Tory has had similar experience of the shop floor. There are several other areas about which few senior Conservatives have first-hand knowledge or expertise, such as education and the social services. In these fields Labour is left to make the running. On the other hand there is a wealth of knowledge among MPs and local leaders about finance, defence, business, agriculture and the law. Similarly some of the discussions about industrial relations in the Conservative cabinet of 1970–4 would surely have been very different if among its members there had been a single figure with the background and prejudices of an Ernie Bevin or, even to pitch it far lower, of a Jimmy Thomas, to remind ministers of how other people reacted.

The uniformity of their backgrounds gives members of the Conservative elite in the House of Commons and the constituencies an unduly restricted frame of reference which limits the party's ability to formulate policies or to put them into operation.

The narrower band of choice exercised by constituency associations in recent years has probably hurt the Conservative party more, through an increase in uniformity, than it has helped it through an increase in ability. Likemindedness can be a hazard to a party that seeks to guide a diverse nation.

Although the Labour parliamentary party has had its own problems as it has moved from an overwhelmingly working-class group to one that has almost as many graduates as the Conservatives, it has always had and continues to have a far wider social, educational, and economic diversity than its opponents, and that has been a genuine strength.

Following the concerted efforts of the 1940s to broaden the social base of the Conservative party, the attempts to attract members of the working class into the higher ranks of the organisation and into the House of Commons have flagged. It is in the interests of good government and probably the electoral advantage of the Conservative party that they should be renewed.

## NOTES

1. *The Industrial Charter* (Conservative and Unionist Central Office, 1947).
2. *Interim and Final Reports of the Committee on Party Organisation* (The National Union of Conservative and Unionist Association, 1949).
3. Ibid., pp. 13–14.
4. *Woolton, Earl of, Memoirs* (London: Cassell, 1959) p. 345.
5. The Harvey Memorandum is reprinted in J. F. S. Ross, *Parliamentary Representation* (London: Eyre & Spottiswoode, 1943) pp. 236–8.
6. Ibid., p. 237.
7. Woolton, op. cit., p. 346.
8. *Interim and Final Reports of the Committee on Party Organisation*, op. cit., p. 15.
9. *Report of the Committee on Financial aid to Political Parties*, Cmnd. 6601 (HMSO 1976) p. 31.
10. J. Ramsden, *The Organisation of the Conservative and Unionist Party in Britain 1910–1930*, Oxford D.Phil. Thesis, 1974. According to Ramsden there was a move towards democratic financing of Conservative associations during the interwar years. But it was not until after 1945 that the decisive steps were taken.
11. D. Butler & D. Stokes, *Political Change in Britain* (London: Second Edition, Macmillan, 1974) p. 359.

# Appendixes

1 Main occupations of Members of Parliament 1918–74 (percentages)

| | Conservative | | | | Labour | | | |
|---|---|---|---|---|---|---|---|---|
| | 1918–35 Average | 1945 | 1950 | 1951 | 1918–35 Average | 1945 | 1950 | 1951 |
| Employers and Managers | 32 | 32½ | 30½ | 32½ | 4 | 9½ | 9½ | 9 |
| Rank and File Workers | 4 | 3 | 3 | 4½ | 72 | 41 | 43 | 45 |
| Professional Workers | 52 | 61 | 62 | 57½ | 24 | 48½ | 46½ | 45½ |
| Unpaid Domestic Workers | – | ¼ | – | – | – | 1 | 1 | ½ |
| Unoccupied | 12 | 3 | 4½ | 5½ | – | – | – | – |
| | 100 | 100 | 100 | 100 | 100 | 100 | 100 | 100 |

(continued)

(continued)

### Conservative

| | 1951 | 1955 | 1959 | 1964 | 1966 | 1970 | Feb. 1974 | Oct. 1974 |
|---|---|---|---|---|---|---|---|---|
| Professional | 41 | 46 | 46 | 48 | 46 | 45 | 44 | 46 |
| Business | 37 | 30 | 30 | 26 | 29 | 30 | 32 | 33 |
| Misc. | 22 | 24 | 23 | 25 | 23 | 24 | 23 | 20 |
| Workers | – | – | 1 | 1 | 1 | 1 | 1 | 1 |
| | 100 | 100 | 100 | 100 | 100 | 100 | 100 | 100 |

### Labour

| | 1951 | 1955 | 1959 | 1964 | 1966 | 1970 | Feb. 1974 | Oct. 1974 |
|---|---|---|---|---|---|---|---|---|
| Professional | 35 | 36 | 38 | 41 | 43 | 48 | 45 | 49 |
| Business | 9 | 12 | 10 | 11 | 9 | 10 | 9 | 8 |
| Misc. | 19 | 17 | 17 | 16 | 18 | 16 | 15 | 15 |
| Workers | 37 | 35 | 35 | 32 | 30 | 26 | 30 | 28 |
| | 100 | 100 | 100 | 100 | 100 | 100 | 100 | 100 |

SOURCE
Data for 1906 and 1910 are based on J. A. Thomas, *The House of Commons 1906–1911* (1958). From 1918 to 1950 J. F. S. Ross provides the data on university education in *Elections and Electors* (1955) and on public school education for Conservatives. The figures for Labour public schoolboys up to 1935 have been calculated afresh for this table. All figures from 1951 onwards are taken from the Nuffield studies. See also C. Mellors, *The British MP 1945–1975* (1978).

2. Public School and University Education of Members of Parliament 1906–74 (percentages).

| | Conservatives | | Labour | |
| | Public School | University Educated | Public School | University Educated |
| --- | --- | --- | --- | --- |
| 1906 | 67 | 57 | 0 | 0 |
| 1910 Jan. | 74 | 58 | 0 | 0 |
| 1910 Dec. | 76 | 59 | 0 | 0 |
| 1918 | 81 | 49 | 3 | 5 |
| 1922 | 78 | 48 | 9 | 15 |
| 1923 | 79 | 50 | 8 | 14 |
| 1924 | 78 | 53 | 7 | 14 |
| 1929 | 79 | 54 | 12 | 19 |
| 1931 | 77 | 55 | 8 | 17 |
| 1935 | 81 | 57 | 10 | 19 |
| 1945 | 85 | 58 | 23 | 32 |
| 1950 | 79 | 62 | 22 | 41 |
| 1951 | 75 | 65 | 23 | 41 |
| 1955 | 76 | 64 | 22 | 40 |
| 1959 | 72 | 60 | 18 | 39 |
| 1964 | 75 | 63 | 18 | 46 |
| 1966 | 80 | 67 | 18 | 51 |
| 1970 | 74 | 64 | 17 | 53 |
| 1974 Feb. | 74 | 68 | 17 | 56 |
| 1974 Oct. | 75 | 69 | 18 | 57 |

SOURCE
As Appendix 1

3 Social and educational composition of British Cabinets 1895–1974[1]

| Date | Party | Prime Minister | Cabinet Size | Aristo-crats | Middle Class | Working Class | Public School | | University educated | |
|---|---|---|---|---|---|---|---|---|---|---|
| | | | | | | | All | Eton | All | Oxbridge |
| Aug. 1895 | Con. | Salisbury | 19 | 8 | 11 | – | 16 | 7 | 15 | 14 |
| Jul. 1902 | Con. | Balfour | 19 | 9 | 10 | – | 16 | 9 | 14 | 13 |
| Dec. 1905 | Lib. | Campbell-Bannerman | 19 | 7 | 11 | 1 | 11 | 3 | 14 | 12 |
| Jul. 1914 | Lib. | Asquith | 19 | 6 | 12 | 1 | 11 | 3 | 15 | 13 |
| Jan. 1919 | Coal. | Lloyd George | 21 | 3 | 17 | 1 | 12 | 2 | 13 | 8 |
| Nov. 1922 | Con. | Bonar Law | 16 | 8 | 8 | – | 14 | 8 | 13 | 13 |
| Jan. 1924 | Lab. | MacDonald | 19 | 3 | 5 | 11 | 8 | – | 6 | 6 |
| Nov. 1924 | Con. | Baldwin | 21 | 9 | 12 | – | 21 | 7 | 16 | 16 |
| Jan. 1929 | Lab. | MacDonald | 18 | 2 | 4 | 12 | 5 | – | 6 | 3 |
| May 1931 | Nat. | MacDonald | 20 | 8 | 10 | 2 | 13 | 6 | 11 | 10 |
| Jun. 1935 | Con. | Baldwin | 22 | 9 | 11 | 2 | 14 | 9 | 11 | 10 |
| May 1938 | Con. | Chamberlain | 21 | 8 | 13 | – | 17 | 8 | 16 | 13 |
| May 1945 | Con. | Churchill | 16 | 6 | 9 | 1 | 14 | 7 | 11 | 9 |
| Aug. 1945 | Lab. | Attlee | 20 | – | 8 | 12 | 5 | 2 | 10 | 5 |
| Oct. 1951 | Con. | Churchill | 16 | 5 | 11 | – | 14 | 7 | 11 | 9 |
| Apr. 1955 | Con. | Eden | 18 | 5 | 13 | – | 18 | 10 | 16 | 14 |
| Jan. 1957 | Con. | Macmillan | 18 | 4 | 14 | – | 17 | 8 | 16 | 15 |
| Oct. 1963 | Con. | Home | 24 | 5 | 19 | – | 21 | 11 | 17 | 17 |
| Oct. 1964 | Lab. | Wilson | 23 | 1 | 14 | 8 | 8 | 1 | 13 | 11 |
| Jun. 1970 | Con. | Heath | 18 | 4 | 14 | – | 15 | 4 | 15 | 15 |
| Mar. 1974 | Lab. | Wilson | 21 | 1 | 16 | 4 | 7 | – | 16 | 11 |
| Apr. 1976 | Lab. | Callaghan | 22 | 1 | 13 | 7 | 7 | – | 15 | 10 |

| Date | Party | Prime Minister | Cabinet Size | Aristo-crats | Middle Class | Working Class | Public School | | University educated | |
|---|---|---|---|---|---|---|---|---|---|---|
| | | | | | | | All | Eton | All | Oxbridge |
| | | Average 22 Cabinets | 19½ | 5 | 11½ | 3 | 13 | 5 | 13 | 11 |
| | | 12 Con. Cabinets | 19 | 7 | 12 | – | 16½ | 7½ | 14 | 13 |
| | | 6 Lab. Cabinets | 20½ | 1½ | 9½ | 9 | 7 | ½ | 11½ | 7½ |
| | | 2 Lab. Cabinets | 19 | 6 | 11½ | 1 | 11 | 3 | 14½ | 12½ |

NOTE

This table is largely based on W. J. Guttsman, *The British Political Elite* (1963). Aristocrats are those who had among their grandparents the holder of a hereditary title. Working class are those whose fathers appear to have had a manual occupation when they were growing up. Schools are classified as Public Schools if members of the Headmasters' Conference.

# 9 Conservatives and Trade Unionists

## Andrew Rowe

### I INTRODUCTION

In February 1974 the determination of a government not to give in to a trade union was one of the issues contributing to its defeat. Several trade union leaders made it clear that they would do all they could to prevent the Conservatives from winning the general election. A few have gone even further and suggested that it will be impossible for a Conservative government to work with the trade unions or vice versa. This is one of those judgements the public statement of which looks rather like a threat. These facts alone would suggest that the Conservative party should take seriously the trade union movement not only in its policies but also organisationally.[1] If we add to them the facts that the Labour party derives about eleven-twelfths of its national income from trade unions, that union block votes account for seven-eighths of the votes at Labour conferences, and that eighteen of the 29 members of the NEC are elected by union votes, the case for an effective Conservative response becomes overwhelming.[2]

The Conservative Trade Unionists organisation is part of that response and this paper seeks to explain what it is and how it works. Part of my task is to make clear also what it is not, since many people, including some Conservatives and some industrial correspondents, have sometimes implied that the CTU is in some way an embryo alternative to the TUC. It is not, of course, and never can be. It is rather a voluntary organisation composed of paid-up members of trade unions who believe in Conservative principles and who seek a Conservative victory at the next general election, but whose priority is activity within their unions.

The CTU believes in free and responsible trade unions and its members work hard for their unions. They also believe, however, that there is plenty of room for argument about where the best interest of trade unions and their members lie politically. For example, they may point to a long series of polls among trade union members declaring their firm opposition to further nationalisation and ask why so many union leaders support it.[3] They may look at the problems posed for free trade unions when a government is the only large employer and ask if it might not be better for trade unionism if the government's share of the economy were cut back relative to the private sector. They may compare living standards here with those in other advanced industrial countries and ask whether the century-old link between the Labour party and the trade unions[4] has necessarily been in the best interests of their members. Looking at voting patterns in successive general elections, they wonder why it is that, with so many trade union members obviously voting Tory, the Labour party can so confidently claim to have the trade union movement behind it at election time. Polls also show stronger belief in union membership than in current union leadership.[5]

Most of the answer is to be found in the history of the two main parties. Despite the fact that many of the laws which allowed trade unions to form and flourish were passed by Conservative governments,[6] it is the fact that the Labour party is the child of the unions—the political arm of organised labour—which has dictated its history so far. Moreover, among union activists, the commitment to socialism, at least in theory, has kept the link secure. It may be true that the link is sometimes one of rhetoric rather than one of substance, but rhetoric is particularly important in the Labour movement. It is one of the more remarkable failures of the Labour party's opponents that it is still possible for union leaders to pretend that Labour governments achieve more, even in economic terms, for trade unionists than Conservative ones.[7] The myth has been sustained partly because, however slow the rate of growth in the general economy, it has at least grown a little each year so that the fairer shares for all implicit in the commitment to a form of socialism did not mean that significant numbers of union members might have to receive less. Further, trade unions are deeply conservative in their practices and habits of mind so that, even without going as far as the family fiefdom of the General and Municipal Workers Union, many major industrial unions have preserved a fairly long, Labour-oriented, line of succession among their leaderships. It is an important paradox that the newer white-collar unions often produce more radical leaderships who, at the moment, frequently lean a good deal further left.[8]

It would be foolish to suggest that this had changed already but the old system is coming under pressure. A combination of the closed shop, the switch in employment from blue to white collar occupations (with a consequent drive by unions such as the Transport and General Workers Union to spread their base) and a realisation by managers and professionals that they need protection too, is sweeping into the unions millions of people who not only have no background of working-class solidarity against 'exploitative' bosses but who have probably joined unions to protect their privileged earnings and status. This increasing unionisation of non-manual workers presents a challenge to the Conservative party as it does to the trade union movement.

The tensions are showing in some of the larger unions and in the competition between unions for merger partners. Some unions, like the Amalgamated Union of Engineering Workers, may break into some of their constituent groups. If they do, they may then float free until they join up with other fragments to form new unions based on skills or earning levels. How long, for example, can TASS (Technical, Administrative and Supervisory Section) be expected to remain part of the AUEW?[9]

Furthermore, there are a number of pressures, including cash flow difficulties, often caused by technological changes reducing membership, which are likely to force mergers. It is already true that sizeable numbers of union staff are recruited directly from graduates and others who seek union employment either for ideological reasons or as a step in their own professional career rather than as a climax to a long period of voluntary service to the union. It seems possible that, if unions grow larger and their management more technical, the gap between a union leadership tempted to look outwards to the wider political scene and the members concerned overwhelmingly with their own problems will grow wider.[10] It is vital that the CTU succeed in mobilising trade union members who are prepared to work hard to secure the sort of official they really want and to mobilise support for non-socialist solutions. Otherwise, the radical left will increasingly dominate the unions.

As unions grow and their influence at least appears to extend into more and more sectors, the general public will become increasingly aware of the need to find acceptable and effective restraints. Already, strikes and go-slows in the Health Service or local government, widely covered by the media, have increased public awareness of the problem. Members, too, will find the bureaucratic restrictions on their activities imposed by their unions increasingly irksome.

Thus the unions are faced with difficulties created by what their early champions would have called success. Furthermore, huge employers, whether government or multi-national corporations, may make union organisation easier but they also wield sanctions capable of making even the largest unions cautious. The organisation of half the country's workforce already, with the promise of many more, certainly boosts the unions' claim to representativeness, but carries with it new problems. For example, they not only have to balance the claims of one section of members against another but, as we saw at the 1978 Labour party conference, there is also the appalling difficulty of balancing what is perceived to be the government's interest against that of the union members.

For the Conservative party, too, the changing union structure presents problems. Should Margaret Thatcher and Jim Prior really encourage activism among people who accept most, if not all, the principles and practices of trade unionism? Can Tories really argue, not only for the closed shop, as a good number of members did at the CTU conference in 1977, but also for the use of sanctions by one group of people in restraint of the trade of another, especially if both vote Conservative? How much of the present practice of trade unions can Conservative trade unionists accept either in the short or the long term? There are Conservatives who will argue passionately that the attempt to build an effective CTU on the basis of loyalty to trade unionism is to build a Trojan horse filled with corporatists who will spill out one dark night finally to subdue the Conservative liberal tradition of individual freedom.

There is no room here to discuss this crucial question properly but many CTU members would, I think, approach an answer as follows. The principle and practice of individuals coming together to secure jointly benefits which would not accrue to them separately have been accepted by Conservatives for over a century. It was indeed the Conservative party which made trade unions legally possible and encouraged them legislatively, even if, for a variety of reasons (some of which are looked at later), they remained unconvincing champions to many wage-earners. Moreover, the same principle has been regularly used by skilled or professional people and by capitalists to further their own interests. Indeed, the absence of effective anti-trust legislation in this country and the blurring of outline between professional associations and trade unions make many of the arguments between supporters and opponents of the closed shop resemble those between pots and kettles.

The closed shop chiefly exists because large numbers of people wish to enter and maintain one at their place of work and because many employers find it convenient to deal with one. The CTU, like Jim Prior, is clear that there are aspects of the closed shop, as at present operated, which are unacceptable and, if unions will not moderate its ill effects upon individuals, legislative action may be required to protect individuals. CTU members would certainly prefer that abuses were modified by action from members within unions rather than by intervention by government, but they readily accept that the government has an overriding responsibility for its citizens.

What is urgently needed in Britain is a new solution. A closed shop is regarded by many trade unionists as such as good thing in itself that they pursue one at their place of work with a single-mindedness which excludes any consideration of personal choice, personal responsibility at work, or the changing conditions in which they work. Skill has long ceased to be the basis for membership but at the same time technology has increasingly put the power to stop an industry or the country into the hands of groups so small as to make a mockery of claims to be representative of the workers, the nation, or even of the majority of the particular union's members. In these circumstances, it is essential that some forward-looking compromise be reached. CTU members believe that no solution will work which is imposed from above but they are anxious to resolve a dilemma which is increasingly burdensome to Conservatives and the country. Jim Prior may have more room to manoeuvre than has sometimes seemed likely, in that public opinion in general seems hostile to some of the effects of the closed shop, including trade union members themselves. Thus, in the Opinion Research Centre poll 74 per cent of the total sample thought it wrong for an employer to sack someone who does not belong to a union, if a closed shop agreement is brought in, and 60 per cent even of active trade unionists thought the same.

CTU members tend to believe that strikes are an undesirable

method of reaching settlements but they also believe that there are occasions on which employers will only negotiate properly under threat of strike. The CTU looks to secure responsible trade union leadership which will use the strike as a weapon of last resort in matters of proper industrial concern and not in pursuit of political aims. The pendulum of opinion about strikes swings relentlessly. Once unofficial strikes were everybody's bugbear, yet any successful attempt to regulate or postpone official strikes will inevitably increase unofficial strikes.

Again, however difficult it may be to draw a dividing line between behaviour acceptable and unacceptable to good trade unionists who are also Conservatives, there is no doubt that with over four million Conservative voters already involved in their unions, there can be no question of withdrawing from them and that therefore many practices which may be difficult to accept in principle have to be accepted in the short term. In many unions, for example, it would probably be fruitless at this stage even to debate the propriety of the block vote at the Labour party conference since it is the foundation of the present establishment, and it is much more important to secure limited objectives which lie within one's grasp than reach, like Tantalus, for the fruit beyond one's scope.

In a party system which has developed the three-line whip and the guillotine to their present effectiveness, MPs' strictures on the corporatist tendencies of trade unions seem somewhat selective. Their problem, too, is to enforce voting discipline. What is needed is to build the CTU to a point where it can press realistically for changes. Who knows, it might end up seeking change in more than just the constitution of trade unions.

II THE DEVELOPMENT OF CONSERVATIVE TRADE UNION ORGANISATION

The Conservative party's history shows at least two previous attempts to organise to meet the challenge of a largely hostile union movement: the Unionist Labour Movement of the inter-war years and the Conservative Trade Unionists' organisation formed shortly after the Second World War; yet Disraeli himself grappled with a problem which still bedevils the CTU: 'I have never been myself at all favourable to a system which would induce Conservatives who are working men to form societies confined to their class'. He wanted, above all, to have constituency associations 'of whom a very considerable majority (would consist) of working men'.[11]

After a number of experiments based mainly in Lancashire, there was formed on 22 July 1919 the Central Labour Committee as a sub-committee of the National Union and a National Labour Organiser was appointed to head a Labour Department at Central Office.

At the very beginning it was clearly hoped that Conservative trade unionists might succeed, if properly organised, in counteracting the use of the political funds for the benefit of the Labour party but as early as 1922 the emphasis had swung towards a contracting-out campaign. Its other great aim was to strengthen the representation of working men at every level in the party including parliament. *Plus ça change* . . .

Throughout its existence, the Central Labour Committee fought a losing battle against the middle-class dominated constituency organisations and by 1939 there were only 113 constituency Labour Committees throughout England and Wales. A further problem which remains with us was the fact that so few effective wage-earners could afford the time and money needed to sustain full participation in the party on terms equal to volunteers working for other sections.

After the war the last remnants of the Unionist Labour Movement were allowed to die and a new organisation was attempted. One of its principal objectives was 'to promote non-political trade unionism'. This time Central Office tried to ensure that the 'Councils of Conservative trade unionists should not be an integral part of the constituency association and formally linked to it by rules'. The attempt was, however, a failure and it became obvious that the trade union organisation had no chance unless it were linked to and cooperative with the constituency associations and agents.

In 1953 the National Union Executive Committee published a report by Sir Edgar Keatinge recommending a reversal of policy and urging that where a constituency had a Divisional Council of Trade Unionists (DCTU) its chairman should be ex officio a vice-chairman of the constituency association. While in theory this was very valuable, in practice it raised fierce opposition in the constituencies. Moreover, as with every innovation in the party, the existence of a DCTU threw extra work upon the agents. As a result more effort was put into the formation of industrial groups and by the mid-1960s it was claimed that there were over 15,000 of them. At the same time the DCTUs were renamed Trades Union Advisory Committees (TUAC). Yet by 1964 the party itself was already running the organisation down and by 1975 the two remaining paid staff took their old age pensions and left. Why?

Partly it was snobbery: snobbery allied to ideology. In many constituencies, the TUAC was regarded as a nuisance, a boring if necessary device for bringing into the fold the kind of person who would not ordinarily fit in with the association. If a trade unionist did fit in well with the association, he or she probably devoted increasing amounts of time to ordinary association work rather than the TUAC because that was where the rewards lay. And most Conservative activists were not only ignorant about trade unions, but also they came from the very groups most obviously threatened by their spread. People of independent means, small businessmen and professionals were ideologically unsympathetic to trade unions. There are examples of constituencies which refused to set up a TUAC because the model rules enjoined upon them the duty of giving it a seat on the executive, and this seems to have been for reasons of snobbery as much as any.

Yet three years after its demise, the organisation was back in business with 270 branches, seven full-time executives, all with union backgrounds, and a new hope and vigour. How was the Conservative trade union organisation re-established, and can it succeed this time where it failed before?

The decision to try to revive the party's trade union organisation owed something to the persistence of the voluntary members of TUNAC (Trades Union National Advisory Committee), including Ron Benson of the NUR, convenor of the shop stewards' committee at York; Tom Ham, ex-president of the Stevedores and Dockers Union; and Fred Hardman, the present national committee chairman. It also owed something to Jim Prior's determination that his activities in relation to trade unions should be backed up by a field force of trade unionists with knowledge and experience in a position to offer him accurate information. It owed most, however, to the chairman of the party, Lord Thorneycroft, who took the decision to re-establish the Central Office machinery. From then on both he and Mrs Thatcher gave the CTU considerable support and Mrs Thatcher appointed John Page, MP for Harrow West, as her liaison officer between the parliamentary party and the CTU. A key step was taken when John Bowis, at that time national secretary of the Federation of Conservative Students, was appointed director of the CTU, responsible to the director of Community Affairs.

To try to answer the question whether this initiative will be successful I look at what we are trying to do and how we do it, and I start with three questions which we are often asked. First, who does the CTU represent and how representative is it? Second, if the Conservative party believes in lessening the involvement in party politics of trade unions, are there dangers in setting up an organisation within them open only to people who are prepared to be attached to the Conservative party? Third, how can the party justify such interference in the internal affairs of an independent trade union?

The CTU represents itself. However often and however realistically it may claim to be the voice of a large minority within trade unions, the truth must be that its elected officers from local to national level represent strictly only the CTU, except in cases where the views of others have been explicitly sought and conveyed on their behalf by the CTU. Yet this is not necessarily a derisory position to be in. When we talk of the CTU, we are not talking of an alternative nor a rival structure to that of the trade unions. We are talking about a voluntary gathering of members of the existing structure who happen to share a number of beliefs. Chief among these, of course, is that the country, including the trade unionists, would benefit from a Conservative government. This is not widely shared by the union leaders themselves, at least in public, and since they have a strong grip upon the union structures and resources, members who wish to challenge the establishment's anti-Tory orthodoxy need to organise themselves to make their potential strength effective. Hence the CTU which, if it can attract its due proportion of able union activists, will become as capable of effecting change as the Protestant reformers became within the late mediaeval church, although, we must hope, not to the point of schism!

In many respects, the CTU is a voluntary organisation more representative of its membership than the unions themselves. It is after all more voluntary than many trade unions. Nobody joins the CTU because he or she must. None can lose a job or face a disciplinary hearing for not belonging. It is at least as democratic. Every voluntary officer in the CTU is elected every year, so that when the national chairman speaks, he is speaking as the representative of all the members and there is no question of his holding his office for life. It must obviously be our aim to ensure that more and more Conservatives become active in their unions until it ceases to be even mildly surprising to find Tories everywhere within their union structures. There are already scores of branch officers and shop stewards in the CTU as our annual conferences show. Equally, we must try to make certain the CTU at every level is represented by effective and successful trade union activists. (The CTU represents its members within the Conservative party and, in that respect, is fully representative.)

It is no use pretending, however, that all is cosy for the CTU within the party itself. It is a great advance that so many candidates and an increasing number of MPs are pleased to claim union membership as part of their credentials, but there is still some way to go before trade union activism is regarded by selection committees as a powerful reason for selecting a parliamentary candidate. Sir Edward Brown and Ray Mawby have carried the torch of Conservative trade unionism into the House of Commons but the years since they were first adopted, in 1963 and 1955, have not seen any considerable trade union figure selected by a constituency and this lack needs to be made good soon if the CTU is to carry real weight within a Tory government. The independence of constituency selection committees seems often incredible to outsiders but is well attested by many unsuccessful candidates.

It is, of course, a chicken and egg problem. In the present Labour-orientated trade union hierarchies, it will be rare for an official to reach the highest levels with declared Conservative sympathies and anything short of that will make selection for a constituency hard to secure. A very great deal will depend on how the next Conservative government handles its relations with the trade unions.

In the meantime, most constituencies need to take much more trouble than hitherto to support (and use) their CTU branch. The Penistone by-election, in which the area CTU put in 200 hours of work, showed how the use of trade unionists to canvass and work in areas which have been traditionally unsympathetic to the Conservative party could achieve impressive results.[12] There is a great deal of work to be done to help the CTU and constituencies work out the best ways of mutual support, but that brings us to the much wider question of how the party organisation should respond to the modern world.

The answer to the second is easier to give on pragmatic grounds than in pure principle. The UK is the only advanced industrial nation in which trade unions are linked exclusively with only one of the great political parties. Norman Atkinson, treasurer of the Labour party, put it explicitly:

> The Labour party is the trade unions and the trade unions are the Labour party. We are an integral part of each other and there has never been an attempt by either part to dominate the other.[13]

There are signs that the Labour party is not always as happy with a relationship which seems to be more one of involvement by the unions in the affairs of the party than vice versa. It was, for example, suggested at the time that Harold Wilson set up the Houghton Committee partly to seek a means of lessening the financial dependence of the Labour party on the unions. Yet, as the government increasingly dominates the employer's side of wage negotiations, it is hard to see the relationship continuing without the unions losing some important freedoms to the government as employer, especially in periods of Labour rule. This provides a respectable ground on which even Labour supporters can stand to criticise the relationship. For Conservatives, the argument is a great deal stronger. While the trade union leaders persist in maintaining automatic links with one political party, even to the point of financing it, members of other parties are entitled to organise to challenge them. It would be as unrealistic to imagine that, if Conservative supporters decide to organise themselves, they would not seek help from their own organisation as it would be to expect Labour members of unions to refuse help from Transport House. The key here is whether any action is undertaken with the best interests of the union at heart or for some other purpose and CTU members believe that there is plenty of room for constructive argument about where the best interests of their fellow union members and of themselves lie. In theory, two outcomes at least are possible. Either the unions will end up as determinedly non-party political as chambers of commerce and many other voluntary organisations, or the existence of political factions within them will be openly recognised and accepted, as they are in other countries. A third possibility would be for union members to be organised in unions according to their political allegiance, but that seems too alien to the British tradition to be likely. I discuss the question of reciprocal influence on the Conservative party later, in the context of finance.

The third question referred to Conservative 'interference' in the internal affairs of trade unions. It is often asked, and is usually taken to mean trying to alter the union's practice to fit an outside body's purposes. The best way to answer this is to look at how such 'interference' might work in practice. If the Conservative parliamentary party or a shadow minister wished, for example, to persuade a union to strike or to postpone a strike in order to affect the result of a general election they could, in theory, ask the national committee of the CTU to advise all its members in that union to work to achieve the agreed end. Unlike the Labour party, on whose National Executive the trade unions are represented and which is, in theory, bound to take heed of its National Executive, the Conservative party has no constitutional relationship with the CTU national committee which could evoke the desired response. If the advice appeared sound, the CTU national committee might agree to recommend it to its member groups, but each of them would have to make an individual decision on whether to accept or not. And what they decide begs the question of how effective any decision could be in relation to the union's policies, even if the CTU were a good deal stronger than it is now. The point is that the members of the CTU are volunteers in only an advisory relationship with the party. They have no power beyond any influence they earn with the quality of their advice. If the party's policy-makers succeed in persuading them to act in a particular way, they still have the task of persuading their fellow trade unionists to agree with them and, in those circumstances, the term 'outside interference' becomes meaningless.

The only other type of issue on which it might be possible for the Conservative policy-makers to persuade the CTU to exert an influence is in the election of union officers. And on this matter the present union leaders are understandably, if erroneously, touchy.

Although many unions have national journals, information about the candidates at their regional or national level elections is often sparse and quite hard for the ordinary member to acquire from sources which he regards as trustworthy. Moreover, since many unions, probably in a tradition dating from their non-party political origins, forbid canvassing, candidates have no opportunity publicly to proclaim their experience or loyalties. There is, therefore, a need for information which is met at present by a haphazard series of devices, such as magazines of the far left[14] urging a slate of candidates or, occasionally, national newspapers doing the same for the centre right. In these circumstances, it is hardly surprising if CTU members ask for help from their fellows in their own union through the central secretariat and, where it is available, *factual* information about the records of all candidates for union office is circulated to CTU members who ask for it. It would be much more satisfactory if the unions themselves organised their elections in ways which ensured that every member had easy access to enough information to make an informed judgment although, even so, many members would want to know, for example, about the voting record of a National Executive member.

## III THE ORGANISATION OF THE CTU

Within the Conservative party, the CTU has an assured place. The rules of the National Union lay down that the national CTU committee is to be regarded as one of its major advisory committees and this is reflected at area and at constituency association level. Every constituency association is, of course, autonomous, but in the 220 which have CTU groups, the guidance of the model rules is followed and the CTU has an automatic place on the constituency executive committee.

There may still be a handful of constituencies which think of trade unionists as I described earlier, but the effect of Margaret Thatcher's constantly repeated appeals to Conservatives to become active in their unions, combined with the spread of union membership, makes these a dying breed. Over 40 parliamentary candidates in England and Wales and some seventeen in Scotland claim union membership now as part of their credentials and the number of card-carrying union members at the April 1978 Central Council meeting was surprisingly high.[15]

Constituency based groups of Conservative trade unionists meeting together regularly serve some useful purposes. For example, they allow, rather as a Trades Council allows, members to discuss issues of common local concern. These may be industrial, such as the effect of incomes policy on wage levels generally, or more general, such as the response of CTU members to an invitation to join a newly-formed branch of the Anti-Nazi League. They are also valuable for organising recruitment drives, social events, rallies, etc. and for the part they play in the local association. Yet despite these activities, local groups of the CTU are not enough. If Conservative supporters are to make their influence felt, groups based on their union or on their industry must also exist. That is why we have so far created at national level the following groups:

| | | |
|---|---|---|
| Teachers | Local Government | Communications |
| Railways | ASTMS | Firemen |
| Post Office | Civil Service | |

Several more have been formed locally or are in the process of formation. This will have increasingly important effects within and without the party. First, within, it will be a rare urban constituency which will be able to sustain a CTU group based on a single union or even group of unions. It is much more likely that a COHSE or NUM CTU group will draw members from quite a wide area, covering several constituencies. If the groups thrive and perform their function properly, they will, for example, have several MPs and candidates to brief on the affairs of their union and their employment. It seems probable that, because such groups correspond with union organisation, they will gradually take up the time and resources of CTU members, except for special efforts, such as local elections or a general election campaign, and the general CTU group will become a kind of holding company for a number of specialist groups. It will remain an essential part of the structure because progress within the Conservative party will still depend, to a large extent, on the contribution made to the local association's affairs.

## IV THE FUNCTIONS OF A SPECIALIST GROUP

What will a CTU specialist group do? So far, we have only limited experience on which to draw, but it seems likely that its functions will include briefing themselves and the Conservative party, at whichever level is appropriate, about the affairs of their union or their place of work. In the past, the party has got into unnecessary trouble because it has had no source of reliable information about the strength of feeling within a union or a shop floor on a particular dispute nor whether the leadership's view is representative of the members, nor whether the public pictures of the issues presented by the press or the union leaders fits the real position. Again, the party has often lacked information about the hopes and fears of union members about such matters as dumping or technological change or the thousand and one issues on which unions pronounce opinions, often more in accord with the political leaning of their research staff than of their members. Good CTU groups can begin to change that.

One particularly vital job for CTU groups in the future will be to elucidate for the Conservative party the tangled skein of inter-union disputes. These are likely to become more bitter and complex as financial pressures force mergers and competition upon unions.

All this is vital because trade unions are now a formidable power within the state, with leaders determined to work against a Tory victory, and because of the Conservative party's need to brief itself about every aspect of their work if it is to live with them successfully. But there is an even more important job to do. As union membership grows, so do the anxieties of many members about the way in which the unions go about some of their business. See for example, responses of union members to a poll in 1977.[16]

|  | Agree % | Disagree % |
|---|---|---|
| Unions have too much power in Britain today. | 68 | 27 |
| Unions are mostly controlled by a few extremists. | 58 | 33 |
| The closed shop is a threat to individual liberty. | 66 | 26 |
| The Labour party should not be so closely linked to the unions. | 57 | 34 |

Hugo Young, political editor of *The Sunday Times*, wrote on 25 June 1978:

One cannot underestimate the high cost of the interim victory over inflation: a steady, often pernicious, usually unchallenged advance of collective over individual rights . . . Since 1974, unions have not only got more power. They have succeeded in suppressing honest outrage about how they sometimes use it.

If a union has this power over the life of its members, is it satisfactory that the disciplinary procedures of most unions allow the union itself to act as judge and jury in its own cause? A recent case in ASTMS illustrates the dangers. The executive had ordered an enquiry into the behaviour of a member accused of conduct 'likely to bring the union into disrepute' and of 'interfering in the affairs of another union'. When the enquiry began, not only did the union executive provide the chairman of the enquiry, but the tribunal under his chairmanship ruled virtually all disputed points of order in favour of the executive, even the central fact that the other union had not only lodged no complaint, but sent witnesses from their own national executive committee to say so. More important still, the proceedings, which had been started as a complaint by the executive against the member, were turned quite arbitrarily by the tribunal into a hearing at which the member was expected to justify his behaviour without the executive feeling bound to establish that there was a proper case to answer. It is right that there should be public anxiety about allegations of corruption in union elections or maladministration but there are rotten apples in most barrels. It is much more worrying when the legitimate operation of normal procedures appears to fly in the face of natural justice.

If trade union members successfully campaigned for reforms to bring their practices up to date and to make their leaders more in tune with members' opinions, trade unions would be strengthened by becoming less disliked by the public as well as more relevant to the members. It might also put them and the TUC in a stronger position to play a full part in the development of a competitive British economy in contrast to their largely negative strategies of the present moment, but it will only come if enough union members seek it from within.

Constructive resolutions demanding change are needed to come up through the union structure for debate at annual conferences and elsewhere and, in this process, the CTU should be able to play a useful part. Speedy action will be needed because of financial pressure on many unions which will create opportunities to look at the rules and structures which should not be missed.

## V FINANCE

Like most voluntary bodies with no capital, the CTU is perennially short of money. To act effectively, CTU groups must be able to act at national level as well as local level and travel is desperately expensive. Union members do not get paid leave nor expenses if they are engaged on CTU business and several CTU loyalists spend substantial sums of their own money on their work for the party.

In these circumstances, the possibility that the political levy could provide support for the CTU as it has in so many unions for the Labour party, is bound to be attractive. There are, however, problems. These do not lie in the legal status of the political fund. The law is careful not to stipulate any party and, indeed, is not even couched in terms which imply that political activity equals party activity, except in the use of the fund to sponsor an MP or candidate. The rules of some unions may raise problems, but the fact that the NUT, for example, until recently sponsored Tory MPs as well as Labour, shows that there is no difficulty for many.

Paradoxically, the problem lies at the other end. The Conservative party has always kept itself carefully aloof from any suggestion that money could buy influence in the party. The largest contributor cannot, by his contribution, achieve a seat at the party conference nor an office at any level within the party. Moreover, the party is not structured to give any group within it power in return for its support. All policy stems from the leader and bodies like the CTU or the party conference are simply invited to offer advice and help. They have no direct control over any party decision. Indeed, the divorce is even wider than this. As the debate over the Conservative party's stance in relation to the Joint Committee Against Racialism emphasised, the party has no corporate identity. It cannot belong to another organisation and it, as a whole, cannot declare an opinion nor receive affiliations from outside. Full affiliation, therefore, of a union to the Conservative party, is not possible. Nevertheless, there is no good reason why a union branch should not decide to contribute from its political fund to a Conservative meeting or other activity and perhaps this will be one way of meeting some CTU expenses, although it could never solve the problem. A union could also act as collecting agent for subscriptions to the CTU.

Whatever happens, the financial future of the CTU is bound up with that of political parties in general and is likely to remain on the agenda of constitutional discussion.

## VI CONCLUSION

This discussion has deliberately avoided the difficult philosophical questions of whether either or both the Conservative party's dominant traditions can come to terms satisfactorily with the corporatist tendencies of the most powerful pressure groups in the country but I hope that this brief account of what the CTU is gives some pointers to what could be done.

The goal is an ambitious one: to break eventually the automatic link between the Labour party and the trade unions. It is important to remember that the link is not quite such a simple one as at first sight appears.[17] From the earliest days, the TUC has eschewed a structural attachment to the Labour party although the last few years have seen the creation of the Liaison committee on which TUC representatives sit with members of the National Executive committee and the parliamentary Labour party. The creation of the Liaison committee was followed by the Social Contract and, at the 1978 TUC conference, by the Trade Unionists for a Labour Victory committee. Indeed, the whole conference resembled nothing so much as a pre-election rally for the Labour party.

The important point to notice, however, is that it is still possible for the TUC to take a step back again and seek to preserve its independence from the Labour party. And it is in connection with the stance of individual unions that the CTU must work. At the moment, it is taken for granted at most union meetings that if politics arise at all, they will be Labour politics. How many union branches, for example, have ever heard a report on CTU activity, let alone on Conservative party activity? Yet many branches expect to hear a report on Labour party operations. Moreover, one-third of the parliamentary Labour party is sponsored by trade unions.

For all practical purposes, it is wishful thinking for Conservatives to imagine that a serious rift will open up (at least for electoral purposes) between the Labour party and any of the large unions for some time to come, but the goal of persuading enough trade union members that Conservative governments may do better for them than the Labour party, and thus of changing the nature of union alignments in this country, remains a proper and, I believe, an attainable one. We believe that a majority of the country and nearly half of trade union members would like to see this done. We also believe that it would be good in the long run for the trade unions to break the link. On the way to the goal, there is much that can be, and is already being, usefully done. Conservative spokesmen, MPs, candidates, students, Young Conservatives, and others are receiving better briefs on industrial matters, including disputes. Conservatives at every level are actually meeting trade union officials and activists in much greater numbers than ever before. The specialist groups are beginning to appear at union conferences, often to a warm welcome from members who had little idea that the CTU existed. More important still, CTU members are beginning to challenge the present leadership in their branch meetings and even, occasionally, at annual conferences. ASTMS's decisions against nationalisation owe something to CTU members (acting as loyal trade unionists first and Conservatives second). If we can spread that kind of attitude and build the self-confidence of Conservatives in their trade unions, the prospects both for successful Conservative government and for fully representative unions enormously increase.

If the CTU can bring both pressure and first-hand understanding of union life to bear on the Conservative party, which often appears quite long on legal and constitutional knowledge but disastrously short on personal experience of union matters, it will have done much of value to strengthen the whole constitution. It was a proud moment for CTU when, on the Post Office Bill recently, it persuaded the party to change its whipping intentions because of advice from UPW members of the CTU. More of that and the union-bashing epithets trotted out so readily by trade union leaders, uneasily aware of the gap between themselves and their members, will become impossible to use.

NOTES

1. In 1975 there were 488 registered trade unions with an average size of 24,000 members. At the end of 1974 there were 11,950,000 members claimed by trade unions of whom 10,364,000 belonged to unions affiliated to the TUC. However, only 111 unions were affiliated to the TUC—see Department of Employment Gazette (November 1976) and the Bullock Report on Industrial Democracy (1977) quoted in R. Taylor, *The Fifth Estate* (London: Routledge Kegan Paul, 1978).
2. In 1976, 59 of the TUC unions were affiliated to the Labour party, accounting for 5,800,069 of the party's total membership of 6,459,127—R. Taylor, ibid.
3. The British Election Study directed by Ivor Crewe and quoted by P. Kellner in the *New Statesman*, 23 June 1978, p. 839, shows that support for more nationalisation among those with 'very' or 'fairly' strong Labour party

identification had fallen from 64 per cent to 50 per cent between 1964 and 1974.

4. MORI poll—*Sunday Times*, August 1977: 57 per cent of union members believed that 'the Labour party should not be so closely linked to the unions'. (354 trade union members out of interlocking quota sample of 2248 electors.)

5. MORI poll (15-19 October 1975)—a probability sample of 3761 adults in 240 constituencies throughout Britain, of whom 29 per cent (1103 people) were trade union members. Of all the trade unionists, 47 per cent believed that 'everyone who works should have to belong to a trade union', but 56 per cent of them believed that 'most trade unions today are controlled by a few extremists and militants' and 66 per cent of them believed that 'trade unions have too much power in Britain today' (72 per cent of non-activists).

6. Repeal of the Anti-Combination Laws—1824.
   Truck Acts—1831.
   Legalisation of Peaceful Picketing—1859.
   The Conspiracy Act (right to strike)—1875.
   The Mines Regulations Act ('Miners' Charter')—1875.
   The Unemployment Insurance Act (benefit a right)—1887.
   The Contracts of Employment Act—1963.
   The Industrial Relations Act (right to join a union and compensation for wrongful dismissal)—1971.

7. Some of the facts, at least, suggest otherwise. In real terms the improvement in average take-home pay in sixteen years of Labour rule is 6 per cent, in sixteen years of Tory rule, 60 per cent.

8. See for example L. Minkin, *New Left Unionism and the Tensions of British Labour Politics*, paper delivered to a conference on Eurocommunism and Eurosocialism at the City University, New York, November 1976.

9. See, for example, the conflict between docker and driver members of the Transport and General Workers Union, where drivers talked of having their own union, quoted in R. Taylor, op. cit. At the same time, Taylor stresses the considerable cohesive strength of the TGWU and it may be that, despite its size and diversity, the TGWU will manage to hold together.

10. But there is, for example, considerable confusion among union members. In the ORC poll of October 1977 (quota sample of 1051 electors, 10-19 September 1977), 67 per cent agreed that 'trade unions should concern themselves only with the pay and working conditions of their members and not with political problems', but 42 per cent agreed with the proposition that 'trade unions should be just as much concerned with politics as with looking after their members' interests'.

11. J. Greenwood, *The Conservative Party and the Working Classes: The Organisational Response*, Working Paper no. 2, Department of Politics, University of Warwick, (June 1974).

12. Penistone by-election, 13 July 1978: Labour 19,424, Conservative 14,053, Liberal 9241. The increased Tory vote on a reduced poll in this highly trade unionised constituency (steel, coal etc,) was in part due to the very active campaign by CTU members in the by-election.

13. World at One, BBC Radio 4 15 June 1978.

14. e.g. In the CPSA elections in 1976 there was a double page spread in the left-wing newsletter canvassing for a whole slate of left-wing candidates. It was

called *Redder Tape* in a direct satire of the official CPSA magazine *Red Tape*.
15. Conservative MPs in 1978 included members of APEX, ASTMS, TGWU, EETPU, NUJ, IPCS, AUT and BALPA.
16. *Sunday Times* MORI poll, August 1977.
17. L. Minkin, op. cit. L. Minkin and P. Seyd, 'The British Labour Party', in W. Paterson and A. Thomas (eds.), *Social Democratic Parties in Western Europe* (London: Croom Helm, 1977).

# 10 Factionalism in the 1970s[1]

## Patrick Seyd

I INTRODUCTION

It is rather unusual to observe Conservatives involved in intense intra-party dispute, but in 1978 press stories of party bureaucrats' responsibilities being amended, of party officers being excluded from 'all-party committees', and of policy documents being 'leaked' were not mere instances of sensational political journalism, but rather were a reflection of serious internal party division usually more common in the Labour party.

Conservatives have continually placed great stress upon party unity. Perhaps the degree of unity has been overstated but nevertheless, whilst differences of opinion have existed, the Conservative party in contemporary times has not suffered from breakaways or expulsions. The party has had its differences of opinion on particular issues but it has maintained its overall unity. Consequently some observers argue that whilst factionalism is apparent in the Labour party, it has no counterpart within the Conservative party. For example, Richard Rose argues that the Conservative party is a party of tendencies rather than factions: that it contains constant sets of political attitudes but lacks groups of organised members united in attitude towards a range of issues over a period of time.[2] The purpose of this chapter is first, to challenge this argument and second, to assert that the incidence of factionalism within the Conservative party has increased since 1964.

## II CONSTRAINTS ON FACTIONALISM

One important reason why party unity has been maintained has been the low priority party members have placed upon ideological discussions. Conservatives tend to deny the existence of any single cohesive body of ideas which might provide the basis for party programmes; instead they rely upon such general guidelines as tradition, intimation, or common sense. Whilst the existence of a Conservative ideology is open to considerable academic debate, the important point when considering intra-party conflict is that the practitioners have placed little emphasis upon its importance. Appeals to an underlying 'Conservatism', except at the most general and superficial level, are rare, thus making it easier for the Conservative party to adapt to changing political circumstances without intense intra-party disputes. Thus in the past it has not experienced the soul-searching over objectives which, for example, affected the Labour party in the 1950s.

Nevertheless the party is not monolithic; tendencies do exist. It is possible to distinguish authoritarian and populist, imperial and nationalist, tendencies. It is common to distinguish the Tory from the Liberal in domestic politics by the stress placed upon collective or individual action in the economic and social fields. The Tory view is of an organic society—a corporate entity with interrelated functional parts and each part operating to preserve the unity of the whole. The state plays a positive role in co-ordinating these various sections, thus achieving the necessary stability, harmony, and order. From this springs the Tory belief in the state's responsibilities in economic policy, such as planning or a prices and incomes policy, and social welfare involving the general Disraelian commitment to the 'welfare of the people'. In contrast, the Liberal view is individualistic, in which the state plays a limited role. Liberal values are those of competition, incentive, and conflict, and the function of the state is limited to 'holding the ring'. Thus the Liberal is concerned to stimulate economic competition, to curb the amount of government expenditure, and to encourage personal initiative by reducing taxation and restricting the universal provision of social welfare.

Whereas revisionist and fundamentalist tendencies in the Labour party have become organised into factions, such bodies are not so common in the Conservative party. Various studies of the voting behaviour of members of the *parliamentary* party between 1945 and

1970 reveal the absence of factions.[3] However, such conclusions about the parliamentary party should not lead on to the generalisation that factionalism is entirely absent from the party. Whilst the incidence of factionalism is low, it nevertheless exists; individual members of the Conservative party[4] have formed groups seemingly with the purpose of winning political support for a range of policy proposals to be adopted by the party leadership. Some instances of group formation with the intention of strengthening a political position which ranges beyond one political issue include the Social Reform Committee (1911–14), the Tory Reform Committee (1943–5), the Monday Club (1961–   ) and Pressure for Economic and Social Toryism (1963–75). I would not, however, include the Bow Group (1951–   ) as a faction since it generally refrains from commitment to an overall set of policies which it wishes to persuade the party to adopt; instead it prefers to adopt a similar position to the Fabian Society, namely publishing worthwhile contributions to the political debate as a stimulant to political discussion rather than the pursuit of a partisan point of view.

The low priority placed upon ideology has already been referred to as a factor explaining party unity. Other factors are party loyalty, which Conservatives feel even to the point of jeopardising their own political careers, [5] and the cohesion within the parliamentary party arising from the similarity of recruitment patterns.[6] These all tend to curb factionalism. There are also important structural factors which limit the extent of factionalism.

First, there is the limited role of the extra-parliamentary party in policy-making. This is especially reflected in the organisation and procedure of the party's annual conference which is carefully managed by a senior group of people within the National Union, the party organisation, and the parliamentary party, who seem more concerned with achieving accord than with reflecting differences of opinion. The restricted constitutional role accorded to the National Union ensures no factional activity in the submission of resolutions for the conference, in choice of resolutions for debate, nor in mobilisation of votes on the floor of the conference. Neither is there factional concern with the election of such personnel as National Union officers or members of the National Union's General Purposes and Executive Committees. Furthermore, the National Union's functional groupings—Conservative Students, Young Conservatives, Women, Trade Unionists and local government councillors—are of limited importance and provide little institutional opportunity for political pressure of a factional nature.

Second, the constitutional relationship between the party leader and the party organisation limits the ability of factions to use the bureaucracy as a separate channel of opinion in which to challenge the parliamentary leadership. The inter-dependent relationship between party leader and senior party bureaucrats stifles factional activities.

Thus the opportunities for factions to mobilise support at alternative points in the Conservative party structure are restricted. In the Labour party, intra-party factional politics lead to pressure upon constituency parties and affiliated trade unions, which can involve the drafting of model resolutions for these bodies to submit to the annual conference, pressure upon party conference delegations, and competition amongst personnel closely related to a factional position for election to institutions of the extra-parliamentary party. In the Conservative party, such factional activity is almost totally absent. But events within the Conservative party during the period since it lost office in 1964 have provided an impetus for factionalism.

## III FACTIONAL UPSURGE

Thirteen years of government naturally produced a sense of satisfaction amongst Conservatives and reinforced their belief that they were the 'natural party of government'. Since 1964 the record of only four years in office shattered that confidence, particularly since first Harold Wilson and then James Callaghan seemed intent on a conservative electoral strategy that threatened Conservative dominance. Paradoxically it seemed increasingly to be the case that the Labour party was adopting the position of the 'natural party of government', whilst the Conservative party adopted the position of 'the party of protest', representing discontented tax-payers or beleaguered whites in the inner cities. This loss of confidence amongst Conservatives was reflected in a more argumentative party in which divisions of opinion hardened into factions.

This argumentativeness has been more difficult to contain as party membership has become more meritocratic. The national expansion of higher education has had its impact. The influx of relatively more university graduates into the party has meant that many of them wish to discuss ideas and policies and are unwilling to accept the party's procedures for dealing with intra-party debate. Furthermore, the general shift in attitudes towards authority within society has had some impact within the party. Party members seem less deferential towards the parliamentarians than used to be the case.[7]

But inevitably in a political system in which Westminster so dominates party activity, it is amongst the parliamentarians that this argumentativeness has been most apparent. The parliamentary party has become increasingly rebellious. Conflict over the issue of entry into the EEC was the major factor, but the shifts in party policies between 1970 and 1974, particularly over industrial affairs, statutory curbs on wages and prices, sanctions against Rhodesia, immigration rules and the imposition of direct rule in Northern Ireland provoked a great deal of dissatisfaction amongst back-benchers. Since 1970 it has become clear that a coherent and identifiable group has emerged within the parliamentary party whose attitudes merge on a range of issues, from opposition to state intervention in the running of the economy, to support for the white Commonwealth.[8] Whereas such a group of back-benchers would become highly organised in the parliamentary Labour party (the two current factions being the Tribune and Manifesto groups), there remains a dislike for such activity by many Conservative back-benchers. Nevertheless, on the issue of entry into the EEC, the supporters and opponents of the Conservative government's policy established organisations. And since 1974 there has been further increase in organised activity amongst Conservative back-benchers.

This rebelliousness amongst back-benchers has reverberated outside the parliamentary party. Dissatisfaction with the Heath government's increasing intervention in the economy stimulated the formation of the Selsdon Group in 1973. The choice of title by this small group of economic liberals was intended as a reminder of the commitments which had emerged from the Conservative shadow cabinet's meeting at the Selsdon Park Hotel in February 1970 and on which that year's election manifesto was based.

The Selsdon Group believes economic freedom is indispensable to political freedom.

The basic principle upon which Conservative policies should rest is that what the public wants should be provided by the market and paid for by the people as consumers rather than taxpayers . . . The function of government should not be to provide services, but to maintain the framework within which markets operate.[9]

Government has three functions only—first, to maintain the value of money (although 'whether the government should have a monopoly of money is a question which has to be faced before very long');[10] second, to maintain the law; and third, to protect the country's foreign policy and defence interests. In other than these areas government direction should be withdrawn in favour of the market as a means of distributing resources and encouraging consumer choice. The group therefore proposes an end to government intervention in prices, wages and dividend controls, regional and locational policies, industrial training and job-creation schemes, employment subsidies, and investment grants and incentives. It believes that the nationalised industries should be reintegrated into the private economy by restructuring their ownership where possible, and by forcing them to raise funds on the private market. For example, the miners would take over and manage locally-organised pits on a profitability basis; so also should the railwaymen have the opportunity to own those parts of the railway system which they wished to run, and any remaining units should be allowed to disappear. No subsidies on services or commodities should be tolerated; thus, for example, transport undertakings should charge the price the market would bear, particularly for bus and air transport. Similarly, the pricing mechanism should operate in the social services. The group argues that 'it is time that the very idea of government running the social services should be abandoned'.[11] Charges should be introduced for medicine and education, and the problem of the low-income earner would be met by reverse income tax or tax credits or, in the case of education, by vouchers. Local authorities should not provide a housing service; all public housing should be automatically transferred to sitting tenants and no new public housing should be built.

Notwithstanding the support for the liberal tendency within the party leadership since Mrs Thatcher's success in 1975, the influence and impact of the Selsdon Group appears limited. It applied pressure on back-benchers in a very orthodox manner by means of meetings in the House of Commons with Conservative shadow spokesmen. Only four back-benchers are members—Nicholas Ridley, Ronald Bell, Richard Body, and Archie Hamilton—although Ian Gow, Rhodes Boyson, and John Biffen are sympathisers. A large number of back-benchers are hostile to the group, regarding members as 'ideological splitters' undermining the chances of a Conservative victory at the general election, and for this reason the group adopted a low public relations profile during 1978. It relies on pamphlets, briefing documents and individual speaking engagements as its only means of pressure within the constituency associations. It has an active membership of only 40 and a total membership of approximately 250. It has remained a small group of activists, with limited funds and no branch organisation, because of its rather academic and intellectual approach to politics and its concern not to be taken over by some fringe group, such as the National Front.

One of the dangers of a formal definition of factionalism in which one concentrates entirely upon organised groupings within the Conservative party to explain the nature of intra-party political behaviour and to assess the distribution of political power, is that significant factors which affect power relationships can be missed. For example, to concentrate merely upon the Selsdon Group might be to underestimate the impact and importance of the economic liberals within the Conservative party. Other institutions and groups not part of the formal structure of the Conservative party are clearly intent upon capitalising on external developments to influence the party in this direction.

Britain's economic problems of the late-1960s produced significant shifts of opinion within both major parties. The difficulties experienced by the 1966–70 Labour government led to a reaction within the Labour party against revisionist social democracy and the reassertion of traditional fundamental beliefs about the importance of state intervention. Support for this trend amongst many of the trade unions resulted in a shift of power within the Labour party—particularly within the annual party conference and the National Executive Committee—which resulted in *Labour's Programme 1973*.[12] A similar shift in opinion away from the social democratic consensus of the early-1960s occurred within the Conservative party. In opposition after 1964 the Conservative party began to reject some of its earlier policy commitments such as economic planning and income policies. This shift was reflected in the party's election manifesto of 1970, but when the Conservative government found it necessary to abandon some of those manifesto commitments and again to intervene to a considerable extent in the running of the economy, it produced another ideological shift and assertion of liberal values stronger than that of the late-1960s.

Mrs Thatcher's election to the party leadership in 1975 was a reflection of Conservative back-benchers' unease at Mr Heath's corporatist tendencies and his indifference towards backbenchers and party activists who challenged his government policies. Mrs Thatcher and Sir Keith Joseph, in overall charge of policy making, have made clear their own commitment to an explicit Conservative ideology, albeit a very specific and restricted one. Sir Keith Joseph announced in April 1974 that after being à Conservative MP for eighteen years he had only now been converted to Conservatism. By this he meant a commitment to reverse 'the ratchet effect of socialism' and return to a market economy of free enterprise and profitability in which the state would enforce competition, limit concentrations of power and restrict the worst excesses of individual selfishness.

The Centre for Policy Studies, founded and directed by Keith Joseph since 1974, exists as a research body to advance the cause of economic liberalism, independent of the Conservative party but clearly intended as a rival research body to the party's Research Department. The Centre's prime function is to service Keith Joseph in his public speeches, primarily on the university undergraduate circuit, but also to popularise the market liberals' case amongst party activists. It is attempting to reach a party political audience whilst the Institute of Economic Affairs concentrates upon an academic readership.

The Selsdon Group is the Conservative advance guard of the Institute of Economic Affairs and the Centre for Policy Studies. But the main effort to popularise these views amongst party activists is carried out by the *Daily Telegraph*, which has adopted a position of strong support for Mrs Thatcher's version of Conservatism. A further carrier of such opinions is the fortnightly newspaper of the National Association for Freedom—*Free Nation*. NAFF, formed in December 1975, represents a wider set of right-wing attitudes covering economic, social, and moral attitudes as well as foreign and defence policy issues. NAFF adopts an authoritarian stance on law and order issues, is pro-white in African affairs, and is anti-Soviet in foreign and defence matters. But it also campaigns for the ideas of the economic liberals and as such *Free Nation*, with a circulation of approximately eighteen thousand, is an important communicator to the party activists.[13] This political position—anti-communist, authoritarian over personal behaviour and liberal in welfare policies—used to be effectively represented by the Monday Club, which grew in the late-1960s into a significant faction actively campaigning at all levels of the party in pursuit of its policies.[14] But in 1972 the group was racked by an internal dispute over its leadership which resulted in loss of membership and almost complete withdrawal from intra-party activity for a period. NAFF emerged in 1975 to fill this political vacuum left by the decline of the Monday Club.

Six months after Mrs Thatcher's election as party leader, the Tory faction within the party reorganised; Pressure for Economic and Social Toryism, and two local groups—the Macleod group based in the north-west of England, and the Social Tory Action Group based in southern England—amalgamated into the Tory Reform Group. The group claims to represent the Disraelian tradition within the Conservative party, with its concern for the two nations in Britain (rich/poor, white/black, suburbia/inner city), requiring compassionate understanding and reform through state intervention. Robert Rhodes James, not a member of the group but a sympathiser, reflects the group's viewpoint when he writes in the group journal:

> The Conservatives still, collectively, give the clear impression that they simply do not understand what poverty, misfortune and unemployment really mean to those who suffer any or all of these afflictions . . . The Conservatives still seem the party of privilege, and not that of opportunity.[15]

The ethos of the Tory Reform Group is of partnership and cooperation between the state and the individual, between capital and labour, rather than confrontation and conflict. Clearly the group is opposed to Thatcher's style of leadership, arguing that the party 'must stand back from stridency',[16] and must reject the 'mouthing of catch-phrases about freedom'.[17] On the issue of race it has directly attacked her by arguing that '. . . to pander to basic fears and instincts in the pre-election atmosphere, as Mrs Thatcher is doing . . . is an old and ugly subtlety'.[18]

The Tory Reform Group believes that the Conservative party should commit itself to more planning and more government expenditure rather than less. The key policy area in which more planning and expenditure is required is the inner city, in order to relieve unemployment and alleviate racial problems. The group is in favour of an incomes policy which would include both statutory wage restraint and Price Commission analysis of company profits. It would help to reduce unemployment by providing temporary subsidies to non-profitable industries, and it would pay higher unemployment benefit to school leavers willing to enter community service schemes. It is very much concerned with partnership in industry rather than conflict, and thus believes in providing tax-incentives to encourage profit-sharing, and also advocates forms of worker participation. It is interesting to note that, whereas George Ward was a Selsdon Group dinner guest, the Tory Reform Group regards such employers as an embarrassment to responsible labour relations. Finally, 'power to the people' is a key theme of the group, and thus it advocates devolution and electoral reform.

Soon after its formation the group became relatively moribund and relied upon its parliamentary sympathisers to provide the group with publicity. However, such publicity was 'double-edged', since the publicists—Peter Walker, Nick Scott and David Knox—were labelled by the press as 'Heath-men' plotting to undermine the new party leader. But in 1978 the group was revitalised by a new set of leaders, primarily university graduates in their thirties. Gerry Wade, ex-chairman of the Greater London Young Conservatives and one of the leading figures in the campaign in the late-1960s to make the Conservative party more democratic, is the new chairman. The group now has a dozen branches, primarily concentrated in university towns, and approximately 1000 members. Whereas the group has been rather better at making fine-sounding but rather banal statements than at making detailed policy proposals, Wade and his new executive are intent on remedying this defect by concentrating research, long-term rather than short-term, on four areas: Europe, constitutional reform (especially electoral reform), industrial relations, and social welfare.

It is noticeable that the Tory Reform Group is not backed up by the same panoply of organisations outside the Conservative party as those reflecting the liberal and authoritarian tendencies. But that may be because parts of the National Union and the party organisation have become involved in the intra-party disputes and have adopted factional positions in a manner unknown in the past. The Tory Reform Group now relies on the support of certain sections of the party—the Federation of Conservative Students, the Young Conservatives, the Conservative Trade Unionists, and particular sections of Conservative Central Office—whilst the

Selsdon Group and the Monday Club are forced into mobilising support through extra-party organisations.

## IV CONCLUSIONS

I have argued that those observers who believe that factionalism is no part of Conservative party politics are wrong; nevertheless, I do believe that a comparison of party factionalism reveals significant differences. Conservative factions are less concerned than their Labour counterparts with strategies for winning positions of political support within the party and more concerned with providing an institutional form of reassurance for those with like-minded opinions. Conservative factions exist to provide some form of meeting-ground rather than to establish a campaign headquarters. Naturally this need to provide collective reassurance is part of all factional activity. Certainly this was the case with the Gaitskellite faction—the Campaign for Democratic Socialism—which provided reassurance to individual revisionists in the constituency parties when their tenets were under attack; but its major concern was to re-establish the dominance of revisionist politics within the party. Admittedly the structures of the Conservative party make it more difficult for factions to mount such campaigns, but it remains possible to use existing procedures to influence the party's deliberations. Only one Conservative faction compares with the Labour factions in terms of intra-party activity, and that is the Monday Club. The Monday Club, before its internal dispute, used the party's procedures in an attempt to impose its views on the party leadership. It initiated resolutions for the party conference, mobilised support in the ballot to choose two resolutions for debate at the party conference, and also concentrated its attention upon parliamentary candidate selection. No other contemporary Conservative faction has adopted any of these techniques for mobilising political support and attention.

Another factor in comparing factional activity is that notwithstanding the injection of a more meritocratic element into the Conservative party, the bulk of members remain uninterested in debating and discussing political ideas and policies. The major response of party members is one of loyalty towards the party leadership irrespective of its policy shifts over time. Factionalism remains of limited importance within the Conservative party because the bulk of the membership places little importance on political argument.

As a consequence, factional activity provides little guidance to the development of Conservative policies. For example, the present dominance of economic liberalism in the party is a reflection of the mood of the electorate rather than the influence of the Selsdon Group or the Centre for Policy Studies. Examination of the electorate's attitudes reveals some popular reaction against certain basic tenets of social democracy, such as state intervention and public expenditure, to which the Conservative party has found it convenient to respond (and stimulate further) whilst in opposition.[19] On the other hand, a study of policy making within the Labour party cannot afford to ignore factional activity. For example, the strength of the organised Left had an impact, via conference decisions and NEC elections, upon the policy commitments of the Labour party in the early-1970s. No such factional impact is apparent in the making of Conservative policies.

NOTES

1. I am grateful to my good friend Lewis Minkin for his usual perceptive comments on an early draft of this paper, and to the University of Sheffield Research Fund for a grant to facilitate certain interviews.
2. R. Rose, 'Parties, Factions and Tendencies in Britain', *Political Studies*, 12(1), (1964) pp. 33–46.
3. S. E. Finer, H. B. Berrington and D. J. Bartholomew, *Backbench Opinion in the House of Commons 1955–1959* (London: Pergamon, 1961). H. Berrington, *Backbench Opinion in the House of Commons 1945–1955* (Oxford: Pergamon Press, 1973).
4. Strictly speaking I mean individual members of local Conservative associations which make up the National Union of Conservative and Unionist Associations, but for the sake of simplicity I use 'the Conservative party'.
5. For example, Sir Anthony Nutting, who resigned in opposition to Eden's Suez policy and made no attempt to justify his position because of the embarrassment it might cause the party.
6. All studies of the parliamentary party reveal that three-quarters of the parliamentarians are recruited from public schools. See C. Mellors, *The British MP* (London: Saxon House, 1978).
7. Criticisms of the party's internal procedures were contained in *Set the Party Free*, produced by the Greater London Young Conservatives in 1969. The interim report of the Chelmer Committee (1972) contained proposals for constituency associations to assess the performance of Conservative MPs. See P. Seyd, 'Democracy Within the Conservative Party', *Government and Opposition*, 10(2), (1975) pp. 219–37.

8. P. Norton, *Intra-Party Dissent in the House of Commons: The Conservative Party in Government 1970–74*, PhD thesis, University of Sheffield (1977). Norton established significant correlation in backbenchers' behaviour in the votes on EEC entry (October 1971), the annual Rhodesian Sanctions Order, the Second Reading of The Northern Ireland (Temporary Provisions) Bill (March 1972), the immigration rules for entry into the UK (November 1972), and on the Amendment to Clause 4 of The Counter Inflation Bill (February 1973).

9. *A Second Selsdon Group Manifesto* (1977) p. 3.

10. Ibid., p. 10.

11. Ibid., p. 7.

12. *Labour's Programme 1973* (Labour Party, 1973).

13. Stephen Eyres, a founding member of the Selsdon Group, is Managing Editor of *Free Nation*.

14. See P. Seyd, 'Factionalism Within the Conservative Party', *Government and Opposition* 7(4) (1972) pp. 464–87.

15. *Reformer*, 2 (Autumn 1977) p. 7.

16. *Reformer*, 1 (Summer 1977) p. 8.

17. Loc. Cit.

18. *Reformer*, 3 (Winter 1977) p. 1.

19. I. Crewe, B. Sarlvik and J. Alt, 'Partisan Dealignment in Britain 1964–1974', *British Journal of Political Science* 7(2) (1977) pp. 150–2.

# 11 Popular Attitudes and Electoral Strategy

Ivor Crewe and Bo Särlvik

The true Conservative course . . . is to stick as closely as possible
to the centre with a slight Right incline.

(Ian Gilmour, *Inside Right*)

A choice not an echo.

(slogan for Senator Goldwater, US Presidential Election 1964).

## I INTRODUCTION

When a major party of government suffers a heavy, unexpected or
repeated defeat at the polls, its inner counsels usually divide into two
familiar groups. On the one side—especially amongst the younger
back-benchers, local activists, and publicists from the media and
universities—are the 'fundamentalists'. Doubly frustrated by the
party's record in, as well as its fall from office, they call for a bold
and imaginative restatement of first principles, a 'choice not an
echo'. On the other side—especially amongst former ministers,
senior back-benchers and long-standing officials—are the 'moderates'. Made wiser by office, they urge caution, counselling
pragmatism rather than doctrine and moderation rather than
extremism. Electoral realities are given priority over purity of
principle. In truth the lines of battle are not as clear-drawn as this,
not least because of the large group of unhappy and bewildered
loyalists caught in the crossfire; but a division roughly along such
lines normally occurs.

The common assumption is that the Conservative party was
similarly divided on going into opposition in 1974. Certainly it

conducted an unusually public discussion of its future electoral and policy options, not only in the normal round of speeches and newspaper articles, but in a number of books.[1] But the debate did not run along quite the usual clear lines. Consider the two following passages written by members of ostensibly different 'sides' of the party:

> There is a very large centre group in Britain making up possibly 80 to 90 per cent of my fellow countrymen and women who have firm views on law and order, morality, personal initiative and responsibility, educational standards and discipline, and national pride. The Conservatives lose elections only when they lose contact with this central group . . . I am not talking about the soft 'centre' or the constantly shifting intellectual consensus; I am talking about the broad range of common basic beliefs that unite the vast majority of the British people.
>
> (Prologue to Rhodes Boyson, *Centre Forward*)

> A party cannot win an election unless it wins the support of a high proportion of the uncommitted voters. And as the common middle ground means the uncommitted voters, anybody who says he is not concerned with that ground is in effect saying that he does not ever want to win an election . . . for the Conservatives there is no alternative to moderation.
>
> (Ian Gilmour, *Inside Right*, p. 141)

The reader of these passages would be forgiven for feeling confused. On the one hand, in these extracts and the rest of their books, Boyson reads like the 'fundamentalist' seeking a return to first principles, Gilmour like the 'moderate' urging electoral realism. On the other hand both writers stress the importance of the 'centre', the 'common middle ground'. Their differences appear to rest not on whether to pursue 'centre' policies (the issue at stake in the Labour party in the 1950s and in the Republican party in 1963–4), but on where and what the 'centre' is. The purpose of this chapter is to clarify the terms of the debate and to bring to bear on it some preliminary evidence from academic surveys and the polls.

II THE CONCEPTS OF MIDDLE GROUND AND COMMON GROUND

To cut through the tangle of military and footballing analogies typically adopted in discussions of this sort, we propose to use the pictorial devices made familiar by Anthony Downs in *An Economic Theory of Democracy*.[2] Imagine a line representing the spectrum of positions that can be taken on any issue, running from far left to far right. On that line can be plotted:

  (i)  the various positions themselves: *the ideological ground*;

 (ii)  the parties' position on the issue: *the campaigning ground*;

(iii)  the position taken by various groups of electors—Conservative and Labour supporters, the uncommitted voter, party activists perhaps—as well as the electorate as a whole: *the electoral ground*.

Thus, although a single line is used for the purposes of display, it represents a number of quite distinct political 'spaces'. As an illustration consider the assumptions that appear to be held by the party 'moderate' who advocates the pursuit of the middle ground (Figure 11.1). In such a situation it would be electorally imperative for the Conservative party to locate itself at point X, i.e. a shade right of Centre, and well to the left of not only its activists but its normal supporters as well. And, as Anthony Downs has persuasively demonstrated,[3] the Labour party would place itself at point Y, just left of Centre, for exactly the same reasons: a middle-of-the-road consensus politics would therefore emerge. But the scene depicted above rests on two crucial assumptions: (a) that uncommitted voters take positions in between, and roughly equi-distant from, those taken by committed voters for the two main parties; and (b) that the electoral ground coincides with the ideological ground; in particular, that the electoral centre therefore coincides with the ideological centre.[4]

FIG. 11.1  The moderative Conservative's picture of the electorate

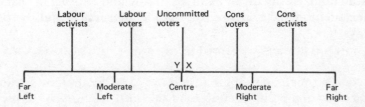

'Fundamentalists' like Boyson, however, would deny both assumptions. Their electoral picture is shown in Figure 11.2.

FIG. 11.2    The fundamentalist Conservative's picture of the electorate

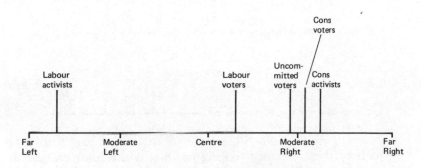

Uncommitted voters have views that come between those of Conservative and Labour voters, but nonetheless views much closer to those of Conservatives. And, more important, the electoral ground is *not* co-terminous with the ideological ground; on most issues it occupies the centre and right-hand side only, leaving the ideological left to a small minority of active socialists in the trade unions and intelligentsia. The correct electoral strategy for the Conservatives, therefore, is to locate themselves firmly on the Right, close to the position of their own activists and usual supporters, with whom the uncommitted voter, in fact, agrees on most things. Party principles and electoral advantage converge.

To speak of the middle or centre ground is one thing; to speak of the *common* ground quite another. The first refers to the *location* of a group of electors (or a party) along an electoral or ideological dimension and is best estimated by a measure of central tendency such as an arithmetic mean. The second refers to the *distribution* of the electors around that location—whether they are concentrated or dispersed—and is best estimated by a measure of dispersion such as a standard deviation. The ground occupied by five groups of electors (A, B, C, D, E) could therefore be described in one of four ways:

1.    common middle ground

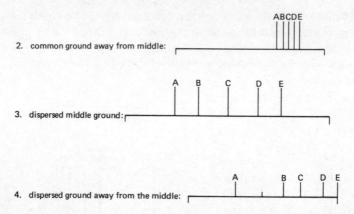

2. common ground away from middle:

3. dispersed middle ground:

4. dispersed ground away from the middle:

Which of these electoral configurations is the most common? Before coming to an answer, it is important to add some refinements to this method of proceeding. First, the 'position' on the line for any group of voters is only the average of a scatter of positions of the individuals composing the group; moreover, the degree of scatter will itself vary across issues and between groups: on nationalisation, for example, there is a greater consensus of view amongst Conservative than Labour supporters.[5] Degree of consensus has an important bearing on electoral strategy: the lower the consensus amongst a party's supporters (or the uncommitted) the more ambivalent about its position the party will need to be.

Secondly, there is no such thing as a true or objective party position. What counts is the electorate's perception of the party's position: this perception might well differ, of course, from that of the party leadership, and will vary not only between but also within groups of electors. Indeed, the degree of agreement within a group about a party's position will itself differ across groups, issues and the party in question.

Thirdly, it is unusual for a single issue to be the exclusive or decisive factor in the way any individual, or the electorate as a whole, votes. For most voters party preference is determined by a complex amalgam of issues, the precise weight of any one being difficult to gauge; and where one issue is of overriding importance it will not be the same issue in every case. Analysis therefore needs to proceed at two levels: we require the configuration for a number of issues combined and we also require configurations restricted to those electors for whom the issue in question is particularly important. And ideally, we should attempt to construct configurations that combine both.

It is also important to appreciate some of the limits to this method of analysis. For one thing, it is difficult to apply to those issues (sometimes described as 'valence' as opposed to 'position' issues) on which the electorate shares a near-identical goal and disagrees only on the relative ability of the parties to achieve it, e.g. a reduction in the rate of inflation, unemployment or strikes. For another, not all 'position' issues are unidimensional: although the issue of nationalisation can be represented by a line running from 'nationalise the lot' to 'denationalise the lot', there would be no obviously correct location for the voter who believed in nationalising some industries but denationalising others. Finally, it must be added that factors other than issues, such as a party's leadership or its overall 'image' play a part in the election outcome and these cannot be analysed in the way we adopt for issues.

There follow two electoral 'pictures', drawn from the October 1974 election, one for the issue of nationalisation and the other for that of the EEC. On both issues the subjects of the October 1974 British Election Study were asked to give their own view, and their preception of each party's position, on the two issues: there was a choice of four positions on each issue, which were scored from one to four, a low score denoting a 'left-wing' position, i.e. support for large-scale nationalisation or for withdrawal from the EEC. Committed Conservative and Labour supporters were defined as those with a 'very' or 'fairly' strong party identification, on the basis of the standard three-category party identification question:[6] there is extensive evidence from the Butler and Stokes, and Essex election surveys that the great majority of such partisans regularly turn out for their party at each election.[7] Three groups of 'uncommitted voters' were distinguished:

(a) *Conservative 'leaners'*, defined as 'not very strong' Conservative identifiers. In October 1974, 55 per cent voted Conservative, 19 per cent defected (4 per cent to Labour) and 25 per cent abstained. In other words, this group is predominantly Conservative but easily persuaded to defect and abstain: further losses of Conservative support would come primarily from this group.
(b) *Labour 'leaners'*, defined as 'not very strong' Labour identifiers. In October 1974, 53 per cent voted Labour, 14 per cent defected (5 per cent to the Conservatives) and 33 per cent failed to vote. Any

Conservative success amongst Labour supporters would first occur in this group, as would Conservative advantage from Labour abstention.

(c) *Liberal 'leaners'*, defined as 'not very strong' Liberal identifiers, of whom 54 per cent voted Liberal in October 1974, 17 per cent Conservative, 8 per cent Labour, and 18 per cent abstained. Conservative gains from a collapse of the Liberal vote at the next election could be expected to come disproportionately from this group.[8]

The two configurations shown in Figures 11.3 and 11.4 are reasonably typical of the kind that support, in turn, the case of the 'moderates' and the case of the 'fundamentalists'.

First, the issue of the EEC: this configuration has two features which support the case of the 'moderates'. First, the five groups of voters are located in the predictable ideological 'order'; indeed, in all but one case with almost equal 'distances' between them. Secondly, the five groups of voters are clustered almost exactly around the ideological centre (the score for the whole electorate was 2.51). The two parties, however, are in very different strategic locations. Labour is perfectly positioned: a shade left of the ideological centre, it is on the moderate side of its own committed supporters, very close to Labour 'leaners' and considerably less distant than the Conservative party from the two other groups of uncommitted voters. Even committed Conservative voters are somewhat less distant from Labour (.49) than from the Conservative party (.73).[9] In these circumstances it is not surprising that in October 1974 the Conservatives lost votes on the EEC: amongst February 1974 Conservative voters who (in October) considered the EEC the most important of all issues, 26 per cent defected or abstained; but amongst those who considered the issue only fairly or not very important, the proportion was 21 per cent.

For an almost exact contrast we now turn to the issue of nationalisation (Figure 11.4). Once again, the five groups of electors are positioned on the line in an ideologically predictable way, but this time they cluster around a point well to the *right* of the ideological centre (the mean position for all respondents is 2.80). And this time it is the Conservative party, not Labour, which finds itself at a clear strategic advantage, being positioned very close to both committed and 'leaning' Conservatives, and considerably nearer than the Labour party to the two other uncommitted groups

Fig. 11.3 The electoral configuration for the EEC issue, October 1974

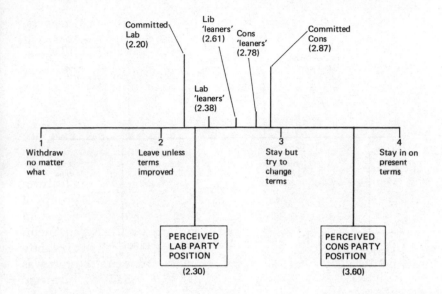

SOURCE
British Election Study, October 1974 cross-section sample.

QUESTION
'It is sometimes said that Britain should try to change the terms of entry into the Common Market and if this is not successful, get out. Which of the following statements on this card comes closest to what you yourself feel should be done?'
1 It is all right for Britain to stay in the Common Market on the present terms
2 Britain must stay in the Common Market but must try hard to change the terms
3 Britain must change the terms and should leave the Common Market unless they improve
4 Britain should get out of the Common Market no matter what.

NOTES
The perceived party positions are based on those of the respondents as a whole. Figures in parentheses indicate the point on the scale at which the group is located. The height of the vertical lines above the horizontal represent the relative size of the electoral groups.

of electors. Analysis of each group's perception of the two parties' positions revealed a similar distorting phenomenon to that found on the EEC issue (see note 9) but on this occasion it was committed

Fig. 11.4    The electoral configuration for the nationalisation issue, October 1974

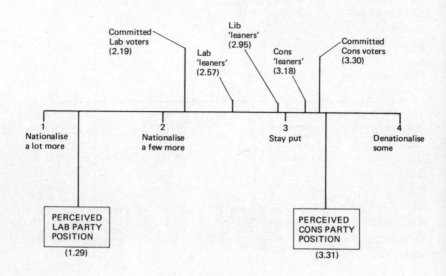

SOURCE
British Election Study, October 1974 cross-section sample.

QUESTION
'There has been a lot of talk recently about nationalisation, that is, the Government owning and running industries like steel and electricity. Which of these statements comes closest to what you yourself feel should be done?'
1  *A lot more* industries should be nationalised
2  Only a *few more* industries should be nationalised
3  *No more* industries should be nationalised but industries that are now nationalised should stay nationalised
4  Some of the industries that are now nationalised should become private companies.

NOTES
The perceived party positions are based on those of the respondents as a whole. Figures in parentheses indicate the point on the scale at which the group is located. The height of the vertical lines above the horizontal represent the relative surge of the electoral groups.

Labour supporters who 'pulled' their party towards their own less fundamentalist position.[10] Just as the Conservatives appeared to lose some votes on the EEC issue, so Labour did on nationalisation: amongst February 1974 Labour voters who (in October) considered nationalisation the single most important issue 24 per cent defected or abstained; but amongst those who considered the issue only fairly or not very important, the proportion was 17 per cent. Thus, on nationalisation the 'fundamentalist' strategy looks, for the Conservatives, the more attractive.

III   THE ELECTORATE'S POSITION ON DIFFERENT ISSUES AND THE IMPLICATIONS FOR A RATIONAL ELECTORAL STRATEGY

But elections are fought on and decided by a host of issues: what are the configurations across them all? Do they generally support the moderate's or fundamentalist's assumptions, or vary by type of issue, or reveal no clear pattern at all? To answer these questions we shall analyse the large number of issue-questions included in the October 1974 British Election Study. Three kinds of issue-questions were asked:

1. *Position-issue questions*: respondents were asked to say to which of four positions on the issues of nationalisation, North Sea oil, social services, and the EEC they felt 'closest' (and, also, perceived the parties as 'closest').

2. *Social trend questions*: respondents were asked for their view on 'some of the general changes that have been taking place in Britain in the last few years'. They could choose one of five answers:

1. Gone much too far
2. Gone a little too far
3. Is about right
4. Not gone quite far enough
5. Not gone nearly far enough

The 'changes' on which judgement was invited included:

1. Equality for women
2. Leniency on law-breakers
3. Pornography
4. Declining respect for authority
5. Equality for coloured people
6. Modern methods of teaching
7. The easier availability of abortion
8. Welfare benefits
9. Cuts in Britain's defence forces

This series of questions was specifically designed to tap 'populist' resentment against modern social trends, especially the decline of traditional conceptions of authority and morality.

3. *Policy questions*: respondents were asked how important it was that the government should, or should not, carry out each of the following policies:

1. Establishing comprehensive schools
2. Repatriating immigrants
3. Increasing state control of land
4. Increasing foreign aid
5. Toughening up measures against crime
6. Getting rid of pollution
7. Encouraging worker-participation
8. Strengthening measures to curb Communist influence in Britain
9. Getting rid of poverty
10. Redistributing wealth
11. Devolving power to regions
12. Protecting countryside
13. Putting more money into Health Service

They could choose one of five answers:

1. Very important that it should be done
2. Fairly important that it should be done
3. It doesn't matter either way
4. Fairly important that it should not be done
5. Very important that it should not be done

It would be both impractical and unnecessary to provide configurations of the kind described for the EEC and nationalisation issues for each of the above. Instead we should ask: how do opinions on these issues cluster, and what are the configurations for the major clusters? A factor analysis (unrotated) of the correlation matrix for all these issues revealed three main 'clusters' (or 'factors' as they are usually termed), of which the heaviest 'loading' (i.e. contributory) issues were as shown in Table 11.1.

The primary cluster—primary in the sense that it accounts for more of the variation in public opinion than any other cluster—is the familiar socio-economic Left-Right division over the distribution of wealth and the ownership of production. The second most important cluster is more difficult to describe concisely: for want of anything better I shall refer to it as 'populist-authoritarian'. The third factor is uncomplicated, consisting of support for (or rejection of) racialist policies. It is possible, of course, to discern additional

TABLE 11.1 Unrotated factor analysis of issue questions, October 1974

| Issue | Factor I<br>Loading on factor | Issue | Factor II<br>Loading on factor | Issue | Factor III<br>Loading on factor |
|---|---|---|---|---|---|
| Nationalisation | ·588 | Measures against crime | ·557 | Repatriation of Immigrants | ·501 |
| Redistribution of wealth | ·578 | Pornography | ·444 | Racial equality | ·457 |
| Welfare benefits | ·570 | Communist influence | ·406 | | |
| Social services | ·564 | Respect for authority | ·383 | | |
| % total variance explained | 17·1% | | 10·7% | | 7·3% |

FIG. 11.5    Electoral configurations for three issue-clusters

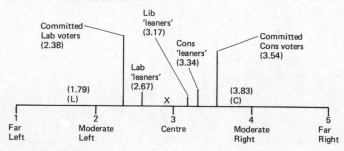

'LEFT-RIGHT SOCIOECONOMIC'

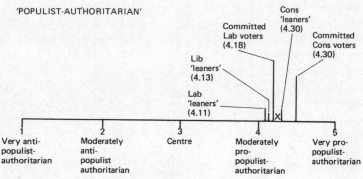

'POPULIST-AUTHORITARIAN'

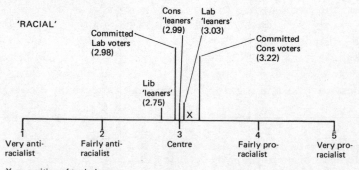

'RACIAL'

clusters of opinions accounting for a smaller proportion of the variance; but the three described above represent the major axes by which public opinion was organised in Britain in October 1974.

How should the Conservative party respond electorally to these three opinion-clusters? Should it take a non-committal and 'moderate' position or boldly follow its ideological instincts? As the electoral configurations in Figure 11.5 show, the answer depends on the particular issue-cluster:

(a) *Left-Right socioeconomic issues.*   Here the electoral configuration conforms almost perfectly to the 'classical' model: committed Labour supporters are furthest to the Left, committed Conservatives furthest to the Right, with uncommitted voters in between. The typical voter is located at almost dead centre. But whereabouts on the Left-Right socioeconomic scale do the two parties stand in the eyes of the electorate? Data on perceptions of the parties' positions are only available for two of the four issues represented by the scale: nationalisation and social services. The perceived positions of the Labour and Conservative parties on these two issues combined are denoted on the first configuration of Figure 11.5 by (L) and (C) respectively. There are a number of features to this configuration worth noting. First, both parties were placed on the 'extreme' side of their own most committed supporters—Labour to the left of theirs, the Conservatives to the right of theirs. Secondly, the committed and leaning supporters of both parties were closer to their own party's position than to that of the other party. Thirdly, it was to the clear advantage of both parties to move towards the ideological centre. A *unilateral* shift towards (but not over and across) the centre would have allowed either party to become the closer of the two parties to the Liberal leaners without becoming more distant from its own more faint-hearted supporters. Nonetheless, the Left-Right socioeconomic configuration of party and voter positions is not perfectly symmetrical. For one thing, the Conservative party is regarded as somewhat closer to the ideological

NOTES

Figures in parentheses indicate the point on the scale at which the group is located (i.e. its combined mean score on the issues). For each group, the score on each issue was standardised, aggregated, and divided by the number of issues. The height of the vertical lines above the horizontal represents the relative size of each electoral group.

centre (being 0.83 away) than Labour is (being 1.21 away). For another, the overall array of electoral groups is skewed fractionally to the right: Liberal leaners place themselves to the right of centre and both committed and leaning Labour supporters are closer to the centre (although to its left) than are their Conservative counterparts. As a result it would take a much smaller change of position for the Conservatives than for Labour to compete effectively for the vote of leaning Liberals or, for that matter, for the vote of uncommitted supporters of the 'opposite' party. On socioeconomic issues the rational electoral course for the Conservatives is clearly to move further towards the ideological centre. Moderation is the party's right course *not* because the electorate occupies common ideological ground but because it is symmetrically dispersed across the *middle* point of the ideological spectrum.

(b) *Populist-Authoritarian issues.*   Here, on the other hand, the electorate clearly does stand on *common* ground: there is almost nothing to distinguish the views of the various electoral groups. But it is ground far to the right of the ideological mid-point: the electoral centre does not coincide with the ideological centre. On the issues that make up this cluster Rhodes Boyson's view of the electorate stands up: 96 per cent of the electorate wanted 'tougher measures to prevent crime'; 82 per cent said that the decline in 'respect for authority' 'had gone too far'; 78 per cent wanted 'tougher measures to prevent Communist influence in Britain' and 64 per cent felt that 'nudity and sex in films and television' 'had gone too far'. The electorate's positioning of the two parties on populist-authoritarian issues, however, must be a matter for speculation, since the British Election Study surveys in October 1974 did not ask respondents about the parties' positions on the issues composing this dimension. There is a small amount of fragmentary evidence from other polls and surveys. For example, each of the monthly Gallup polls from January to May 1978 asked 'Which parties do you think are particularly good at maintaining law and order': over the five months combined 42 per cent chose the Conservatives, 30 per cent Labour.[11] In February 1974 the British Election Study asked 'When it comes to dealing with Communists in trade unions, which, if any, of the parties do you think is best?': 40 per cent said the Conservatives, 25 per cent Labour. Thus the Conservatives are almost certainly regarded as closer than Labour to the electoral groups in the populist-authoritarian configuration, but *how* close is impossible to judge. It is possible, for example, that the electorate regards both parties as so remote on these issues that, much in the way that long perspective forecloses the gap between distant objects, little significant difference between the parties is discerned. But whatever the perceived party positions on this dimension, the Conservative party would appear to have much to gain electorally and little to lose by following its heart and establishing itself firmly as the party of discipline, order and morality.

(c) *Racial Issues*.    Here the electoral configuration is different yet again: the electorate congregate on common ground which *is* at the ideological mid-point. The ideological and electoral centre coincide. (It is worth noting, however, that the electoral groups are not located in 'ideological order': Liberal leaners are a shade to the left of committed Labour supporters, and Conservative leaners are fractionally to the left of Labour leaners.) Once again, unfortunately, no data exist on where the electorate places the parties on the two racial issues. It is true that recent opinion polls, especially since Mrs Thatcher's remarks in January 1978 about 'swamping', have extensively covered public opinion on immigration, and on first reading suggest that the Conservatives are much the more popular party on the issue. For example, between February and May 1978 Gallup asked 'Which parties do you think are particularly good at controlling immigration?'; over the four months combined 53 per cent replied Conservative, 23 per cent Labour. There is also patchy but fairly convincing evidence that Mrs Thatcher's remarks served to distinguish more clearly the major parties' policies on immigration control, to the Conservatives' benefit.[12] But the significance of such findings should be assessed with caution. Immigration is only one aspect of the racial issue; the same Gallup polls as those referred to above also asked 'Which parties do you think are particularly good at improving race relations?'; 27 per cent said the Conservatives, 35 per cent said Labour. The rational electoral strategy for the Conservatives (and Labour) therefore appears to be to stick to the centre, certainly to avoid a Powellite line on the repatriation of immigrants or on the dismantling of race relations legislation.

## IV FURTHER CONSIDERATIONS ON AN ELECTORAL STRATEGY FOR THE CONSERVATIVE PARTY

It would be simple to end at this point with the conclusion that both the 'moderates' and 'fundamentalists' are right: the Conservative party's optimal appeal to the electorate would combine moderation on the conventional bread-and-butter issues with a firm reassertion of traditional values on the more exotic authoritarian-populist issues (except race). Indeed, such a strategy would have the additional advantages of appealing to the party faithful, satisfying both the moderate and fundamentalist camps, at least in part.

Such a conclusion assumes, however, that both types of issue are of roughly equal importance in an election, whereas the normal view is that they are not. In the final analysis, it is said, bread-and-butter issues are the more decisive: it is on these that the parties campaign and the voters decide. Come an election the emotion generated by such matters as crime, immigration, pornography and abortion evaporates—just as it did on 'Communist influence' and 'Who Governs?' in the February 1974 campaign. Thus, the argument goes, it remains in the Conservative party's electoral interests to abide by convention, avoid 'emotive' but essentially peripheral issues, and take a cautious and pragmatic line on the traditional but still salient socio-economic issues. The 'moderate' strategy should take precedence.

But is voting quite as unaffected by populist-authoritarian sentiments as the moderates are suggesting? Careful examination of polls and surveys suggests that the electoral importance of at least some of these issues—in particular race and law and order—can be underestimated. The basis for regarding social and economic issues as of almost exclusive importance when it comes to voting appears to rest on figures given by the monthly polls. For example, Gallup always asks 'What would you say is the most urgent problem facing the country at the present time?' followed by 'And what would you say is the next most urgent problem?'. The results since the October 1974 election are shown in Table 11.2.

On this evidence both immigration and law and order, although slowly growing in importance over the past four years, run a long way behind inflation, unemployment and a host of other 'conventional' economic and social issues. But in recent years Gallup have also asked an additional question on the relative importance of issues, which is close-ended and asks, simply, 'How important

TABLE 11.2  The Relative Importance of Issues, 1975–78 (in answer to open-ended questions)

| Issue | Most Important | | | | Next or Next most Important | | | |
|---|---|---|---|---|---|---|---|---|
| | 1975 %[2] | 1976 % | 1977 % | 1978 (up to Oct) % | 1975 % | 1976 % | 1977 % | 1978 (up to Oct) % |
| Prices/cost of living | 62 | 50 | 46 | 29 | 77 | 68 | 65 | 47 |
| Unemployment | 10 | 18 | 20 | 30 | 31 | 43 | 41 | 48 |
| Strikes/labour relations | 7 | 3 | 9 | 6 | 18 | 9 | 18 | 13 |
| Other economic | 6 | 10 | 7 | 7 | 11 | 16 | 15 | 14 |
| Law and order | – | 1 | 1 | 5 | 2 | 4 | 6 | 10 |
| Immigration | – | 3 | 1 | 5 | – | 10 | 5 | 14 |
| Other[1] | 12 | 12 | 14 | 15 | 46 | 40 | 40 | 41 |

NOTES

1. Mainly: housing, health, pensions, social security benefits, education, productivity, energy.

2. The annual percentages are an average of the monthly observations

SOURCE

Gallup Political Index, 1975 to 1978

TABLE 11.3 The relative importance of issues, Jan–May 1978 (in answer to a close-ended question)

| Issue | Rank Order | % saying extremely important | Issue | Rank Order | % saying extremely important |
|---|---|---|---|---|---|
| Maintaining law and order | 1 | 82 | Increasing pensions | 8 | 47 |
| Controlling inflation | 2 | 77 | Improving labour relations | 9 | 45 |
| Reducing unemployment | 2 | 77 | Improving race relations | 10 | 38 |
| Controlling immigration | 4 | 64 | Improving national unity | 11 | 36 |
| Reducing taxation | 5 | 55 | Creating a fairer society | 12 | 34 |
| Protecting freedom of speech | 6 | 51 | Building more houses for owner-occupation | 13 | 29 |
| Protecting people's privacy | 7 | 50 | | | |

NOTES
The percentages are the mean of the five observations for the months January to May 1978.
The answer categories were: Extremely important/Quite important/Not very important/Not at all important/Don't know.
SOURCE
Gallup monthly polls, January to May 1978

would you say . . . is at the moment?'. The results are shown in Table 11.3

On the evidence of these figures law-and-order emerges as the single most important issue to the public, and the control of immigration fourth most important. Why should the importance of these two issues differ by so much, in terms of both absolute percentages and rank order, in response to the two questions? One possibility is that the different phrasing is responsible. But a more intriguing possibility is that, unlike the first question, the second offers a 'prompt': it reminds the respondent of the existence of the issue, and to some extent 'legitimises' it. It is usually assumed that the respondent's true feelings are more likely to be expressed in answers to open-ended rather than close-ended questions, the fixed categories of the latter being regarded as imposed and artificial. But the argument can be reversed: given that election campaigns 'impose' issues on the electorate, answers to the close-ended question might be the more reliable guide to the relative impact of issues on voting decisions. A further, reinforcing, piece of evidence drawn from the British Election Study should also be considered. Respondents were asked to say which of the statements in Table 11.4 should be 'the most important general aim of a government'.

As the table shows, the maintenance of law and order (chosen by 25 per cent) was a close runner-up to the raising of living standards (30 per cent) amongst the electorate as a whole, and more or less level-pegging amongst two of the three 'uncommitted' groups, the Conservative and Liberal 'learners'. (In passing it is also worth noticing that private enterprise was bottom or next to bottom of the list for everybody other than committed Conservatives.) Thus the evidence that law and order—the core of the authoritarian-populist syndrome—and immigration could be crucial election issues cannot be lightly dismissed.

But even if populist-authoritarian and racial issues are less salient than socio-economic issues for the electorate taken as a whole, they are still the most important considerations for a minority. Indeed, the electorate can be regarded as a collection of such minorities (or 'issue-publics', as we shall call them) for each of whom a different issue assumes primary importance. Similarly, each electoral group, from committed Labour supporters to committed Conservatives, is composed of various issue-publics. These must be taken into special account in any rational electoral strategy: in particular, where views differ between those for whom the issue is important, and

TABLE 11.4 The Most Important General Aim of Government

| | All respondents % | Committed Labour voters % | Labour 'leaners' % | Liberal 'leaners' % | Cons 'leaners' % | Committed Cons voters % |
|---|---|---|---|---|---|---|
| Maintaining law and order | 25 | 20 | 18 | 26 | 24 | 33 |
| Raising everybody's standard of living | 30 | 34 | 26 | 24 | 27 | 27 |
| Achieving greater equality | 18 | 24 | 29 | 19 | 14 | 8 |
| Protecting individual liberty | 12 | 7 | 8 | 21 | 20 | 15 |
| Protecting the weakest and worst off | 10 | 14 | 13 | 4 | 8 | 5 |
| Promoting private enterprise | 6 | 1 | 6 | 6 | 6 | 13 |
| Total | 100 | 100 | 100 | 100 | 100 | 100 |

NOTES
The six answer categories were ordered differently in the questionnaire. The full question was: 'Looking at this list, could you say what the *most* important *general* aim of a government should be?'.
SOURCE
British Election Study, October 1974 cross-section sample.

those for whom it is not, the vote-conscious party will pay more attention to the former. Figure 11.6 reveals that positions on an issue can clearly differ between those who are and those who are not relatively concerned about it. For example, Labour, Liberal and Conservative 'leaners', for whom nationalisation was an important issue, all took up a somewhat more right-wing stance than those leaners for whom the matter was one of relative indifference. The electoral implication is that Conservative party can afford that much more, and Labour that much less, to maintain their respective right and left positions on the issue. On social services, however, views hardly differ between those for whom the issue is or is not important (except amongst committed Labour supporters, the concerned taking a markedly more left-wing position than the indifferent). The issues that best illustrate the importance of paying special regard to issue-publics, however, are immigration and Communist influence in trade unions. As Figure 11.6 shows, in every electoral group those for whom immigration was 'very important' clearly took a more hard-line anti-immigrant position than those for whom the issue was of little concern; moreover, this was especially true of the *uncommitted* voters. The pattern is similar in the case of Communist influence in trade unions: those to whom the matter was salient took a markedly tougher anti-Communist line. And once again, it is two uncommitted groups of voters—Labour and Liberal 'leaners'—who take a particularly large leap to the Right if they consider the issue important. It needs to be stressed that immigration is only part of the set of issues described as 'racial'; similarly, anti-Communism is only one of the four issues making up 'populist-authoritarianism'. Nonetheless, these two cases do raise the possibility that the fundamentalists' electoral strategy of robustly right-wing rhetoric on non-economic issues is based on stronger grounds than was first apparent.

There are two additional electoral advantages to the Conservative party from emphasising a fundamentalist position on populist-authoritarian issues. The first is that opinion on such issues, not only amongst the electorate as a whole but within each group of voters, is considerably more *homogeneous* than it is for socio-economic issues. This is clearly shown in the standard deviation scores set out in Table 11.5. The second electoral benefit to the Conservatives arises from the *intensity* of opinion that seems to be associated with some of these issues: as Table 11.6 shows, the proportion opting for an 'extreme' answer was considerably greater for populist-

F IG. 11.6   Electoral configurations on nationalisation, social services, immigration and Communist influence in trade unions, by importance of issue, 1974.

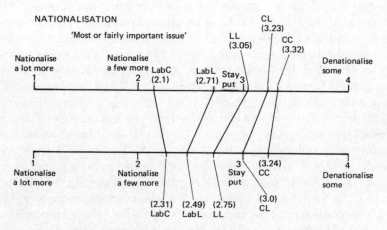

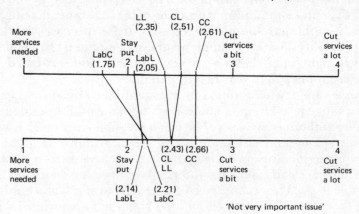

IMMIGRATION

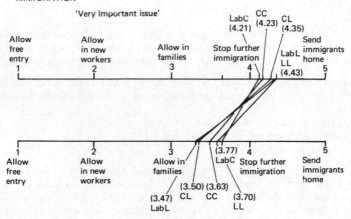

'Very Important issue'

Allow free entry 1 · Allow in new workers 2 · Allow in families 3 · Stop further immigration 4 · Send immigrants home 5

LabC (4.21) · CC (4.23) · CL (4.35) · LabL LL (4.43)

Allow free entry 1 · Allow in new workers 2 · Allow in families 3 · (3.77) LabC · Stop further immigration 4 · Send immigrants home 5

(3.47) LabL · (3.50) CL · (3.63) CC · (3.70) LL

'Not very important issue'

COMMUNIST INFLUENCE IN TRADE UNIONS

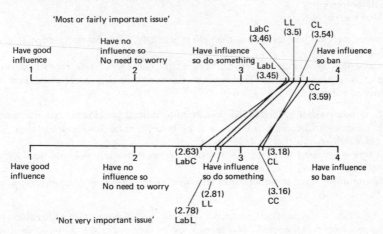

'Most or fairly important issue'

Have good influence 1 · Have no influence so No need to worry 2 · Have influence so do something 3 · Have influence so ban 4

LabC (3.46) · LL (3.5) · CL (3.54) · LabL (3.45) · CC (3.59)

Have good influence 1 · Have no influence so No need to worry 2 · (2.63) LabC · Have influence so do something 3 · (3.18) CL · Have influence so ban 4

(2.81) LL · (3.16) CC · (2.78) LabL

'Not very important issue'

SOURCES

Nationalisation and social services: British Election Study, October 1974 cross-section sample; immigration: British Election Study, February 1974 wave of 1970–February 1974 panel sample; Communist influence: February 1974 cross-section sample.

NOTES

The question on nationalisation is given in Figure 11.4. The question on social services was: 'Now we would like to ask what you think about social services and benefits. Which of these statements do you feel comes closest to your own views?'

1. Social services and benefits have gone much too far and should be cut back a lot.
2. Social services and benefits have gone somewhat too far and should be cut back a bit.
3. Social services and benefits should stay much as they are.
4. More social services and benefits are needed.
5. Don't know, no view.

'When you were deciding about voting, how important was the question of social services and benefits (nationalisation) (Communist influence in trade unions)—the most important single thing, fairly important, or not very important?'
The question on immigration was: 'Which statements come closest to what you yourself feel should be done about immigrants?'

1. Assist in sending immigrants home.
2. Stop further immigration but allow immigrants already here to stay.
3. Allow in the immediate families of immigrants here and a few skilled workers.
4. Allow in new workers and their families.
5. Allow free entry.
6. Don't know, no view.

'How strongly do you feel about this—very strongly, fairly strongly, or not very strongly?'
The question on Communists was: 'There has been some talk recently about Communists in trade unions. Which of the statements on this card come closest to what you yourself feel?'

1. Communists should be banned from holding official positions in trade unions.
2. Even though Communists should not be banned, something must be done to reduce their influence in trade unions.
3. There is no need to worry about Communists in trade unions because their influence is rarely important.
4. Communists have some influence in trade unions and it is generally good.
5. No view/don't know.

In the case of nationalisation, social services, and Communist influence, respondents were divided into those who considered the issue not very important and those who considered it either fairly important or the most important single issue (the latter category contained too few cases for separate analysis). In the case of immigration we have contrasted those who considered the issue 'very important' with those who considered it 'not very important', omitting those in the 'fairly important' category from the analysis.

TABLE 11.5   Homogeneity of opinion of types of issue

| | All electors | Committed Cons voters | Cons 'leaners' | Liberal 'leaners' | Labour 'leaners' | Committed Labour voters |
|---|---|---|---|---|---|---|
| Socio economic Left-Right issues | 1.13 | 1.09 | 1.17 | 1.03 | 1.16 | 1.08 |
| Populist-authoritarian | 0.96 | 0.85 | 0.91 | 0.95 | 0.97 | 0.77 |
| Racial issues | 1.17 | 1.15 | 1.16 | 1.05 | 1.17 | 1.20 |

NOTE
The figures in the table are the mean standard deviation scores of an electoral group for the set of issues making up each of the three 'types' of issue.

TABLE 11.6   Proportion opting for 'extreme' answers on different kinds of issue.

| % choosing 'extreme' answer category on: | All electors % | Committed Cons voters % | Cons 'leaners' % | Liberal 'leaners' % | Labour 'leaners' % | Committed Labour voters % |
|---|---|---|---|---|---|---|
| Socioeconomic Left-Right issues[1] | 32 | 32 | 30 | 22 | 31 | 34 |
| Populist-authoritarian issues | 59 | 70 | 57 | 49 | 50 | 56 |
| Racial issues | 24 | 25 | 20 | 18 | 26 | 26 |

NOTE.

An 'extreme' answer was defined as either of the two end categories of answer for any of the questions. Thus, 'Gone much too far' and 'Not gone nearly far enough' were the 'extreme' responses to social trend questions; 'Very important that it should be done' and 'Very important that it should not be done', the 'extreme' responses to the policy questions, and so on. Two of the issues-nationalisation and social services-were measured by four-category, not five-category questions. This will have slightly *inflated* the proportion of 'extreme' answers on these questions.

authoritarian than for socio-economic (or racial) issues. On populist-authoritarian issues, therefore, uncommitted voters share a similiar set of strong opinions; on socio-economic issues, on the other hand, their views are mixed and less deeply felt. It is on the latter, therefore, that the Conservatives (and Labour, of course) need to fudge, and on the former that they can be bold and clear. It is precisely on that set of issues where the Conservative party is the closer of the two parties to the uncommitted voter that it can also afford to be most assertive. But to this conclusion one important qualification needs to be made: as both Tables 11.4 and 11.5 show, the electorate is as divided and moderate on *racial* issues as it is on socioeconomic matters. For the second time in this analysis, therefore, there emerge good reasons for the Conservative party to take a much more cautious and ambivalent line on race than on the other non-economic issues. The 'fundamentalist' electoral strategy looks more promising for matters of order and traditional morality than it does for the tricky, double-edged issue of race.

There is also a good deal of circumstantial evidence from beyond polls and surveys—indeed perhaps masked by polls and surveys— that populist-authoritarian issues arouse unusually strong emotions. It is these issues which appear to crop up particularly often in anonymous, private, or informal settings which are not thought subject to the sanction of respectable or fashionable opinion—in pubs and clubs, in the conversation of families and friends, in unsigned letters and graffiti, and so on. Not surprisingly, if intensely-held but non-respectable opinions are given a sudden legitimacy through endorsement by a leading public figure—as happened after Enoch Powell's 'rivers of blood' speech—a wave of popular feeling will make itself felt, to the potential benefit of the Conservative party. In this respect it is interesting to note that two recent investigations of the impact of the immigration issue on the 1970 election have concluded that the Conservatives gained a distinct and perhaps decisive increment of the vote.[13]

Much of the material presented in this paper will come as no surprise to those familiar with the extensive literature on the 'radical right', the 'working-class authoritarian', the 'tough/tender-minded' distinction and, more recently, the differences between those with 'acquisitive' and 'post-acquisitive' values.[14] Countless academic surveys and polls have revealed the existence in Britain of majorities—ranging from substantial to overwhelming—in favour of the authoritarian reassertion of traditional ideas of morality and the national interest. The same surveys also show, consistently, that public opinion on these matters is largely independent of party preference or social class (although not level of education) and thus of opinion on the issues of economic management, distribution and ownership which have traditionally dominated election campaigns. In a large number of policy areas—foreign affairs, defence, crime, minority rights, sexual morality—the majority view aligns with Conservative rather than Labour instincts.

## V CLOSING REMARKS

The puzzle is why the Conservative leadership has not exploited its electoral advantage to a greater degree. To do so would not, of course, be without political risks, notably the alienation of its liberal wing, and the possibility that the party would acquire an old-fashioned and dour image which would in turn be electorally damaging. Failure to mine this electoral seam probably stems from other factors: partly from the personal views of the three (four?) leaders preceding Margaret Thatcher, more probably from the availability of other sources of electoral support. Simplifying drastically, right-wing parties seeking to win elections in highly industrialised societies depend on attracting substantial working class support through one or more of the following means: (i) by offering the more promising economic prospect; (ii) by exploiting the residual pockets of pre-industrial values (the 'deferential' vote); or (iii) by offering the more attractive leader. The first option clearly remains, although Britain's disappointing economic record under successive governments of both parties, as well as the currently dim prospects for sustained economic growth, make it considerably more tricky than in the 1950s or 1960s. The second option is barely available as the 'deferential' vote appears to have dwindled to tiny proportions. And, judging by the polls, the third option must remain in temporary abeyance until the relative fortunes of the two parties in this respect is reversed. In these circumstances the resort to populist-authoritarian issues must seem the logical electoral strategy to the Conservative party.

NOTES

1. See, for example, Ian Gilmour, *Inside Right: A Study of Conservatism* (London: Hutchinson, 1977); Rhodes Boyson, *Centre Forward: A Radical Conservative*

*Programme* (London: Temple Smith, 1978); William Waldegrave, *The Binding of Leviathan* (London: Hamish Hamilton, 1978) and Maurice Cowling (ed.), *Conservative Essays* (London: Cassell, 1978).

2. Anthony Downs, *An Economic Theory of Democracy* (New York: Harper & Row, 1957).

3. Ibid, ch. 7.

4. The argument that both parties would position themselves near the mid-point strictly depends on a series of additional—but realistic—assumptions, the most notable being (a) that few committed voters or activists will abstain in protest at their party's central location; and (b) that there are approximately equal numbers of committed Labour and committed Conservative voters.

5. The standard deviation of opinions was .63 amongst Conservative identifiers and .82 amongst Labour identifiers.

6. The full wording of the question is: 'Generally speaking do you think of yourself as Conservative, Labour, Liberal (in Scotland/Wales: Nationalist/ Plaid Cymru), or what?'
This is followed by: 'Would you call yourself a very strong Conservative (Liberal, etc.), fairly strong or not very strong?' (Respondents answering 'no' or 'don't know' to the first question were asked: 'Do you generally think of yourself as a little closer to one of the parties than the others?' If they then mentioned a party they were automatically defined as 'not very strong' identifiers.)

7. See Ivor Crewe *et al*, 'Non-Voting in British General Elections 1966–October 1974' in Colin Crouch (ed), *British Political Sociology Yearbook*, vol 3, p 90.

8. There are other ways of defining the uncommitted voter. If defined as, e.g. those who defected from the Conservatives between February and October 1974 or, alternatively, those who voted Conservative in 1966 and 1970 but not in either of the two 1974 elections, the results turn out to be very similar to those presented in this paper although, of course, by using this definition it would not be possible to distinguish the partisan direction in which uncommitted voters leaned.

9. The position of the two parties is based on the perceptions of the electorate as a whole. As the following figures show, perceptions of the two party positions did differ between electoral groups: for example, committed Conservatives 'pulled' the Conservative party towards them and 'pushed' the Labour party away, such that they perceived themselves a fraction closer to their own party.

| | Perception of Conservative party position on EEC (mean score) | Perception of Labour party position on EEC (mean score) | Relative closeness to Con/Lab party |
|---|---|---|---|
| Committed Conservative supporters (2.87) | 3.48 | 2.21 | .05 to Con |
| Conservative 'leaners' (2.78) | 3.58 | 2.33 | .35 to Lab |
| Liberal 'leaners' (2.61) | 3.53 | 2.39 | .70 to Lab |

9 (*Continued*)

| | Perception of Conservative party position on EEC (mean score) | Perception of Labour party position on EEC (mean score) | Relative closeness to Con/Lab party |
|---|---|---|---|
| Labour 'leaners' (2.38) | 3.70 | 2.40 | 1.30 to Lab |
| Committed Labour supporters (2.20) | 3.67 | 2.33 | 1.34 to Lab |
| All respondents (2.51) | 3.60 | 2.30 | .88 to Lab |

NOTES

High scores = pro-EEC, low scores = anti-EEC
Figures in parentheses are scores for respondents' own position. 'Relative closeness' is calculated by subtracting distance from one party from distance from the other party.

10. The figures were as follows:

| | Perception of Conservative party position on nationalisation (mean score) | Perception of Labour party position on nationalisation (mean score) | Relative closeness to Con/ Lab party |
|---|---|---|---|
| Committed Conservative supporters (3.31) | 3.29 | 1.10 | 2.19 to Con |
| Conservative 'leaners' (3.18) | 3.25 | 1.12 | 1.99 to Con |
| Liberal 'leaners' (2.93) | 3.30 | 1.28 | 1.28 to Con |
| Labour 'leaners' (2.57) | 3.22 | 1.44 | 0.48 to Con |
| Committed Labour supporters (2.19) | 3.36 | 1.47 | 0.45 to Lab |
| All respondents (2.79) | 3.31 | 1.28 | 0.99 to Con |

NOTES

High scores = anti-nationalisation, low scores = pro-nationalisation. Figures in parentheses are scores for respondents' own position. 'Relative closeness' is calculated by subtracting distance from one party from distance from the other party.

11. See *Gallup Political Index*, nos 211–15, February to June 1978. It should be added that these figures cannot be explained as simply a reflection of the Conservatives' greater overall popularity: the average Conservative lead over Labour in the Gallup polls for this period was only 3.6 per cent. An August 1978 MORI poll, published in the *Daily Express*, produced a similar result: 42 per cent thought the Conservatives 'had the best policies' on law and order: 24 per cent thought Labour had.

12. A Gallup Poll in February 1978, conducted shortly after Mrs Thatcher's remarks, asked 'If the Conservatives/Labour won the next general election do you think there would be more or less immigration, or wouldn't things change?' The figures were:

|  | Under Con Govt | Under Lab Govt |
|---|---|---|
| More | 6 | 25 |
| Less | 71 | 13 |
| No change | 14 | 54 |
| Don't Know | 9 | 9 |
|  | 100 | 100 |

The same pair of questions was asked of nine other 'items'—unemployment inflation, taxation, etc. On no other item was there such a consensus of view about Conservative policy or such a low proportion of 'Don't knows'.

13. See Donley Studlar, 'Policy Voting in Britain: The Coloured Immigration Issue in the 1964, 1966 and 1970 General Elections', *American Political Science Review* 72(1) (March 1978) pp 46–64; and W. L. Miller, 'What was the Profit in Following the Crowd? Aspects of Labour and Conservative Strategy since 1970', paper presented to PSA Conference, March 1978, University of Warwick.

14. On the 'radical right' see Daniel Bell (ed.) *The Radical Right* (Garden City, NY: Doubleday, 1964) and Seymour Martin Lipset and Earl Raab, *The Politics of Unreason* (London: Heinemann, 1970); on working class authoritarianism see S. M. Lipset, 'Democracy and Working Class Authoritarianism', *American Sociological Review*, 24 (1959) pp 482–502; on 'tough' and 'tender-minded' personalities see H. J. Eysenck, *The Psychology of Politics* (London: Routledge & Kegan Paul, 1954) and on acquisitive and post-acquisitive values see Ronald Inglehart, *The Silent Revolution* (Princeton, New Jersey: Princeton University Press, 1977).

# Select Bibliography

P. Abrams and A. Little, 'The Young Activist in British Politics' *British Journal of Sociology*, 16 (1965) 315–33.

F. Bealey, J. Blondel, W. McCann, *Constituency Politics* (Faber, 1965).

S. Beer, *Modern British Politics* (Faber, 1965).

R. Behrens, 'Blinkers for the Carthorse: The Conservative Party and the Trade Unions 1974–78', *Political Quarterly*, 49 (1978) 457–66.

A. Beichman, 'The Conservative Research Department: The Care and Feeding of Future British Political Elites', *Journal of British Studies*, XIII (1974) 92–113.

H. Berkeley, *Crossing the Floor* (Allen & Unwin, 1972).

H. Berrington, *Backbench Opinion in the House of Commons, 1945–1955* (Pergamon, 1973).

R. Blake, *From Peel to Churchill* (Fontana, 1972).

Lord Blake and John Patten (eds.), *The Conservative Opportunity* (Macmillan, 1976).

G. Block, *A Sourcebook of Conservatism*, Conservative Political Centre (1964).

J. Blondel, 'The Conservative Association and the Labour Party in Reading', Political Studies xx (1958) 101–19.

S. Brittan, *The Treasury under the Tories, 1951–64* (Penguin, 1964).

Lord Butler, *The Art of the Possible* (Hamish Hamilton, 1971).

Lord Butler (ed.), *The Conservatives: A History from their Origins to 1965* (Allen & Unwin, 1977).

D. E. Butler and M. Pinto-Duschinsky, *The British General Election of 1970* (Macmillan, 1971).

D. E. Butler and D. Kavanagh, *The British General Election of February 1974* (Macmillan, 1974).

——, *The British General Election of October 1974* (Macmillan, 1975).

D. E. Butler and D. Stokes, *Political Change in Britain* (Macmillan, 1969).

R. Churchill, *The Fight for the Tory Leadership* (Heinemann, 1964).

D. H. Close, 'The Growth of Backbench Organisation in the Conservative Party', *Parliamentary Affairs*, XXVII, 4 (1974) pp. 371–83.

M. Cowling (ed.), *Conservative Essays* (Cassell, 1978).

I. Crewe, and B. Sarlvik, and J. Alt, 'Partisan Realignment in Britain 1964–1974' *British Journal of Political Science*, 7 (1977) pp. 129–90.

A. D. R. Dickson, 'MPs Readoption Conflicts: their Courses and Consequences', *Political Studies*, XXIII (1975) 62–70.

R. Eccleshall, English Conservatism and Ideology, *Political Studies*, XXV (1977) pp. 62–83.

L. P. Epstein, 'Politics of British Conservatism', *American Political Science Review*, XLVIII (1954) pp. 27–49.

——, 'British MPs and their Local Parties: the Suez Cases', *American Political Science Review*, LIV, 1960, 374–91.

L. Fairlie, 'Candidate Selection Role perceptions of Conservative and Labour Secretary/Agents', *Political Studies*, XXIV (1976) pp. 281–95.

S. E. Finer, H. Berrington and D. J. Bartholomew, *Backbench Opinion in the House of Commons 1955–1959* (Pergamon, 1961).

N. Fisher, *The Tory Leaders: Their Struggle for Power* (Weidenfeld & Nicolson, 1977).

——, *Ian Macleod* (Andre Deutsch, 1973).

P. Foot, *The Rise of Enoch Powell* (Penguin, 1969).

R. C. Frasure, 'Backbench Opinion Revisited: the Case of the Conservatives', *Political Studies*, XX (1972) pp. 325–8.

R. C. Frasure and A. Kornberg, 'Constituency Agents and British Party Politics', *British Journal of Political Science*, 5 (1975) pp. 459–76.

Andrew Gamble, *The Conservative Nation* (Routledge & Kegan Paul, 1974).

I. Gilmour, *The Body Politic* (Hutchinson, 1969).

——, *Inside Right: A Study of Conservatism* (Hutchinson, 1977).

H. Glickman, 'The Toryness of English Conservatism', *Journal of British Studies*, I (1961) pp. 111–43.

P. Goodhart, *The 1922: the Story of the 1922 Committee* (Macmillan, 1973).

Lord Hailsham, *The Conservative Case* (revised edition 1969).

N. Harris, *Competition and the Corporate Society* (Methuen, 1972).

J. Hoffman, *The Conservatives in Opposition* (London: MacGibbon & Kee, 1964).

R. T. Holt and J. E. Turner, *Political Parties in Action: the battle of Barons Court* (Collier-Macmillan, 1968).

D. Hurd, *An End to Promises: Sketch of a Government 1970–1974* (Collins, 1979).

R. J. Jackson, *Rebels & Whips* (Macmillan, 1968).

R. R. James, *Memoirs of a Conservative: J. C. C. Davidson's Memoirs and Papers, 1910–37* (Weidenfeld & Nicolson, 1969).

——, *Ambitions and Realities: British Politics 1964–70* (Weidenfeld & Nicolson, 1972).

B. Jessop, *Traditionalism, Conservatism and British Political Culture* (Allen & Unwin, 1973).

A. King, 'How the Conservatives evolve Policies', *New Society* (20 July 1972).

Z. Layton-Henry, 'The Young Conservatives, 1945–70', *Journal of Contemporary History*, VIII (1973) pp. 143–56.

——, 'Constituency Autonomy in the Conservative Party', *Parliamentary Affairs*, XXIX (1976) pp. 396–403.

——, 'Race, Electoral Strategy and the Major Parties', *Parliamentary Affairs*, XXXI (1978) pp. 268–81.

——, 'Democracy and Reform in the Conservative Party', *Journal of Contemporary History*, 13 (1978) pp. 653–70.

J. Lees and R. Kimber, *Political Parties in Modern Britain* (Routledge & Kegan Paul, 1972).

T. F. Lindsay and M. Harrington, *The Conservative Party 1918–1970* (Macmillan, 1974).

R. T. McKenzie, *British Political Parties* (London: Mercury Books, 2nd revised edition, 1963).

R. T. McKenzie and A. Silver, *Angels in Marble* (Heinemann, 1968).

L. W. Martin, 'The Bournemouth Affair: Britain's First Primary Election', *Journal of Politics*, XXII (1960) pp. 654–81.

C. Mellors, *The British MP* (Saxon House, 1978).

N. Nicholson, *People and Parliament* (Weidenfeld & Nicolson, 1958).

E. Nordlinger, *The Working Class Tories* (MacGibbon & Kee, 1967).

P. Norton, *Conservative Dissidents: Dissent within the Parliamentary Conservative Party, 1970–1974* (Temple Smith, 1978).

N. Nugent and R. King, *The British Right* (Saxon House, 1977).

N. O'Sullivan, *Conservatism* (Dent, 1976).

F. Parkin, 'Working Class Conservatives: A Theory of Political Deviance', *British Journal of Sociology*, XVIII (1970) pp. 278–90.

M. Parkinson, 'Central Local Relations in British Parties: a Local view', *Political Studies*, XIX (1971) pp. 440–6.

M. Peston, 'Conservative Economic Policy and Philosophy', *Political Quarterly*, XLIV (1973) pp. 411–24.

M. Pinto-Duschinsky, 'Central Office and Power in the British Conservative Party', *Political Studies*, XX (1972) pp. 1–16.

——, 'Stratification and Policy in the British Conservative Party', *American Behavioral Scientist*, XVII (1973) pp. 285–92.

R. M. Punnett, *Front-Bench Opposition* (Heinemann, 1973).

J. Ramsden, 'The Changing Base of British Conservatism' in C. Cook and J. Ramsden (eds.) *Trends in British Politics since 1945* (Macmillan, 1978).

——, *The Age of Balfour and Baldwin 1902–1940* (Longmans, 1979).

A. Ranney, *Pathways to Parliament* (Macmillan, 1965).

R. Rose, 'Tensions in Conservative Philosophy', *Political Quarterly*, XXXII (1961) pp. 275–83.

R. Rose, 'The Bow Group's Role in British Politics', *Western Political Quarterly*, XIV, 4 (1961) pp. 865–78.

——, 'The Policy Ideas of English Party Activists', *American Political Science Review*, LVI (1962) pp. 360–71.

——, 'Parties, Factions, and Tendencies in Britain', *Political Studies*, XVII (1969) pp. 413–45.

——, *The Problem of Party Government* (Macmillan, 1974).

——, '*Studies in British Politics* (3rd edition) (Macmillan, 1976).

A. Roth, *Enoch Powell—Tory Tribune* (Macdonald, 1970).

M. Rush, *The Selection of Parliamentary Candidates* (Nelson, 1969).

T. Russel, *The Tory Party* (Penguin Books, 1978).

J. E. Schwarz, 'The Impact of Constituency on the Behaviour of British Conservative MPs', *Comparative Political Studies*, VIII (1975) pp. 75–89.

J. E. Schwarz and G. Lambert, 'Career Objectives, Group feeling and Legislative Party Voting Cohesion: the British Conservatives 1959–68, *Journal of Politics*, XXXIII (1971) pp. 399–421.

D. E. Schoen, *Enoch Powell and the Powellites* (Macmillan, 1977).

P. Seyd, 'Factionalism within the Conservative Party: the Monday Club', *Government & Opposition*, VII (1973) pp. 464–87.

——, 'Democracy within the Conservative Party', *Government & Opposition*, X (1975) pp. 219–37.

D. Studlar, 'British Public Opinion, Colour Issues and Enoch Powell', *British Journal of Political Science*, 4 (1974) pp. 371–81.

D. Urwin, 'Scottish Conservatism: a Party Organisation in Transition', *Political Studies*, XIV (1966) pp. 145–62.

W. Waldegrave, *The Binding of Leviathan* (London: Hamish Hamilton, 1978).

D. J. Wilson, 'Constituency Party Autonomy and Central Control', *Political Studies*, XXI (1973) pp. 167–74.

——, *Power and Party Bureaucracy in Britain* (Saxon House, 1975).

D. J. Wilson and M. Pinto-Duschinsky, 'Conservative City Machines: The End of an Era', *British Journal of Political Science*, 6 (1976) 239–44.

Peter Walker, *The Ascent of Britain* (Sedgwick & Jackson, 1977).

Lord Woolton, *Memoirs of the Rt. Hon. Earl of Woolton* (Cassell, 1959).

# Index

# BEASTS OF NO NATION

# BEASTS
# OF NO NATION

## Uzodinma Iweala

JOHN MURRAY

© Uzodinma Iweala 2005

First published in Great Britain in 2005
by John Murray (Publishers)
A division of Hodder Headline

1

Quotation from Rimbaud, *Une Saison en Enfer* taken from *Rimbaud: Complete Works,*
*Selected Letters,* trans. Wallace Fowlie, University of Chicago Press, 1966.
Reproduced with permission from the University of Chicago Press.

A CIP catalogue record for this title is available from
the British Library

Hardback ISBN 0 7195 6752 1
Trade paperback ISBN 0 7195 6843 9

Typeset in 11/17.5pt Meridien by Servis Filmsetting Ltd, Manchester

Printed and bound in Great Britain by Clays Ltd, St Ives plc

Hodder Headline policy is to use papers that are natural,
renewable and recyclable products and made from wood
grown in sustainable forests. The logging and
manufacturing processes are expected to conform to the
environmental regulations of the country of origin.

John Murray (Publishers)
338 Euston Road
London NW1 3BH

For those who have suffered

Je parvins à faire s'évanouir dans mon esprit toute
l'esperance humaine. Sur toute joie, pour l'étrangler,
j'ai fait le bond sourd de la bête feroce.

*I was able to expel from my mind all human hope. On
every form of joy, in order to strangle it, I pounced
stealthily like a wild animal.*

Rimbaud, *Une Saison en Enfer*

It is starting like this. I am feeling itch like insect is crawling on my skin, and then my head is just starting to tingle right between my eye, and then I am wanting to sneeze because my nose is itching, and then air is just blowing into my ear and I am hearing so many thing: the clicking of insect, the sound of truck grumbling like one kind of animal, and then the sound of somebody shouting TAKE YOUR POSITION RIGHT NOW! QUICK! QUICK QUICK! MOVE WITH SPEED! MOVE FAST OH! in voice that is just touching my body like knife.

I am opening my eye and there is light all around me coming into the dark through hole in the roof, crossing like net above my body. Then I am feeling my body crunched up like

1

one small mouse in the corner when the light is coming on. The smell of rainwater and sweat is coming into my nose and I am feeling my shirt is so wet it is almost like another skin. I want to be moving but my whole bone is paining me and my muscle is paining me like fire ant is just biting me all over my body. If I can be slapping myself to be making it go away I am doing it, but I cannot even move one finger. I am not doing anything.

Footstep is everywhere around me and making me to think that my father is coming to bring medicine to stop all of this itch and pain. I turn onto my back. The footstep is growing louder, louder, louder until I am hearing it even more than my own breathing or heart beating. Step slap, step slap, step slap, I am hearing getting louder, louder, louder and then shadow is coming into the light from under the door.

Somebody is knocking. KNOCK KNOCK. But I am not answering. Then they are angrying too much and just kicking so the whole of this place is shaking and the roof is falling apart small small so that more light is coming in. And the wood everywhere is cracking until I am hearing PING PING and seeing screw falling from the door into bucket near my feets. The sound is fighting the wall, bouncing from here to there, through the net of light, until it is like the sound is pushing the door open so there is so much brightness. BRIGHTNESS! So much brightness is coming into my eye until I am seeing purple spot for long time. Then I am seeing yellow eye belonging to one short dark body with one big belly and leg thin like spider's own. This body is so thin that his short is just blowing around his leg like woman's skirt and his shirt is looking like dress the way it is hanging from his shoulder. His neck is just struggling too much to hold up his big head that is always moving one way or the other.

I am looking at him. He is looking at me. He is not surprising at all to be seeing me even if I am surprising for him, but his face is falling and becoming more dark. He is sniffing like dog and stepping to me. KPAWA! He is hitting me.

Again and again he is hitting me and each blow from his hand is feeling on my skin like the flat side of machete. I am trying to scream, but he is knocking the air from my chest and then slapping my mouth. I am tasting blood. I am feeling like vomiting. The whole place around us is shaking, just shaking rotten fruit from the shelf, just sounding like it will be cracking into many piece and falling on top of us. He is grabbing my leg, pulling it so hard that it is like it will be coming apart like meat, and my body is just sliding slowly from the stall out into the light and onto the mud.

In the light, my breath is coming back and using force to open my chest to make me to coughing and my eye to watering. The whole world is spreading before me and I am looking up to the grey sky moving slowly slowly against the top leaf of all the tall tall Iroko tree. And under this, many smaller tree is fighting each other to climb up to the sunlight. All the leaf is dripping with rainwater and shining like jewel or glass. The grasses by the road is so tall and green past any colour I am seeing before. This is making me to think of jubilating, dancing, shouting, singing because Kai! I am saying I am finally dead. I am thinking that maybe this boy is spirit and I should be thanking him for bringing me home to the land of spirits, but before I can even be opening my mouth to be saying anything, he is leaving me on my back in the mud.

I can see the bottom of truck parking just little bit away from me. Two truck is blocking up the whole road and more are parking on the roadside. The piece of cloth covering them is so torn up and full of hole and the paint is coming off to showing so much rust, like blood, making me to thinking the truck is like wounding animal. And around all the truck, just looking like ghost, are soldier. Some is wearing camouflage, other is wearing T-shirt and jean, but it is not mattering because all of the clothe is tearing and having big hole. Some of them is wearing real boot and the rest is wearing slipper. Some of them is standing at attention with their leg so straight that it is looking like they do not have knee. Some of them is going to toilet against the truck and other is going to toilet into the grasses. Almost everybody is carrying gun.

The boy who is hitting me is running to the first truck.

When he is reaching the door, he is bending down with his back so straight and his leg so straight. Only his head is moving back and forward, left and right, on his neck. Then he is standing up and suddenly, quick just like that, the door of the truck is swinging open and hitting the boy right in his big belly and he is just taking off like bird, flying in the air, and landing on his buttom in hole of water in the road. There is sound coming from all the other soldier. It is laughing sound.

I am lying here even if I am wanting to get up because my body is just paining me and I am fearing that if I am moving, somebody will be doing something very bad to me.

A man is coming down from the truck. He is looking like the leader. I am staring at the man and his jacket that is coming apart into many green string moving back and forward each time he is breathing in or out. He is wearing glove so dirty they are almost yellow or brown and his cap that he is holding in the sweaty place under his arm is flopping down because it is soaked almost all the way with his sweat.

I am watching him move from truck to truck. The truck is so old that the paint is falling off and the tyre is so low that when he is kicking them, they are pressing in and out. All the other soldier is following each movement he is making; even all the one holding their gun ready to shoot is shifting his head to be watching him looking at every truck. He is moving slowly like important person to make sure that everybody looking at him is knowing he is chief. All of the other soldier is staring at him like he is king. I am staring also.

By the time this leader man is leaving the last truck, they are surrounding him and all of them are moving the same way he is moving. They are following him to me. Their shadow is surrounding me and their leg is like cage around me. Nobody is saying one word and the man is chewing the inside of his cheek just looking at me like I am ant or some insect like that. He is saying, so who is finding this thing? But nobody is answering.

Then he is saying louder, why is this thing here on the ground?

The boy who is finding me is now coming back from my shack with some banana just as black as the road. He is wiping fruit from his mouth with his hand and walking to this big man who is saying to him, Strika. Is it you who is finding this thing? And the little boy is nodding his head very hard like he is happy that the man is knowing it is him.

Enh! Strika? Is it you, the man is saying. Heyeye! Hmm! he is shouting and then he is turning to the other soldier and cursing them. So you mean of all of you GROWN MEN only this boy – one skinny little thing like this – is finding this thing here.

I am not moving and the leader man is throwing up his arm to the sky. He is shouting, where are you finding him, so hard that his voice is becoming high and sounding like it is sticking in his throat. Strika is pointing his arm at the shack. Is that right, the man is saying and shaking his head like he cannot be believing it at all at all. SSSSS! He is shouting, you. Where is Luftenant? Luftenant. LUFTENANT! And another voice is answering, he is in the bush.

The grasses is shaking and man is coming from there holding his trouser up with one hand and holding his gun with the other. His yellow skin is shining like gold and sweat is shining on his beard. He is running to us and stopping when he is coming to be looking at me like he is confusing too much. Then he is saluting very lazy, not like everybody else who is looking like they are not even able to bend anything.

Commandant Sah! he is shouting in voice that is even sounding like somebody whining. This man Commandant is saying, come here. Come here, until Luftenant is moving closer to Commandant who is shouting, JUST WHAT ARE YOU DOING? Luftenant is not saying anything. You don't know? Please Sah. I was shitting in the bush. And Commandant is grabbing Luftenant's ear until the man is squeezing his face with so much pain. Open your ear and listen to me well well, Commandant is saying. If you are wanting to shit, you are not shitting on my time. Who are you? Just running into the bush like woman. If you are wanting to shit, you should be shitting right here on the road. You are not leaving this road for anything. Are you understanding me Luftenant? He is nodding, yes yes, and all the other soldier are trying not to be laughing by stomping their feets and coughing or pretending to sneeze.

Can you be telling me what this is, Commandant is saying and pointing to me. Why are you leaving Strika to bring him out?

Oh God. What am I doing, Luftenant is saying. He is spy oh. It is ambush oh. Let's just kill him and clear from this place.

SHUTUP YOUR MOUTH, Commandant is shouting. Who and who is asking you to speak? Idiot. If anybody is coming here, we will deal with them proper.

Then everybody is starting to laugh, even Commandant, and while this is happening I am seeing how Luftenant is looking like he is wanting to be killing Commandant. He is grumbling to himself and making his hand into fist.

Commandant is kneeling next to me and smiling so I am seeing how his teeths is in his mouth anyhow, just yellow with gap here and there. His gum is black and his eye is so red. His nose is coming out into a very round bulb at the tip which is sticking over his fat brown lip. He is stretching his glove to my face, grabbing it hard but also soft like he is caring for me, and then he is looking at all of the blood, and dirt, and mosquito bite, and mud I am having on me from dragging in the road. He is clicking his tongue and saying to Strika, are you trying to eat this one or what. And Strika is shaking his head no. Since he is finding me I can never hearing this boy speak.

By now I am knowing who is Strika and Commandant and Luftenant. But there are so many person who is just not saying anything at all that I am wondering if they are even knowing how to speak. Commandant is turning to me. Do you want some water, he is saying softly but I am not answering because I am floating on top of my body and just watching. The world is changing into many colour around me and I am hearing the people speaking but it is like different language. I am floating away like leaf in water until KPWISHA! I am feeling cold and more wet and then how my body is so heavy all around me.

Strika, Commandant is saying. Go and bring more water. Strika is running to the last truck and jumping up. Then Commandant is saying to me, are you hungry? Are you thirsty? And because I am feeling much better and my head is feeling more clear, I am touching my belly and nodding my head yes.

He is saying, well that is no problem. If you are wanting food, you will eat. And if you are wanting drink, you will drink but that is having to wait until you are telling me your name. How can I be sitting down to eat with a man who I am not knowing his name? Are you hearing me? I am nodding to him again but word is not able to be coming from my mouth.

You are having name is it not, he is saying and sticking his

9

face into my own face. I am trying hard to remember, to be squeezing my thought for my name, but I am not getting anything. Now Commandant is getting angry and pointing to himself. My name is Commandant. Everybody is always calling me Commandant. What is everybody always calling you?

I am shaking my head trying to remember as Commandant is just reaching to his belt and showing me one black gun like that. I am wanting to cry and I am feeling like I am having to go to toilet, but I am knowing if I am doing this, he will be killing me just like that so I am shaking my head and looking at his red eye until I am remembering just like that how in my village everybody is calling me Agu because that is what my father is calling me. I am whispering Agu, my name is Agu, because it is hard for me to be talking and then I am seeing how Commandant is taking his hand from his gun and smiling. Agu enh? They are calling you Agu. Well, that is what I will be calling you, he is saying. And I am breathing again and my head is not hurting so much because I am thinking, Glory be to God in the Highest I am still living.

Commandant is having smile crawling slowly onto his face and he is turning to his soldier and saying, see this one on the road. Do you see him? And they are all shouting, YES YES while Commandant is touching his beard and using his fingernail to pick all the scab and cut from between the hairs. He

10

is looking from soldier to soldier and everybody is staying quiet.

BRING WATER EHN! he is just shouting and Strika is handing him one small blue jerry can with red top. Commandant is taking one dirty handkerchief from his breast pocket and wetting it with some water. Then he is grabbing the back of my head and rubbing my face saying, well, if you are going to be eating with man, then you are having to be clean. I am feeling the water in all my scratch, bite, and cut and it is stinging me too much. I am wanting to shout but he is smiling with his tongue in his teeths like he is finding and cleaning old treasure. I am so thirsty. I am grabbing the can but Commandant is lifting it high into the air and pouring it onto my face and into my mouth. It is tasting of plastic and kerosene. It is having small small grain of sand in it but I am managing. It is making me to feel somehow good.

Luftenant is snorting and stomping his feets. Commandant is saying to me, why are you just lying by the roadside like one dead rat. Luftenant thinks you are a spy. Is it so?

Luftenant is saying something under his breath and staring at me like he could be chopping me to many piece right there. So what is your business here, Luftenant is shouting at me.

SHUTUP YOUR MOUTH! Commandant is shouting at him. Who is asking you to be opening this your stupid mouth anyway? And then he is talking to me and saying, so what is

11

it that you are doing here in one small small stall just waiting. You should be telling me. Are you spy? If you are not speaking then heyeye! And he is taking one knife from its container on his leg. It is having black handle and black blade excepting the edge which is just shining so sharp it is looking like it can even cut hair right down the middle. The shine is blinding my eye and making me to fear. Otherwise, he is saying, I will just be giving you to Luftenant. Just look at him. I am not even knowing what he will be doing to you. Better you just tell me and I will be helping you.

I am blinking because of the sharpness of the knife. Looking at it is making me to feel like my tongue is cutting loose and just readying to say this and that. My father is telling me to run, I am saying to Commandant. Run far far so the enemy is not catching you and killing you. And then I am just hiding in the bush and running this way and that way not knowing anything.

Luftenant is snorting again.

Enh. Hmm. Is that so? Commandant is asking me. Where is this your father? And the other soldier is leaning forward until I am feeling like they are putting their eye on me, until their stare is just feeling like insect bite.

I am not knowing, I am saying and trying very hard not to be crying so these people are not thinking I am fool. He is saying that he will find me.

Commandant is sucking in his lip and touching my face softly softly. He is taking my hand and pulling me onto my feets. Do you want to be soldier, he is asking me in soft voice. Do you know what that is meaning?

I am thinking of before war when I am in the town with my mother and I am seeing men walking with brand-new uniform and shiny sword holding gun and shouting left right, left right, behind trumpet and drum, like how they are doing on parade and so I am nodding my head yes.

If you are staying with me, I will be taking care of you and we will be fighting the enemy that is taking your father. Are you hearing me? He is stopping and licking his lip. Are you hearing me? Everything will be just fine, he is saying with his lip so close to my ear that I am hearing his saliva in his mouth. I am looking and seeing his smile and feeling his hand on my face touching me softly. I am seeing all of the soldier with gun and knife and then I am thinking about my father just dancing like that because of bullet.

What am I supposed to be doing?

So I am joining. Just like that. I am soldier.

Luftenant is saying don't think. Just let it happen. He is saying that the second you are stopping to think about it, your head is turning to the inside of rotten fruit.

Commandant is saying it is like falling in love. You cannot be thinking about it. You are just having to do it, he is saying.

And I am believing him. What else can I be doing?

They are all saying, stop worrying. Stop worrying. Soon it will be your own turn and then you will know what it is feeling like to be killing somebody. Then they are laughing at me and spitting on the ground near my feets.

We are stopping on the road and Strika and myself are just sitting in the back of one truck kicking the air with our leg and sweating with the sun. The wind is blowing softly in my ear and on my skin and I am looking at Strika and thinking all of the things I am learning as a soldier. I am learning to march, left right, left right; how to hide in the bush and stay very still so nobody can be seeing where I am, how to be walking one foot in front of the other so nobody is hearing me; running, jumping, rolling around on the ground and singing all of the soldier song that we are singing when we are working or marching. I am liking the older men and how they are carrying gun and always looking so tough like they are in movie and I am trying to be acting like them, but sometimes I am thinking of my home and my mother and father and sister and I am sadding. And I am thinking about Strika and asking myself why he is not even saying one word in this whole time I am soldier. If I am asking him question, then he is only shaking his head yes or no. So I am asking him all the time, even now while we are just sitting here waiting, are you Strika, and he is nodding yes. Are you having parent, and he is shaking his head no. Are you liking plantain? Nodding yes. Fish? Yes. Pear? Yes. Are you stupid? No. Why are you not talking talking? No answer. What is it like to be killing somebody? No answer. Strika! He is looking at me.

And then one scout they are calling Hope is shouting and running up the road. He is coming from the bush and yelling, they are coming oh! They are coming again! And as he is running he is tripping on himself running up the hill and all his muscle are moving even after he is stopping so he cannot be standing still. His gun is banging against his back like it is beating him to run faster, faster, faster, and I am laughing because he is looking not just like madman but mad horse.

Commandant is exciting softly softly when he is seeing the scout running for his life up the hill. Enh! he is saying and I am watching how he is folding his hand together and how his lip is just crawling to be smiling. Commandant is starting to sweating and I am seeing how his shirt is also soaking through with sweat. Luftenant is leaving him alone and looking like he is trying to find somewhere to be hiding. Commandant is thinking and I am liking to watch him thinking. He is putting his one hand in all of his big hairs and the other to be picking his beard and walking up and down backward and forward like he is in cage even if we are really standing outside in the open air. Then he is shouting order. Move this truck across the road! Park this truck here! Everybody take your position! You in the bush, speed up speed up! Quick. Quick quick. And we are all moving very quickly to do all the thing he is saying. We are causing so much confusion and chasing the small small animal from the bush onto the road. Lizard and bush rat and frog, they are all running and hopping and jumping. They are running around the road like chicken with no head just looking for place to be hiding. Strika is jumping up and down and grabbing his machete and then running to behind the tyre of the truck blocking the road. I am following him because I am not knowing where to go, but I am putting myself behind the back wheel because there is not even enough space for two of us behind one wheel. Everybody is moving, rushing, jumping, hiding, and making noise until just like that it is quieting everywhere and it is only looking like truck is breaking down on the road. Even before the war, this is always happening, and now it is happening even more because war is making it very hard to be fixing anything.

I am sitting behind this tyre, holding knife and waiting. I am watching mosquito everywhere moving around in circle like they are also waiting for something. If they are coming near to me, then I am beating them with my hand but it is not doing anything. There are so many.

I am looking out from behind my tyre and down the road the air is shaking just like still water if you are throwing rock into it. And then I am seeing small small truck moving closer, moving slowly slowly like cow. They are not even thinking anything is wrong and I am almost laughing and almost dying because my heart is beating so so fast and I am thinking about what is going to happen. They are not even knowing we are here and are just coming to us like idiot.

The first truck is stopping some metre from where I am hiding. I am looking around the tyre into the eye of the driver. His window is shining with so much sun, but somehow is still looking dark. Next to him, one man with uniform is making sign. His face is scrunching up with fear and it is looking like his lip is pulling down all of his face, his nose, his eye, his eyebrow. They are looking at each other and then the driver is just disappearing behind the steering wheel. I am remembering the soldier who are coming to my village and I am holding my machete closer. I am liking how it is feeling in my hand, like it is almost part of my body. I am looking at the man and looking at Strika and I am saying to myself if it is time to be killing, I am ready, but I am putting my hand between my leg because I am feeling like I need to be going to toilet. My heart is beating BUMP BUMP. BUMP BUMP. And I am finding it hard to be breathing, but still I am saying God will be helping me. I am ready.

I am watching.

The enemy is not even trying to fight and is just looking too tiring to even be thinking anything like fight fight, wahala wahala. Even if they are not yet seeing us soldier anywhere on the road, they are just jumping down from their truck looking like they are going to cry. PLEASE DO NOT SHOOT US! the

19

man in the uniform is shouting. We are not having any weapon, or any food, or any money, or any ammo. ANY-THING! PLEASE JUST LET US GO!

I am counting them. They are only twenty, and they are looking like they are already dead. Blood is just covering all of their clothe and skin, sometimes even their eye, but I cannot be knowing if it is their blood or another person's blood. And they are even walking so slow like old man with walking stick.

The head man of the enemy is shouting, see. See. Our hand is up and we are not having gun. No weapon at all.

There is silence and then I am hearing Commandant shouting from the grass by the road, number one: This territory is belonging to all of us rebel. You are trespassing. Number two: Take off all your clothe and put them on the road. Number three: Lie down with your face on the ground and your hand stretching all the way out. If you are not doing this in ten second, we will be shooting you dead. Are you understanding me?

I am watching the enemy looking at each other and I am counting one, two, three, four, all the way up to ten, but they are not taking off their clothe. Then I am hearing KPWAP like one million people clapping and then KPWING when bullet is hitting the metal door of the enemy truck. The enemy is looking at each other and whispering until Commandant is shouting from the bush, COME ON! I SAID OFF YOUR

CLOTHE! EVERYBODY TAKE OFF YOUR CLOTHE RIGHT NOW!

Then the enemy is taking off their clothe very fast, just ripping the shirt and ripping the trouser and throwing it to the ground. Their body is just shining with sweat in the sun, and the mosquito is coming to them slowly slowly. Some of them are having underwear full of hole covering their thing and others are having to use hand to be keeping everybody from seeing it.

LIE DOWN! Commandant is shouting. Put your hand on the ground. They are lying down and I can see the tear on the face of one enemy. He is coughing and sniffling and whispering. I think he is saying, I am not wanting to die. Please God. I am not wanting to die, but I am too far away to be hearing him. I think this is what he is saying and I am looking at him and even feeling sorry for him, but then I am remembering my father.

Commandant is coming out of the bush smiling and sweating and holding his gun ready to shoot anybody who is not following his order. Behind him everybody else is coming from the bush from all side until there is not even any one place for the men to be running. Strika is coming out from behind his wheel so I am following him. He is collecting all of the enemy uniform and taking them to the truck.

The mosquito is getting closer. Closer.

Who is the leader, Commandant is shouting, but nobody is answering. He is walking up and using his weapon to touch the enemy who is talking first and begging begging PLEASE DO NOT SHOOT US! You. Where are your weapon? he is shouting. Get up. Where are they?

The man is saying, we don't want trouble oh. We don't have any weapon. But Commandant is saying, Oho! This enemy dog is not wanting trouble, and everybody, excepting me and Strika who is never making any noise, is laughing, kehi, kehi, kehi like it is the best joke in the world.

Then Commandant is kicking this enemy man in the stomach very hard and the man is just dropping onto his knee and vomiting all over the ground.

Commandant is shouting, search the truck. Search the truck! and three soldier are running to search the truck. Then Commandant is telling me, Agu. Come here enh. Come here right now. And then he is telling the enemy chief to kneel down even though the man is already kneeling down and vomiting. I am standing in my place and I am just fearing. I am not wanting to be killing anybody today. I am not ever wanting to be killing anybody.

Bloody fool, he is saying to me. Come here and bring that machete. But I am still not moving. Commandant is stepping to me and grabbing my neck. You idiot, he is shouting. Come here! Come here right now! He is dragging me to the enemy soldier. Do you see this dog! he is shouting. You want to be a soldier enh? Well – kill him. KILL HIM NOW!

I am starting to crying and I am starting to shaking. And in my head I am shouting NO! NO! NO! but my mouth is not moving and I am not saying anything. And I am thinking if I am killing killing then I am going to hell so I am smelling fire and smoke and it is harding to breath, so I am just standing there crying crying, shaking shaking, looking looking. Then I am seeing, just like that, one enemy soldier is trying to run for the bush. His thing is just bouncing up and down and his buttom is slapping until I am hearing gunshot and then seeing his flesh from his leg scattering on the road. He is falling to the ground but he is not even saying anything, not screaming or crying or shouting, but he is still moving, just dragging his naked body with his arm and one leg like he can still be running away. Nobody is even looking at him anymore, but I am hearing the sound of his moving and it is sounding like lizard scratching on the roof. I am shaking and holding my thing. I am wanting to vomit.

Nobody is moving. Commandant is yelling, ANYBODY WHO IS TRYING TO RUN AWAY WILL NOT BE HAVING LEG TO RUN WITH. UNDERSTAND?

Please Sah. Please oh. We are not doing anything, the enemy man is saying from the ground and looking like cow because he is putting his hand for ground and just breathing

23

like cow is making noise. Please Sah, and his tear is running down his face. They are mixing with his sweat and he is blinking so much. Please now Sah. Don't just kill us oh. Just take us. Make us POW. Please oh. We don't have anything.

Sah, one of the men is jumping down from the enemy truck and shouting to Commandant who is looking up from the enemy chief and watching the soldier throw down four gun, two big two small. They are opening up their hand to be showing that they are not finding anything else. Commandant's eye is flashing and he is slapping the enemy soldier with the back of his hand.

You are a LIAR! he is shouting and hitting him again and again and again. LIAR and idiot. Stupid somebody.

I am watching the man as he is just falling onto his hand and knee and spitting blood onto the road. Commandant is kicking him and I am hearing KWUD KWUD knocking inside my head. He is opening his trouser and pulling out his thing and saying to me, see Agu. See how we are dealing with this enemy. And I am hearing hsssss and seeing how Commandant is squeezing his eye and mouth and teeths while he is just going to toilet all over the enemy man.

Ahhh, he is saying when he is closing his trouser and everybody is laughing kehi kehi kehi. See this bloody goat. Get up you bloody fool! Kneel. Come on. Kneel.

None of the other enemy is even looking up from the

ground. Some of them is going to toilet and making the whole air to stink. I am spitting because there is too much saliva in my mouth.

Kill him, Commandant is saying in my ear and lifting my hand high with the machete. Kill him oh.

The enemy is saying to me, please don't kill me oh. Please I beg enh. Please. God will bless you. And each time he is talking he is spraying saliva and blood everywhere. Then he is starting to piss and he cannot even be stopping himself.

See this man, Commandant is saying, look at him. He is not even man. He is just going to toilet like sheep or goat or dog. He is grabbing my neck and whispering into my ear, kill him now because I am not having the time oh. If you are not killing him, enh. Luftenant will be thinking you are spy. And who can know if he won't just be killing you. He is squeezing my hand around the handle of the machete and I am feeling the wood in my finger and in my palm. It is just like killing goat. Just bring this hand up and knock him well well.

He is taking my hand and bringing it down so hard on top of the enemy's head and I am feeling like electricity is running through my whole body. The man is screaming, AYEEIII, louder than the sound of bullet whistling and then he is bringing his hand to his head, but it is not helping because his head is cracking and the blood is spilling out like milk from coconut. I am hearing laughing all around me even as I am watching him trying to hold his head together. He is annoying me and I am bringing the machete up and down and up and down hearing KPWUDA KPWUDA every time and seeing just pink while I am hearing the laughing KEHI, KEHI, KEHI all around me.

Then I am hitting his shoulder and then his chest and looking at how Commandant is smiling each time my knife is hitting the man. Strika is joining me and we are just beating him and cutting him while everybody is laughing. It is like the world is moving so slowly and I am seeing each drop of blood and each drop of sweat flying here and there. I am hearing the bird flapping their wing as they are leaving all the tree. It is sounding like thunder. I am hearing the mosquito buzzing in my ear so loud and I am feeling how the blood is just wetting on my leg and my face. The enemy's body is having deep red cut everywhere and his forehead is looking just crushed so his whole face is not even looking like face because his head is broken everywhere and there is just blood, blood, blood.

I am vomiting everywhere. I cannot be stopping myself. Commandant is saying it is like falling in love, but I am not knowing what that is meaning. I am feeling hammer knock-ing in my head and chest. My nose and mouth is itching. I am seeing all of the colour everywhere and my belly is feeling empty. I am growing hard between my leg. Is this like falling in love?

Then I am falling down on the road and just watching as they are killing everybody, just cutting arm and using it to beat somebody else's head. And I am watching the man with his leg shot still scratching down the road as if he can be going somewhere. His leg is leaving trail like leaking car. And I am seeing mosquito everywhere flying in circle all around us.

I am not bad boy. I am not bad boy. I am soldier and soldier is not bad if he is killing. I am telling this to myself because soldier is supposed to be killing, killing, killing. So if I am killing then I am only doing what is right. I am singing song to myself because I am hearing too many voice in my head telling me I am bad boy. They are coming from all around me and buzzing in my ear like mosquito and each time I am hearing them, they are chooking my heart and making my stomach to turn. So I am singing,

*Soldier Soldier*
*Kill Kill Kill.*

*That is how you live.*
*That is how you die.*

This is my song that I am singing all of the time wherever we are going to be reminding myself that I am only doing what soldier is supposed to be doing. But it is never working because I am always feeling like bad boy. So I am thinking how can I be bad boy? Me, bad boy – somebody who is having life like I am having and fearing God the whole time.

I am learning how to read very early in my life from my mother and my father. When I am very small, before even my sister is born, I am always sitting with my mother on the floor of the kitchen and watching her washing all the plate. In the evening, I am always sitting on the floor just watching her with her buttom sticking high into the air and her breast touching her knee while she is working to make the kitchen so clean that not even fruit fly is wanting to put its egg inside.

I am liking to read so much that my mother is calling me professor. I am pulling her dress and she is saying to me, two more minute professor. Only two more minute. Then she is locking the door and holding my hand as we are walking to the main house. Inside, my father is always just sleeping sleeping or listening to his radio, so we would be moving quietly, getting the matches from the wood table in the middle of the room and lighting the lamp just in case they are taking the light. All of this is making me to agitate because it is taking so long until finally she is coming to the bookshelf and pretending to search for just the right book. The shelf was having many book of different size and different colour – some red, some yellow, some blue, and some brown, but the one I am always wanting her to pick, the only one that I am wanting to hear is the one that is holding all of the other book up, the big white Bible. I was so small and the book was so big that I am almost not even able to be carrying it. But I was enjoying how the cover is so soft, and how the letter saying HOLY BIBLE was made of gold. This was my favourite book because of how it is looking and because of all the story inside of it. Whenever my mother is touching it, I am shouting, that one, that one and she is saying, shhh don't be so loud or you will be waking your father. I was always sitting in her laps on our favourite chair and we are staring at the small small letter on the page. She was reading over my shoulder and I am feeling her lip moving in my ear as she was saying each word. My mother is reading very very slowly because she is not schoolteacher like my father who is knowing too much about book. She is not going to school for long enough like my father, but she was always saying, I am knowing enough to read the only book that is mattering. This is why Pastor is liking her so much.

She is reading to me about how Cain is killing his brother Abel, and how God is visiting Abraham, and about Jonah living in the fish. She was also reading about how God is making Job to suffer very much, but how he is rewarding him at the end, and how David is killing Goliath. Each time she is reading this story I would be thinking in my head that I am standing here looking at how all the army is shining with gold and bronze in the sun and how Goliath is laughing until David is cutting off his head. I am seeing all of these thing when she is reading and thinking that I am wanting to be warrior. And all the time my mother is reading I am pointing to each word and asking what is that what is that so she can be telling me and I can be learning. We were doing this every evening until my mother is saying, okay Agu it is enough now. My eye is tired.

When my mother is not there, I was going to the shelf to be reading The Bible myself. My mother was still reading to me every night, but I was also able to be reading by myself, and soon, when my father was coming back from work to be sitting in his short and singlet listening to the radio in his favourite chair, I was sitting with him and not my mother and I would be reading to him what I am teaching myself from The Bible. I was wanting to show him that I am big enough to be going to school so I can be learning everything that he is knowing that is making everybody in the village to like him so much. I was always asking him every day, tomorrow can I be going to school? Tomorrow can I go to school, and he was always saying to me just wait just wait. Enh. Agu! Why are you wanting to grow so big so fast? Then I would be going to my mother to be begging her to help me go to school. I was wanting to go so much that each time I would be crying to her to make my father take me to school and she is saying to me that if I am crying like this then at school they will just be laughing at me. So, when my father is coming home, I was first asking him how is his own school that he is teaching and then I was asking him if I am big enough and he was telling me to take my right hand and put it over my head to touch my left ear, but I was too small to be doing that so he was telling me Agu you are not ready yet.

Until one day, I am running to my father and saying, look and then taking my hand over my head and touching my ear. He is smiling and saying, okay, and then the next day we are going to the primary school where everybody is wearing uniform that is red short and white shirt if you are boy and red skirt and white shirt if you are girl. I was looking at all of them holding one red notebook and Biro in their hand and standing in line not making any noise. The boys were all having head shaved and the girls were all having plaits so that everybody is looking the same. I wanted to be wearing uniform and carrying red notebook and Biro too much so I was just standing there agitating.

My father was taking me to Mistress Gloria who is the head

teacher and asking her if I can be going to school but she was asking, this one? Isn't he too small? And I was looking at how Mistress Gloria is having very fat belly and big cheek and I wanted to be saying, I am only too small because you are so big, but my father is saying, no. He is not small and Mistress Gloria is having to take me in.

Because my father was schoolteacher and my mother is always reading to me from The Bible, I was already reading when the other children are just trying to learn. I was the smartest person in my class, so smart that the only thing I am having to learn is writing. Mistress Gloria was seeing how smart I am and she is moving me up with the other people in primary one so I was just sitting on a bench with people bigger than me. When all of the other student are having their leg touch the ground while they are sitting, my own was just swinging back and forward in the air.

The school is just one big building with blackboard at the front of the classroom. This is where Mistress Gloria is standing when she is teaching lesson. All of the class are having their lesson in this one room so that Mistress Gloria was teaching every class up to primary six. She was always holding one large wooden ruler that she would be using to hit you on the head if you are not behaving well. Sometimes during the day we are having quiet time where the younger people is having to put their head down on their desk and all the older one is having to copy their lesson in their notebook. I am always doing my lesson at home so during quiet time I am sitting and thinking about different thing. I always liked thinking about everything that I am reading in book until it is time to play. Even though I am learning with the older children, I am always playing with all my mates. I am having one very good friend who is having Engineer for father so they are some of the rich people in the village. My friend's name was Dike. He was tall past me even if we are the same age, but he was still my best friend.

But these thing are before the war and I am only remembering them like dream. I am seeing my school and all of my friend. I am seeing Mistress Gloria and her curly black wig of hairs that she was always shifting around because it is not staying on her head well well. Some people were hating Mistress Gloria and always making fun of her by pushing out their belly big and walking around like fat goat, but I am liking Mistress Gloria and she was liking me. She was always saying to me softly when I was leaving the classroom after helping her to clean up, Agu make sure you study book enh? If you are studying hard you can be going to the university to be Doctor or Engineer.

All of this thing that she was always telling me are making me to happying because I was seeing how the Doctor and the Engineer is being treated. I was putting all this thing in my head and remembering them but not letting them be taking up too much of my time as I am young. So after talking with her like this each day, I was then going to play with all my friend in the schoolyard. I was having many friend in my village because all of the other children were thinking that I am nice boy and also I am the best at all of the game and all of the lesson we are learning. So they were all liking me and wanting to be my friend, but the person who was really liking me and who I was really liking was my best friend Dike. We are always doing everything together in the village. So after going from Mistress Gloria, I was going with Dike to be going behind the school-yard with some of the other boy to be playing football in the dust with one flat ball that is never very good to kick or we are having the race that I am always winning and I was flying up and down the schoolyard even if I am only wearing slipper. I am liking school very much and always thinking about going until the war is coming and then they are stopping school because there is no more Government.

I am always going to Church every Sunday where I am first going to the Sunday school to be sitting outside under the shade of one big tree in the church compound with all of my mate and sometimes, if she is not causing too much trouble, my sister, to be listening to the women reading us more story from The Bible about Jesus and Joseph and Mary and telling us that we should watch out so that we are taking the hard road and not the easy road. And then we are saying prayer for forgiveness and the Our Father and also singing many song because God is liking music more than just talking so if we are singing then he is listening to us well well. They are always telling us that God is liking children so much, that he is always watching us. Sometimes after Sunday school is finishing I am going into the big grey Church and sitting with my mother and father who are dressing in their nice clothe and listening to Pastor shouting and sweating. I am feeling how the wood is chooking my buttom with splinter and how the fan above us is shaking so much that it is looking like it was going to fall and be cutting off my head. I was always watching how the women would be dancing well well so that their clothe is shaking and they are having to tie it and tie it again and singing very loud when it is time to put their money in the collection plate. And the men are just shuffling their feets and bowing their head so their chin is touching their chest.

And on Sunday there are other thing that we are doing in my village. When there is no school and no chore, all my friend and me are making all kind of game to be playing. Sometimes we are playing that we are grown up and doing grown-up thing like driving car and flying plane, or being Doctor or Boatman. And sometimes, we are playing that we are soldier like we are sometimes seeing in movie and taking stick and using them as gun to be shooting at each other and falling down each time to pretending we are dead. And each time we are playing all this game we are having so much fun and laughing and running and yelling all up and down the road of the village. All the small small children are watching us and wanting to be like us and even the grown people are watching us and even if they are yelling at us to stop making so much noise, I am knowing from the way that they are shouting through their teeths they are trying not to be smiling because they are also wanting to be just like us. So we were playing all this game then and thinking that to be a soldier was to be the best thing in the world because gun is looking so powerful and the men in movie are looking so powerful and strong when they are killing people, but I am knowing now that to be a soldier is only to be weak and not strong, and to have no food to eat and not to eat whatever you want, and also to have people making you do thing that you are not wanting to do and not to be doing whatever you are wanting which is what they are doing in movie. But I am only knowing this now because I am soldier now.

So I am singing to myself,

> *Soldier Soldier*
> *Kill Kill Kill.*
> *That is how you live.*
> *That is how you die.*

And I am remembering to myself that I am doing all of this thing before I am soldier and it is making me to feel better. If I am doing all of this good thing and now only doing what soldier is supposed to be doing, then how can I be bad boy?

It is morning again, like all the other morning. The sun is just jumping up up into the sky so quickly that we are not even having any time before we are just sweating sweating everywhere. There are many tree around us, but they are all too far away to be giving any shade. I am crushing the grasses under my feet and just looking at how all of our footprint from the day before is everywhere. They are drying in the mud so it is looking like somebody is playing football here the night before, but I am knowing that this is never happening because nobody is playing football anymore during the war.

My feets is paining me. My leg is paining me. My knee is hurting because we are training very hard now. All the time

41

just training training. They are telling us to run up and down so we are running up and down like we are running race when I am schoolboy. They are telling us to be crawling on the grasses and to be running zigzag to be dodging pretend bullet. I am hot and my body is too tired. I am not feeling good at all at all.

I am not liking this field even if Commandant is loving it because he says it is taking away insubordination. I am not liking everything Commandant likes even if I am supposed to be liking it. But I am liking his shiny forehead and his big nose that is covering his whole face and even his top lip. I am liking his moustaches and his big black beard, and I am liking how he is squeezing his chin and all of its hairs in his fist when he is thinking very hard. I am wanting beard so I can be doing that. Maybe then I will be feeling older and I won't be tireding all the time. If you are seeing Commandant, you will be knowing that he is just very big man even though this war is coming to make most men small like children and children small like baby. He is so tall that looking at him is like climbing tree, so big that if he is standing next to you, then his shadow is blocking the sun. He is so strong that I can be seeing the vein on his arm. It is funny to be watching him moving also because he is walking like his leg is wooden pole that is not bending for anything. Before the war, this is how I am seeing soldier moving when they are parading in the town near my village so I am knowing he is real soldier. Even when we are running his leg are moving this way and it is making me to want to laugh at him, but nobody is laughing at him because that is annoying him. He is beating people who annoy him and one time he was even killing one man who just annoyed him too much. We are leaving that man somewhere on the roadside with one big hole in his head and his eye wide open.

As we are standing in this field, Commandant is walking in front of us and shouting, are we soldier? We are saying, yes Sah! Are we army? Are we strong and proud? And we are saying, yes Sah! Yes Sah! and he is smiling but I am knowing that he is not believing what we are saying because sometimes he is talking to himself that we are hopeless and only good enough to be thrown into battle and die.

I am not knowing why he is so angry with us all of the time for not acting like real soldier. We are not even looking like real soldier. There are almost one hundred and twenty of us standing at attention but none of us is even wearing the same dress. Some of us is wearing green camouflage like real soldier are doing, but our own is just fulling with hole and having thread just blowing this way and that in the wind. If we are killing soldier or finding it on any dead body, then person is always quarrelling and sometimes even fighting to be stealing it. Other soldier is wearing black trouser and black shirt with red stripe on the arm which is the uniform that the police is wearing before the war. This uniform is not as good because it is making you too hot in the sun and it is making you too easy to see in the daytime, but that is not mattering to anybody. People are just wanting to wear anything that is looking like uniform. I am not even having one uniform because I am too small. I am just wearing my short and shirt that I am taking from village we are looting one day. I was really wanting trouser to be stopping the mosquito from biting me on the leg, but I am not finding any small enough for me to be wearing. Anyway, I am really liking my shirt even if it is dirty and I am having to fold the sleeve a whole six time. I am liking it even if it is too big so it is coming down over my short.

Sometimes I am thinking, if army is always having one uniform for its soldier to wear and we are not all wearing the same uniform, then how can we be army. And if army is made of soldier, and we are not army then how can we be real soldier. This is why I am not knowing why Commandant is always so angry with us.

Commandant is saying we are going to raid one village. Where is the village, I am asking to myself. And what are we to be taking from them? I am not knowing but I am not going to be asking or he might be beating me. Then he is saying to us if we are hating the enemy and each time we are answering, YES SAH! We are stomping the ground and sometimes even jumping up in the air. He is saying to us if the enemy is killing our mother and our father and burning our house and we are answering softly, yes Sah, because we are all thinking of all the place and person we are leaving behind. I am thinking of my mother and my sister who are running away. I am not knowing if they are dead or alive or if I can even be knowing what they are looking like if I am seeing them today. Every time we are seeing woman or girl, I am looking at them well well to be knowing if they are my mother or my sister.

Commandant is shouting at us to be ready for fourteen hundred hours. I am thinking that this is very funny and I am wanting to laugh. Everybody is knowing that the day is not having fourteen hundred hours and I am looking down the line of soldier to see if Strika is also thinking it is funny. He is leaning forward to look at me, sticking out his tongue and opening his mouth wide. I am wanting to laugh but instead I am sucking in my belly and holding my breath. Commandant is raising his head high until his face is shining like it is made of metal. DISMISSED! he is shouting at us and then he is walking off to the tree and the path that is leading to the many hut we are living in. Some of the men are following Commandant, swinging their gun onto their back and walking quietly quietly. Some of these soldier, everything he is doing, they are doing. Everything he is saying, they are doing. Some other men is holding their gun by the front and letting the end to be dragging in the ground like plough when the men is going to find shade to be resting in. I am going to find Strika.

I am finding him sitting under tree far away from the other men, holding stick and scratching picture into the dry ground. Over and over again he is drawing the same picture of man and woman with no head because their head is rolling away on the ground. Strika, I am calling to him, and he is looking up at me. No noise from him. He is not saying anything, I am telling myself. Since I am becoming soldier, I am never hearing the sound of his voice, but now, I am knowing now what is his problem. His picture is telling me that he is not making one noise since they are killing his parent. I am not believing him the first time he is telling me this, and every time I am trying to get him to say something or at least be making one sound from his mouth. I am feeling sad for him. I am getting used to it; this is how he is behaving from the very beginning. Strika is moving to one side so I can also be sitting in the shade next to him. Because I am tall more than him, I am knowing that I am older, but nobody is really telling how old they are anymore. All we are knowing is that, before the war we are children and now we are not. I am looking at Strika and how his skin is just brown in some place and black in other place, looking just like camouflage dress everybody is wearing. I am laughing when I am seeing him and saying to him, ha ha. Kehi kehi kehi. Strika is looking like shirt.

On the ground he is writing HUNGRY and I am wanting to say to him, I am hungry too. I am hungry too, but the word are not coming out of my mouth. There is no food left for anybody in the camp. Strika is putting his head on my leg and licking his cracking lip. The blood on them is dry and shiny, making his lip to look like he is swallowing red paint. I am touching his forehead with my hand and then I am touching my own to be seeing if he is hotter than me, but we are the same hotness. He is not having fever and I am not having fever. We are just tired. Strika is punching the air above his head. We are not wanting to fight. We are tired of fighting. I am saying to him, one day there will be no more war and we can be living together in a house and eating all of the food we are wanting to eat. Are you hearing me? He is not acting like he is hearing anything I am saying because he knows it is lie. We will always be fighting war, but sometimes it is nice to be thinking that there is something else for our future.

Luftenant is shouting IT IS FOURTEEN HUNDRED HOURS and I am hearing the voice of Commandant saying, come on! Get ready! Time to go. Time to go.

And then we are loading the truck on the road near to our hut and building. Even the truck is not wanting to go. They are not sounding good at all at all. The engine is coughing and spitting like sick old man. The back of the truck is having long wooden seat that is chooking you with splinter if you are even luckying enough to getting seat. And if you are not luckying, then when the truck is moving, your head is moving from side to side with the bump in the road and you are feeling like you have been in battle before the killing even starts. Commandant is having smaller truck for himself which I am liking better because it is giving more comfort. Sometimes, if we are making him to happy, he is taking Strika and me to be riding in, but this is only sometimes. Most of the time, we are having to ride in the big truck with the other soldier.

Commandant is dividing people like this, you. Come with me. You, go with Luftenant. You come with me. You go with Luftenant. I am standing next to Strika when he is putting person here and there because I am wanting to be in the same group as Strika. And also I am wanting to be in the same group as Commandant because he is real soldier and making people to behave more like soldier than Luftenant. Commandant is choosing. One of the people he is taking is Strika and one of the person he is not taking is me. I am wanting to be with Strika and Commandant, but of course the thing you are wanting most is always the thing that is not happening. I am not wanting to be with Luftenant and I am not wanting to ride in his truck.

I am not liking Luftenant because he is coward. I am knowing he is coward because his skin is looking very light and yellow like one of his parent is white man. I am not knowing if it is his mother or father that is white because, most of the time, I am wondering if he is even having mother or father. One time I am hearing him say that before the war he is selling shoe, but that is only because he is not having chance to go to school; and I am hearing him say also that his mother and his father are dying in car crash when he is young and that is how he is ending up selling shoe in the market. I am not believing him and I am thinking that no other soldier is believing him. I think he is being born to sell shoe and that he is only Luftenant of rebel because he is bribing somebody to be giving him this rank. I am knowing it because one day after Commandant is abusing him for not fighting, I am hearing him grumbling that he is becoming Luftenant because he is thinking that officer is not having to fight. Whenever he is near Commandant, he is acting like one scared dog and not even speaking. And in battle, he is never coming to the front and always staying at the back where he is trying to tell people what to be doing. Always, he is hiding behind the truck or anything that is giving him protection from the bomb and the bullet. I am even seeing him use dead body for protection, but I am also seeing other people doing the same thing so I am not too angry about that. Still, I am not wanting to be with Luftenant because I am fearing that I will be dying too quickly and then I will never be seeing my family again.

I am angrying that Commandant is not taking me and Strika

together and I am fighting very hard to get into the back of truck first so at least I am not having to stand and be too too tired wherever we are going to raid. I am finding my seat in the corner where I am having wood wall on one side. This way no one can be pushing me this way or that way. No one will be making me to get up.

The road is going on and on. I am looking through the wooden board to where the tree is moving by like it is running and I am seeing the road, which is moving like black river carrying us to far away. I am feeling the cold air on my body that is pushing away all the heat from all of the body on this truck so I am not sweating as much. And my head, it is moving from side to side so much that I am having to use my hand to be holding it in one place. Hunger is attacking me because I am not eating anything since so long. Sleep is attacking me because the truck is just rocking back and forward and back and forward with all of the bump in the road. Sleep is attacking me and I am beginning to think of my village. It is so long since I am even seeing it in my dream.

All the truck is stopping. We are here at one junction and everybody is getting down, but I am the last to get down because I am the first to be sitting in the truck. As soon as I am jumping down into the outside, I am starting to sweating and it is sticking to my skin like million shiny insect. I am brushing the sweat away but it is only making my hand wet and to be smelling like wet mud. Everybody is stretching his body this way and that way and Commandant is shouting to us, THE BLOOD MUST FLOW!, and we are all saying back, YES SAH!

Commandant is walking up and down and folding his hand one on the other and just looking around. He is putting his hand in his hairs and also holding his beard and this is making me to fear somehow. I am wondering if he is knowing where we are going or how we are going to be getting there.

I am looking behind me down this hill at the land that is stretching for kilometre and kilometre. Everything is green because this is the south of the country and we are having many tree. These tree are very fat because they are having so much water to drink. From the top of this hill, I am seeing through the tall grasses by the roadside to where the land is meeting the sky. I am not knowing where the hill is stopping or the bottom of the cloud is beginning because it is so far away that all of this is happening. I am seeing many many tree, too many tree that it is making me to wonder if God is planting all of the tree he can think of in this part of the country. Maybe He is running out before He is getting to the north where government is and this is why they are angrying at us and wanting to kill us, because God is forgetting them. From this hill it is looking like you can just be jumping into the top of the tree

51

for them to catch you, but I am knowing that that cannot happen. One day one soldier from our group is jumping off tall rock because he is saying he is finding heaven in all of the tree. I am thinking that he was madding in the head. I am not knowing if he is finding heaven, but I am not wanting to try it for myself to be finding out.

Nobody is telling me the name of these tree, so I am making it up. I am only knowing the Iroko tree so I am calling those one when I am seeing them. But some of the tree are shorter than the Iroko tree and I am calling these one the children of the forest. There are tree with leaf that are having five point so I am calling them the star-leaf tree because it is like their leaf is becoming the star in the sky when they are falling. I know because when this leaf is falling to the mud, it is becoming yellow like the colour of star. And there is some smaller tree with vine that is strangling them. I am calling these tree the slave tree because they are slave to the vine that is using them to climb up to the sun. If I am tree, then I will be liking to be like the Iroko because they are so tall and strong that nothing is bothering them, but I am thinking that I am more like slave tree because I can never be doing what I want.

I am not wanting to fight today because I am not liking the gun shooting and the knife chopping and the people running. I am not liking to hear people scream or to be looking at blood. I am not liking any of these thing. So I am asking to myself, why am I fighting? Why can I not just be saying no? Then I am remembering how one boy is refusing to fight and Commandant is just telling us to jump on his chest, so we are jumping on his chest until it is only blood that is coming out of his mouth.

Commandant is saying, form rank. You who are going with me and you who are going with Luftenant. We are forming them but they are not even straight. My leg is shaking shaking. Everybody's leg is just shaking shaking because nobody is liking to be standing on the main road like that. Even Commandant is fearing because he is turning his head from side to side and looking down the road one way and then up the road the other way. He is looking up to the sky and I am knowing that he is thinking about how government is some-times flying plane or helicopter to be dropping bomb and fire on everybody. He is speaking very fast when he is shouting, TENSHUN! and we are all shouting back, YES SAH! This village is between these two road, he is shouting, so people with me will be attacking from one end when people with Luftenant is attacking from the other. That way there is not even any place for these dog to be running. We will be killing them like they are killing us and we will be stealing from them what they are stealing from us. We are shouting back to him, YES SAH!

He is taking his people, one of them is Strika, but he is leaving me to be going with Luftenant and Rambo. I am liking Rambo and wanting to be wearing red bandanna like that on my head like he is wearing to be keeping the sweat from pouring into his eye when he is busy killing killing. Nobody is knowing why he is getting the name Rambo but I am knowing of the movie and how that man is very tough and mean and I am thinking to myself, yes, yes this Rambo is very tough and also mean, but he is also very smart. I am liking the way his eye is so sharp that they are seeing everything each time we are in battle. He is dodging bullet and bomb and all of the thing that are killing people. Sometime I am wondering if he is having his own juju to be making him live without fearing death, but I am not wanting to ask him or he will be laughing at me. I am knowing that if I am staying with him then at least I am surviving, so it is not making me to feel too so mad that I am having to go with Luftenant this time.

There is not enough gun for each person to be having one and so I am not having gun. Anyway, Commandant is saying that I am too small to be carrying gun because small person is not holding gun well well and just bouncing up and down when they are shooting. Instead he is giving me knife. But everybody is getting gun juice. Everybody is always wanting gun juice because it is drug and making life easy easy. Gun juice is making you to be stronger and braver. It is making your head to hurt and it is tasting like bullet and sugar cane. I am not liking how it is the colour of oil and the colour of black paint or water in the gutter but I am struggling to get my own so I can be putting it in my mouth. It is tasting like licking rock and it is tasting like eating pencil but it is also tasting like licking sweet. My throat is burning like the fire of gun, but it is also sweeting like sugar cane. I am wanting more gun juice.

My belly is growing like hungry dog because the gun juice is making it to be that way. I am feeling hungry and I am not feeling hungry. I am wanting to vomit and I am not wanting to vomit but I am thinking let me not be vomiting because I am not even eating very much food so if I am vomiting there is nothing staying inside my stomach to be giving me energy.

Commandant is shouting but I am hearing him like he is speaking through one big bag of cotton. He is saying, let us pray, let us pray and then he is asking the Lord to be guiding us in everything we are about to be doing. I am thinking that we should not even be asking God for anything because it is like He is forgetting us. I am trying to forget Him anyway even if my mother would not be happying with me. She is always saying to fear God and to always be going to church on Sunday, but now I am not even knowing what day is Sunday. I am saying bye to Strika and watching him walking away with Commandant. I am just waiting for the gun juice to start to working so I am not having to think as much anymore.

We are walking down into the valley and down into the bush so I am feeling like animal going back to his home. My forehead is heating up and my hand is hot and I am finding it hard to be breathing, like the air is water, like in the place the cloud is borning before they are bringing rain. I am hearing water and I am thirsty and wanting to drink but the stream we are coming to is having too much mud. Anyway, it is not mattering. I am putting my head in the water and when I am bringing it out the sky is many different colour and I am seeing spirit in the cloud. Everybody is looking like one kind of animal, no more human. Nobody is having nose or lip or mouth or any of the thing that is making you to remember somebody. Everything is just looking like one kind of animal and smelling like chicken or goat, or cow.

Across the stream, I am feeling in my body something like electricity and I am starting to think: Yes it is good to fight. I am liking how the gun is shooting and the knife is chopping. I am liking to see people running from me and people screaming for me when I am killing them and taking their blood. I am liking to kill.

Across the stream, I am feeling like man with big muscle and small head and I am thinking that nothing can be stopping me and nothing can be slowing me down – not even the hill we are climbing. I am like leopard hunting in the bush and I am feeling like I am going home.

All of the leaf is red and dripping and all of the plant is too thick. The bush is chooking me with its branch and it is trying to trip me with its root, but I am running running through all of the colour of this world, through all the tree, through all the flower. If I am falling on my knee it is not mattering because I am getting up and running, running, running. Nobody is knowing we are coming here, coming just like cloud when you are not even expecting it.

On the path, I am feeling wet mud between my toe and the grasses like knife on my ankle. I am saying prayer to God but all my word is going to Devil. Help me to be doing the thing you want me to do I am saying but I am only hearing laughter all around me in the tree and in the farm we are passing, many farm that is having no more yam or cassava because there is nobody staying to be growing them.

And on the path, we are coming to the edge of this village where there are the poor person house made of mud and tin and wood. There is nobody living inside so we are tearing them down and setting the thatch roof on fire and then we are moving on to more house. Each person is taking house and saying this is my house and everything that is in it is belonging to me. I am running to the smell of smoke in one house that is having wall of cement with breaking-up glass on top to be keeping away the terrible people like Commandant and Luftenant.

Person in this house is trying to keep safe behind iron gate but we are pushing it pushing it until it is opening with big scream like it is not wanting to be opening at all at all. There is soft dirt under my feets and tall green tree with orange and mango. Every building here is painting green even if it is fading but they are rising from the grasses with white window like bone inside them.

Far away, I am hearing screaming and gunfire and my head is growing smaller and my body is growing bigger. I am wanting to kill; I don't know why. I am just wanting to kill. I am seeing animal and I am wanting to kill it. I am raising my machete and then I am seeing. I am shouting, STRIKA! because I am almost chopping him. He is looking like dog to me, but we are hugging in all of the screaming and the gunfire and I am feeling his head and he is feeling my head and then we are going together through all of the changing colour to the main house of this compound.

In the main house, there is no food, nothing to lick, nothing to chop, nothing. Breaking glass is everywhere like someone is coming here before. All of the chair is breaking but there is still picture on the wall, and there are plastic flower lying on table.

So many door from this room. They are leading down hallway. The smell of shit and piss is all around us. At the end of the hall, soldier is breaking down door, KPWAMA, KPWAMA, they are kicking and knocking it with machete until the wood is breaking.

In the room, I am looking up and seeing – sky. There is nothing to be keeping out the rain or God from watching what it is we are doing. The sun is coming loose like someone is cutting it and it is bleeding red and yellow and purple and blue above us. In the corner, there is desk being eaten by termite and in the other corner is bed smelling like chicken and goat. I am wanting to kill. We are all wanting to kill.

Under the bed there is woman and her daughter just hiding. She is looking at us and worrying worrying so much it is looking like somebody is cutting her face with knife.

She is smelling like goat and we are wanting to kill her so we are dragging her out, all of us soldier but she is holding her daughter. They are holding each other and shaking like they are having fever. They are so thin more than us and the skin is hanging down like elephant skin so I am knowing she is fat before this war is coming and making rich and fat like poor and thin. The girl is so shrinking, she is almost like unborn baby – I am knowing because I have been taking them from their mother's belly to be seeing who is girl and who is boy. Are you my mother, I am saying. Are you my sister? But they are only screaming like Devil is coming for them. I am not Devil. I am not bad boy. I am not bad boy. Devil is not blessing me and I am not going to hell. But still I am thinking maybe Devil born me and that is why I am doing all of this.

But I am standing outside myself and I am watching it all

happening. I am standing outside of myself. I am grabbing the woman and her daughter. They are not my mother and my sister. I am telling them, it is enough. This is the end.

And now the woman is praying to God, please take my daughter safely to heaven. Forgive her sin. You are saying blessed is the children and who is living in you. They are never seeing death. Am I wronging You? I am trying to live for You. Please Lord I am begging to You. I am laughing laughing because God is forgetting everybody in this country.

Strika is pulling down his short and showing that he is man to this woman while I am holding her one leg and another soldier is holding the other. She is screaming, DEVIL BLESS YOU! DEVIL BORN YOU! But it is not Devil that is borning me. I am having father and mother and I am coming from them.

She is still screaming screaming, AYIIIEEE, like it is the creation of my village when long ago great warrior and his army are just fighting fighting enemy in the bush near my village. They are fighting for many day, but nobody is winning until finally they are growing tired and saying, let us stop. Let us stop. So they are stopping and feasting together, enemy with enemy, and rejoicing well well until they are going to sleep. But in the night enemy is attacking warrior and wounding him until he is running away into the bush. It is at this time that he is falling down by this river and almost dying, but the goddess of the river is coming to help him and make him better. She was the most beautiful thing to be seeing in the whole world so when the warrior is waking up to see her he is saying Kai! and falling in love right there. Then, because he is loosing from his own village he is saying well I will just marry this beautiful woman so that we can be having some children which is exactly what he is doing at the time. When the woman is having her baby, she is having twin boy, very strong because of their father being warrior and their mother being goddess. Also, because of their mother being goddess, they could be changing from one animal to the other. So sometimes they are changing into monkey to be climbing into the tree and getting the best fruit and sometimes they are changing to bird to be seeing the whole world. And they are loving each other so much until one day they are changing into different animal. One is becoming ox to be going to the river to drink because he is thirsty and the other is becoming leopard so that he can be hunting in the bush. Leopard was hunting hunting, but he is not finding anything to be killing so he is coming back to find his mother and his father. When he is coming to the river, he is seeing this ox just standing there drinking and he is saying, oho I will be killing this thing and bringing food back for my family to be eating. He is coming to Ox very quietly until he is so close he is biting Ox on the neck, but at the same time Ox is fighting him and chooking him in the heart with his two big horn. Since they are wounding, they are changing back into human being and seeing that they are brother and not enemy so they are crying crying until they are dying right there and their blood is just running into the river and turning it to brown. Their mother and their father are coming back and finding them dead just like that and the mother is screaming AYIIIEEE and crying and saying that she is needing to get away from this place where her children are dead because it is abomination. So, they are moving up the hill to where the square of the village is now and having more children, but every year, goddess and warrior are coming back to this river with all of the rest of their children to be visiting the place where their son is dying.

AYIIIEEE! woman is just looking at me and screaming. And I am shouting, SHUTUP! SHUTUP! SHUTUP! This woman is enemy. She is killing my family and burning my house and stealing my food and making my family to scatter. And this girl is enemy. She is killing my father and making me to run from my home. I am pulling the girl but she is not letting go of her mother's arm. She is holding holding her so the two of them are like one animal. I am with Strika and we are pulling the girl, pulling until her leg is cracking but she is not letting go. She is screaming and I am seeing her breath is coming out from her mouth, just coming out and coming out. Then Strika is taking his knife high above his head and chopping and everybody is coming apart.

The girl is having no more hand.

She is not screaming or shouting or making any noise. She is just having no more hand. Commandant is saying that she is enemy, she is stealing our food, and killing my family because she is enemy. I am jumping on her chest KPWUD KPWUD and I am jumping on her head, KPWUD, until it is only blood that is coming out of her mouth.

You are not my mother, I am saying to the girl's mother and then I am raising my knife high above my head. I am liking the sound of knife chopping KPWUDA, KPWUDA on her head and how the blood is just splashing on my hand and my face and my feets. I am chopping and chopping and chopping until I am looking up and it is dark.

Another night.

$T$ime is passing. Time is not passing. Day is changing to night. Night is changing to day. How can I know what is happening? It is like one day everything is somehow okay even if we are fighting war, but the next day we are killing killing and looting from everybody. How can I know what is happening to me? How can I know?

Everything is inside out like my shirt I am wearing. Sometimes I am seeing thing in front of me when we are walking or drilling or killing, and sometimes I am seeing thing that I am knowing is coming from before the war, but I am seeing it like they are coming right now. If person is dancing or singing in the camp just to be doing something to not be thinking about war then I am closing my eye and seeing how when I am in my village we are loving so much to dance. We are dancing too because it is how we are learning to become men. Young person is having to spend one whole year learning all the dance that is turning you to man, and if you are not learning, then nobody is thinking that you are man.

If I am seeing celebration in my village it is because I am closing my eye and seeing how everybody is coming to the village square and the men are standing to one side while the women and children and boy who are not dancing are standing on the other. It is starting in the morning when the air is still cool and it is fulling of the smoke from everybody's morning fire. I am remembering how the village square is always being swept clean by all the dancer and how the broom is making line in the sand from the chief's house all the way to the grey wall of the church.

Every year this is happening, my mother is grumbling, it is not good to be celebrating any spirit but God because He is jealous and will be punishing you. But she was still tying her white cloth around her body and wrapping her head in white cloth to be joining the other woman cooking the whole night in the compound of the village chief. And when she is grumbling like this, my father is saying, God is knowing that we are only worshipping him truly, but there are other spirit that we must also be saying hello to.

In the morning, the whole village was standing in the square and wearing their white cloth. I was always looking at all the woman and how they are shutting their eye from tiredness and how the men who are standing are jumping and shaking like they are wanting to be dancing again. Then I am looking to the drummer who are sitting and cracking their finger and putting their ear on the goatskin of their drum just listening to what the drum is wanting to say. And the air was tighting like top of the drum and everybody in the whole place was just agitating.

Everyone is just standing around and agitating when each noise is coming and thinking, is this the time, is this the beginning, but the beginning was never coming when you are thinking. Everybody is just stopping to wait and talking talking about this and that when KPWOM! the first drum is beating and AYIIIEEE! then first dancer is shouting out to be telling everyone to shut up and just be watching. All the dancer is dancing the Dance of the Warrior and they are coming out wearing bell on their ankle and carrying machete that they are making from wood. All of the mask on the face is painting with colour bright like sunrise, colour that is dancing almost as much as they are dancing when the drum is beating and the bell is ringing. They are wearing grass hat that is just talking like the wind in the grasses when they are jumping this way and that way pretending to be fighting until dust is flying everywhere and making people to have catarrh too much.

Then all the dancer is disappearing just like that and everybody was sweating and shouting and smiling before we are feasting on yam with red palm oil, and fish, and meat, and egg with pepper that are making the mouth to be feeling fire so you are having to drink so much water. At this time, the women are talking to themself and the men are talking to themself and the children are playing. But me, I am wanting to dance too much so I am trying to be repeating the dance I am seeing.

And before you are even ready, KPWOM! AYIEEE! And all the dancer is coming back to be dancing the Dance of the Goddess in mask of white chalk and blue paint on their body and blue cloth around their waist. No drum is beating this time, but the women of the village are singing loudly loudly the song of the river goddess while the men are watching and moving from one foot to the other foot.

And in the afternoon, we are eating some more pounded yam and soups with goat meat and oxtail, or rice with chicken and plantain, or roasted maize and salad with leaf fresh from the farm, but nobody is really jubilating because the song is so sweet that it is making you to want to cry, and if you are talking then you are disturbing how sweet it is.

When evening was finally coming and the sun is setting so

the only light is coming from the torch burning in the village square, we are dancing the Dance of the Ox and Leopard. All the dancer was shining with oil and sweat and their feets stomping the ground and their dress is shaking grasses all over the ground. In the orange light, they are looking like spirit themself just dancing in ox-head mask with sharp horn colouring red and white, and also leopard mask with sharp teeths colouring red and white. I am liking this dance the best, how the ox and leopard are just running at each other and falling back, running and falling back, and snapping their arm and their leg, throwing their head from this side to that side until the end of the dance when so much sweat is running down their arm it is looking like the colour of blood in the orange light.

With all of the song from the day sounding in the air above us, the whole village was collecting all our torch, picking up the fire from the square and walking down the road past all of the compound, down to where the path is cutting through palm grove and down to the river. Everybody is rushing rushing because mosquito was biting us and also to be seeing who the head boy cutting the ox will be.

By the river, tied to one palm tree by its horn and its leg an ox was always waiting and stomping and making long low noise that are making you to sadding very much in your heart. The whole village was watching as all the dancer is dancing in the shallow river until the whole water is shining with small small wave. Then the top boy is going to the village chief and kneeling before him while the other leopard and ox dancer are dancing around and around him. The chief is giving him real machete and saying something into his ear until the boy is going and chopping one blow into the neck of the ox. Blood is flying all over his body and he is wiping it from his mask with his hand. Then he is putting his hand where he is cutting and collecting the blood to be rubbing on his body. When he is finishing, all the other is doing the same until everyone is covering in so much blood. They are spinning and spinning in their leopard mask or ox mask until KPWOM! the drum is sounding.

Everybody is knowing that to be killing masquerade you are removing its mask.

All of the dancer is removing their mask.

All of the spirit are dying and now all the boy is becoming men.

I am opening my eye and seeing that I am still in the war, and I am thinking, if war is not coming then I would be man by now.

If I am closing my eye, I am seeing the rainy season and how, in my village, they are saying it is always bringing change too fast. You can be starting in one place with one plan and then finding that the whole world is washing away beneath your feets. You can be walking on road and finding that you are swimming in river. You can be starting day all dry and warm and then be finishing with your clothe like another skin on your body. Nothing is ever for sure and everything is always changing.

It is not like one day I am going to sleep and the next day I am waking up and there is war, but it still is not like we are having time to prepare for this war because everything was still happening so fast that we were not even knowing what really happened.

One day, they are closing school because there is no more government. Part of me is feeling sad because I am liking to be in school and learning. Part of me is also happy because sometimes sitting in the hot classroom and just sweating while everybody else is making noise and all of the younger people are crying is making me to angry. Anyway, we are not having anything to be doing so early one morning I am going to Dike's house because I am knowing he was always waking up early. I went to be standing outside waiting for him because his mother is not liking us to disturb her so early in the morning and I am waiting, waiting, waiting, waiting for so long until the sun is full in the sky and the chicken are starting to fighting each other and quarrelling over the insect and rubbish in the gutter. I was waiting but no one was coming out.

So I was just standing outside Dike's house just watching and looking at how big and nice his house is. It is having nice paint that is always looking fresh, and window that is always looking washed, and also the compound around the house is looking very fine because someone is always cutting the grasses and his father is making sure that nobody is leaving rubbish inside the compound so there is nothing like chicken or goat coming to be eating and messing up the place. I was always wanting to go inside the house but I am knowing not to because Dike's mother is not wanting me inside to be messing up the place with my dirty shoe.

But this time I am standing outside of Dike's house, I am not hearing any of the normal sound like music or singing or crying or shouting coming from inside. I am running around trying all of the door and beating on the iron bar of the window with my hand, but they are locking tight which is not normal because someone was always home at his house. This was making my belly to feel big and too small because Dike is my best friend at this time and I am hoping that something bad is not happening to him or his family. So, I am sitting on the verandah and not knowing what to be doing to solve this problem.

As I was just sitting is when the cook for Dike's house is coming out from the boy's quarter in the back and asking me what I am doing this morning and why I am sitting on the verandah if this is not my house. If you had been looking at my face, you would have been seeing so much happiness because I am now believing that nothing is wrong and maybe they are just going somewhere and will be coming back later. I was looking up because of the voice of the cook, but he was looking sad even though he was smiling because his eye is having red colour and bending down at the edge like he is crying too much. His clothe are having many wrinkle and stain on them like he is fighting food instead of cooking it and also his hand which he is putting on my head are smelling so much of chicken and other nice meats.

He was telling me that Dike and his mother are leaving the last night to meet his father where they are staying in faraway town. I was just looking. Sometimes when you are hearing what you do not want to be hearing then everything in your body stops to working and all you can be doing is looking because unless you are blind then your eye never stop looking. That is how I am looking because my mouth is not working enough for me to speak and even my leg are hardly working for me to move.

Papa said they should just be leaving before war is coming to mess this place up, he is saying to me and I am just looking, but in my head I was feeling so angry because Dike was not telling me if he was leaving. And at all time, we are telling each other all thing because we are best friend almost like brother.

So now I was sitting not knowing what to be doing with my day as there was no school and no Dike. I was feeling like somebody is coming to take everything that I like and just make me to sad. And I am watching the cook, who even though he was still smiling, was also looking sad because he was complaining. Even since I go cook them this food, for all this time. Madam can't even leave nothing for me to find my own way home. Because I no have money like Madam does it mean I no have family to go for find, he was saying to me.

He was sitting next to me and stretching his leg out in front of us so that I am seeing his leg and how they are full of mosquito bite and other dark spot. It was making me to feel somehow in my head and belly when I am looking at it.

I am saying, sorry sorry oh, but he was not even listening to me because he is too busy talking to himself.

Devil bless Madam. Only bad thing go happen to her from now on, he was saying and shaking all the fly away from his head and feets.

Then because I was still feeling angry in my head, and because the cook is acting like madman, I was thinking to be going home. And as I am walking on the road that is going to my home, I am seeing only the feets of all the other people who were living in or had come back to the village because my anger was weighing my head forward. So because of this I am not greeting the older people as I should be doing but nobody was saying anything to me because they were all having their own worry and I was just going on my way until the old woman who is always sitting on her chair selling groundnut that nobody is buying because person are fearing that she is some sort of witch was saying, you are not wanting to greet me? These young person not behaving well anymore, just acting like animal. But it is okay. Trouble go follow you.

And I am remembering that woman even now because I am thinking what she is saying is why my life is so bad.

Behind my eye I am seeing how one day, the younger children began to be growing thinner. Their belly are becoming rounder because other part of their body was growing smaller. When they are running around in the village they are having to hold their clothe to their body because even the elastic was not tighting their trouser enough. My sister was looking this way with her neck and her arm and leg becoming less strong. She was becoming slower in everything she was doing. When she was washing the plate, her head was tipping to her chest and her arm was becoming harder for her to move so that too much water would be splashing in every different direction and causing my mother to scream. But really, even though she was screaming on us all the time, I am knowing inside my head, also because I am hearing her praying, that she is fearing and feeling sad that we are so thin.

Then the people started coming back and everything was changing. The first one that were coming are looking okay. You could see from how their eye is looking this way and that they are fearing, like they are waiting for some animal to jump out from the bush. But when they were coming, they are coming in their car which were filling with more of thing they are owning than with people. Electrician is coming with their electrical thing. Tailor with all of their clothe. Banker with all of his money.

And when they started coming on transport and bus, there were so many women and their children, so many new people that every day everyone from the village is getting dressed very early to go and be waiting at the bus stop and car park to be watching for which relative is returning home and also to be praying that everyone is returning safely.

And then they are taking the light, but it is not changing how we are living too much. My mother is never using electricity to cook and my father's radio is using battery, so we are living like normal. My father was still going into town because his school is still meeting, but then one day, my mother is waking to find me and my father sitting together and looking at how the iron he is heating in the fire is just burning his shirt. The spot was just looking brown and crinkly, making the shirt to look like toilet paper. My father was looking to cry and biting his lip. He is wiping sweat from his forehead with the back of his hand and using his rappa to be cleaning his finger.

They are telling me not to be coming anymore. There is no more school, he is saying through his shirt he is holding up to his mouth. I am wanting to cry for him because I am knowing that he is never crying himself. I am wanting to open my mouth and scream so that everybody is waking up and listening to all of the trouble this war is bringing, but my mother and my father are keeping quiet so I am keeping quiet also.

My mother was just standing facing the compound. Her own clothe was wrapped under her armpit just where the hairs is sticking together from the sweat of her sleep. She is not turning around to us but she is not stepping away or even holding the iron bar on the verandah to be helping her stand up. My father is touching his beard and asking what are we going to do and then he is just looking at my mother's back.

She is saying, stop looking at me and start praying. God is always helping you if you are asking Him. Then she is walking to the kitchen and leaving me and my father just sitting and staring at all the plant in the compound. My father is putting his head in his shirt and saying nothing. I am confusing. How can my father just be sitting there looking like goat that is ready to die? I was getting up to get water for my bath and leaving my father there for the whole day. He was just sitting and not even saying one word to anyone, not even to my sister who is always making him to laugh and be talking talking. I am not knowing if he is going to bed that night because he was still sitting there when I am coming to lock the gate and hang the key.

And then one day, when I am sweeping the parlour, just bending over and using broom to get all of the dust from each corner of the room, my father is rushing into the room sweating like he was running very fast. I am seeing how the sweat is just soaking through his shirt and making his face to shine and I am standing there looking at him wondering what is happening that is making him to look like this. My father is shouting to me, get up! Come on, we are having to go to the church NOW! And I am wondering what it is that is happening because it is not even Sunday. I am wanting to go and change into something but my father is saying to move quick quick and to get my mother so we can be going to church. I am moving quickly and running out to the kitchen where my mother was just humming over one pot of stew, but when she is seeing me, right away she is thinking that something is wrong and so she is running to meet my father on the verandah where he is waiting. And then they are shouting and I am hearing my mother saying, heyeye! The war is come oh! War is coming.

I am asking if I can be going with them to the church and they are saying yes, so my father is carrying my sister who is sleeping because she is having nothing better to do and I am walking with my mother up the path of my village to the church. Even before we are getting inside, I am hearing voice that are even too loud to be coming from service. People are shouting and talking too loud and I am not even able to hear one sentence that anybody is speaking. When we are getting inside the church, the whole place was too hot and smelling like animal because there is no electricity and all the fan cannot be moving round and round to be bringing some air. Everybody in the village was trying to fit into the church so some people are standing on the bench, and other people are leaning on the wall, and everybody is just sweating because it is like we are one million cow just being put in the same space to be living. I am seeing so many people – even people who are not coming to this church, just talking talking and shouting shouting like something bad is going to happen. Pastor and the Chief are standing at the front of the church and shouting but because there is no microphone nobody was really hearing them and everybody was talking over their talking. Pastor is just getting angry and running to one big drum set that is there and beating the cymbal well well until the whole place is sounding KWANG! KWANG! KWANG! We are all shutting up. We are all shutting up except for the sound of too many people breathing.

Pastor was not even wearing his white robe when he is walking around at the front of the church. Instead, he was just wearing one blue shirt and trouser and also one cap to be covering his bald head. He was shouting shouting, DO YOU HEAR! WE CANNOT JUST BE SITTING HERE LIKE COW UNTIL THEY ARE BRINGING THE WAR! It is saying in The Bible that God is only helping those who are helping themselves. Isn't God protecting the Israelites when they are having to leave their own home? So let us be pleasing God and leaving until the fighting is no more in our area. Otherwise they will just be killing killing all of us and then what will we be doing? I am laughing in my head even though my heart is beating fast fast with all of this talk of killing because I am thinking how my father is saying that Pastor is thinking he can be talking so much because he is having his Reverend Doctorate that is making him doctor of talking.

Then the Chief was getting up and wearing his red cap and his black shirt and saying, yes. Yes Pastor is right. We should be leaving. They are telling me that UN is coming to help us go, so when they are coming, we will be going with them. Tomorrow, at least all of the women and the small small children will be going with them first and then after we are making sure that everything is okay with all of the thing we are owning then the men can be finding their way to safety. Am I making it clear?

And then there was shouting shouting, WHO IS UN? WHAT ABOUT MY FARM? AND MY GOAT? AND WHAT ABOUT

ALL MY BOOK? OR MY CAR? ENH! WHAT ABOUT ALL OF THESE THING! the voice are just coming from all of the different place in the church and every time somebody is shouting one thing then every head is turning to that direction to be seeing what it is they are shouting. There was too much grumbling and it was making my head to hurt so I am just standing near to my mother and my father and trying to be making sure that I am not annoying anybody. When we are finishing, everybody is leaving the church and nobody is even remembering to say a prayer because everybody is fearing how the fighting is coming too too near. I am not hearing anything, but my father who is already surviving one war is saying that you will know when war is coming if you are seeing airplane and hearing GBWEM GBWEM which is meaning that they are shelling and bombing.

That night my mother is making a big dinner of all my favourite food which is rice and stew with so much meats, but nobody, not even my father who can be eating three whole plate and even going back for more is able to be eating anything at all at all. After dinner, I am clearing the table and stacking all the plate in one corner because it is even too dark to be washing and when I am coming back to the house I am seeing my mother like one dark spot and the light from the lamp was all around her while she was just packing food into many small bag. I was going to her and tapping her on her elbow to be asking, where we are going to go? And she is saying to me, we are going where we will be going and we will be getting there when we are getting there. I am not even knowing what she is meaning when she is saying this kind of thing, but then I am asking her if she is fearing, and she is looking back at me and bringing me close and hugging me so that my head is resting in her breast. Why should I be fearing Agu? Enh, she is saying. Aren't you remembering that the Lord is protecting everybody and making sure that nothing bad will ever be happening to us? Now go and get ready for bed okay. And don't be forgetting to pray. No matter what is happening remember that God is only remembering those who are praying.

So I am running through the hallway and into the room I am sharing with my sister and when I am getting there I am seeing that she is putting one knife under her bed. What is this for, I am asking her while I am looking at it with lamp and she is saying, for the enemy if they are coming, and then turning her head to be facing the wall. And I am laughing small small even if I am fearing because sometimes my sister, even though she is young, is trying to be too smart.

I was lying down to be sleeping in my own bed, but my whole body was just feeling so hot and everywhere was itching too much like ant is biting me. I am trying to sleep, trying to sleep, but I was not even closing my eye. It was like

I am waiting for Father Christmas, and I am just lying there until the middle of the night when I am hearing my mother and my father talking. What do you mean you are not coming, my mother is saying to my father and I am hearing my father saying back, how can Agu be coming with you if we are supposed to be the men of this village? What is that looking like if everybody is staying to make sure their house is all right and we are just running from place to place? Enh? That is not right. And my mother is saying back to him, no. No. Just remove that thought from your head. God forbid such thing enh. And my father is saying, you are not understanding anything here. And my mother is saying what if you are going and dying, then what am I doing? Do you want me to be sitting by the roadside like some woman with no sense who is just pulling out her hairs and trying to sell it? Then my father is just shouting Wait now! It is my duty and it is his duty as my first son to be – before my mother is shouting YOUR SON THIS AND THAT! Sometimes I am thinking that you are having no sense at all. Let me just be taking him with me enh. If there is war and everybody is dying, then who is even going to say anything if he is not staying around?

My belly was starting to tight too much because I am lying and thinking that I am not wanting to be seeing all the killing but I am also knowing that I cannot just be leaving my father alone here and running off otherwise all of the other men will be laughing at him. So I am just staring at the roof and listening to the rainwater going PAH PAH PAH on the roof and to the lizard that is trying to find place to hide from the heavy rain, but I am not sleeping because I am fearing too too much.

The next morning my father is waking me but I am so so tired and his face was just looking too tired also. He was moving around too fast and just agitating everywhere. I am asking him, where are we going and he is saying, don't worry. Don't worry.

Later, we are all walking to the centre of the village with my mother and sister just carrying this small load and that small load that they are taking with them. So many person was standing there that it is looking like how it is looking during the festival, only nobody is smiling at all. Each family was just staying in one corner and you are seeing all of the mother with their small small children just sitting next to one red-and-white-striped bag that was holding everything they can be taking at one time. And we were just waiting, waiting until the rain is starting to fall onto everything and sticking to it like million tiny insect. Everybody was trying to get into one building or another building in the village square to be waiting and everybody was just looking sad. The men are looking tired and the women are fearing. It is only the small small children that are not knowing what is happening.

Late in the afternoon we are hearing all of many truck rumbling up, big white truck with the letter UN in black on the side. Soldier in blue helmet and green camouflage is just jumping down from the truck even as they are moving and their tyre is just chewing up the whole ground. They are shouting to just remain in order, and then they are shouting at us to load up onto all the truck and I am looking at my father who is helping my mother to be carrying one bag to the truck with all of the other women and their children. I am seeing how my father's mouth is just being pulled down at the edge, and I am seeing how he is not even wanting to be letting go of my sister or my mother. My mother is touching me and holding me and telling me to remember to be praying praying all the time and not to be worrying, that we will be seeing each other soon. I am seeing my father pushing my mother onto the truck and then I am remembering how her hand is feeling in my own hand and then I am remembering standing with my father while she and my sister are just going away on the truck and that is the last time I am ever seeing them.

And I am seeing behind my eye how it is just men and boy in the village sadding too much because war is taking everything away from us. Nothing in the village is the same without women cooking food and selling groundnut and talking talking so all of the men are just staying quietly quietly like somebody is dying. I am seeing all of this and I am seeing how one day, I was not seeing excepting light that was pushing through hole in the roof but it was not enough. The whole place was so hot and I am sweating too much. My short was soaking through and my shirt was touching my body like skin. How many of us are there just sitting in this place? I am not knowing but I am thinking maybe ten or fifteen or even more. There are too many that our fear is just smelling and the whole room is just tasting like salt. Outside I am hearing bullet everywhere and shouting and screaming.

I am asking my father, will they be killing us? Will they be killing us?

Somebody was slapping my face and saying SHUTUP. Is it my father who was slapping me? It is so dark, but I am knowing it is not him. My mouth was filling with blood and I am knowing the colour of blood is red just red everywhere. I was wiping my mouth with my arm but my sweat was making my lip to sting too much. I was wanting to see, but the only light that was here is coming through small small hole in the ceiling. The door was locked and I am trapped. We are all trapped because of the bullet outside.

I am hearing my father's voice, look. You can be dying now or dying later. It is all the same. Are you wanting to sit here until they are coming to burn us to ash? Enh? Remember now, you can only be dying once. If you are not dying standing anyway, you will be walking on your knee with all the ancestor. I am knowing that this is bad thing because if you are walking on your knee then you are always having to look up when somebody is talking to you and if they are talking to you then their spits will just be flying into your face. A voice is saying, I am rather to be living now inside than to just be dying like animal outside. And people are whispering, yes, yes. And my father is whispering, then your son will be spitting on your grave enh.

And more people are whispering, yes yes. It is true. It is true.

Are we ready?

Nobody is saying anything at all, but I am hearing machete scraping the floor. Outside it is still sounding of bullet and laughing like goat chewing on metal. I am fearing so much that my feets is feeling like they are belonging to the man standing next to me. And my hand is feeling like they are being carved from stone. My father was telling me that when we are going out I should just be running running. Running in the other direction. It is okay, he is saying. It is okay. If you are running fast, then the enemy won't be seeing you. I am asking to him if we are going to die but he is not saying anything. It is all quiet except for everybody breathing like cow or goat in the pen. Will we die, I am asking? Will they be killing us? I am having another slap on my face.

Bullet was just sounding so loud and there was so much screaming and shouting and laughing. They are finding us.

Somebody was groaning and mumbling that they will be using our body after they are killing us. They will just be loading us onto one truck, bleeding like that so our blood is dripping from the edge and flying off into the wind. And they will be driving us into the bush so we cannot even be buried in our own village and just leaving us for the animal to be eating like that. Another person is saying that they will be playing with our body and using our intestine as whip to be whipping each other and cutting off our hand and holding them to be shaking each other. One more voice was saying, they are the Devil, I am seeing it with my own eye. They are looking like monster with half face, long fingernail, and sharp teeths. He is saying they are looking like the Devil because you cannot even be living long enough to see them, and if you are living, then you are already becoming Devil like them.

Shutup! Shutup! There is no time, somebody is shouting and then I am hearing another person counting, one, two, three and the door is opening to let in so much light that is blinding me. I am not seeing anything anymore, just white light everywhere. I am hearing everybody sucking in breath and I am sucking in breath too. The air is smelling of burning wood and gunpowder and gasoline. I am hearing more shouting and then I am hearing my father saying run. RUN! RUN! AGU RUN! and I am saying, I am running if the other man is not having my leg but then somebody is pushing me and I am just running. I am seeing soldier with black face and big white smile. I am seeing bullet making my father to dance everywhere with his arm raising high to the sky like he is praising God. I am hearing terrible laughing and I am running, running, running through the mud but the mud is trying to hold me. I am smelling how it is smelling like the butcher shop and I am hearing, THEY ARE KILLING ME OH! JESUS CHRIST HELP ME! HELP ME! I am seeing man running with no head like chicken, and I am seeing arm and leg everywhere. Then everything is just white and all I am hearing is step slap, step slap, step slap, and the sound of my own breathing.

All of this is really happening to me? It is all happening like it is happening again and I cannot even be believing it.

I am opening my eye and seeing how everywhere is dark in some place and orange with fire and lamp in other place. I am seeing men lying everywhere with gun lying next to them. My heart is beating beating, so fast. I am feeling thirsty.

We are at the camp and I am watching how the sun is just dropping down behind the hill like it is not wanting to be seeing us anymore. All the colour is leaking out of it and looking like flame from hell all over, eating up the top of all the tree, making all the leaf bright bright. Suddenly it is night. The earth is changing from bright orange to black and I am seeing steam rising up from some darkness, just chasing the sun away.

At this time, I am thinking all the building of this camp we are living in is not just the terrible place that we are to be sleeping but are looking almost like simple village house made of palm wood and thatch. I am looking and thinking that if we are not having war, then this place would be too nice to be looking at. All the palm tree, so kind to us, giving us oil and wine, is stretching high up to where they are brushing the sky clear of cloud after it is raining. And when the night is coming, I am thinking the bird and animal should just be singing back and forward to each other before they are going to be sleeping.

But we are coming here and bringing the war. When we are coming here, we are stripping all the palm tree to build our shelter and because there is no more place to rest all the bird is flying away. The night is now too quiet because we are so hungry that we are eating everything that is making noise. And those thing that we are not catching stopped to making noise so they are not getting eaten. Behind this camp, there is also stream that was just shining in the clear sunshine and smelling so fresh with life that you are even seeing how the fishes is enjoying and the frog and their baby is acting like they are in heaven, but we are emptying our rubbish and using this place for washing ourself and going to toilet so it is becoming terrible to look at.

I am just watching as they are unloading all the thing that we are looting from different village off all the truck. I am watching as the sun is leaving small by small from the sky and how all the colour is making truck driver's skin to be shining when they are going into the engine to make sure that they are running well well for the next day. And in the small small light, they are coming out just shining with oil even if it is getting dark. Still if I am looking too hard they are beginning to disappear like ghost. All I am seeing is their eye blinking like all the firefly that are one time living in this area. They are walking to the stream to wash off and their singing is making me to feel somehow at ease. I am stretching my leg out in front of me and placing my hand behind my head.

Every night they are making fire and soldier is sitting down and talking. After some time I am getting up to go and sit with them around the fire. It is warm and it is making me to feel a little bit okay and I am happying to be back at the camp because it is nice here – at least nicer than having to be in place with all of its screaming people that you are killing all the time. And here, I am relaxing because there is no enemy that I have to be watching out for if they are wanting to kill me. But I am sitting here listening to the other men talking and breathing and breathing and somehow looking alive. When it is so, we are really all just waiting to die, I am still sadding too much. I am not liking to be sad because being sad is what happens to you before you are becoming mad. And if you are becoming mad then it is meaning that you are not going to be fighting. So I cannot be sad because if I cannot be fighting, then either I will die, or Commandant will be killing me. If I am dead, then I will not be able to be finding my mother and my sister when this war is finishing. I am thinking to myself of all the thing that I will do when the war is over and I am alive. And I am thinking that when it is over, I can be going to university to study. I think I am wanting to be Engineer because I like how mechanic is always doing thing to the truck and I like to be watching even though there is no chance for me to try what they are doing. And sometimes I am thinking that I want to be Doctor because then I will be able to be helping people instead of killing them and then maybe I will be forgiven for all my sin. I am thinking that if I am both Doctor or Engineer, these people are the one who are the big men. I know because the richest man in our village – even though he was old and died before the war is coming – he was Doctor and he was always having little monies to be giving out to people who are asking him. He was also big man with fat stomach because he was having lots of monies to be eating a lot of thing here and there. So also when I am big man, I know that I can be reading my book without anyone troubling me like they used to be troubling me before and nobody will be able to say anything to me. I will be saying all the thing to person, telling them to do this and do that and making sure that they bow their head and only look at the ground when they come to greet me, also making sure that they bring me my water when I want it or that they are bringing me my food when I want it. And I will be fat because big men are always fat; they are always having so much to eat. And I will be eating all the food until my stomach is full and then I will be eating even more until my stomach is so full that I will not be able to see my feets even if I am stretching my neck all the way forward. I think that this will be fine because if I am ever not able to eat for long period of time then at least I will not be turning into ghost like we are turning into because of war.

Then I will go back to church. I will go back to church to ask God for forgiveness every day. And I will go back to church and sit on the bench under the fan that one day will just be falling and crushing me and I will not even be minding the splinter that is chooking into my leg because I will be paying attention to Jesus. I won't even be moving my eye from the statue of Jesus and instead I will just be sitting there watching him and watching him until one day he will be telling me that it is okay.

I am smelling food that they are cooking that is making me so hungry. What should I do? When we are killing people, their blood is getting all over the food we are stealing from them. It is getting all over their animal and vegetable. We are finding farmer and his goat on the road and we are killing him. Now I am not knowing what is farmer and what is goat. And the yam, they are having blood on them. And the rice, they are having blood on them. All the other soldier are saying that since they are boiling it that nothing will be happening to us, but I am not thinking you can be boiling away the blood of farmer even if you are boiling rice or yam forever. But I am hungry and I am eating vegetable and fruit and rice and meats and I am not thinking anymore. I am only eating. When we are eating, we are not speaking. We are so hungry and just eating and eating until we are so full all we can be doing is sleeping sleeping.

We are going to be sleeping in our four building that we are making them of stick and palm thatch. They are not even having any wall, just roof to keep the rain from beating us, so all of the insect is coming up to us in the night. There is not enough room for all of us under these building, so some soldier is sleeping outside and where the rain can be falling on them. No animal is coming up to eat anybody because they are all gone away. They are so afraid of us that they are not wanting to come back.

We are all lying down to sleep, but I am not sleeping. I cannot be sleeping. I can never be sleeping. I am just listening listening. No noise. Then I am hearing one boy talking talking. We are calling him Griot because he is always telling story when we are falling asleep. This is story he is telling:

I was just with my mother when the war is coming, he is saying. This is how he is starting every night when we are trying to be sleeping. We are just in the market to get some food because we are having no food to eat, not even the skin of cassava. I was just in the market when I am hearing GBWEM! I am just hearing one blast and the whole ground began to shaking shaking. And then those government pilot, they are just coming in low with their screaming plane and I was covering my ear but the drum were just beating BOTU BOTU BOTU because the pilot was shooting TAKA TAKA TAKA and everybody is running this way and that way. This one is hiding under wheelbarrow. That one is hiding in church. This one is jumping in gutter. I am not knowing where to be hiding so I am just running running up and down the road. I am hearing another GBWEM landing right next to me. And then I was feeling fire on my body but I wasn't burning. When I am looking up, I am seeing people hanging from tree like piece of meat. Head just hanging like coconut before it is falling off. Ah ah. Nah wah oh!

No noise.

But not for too long because he is starting again. He is saying, my mother. My mother. Heyeye now. My mother is dead. All of her meats just hanging from tree. Then he is coughing and beginning to shake – I am hearing him moving on the ground where he is lying.

And then there is boy we are calling Preacher who is not coming from village. He is coming from the bush. He is twisting around in his sleeping and singing song I am never hearing before. Thou art worthy. Thou art worthy oh Lord, he is singing in his deep voice that is making me to fear because it is sounding like it is coming from nowhere, from spirit. Preacher is having Bible that he is using as pillow sometimes. That is why we are calling him Preacher. His Bible is so tattered that it is not even staying together by itself anymore and he is having to hold it together with piece of old shirt. He is keeping it in his pocket with his knife and his extra bullet.

But he is asleep and singing, thou art worthy. Thou art worthy oh Lord, over and over again. I am not asleep, and I am now singing with him even if I am not knowing all the word. For thou has created. All thing and for thy pleasure. They a-a-are and were created. Thou art worthy, because the song keeps going round and round and round again and again.

But then there is light shining in my face and when I am opening my eye it is blinding me. I am stopping to breathing because I am seeing Strika's face looking like spirit or demon. His skin is looking somehow like burned-up wood or charcoal and it is sticking tight to his face so his whole cheek is sticking out sharp sharp. I am saying, leave me. Leave me alone. But then I am looking in his eye and the way that he is trying to tell me that I should not be lying here and that I should be hurrying up – Commandant is wanting to see me right now. I am not liking it when Commandant is wanting to see me, but I am having to go otherwise it will be making him to angry. I am getting up, but it is not easy to do this. And when I am standing up I am stretching my body and watching as Strika is going back quickly to his own place where he is sleeping which is under one of the truck with all of the truck driver. Then, I am picking up my knife that I am having with me because I am never leaving my knife just in case the enemy is coming and I am stepping over people's head and feets to be getting to where Commandant is staying. The way I am walking through the darkness, I am like animal in the night. Tonight it is all so quiet and I am thinking it is because of the killing we are doing. I am walking this way and just stepping over people and stepping around them and their gun and knife trying not to be waking them up so that there will not be any kind of trouble.

Then I am walking past the other soldier to Commandant's own quarter and just watching him through his mosquito net as he is moving back and forward. He is the only one with mosquito net. I am seeing the shadow that he is making as he is moving around his room and I am thinking that only big man can be making such big shadow.

When I am reaching the shack, I am looking through the net and seeing Commandant. They are calling him the man who is driving the enemy to madness. He is fighting in many battle even if he is only young man, so he is always telling story of people who are treating death like lover and child who can kill before they can even speak. And he is always saying that he is seeing thing that are making even the Devil fall to his knee and be begging for mercy. He is always saying that he is eating people, but it is not tasting too good. And he is saying he is seeing people eat people like they are real meats.

I am waiting outside in the darkness making myself ready for when I go in. So I am thinking as many good thing I can think because if you are thinking good thing, nothing bad is happening to you.

Each time I am going to Commandant, I am feeling that I should not go in because I am knowing what he is wanting to do to me. I am thinking that each time I should be telling him that I do not want to fight anymore and that he should let me go and become refugee so that at least I will not be having to kill people. But I know that if I am saying this to him, he will be doing the same thing he is doing when he is not happy which is smiling and licking his teeths with his tongue. Then he will just laugh but it will be angry laugh that he is doing when he is thinking somebody is becoming spy.

Commandant is sitting on the floor with all of his map lying next to him. Even though I am standing at the doorway for long time, he is not looking up at me. I am coughing to be letting him know that I am here, but he is still not looking at me and instead he is looking so tired, just like the rest of us because he is not wearing his dress uniform. He is having only one rappa tied around his waist and between his leg and dirty shirt on. And he is kneeling down on the ground wiping sweat from his head with that same dirty white handkerchief that I am always seeing him using for everything he is doing. It is even looking like he is talking to himself because of all of the thing that he is trying to look at though the light is not bright enough for me to even be seeing my hand if I am holding them up in front of me. When he is on the ground, he is not looking so good because he is having all his finger in his mouth and is rubbing the top of his bald head with the other hand.

What is taking you so long, he is saying to me before I am coming in. Then he is saying, sit down, pointing to cot in the corner of the room. He is Commandant so he is always getting cot to sleep on while the rest of us is sleeping on whatever there is to be sleeping on – if you are lucky it is mat, but mostly it is the ground. Even so, it is not changing anything of what I am thinking while I am standing at the door because I am not liking at all at all how his room is smelling – like animal house after animal is passing the food he is eating – or how this smell is making my nostril to sting like I am breathing in something very sharp like metal. I am also not wanting to move because I am fearing that I am in trouble even if I am not doing any-thing wrong today. I am moving myself slowly slowly around the edge of the hut, feeling the branch of the thatch chooking into my buttom as I am sliding along to the cot. By the time I am reaching the cot and sitting down, he is still looking at the map and taking Biro to be drawing out thing even if it is so dark he is hardly seeing. I am also thinking as I am rubbing the mud off my feets and then folding my arm up in my lap how it is strange that all of these men are always looking at this whole country on map and acting as if it is piece of meat they can just be dividing by cutting it with knife.

Commandant is just coughing and rubbing his head and arm and talking to himself before finally he is blowing out the candle one by one by one until all the room is dark. When he is finished, I am looking through the mosquito net to where I can see the fire outside. It is very low now but still I am wanting to be outside where the other soldier is sleeping, where Griot is talking and Preacher is singing, but I am not saying this to Commandant. He is telling me, take off your clothe.

I do not want to be taking off my clothe but I am not saying so because Commandant is powerful more than me and he is also sometimes giving me small small favour like more food or protection and other thing like shirt or trouser for doing this thing with him. It is making me to feel a bit better when he is giving me these thing because I am knowing that he can be doing what he is wanting to do with me and not giving me anything after. I am hearing him walk over to me where I am sitting on the cot. He is taking off my clothe for me and then he is sitting down next to me and breathing hard, but not like he is running very hard and trying to catch his breath, a different breathing in my ear that I am not liking to listen to at all at all. Then he is beginning to touch me all over with his finger while he is breathing just even harder. But each time he is doing this to me, he is telling me, it is what commanding officer is supposed to be doing to his troop. Good soldier is following order anyway and it is order for you to let me touch you like this. I don't want to be good soldier, but I am not saying that. I don't want to be soldier at all. I don't want his finger creeping all over my body. I don't want his tongue to be touching me and feeling like slug should be feeling if it is on your body. I don't want it on my back and even on my leg. And I am thinking it is not good for Commandant to be doing this to me. But I am not saying any of this. I am not saying anything at all. It is making me to angry and it is making me to sad, the thing that he is doing to me. I am knowing that I am not the only one he is doing this to and that is not making me to happy.

Commandant is touching me and bringing my head to where he is standing at attention. As he is doing it, and I am smelling his smell and feeling how much it is making me to want to vomit, I am thinking about the very first time he is doing this and yelling to me, touch his soldier. It is seeming like so long long ago but this is not mattering because each time it is still feeling like the very first time. This first time I am even lucky because we are not in place like this and there is bed that is not cot. But even so, that time he was telling me to kneel down on the floor and then he is removing his belt and I am fearing so much that I am doing something wrong and that he is going to beat me so hard for what I am doing even if I am not knowing what it is. That time he was saying, relax. I am not punishing you. Then he is saying, remove your clothe.

So I was removing them. And then, after making me be touching his soldier and all of that thing with my hand and with my tongue and lip, he was telling me to kneel and then he was entering inside of me the way the man goat is sometimes mistaking other man goat for woman goat and going inside of them. If you are watching it, then you are knowing it is not natural thing. But me, I was not struggling because I am knowing that he will be killing me if I am struggling and since I am not wanting to die, I just let him to be moving back and forward even though it is hurting me so so much. That first time because we are still having food and thing, he was putting palm oil all over me to make everything easier, he is saying, so it will not be paining me so much. Sometimes if palm oil is not enough, my buttom is burning like it has fire in it.

That first time after he is finishing and I am leaving him, I was going to lie down but I could not. I was asking Strika whether his own was hurting so much the first time, and he was drawing me picture in the mud of man bending down with his hand on the ground and gun and bullet shooting up his buttom. The picture was very funny, but I am not smiling. I was feeling I can never be smiling again. I was deciding that it was time for me to leave because I felt that I was bleeding and I did not want to be bleeding in front of him or the other soldier otherwise they might be laughing at me and calling me woman. So, that time I am leaving him in the darkness of the room where we are sleeping and taking the lantern and going on my way to find the stream. This time I am not even fearing because I am so angry and confusing in my head about what was happening that I am just walking along the path not even thinking that there is any animal or spirit or the Devil to come and get me. And when I am reaching the stream, I am letting myself to fall in backward with my buttom first, and then I am feeling the water rising up to my chest and all around my face. If I was brave boy, then I would have been swallowing water or rock or something that would have made me to stop breathing and sink right to the bottom where I would just be staying forever, but I am not wanting to die this way because the ancestor will not be letting you to come and live with them. Instead your spirit will just be living wherever you are leaving your body. I was staying under and holding my breath and then trying to open my mouth but each time I was becoming afraid and swinging my arm and scaring the frog to be making too much noise.

That first time, I am walking back to my camp in the darkness with all the ancestor making noise in my head, with my feets going this way and that into the thorn because it was hurting me too much to walk straight. I was tripping and pounding and trying to keep the lamp from falling unless Commandant would beat me because the lamp is very costly. It is taking me so long to be getting back to the building where Strika was sleeping that by the time I am returning, I am finding Strika sleeping on his mat. I was not knowing where my own mat was, so I just started lying down on the concrete beside him. Then I was feeling his arm around me even though he is not opening his eye to be showing that he is awake. I was not sleeping and was watching him the whole night, shifting, sucking his finger, grabbing his thing, and beating the air with his hand. When the morning was just coming around, I began to be feeling tired and sleepy even more than I was feeling the pain in my buttom and also in my head so I slept. I must have been sleeping for long time because when I am waking, Strika was gone, leaving only scratching in the ground next to me saying, God will punish him.

But now he is doing the same to me over and over and over and I am used to it somehow even though it is also making me to feel as if I am still feeling it for the first time. He likes to be whispering to me as if I am woman and this time when he is finishing, he is running his hand up and down my back to wipe away the sweat, and then he is rubbing my head like I am still little boy. He is quieting when we are finishing, so quiet I can hear him cleaning himself with his handkerchief and then sitting back down on the cot.

When he is finishing this time, the light from the fire is still showing through the mosquito net and Commandant is sitting at the edge of the bed with his hand between his leg. He is rocking back and forward and I am trying to know what he is thinking. I am holding my own hand against my buttom and pressing it to stop the pain. And I am putting my head down in his pillow which is smelling of sweat and having little splinter of chewing stick sticking out from inside it. This his cot is not even strong enough to be holding both of us and is creaking with every breath he is taking. My tongue is shifting back into my mouth because I am afraid that I will be biting it off to stop the pain. He is taking deep breath and sucking in all of the shadow in the room like they are food to him.

Agu, he is saying. But he is so tired his word is dragging instead of jumping off of his tongue. Do you want to know something? Let me tell you something.

I am not wanting to know anything he is telling me. I am not wanting to be hearing his voice even if it is only sounding like dull knife because he is so tired. I am not wanting to hear him breathing or to be smelling the anger or worry in his breath. All of this is making me to want to take the fire from outside and be swallowing it so that it is burning out my inside and making me empty shell. But I am saying Sah! Yes Sah! He is putting his hand on the back of my head and I am swallowing hard. The spit is growing in my mouth and I am drooling on the pillow. He is looking at my back, and I am feeling his eye all up and down my naked body. I can feel his stare crawling on my skin like many ant that is moving slowly slowly on the land and eating the world to many piece in one million tiny bite. I am turning and looking at him from the corner of my eye. Even though the room is not having too much light, I am seeing his eye with the red and it is making me to think he is demon. The light is making his nose to sharp more and his lip to shine too much with saliva from his tongue so he is just looking like he is eating very good meal.

Agu. I am not bad man, he is saying softly and putting his hand on my back.

My tear begin to running down my face and are mixing with my spit in the pillow. I want to be telling him that I cannot be fighting anymore, that my mind is becoming rotten like the inside of fruit. But I am knowing that if I am saying anything like this, he will be slapping me the way he is always slapping all the other soldier – until their bloody teeths is cutting his hand. I am biting into the pillow so I will not be making any noise. I am feeling the wooden splinter digging into the top of my mouth and tongue. I am wanting to leave.

Commandant is dragging his finger down the back of my neck and letting them dance and drum on the bump of my back. They are feeling like many drop of hot hot boiling water. Then he is closing his hand around my own hand and moving them away from my buttom.

Don't worry, he is saying. It will be okay.

We are leaving this place and before we are leaving we are tearing it all down. Tearing it all down. The morning is cool and it feels nice on my skin. And if there is no war and we are normal person and not soldier, we are jubilating and saying, how nice the morning feels. How nice it is before the sun is coming out from all the cloud. We are all waking up and walking around stretching our arm and leg, and we are all hungry. Nobody is eating. Everyone here is doing zero zero one. I am not knowing what this is meaning before I am soldier, but now I am knowing that it means no breakfast, no lunch, only dinner. If you are wanting to eat when it is not dinner, then you are having to keep your dinner from before to be eating the next day. Or if we raiding or finding farm, then we can be eating.

We are all knowing what to do when it is time to be leaving. Food is going in one truck. Kerosene and fuel is going in another truck, and everybody is making sure he is having his own gun or knife because if you are losing this gun or knife, then Commandant will be losing you.

So this is what we are doing, loading this and loading that until finally we are pulling all of the building into one pile of palm and wood and so before we are leaving the camp, we can be burning it all up. Burning it all up. Commandant is saying, quick. Tear it down. Make the pile. We are not wanting to leave any nice place for Government to be using if they are coming this side. Soldier is getting kerosene ready from one jerry can and pouring it all over all the palm that is just lying there like dead thing, and then Commandant is coming to me with match and saying to me, you should be lighting the fire. Commandant is making it big honour to be lighting the fire and I am knowing that he is giving it to me only because I am saluting his soldier for him. I am liking very much to be setting fire but it is still not making me like what he is doing to me last night. Nothing he is giving me is ever making me to like that, but I am not saying it or he will be beating me.

I am taking the match from Commandant and striking them well well until I am hearing SHHKA and seeing the fire on the

112

end of the matchstick. The smell is coming into my nose and making me to want to sneeze. I am holding the match, holding the match until the fire is just eating up the stick and then I am throwing it like that into the pile. The whole place is bursting into big flame but no GBWEM! like if they are bombing or shelling. It is still very hot and still rising up quick quick until everything is burning burning. The flame is having the colour of sunset, just orange everywhere but everything it is touching it is only making them black so quick that there is nothing nice to be looking at. I am not liking the way this orange is just making black smoke to be flying everywhere and if you are looking through it, it is making everything to move back and forward even if it is standing still.

We are all watching for some while and drinking in the smell of the smoke rising up up to the sky. I am watching all the other soldier around us and how everyone is staring at the fire growing bigger and bigger until it is becoming to be very hot and we were also not wanting to be waiting around because the smoke is now beginning to get into our chest and making us to cough and getting into our eye and making us to cry.

Then we are lining up and I am next to Strika waiting to take my place in the truck and watching all the other soldier load up quick quick until the weight is making all the truck to groaning like wounded beast. We are waiting, but before we are getting in, Commandant is coming over and we are saluting him. He is saying to us, no. No. You two are bodyguarding me today. You will be riding in my own car with me.

There are so many of us to be sitting on one seat of Commandant's truck, but we are all squeezing in. Driver is sitting behind the wheel. I am sitting next to driver, Strika is sitting next to me, and Commandant is sitting next to the other door. Inside of Commandant's truck is so nice past anything that all the other soldier are even having. His seat is not made of wood but cushion so it is feeling very nice on your buttom when you are sitting on it. He is having button to be bringing down the window and you can even be turning on the radio when you are driving so we can be listening to music. Driver is turning it on and we are all moving our head up and down like lizard and tapping our finger to the song.

But I am looking out the window too and seeing how thing is just flashing by so fast, WHOOSH there is tree, WHOOSH there is house, WHOOSH there is person, and I am thinking that everything is moving so fast, I will be old man before the war is over. I am knowing I am no more child so if this war is ending I cannot be going back to doing child thing. No. I will be going back to be teachering or farming, or Doctor or Engineer and I will be finding my mother and my sister, but not my father because he is dying in this war.

My thinking is like the road, going on and on, and on and

on, until it is taking me so far far away from this place. Sometimes I am thinking of my life far far ahead and sometimes I am thinking of all the life I am leaving behind. And then I am looking at Commandant and Strika and I am also thinking to myself that both of them are looking so peaceful and beautiful like how we are looking before the war, like how we are being after the war, but not like now. Now we just be looking like animal.

Driving driving and walking walking and driving driving and walking walking and fighting and soldiering and running from road into bush and bush onto road. That is all we are doing. That is the only thing we can be doing until one day we are coming to one town. Commandant is calling it his town because he is living here as soldier sometimes before this war is starting. I am seeing sign that is saying, Welcome to the Town of Abundant Resources. I can read so I am knowing what welcome is meaning. I am knowing what town is meaning. And I am knowing what is abundant resources. But still I am wanting to know what this sign is meaning for us. I am wanting to ask somebody but I am not saying anything. No word is coming out of my mouth.

As we are standing on this road, I am seeing the breezes and feeling the grasses. I am mixing up, but I am knowing always to be keeping my mouth closed. I am not saying anything, but I am thinking nothing is easy. I am not happying anymore. I am not happying ever again.

Before we are coming here, Commandant is telling me how his town is fine past any other town, that this place is like paradise they are always talking about in Bible. In this place, he is saying, in this place enh. Everything is so fine. If you are looking from the top of hill, you are seeing how all the house is having different colour roof, red, green, blue, yellow, orange so the whole place is just looking like field of flower stretching all the way up to the river which is shining shining. Ah, this river is shining so bright at the end of the town like one big piece of tin lying on the ground. We are always saying, he is saying, that in this place, maybe one day, big bird will just be coming down and carrying it off because he is thinking it is tin and not water. And ah ah! Agu, we are always having light all the time, and water and so many foods to be eating like chicken, and cow, and goat, and vegetable, and fruit, any kind fruit you are wanting because trader is always bringing everything he is having to this place to be selling. There is nothing they are not selling in this place. If you are wanting beautiful clothe, you can have clothe. If you are wanting beautiful wood, you can have wood, and jewellery – gold and silver. It is all here. We are having it all. But that is not even what I am really liking.

He is saying, the best thing this town is having is all the womens. Ah, woman in this place is just too beautiful. If you just see woman here, before you are even knowing it, your soldier is standing at full tenshun. They are having breast big like pillow and so nice and round that their clothe is even rejoicing to be holding them. And they are having buttom that is just rounding so nice that anytime they are sitting down, chair is also rejoicing. They are knowing well well how to make man feel so good with their kissing and loving. He is saying, kai! the last time I am in this place, enh! I am having four womens in one day until my soldier is hurting too much for me to even be easing myself.

You cannot even be knowing how nice this place is. It is just too nice, he is saying. And I am looking at him with my eye so open. So he is saying to me, why are you looking at me with your eye open like that? Enh? You think it is lie? Agu, enh, you think it is lie?

Let me be telling you how town is coming to this place, he is saying. Long long ago, he is saying, but not so long ago that there is no human but before human is really travelling from one village to the next village, there was trader who was just

119

trading small small clothe in his own village. He is greedy man just trying to make his money from anything he is having, so all of the people in his village are living very poor and he is the only one living rich with the biggest compound, the most yam, and the most wife and child than anybody in his village – even the chief.

So one day there was small famine in the whole of the village, not too big but big enough that people are beginning to hungry too much and since it is famine, the land is not even giving anything for them to be eating because the land is hungry itself. So they are coming to the richest Cloth seller, all of them the whole village in their brown rag and their dry skin. And they are asking him in one big voice that is just weak even though there are so many of them, Please Papa. Please give us food you are storing because we are so hungry and you are so rich. And the Cloth seller was sweating and looking to his storage and then looking to everybody in the village and saying, why are you asking me for my yam? Are any of you helping my family and me when I am harvesting them? And then all of the village people were hmmming and ahahing between themself because it is all of their monies that is making this man to be so rich that he can be planting so many yam. So everybody in the village was just angrying at this Cloth seller and shouting that he is not having any heart, and attacking him and his family until the man – who was also coward – is just running running, leaving his family to all the angry people agitating for food.

He was travelling, travelling, travelling through the bush looking left and right, walking for many many day, too many day. No food. No water. All his clothe tearing by the bush and his feets cutting with root and rock in the road until one day he is finding one old woman lying on the road. The woman was having only one eye and no teeths so that you are not even hearing what she is saying too much of the time. Cloth seller was seeing that she is smelling of food so he was going to her and saying, Mma. Please Mma. Help me. I am just small trader leaving his village for trading but robber on the road is attacking me and now I am having nothing, not even one drop of water to drink. The old woman he is talking to is witch and she is saying to him, don't worry. If you are helping me to do something, then I will be giving you anything you are wanting. Normal, this man is not really helping to anybody and just trying to help himself, but this time he is hungrying so much that he is listening well well.

Witch is saying, I am old woman just too weak to be moving from my place under this nice tree, but my house is not too too far. Go into my house and be bringing yam pottage I am making but do not be eating any of it until you are here. So Cloth seller was following what Witch is saying and finding her hut in the middle of bush. It was smelling so bad like refuses all around and the whole mud of the hut is melting back into the ground because she is only having one leg and not able to be fixing it all the time like you are always having to fix mud hut. He was also smelling yam pottage so he was going into the hut and finding in the middle, on the fire, big bowl of it. At this time, he was hungrying so much that he is sitting down and eating some food for himself. When he was finishing, he was fulling so much that he is lying down his head on the ground and sleeping.

When he is waking up, he was seeing that there was not even very much yam pottage left, so he is very shameful and picking up the pot from the fire and rushing back to Witch thinking, oh my God! What can I be doing? What can I be doing? When he is getting to the place he is leaving Witch, he is saying to her before she is even having chance to speak, Mma please. I am so sorry I am just spilling yam pottage onto the ground that is why there is only small small food left. Please be forgiving me because I am not meaning to do you any harm. Witch is looking at him and saying to him, are you eating well? And he is answering, yes well well. The food is very good, before he is even knowing what he is saying. Then she is looking up at him and saying ah ah liar. You know that I am Witch and watching you with my one eye I am leaving in my house. And she was shouting on the man. But Cloth seller was saying to Witch, I am travelling for too many day and I am so hungry and tired. Please. Please. Please. Witch was saying, that is fine since you are helping me at least have some food. I am sorrying for you and will be giving you one wish before you are moving on. What is it that you are wanting most in this world?

Cloth seller was just thinking, even having his mouth to watering more when he is hearing this woman saying this thing. How can she, he was asking himself, how can she be asking me this? Then he is saying to her, I can be having anything that I am wanting in this whole world? Anything? And she is saying, yes. Anything. So the man is remembering all of the nice thing he is leaving in his village. All of the nice clothe and food, the nice bed and other thing and then he was saying to her, Mma. Please. If you are giving me anything in the world, then I am wanting all the richness that you can be having in this world. Witch was angrying. She is saying, foolish somebody. Stupid man. All you are thinking about is what you are wanting. She was angrying so much that she is getting up and hopping on her one foot. She is shouting, go on your way. In small small while you will be finding river. Lie down by this river and make your bed and when you are waking up, you will be having everything you are ever wanting.

He is not even saying one more word to Witch. Cloth seller was rushing off into the bush and after some little time was coming to the bank of great river that was just shining silver with all the sun. He was kneeling down and laughing to himself because he was almost having all of the rich in the world. Then he is finding one rock for his pillow and even though he was too too happy to be sleeping, he was putting his head down and finally, after some time, falling asleep.

This Cloth seller is never waking up. Instead, he is becoming the market and having everything that anybody can ever be wanting. That is why you can be standing above this town and seeing how it is looking like man lying near the river. And that is why they are saying, you can never be trusting anybody or anything in this town. It is the market. It is having everything but nothing is ever really how it is looking.

Commandant is telling this to me and I am stopping to open my eye wide wide. I am looking this way and that, just seeing how all of the soldier is agitating and agitating. They are talking about all food and drink and womens they will be finding for this place. As we are moving down the hill into the town, I am seeing market stretching forever and ever swallowing up all of the house and building in this town. Everywhere, the street is full of refuses which are lining the road up and down and smelling like dead body rotting. I am seeing animal leg and head and it is making me to want to vomit even if I am seeing not just dead animal body but dead human body before. This one on the road is making my belly to be turning over.

Everywhere we are going, we are seeing refuses, dead animal, and people everywhere. All of the house, if they are looking fine from far away, they are not looking fine anymore close up. They are all looking like old man and woman who is wanting to fall down. Bullet hole is everywhere like bullet is locust and just making their nest in anything around, even concrete. And now, I am seeing how there is small small crater here and there. Sometimes you will just be looking as you are driving – house, house, house, no house, and where there is no more house, the ground is looking like somebody is pressing thumb into it, only the thumb is like giant's thumb. In these place, everything is sometimes shining with broken glass and sometimes you are still smelling the smokes from the rubbles. I am looking to see if anybody but me is looking at this kind thing, but I am the only one looking and thinking, KAI! this is just too very bad. They are all just thinking about all of the drink and woman that we can be getting in this place. I am too young to be knowing about these thing even if I am knowing from how the men are talking about woman that I am really wanting one to be making my soldier feel good. I am wanting one, but not like how we are getting them in battle.

If this town was big place for all of the trader to be buying and selling this and that, I am not seeing it. The market is empty. The whole place is just empty. Too many of the roofs is just falling and showing bullet hole inside of them making me to thinking, how much person are dying here every day? So so much because they are not enough people to be burying all of the dying people. They are just throwing them into the street like refuses.

We are getting out of all the truck and walking, looking for some good thing. I am not knowing if Commandant is telling everybody about all the thing we should be finding in this place. I am thinking he is not because they should be madding since we are not finding any good thing. We are walking through the market and finding nothing. And when we are walking out of the market, we are still finding nothing.

I am looking left to right and left to right at the compound on each side. There is nothing like what Commandant is saying here even if I am beginning to see that there is more life here than I am first thinking. First, I am seeing bony cat licking dusty old chicken bone on the ground. The bone is so dry that it is even looking like rock, like it should be breaking the cat's teeths, but the cat is not minding so much because it is at least feeding small small on the thing it is finding. All of us is then going around one corner and I am finally seeing few person walking around. These people are acting like soldier is nothing new or real to them in this place where in other place everybody is fearing us. I am thinking, what if they are not seeing me? What if they are not seeing us? What if we are dying and becoming spirit? What if they are spirit because they are all looking the same? The people are all looking the same, and I am not knowing who is old and who is young or who is man and who is woman. I am thinking to myself, this place is making me to confuse too much with its kind of people.

I am following behind Commandant and Luftenant and Rambo and Strika. All the other soldier is following behind me. We are turning onto one road that is only just wide enough for us to be moving one man behind the next man, one truck behind the next truck. On each side of us there is building with two or three floor and as we are walking, woman is just looking down at us and I am seeing how they are just holding cloth around their breast like that. Commandant and Luftenant and Rambo and everybody is looking round and round and licking their lip like this is the best thing we are ever seeing. All of the building is behind wall that is crumbling but they are each having gateman or woman just sitting with stick and looking at us, not smiling. I am hearing one man shouting loud, enhen now! Don't worry. Don't worry baby! We are coming back for you!

It is some time that we are walking and driving like this until Commandant is saying, enhen, and we are stopping in one place. The place we are coming to is just one house that is having no guard or anybody at the gate. We are opening the rusty gate and they is screaming so loud. Behind the gate is one compound where person is not coming for long long time.

I am knowing because the grasses are growing very high. I am wondering why Commandant is bringing us here when suddenly I am seeing gun, big gun, the biggest gun I am ever seeing, so big that they are coming with seat so you can be sitting down when you are shooting them. Next to them is big triangle of bullet, bullet even bigger than my arm. These gun are standing on wheel even bigger than my whole body and it is making me to want to go and touch them. All of these bullet and gun is rusting like nobody is even using them for too long. None of us is seeing such thing before.

Commandant is yelling, TENSHUN and I am seeing that now all of us is standing here and all of us is forming tenshun very quickly. Then, Commandant is saying to us that we should be behaving ourself and looking sharp and resting well well that we will be knowing what is happening in some time. Everybody is listening, but nobody is really understanding what he is saying about moving to the front and fighting the enemy in this place or that place because I am never seeing this place or that place for my whole life. Anyway, it is not mattering too much because I am just following order and not having to do anything else. After he is shouting on us like this, he is telling us to dismiss and make our camp.

The rest of the soldier are now going every this way and that way to be seeing what is in this kind of place that we are never seeing before. I am wanting to go especially to all the big gun so I can be seeing if I can sit in them and look at the sky to be shooting, but Commandant is telling me and Strika, follow me. We are going, and he is walking to one house, the only house remaining in this compound.

We are opening the door of this house into room with sunlight that is having many window with all of the glass gone. I am knowing immediately that this place is school because I am seeing bench, and table, and blackboard, only every place is having so many many map with green pin, and yellow pin, and blue pin, and white pin, everywhere. These map is covering every place on the wall and table and also sometimes the floor. My head is spinning this way and that way because I am feeling like I am inside the world and I am looking at how everything must look from the inside instead of outside. It is not map of the world, but map of my country so everywhere is name of place I am hearing sometimes there is fighting or place where I am hearing there is the enemy one day and no enemy the next day but I am not knowing that everywhere there is war. I am looking at this pin and that pin and thinking, if I am to run away where can I be running to? Where can I be running to? War is everywhere. My heart is beating so fast and I am sweating so much. I am wanting to sit down.

Suddenly, I am standing here in this room but I am also standing in my classroom in the shadow, in the corner like what is happening when you are talking too much or if you are not doing your lesson proper. I am seeing all of the face I am knowing from home all sitting there and doing work and then I am looking at the woman who is writing lesson on the board. She is stepping like she is having limp but her body is looking like Mistress Gloria. She is writing, I will not kill, I will not kill. I will not kill, and everybody is writing in their book, I will not kill, I will not kill excepting me because I am not having book. Then the teacher is turning around and looking at me and I am fearing because she is having the face of that woman I am killing with blood everywhere on her face and in her eye. She is saying to me, are you not understanding our lesson, even while she is walking to me with one sharp machete that is shining like the river is shining. When she is coming near to me, all of the face of the child are only the girl that they are using anyhow, that Strika is killing. I am starting to want to scream.

AGU!

I am hearing my name and then everything is map and I am standing inside the world looking at Commandant just looking at me. I am saying, yes Sah! Yes Sah! I am shouting and standing tenshun and trying to look like I am prouding and strong.

He is saying to me, what is wrong? What is wrong? But I am not answering. My mouth is shut. Then he is saying, come on. Let us leave this place.

Outside it is getting dark, but the whole compound is starting to grow with noise because they are preparing meal. Each one soldier is talking to the next, talking talking. I am listening to them, but I am also thinking of all of the map and all of the fighting that is going on in this whole world and I am fearing for my life. I am thinking if there is even any way to be getting out.

When it is dark, we are not even lighting match or the enemy may be finding where we are and sending helicopter and plane to be bombing and shooting us. Everywhere is just black, but you are hearing voice just talking or singing like spirit in the night. Everywhere you are going you are hearing different talking, different story, different song. We are not just like army now, we are like school or family is what I am thinking. Each person is finding his own best friend and they are going off to this corner or that corner. I am walking around to be seeing if I can find Strika, but each step I am taking is so slow and each time I am stepping I am having to put my hand in front of me to be finding my way. This darkness is so full like it is mother's hug. Heya! I am remembering my mother and how she is so good to me that each time she is hugging me that is all I am needing to see the dark skin of her arm holding me close to her and I am knowing that the life I am living is so good. This kind of dark is making me to feel like I am turning inside out, so all of my thought is floating outside of me and all of my clothe is inside of me. I am walking with my hand stretching out in front of me because I am trying to catch all of those thought that is floating around me so I can make sure no part of me is missing.

I am walking in the direction I am remembering where is the building. As I am walking to the building, I am hearing sound from before the war when I am in school, sound of laughter and sound of crying and sound like the game we are playing during school break. I am hearing sound of pencil writing on paper and sound of chalk writing on blackboard and how eraser is sounding when I am beating it on the stone to be removing the dust. I am hearing how all the girl is tearing paper to be passing note back and forward and how all the boy is just whispering this answer and that answer so we can be beating all the girl. I am hearing sound of lizard watching us from the wall and mosquito entering the classroom making it so hard to be hearing what the teacher is saying. I am hearing the sound of Dike chewing gum or licking sweet when we are not supposed to be eating anything. I am hearing sound of my sandal tapping on the ground when I am doing my maths until Mistress Gloria is telling us, lesson is over and now it is time to go home. I am hearing the prayer we are saying each day at the end of all the lesson, please God help me to use what I have learned for the good of all when I go home. I am hearing all of this thing and it is making me to sad.

Commandant is smoking cigarette on the step of the house

when I am walking up. He is alone and staring up to the sky. Each time he is smoking, he is holding his cigarette down so that nobody can be seeing the light. I am hoping he is not seeing me or saying anything to me even though I am coming right close to him, but then it is like he is animal knowing something is there even if he is not seeing it and he is shouting AGU! AH AGU! WHAT ARE YOU DOING? JUST COME HERE RIGHT NOW. And when I am coming he is saying softly softly sit down sit down. So I am sitting down but is like he cannot even be seeing that I am sitting there next to him, like the darkness between us is too much. I am just drinking the smoke from his own cigarette and wishing that I had not been giving my own away for small small biscuit because I am still so hungry. After he is finishing smoking his cigarette to the end, until the spot of fire is just disappearing and his face is not shining orange anymore, he is putting his hand on my head and rubbing his rough hand on the back of my neck. Sometimes Agu, I am thinking he is saying to me, sometimes I am feeling sorry for you. I am looking at him but I cannot be seeing anything on his face because it is too dark. But he is not saying, sometimes Agu, I am feeling sorry for you. I am wishing he is saying something like that, but he is never saying anything like that to me. He is moving closer to me and I am slowly moving away from him and we are doing this on the verandah of the school building until Luftenant is calling out to us, Commandant Sah. Is that you? And is that Agu? Commandant is saying, let us go. Hmm. If you are my body-guard, then if I am going, you are also going. Is it not so?

Commandant is saying we are going out this night. He is saying to all the soldier, half of you come on, let us go, and then dividing us into half. To the other half, he is saying, you should be staying here. When they are grumbling, he is saying, don't worry. There is enough woman so that they will still be here tomorrow. Relax yourself enh. I am walking with Commandant and Luftenant as they are talking about drink and money and womens and talking talking about how nice it is. We are moving very slowly in the road because we cannot be using any light. Around me, all the men are smelling hungry, like they will be chopping something sweet very soon. Even if I have been eating too much food this night, my stomach is feeling hungry and more hungry each time we are turning one corner on the road. There is no way to be seeing where we are going at all at all. No house is having light. No house is even having lamp or candle, and the whole place is like death's hometown.

We are stopping beside wall of concrete, the wall of one compound. Commandant is stamping his feets on the ground and spitting between his boot and cursing. There is woman at the gate just sitting on stool with her head in her hand and dog that is grumbling at her feets when we are coming close. She is shining torchlight very quickly in our eye and saying, so you have come enh? One other man is saying, why are you so angry Sista? And then she is looking at me and saying, child is not coming for this place. Stupid woman, I am starting to abuse her, but Commandant is hitting my head and saying, he is my own bodyguard. She is nodding and spitting at me and it is landing just next to my feets but it is not touching me. Devil bless you she is saying, but I am just walking by.

Inside of the compound is smaller than where we are camping, but there is large house inside. I am hearing the sound of generator in this compound, but I am not seeing any light anywhere. We are entering into the house, into room that is just having blue light everywhere. All of the table and chair and everything is just looking blue, and even my skin and Commandant's skin is looking blue and black like we are already dead. Woman is coming up to us and her eye is shining like blue diamond. She is limping so when she is stepping this way and that way her slipper is just making step slap like she is beating the floor because she is angry with it. Every time she is stepping, all the fly is jumping from the table and drink and cup that are just everywhere making whole place to be smelling of beer and alcohol. Also, from the corner of the room behind big tower of bread loaf piled high on each other to the roof like cement block is coming the smell of burning meat and nice-tasting stew. From the roof is hanging flag of different beer and mineral like they are country that everybody should be visiting. They are not flying back and forward like normal flag and instead are just hanging down like they are not even wanting to be on the wall. On all of the window there is heavy board and heavy black cloth making sure that there is no light even allowed to come out, but because there is no open window, the whole place is just heating too much. We are all filling up the room and just looking. I am hearing this sound like mosquito that is when I am looking up and seeing Television. TELEVISION! In this war! Can you imagine? There is no sound coming from it, but one movie is playing. I am having to try and hear what they are saying but I am seeing police officer and woman who is looking like prostitute shouting at each other on the screen. A whole television! I am never even seeing anything like this since war is starting.

Mma. Bring something that will satisfy soldier, Commandant is shouting at the woman and the other men are just laughing. Bring beer! Bring mineral! Bring it all! Commandant is shouting.

It is only now that I am seeing woman who is looking very young and very nice just sitting on one stool in the back of the room. The Madam is shouting at her, get up you lazy idiot can't you see we are having guest and this young woman is getting up and going to the cooler. She is bending down so her buttom is just rising high into the air. I am seeing Commandant and the other men now just looking looking and not even moving their eye from this buttom like it is piece of cooked meat. Then they are laughing to each other, heye! Ekaa ekaa ekaa. Heye! Kehi, kehi, kehi. When the girl is turning around I am seeing how sweat is just soaking her white head tie which is really looking blue because of the light. She is breathing out and opening her mouth so that her lip are blowing small bubble of spit into the air. It is all warm, she is saying. No ice to be cooling it, and Commandant is angrying, no ice. How can that be enh? Because of war, the woman is saying. Ah ah! War no stop you from making ice. Bring the drink. We will be drinking it even if it is warm, Commandant is saying. And when the girl is coming over, it is like he is just changing so when she is near he is sticking his hand out to be touching her all over. Baby, he is saying, baby, I love you when he is touching her buttom. She is not liking it. The other men are just laughing laughing and looking at her breast which is even showing because there is so much sweat in her shirt. I am looking at her breast also and my soldier is becoming to stand at tenshun which is making me to feel good and it is not making me to feel good. Madam, I am saying to this young woman while they are laughing and now drinking their warm drink, Madam be bringing us some breads. The woman is sucking in her teeths at me. Is this war just making you to have no respect for your elder? This small thing borned yesterday trying to order me around. Enh! You this small thing. I can be your mother! The men are laughing so loud that the fly is jumping in the blue light, but she is still getting breads and bringing it back. When she is coming back, Commandant is even grabbing her breast and she is slapping him on the hand but he and the men are still smiling.

The big Madam is just watching from one corner until she is growing angry and saying if it is woman you are wanting, leave this one. I am having plenty plenty womens in the back if you are having plenty plenty money to be giving me. And just like that they are all getting up and following the big Madam through door in the back of the room just leaving me to be sitting here with the warm drink and this breads that the young woman is throwing at me. I am waiting. Ten minute. Twenty minute just staring at the television and the movie with policeman and prostitute. I am chewing my breads and also watching the young woman who is coming over to collect the bottle on the table. I am looking at her breast and wanting to touch her buttom like Commandant is doing, but as soon as I am even bringing up my hand to be touching her, she is looking at me like she will be beating me to death and sucking in her teeths so I am putting my hand down. Then I am getting so hot because there is not even one bit of air in this room and I am going outside to be catching some breath.

When I am sitting outside in the dark, under the window, I am hearing all of these noise coming from inside sounding just like Commandant when he is entering me. I am hearing these thing and it is making my soldier to become very hard and I am not knowing what to be doing. I am touching it very softly through my short and it is feeling very good, so I am touching it some more whenever I am hearing the man and woman making more sound from the room. My hand is just moving up and down and up and down like it is not even part of my body anymore and I am thinking to myself of how I will be touching breast and leg. All of this thing is making my eye to close and my heart to beat fastly and I am liking it and doing it so much until I am just hearing one scream, AYIIIEEE!!!! SHE HAS KILLED ME OH!

And then I am hearing all of this footstep running this way and that in house so I am stopping to touch myself and I am running inside to the room with the blue light where I am finding that all of the soldier are coming out of their room just looking like something is confusing them. Then I am seeing how Luftenant is just holding the wall and having blood to be coming from his mouth shining black in the blue light. I am looking at him and thinking whatever it is that is happening is good for him, but then I am seeing how his face is looking like all the bad thing in the world is paining him and I am sorrying small small. All of the other soldier is coming up to him and they are holding him by one arm or the other arm and helping him to sit down in chair. Commandant is coming out of the back door only wearing his short and his soldier is still at full tenshun when he is yelling, WHAT IS IT THAT IS HAPPENING! Everybody is looking at Luftenant and then looking at woman who is also coming out of the room after Luftenant. She is bleeding from her body where it is looking like somebody is beating her in the head and beating her in the mouth. She cannot even be walking at all so she is holding the wall when she is trying to move and also holding one hand to her neck. Nobody is knowing what to do until the Madam is coming out and asking what is happening. And then the other woman are coming out from their room, some of them wearing one cloth and trying to cover their body while other is just walking out like that, naked, like it is no problem to be walking around with no clothe.

All of the soldier are looking at Luftenant who is pointing to his stomach. What is happening, one man is asking. And then they are lying Luftenant on the table under the television and making him to stretch out. KAI! someone is shouting. Enh? another is saying and they are all looking down at Luftenant's body. I am going over to see what I can be seeing, and then I am seeing how he is just having one knife sticking out from his belly just like that. It is making me to grab my own belly just to be making sure that everything is still there. Luftenant is not even screaming anymore. He is just shaking shaking on the table and mumbling to himself like he is madman.

Commandant is shouting, WHO IS DOING THIS? And then the Madam is coming and saying, heyeye now! What is happening here oh? She is looking at her girl who is just bleeding and crying, and holding her throat, and coughing, he is just grabbing my neck and beating me, so what am I supposed to be doing. I am only small girl. How can I be stopping him from doing anything? So I am just seeing this knife that he is having in his trouser and I am using it and just chooking him to get him off of me. I am not knowing it is going to be like this. I am watching how Commandant's face is darking and how the whole room is smelling of fear and sweat. I am thinking that he will be telling us to be grabbing this woman and shooting her, but he is not even opening his mouth. He is just standing there and looking around us and then at Luftenant who is lying shaking shaking on the table. COME ON! Everybody just get up! Get him up! Let us be getting out of here, he is saying and looking at the big Madam who is just holding her girl and using cloth to be wiping the blood from her face. No woman is even saying anything because they are fearing too much. COME ON! MOVE QUICK! Commandant is shouting and then he is going into the back room to be getting his clothe on and all of the other soldier are taking turn to be doing the same. Then we are picking up Luftenant and carrying him out of this building and into the night. The woman at the gate is sleeping like she is not even knowing anything is happening at all inside and nobody is telling her anything because the men are just trying to be keeping their soldier between their leg and their trouser from falling down.

A whole three day we are staying here and Luftenant is not getting better. Every day somebody is washing his stomach with cloth and water and soap, but it is not doing anything and he is just shivering in the night. We are keeping him in the building in our camp because that way the mosquito is not getting to him as easily, and since it is not too many people walking this way and that we are not having to worry that the building will be falling down. Three whole day somebody is watching him on and off and on and off but he is never speaking anymore and his face is just growing too white.

We are kneeling around his bed, squeezing brown water onto his face and shining kerosene lamp into his eye. And his eye is so wide we are seeing through to the back of his head. All the morning, he is just groaning and moaning like his spirit is fighting to be let free from his body and all the evening, he is shaking and shivering like it is so cold even though the night is so hot that we are all sweating. We are just watching him like this for all this time and everybody is not saying anything.

It is taking Luftenant three whole day to be dying, and then he is dying when the moon is full and the night is shining like silver. We are dumping his body in the gutter – me, Strika,

Commandant, and Rambo, but before that, Rambo is just taking his clothe because Commandant is saying that Rambo is new Luftenant. Then we are leaving his body for the cat and dog and maggot and worm to eat. We are leaving him and I am thinking that he is getting his wish not to be fighting anymore, and I am fearing because I am seeing that the only way not to be fighting is to die. I am not wanting to die.

It is night. It is day. It is light. It is dark. It is too hot. It is too cold. It is raining. It is too much sunshine. It is too dry. It is too wet. But all the time we are fighting. No matter what, we are always fighting. All the time bullet is just eating everything, leaf, tree, ground, person – eating them – just making person to bleed everywhere and there is so much blood flooding all over the bush. The bleeding is making people to be screaming and shouting all the time, shouting to father and to mother, shouting to God or to Devil, shouting one language that nobody is really knowing at all. Sometimes I am covering my ear so I am not hearing bullet and shouting, and sometimes I am shouting and screaming also so I am not hearing anything but my own voice. Sometimes I am wanting to cry very loud, but nobody is crying in this place. If I am crying, they will be looking at me because soldier is not supposed to be crying.

All the time, we are sick and going to toilet, shitting water. We are hungry too and living off anything we can find. Lizard, we are eating them. Insect, we are eating them or even better, if we are finding them, we are eating rat and every other kind of bush animal. Sometimes we are eating this leaf or that leaf, but leaf is what is always making my belly to turn so I am not eating it so much. Meat is also making my stomach to turn because we are not able to use too much fire to cook it because if we are using too much fire, then the enemy will be seeing us and shooting us dead from where they are hiding. I am always hungry, so hungry that I am always dreaming of chicken and how I will be eating it, how I will be crunching its beak and eating even the feather. I am so hungry I can be eating wood if it is making me to hungry less, but it is only hurting my belly and making me to vomit and shit. I am so hungry I can even be eating my skin small by small if it is not making me to bleed to death. I am so hungry that I am wanting to die, but if I am dying then I will be dead.

But there is so much bombing and bombing and shelling and shelling and sending helicopter to come and shine light on us and kill us. All the time, the ground is shaking and the tree is shaking and the air is smelling of smoke or the air is beating in your ear BOTU BOTU BOTU and you are not even having one second to be thinking anything. So much time pass us now. I am not seeing road or village or woman or children for too long. I am only seeing war, one evil spirit sitting in the bush just having too much happiness because all the time he is eating what he wants to eat – us – and seeing what he is wanting to see – killing – so he is just laughing GBWEM! GBWEM! GBWEM!

All of our truck is gone, just bombed away, so we are having to walk everywhere now, and there is not so many of us anymore. People are just dying like this every day. Onc boy named Hope is dying, just burning up in the fire of bomb that is hitting truck. One man we are calling Dagger is dying because he is stepping on mine and it is just chewing his whole body to many piece like termite is chewing wood. And Griot is dying from malaria making him to shaking shaking, and Preacher is dying holding his Bible in one hand and his leg in the other screaming to God, come take me come take me. People are dying just like that every day. Everyone I am knowing is dying. And even all the soldier whose name I am not knowing is dying. In the middle of this war, I am even missing some of them. I am even missing some of them.

Commandant is helping some people to be dying. Already he is shooting three people he is calling traitor, including Driver who is trying to run away because he is having no more truck to be driving. After Commandant is shooting Driver, he is laughing laughing and talking to himself and not even listening to anyone. Not even Rambo who is new Luftenant. When I am seeing all of this, all of this bombing bombing, killing killing, and dying dying, I am thinking to myself that now, as we are in this bush, only ant is still making and living. I am wishing I am ant.

Now we are just living underground in trench that we are digging in the red mud and just living inside it like one kind of snake or rat. When it is dry, we are happying because there is no water anywhere and we can just be fighting war. When it is raining, ah! It is so terrible. So terrible. It is like living in gutter. Sometimes water is coming up to my belly and I am just looking at my reflection staring at me everywhere I am going. We are staying in this place for too long. I am tired and hungry and I am wanting to leave.

There is so much mist that is wrapping around people like extra shirt. No shooting still for today and I am wanting to think, HEYA! WAR IS OVER! WAR IS OVER! but then I am thinking, is it really over? This whiteness that is hanging around all of us and making it hard to breathing is making me to feel like somebody is wanting to fly into my chest and close my nose with cotton. My feets are staying in the water all night so I am feeling they are curling at the end like the feets of rat. Some of the men are sleeping and hugging themself against the wall of the trench with their shirt on their head to be protecting them from the rain. They are shivering because there is cool wind that is coming through the whole place. It is hard not to be stepping on them because they are just appearing quickly quickly from the mist. One second everything is all white around me and then I am kicking foot that is just appearing and the man is screaming in his sleep but not waking up. I am learning to see where the heat from body is making it less thick so I am walking carefully when I am seeing this. Some of the men are awake because they are on guard all night and I am moving gegerly gegerly to not be disturbing them.

Strika is standing outside Commandant's HQ which is only just the trench, but with one blue cloth covering with leaf so he is not getting as wet as the rest of us. Strika is holding gun that is so heavy in his hand it is pulling the right side of his body to the ground. We are looking at each other for long time and then I am bringing my hand to be beating away the mist. I am not liking Strika's eye because they are too red and his teeths because they are too brown and his head because it is big, but he is my friend even if he is looking ugly. He is giving me the gun and then walking past me.

I am stepping inside HQ to see Commandant sleeping on his crate with his back against the mud wall and his boot stretching into the muddy water. Cigarette and ash is floating in the water around him and the whole room is smelling of smoke. I am taking deep breath to be drinking it all in because it is somehow making my body to full so I am not feeling as hungry.

His beard is growing so thick now that it is almost covering his whole chin and cheek. When is breathing out, the hairs is shaking with his breath. Commandant is looking like wild man and behaving like madman. I am thinking of him running naked through the bush with only his big beard reaching down to his feets and it is making me want to laugh but I am too hungry. Laughing is making my belly to hurt too much. Commandant is fearing the other soldier so much now that he is saying it is always good to be sleeping with one eye open. That is why either Strika or myself is always standing outside when he is sleeping. I am his one eye. Strika is his other.

Come on. Out of my way, Rambo's head is following his voice out of the mist while his spit is spraying onto my face. He is stepping from the whiteness to stand right in front of me. I am seeing him with his gun hanging on his shoulder. My belly is tighting and my neck is becoming stiff. I am holding the gun Strika is giving to me.

Commandant is sleeping, I am saying to Rambo. Well wake him up, he is saying back. I am stepping in front of him and kicking water in his boot. He is tiring so don't be bothering him, I am saying. My leg is shaking shaking and my feets are too too cold. Out of my way, Rambo is saying again and stepping right so I am holding my gun tighter and stepping in front of him. His boot is squishing the mud. No he is resting, I am saying.

Rambo is bending down so I am seeing his face and his beard that is growing thick and black. Listen you small boy. Get out of the way. We are not playing game. I am not remembering the last time I am playing game.

What is all of this noise, Commandant is saying. Sah it is me, Rambo is answering. Idiot can't you see I am sleeping. Enhen now Sah I can see. Then shutup and go back to your post. No Sah I am not doing that anymore Sah. And why not? Because we are leaving Sah. WHO AND WHO IS LEAVING? Commandant is shouting and then I am hearing him laughing quietly to himself from the shadow of his HQ.

In front of me, Rambo is swallowing so hard that I am feeling it in my own throat. And from the back of the HQ, Commandant's laughing is growing louder and louder until I am feeling him standing right behind me. He is pushing me aside with his arm and I am hitting rock in the wall. My shoulder is beginning to hurt. Who is leaving. Idiot. Go back to your post. You are leaving when I say leave. Understood? No Sah, never, Rambo is saying. We are going, Rambo is saying. I no want trouble oh, he is saying. Who is this we enh, Commandant is saying and laughing. You are the only one stupid enough – I AM GOING one voice is shouting. I AM GOING TOO. AND ME, AND ME, AND ME the voice keep yelling from the mist softer and softer until the farthest person is shouting small small, saying and me. Rambo is sliding his finger to the trigger of his gun and I am sliding my finger to my own trigger because I am fearing what Commandant will be doing to me if I am not protecting him, but then I am remembering how much he is hurting me when he is chooking me and I am saying never. Never will I feeling sorry for him. Never will I be helping him. I am lowering my gun.

See! We are going, Rambo is shouting to Commandant. Then he is just taking his gun and shooting him. Only one shot just right in the chest and I am seeing Commandant looking down to his chest with his whole mouth open like he is screaming. But no sound is coming out. He is not saying anything. And then his body is just falling and making the water that is running down the trench red like that.

Rambo is stopping his shaking and is puffing out his chest. Rambo is looking at me and I am looking at him. He is looking at me for long time and then he is just turning and climbing up wall and I am hearing his boot crunching the leaf near my head. Then I am looking up and hearing how all of the soldier is climbing up out of the trench and I am hearing Rambo shouting, COME ON! COME ON QUICK QUICK QUICK!

MOVE FAST OH! MOVE WITH SPEED! HOME HOME! WE ARE GOING HOME! I am looking at Commandant and then I am climbing out of the trench. I am tired and hungry and I am wanting to go home.

Commandant is dead. It was so easy to be killing him. Why we are not doing it before I am not knowing, but I am not wanting to think about that right now. I am tiring too much.

We are walking the whole night on this road, left right, left right, left right, left right and carrying everything we are having, gun, knife, clothe, but that is it because we are not having anything else. How can we be having anything else if we are staying in the bush for so long? I am so tired that it is hard for me to move my leg, but I am following Rambo. So are all the other, just following following even if Rambo is not having map like Commandant. No one person is even marching, left right, left right, like soldier and instead they are just walking almost right almost left, dragging this foot and that foot on the ground. My slipper is sticking to my feets because they are so worn down and almost spoiling, and my feets are paining me because my skin is just rotting and peeling away from too much time standing in the water in the trench. I am feeling like I am always walking on nail and I am wanting to stop to be resting but nobody is stopping. Strika is not stopping even if his face is cracking everywhere and all his body is just shaking shaking the whole time so I am just moving on almost left almost right, and saying that if he is doing it then I am also doing it. Sometimes I am falling to the back and then I am getting to fear very much because the man fronting me is like shadow, not person, so I am running to the front which is making my leg to pain even more. I am wishing that I am having boot or canvas shoe so my feets is not hurting. Or even I am wanting to be having car to be driving away so when we are walking I am always hearing car in my head and it is making me to look from side to side for car that is coming to rescue me and take me home. No car. I am thinking I am car and trying to make my feets to move like wheel that is never stopping, but I cannot. I am hungry and I want to stop and rest and eat.

Wherever we are going the moon is following us. It is so big and so bright that we are not using any torch to be seeing, so nobody is fearing that the enemy can be seeing us from wherever they may be hiding in this bush. They cannot see us if we are not having torch because we are invisible unless they are bringing helicopter to be beating the air BOTU BOTU and to be shining their bright light on the road. I see tree and its shadow. I see rock and its shadow and then I am saying let me just make it to that tree or to that rock. My eye is becoming used to the light and I am beginning to see more of everything that is around – each tree, each rock, each piece of rubbish or plant growing alone in the mud of the road. Wherever we are going it is only the moon shining and it is making the whole place to be looking like it is glass and will just break if you are touching it too hard. I am not liking this at all at all. If something is making of glass, then it is looking nice and beautiful, but it is also looking dead even if it is really having life. Everything here is looking dead when it is really alive. The grass on the side of the road, the tree behind the grasses, my arm or leg, Strika's face, Rambo's neck – they are all looking dead and making me to wonder how all of these dead thing can even be living. I am seeing each thing on the road – I am seeing them all stiff like glass but I am not able to be seeing through them and I am knowing that the world is full of people and thing even if we are trying to look like they are not there.

I am hearing song. Someone is singing it. It is old song that my mother was singing all the time she is cooking or washing.

A song! A song! I am not even hearing music for so long not even from bird. Hearing this music is making my whole skin to burn and I am wanting to scratch myself, my whole self, all over. I feel like I am wanting to dance but is my body even remembering how? I don't think so. I am sadding because of this. What is happening to the music and all the song we are having? I don't know. I don't know.

I am walking faster because I am trying to see who it is that is singing the song so I can be standing next to him and feeling this music. I am walking from this person to that person but I am not seeing any sort of sound coming from their mouth. I am feeling like I should be going to that person who is singing and taking all of the sound so I can be having it for myself to be keeping in my pocket for whenever it is getting to be too too bad, but the sound I am looking for is coming from nowhere. I don't mind at all, because the song is making my body to move and I am not having to think anymore. I am having to think of other thought that are just jumping into my head. I am not even minding the gun that is making my whole back to hurt even though it is very heavy. I am thinking of home. How many time am I thinking of my home when we are in the bush? How many time am I seeing all of the people that I am growing up with running around in my head like child running around after school, running to the house, running to the church, running to the market like there is no war and everything is just fine? In my head, all of the people that I am seeing in my home are too too happy and I am thinking, if this is how they are living, why am I staying here to just be walking to someplace not even knowing if I am to be living or dying. I don't know. I don't know.

We are tiring so so much, but we are trying to reach some place. Where is this place? I am not knowing, but I am knowing that Rambo is saying we should not be stopping. So we are not stopping and we are walking through the whole night into the day. The sun is rising behind us so all our shadow is growing front from our feets and making the road ahead very dark which is making it harder to be taking each next step. On this road, it is so empty and I am thinking where have all the people gone because I am not liking the quiet and I am not liking how the only sound in the daytime is the sound of my slipper hitting my own feets, the sound of my breathing so hard every time this is happening because it is paining too much. I cannot be stopping and so I keep walking. I am picking one noise, even if it is just one person moaning, and I am saying that I should be catching that noise so each time the noise is getting softer, I am walking faster to be catching it wherever it is going. They cannot be leaving me behind because I am not knowing where I would be going to in this bush. Just imagine if they are leaving me for the bush and then

I am being eaten by animal or other soldier who is sacrificing me to be winning this war. I am thinking about the kind of animal that will be following me if they are leaving me. It is having the body of lion and the head of soldier with helmet and eye that are looking like bullet and teeths that are looking like knife to be chewing me up. Its tail is like gun and its breath like fire that is cooking me well well before it is sitting down to be eating all of the burning part of my body. When this is coming to my head, I am hurrying up my step so that I am not being the last one in the line.

My sweat is burning my eye away. Now it is so hot because the sun is beating on my back and making my gun to warm so much that it is feeling like hot iron on my back. I know it is making mark and burning my back so I am like cow and belonging to one owner which is gun. I am sadding when I am feeling this gun in my back because I am thinking that first when this war is starting, I am wanting gun because I can be using it to protect myself. At this time, gun is belonging to me and it is going wherever I am carrying it but now it is just riding on my back like it is king and I am servant to be doing whatever it says. If it is saying go right, then my body is walking to the right even if I am struggling to go left, and if it is saying for me to stop then I am stopping to catch breath and if I am going down the hill with the other men then it is saying go faster and it is pushing me down the hill just like that. I am not liking this at all at all and I am wanting to be throwing gun away into the bush, but if I am throwing gun away then Rambo will be throwing me away because gun is more important than me. I am always remembering this.

The road is too long, but sometimes it is nice to be looking at. I am liking how it is just rising up and down like one animal, how it is moving with the land that it is sitting on. If you are seeing this road in sunshine, then you will be knowing how great it is and how all of the tree is even respecting it and not trying to grow in it. It is only small small thing on the road that are not respecting it, like small plant and sometimes small animal here and there that is getting run over by car and being left there for long time. I am fearing because there is nothing on road excepting us and these small plant that is not respecting road, and if they are not respecting road and road is killing them, then because we are not respecting road from going to toilet and spitting everywhere on it, I am fearing that it may be killing us soon also.

When we are walking, my mouth is tasting of salt, of so much salt that I am not liking the way that salt is tasting anymore. It is making me to thirsty so much and this is even worse than to be hungrying so much because it is making my head to turn from one place to another and the whole world is just spinning round and round me like I am walking in circle. One time I am seeing Strika in front of me walking slowly slowly then the next time I am seeing him behind me walking fastly fastly. This is making me to think am I mad.

We are moving always moving because that is what we are doing and watching all the thing on the road passing us by. House, tree, school, empty car all burned up, refuses, all passing us, but still we are not seeing person. We are coming into another village but it is just small, not even really village. It is only just house on each side of the road, and it is empty, nothing there excepting the refuses. Person is running away from us like we are sickness, like we are the most evil thing to be on this earth. I am looking at road that is cracking in many place like somebody is just taking it and stretching it until you are seeing the red mud bleeding from underneath. And everywhere there is rubbishes just moving along the road like they are people just moving moving when they are having nothing to be doing. We are just moving until Strika is stepping on piece of breaking-up bottle glass and falling down. He is not saying word, not even crying or screaming. It is not even like he is feeling any pain, but I am feeling pain for him and it is making me to want to shout and yell. The other soldier are just walking by us and not even looking at us. Strika. Strika, I am saying. We are having to go or they will be leaving us. But he is not listening to me. Instead he is just taking his foot and picking away all of the skin until the glass is just coming out from his foot. Then he is just licking his finger clean of all the blood and the dust but making sure to not be touching any of the sore that is on his lip. He is stretching his hand out to me and we are getting up and walking. One step. Two step. He is falling down. Why is Strika doing like this? We have to be going now but he is not getting up. Get up! He is just looking at me and coughing until he is spitting onto the ground next to him, blood and spit, so much blood. I am asking Strika to be getting up but he is not listening and he is not getting up. His lip is moving but there is no noise coming out. I am looking at him. His face is just shining shining like he is sweating so much but there is no sweat coming out. I am kneeling down on the road next to him just watching all the other soldier walking away from us. I am feeling his heart that is just beating beating like whole village is stomping on the ground. Ah ah! Strika, I am saying. Ah ah! What is happening? But no word is coming from his mouth. His eye is blinking, my eye is blinking and I am seeing him crumpling up. I am getting up and pretending to be walking away. Don't leave me, he is saying and looking at me. And I am shouting at him, come on! Get up and stop this thing you are doing! I am hearing, don't leave me. Please Agu. Don't just be leaving me.

Strika is saying something. Enh! Strika is saying something! I am stopping to move, turning around and looking at him and he is looking at me but it is like he is not even seeing me.

I am bending down to him and seeing his body which is almost just disappearing beneath his clothe. His face is just looking so terrible because all of his skin is just coming away, and his eye is rolling up into his head and showing yellow and red everywhere like going to toilet and blood. Strika is just looking like one piece of refuses on this road. I am trying to be crying, but no tear is coming out from my eye, and I am trying not to be fearing, but Strika – Strika is my brother and my family and the only person I can be talking to even if he is never talking back until now. I am watching him and then I am looking up because I am not hearing all the other soldier walking on this road. I am not wanting to be left behind. I am not wanting to leave Strika behind. Strika, I am calling his name. Strika, but he is not answering. He is not saying anything. I am saying Strika? Strika? Strika?

Nothing is the same anymore. I am not being able to be sleeping at all when it is time to sleep. Each time I am lying down my head, some voice inside of me is shouting and starting to make too much trouble so I cannot even be closing my eye. And all of the time this is happening I am fearing that I am not knowing myself anymore. If it is day, I am sitting and staring at the sun like it is the only thing to look at in this world. I am watching how sometimes it is bright and other time it is like it is just struggling too much to be shining and I am wanting to ask it why it is even thinking to shine on this world. If I am sun, I will be finding another place to be shining where people are not using my light to be doing terrible terrible thing. At night I am staring at the moon and looking to see if a man is smiling. They are saying man is living there and smiling, but I am never finding anything at all. Nobody is smiling in this place. If it is night, if it is day, nobody is smiling.

So many time I am saying to myself that I will be running away, far far away to where no one can be finding me or seeing me and I will be staying there to the end of time when God is coming to judge the dead and the living. So many time I am telling this to myself, but when I am getting up to go and run away, I am thinking about all the animal and the spirit in the bush, and I am remembering the map which I am seeing in the town and thinking to myself, how can I be running if I am not knowing the way to be taking me away from the war. All I can be doing is sitting here and dreaming about how my leg will carry me far and fast like I am standing and it is the world that is moving to help me. I am dreaming this so many time but I am waiting for it to happen.

One day we are on the road and then we are just hearing some noise like truck and then we are scattering into the bush, all of us to one side just moving moving quickly into the shadow of all the tree and leaf, just stepping on this branch and that rock running running so that whoever it is will not be seeing us and maybe killing us. I am running

running and not looking at where I am putting my feets until KPWAWA, I am just hitting something and my body is falling down KPWOM just like that on the ground. My knee is paining me because I am falling hard and I am looking down to be seeing what is tripping me too easily. I am seeing one dead body just lying on the ground as if he is sleeping. The man is stiff and his whole belly is big like he is fulling of gas. It is so big that it is pressing on the button of his uniform until it is looking like it is going to pop. I am just looking down at this man because something is telling me in my head that this is meaning that we are getting closer to the war.

One soldier is also seeing this dead body and then he is coming and kneeling down next to him and unbuttoning the shirt. There is insect all over. Shiny beetle with silver on its back and little white maggot is just crawling up and down this dead man's chest. Then the man is turning the body over and taking off the shirt and rolling it up and putting it under his arm. He is going to the leg and removing the boot from it and putting his own slipper on the man's feets. He is looking at me and smiling and showing his brown teeths and then he is quickly running away to be joining the other soldier. I am watching him running away and I am wanting to be getting up and running after him because I do not want to be staying in this place with one dead body. But my leg is not getting up. I am just thinking thinking and I am asking to myself, why, if I am killing man and woman and beating them until their blood is just covering my whole body, if I am seeing my friend just sitting down by the road and shaking like Devil is possessing him, why am I wanting to cry and vomit if I am only seeing dead body?

And then I am thinking of all the thing I am doing. If they are ordering me KILL, I am killing, SHOOT, I am shooting, ENTER WOMAN, I am entering woman and not even saying anything even if I am not liking it. I am killing everybody, mother, father, grandmother, grandfather, soldier. It is all the same. It is not mattering who it is, just that they are dying. I am thinking thinking. I am thinking that I cannot be doing this anymore.

Then I am getting up from where I am sitting and wiping the mud on my hand onto my short. I am looking at my gun and I am saying to it, I am not needing you anymore. Just stay where you are. My shoulder that it is always sitting on is hurting so much but I am feeling it jubilating because it is not having to be obeying gun anymore.

Nobody is seeing me as I am getting up and walking through the tree right to the road. I am feeling breezes to my back that is pushing me to walk far far away from here and I am moving quickly quickly onto the road where I am just walking walking walking to where the sun is setting. I am looking at it and wanting to catch it in my hand to be squeez-ing until the colour are dripping out from it forever. That way everywhere it is always dark and nobody is ever having to see any of the terrible thing that is happening in this world.

In heaven, I am thinking it is always morning. It is not mattering when I am waking up, there is always the feeling of warmness from the sunlight that is coming in through the window, and the sound of bird singing outside in the tree, and the sound of the cock shouting KROO KROO, and the smell of smoke coming from where they are making fire. Everything is new. Everything is fresh. That is how I am feeling each time I am waking up in this place.

I am not knowing how long I am staying here, but I am staying here for long time – some week, some month – I am not knowing. All I am knowing is how it is feeling here. From my window, if I am standing on my bed, I can be seeing ocean and hearing how it is just grumbling. And all the time I can be hearing the wind talking when it is blowing through the coconut palm that is standing at tenshun in front of the ocean. Every morning I am getting up and I am going to walk in the sand that is rubbing the skin between my toe until that skin is becoming very red. And every morning I am looking very closely at everything that is here and seeing how crab is running in the sand, and mushroom is growing on the palm-tree trunk. Sometimes I am seeing how ant is eating up the coconut that is falling and how new plant is just growing everywhere in this place. When I am seeing this, I am thinking everything is so nice. Everything is so good.

I am not having to worrying about anything from war, like bombing or shelling, or dying. At night, we are sleeping inside with fan instead of outside in heat or rain. They are giving us much of food and telling us that we can be sitting down to eating it at the table in room with wall that is painting blue and floor that is just white. They are giving us as much food as we can even be wanting. We are not having to ask if we are wanting more. They are just letting us to take it. Plantain, rice, meats, chicken, fishes – anything we are wanting we are having. Sometimes I am eating even if I am not hungrying too much because I am fearing that the food is finishing and I will not be eating any for the next day.

Now, I am strong again. My arm and my leg is carrying me

again and when I am walking my bone is not cracking and the whole place is not spinning around and around anymore. I am wearing new clothe – one new shirt that is white with black stripe across my chest and new trouser that is blue and fitting me well well. I am liking it very much because it is clean and dry and it is not having any hole from bullet or blood from the last person who is wearing it. When I am finishing my bath in the morning, I am rushing rushing to be putting on my clothe so everybody can be seeing how I am looking so fine when I am wearing them.

They are giving me one room for myself where I am having whole bed, and my own table right under the window for the sunlight to be warming. They are giving me all of the book I can be wanting to read because I am telling Amy that my father is schoolteacher and that before the war I am always reading whatever I can. They are even giving me as much paper as I can be wanting and telling me to write or draw whatever I am wanting to draw, so I am drawing picture of school so I can be finishing and becoming Doctor and Engineer.

There is priest who is coming every Wednesday and Sunday in his black clothe and white collar. He is calling himself Father Festus so we are calling him that. He is very thin, but he is having fat cheek that is folding on each other and hanging to the ground and nose that is covering his whole mouth. He is always wearing sunglass so I am never seeing his eye. Sometimes I am even wondering if he is having eye. He is saying, turn to God. Pray to the Almighty so he can be forgiving you. Confession and Forgiveness and Resurrection, Father Festus is always saying, these are the only thing you are needing to be giving The Life to your life.

I am always thinking Confession and Forgiveness and Resurrection, I am not knowing what all this word is meaning. They are not making any sense to me anytime he is saying them. The only thing that is making sense to me is memory that I am having of another boy – Strika – sleeping next to me, so close because we are the only people protecting each other from all of the thing trying to kill us. I am remembering sound of people coughing and screaming, and the smell of going to toilet and dead body everywhere. This is the only thing that I am knowing. So, I am asking Father Festus about Confession and Forgiveness and Resurrection and he is saying to me, above all my boy, be having faith in God and trusting in him because he is helping you to understand this thing. Are you having Bible?

Yes I am having Bible, but I am using to be holding my drawing down on my desk so the fan is not throwing them everywhere.

Even if I am not understanding all the thing he is saying, I am still listening because he is saying that God is still alive in this place. I do not know if I am believing him, but I am liking to hear it.

And every day I am talking to Amy. She is white woman from America who is coming here to be helping people like me. Her teeths is too small and her tongue is too big for her mouth so she is speaking through her nose, but her nose is too small so sometimes it is troubling me too much to be hearing what she is saying. Most of the time she is not even saying anything and is sitting across from me in her chair. She is sitting in her chair and I am sitting in my own chair and she is always looking at me like looking at me is going to be helping me. She is telling me to speak speak speak and thinking that my not speaking is because I am like baby. If she is thinking I am baby, then I am not speaking because baby is not knowing how to speak. But every time I am sitting with her I am thinking I am like old man and she is like small girl because I am fighting in war and she is not even knowing what war is.

She is always saying to me, tell me what you are feeling. Tell me what you are thinking. And every day I am telling her the same thing, I am thinking about my future. What is your future, she is asking to me. And I am saying I am seeing myself becoming Doctor or Engineer and making too much money so I am becoming big man and never having to fight war ever again. And sometimes I am telling her, I am hearing bullet and scream in my ear and I am wanting to be dying so I am never hearing it again. I am wanting to lie down on the warm ground with my eye closed and the smell of mud in my nose, just like Strika. I am wanting to feel how the ground is wet all around my body so that if I am sweating, I am feeling like it is the ground sweating through me. And I am wanting to stay in this same place forever, never moving for anything, just waiting waiting until dust is piling on me and grasses is covering me and insect is making their home in the space between my teeths. I am telling her that I am thinking one Iroko tree will be growing from my body, so wide that its trunk is separating night and day, and so tall that its top leaf is tickling the moon until the man living there is smiling.

I am saying to her sometimes, I am not saying many thing because I am knowing too many terrible thing to be saying to you. I am seeing more terrible thing than ten thousand men and I am doing more terrible thing than twenty thousand men. So, if I am saying these thing then it will be making me to sadding too much and you to sadding too much in this life. I am wanting to be happy in this life because of everything I am seeing. I am just wanting to be happy.

When I am saying all of this, she is just looking at me and I am seeing water in her eye. So I am saying to her, if I am telling this to you it will be making you to think that I am some sort of beast or devil. Amy is never saying anything when I am saying this, but the water is just shining in her eye. And I am saying to her, fine. I am all of this thing. I am all of this thing, but I am also having mother once, and she is loving me.

# ACKNOWLEDGEMENTS

My thanks to The Kagan Fellowship Committee and the Mellon Program for their generosity.

My love and thanks to my advisor – Jamaica Kincaid – for everything. Your excitement, motivation, and guidance are much appreciated. Without you, this never would have happened. My first writing teacher – Patricia Powell – for giving me the chance to explore and taking the time to show me what writing is about. Without you, this never would have happened. My family – Mommy and Daddy for understanding and continuing to understand what this means to me. Onyi, Oke, and Uch for listening to my ideas (and tolerating my never washing the dishes). Uncle Chi-Chi and Auntie Uju for housing and feeding me for the summer. Uncle Chude and Dayo for keeping me on track with my work. Uncle Amaechi for the jokes and the suya. And to my grandparents and all of my other uncles, aunties and cousins for their love and companionship. Simi and Auntie Kaine for believing in me, taking care of me, and helping me to understand what it means to be from where we are from. My friends – all of you who had nothing but good things to say without even reading a word of what I wrote. Nina for her unflagging support and for editing and proofreading up a storm (it's finally finished). Ian for being a huge role model (when I grow up, I want to be *almost* just like you). Adeline, Benita, Elliot, Robin, and Thenji for entertaining my thoughts (stay as you are forever). The Chateau for being there and for dealing with me (burn the videotape). And to Aaron and Ismael because you are who you are to me. My agents, Jeff and Tracy – you are wonderfully kind and patient. My editors, Anya and Tim – you are wonderfully kind and patient.

I am deeply indebted to all of you.

# Let's Study Greek

# Let's Study Greek

by
CLARENCE B. HALE

MOODY PRESS

CHICAGO

ISBN: 0-8024-4666-3

*Printed in the United States of America*

# CONTENTS

## Preface to the Revised Edition

In this edition several changes have been made in the 1959 arrangement of the book. The number of lessons has been reduced from 54 to 50.

Declensions are presented as having five cases instead of eight, since in the author's experience there seemed to be very little advantage in using the term *ablative* in addition to *genitive*, and the terms *instrumental* and *locative* in addition to *dative*.

One verb, πιστεύω, has been selected to represent the regular inflection of the omega verb.

The exercises have been expanded by including excerpts from *The Greek New Testament*, edited by Kurt Aland et al. (3rd ed. [New York: United Bible Societies, 1975]), used by their kind permission. Also included are excerpts from papyri and inscriptions cited for the most part by James Hope Moulton and George Milligan in *The Vocabulary of the Greek Testament Illustrated From the Papyri and Other Non-literary Sources* (Grand Rapids: Eerdmans, 1949).

Type faces larger than those employed in the second edition may aid the beginning student.

*A Greek-English Lexicon of the New Testament and Other Early Christian Literature*, (2nd ed., revised and augmented by F. Wilbur Gingrich and Frederick W. Danker [Chicago: U. of Chicago, 1979]) has been consulted frequently.

The author wishes to thank his wife for her patience and accuracy in typing the manuscript, and the editors, typesetters, and proofreaders of Moody Press for their careful work.

# Lesson 1

### 1. IMPORTANCE OF THE GREEK LANGUAGE

You are beginning the study of one of the most important languages in the world. Its importance lies not in the number of people who now use it, for the kind of Greek presented in these lessons is no longer spoken, written, or read as an instrument of modern communication. Its importance lies rather in the literature that it has preserved from Homer on, of which the most widely known part is the New Testament. Its importance lies also in the contributions it has made and is making to the vocabulary of the English language. A large and increasing proportion of the entries in our unabridged dictionaries are words derived from Latin and Greek, in many instances terms coined to label scientific discoveries. As you make progress in mastering this language, you will also increase your understanding both of the English language and of the Greek New Testament.

### 2. IMPORTANCE OF LEARNING THE GREEK ALPHABET

The first step in the study of Greek is to learn the alphabet. Learning the names, the order, and the sounds of the Greek letters will do several things for you. The barrier of strangeness between you and Greek will begin to crumble. When you see Greek letters or their names, you will experience the pleasure of recognition. When you wish to look up a word in a Greek-English lexicon, your knowledge of the order of the letters in the alphabet will enable you to find the word and to learn its meaning. When your teacher pronounces a Greek word slowly, you will have some idea of how it looks when written down. Although you will not be expected to speak this language or to understand anyone else who is speaking it, still it is often necessary in class to talk about Greek words and phrases. A knowledge of the sounds of the letters is needed for those discussions.

### 3. THE GREEK ALPHABET

| Forms | | Names | Sounds | Forms | | Names | Sounds |
|-------|---|-------|--------|-------|---|-------|--------|
| A | α | alpha | *palm* | M | μ | mu | *m*oon |
| B | β | beta | *b*ig | N | ν | nu | *n*o |

1

| | | | | | | | | |
|---|---|---|---|---|---|---|---|---|
| Γ | γ | gamma | go (but before γ, κ, or χ as a*n*gle, a*n*chor, i*n*k) | Ξ | ξ | xi | brea*ks* |
| Δ | δ | delta | *do* | Ο | ο | omicron | *o*n |
| Ε | ε | epsilon | *e*nd | Π | π | pi | *p*ull |
| Ζ | ζ | zeta | lea*ds* | Ρ | ρ | rho | *r*un |
| Η | η | eta | ch*a*os | Σ | σ,ς | sigma | *s*ee |
| Θ | θ | theta | weal*th* | Τ | τ | tau | *t*o |
| Ι | ι | iota | s*i*n or mach*i*ne | Υ | υ | upsilon | s*u*r in French or *ü*ber in German |
| Κ | κ | kappa | *k*ing | Φ | φ | phi | *phi*losophy |
| Λ | λ | lambda | *l*amb | Χ | χ | chi | *ch*aos |
| | | | | Ψ | ψ | psi | cu*ps* |
| | | | | Ω | ω | omega | *o*cean |

## 4. CLASSIFICATION OF LETTERS

a. *Vowels.* The vowels are α, ε, η, ι, ο, υ, ω. Notice their lengths:

| Always short | Either long or short | | Always long |
|---|---|---|---|
| ε | long | ᾱ, ῑ, ῡ | η |
| ο | short | ᾰ, ῐ, ῠ | ω |

b. *Consonants.* The letters that are not vowels are consonants.

## 5. DIPHTHONGS

a. *Proper diphthongs* are combinations of two vowels pronounced in rapid succession. They are pronounced like the underlined letters in the English words below.

αι *ai*sle

αυ s*au*erkraut
ει *ei*ght or h*ei*ght
ευ *e* (in let) plus *oo* (in soon): *e-oo*

ηυ *a* (in l*a*te) plus *oo* (in soon): *a-oo*
οι t*oi*l
ου thr*ou*gh
υι w*ee*k

b. *Improper diphthongs* consist of α, η, or ω and a small iota written underneath: ᾳ, ῃ, ῳ. This small letter is called *iota-subscript*. The improper diphthongs are pronounced exactly like long ᾱ, η, and ω respectively.

c. *Length of diphthongs and syllables.* All diphthongs are long, and all syllables containing diphthongs are long with certain exceptions (number 411).

2

## 6. BREATHINGS

Every Greek word beginning with a vowel must have either a rough or a smooth breathing with the initial vowel or diphthong. The rough breathing is pronounced like the aspirated *h* in English and is written like an introductory single quotation mark ( ' ); the smooth breathing is pronounced with no change in the sound of the vowel or diphthong involved and is written like an apostrophe ( ' ). ὅτι (hoti), ὦ (oh), εὗρον (heooron), οἴνους (oinous), εἰ γὰρ λέγει (ei gar legei). Notice (1) that both breathings and accents are placed on the second vowel of diphthongs, (2) that a circumflex accent is placed above its accompanying breathing, and (3) that other accents follow their accompanying breathings.

## 7. ACCENTS

Three accents are used in spelling Greek words: acute ( ´ ), circumflex ( ˜ ), and grave ( ` ). Only the last three syllables are ever accented.

## 8. EXERCISES

a. Learn the letters of the alphabet so well that you can repeat their names in correct order in thirty seconds.

b. Practice writing the small letters.

c. Be able to recognize the capitals.

d. Pronounce the following Greek words. Notice their similarity to familiar English words. What do you notice about the positions of the breathing marks? You need not memorize these words or their meanings, but familiarity with the sounds of the Greek letters will be very helpful.

1) φωνή:  sound (cf. *phone*)
2) ἀπόστολος:  apostle
3) ἄγγελος:  angel, messenger
4) καρδίᾱ:  heart (cf. *cardiac*)
5) φόβος:  fear (cf. *phobia*)
6) Μᾶρκος:  Mark
7) Νικόδημος:  Nicodemus
8) Πέτρος:  Peter
9) Ῥώμη:  Rome
10) ὕδωρ:  water (cf. *hydro-*)
11) ἐπιστολή: epistle, letter
12) μαργαρίτης:  pearl (cf. English *Margaret* and Spanish *Margarita*)
13) Γαλατίᾱ:  Galatia

3

14) Φίλιππος: Philip

15) ἔξοδος: departure (cf. *Exodus*)

e. Look up the meanings of the following words in the Greek-English vocabulary at the end of this book.

| | |
|---|---|
| 1) λαμβάνω | 4) ἔρχομαι |
| 2) θάνατος | 5) τίθημι |
| 3) ζωή | 6) δίδωμι |

f. Look up in the Greek-English Vocabulary the three words that this lesson has not presented. Then read the Greek aloud and translate:

Ἐγώ εἰμι τὸ (the) Ἄλφα καὶ τὸ Ὦ. . . .

The source of this excerpt is listed on page 244.

# Lesson 2

## 9. GREETINGS

Πέτρος βλέπει ἄνθρωπον, καὶ ὁ ἄνθρωπος βλέπει Πέτρον.

"χαῖρε, Μᾶρκε," λέγει Πέτρος.

"χαῖρε, Πέτρε," λέγει ὁ ἄνθρωπος Μᾶρκος.

ὁ ἄνθρωπος Μᾶρκος ἔχει ἀδελφὸν Νικόδημον. Πέτρος βλέπει καὶ τὸν ἀδελφὸν Νικόδημον, καὶ ὁ ἀδελφὸς βλέπει 5 Πέτρον.

"χαῖρε, Νικόδημε," λέγει Πέτρος.

"χαῖρε, Πέτρε," λέγει Νικόδημος.

Πέτρος καὶ ἔχει ἀδελφὸν Φίλιππον. Φίλιππος βλέπει καὶ τὸν ἄνθρωπον Μᾶρκον καὶ τὸν ἀδελφὸν Νικόδημον. 10

"χαῖρε, Μᾶρκε," λέγει Φίλιππος.

"χαῖρε, Φίλιππε," λέγει Μᾶρκος.

"χαῖρε, Νικόδημε," λέγει Φίλιππος.

"χαῖρε, Φίλιππε," λέγει Νικόδημος.

## 10. VOCABULARY

ἀδελφέ: brother (used in direct address)
ἀδελφόν: brother (direct object of verb)
ἀδελφός: brother (subject of verb)
ἄνθρωπε: man (used in direct address)
ἄνθρωπον: man (direct object of verb)
ἄνθρωπος: man (subject of verb)
βλέπει: sees, looks at, watches
ἔχει: has
καί: and, also, too
καὶ . . . καὶ . . .: both . . . and . . .
λέγει: says
Μᾶρκε: Mark (used in direct address)
Μᾶρκον: Mark (direct object of verb)
Μᾶρκος: Mark (subject of verb)
Νικόδημε: Nicodemus (used in direct address)
Νικόδημον: Nicodemus (direct object of verb)
Νικόδημος: Nicodemus (subject of verb)
ὁ: the (used with masculine singular subject)

5

Πέτρε:  Peter (used in direct address)
Πέτρον:  Peter (direct object of verb)
Πέτρος:  Peter (subject of verb)
τόν:  the (used with masculine singular direct object)
Φίλιππε:  Philip (used in direct address)
Φίλιππον:  Philip (direct object of verb)
Φίλιππος:  Philip (subject of verb)
χαῖρε:  greetings, hail, welcome, good morning, farewell, good-bye,
    rejoice

## 11. SENTENCES

A sentence is a group of words expressing a complete thought.

*Πέτρος βλέπει τὸν ἄνθρωπον.*
*Peter sees the man.*

*ὁ ἄνθρωπος ἔχει ἀδελφόν.*
*The man has a brother.*

It may ask a question, express an exclamation, give a command, or make a statement. All the sentences in this lesson are statements or greetings (exclamations or commands).

## 12. NOUNS

A noun is the name of something.

*Πέτρος ἔχει ἀδελφόν.*
*Peter* has a *brother.*

There are six Greek nouns in this lesson.

## 13. NUMBER

A noun representing one thing is *singular* in number. A noun representing more than one thing is *plural* in number.

*Brother*: singular                    *Brothers*: plural

## 14. GENDER

The Greek language has three grammatical genders: *masculine*, *feminine*, and *neuter*. Often there is no correspondence between the grammatical classification and the sex of the object represented, and no satisfactory explanation can be given for this lack of correspondence.

*ὁ ἄνθρωπος*: *the man*

Here gender and sex are both masculine. All the Greek nouns used in this lesson are masculine. Feminine and neuter nouns will appear in later lessons.

6

## 15. VERBS

A verb is a word or group of words used with or without controlling nouns to make a statement, to ask a question, or to give a command. All the verbs in this lesson are used to make statements or express greetings.

ὁ ἄνθρωπος *βλέπει* Πέτρον.   "*χαῖρε*, Μᾶρκε," *λέγει* Πέτρος.
The man *sees* Peter.         "*Good morning*, Mark," *says* Peter.

## 16. SUBJECTS

A noun with whose number the verb has to agree is the subject of that verb. Not all verbs have nouns as subjects.

βλέπει. *He* sees. (*She* sees. *It* sees.)

The subject of βλέπει is here indicated somewhat vaguely by the verb ending -ει.

"χαῖρε, Μᾶρκε."
"Good morning (*You* rejoice!), Mark."

The subject of χαῖρε is shown by the ending to be one person directly addressed. The addition of Μᾶρκε tells us who this person is. Μᾶρκε, however, is not the subject, but rather a form used in direct address.

*Πέτρος* βλέπει τὸν ἄνθρωπον.
*Peter* sees the man.

In this third example the noun Πέτρος is the subject, and βλέπει agrees with it.

## 17. DIRECT OBJECTS

A direct object is a word or several words representing what receives the action of the verb immediately.

Πέτρος βλέπει *τὸν ἄνθρωπον*.
Peter sees *the man*.

## 18. APPOSITIVES

An appositive is a word added to explain another word. It is generally in the same case as the word which it explains.

ὁ ἄνθρωπος ἔχει ἀδελφόν, *Πέτρον*.
The man has a brother, *Peter*.

## 19. GRAMMATICAL FUNCTIONS AND INFLECTIONAL FORMS

The functions of subject and direct object of a verb are fulfilled nearly always in English by the same form of a word. So we distinguish the subject from the direct object by the order of the words in the sentence.

*Peter* sees *the man*.        *The man*    sees    *Peter*.
(Subject)   (Direct Object)    (Subject)       (Direct Object)

Only a few pronouns have different forms for these two functions, as "I" and "me," and "he" and "him."

*I*    see    *him*.        *He*    sees    *me*.
(Subject)   (Direct Object)    (Subject)    (Direct Object)

In Greek, however, masculine and feminine nouns have forms by which the subject may be distinguished from the direct object. So for the Greeks it was possible to arrange the words of a sentence in almost any order they wished. The English order was used in number 9 only because this is the first reading exercise. Other patterns will be used in subsequent lessons.

Πέτρος βλέπει Φίλιππον.     Φίλιππος βλέπει Πέτρον.
Peter  sees  Philip        Philip  sees  Peter.
(Subject)   (Direct Object)    (Subject)       (Direct Object)

Φίλιππος and Φίλιππον as well as Πέτρος and Πέτρον are *inflectional forms*. Their endings, -ος and -ον, are interchangeable as the grammatical pattern requires.

## 20. CASE: NOMINATIVE SUBJECT

The nouns in number 19 that serve as subjects of verbs are in the *nominative case*.

## 21. CASE: ACCUSATIVE DIRECT OBJECT

The nouns in number 19 that serve as direct objects of verbs are in the *accusative case*.

## 22. CASE: VOCATIVE OF DIRECT ADDRESS

When a masculine noun such as those in number 9 is used to address someone directly, it frequently has the ending -ε in the singular. This is the *vocative of direct address*.

"χαῖρε, *Μᾶρκε*," λέγει Πέτρος.
"Good morning, *Mark*," says Peter.

## 23. THE DEFINITE ARTICLE

In English the definite article is the limiting word "the" and is always spelled the same way. In Greek the form changes to correspond with the gender, number, and case of the noun with which the article is used.

ὁ ἀδελφὸς βλέπει τὸν ἄνθρωπον.
*The* brother sees *the* man.

## 24. THE INDEFINITE ARTICLE

In English the indefinite article is a limiting word having two forms, "a" and "an." In Greek there is no single equivalent. Often, but not always, a Greek noun without a definite article may be translated by an English noun preceded by an indefinite article.

Πέτρος βλέπει ἀδελφόν.
Peter sees *a brother.*

But Πέτρος is obviously not translated *a Peter.*

## 25. EXERCISES

a. Read number 9 aloud following your teacher's example.

b. Translate number 9 into English.

c. Write in Greek, not putting the subject first in the sentence.

   1) Peter sees a man.
   2) Philip has the brother.
   3) The man sees the brother and Peter.
   4) The brother sees Philip.
   5) "Good morning, Mark," says Nicodemus.

d. Translate orally, using the pattern indicated for each group of sentences.

   1) Peter sees a brother.
      Peter sees a man.          Subject—verb—direct object
      Peter sees Nicodemus.
   2) Peter sees Philip.
      Peter sees the brother.    Verb—subject—direct object
      Peter sees the man.
   3) Peter sees Mark.
      Peter has the man.         Verb—direct object—subject
   4) Mark says, "Man!"
      Mark says, "Brother!"      Direct object—subject—verb
      Mark has a brother.
   5) Mark has a man.
      Mark has Philip.           Direct object—verb—subject
      Mark has Nicodemus.

e. Fill in the blanks as you read aloud.

   1) Φίλιππος ἔχει ἀδελφ ____.

2) Φίλιππ ——, βλέπει Πέτρον Μᾶρκος.

3) ἀδελφὸν ἔχ —— Πέτρος.

4) τ —— ἄνθρωπον καὶ τὸν ἀδελφ —— βλέπει Νικόδημος.

f. Notice carefully the following English words related to Greek words in the vocabulary of this lesson.

1) *anthropo*logy: "science of *man*."
2) *Peter*: a proper name meaning "*stone*."
3) Phil*adelphi*a: a proper name meaning "love of *brothers*."
4) *Philip*: a proper name meaning "*lover of horses*."
5) *Philip*pians: people who lived at *Philippi*, a city founded by Philip of Macedon.

g. Read the Greek aloud and then translate:

1) . . . Χαῖρε, ῥαββί (Rabbi) . . . .
2) . . . ὁ Πέτρος βλέπει τὸν μαθητήν (disciple) . . . .
3) . . . κἀκεῖ μνησθῇς ὅτι (and there you remember that) ὁ ἀδελφός σου (your) ἔχει τι κατὰ σοῦ (something against you) . . . .

The sources of these excerpts are listed on page 244.

# Lesson 3

## 26. THE MENU IS FRUIT

"Μᾶρκε, ἔχεις ἄρτον;" λέγει Πέτρος.

"οὐκ ἔχω ἄρτον, Πέτρε." λέγει Μᾶρκος.

"Πέτρε καὶ Φίλιππε, ἔχετε ἄρτον;" λέγει Νικόδημος.

"οὐκ ἔχομεν ἄρτον· ἔχομεν καρπόν." λέγουσι Πέτρος καὶ
Φίλιππος.                                                                                    5

"Μᾶρκος καὶ Νικόδημος οὐκ ἔχουσι ἄρτον καὶ καρπόν,
Φίλιππε," λέγει Πέτρος. "φέρε τὸν καρπόν."

"ἐσθίομεν καρπόν· ἐσθίετε καρπόν, Μᾶρκε καὶ Νικόδημε,"
λέγουσι Πέτρος καὶ Φίλιππος.

"φέρε τὸν καρπόν, Πέτρε," λέγει Φίλιππος, "Μᾶρκος καὶ      10
Νικόδημος ἐσθιέτωσαν καρπόν."

"φερέτω Πέτρος τὸν καρπόν," λέγει Μᾶρκος.

καρπὸν ἐσθίουσι.

## 27. VOCABULARY

ἄρτον: bread, loaf of bread (accusative singular of ἄρτος)

ἐσθίετε: eat! (second plural present imperative active), or you are
    eating, you do eat, you eat (second plural present indicative
    active)

ἐσθιέτωσαν: let them eat! (third plural present imperative active.
    This is a command, not a permission.)

ἐσθίομεν: we are eating, we do eat, we eat (first plural present
    indicative active)

ἔχεις: you are having, you do have, you have (second singular
    present indicative active)

ἔχετε: you are having, you do have, you have (second plural present
    indicative active)

ἔχομεν: we are having, we do have, we have (first plural present
    indicative active)

ἔχουσι: they are having, they do have, they have (third plural
    present indicative active)

ἔχω: I am having, I do have, I have (first singular present indicative
    active)

καρπόν: fruit (accusative singular of καρπός)

11

λέγουσι: they say, they ask (third plural present indicative active)
λέγει: he says, he asks (third singular present indicative active)
οὐκ: not
πιστεύω: I believe, trust
φέρε: bring! carry! (second singular present imperative active)
φερέτω: let him bring! let him carry! (third singular present imperative active)
Greek question mark (;),     Greek semicolon (·)

## 28. TENSE: PRESENT

All the verbs in this lesson represent an action as going on at the moment of speaking or writing. In Greek the emphasis on the progressive nature of the action is greater than on the present time.

| | |
|---|---|
| *λέγουσι.* | *ἐσθίετε καρπόν.* |
| *They are saying.* | *Eat* fruit! (as you are doing). |
| | *Go on eating* fruit! |

These verbs are in the *present tense*, which represents an action or a state as continuing or as being repeated in present time.

## 29. VOICE: ACTIVE

All the verbs in this lesson represent an action as performed by the subject.

| | | |
|---|---|---|
| *ἔχεις ἄρτον;* | *Φίλιππος ἔχει ἀδελφόν.* | *φέρε καρπόν.* |
| *Do you have* bread? | *Philip has* a brother. | *Bring* fruit. |

These verbs are in the *active voice*.

## 30. MOOD: INDICATIVE

Some of the verbs in this lesson make a statement or ask a question.

| | |
|---|---|
| *οὐκ ἔχω ἄρτον.* | *ἔχετε ἄρτον;* |
| *I do* not *have* bread. | *Do you have* bread? |

These verbs are in the *indicative mood*.

## 31. MOOD: IMPERATIVE

Other verbs in this lesson express a command.

| | |
|---|---|
| *φέρε τὸν καρπόν.* | *ὁ ἄνθρωπος φερέτω τὸν καρπόν.* |
| *Bring* the fruit. | *Let* the man *bring* the fruit. |

These verbs are in the *imperative mood*.

## 32. NUMBER

Verbs like nouns may be singular or plural. With verbs the number indicates whether the subject of the verb is singular or plural.

Singular: ἔχω.                Plural: ἔχομεν.
      *I have.*               *We have.*

## 33. PERSON

If the subject of a verb is the person or the group of persons *speaking*, the verb is in the *first person*. If the subject of a verb is the person or the group of persons *spoken to*, the verb is in the *second person*. If the subject of a verb is the person or the thing or the group *spoken of*, the verb is in the *third person*.

|  | Indicative | Imperative |
|---|---|---|
| First Sing.: | ἔχω.<br>*I have.* | (There are no first person<br>imperative forms.) |
| First Pl.: | ἔχομεν.<br>*We have.* |  |
| Second sing.: | ἔχεις.<br>*You have.* | ἔχε.<br>*Have!* |
| Second Pl.: | ἔχετε.<br>*You have.* | ἔχετε.<br>*Have!* |
| Third Sing.: | ἔχει.<br>*He (she, it) has.* | ἐχέτω.<br>*Let him (her, it) have!* |
| Third Pl.: | ἔχουσι.<br>*They have.* | ἐχέτωσαν.<br>*Let them have!* |

## 34. CONJUGATION

All this information about the verb can be briefly summed up by the following tabular arrangement called the *conjugation* of the present indicative active and the present imperative active. A conjugation is the inflection or paradigm of a verb. Since πιστεύω follows a clearly regular scheme in all its tense systems, it will be used in this book as the pattern of an omega verb, that is, one whose first person singular present active indicative ends in omega. Other kinds of conjugations will be illustrated by other verbs.

### Present Active
### Indicative

|  | Singular | Plural |
|---|---|---|
| First person | πιστεύω | πιστεύομεν |
| Second person | πιστεύεις | πιστεύετε |
| Third person | πιστεύει | πιστεύουσι |

### Imperative

|  |  |  |
|---|---|---|
| First person |  | (No first person forms) |

13

| Second person | πίστευε | πιστεύετε |
| Third person | πιστευέτω | πιστευέτωσαν |

In learning a paradigm, a student can save time by observing what remains the same and what changes as he reads through the inflection. Every one of the ten items just given has the stem πιστευ-. To this stem are added for the indicative:

| -ω: I | -ομεν: we |
| -εις: you (sing.) | -ετε: you (pl.) |
| -ει: he, she, it | -ουσι: they |

and for the imperative:

| -ε: you (sing.) | -ετε: you (pl.) |
| -έτω: let him, let her, let it | -έτωσαν: let them |

Of the ten items in these lists -ετε appears twice. By itself πιστεύετε is ambiguous. A context is needed to determine whether the form is indicative or imperative. The other eight items, however, carry specific meaning.

All of these endings will be used with many other verb stems, so it will not be necessary to learn ten new forms for each new omega verb encountered. These endings can be combined with ἐσθι-, ἐχ-, λεγ-, and φερ- as well as with πιστευ-. Consequently, by learning five stems and ten endings, a total of fifteen items, the student has at his command fifty possible Greek forms.

## 35. SYLLABLES: NUMBER IN EACH WORD

To describe the location of an accent we must understand something about syllables. A Greek word has as many syllables as the sum of its diphthongs and separately pronounced vowels.

ἄνθρωπος has three separately pronounced vowels and therefore three syllables. ἔχουσι has one diphthongs and two separately pronounced vowels and therefore three syllables.

## 36. SYLLABLES: NAMES OF THE LAST THREE

The last syllable of a Greek word is called the *ultima* (ἔχου/σι); the next to the last, the *penult* (ἔ/χου/σι); the second from the last, the *antepenult* (ἔ/χουσι).

## 37. SYLLABLES: LENGTH

If the vowel or the diphthong in a syllable is long, the syllable is long. Otherwise, the syllable is short.

## 38. ACCENT: RECESSIVE

The accent of the verbs presented in this lesson backs up as far from

14

the ultima as it can. If the ultima is short, an acute accent stands on the antepenult where the verb has as many as three syllables.

βλέπετε, ἔχομεν, ἔχουσι, λεγέτωσαν.

Even if the ultima is short, the accent stands on the penult, of course, if the verb has only two syllables.

βλέπε, ἔχε, λέγε, φέρε, χαῖρε.

If the ultima is long, an acute accent stands on the penult.

βλέπω, φέρεις, ἔχει, βλεπέτω.

## 39. EXERCISES

a. Read number 26 aloud imitating your teacher.

b. Translate number 26 into English.

c. Write in Greek:
1) I see bread.
2) I bring bread.
3) I eat bread.
4) Nicodemus says, "I see fruit, I bring fruit, I eat fruit."
5) Mark says, "We have a man, we bring the man, we do not eat the man."
6) Is Peter saying, "Welcome"?
7) Nicodemus and Mark are asking, "Do Philip and Peter have a man?"
8) Philip and Peter say, "We do not have a man, Nicodemus and Mark."

d. Translate orally:
1) I eat fruit.
2) You eat fruit, Peter.
3) Philip eats fruit.
4) We eat fruit.
5) You eat fruit, Mark and Nicodemus.
6) Peter and Philip eat fruit.
7) Eat fruit, Nicodemus!
8) Let Nicodemus eat fruit!
9) Eat fruit, Mark and Nicodemus!
10) Let Peter and Philip eat fruit!
11) -20) (Substitute "bring" for "eat" in 1)-10).)

e. Accent the following verb forms in accordance with principles of recessive accent.
1) εχουσι

15

2) βλεπετωσαν
3) λεγετε
4) φερομεν
5) ἐσθιε
6) ἐσθιετω
7) ἔχεις
8) λεγω
9) πιστευετω
10) πιστευε

f. Read the Greek aloud and then translate:

1) . . . Διὰ τί (Why) . . . κοιναῖς χερσὶν (with unclean hands) ἐσθίουσιν τὸν ἄρτον;

2) τίς φυτεύει ἀμπελῶνα (Who plants a vineyard) καὶ τὸν καρπὸν αὐτοῦ (of it) οὐκ ἐσθίει;

The sources of these excerpts are listed on page 244.

# Lesson 4

### 40. A REAL DINNER THIS TIME

"ἔχομεν δεῖπνον ἐν τῷ κήπῳ, Φίλιππε καὶ Πέτρε;" λέγει
τὸ τέκνον Νικοδήμου. Νικόδημος γὰρ τέκνον ἔχει.

Πέτρον καὶ Νικόδημον καὶ τὸ τέκνον καὶ Μᾶρκον ἐκ τοῦ
οἴκου Φίλιππος πέμπει.

"δοῦλε," Φίλιππος λέγει, "φέρε τὸν ἄρτον Πέτρου καὶ τὸν    5
ὄνον Μάρκου ἐκ τοῦ οἴκου."

"ἐσθίεις τὸ ἀρνίον, Φίλιππε;" λέγει ὁ δοῦλος Φιλίππου.

"φέρε τὸ ἀρνίον εἰς τὸν κῆπον. ἐσθίομεν γὰρ ἀρνίον,
δοῦλε," λέγει Φίλιππος.

ἐκ τοῦ οἴκου Φιλίππου φέρει ὁ δοῦλος τὸν ἄρτον καὶ τὸν    10
οἶνον καὶ τὸ ἀρνίον.

"Πέτρε, ἔχεις ὀψάριον;" λέγει τὸ τέκνον.

"οὐκ ἔχω ὀψάριον, τέκνον," λέγει Πέτρος.

"ὀψάριον ἔχει Φίλιππος;" λέγει τὸ τέκνον.

"οὐκ ἔχει Φίλιππος ὀψάριον," λέγει Πέτρος.    15

"πίνομεν τὸν οἶνον Μάρκου ἐκ τοῦ ποτηρίου," τὸ τέκνον
λέγει. "οὐ πίνομεν τὸν ἄρτον. ἐσθίομεν γὰρ τὸν ἄρτον."

"δοῦλε, φέρεις δεῖπνον καλόν," λέγει Νικόδημος.
"Φίλιππε, ἔχεις δοῦλον καλόν."

Φίλιππος πέμπει τὸν καλὸν δοῦλον ἀπὸ τοῦ κήπου, καὶ ὁ    20
δοῦλος φέρει καρπὸν καλὸν εἰς τὸν κῆπον Φιλίππου.

τὸν καλὸν καρπὸν Φίλιππος βλέπει καὶ λέγει, "Νικόδημε
καὶ Μᾶρκε καὶ ἀδελφὲ Πέτρε καὶ τέκνον καὶ δοῦλε, ἐσθίετε
τὸν καλὸν καρπὸν τοῦ δούλου."

"ἔχομεν δεῖπνον καλὸν ἐν τῷ κήπῳ Φιλίππου," τὸ τέκνον    25
Νικοδήμου λέγει.

### 41. VOCABULARY

ἀπό:  from, away from.
ἀπὸ τοῦ κήπου:  away from the garden
ἀρνίον, τό:  lamb, little lamb
γάρ:  for (generally put as the second word in its clause)
δεῖπνον, τό:  dinner, supper
δοῦλος, ὁ:  slave, bondslave

17

εἰς:  into, to
εἰς τὸν κῆπον:  into the garden
ἐκ (ἐξ before vowels):  from, out of, from within
ἐκ τοῦ οἴκου:  out of the house
ἐκ τοῦ ποτηρίου:  out of the cup
ἐν:  in, within, among, with, by means of, with the help of
ἐν τῷ κήπῳ:  in the garden
καλόν:  beautiful, good, excellent, fair, noble
κῆπος, ὁ:  garden
οἶκος, ὁ:  house
οἶνος, ὁ:  wine
οὐ:  not (used before a word beginning with a consonant)
οὐκ:  not (used before a word beginning with a vowel having a
      smooth breathing)
ὀψάριον, τό:  fish
πέμπω:  I send
πίνω:  I drink
ποτήριον, τό:  cup
τέκνον, τό:  child
τό:  the

## 42.  METHOD OF INDICATING GENDER IN VOCABULARIES

In the vocabulary just given and in all following vocabularies the
gender of nouns is shown by the gender of the definite article which is
added.

"ἄρτος, ὁ:  bread" is a masculine noun.
"δεῖπνον, τό:  dinner, supper" is a neuter noun.

## 43.  CASE: GENITIVE OF POSSESSION

In the following expressions the italicized words indicate possessors.

τὸ τέκνον *Νικοδήμου*      τὸν καλὸν καρπὸν *τοῦ δούλου*
the child *of Nicodemus*      *the slave's* good fruit

τὸν οἶνον *Μάρκου*    ὁ δοῦλος *Φιλίππου*    τὸν ἄρτον *Πέτρου*
*Mark's* wine        *Philip's* slave        *Peter's* bread

These Greek words, ending in -ου and shown by the context to
indicate possession, are called *genitives of possession.*

## 44.  CASE: GENITIVE OF SEPARATION OR SOURCE

In number 40 the nouns in the phrases ἐκ τοῦ οἴκου and ἀπὸ τοῦ
κήπου name things from which there occurs separation by the action
of the verb. The words ἀπό, *away from,* and ἐκ, *out of,* state the ideas
of separation.

18

ὁ δοῦλος φέρει τὸ ἀρνίον ἐκ τοῦ οἴκου.
The slave brings the lamb *out of the house.*

In this sentence it is clear that the house is the source from which the slave brings the lamb.

Because in number 40 the nouns οἴκου and κήπου end in -ου and because at the same time the immediate contexts have words expressing the idea of separation or source, these nouns are called *genitives of separation or source.*

## 45. CASE: DATIVE OF PLACE

In number 40 the noun in the phrase ἐν τῷ κήπῳ, *in the garden,* names the place in which the dinner is served. Because κήπῳ ends in -ῳ and because at the same time the immediate context has a word expressing the idea of location, this noun is called a *dative of place.*

## 46. PREPOSITIONS

In number 40 ἀπό, *away from,* εἰς, *into,* ἐκ, *out of,* ἐν, *in,* have been used with nouns. These words are called prepositions. Their function is to help show the relation which the accompanying noun has to its context. The inflectional ending of the noun limits the noun to some extent, but the preposition adds a stricter limitation.

## 47. RÉSUMÉ OF INFLECTIONAL FORMS USED THUS FAR

For masculine nouns the following inflectional endings have been used.

| | |
|---|---|
| Nominative | -ος |
| Genitive | -ου |
| Dative | -ῳ |
| Accusative | -ον |
| Vocative | -ε |

The endings for neuter nouns are the same as those for masculine nouns except in the nominative and vocative.

| | |
|---|---|
| Nominative | -ον |
| Genitive | -ου |
| Dative | -ῳ |
| Accusative | -ον |
| Vocative | -ον |

## 48. SINGULAR FORMS OF THE SECOND DECLENSION

Both the masculine and the neuter nouns used so far belong to the *Second Declension.* A *declension* is an inflection or a paradigm of a noun, an adjective, or a pronoun. Adjectives and pronouns will be studied later. Only singular forms have been used.

|   |   | Masculine |   | Neuter |
|---|---|-----------|---|--------|
| N |   | ἀδελφός |   | τέκνον |
| G |   | ἀδελφοῦ |   | τέκνου |
| D |   | ἀδελφῷ |   | τέκνῳ |
| A |   | ἀδελφόν |   | τέκνον |
| V |   | ἀδελφέ |   | τέκνον |

| N | ὁ | δοῦλος | τό | ποτήριον |
|---|-----|--------|------|----------|
| G | τοῦ | δούλου | τοῦ | ποτηρίου |
| D | τῷ | δούλῳ | τῷ | ποτηρίῳ |
| A | τὸν | δοῦλον | τό | ποτήριον |
| V | — | δοῦλε | — | ποτήριον |

## 49. ACCENT: PERSISTENT

Unlike the accent of verbs, which recedes as far from the ultima as the length of the ultima permits (see number 38), the accent of nouns tends to stay where it is in the nominative form. For this reason the accent of nouns is called *persistent*. Notice the position of the accent in the preceding paradigms.

καρπός is accented like ἀδελφός.
ἀρνίον, Πέτρος, and ἄρτος are accented like τέκνον.
δεῖπνον, κῆπος, οἶνος, and οἶκος are accented like δοῦλος.
ἄνθρωπος, ὀψάριον, and Φίλιππος are accented like ποτήριον.

In all of these examples in number 48 except ποτηρίου and ποτηρίῳ the accent remains on the same syllable throughout the paradigm. In those two exceptions the long ultima draws the accent from the antepenult to the penult. An acute accent on the ultima, as occurs in some forms of καρπός and ἀδελφός, is changed to a grave accent when another word follows without intervening punctuation. Enclitics (number 169) are exceptions to this principle.

For the present these paradigms may be consulted in placing accents on nouns.

## 50. EXERCISES

a. Read number 40 aloud to increase your fluency in pronouncing Greek. This control of the language will make the gospels much more vivid when you come to study them.

b. Translate number 40 into English.

20

c. Write in Greek:

1) I do not drink wine.
2) You (sing.) do not drink good wine.
3) He does not drink good wine in the garden.
4) We eat fruit.
5) You (pl.) eat dinner.
6) Eat (pl.) the lamb in the house.
7) They bring the good bread.
8) Bring (sing.) the fish away from the slave.
9) From (out of) the house I see the garden.
10) Out of the cup we drink in the garden.

d. Translate orally:

1) We see Peter.
2) We do not eat Peter.
3) You (pl.) have a little lamb.
4) You (pl.) say, "Drink, little lamb."
5) The little lamb drinks.
6) The little lamb does not drink wine.
7) Send (sing.) the fish into the garden.
8) Send (pl.) the child into the garden.
9) Carry (sing.) the cup into the house.
10) Carry (pl.) the cup out of the house away from Philip.

e. Translate the English words in parentheses so as to fit the sentence in which each stands, for example,
ὁ δοῦλος (Philip's) ἐσθίει δεῖπνον.
ὁ δοῦλος Φιλίππου ἐσθίει δεῖπνον.

1) τὸ ἀρνίον (Peter's) βλέπει τὸ τέκνον.
2) πίνετε ἐν τῷ κήπῳ (the child's).
3) ἔχομεν τὸν ἄρτον (the man's).
4) πέμπε τὸν δοῦλον ἀπὸ (the fruit).
5) βλέπουσι τὸν ἄνθρωπον ἐν (the house).
6) πίνεις ἐκ (the cup).
7) τὸ γὰρ ποτήριον πέμπομεν εἰς (the garden).

f. Read the Greek aloud and then translate:

1) . . . ὕπαγε (go) εἰς τὸν οἶκόν σου (your).
2) . . . λέγει ἡ μήτηρ τοῦ Ἰησοῦ (the mother of Jesus) πρὸς αὐτόν (to him), Οἶνον οὐκ ἔχουσιν.
3) . . . Διὰ τί (Why) μετὰ τῶν τελωνῶν καὶ ἁμαρτωλῶν (with the tax collectors and sinners) ἐσθίετε καὶ πίνετε;

21

4) δοκιμαζέτω δὲ ἄνθρωπος ἑαυτόν (But let a man be examining himself, καὶ οὕτως (in this way) ἐκ τοῦ ἄρτου ἐσθιέτω καὶ ἐκ τοῦ ποτηρίου πινέτω. . . .

The sources of these excerpts are listed on page 244.

# Lesson 5

## 51. DOCTOR LAZARUS

πυρετοὺς ἔχουσι Πέτρος καὶ Φίλιππος καὶ τὰ τέκνα Μάρκου καὶ Νικοδήμου. ἄρτον καὶ ἀρνίον οὐκ ἐσθίουσι. τοῖς τέκνοις καὶ τοῖς ἀνθρώποις ἄρτους καὶ ὀψάρια οἱ δοῦλοι φέρουσι. οὐκ ἐσθίουσι καὶ οὐκ ἰσχύουσι ἐσθίειν καὶ πίνειν ὅτι πυρετοὺς κακοὺς ἔχουσι. 5

θεραπεύειν πυρετοὺς ἰσχύει ὁ δοῦλος Λάζαρος. τοὺς κακοὺς πυρετοὺς τῶν ἀνθρώπων καὶ τῶν τέκνων θεραπεύειν ἰσχύσει. θεραπεύσει τοὺς κακοὺς πυρετούς.

Φιλίππῳ Λάζαρος λέγει, "θεραπεύσω τὰ τέκνα καὶ τοὺς ἀνθρώπους." 10

Φιλίππῳ δουλεύει Λάζαρος. Λάζαρον ἀπολύσει Φίλιππος ὅτι τοὺς κακοὺς πυρετοὺς θεραπεύειν ἰσχύει ὁ δοῦλος. ὅτι Φίλιππος τὸν καλὸν δοῦλον Λάζαρον ἀπολύσει, οὐ δουλεύσει Λάζαρος Φιλίππῳ.

λέγει Φίλιππος τῷ καλῷ δούλῳ Λαζάρῳ, "Λάζαρε, ἀπολύσω 15 τὸν καλὸν δοῦλον. οὐ δουλεύσεις Φιλίππῳ."

## 52. VOCABULARY

ἀπολύω: I release, set free, let go
ἀπολύσω: I shall release, etc.
δουλεύω: I serve as a slave, am a slave to (with dat. dir. obj.)
δουλεύσω: I shall serve as a slave, etc. (with dat. dir. obj.)
θεραπεύω: I treat, cure, heal
θεραπεύσω: I shall treat, etc.
θεραπεύειν: to treat, etc.
ἰσχύω: I am able, strong, powerful, I can
ἰσχύσω: I shall be able, etc.
κακός: bad, evil, wicked, dangerous
καλός: beautiful, good, excellent, fair, noble
Λάζαρος, -ου, ὁ: Lazarus
ὅτι: because, that
πυρετός, -οῦ, ὁ: fever

23

## 53. METHOD OF INDICATING THE DECLENSIONAL PATTERN OF NOUNS IN VOCABULARIES

The vocabulary entry "πυρετός, -οῦ, ὁ: fever" by the part "-οῦ" indicates that the second inflectional form is πυρετοῦ. With this start we can go on to use the pattern of declension used for ἀδελφός, δοῦλος, and ἄνθρωπος.

## 54. CASE: DATIVE OF INDIRECT OBJECT

You will remember that the ending -ῳ plus the use of the preposition ἐν (ἐν τῷ κήπῳ, *in the garden*) determined the construction. But in number 51 we have *Φιλίππῳ Λάζαρος λέγει*, Lazarus says *to Philip*. By grammatical tradition this is called a dative of *indirect object*. What Lazarus says is the direct object of the verb λέγει. Philip receives the action of this less immediately than the words that are spoken.

## 55. CASE: DATIVE OF DIRECT OBJECT

In number 51 Φιλίππῳ is used in another construction.

*Φιλίππῳ δουλεύει Λάζαρος.*
Lazarus is a slave *to Philip.*

Since Φιλίππῳ receives the action of the verb immediately, it is the direct object of δουλεύει although not in the accusative, but in the dative case.

## 56. PLURAL FORMS OF SECOND DECLENSION NOUNS AND OF THE DEFINITE ARTICLE

Until this lesson only singular nouns and articles have been used. In this lesson the plural endings of the second declension have all been used, and the masculine and neuter forms of the definite article. Two complete paradigms follow.

| | A Masculine Noun | | | A Neuter Noun | | |
|---|---|---|---|---|---|---|
| | Singular | | Endings | Singular | | Endings |
| N | ὁ | ἄνθρωπος | -ος | τὸ | τέκνον | -ον |
| G | τοῦ | ἀνθρώπου | -ου | τοῦ | τέκνου | -ου |
| D | τῷ | ἀνθρώπῳ | -ῳ | τῷ | τέκνῳ | -ῳ |
| A | τὸν | ἄνθρωπον | -ον | τὸ | τέκνον | -ον |
| V | | ἄνθρωπε | -ε | | τέκνον | -ον |

| | Plural | | Endings | Plural | | Endings |
|---|---|---|---|---|---|---|
| N | οἱ | ἄνθρωποι | -οι | τὰ | τέκνα | -α |
| G | τῶν | ἀνθρώπων | -ων | τῶν | τέκνων | -ων |
| D | τοῖς | ἀνθρώποις | -οις | τοῖς | τέκνοις | -οις |
| A | τοὺς | ἀνθρώπους | -ους | τὰ | τέκνα | -α |
| V | | ἄνθρωποι | -οι | | τέκνα | -α |

Notice the accent of ἄνθρωποι. In number 49 we observed that a long ultima draws the accent from the antepenult to the penult in the inflection of words having persistent accent. Now we must learn that a final -οι is not considered long in placing accents on nouns and adjectives.

## 57. ADJECTIVES

An adjective is a word that describes or qualifies the meaning of a noun or pronoun. The definite article is an adjective.

| καλὸς δοῦλος | ὁ δοῦλος | ὁ καλὸς δοῦλος |
|---|---|---|
| a *good* slave | *the* slave | *the good* slave |

## 58. AGREEMENT OF ADJECTIVES

Adjectives agree with the nouns or pronouns that they modify by having the same gender, number, and case.

| καλῷ δούλῳ | τὰ τέκνα | τοὺς κακοὺς πυρετοὺς |
|---|---|---|
| for a *good* slave | *the* children | *the dangerous* fevers |

## 59. ADJECTIVES OF THE SECOND DECLENSION

The adjectives used thus far belong to the second declension in their masculine and neuter forms. Consequently, they employ the same endings as the nouns that they modify.

τοὺς κακοὺς πυρετούς
τῶν καλὰ τέκνα
τῶν καλῶν ἀνθρώπων
δούλοις κακοῖς
οἱ καλοὶ κῆποι

The agreement of nouns and adjectives will not always involve the rhyming of endings. In later lessons nouns and adjectives of different declensions and of different endings will be used together.

## 60. TENSE: FUTURE

The verb forms used before this lesson have all belonged to the present tense. In this lesson the following verb forms are not in the present tense.

| ἀπολύσει | θεραπεύσει |
|---|---|
| ἀπολύσω | θεραπεύσω |
| δουλεύσει | ἰσχύσει |
| δουλεύσεις | |

These are future forms and are to be recognized by the sigma just before the personal endings.

| ἀπολύσει | θεραπεύσω |
|---|---|

The *future tense* represents an action as going on, or as about to occur, after the moment of speaking or writing.

## 61. FUTURE INDICATIVE ACTIVE COMPARED WITH PRESENT INDICATIVE ACTIVE

| Present | Future |
|---|---|
| πιστεύω | πιστεύσω |
| πιστεύεις | πιστεύσεις |
| πιστεύει | πιστεύσει |
| πιστεύομεν | πιστεύσομεν |
| πιστεύετε | πιστεύσετε |
| πιστεύουσι | πιστεύσουσι |

All the new verbs in this lesson form their future active indicative as πιστεύω does, but the verbs given in lessons 2, 3, and 4 do not follow this pattern and will be explained later.

## 62. PRESENT INFINITIVE ACTIVE

The form θεραπεύειν is a present active infinitive translated *to heal* or *heal*, depending upon the English verb introducing the infinitive in the translation. It may be called a *complementary infinitive* since it completes the idea in ἰσχύω. It is really a direct object of ἰσχύω.

ἰσχύω θεραπεύειν.
I am able *to heal*, (or) I can *heal*.

All the verbs given thus far and form their present active infinitive by adding -ειν to the present active stem.

| Indicative | Infinitive |
|---|---|
| βλέπω | βλέπειν |
| ἐσθίω | ἐσθίειν |
| πίνω | πίνειν |
| πιστεύω | πιστεύειν |

## 63. CAUSAL CLAUSES

A clause introduced by ὅτι may in a suitable context indicate the reason for the statement to which the clause is subordinate.

Φίλιππος τὸν δοῦλον ἀπολύει ὅτι ὁ δοῦλος τέκνα θεραπεύει.
Philip releases the slave *because the slave heals children*.

## 64. EXERCISES

a. Read number 51 aloud trying to group together the words that are grammatically allied. This should help you to understand what you are reading.

b. Translate number 51 into good English.

c. Write in Greek.

1) I shall let the slave go.
2) You will let the slave go, Peter.
3) She will let the slave go.
4) We are letting the slave go.
5) You are letting the slave go, Mark and Nicodemus.
6) They are letting the slave go.
7) Serve as a slave to Philip, Lazarus!
8) Will you be a slave to Philip, Lazarus?
9) I will not be a slave to Philip, Peter.
10) I can not be a slave to Philip, Peter.
11) Will you be able to be a slave to Philip, Nicodemus?
12) Cure Philip, Lazarus!
13) Good morning, Philip.

d. Translate the following forms and give their corresponding present forms.

1) ἀπολύσομεν
2) δουλεύσετε
3) θεραπεύσουσι
4) ἰσχύσεις
5) θεραπεύσομεν
6) δουλεύσουσι
7) ἀπολύσετε
8) θεραπεύσεις
9) δουλεύσομεν

10) ἀπολύσει
11) ἰσχύσουσι
12) θεραπεύσετε
13) ἀπολύσουσι
14) ἰσχύσομεν
15) ἰσχύσετε
16) δουλεύσει
17) ἀπολύσω
18) δουλεύσεις

e. Read the Greek aloud and then translate:

1) Ἔστιν παιδάριον ὧδε ὃς (There is a lad here who) ἔχει πέντε (five) ἄρτους κριθίνους (made of barley flour) καὶ δύο (two) ὀψάρια . . . .

2) Νῦν (now) ἀπολύεις τὸν δοῦλόν σου (your) . . . .

3) . . . Ὁ μείζων (The older) δουλεύσει τῷ ἐλάσσονι (the younger) . . . .

The sources of these excerpts are listed on page 244.

27

# Lesson 6

## 65. VOCABULARY IN LESSONS 2-5

You should know all these words perfectly.

| NOUNS | PREPOSITIONS | CONJUNCTIONS |
|-------|--------------|--------------|
| ἀδελφός | ἀπό | γάρ |
| ἄνθρωπος | εἰς | καί |
| ἀρνίον | ἐκ | ὅτι |
| ἄρτος | ἐν | |
| δεῖπνον | | |
| δοῦλος | | |
| καρπός | VERBS | ADJECTIVES |
| κῆπος | | |
| Λάζαρος | ἀπολύω | κακός |
| Μᾶρκος | βλέπω | καλός |
| Νικόδημος | δουλεύω | ὁ |
| οἶκος | ἐσθίω | τό |
| οἶνος | ἔχω | |
| ὀψάριον | θεραπεύω | |
| Πέτρος | ἰσχύω | |
| ποτήριον | λέγω | ADVERBS |
| πυρετός | πέμπω | |
| τέκνον | πίνω | οὐ |
| Φίλιππος | πιστεύω | οὐκ |
| | φέρω | |
| | χαῖρε | |

Note: Some of these words will be used with meanings different from those given so far. Whenever the context seems to require a new meaning, look in the Greek-English vocabulary in the back of the book.

## 66. TECHNICAL TERMS DEFINED OR ILLUSTRATED IN LESSONS 1-5

These terms will be used constantly as long as you study Greek. Know them well!

| | |
|---|---|
| Accent | Improper Diphthong |
| Accusative | Indefinite Article |
| Active Voice | Indicative Mood |
| Adjective | Inflectional Form |
| Agreement | Nominative |
| Alphabet | Nouns |
| Antepenult | Number |
| Appositive | Penult |
| Breathing | Persistent Accent |
| Case | Person |
| Causal Clause | Preposition |
| Conjugation | Present Infinitive Active |
| Consonant | Present Tense |
| Dative | Proper Diphthong |
| Declension | Recessive Accent |
| Definite Article | Sentence |
| Direct Object | Subject |
| Future Tense | Syllable |
| Gender | Ultima |
| Genitive | Verb |
| Grammatical Function | Vocative |
| Imperative Mood | Vowel |

# 67. INFLECTIONS IN LESSONS 2-5

## SECOND DECLENSION

| | | | |
|---|---|---|---|
| ὁ | ἄνθρωπος | τό | τέκνον |
| τοῦ | ἀνθρώπου | τοῦ | τέκνου |
| τῷ | ἀνθρώπῳ | τῷ | τέκνῳ |
| τὸν | ἄνθρωπον | τό | τέκνον |
| | ἄνθρωπε | | τέκνον |

| | | | |
|---|---|---|---|
| οἱ | ἄνθρωποι | τά | τέκνα |
| τῶν | ἀνθρώπων | τῶν | τέκνων |
| τοῖς | ἀνθρώποις | τοῖς | τέκνοις |
| τοὺς | ἀνθρώπους | τά | τέκνα |
| | ἄνθρωποι | | τέκνα |

## PRESENT INDICATIVE ACTIVE

| | |
|---|---|
| πιστεύω | πιστεύομεν |
| πιστεύεις | πιστεύετε |
| πιστεύει | πιστεύουσι |

## PRESENT INFINITIVE ACTIVE

πιστεύειν

## PRESENT IMPERATIVE ACTIVE

πίστευε                  πιστεύετε
πιστευέτω           πιστευέτωσαν

## FUTURE INDICATIVE ACTIVE

πιστεύσω              πιστεύσομεν
πιστεύσεις            πιστεύσετε
πιστεύσει             πιστεύσουσι

## 68. OBJECTIVE TESTS

a. Select the Greek item at the right that illustrates the technical term at the left.

1) Accented
Antepenult

  a) κακός
  b) πέμπειν
  c) ὀψάριον
  d) δοῦλος
  e) ἄρτος          1.( )

2) Improper
Diphthong

  a) ῳ
  b) οι
  c) ει
  d) η
  e) ιο          2.( )

3) Preposition

  a) γάρ
  b) εἰς
  c) οὐκ
  d) ὅτι
  e) τόν          3.( )

4) Smooth Breathing
and Circumflex
Accent

  a) ὅτι
  b) ἄρτος
  c) ἀρνίον
  d) οὐ
  e) οἶκος        4.( )

5) Agreement of
Noun and
Adjective

  a) οἶνος κακός
  b) οἴνου κακός
  c) οἴνῳ κακοί
  d) οἶνον κακῷ
  e) οἴνων κακόν   5.( )

6) Grammatical Gender
Differing from
Natural Gender

  a) ὁ ἀδελφός
  b) τοῦ ἄνθρώπου
  c) τῷ τέκνῳ
  d) Λάζαρον
  e) τὰ ποτήρια   6.( )

| 7) Imperative Mood | a) λέγει |  |
|---|---|---|
|  | b) φέρε |  |
|  | c) πίνειν |  |
|  | d) δουλεύουσι |  |
|  | e) βλέπεις | 7.( ) |
| 8) Vocative Case (Choose among the italicized words.) | a) ἀπὸ τοῦ *οἴκου* |  |
|  | b) ἐκ τοῦ *κήπου* |  |
|  | c) τὸ ἀρνίον τοῦ *τέκνου* |  |
|  | d) εἰς τὸ *ποτήριον* |  |
|  | e) οὐ βλέπει, *Φίλιππε* | 8.( ) |
| 9) Recessive Accent | a) Νικόδημε |  |
|  | b) Λάζαρον |  |
|  | c) Φίλιππος |  |
|  | d) θεραπεύω |  |
|  | e) ποτήριον | 9.( ) |
| 10) Long Syllable | a) ἐν |  |
|  | b) ὁ |  |
|  | c) γάρ |  |
|  | d) οὐ |  |
|  | e) ἐκ | 10.( ) |

b. Make each of the following a meaningful expression by filling each blank with an appropriate inflectional ending.

1) θεράπευ _____ τὰ τέκνα Λάζαρος.
2) θεράπευ _____ τὰ τέκνα, Λάζαρε.
3) θεραπεύσ _____ τὰ τέκνα, Λάζαρε;
4) ἰσχύσει θεραπεύ _____ τὰ τέκνα;
5) δουλεύομεν Πέτρ _____.
6) βλέπε, Μᾶρκ _____, τοὺς καρπούς.
7) φέρετε τὸ δεῖπν _____ εἰς τ _____ κῆπον.
8) τὰ ποτήρι _____ τοῦ οἴν _____ οὐκ ἔχουσι οἱ δοῦλοι.
9) τὰ ἀρνία βλεπέτωσαν οἱ ἀδελφ _____.
10) ἐκ τ _____ οἴκ _____ καὶ ἀπὸ τ _____ κῆπ _____ φέρομεν τὰ δεῖπν _____.

## 69. URGENT BUSINESS INTERFERES WITH DINNER

(This little story uses just about all you have learned so far. If you have mastered all the lessons before this review, you should be able to translate this exercise at sight with a little study.)

Πέτρος καὶ Φίλιππος: "ἐν τῷ οἴκῳ δεῖπνον καλὸν ἐσθίομεν. ἐν τῷ κήπῳ ἀνθρώπους βλέπομεν. Νικόδημον καὶ Μᾶρκον βλέπομεν. λέγομεν τοῖς ἀδελφοῖς, 'χαίρετε (plural of

31

χαῖρε), ἄνθρωποι καλοί. χαῖρε, Νικόδημε. χαῖρε, Μᾶρκε.᾽
φέρομεν τοὺς καλοὺς ἀδελφοὺς εἰς τὸν οἶκον καὶ λέγομεν,　　5
'ἰσχύσετε ἐν τῷ οἴκῳ δεῖπνον ἐσθίειν.'"

　　Νικόδημος καὶ Μᾶρκος: "οὐκ ἰσχύσομεν ἐσθίειν, Πέτρε
καὶ Φίλιππε, ὅτι κακοὺς δούλους ἀπὸ τοῦ κήπου πέμπομεν. οἱ
γὰρ δοῦλοι τοῖς καλοῖς τέκνοις ποτήρια οἴνου φέρουσι. οὐ
φέρει οἶνον τοῖς τέκνοις ὁ καλὸς δοῦλος Λάζαρος. θεραπεύει　　10
πυρετοὺς ὁ καλὸς Λάζαρος. τὸν καλὸν δοῦλον Φίλιππος
ἀπολυέτω. τὰ τέκνα καὶ οἱ δοῦλοι καλῶν ἀνθρώπων ὀψάριον
καλὸν ἐσθίουσι καὶ οὐ πίνουσι κακὸν οἶνον. οἶνον κακὸν
κακοὶ δοῦλοι πινέτωσαν. οἴνῳ γὰρ καὶ οὐκ ἀνθρώποις δοῦλοι
κακοὶ δουλεύουσι. ὁ γὰρ κακὸς οἶνος τούς κακοὺς δούλους　　15
οὐκ ἀπολύσει."

　　Πέτρος καὶ Φίλιππος: "ἀπὸ τοῦ οἴκου καὶ ἀπὸ τοῦ κήπου
καὶ ἀπὸ τῶν τέκνων τοὺς κακοὺς δούλους πέμπετε. λέγετε τοῖς
κακοῖς τέκνοις, 'ἐσθίετε ἄρτον καὶ ἀρνίον καὶ καρπὸν καὶ
ὀψάριον.'"　　20

　　Νικόδημος καὶ Μᾶρκος: "χαίρετε, Πέτρε καὶ Φίλιππε."
　　Πέτρος καὶ Φίλιππος: "χαίρετε, Νικόδημε καὶ Μᾶρκε."

# Lesson 7

## 70. TABLE TALK

σὺν τοῖς ἰδίοις ἀδελφοῖς, Πέτρῳ καὶ Φιλίππῳ, ἐσθίει ἀρνίον καὶ ὀψάριον Μαρίᾱ. περὶ τοῦ ἐλευθέρου Λαζάρου λέγουσι.

Πέτρος: "οὐκέτι δουλεύσει Φιλίππῳ ὁ ἐλεύθερος Λάζαρος."

Μαρίᾱ: "πάντοτε τοὺς πυρετοὺς τῶν τέκνων θεραπεύει;" 5

Φίλιππος: "ναί. δικαίᾱν γὰρ καρδίᾱν ἔχει Λάζαρος."

Πέτρος: "καὶ νῦν δωρεὰς ἔχει ὁ μακάριος Λάζαρος."

Φίλιππος: "χρείᾱν δωρεῶν ἔχει ὅτι οὐκέτι ἐν τῷ οἴκῳ Πέτρου καὶ Φιλίππου σὺν τοῖς δούλοις ἐσθίει."

Μαρίᾱ: "Νικόδημος καὶ Μᾶρκος Λαζάρῳ δωρεὰς πέμ- 10 πουσι;"

Πέτρος: "ναί, ἀλλὰ πέμπουσι τοὺς ἰδίους κακοὺς δούλους ἀπὸ τῶν ἰδίων μακαρίων τέκνων."

Μαρίᾱ: "δικαίᾱς καρδίᾱς ἔχουσι πάντοτε οἱ ἀδελφοί."

Φίλιππος: "παρρησίᾱν νῦν ἔχει ὁ μακάριος Λάζαρος. 15 παρρησίᾳ λέγειν ἰσχύει."

Μαρίᾱ: "παρρησίᾱν καὶ ἔχομεν, ἀλλὰ οὐκ ἔχουσι δοῦλοι."

Πέτρος: "ἀλλὰ ἔχουσι αἱ καρδίαι καλῶν δούλων δικαίᾱν ἐπιθυμίᾱν παρρησίᾱς."

Φίλιππος: "ναί, ἀλλὰ ἐπιθυμίᾱν οἴνου ἔχουσι αἱ καρδίαι 20 κακῶν δούλων."

Μαρίᾱ: "τὸν μακάριον καὶ ἐλεύθερον Λάζαρον, ἀδελφοί, εἰς τὸν ἴδιον οἶκον φέρετε."

Πέτρος καὶ Φίλιππος: "ἔχομεν ἐν ταῖς ἰδίαις καρδίαις καὶ ἐπιθυμίᾱν καὶ χρείᾱν λέγειν σὺν Λαζάρῳ. ἰσχύσεις βλέπειν 25 Λάζαρον. ἰσχύσομεν φέρειν τὸν ἐλεύθερον Λάζαρον καὶ λέγειν παρρησίᾳ περὶ τῶν δωρεῶν."

## 71. VOCABULARY

ἀλλά: but
δίκαιος, -ᾱ, -ον: righteous, just
δωρεά, -ᾶς, ἡ: gift
ἐλεύθερος, -ᾱ, -ον: free
ἐπιθυμίᾱ, -ᾱς, ἡ: longing, desire

33

ἴδιος, -ᾱ, -ov: one's (my, our, your, his, her, its, their) own, belonging to one's self

καρδίᾱ, -ᾱς, ἡ: heart

κοσμος, -ου, ὁ: universe, world, earth

μακάριος, -ᾱ, -ov: happy, blessed

Μαρίᾱ, -ᾱς, ἡ: Mary

ναί: yes

νῦν: now

οὐκέτι: no longer, no more

πάντοτε: always, at all times, at any time

παρρησίᾱ, -ᾱς, ἡ: freedom (of speech), confidence, boldness, openness

παρρησίᾳ (dat. of παρρησία used as an adverb): freely, frankly, plainly

περί: (with gen. in figurative sense) around, about, concerning

σύν: (with dat.) with

χρείᾱ, -ᾱς, ἡ: need, necessity

## 72. PARADIGMS OF THE FIRST DECLENSION

Until this lesson all the nouns have belonged to the second declension and have been either masculine or neuter in gender. In this lesson the nouns δωρεά, ἐπιθυμίᾱ, καρδίᾱ, Μαρίᾱ, παρρησίᾱ, and χρείᾱ belong to the first declension and are feminine in gender. It will be noticed that all of these nouns end in -ᾱ preceded by ε or ι. When as in these examples the stem of a first declension noun ends in ε, ι, or ρ followed by α in the nominative singular, the following pattern prevails.

|     | Singular | Plural | Endings | |
| --- | --- | --- | --- | --- |
| N V | καρδίᾱ | καρδίαι | -ᾱ | -αι |
| G | καρδίᾱς | καρδίῶν | -ᾱς | -ων |
| D | καρδίᾳ | καρδίαις | -ᾳ | -αις |
| A | καρδίᾱν | καρδίᾱς | -ᾱν | -ᾱς |
| N V | δωρεά | δωρεαί | | |
| G | δωρεᾶς | δωρεῶν | | |
| D | δωρεᾷ | δωρεαῖς | | |
| A | δωρεάν | δωρεάς | | |

## 73. PARADIGM OF THE FEMININE OF FIRST AND SECOND DECLENSION ADJECTIVES

The feminine forms of the adjectives introduced as new vocabulary in this lesson (δίκαιος, ἐλεύθερος, ἴδιος, and μακάριος) have the same endings as the feminine nouns discussed in number 72.

|  | Singular | Plural |
|---|---|---|
| N V | δικαίᾱ | δίκαιαι |
| G | δικαίᾱς | δικαίων |
| D | δικαίᾳ | δικαίαις |
| A | δικαίᾱν | δικαίᾱς |

The accent of the genitive plural is not a circumflex on the ultima as in number 72. In number 56 we learned that a final -οι is not considered long in placing accents on nouns and adjectives. δίκαιαι illustrates that fact that a final -αι is viewed in the same way.

## 74. COMPLETE PARADIGM OF A FIRST AND SECOND DECLENSION ADJECTIVE

The following paradigm gives the pattern for adjectives of this declension whose stems end in ε, ι, or ρ.

### Singular

|  | Masculine | Feminine | Neuter |
|---|---|---|---|
| N | δίκαιος | δικαίᾱ | δίκαιον |
| G | δικαίου | δικαίᾱς | δικαίου |
| D | δικαίῳ | δικαίᾳ | δικαίῳ |
| A | δίκαιον | δικαίᾱν | δίκαιον |
| V | δίκαιε | δικαίᾱ | δίκαιον |

### Plural

|  | Masculine | Feminine | Neuter |
|---|---|---|---|
| N V | δίκαιοι | δίκαιαι | δίκαια |
| G | δικαίων | δικαίων | δικαίων |
| D | δικαίοις | δικαίαις | δικαίοις |
| A | δικαίους | δικαίᾱς | δίκαια |

There is no distinct vocative form except in the masculine singular.

## 75. METHOD OF INDICATING IN THE VOCABULARY THE DECLENSIONAL PATTERN OF AN ADJECTIVE

The vocabulary entry "δίκαιος, -ᾱ, -ον" is an abbreviated way of giving the nominative singular forms as written out in full in number 74. This style of entry will be used from now on.

## 76. COMPLETE PARADIGM OF THE DEFINITE ARTICLE

Since some of the feminine forms of the definite article have been used in number 70, it will be helpful to see all the forms at once.

Note: Although ὁ, ἡ, τό usually means "the," rather often a definite article may have the force of a *possessive adjective*.

Πέτρος βλέπει τὸν ἀδελφόν.
Peter sees *his* brother.

|   | Masculine | Singular<br>Feminine | Neuter |
|---|---|---|---|
| N | ὁ | ἡ | τό |
| G | τοῦ | τῆς | τοῦ |
| D | τῷ | τῇ | τῷ |
| A | τόν | τήν | τό |
| V | None | None | None |

|   |   | Plural |   |
|---|---|---|---|
| N | οἱ | αἱ | τά |
| G | τῶν | τῶν | τῶν |
| D | τοῖς | ταῖς | τοῖς |
| A | τούς | τάς | τά |
| V | None | None | None |

## 77. CASE: OBJECTIVE GENITIVE

In number 70 occur the following expressions: (line 7) χρείαν δωρεῶν, need *of gifts*, (lines 16, 17) ἐπιθυμίαν παρρησίας, desire *of freedom* (to speak), (line 18) ἐπιθυμίαν οἴνου, desire *of wine*. The italicized Greek words express direct objects of verbs implied by the nouns which the genitives modify. "Need of gifts," for example, implies that someone *needs gifts*. Hence the term *objective genitive* is used.

## 78. CASE: DATIVE

a. *Of Association.* At the beginning of number 70 occurs the phrase σὺν τοῖς ἰδίοις ἀδελφοῖς, with *her own brother*. This expression will be called a *dative of association*. The meaning of σύν, *with*, explains the idea of association.

b. *Of Manner.* In the sentence παρρησίᾳ λέγειν ἰσχύει Λάζαρος, Lazarus can speak *freely*, the italicized Greek word expressed the way in which Lazarus can speak. παρρησίᾳ will be called a *dative of manner*.

## 79. POSITION OF ADJECTIVES: ATTRIBUTIVE

In the expression σὺν τοῖς ἰδίοις ἀδελφοῖς, with *her own* brothers, the position of ἰδίοις between the noun and its definite article is described as *attributive*.

## 80. EXERCISES

a. Read number 70 aloud.

b. Translate number 70 into English.

c. Match the adjectives in list 2 with the nouns in list 1 so that the two words will agree.

List 1                     List 2

1) χρείαις        α) τά          λ) δικαίαις
2) τέκνῳ          β) δικαίᾶς     μ) μακάριε
3) παρρησίαν      γ) ἰδίαν        ν) ἴδιοι
4) πυρετούς       δ) μακαρίων    ξ) ἐλεύθεραι
5) Μαρίᾳ          ε) ἴδιος
6) ποτηρίων       ζ) ἐλευθέρᾱ
7) καρδιῶν        η) δικαίῳ
8) ὀψάρια         θ) καλῶν
9) ἐπιθυμίᾱς      ι) ἰδίᾳ
10) κόσμος        κ) κακούς

d. Translate orally the italicized words:

1) *His own gifts* are here.
2) The price *of the gifts* was high.
3) We serve *a free man.*
4) You came *with happy Mary.*
5) Let's talk *about our own needs.*
6) *Noble brother*, listen!
7) Do you see *the happy children?*
8) He cannot heal *his own fever.*
9) These brothers are *free.*
10) What desires do you have *in your own just hearts?*

e. Conjugate in the present indicative and imperative active to increase your oral facility.

1) ναί, πάντοτε λέγω παρρησίᾳ.
2) νῦν, οὐκέτι λέγω περὶ χρειῶν.
3) ἀλλὰ νῦν λέγω περὶ τοῦ κόσμου.

f. Conjugate in the future indicative active to increase your oral facility.

1) οὐκέτι θεραπεύσω πάντοτε πυρετούς.
2) ναί, ἀπολύσω τοὺς δούλους Μαρίᾱς.
3) νῦν δουλεύσω Μαρίᾳ.

g. Translate the Greek sentences in *e* and *f* into English.

h. Notice carefully the following English words related to new Greek words in this lesson.

1) Theo*dore*: a proper name meaning *gift* of God.

2) *idio*m:  a way of speaking peculiar to a group of people, *their own way* of speaking.
3) *cardia*c:  related to the *heart*.
4) *Mari*olatry:  veneration of *Mary*, the mother of Jesus.
5) *peri*meter:  the distance *around* a geometric figure.

i. Read the Greek aloud and then translate.

1) Οὐκ εἰμὶ ἐλεύθερος;
2) καὶ ὁ κόσμος παράγεται (is passing away) καὶ ἡ ἐπιθυμίᾱ αὐτοῦ (its) . . . .
3) When in A.D. 67 the freedom of the Greeks was proclaimed at the Isthmian games, the Emperor Nero was described in this way: ὁ παντὸς (all) κόσμου κύριος (lord) Νέρων.

The sources of these excerpts are listed on page 244.

# Lesson 8

## 81. FOR OLD TIMES' SAKE

ἐν χρόνῳ μικρῷ πέμπει ἀπὸ τοῦ οἴκου Φιλίππου εἰς τὸν
οἶκον Λαζάρου ἄγγελον Πέτρος.

"χαῖρε, Λάζαρε," λέγει ὁ ἄγγελος.

"χαῖρε, ἄγγελε," λέγει Λάζαρος.

"μνημονεύουσι Μαρίᾱ καὶ Πέτρος καὶ Φίλιππος," λέγει ὁ      5
ἄγγελος, "τὸν χρόνον ὅτε ἦς μικρὸς δοῦλος. τότε ἦτε ὁμοῦ
πάντοτε, Μαρίᾱ καὶ Πέτρος καὶ Φίλιππος καὶ Λάζαρος.
ἐλπίζουσι βλέπειν πάλιν Λάζαρον ἐν τῷ οἴκῳ Φιλίππου καὶ
πάλιν ἐσθίειν σὺν Λαζάρῳ καὶ λέγειν περὶ τῶν χρόνων ὅτε
ἦσαν τέκνα ἐλεύθερα καὶ ὅτε ἦς μικρὸς δοῦλος."              10

"λέγε Μαρίᾳ καὶ Πέτρῳ καὶ Φιλίππῳ," λέγει Λάζαρος,
"'μνημονεύω ὅτε ἤμην μικρὸς δοῦλος, ὅτε ἠσθίομεν ὁμοῦ, ὅτε
ἰσχύετε λέγειν παρρησίᾳ, ἀλλὰ ὅτε ἴσχυον λέγειν παρρησίᾳ.
μνημονεύετε ὅτι εἴχομεν δεῖπνον ἐν τῷ κήπῳ; τότε ἄρτον καὶ
ὀψάριον ἤσθιον, ἀλλὰ οὐκ ἔπινον οἶνον. μακάριοι ἦμεν.'"     15

τότε πάλιν εἰς τὸν οἶκον Φιλίππου τὸν ἄγγελον Λάζαρος
πέμπει.

τότε Λάζαρος μνημονεύει τοῦ χρόνου ὅτε ἦν μικρὸς
δοῦλος καὶ ὅτε ἦν τέκνον ἐν τῷ οἴκῳ Φιλίππου.

"ἀρνίον μικρὸν εἶχε Μαρίᾱ," λέγει Λάζαρος. "ἦμεν τέκνα   20
ὁμοῦ. ἤμην μακάριον τέκνον ἐν τοῖς χρόνοις ὅτε τὸ ἀρνίον
Μαρίᾱς ἤσθιε σὺν Πέτρῳ καὶ Φιλίππῳ καὶ Λαζάρῳ. ἐλπίζω ὅτι
μνημονεύει πάλιν Μαρίᾱ τοῦ ἀρνίου, καὶ ἐλπίζω λέγειν
παρρησίᾳ σὺν Μαρίᾳ καὶ τοῖς ἀδελφοῖς Μαρίᾱς περὶ τῶν
μακαρίων χρόνων."                                           25

## 82. VOCABULARY

ἄγγελος, -ου, ὁ:  angel, messenger
εἰμί:  I am
ἐλπίζω (future will be given later):  I hope, hope for
ἦμεν:  we were
ἤμην:  I was
ἦν:  he (she, it) was
ἦς:  you (sing.) were

ἦσαν: they were
ἦτε: you (pl.) were
μικρός, -ά, -όν: small, little, short
μνημονεύω: I remember (followed by accusative or more frequently
    by genitive direct object)
ὁμοῦ: together
ὅτε: when, while
πάλιν: again, back
τότε: then, at that time
χρόνος, -ου, ὁ: time, a period of time, a while

## 83. CASE: GENITIVE USED AS A DIRECT OBJECT

In number 81 genitives are twice used as direct objects of the verb
μνημονεύω. This construction will be found with several other verbs.

## 84. TENSE: IMPERFECT

In this lesson a new tense has been used. Such forms as εἶχε, ἔπινον,
ἦν, ἦσαν, ἤσθιον, ἰσχύετε, and ἴσχυον belong to the *imperfect
indicative active*. This new tense belongs to the present system of the
Greek verb but has different endings. The imperfect represents an
action or a state as continuing or as being repeated in past time. It
may be translated in several ways.

ἤσθιον: I was eating.
       I used to eat.
       I continued to eat.
       I kept on eating.
       I ate and ate and ate.
       I ate repeatedly.

## 85. PARADIGMS OF THE IMPERFECT INDICATIVE ACTIVE

a. πιστεύω      ἐπίστευον      ἐπιστεύομεν
               ἐπίστευες       ἐπιστεύετε
               ἐπίστευε        ἐπίστευον

The ε at the beginning is called an *augment*, that is, an increase in
the length of the word as compared with the corresponding form
in the present tense. Since this ε adds a syllable to the word, it is
called *syllabic augment*.

    After ἐπιστευ- the next letter is always either *o* or *ε*. This vari-
ation is referred to as the *variable* or *thematic vowel*. After the
variable vowel come the personal endings: -ν, -ς, -, -μεν, -τε, -ν.

b. ἐσθίω        ἤσθιον        ἠσθίομεν
               ἤσθιες        ἠσθίετε
               ἤσθιε         ἤσθιον

The η does not add a syllable to the word, but it does add length to the first syllable. For this reason, the lengthening of the ε in ἐσθίω to η in ἤσθιον is called *temporal augment*, that is, an increase in the time necessary to pronounce the first syllable.

c. ἀπολύω

| ἀπέλυον | ἀπελύομεν |
|---------|-----------|
| ἀπέλυες | ἀπελύετε |
| ἀπέλυε | ἀπέλυον |

Notice that the augment is placed between the prepositional prefix ἀπό and the verb λύω and that the *o* in ἀπό is elided (omitted) before the augment.

d. ἔχω

| εἶχον | εἴχομεν |
|-------|---------|
| εἶχες | εἴχετε |
| εἶχε | εἶχον |

In ἔχω the ε is lengthened to ει in εἶχον. This is another form of temporal augment. Whether η or ει is used as an augment of ε must be learned by observation.

e. ἰσχύω

| ἴσχυον | ἴσχύομεν |
|--------|----------|
| ἴσχυες | ἴσχύετε |
| ἴσχυε | ἴσχυον |

Here a short ι in ἰσχύω is made a long ι in ἴσχυον.

f. εἰμί: I am

| ἤμην | I was |
|------|-------|
| ἦς | you were |
| ἦν | he (she, it) was |
| ἦμεν and ἤμεθα | we were |
| ἦτε | you were |
| ἦσαν | they were |

This verb is being introduced in the imperfect because of certain difficulties in the present and future. For now it will be best to memorize these forms since they are commonly used. The points in which this verb differs from the other paradigms just given will be better understood after -μι verbs have been studied. ἤμην and ἤμεθα are middle forms in common use in the New Testament. ἤμεθα and ἦμεν have the same meaning.

## 86. A REFERENCE LIST OF THE VERBS GIVEN SO FAR

| Present | Imperfect |
|---------|-----------|
| ἀπολύω | ἀπέλυον |
| βλέπω | ἔβλεπον |
| δουλεύω | ἐδούλευον |
| εἰμί: I am | ἤμην |

41

| | |
|---|---|
| ἐλπίζω | ἤλπιζον |
| ἐσθίω | ἤσθιον |
| ἔχω | εἶχον |
| θεραπεύω | ἐθεράπευον |
| ἰσχύω | ἴσχυον |
| λέγω | ἔλεγον |
| μνημονεύω | ἐμνημόνευον |
| πέμπω | ἔπεμπον |
| πίνω | ἔπινον |
| πιστεύω | ἐπίστευον |
| φέρω | ἔφερον |

## 87. DEFINITE TEMPORAL CLAUSES

A definite time may be described by a clause introduced by ὅτε, *when*, and using a verb in the indicative.

*ὅτε ἔβλεπε Μαρίᾱν, μακάριος ἦν Λάζαρος.*
When he used to see Mary, Lazarus was happy.

## 88. CASE: NOMINATIVE IN THE PREDICATE

In previous lessons the nominative case has been used to indicate the subject of a verb. In this lesson the nominative has been used after forms of εἰμί: *I am*.

*Μαρίᾱ καὶ Λάζαρος ἦσαν τέκνα.*
Mary and Lazarus were *children*.

*μικρὸς Λάζαρος ἦν δοῦλος.*
Little Lazarus was *a slave*.

This usage is called the *predicate nominative*.

## 89. CASE: DATIVE OF TIME

In number 45 the dative of place has been explained as showing where an action belongs in spatial relationships. This case may show also where an aciton belongs in temporal relationships.

*ἐν χρόνῳ μικρῷ πέμπει ἄγγελον.*
In a little while he sends a messenger.

## 90. EXERCISES

a. Read number 81 through silently, trying to understand as much as possible while your eye first follows the lines without jumping back. Then reread if necessary.

b. Translate number 81 into good English.

c. In translating the sentences below notice that a Greek verb in the future tense should be indicated in the corresponding English by *should* and *would* (not *shall* and *will*) when this Greek future is in a clause subordinate to an imperfect verb, for example:

ὁ ἄγγελος ἔλεγε ὅτι δουλεύσουσι οἱ ἀδελφοί.
The messenger was saying that the brothers *would serve*.

1) Λάζαρον ἀπέλυε Φίλιππος ὅτε τέκνα ἐθεράπευε Λάζαρος.
2) ὅτε δουλεύσομεν τοῖς ἀνθρώποις ἐν τῷ κήπῳ, ἰσχύσομεν ἐσθίειν τοὺς καρποὺς τοῦ κήπου.
3) ἐλέγομεν ὅτι οὐκ ἠσθίομεν τοὺς καρποὺς καὶ οὐκ ἐπίνομεν τὸν οἶνον Πέτρου.
4) ἠλπίζετε ὅτι οἶνον οὐκ ἰσχύσουσι πίνειν οἱ δοῦλοι;
5) ναί, ὅτι ἔπινον οἱ κακοὶ ἄνθρωποι, ἠλπίζομεν ὅτι οὐκέτι δουλεύσουσι οἴνῳ.
6) Μᾶρκε, ἔφερες ὀψάριον Νικοδήμῳ;
7) ναί, ἔφερον ὀψάριον καὶ ἄρτον τῷ ἀδελφῷ καὶ ἔπεμπον τοὺς καρποὺς ἐκ τοῦ κήπου.
8) ἔπεμπες ποτήρια οἴνου τοῖς τέκνοις;
9) οὐκ ἔπεμπον, οὐ γὰρ ἴσχυον πίνειν οἶνον.
10) Μᾶρκε καὶ Νικόδημε, ὅτε ἦτε μικρὰ τέκνα, ἰσχύετε μνημονεύειν πάντοτε τὰς ἰδίας χρείας;
11) ὅτε ἦς ἐν τῷ οἴκῳ, ἔβλεπες τὰ ἀρνία;
12) ἤλπιζε ὁ ἄγγελος ὅτι ἦτε μακάριοι.
13) ναί, ἤμην μακάριος τότε καὶ ἦμεν μακάριοι πάντοτε.
14) ἤμην σὺν Μαρίᾳ, τότε γὰρ ὁμοῦ ἦμεν πάντοτε.
15) ἦν ἐλευθέρᾱ, ἀλλὰ δοῦλος ἤμην.
16) ἦτε οἱ ἀδελφοὶ Μαρίᾱς.

d. Put the finite verbs of the following in the imperfect.

1) ἐλπίζουσι βλέπειν τοὺς ἀγγέλους.
2) μνημονεύετε τὸν χρόνον ὅτε ἀπολύσομεν τὸν καλὸν δοῦλον.
3) ἔλπιζε πέμπειν τὰς ἰδίᾱς δωρεάς.
4) λέγει παρρησίᾳ περὶ τῶν ἐπιθυμιῶν Πέτρου.
5) λέγουσι Μαρίᾱ καὶ τὸ τέκνον περὶ τῆς παρρησίᾱς Λαζάρου.

e. By combining the personal endings in list 2 with the stems in list 1 form at least fifteen finite verbs. Add correct accents, and translate.

| List 1 | List 2 |
|---|---|
| ἤλπιζ____ | -ε |
| ἐμνημονευ____ | -ες |
| ἔφερ____ | -ετε |

```
εἴχ——              -ομεν
ἤσθι——             -ον
ἄπελυ——
ἴσχυ——
```

f. Notice carefully the following English words related to new Greek words in this lesson.

1) *angel*: a heavenly *messenger*.
2) *mnemo*nic: related to *memory*.
3) *chrono*logy: the study of the measurement of *time*.
4) *micro*scope: an instrument by means of which one is able to see very *small* objects.
5) *palin*genesis: a being born *again*.
6) syn*chrono*us: occurring at the same *time*.

g. Read the Greek aloud and then translate:

1) . . . ὅ (that which) . . . βλέπει τίς (who) ἐλπίζει;
2) . . .῎Ετι (still) χρόνον μικρὸν μεθ᾽ ὑμῶν (with you) εἰμι. . . .
3) μνημονεύετε τῆς γυναικὸς Λώτ (Lot's wife).
4) ἦσαν ὁμοῦ Σίμων Πέτρος καὶ Θωμᾶς . . . καὶ Ναθαναήλ. . . .
5) Χαίρετε ἐν κυρίῳ (the Lord) πάντοτε· πάλιν ἐρῶ (I will say), χαίρετε.

The sources of these excerpts are listed on page 244.

# Lesson 9

## 91. BACK TO SLAVERY FOR LAZARUS

ὅτε ἤσθιον δεῖπνον ἐν τῷ οἴκῳ Λάζαρος καὶ Μαρίᾱ καὶ οἱ ἀδελφοὶ Μαρίᾱς, ἀπὸ τοῦ κήπου ἀπέλυσε τὸ ἀρνίον Μαρίᾱς κακὸς γεωργός. ἐν τῇ σκοτίᾳ τὸν γεωργὸν οἱ δοῦλοι Φιλίππου καὶ Πέτρου οὐκ ἔβλεψαν, ἀλλὰ ἤκουσαν τοῦ ἀρνίου, καὶ ἔλεγον τῷ ἀνθρώπῳ.                                                         5

ἐν τῷ οἴκῳ ἔλεγον οἱ δοῦλοι Φιλίππῳ καὶ Πέτρῳ, "ἠκούσαμεν ἄνθρωπον ἐν τῷ κήπῳ.

"'ἀπέλυσας τὸ ἀρνίον;' ἐν τῇ σκοτίᾳ ἐλέγομεν.

"'ναί, ἀπέλυσα,' ἠκούσαμεν. 'ἀλλὰ οὐκ ἐβλέψατε ὅτε ἀπέλυσα τὸ ἀρνίον. νῦν ἐλπίζω φέρειν τὸ ἀρνίον εἰς τὸν ἴδιον     10
οἶκον. χαίρετε, δοῦλοι.'"

ὅτε τοὺς δούλους ἤκουσε Μαρίᾱ, οὐκέτι μακαρίᾱ ἦν. τότε οὐκέτι μακάριος ἦν Λάζαρος ὅτι οὐκέτι μακαρίᾱ ἦν Μαρίᾱ.

"σήμερον ἐν τῷ κήπῳ ἔβλεψα ἄνθρωπον μικρόν. ἔβλεπεν τὸ ἀρνίον," ἐμνημόνευσε δοῦλος. "οὐκ ἦν δοῦλος, ἀλλὰ ἦν     15
ἐλεύθερος."

τότε Λάζαρος κακοῦ μικροῦ γεωργοῦ ἐμνημόνευσε.

"ἐλπίζω σήμερον βλέψαι καὶ φέρειν πάλιν τὸ ἀρνίον Μαρίᾳ," ἔλεγε Λάζαρος. "χαῖρε, Μαρίᾱ. χαίρετε, ἀδελφοί. χαίρετε, δοῦλοι."                                                            20

οὐκ ἴσχυε Λάζαρος βλέψαι ἐν τῇ σκοτίᾳ, ἀλλὰ ἐμνημόνευσε τὸν οἶκον τοῦ κακοῦ γεωργοῦ. ἤλπιζεν ἰσχύειν βλέψαι τὸ ἀρνίον ἐν τῷ οἴκῳ τοῦ γεωργοῦ.

μετὰ μικρὸν χρόνον ἔβλεψε Λάζαρος τὸ ἀρνίον ἐν τῷ οἴκῳ τοῦ γεωργοῦ. ἀλλὰ ἤκουσεν Λαζάρου ὁ γεωργὸς σὺν τοῖς     25
ἰδίοις δούλοις. ἔπεμψεν ἐκ τοῦ οἴκου καὶ περὶ τὸν οἶκον τοὺς ἰδίους δούλους.

"βλέψατε· φέρετε Λάζαρον εἰς τὸν οἶκον, δοῦλοι," ἔλεγεν ὁ γεωργός. μετὰ μικρὸν χρόνον εἰς τὸν οἶκον Λάζαρον φέρειν ἴσχυσαν.                                                              30

"βλέψον τοὺς δούλους, Λάζαρε," ἔλεγε ὁ γεωργός. "οὐ γὰρ ἰσχύσεις φέρειν τὸ ἀρνίον πάλιν Μαρίᾳ. οὐ λέγω, 'ἀπολυσάτωσαν Φίλιππος καὶ Πέτρος Λάζαρον.' ἀλλὰ λέγω, 'δουλευσάτω Λάζαρος τῷ γεωργῷ. δοῦλοι, μνημονεύσατε, ἔξομεν πάντοτε Λάζαρον.'"                                                        35 ὅτε ὁ κακὸς γεωργὸς παρρησίᾳ ἔλεγεν, οὐκέτι ἐλεύθερος ἦν Λάζαρος, ἀλλὰ ἤλπιζεν ὅτι μνημονεύει Μαρίᾱ τοῦ ἀρνίου καὶ Λαζάρου.

## 92. VOCABULARY

ἀκούω, ἀκούσω, ἤκουσα:  I hear, listen (followed by acc. or gen. direct object)

γεωργός, -οῦ, ὁ:  farmer, vinedresser

μετά:  (with gen.) with; (with acc.) after

μή:  not (used with imperatives)

περί:  (with acc. in local sense) around, about

σήμερον:  today

σκοτίᾱ, -ᾱς, ἡ:  darkness, dark

## 93. TENSE: AORIST

This lesson introduces the aorist tense, which indicates the simple occurrence of an action. In the indicative the occurrence is usually understood to be in past time, but even in the indicative the chief emphasis is on the point-like quality of the action rather than on its past time. In the subjunctive, optative, and imperative moods there is no indication of past time. It is important, therefore, from our first acquaintance with this tense to form the habit of thinking in terms of simple occurrence rather than of past time. Several translations of the aorist are possible.

ἤκουσα: I heard (on one occasion).
I did hear.
I began to hear.

## 94. PARADIGMS OF THE FIRST OR SIGMATIC AORIST INDICATIVE ACTIVE

a. πιστεύω:

| | |
|---|---|
| ἐπίστευσα | ἐπιστεύσαμεν |
| ἐπίστευσας | ἐπιστεύσατε |
| ἐπίστευσε | ἐπίστευσαν |

As in the imperfect, πιστεύω has syllabic augment in the aorist. To the augmented stem ἐπιστευ- is added the tense suffix -σα- (except in the third person singular where -σε is used). The sigma in the suffix accounts for the designation *sigmatic*. To the suffix are added the personal endings: -, -ς, -, -μεν, -τε, -ν.

b. ἀκούω:

| | |
|---|---|
| ἤκουσα | ἠκούσαμεν |
| ἤκουσας | ἠκούσατε |
| ἤκουσε | ἤκουσαν |

These forms have temporal augment.

c. βλέπω      ἔβλεψα      ἐβλέψαμεν
               ἔβλεψας      ἐβλέψατε
               ἔβλεψε      ἔβλεψαν

Here the syllabic augment is used. To the stem ἐβλεπ- is added -σα- or -σε with the result that ἔβλεπσα is written with -πσ- combined as -ψ-. πέμπω follows this pattern.

d. ἀπολύω      ἀπέλυσα      ἀπελύσαμεν
               ἀπέλυσας      ἀπελύσατε
               ἀπέλυσε      ἀπέλυσαν

Here as in the imperfect indicative (see number 85c) the augment is inserted between the prepositional prefix and the verb stem: ἀπο-ε-λυσα. Then the vowel -ο- in ἀπο- is elided. The tense suffix -σα- and the personal endings are the same as in the two previous paradigms.

## 95. PARADIGMS OF THE FIRST OR SIGMATIC AORIST IMPERATIVE ACTIVE

a. πιστεύω:      πίστευσον      πιστεύσατε
                 πιστευσάτω      πιστευσάτωσαν

b. ἀκούω      ἄκουσον      ἀκούσατε
               ἀκουσάτω      ἀκουσάτωσαν

It is quite important to notice that the aorist imperative has no augment. *Only the indicative mood has augment.* The ending -σον requires attention in memorizing since it does not have the suffix -σα-. The accent is recessive in the imperative as it is in the indicative.

c. βλέπω      βλέψον      βλέψατε
               βλεψάτω      βλεψάτωσαν

d. ἀπολύω      ἀπόλυσον      ἀπολύσατε
               ἀπολυσάτω      ἀπολυσάτωσαν

## 96. DISTINCTION BETWEEN PRESENT AND AORIST IMPERATIVES

Just as the present indicative indicates continued or repeated action, the present imperative commands an action that is intended to be kept in progress or to be repeated. The aorist, on the other hand, whether indicative or imperative, emphasizes point action. The aorist may put the spotlight on the beginning of the action, on the effect of the action, or on the action as a whole, but not on its progress or its repetition.

βλεψάτω.
Let him begin to look.

βλεπέτω.
Let him keep on looking.
Let him look repeatedly.

μὴ βλεπέτω.
Let him not keep on looking.
Let him stop looking.

No example of μή with the aorist imperative will be given since prohibitions of this kind were as a rule expressed by μή with the aorist subjunctive. The subjunctive will be studied later (number 311).

## 97. FIRST OR SIGMATIC AORIST INFINITIVE ACTIVE

a. πιστεύω: πιστεῦσαι
b. ἀκούω: ἀκοῦσαι
c. βλέπω: βλέψαι
d. ἀπολύω: ἀπολῦσαι

The ending of the aorist infinitive active is -σαι. The accent falls on the penult, an acute on a short syllable and a circumflex on a long syllable. The principle of recessive accent does not apply to infinitives. Notice that the aorist infinitive has no augment.

## 98. N MOVABLE

In the statement ὁ Φίλιππος ἀπέλυσεν τὸ ἀρνίον the verb is a third singular aorist indicative active of ἀπολύω. But it has at its end a letter not shown in the paradigm. This letter is called ν *movable*. The ν movable is sometimes used at the end of (1) third singular verb forms ending in -ε, and (2) any word ending in -σι, -ξι, or -ψι.

λύσουσιν
ἔβλεπεν

## 99. FUTURES OF VERBS WHOSE STEMS END IN CERTAIN CONSONANTS

a. Verbs in π, β, or φ. Just as βλέπω forms its aorist ἔβλεψα by combining π and σ into ψ, this verb forms its future also by using this same combination.

| Present | Future |
|---------|--------|
| βλέπω | βλέψω |
| πέμπω | πέμψω |

Similarly β or φ may join with σ to form ψ.

b. Verbs in κ, γ, or χ. When σ is added to a verb stem ending in κ, γ, or χ, the result is ξ. The future of ἔχω is ἕξω. The rough

48

breathing is an irregularity that should be carefully noted, but it will not be explained here.

c. Verbs in τ, δ, or θ. The letters τ, δ, and θ are dropped when σ is added. (This is not illustrated in the future tense until number 209. There we learn that the future of πείθω is πείσω.)

## 100. PRINCIPAL PARTS OF GREEK VERBS

The following forms of πιστεύω are its principal parts. Each is an indicative in the first person singular. The tense and voice are given in parentheses.

| | |
|---|---|
| a. πιστεύω | (present active) |
| b. πιστεύσω | (future active) |
| c. ἐπίστευσα | (aorist active) |
| d. πεπίστευκα | (perfect active) |
| e. πεπίστευμαι | (perfect middle and passive) |
| f. ἐπιστεύθην | (aorist passive) |

The first three of these have been introduced for πιστεύω and several other verbs. Eventually you will be able to develop any form (with few exceptions) of a Greek verb if you know its principal parts.

For several lessons the principal parts of all verbs will be given in the vocabularies as far as they have been introduced.

## 101. EXERCISES

a. Translate number 91.

b. Become thoroughly familiar with the principal parts of the following verbs as listed in this summary. Some of the blank spaces in this list will be filled by information appearing in later lessons.

| Present | Future | Aorist |
|---|---|---|
| ἀκούω | ἀκούσω | ἤκουσα |
| ἀπολύω | ἀπολύσω | ἀπέλυσα |
| βλέπω | βλέψω | ἔβλεψα |
| δουλεύω | δουλεύσω | ἐδούλευσα |
| ἐλπίζω | — | ἤλπισα |
| ἐσθίω | — | — |
| ἔχω | ἕξω | — |
| θεραπεύω | θεραπεύσω | ἐθεράπευσα |
| ἰσχύω | ἰσχύσω | ἴσχυσα |
| λέγω | — | — |
| μνημονεύω | — | ἐμνημόνευσα |

| πέμπω | πέμψω | ἔπεμψα |
|-------|-------|--------|
| πίνω | — | — |
| πιστεύω | πιστεύσω | ἐπίστευσα |
| φέρω | — | — |

c. Find in list 2 a correct translation for each Greek form in list 1.

### List 1

1) πεμψάτωσαν
2) ἐμνημόνευεν
3) ἴσχυσε
4) θεραπευέτω
5) ἔλπισον
6) ἐδουλεύετε
7) ἐβλέψατε
8) ἄκουε
9) φέρειν
10) μὴ ἐχέτωσαν

### List 2

α) Keep on listening.
β) To carry and carry.
γ) They will hope.
δ) She used to be able.
ε) You took one look.
ζ) You used to be slaves.
η) Begin to hope.
θ) Go on hoping.
ι) She was remembering.
κ) He remembers.
λ) Let them start to send.
μ) They are about to send.
ν) He became able.
ξ) She will be able.
ο) Let us heal.
π) Let it heal repeatedly.
ρ) Let them stop holding.

d. Complete each of the following sentences with the proper form of ὁ γεωργός or ἡ σκοτίᾱ as the context seems to require.

1) πέμπετε _____ μετὰ τῶν ἀδελφῶν.
2) ἐν _____ ἦσαν οἱ καλοὶ ἄγγελοι;
3) ἐκ _____ ἐβλέψαμεν τὰς δωρεὰς περὶ _____.
4) πυρετοὺς _____ μὴ θεραπευέτω μετὰ μικρὸν χρόνον.
5) σὺν _____ ἐν _____ ἦμεν πάντοτε μακάριαι.
6) μὴ πίνε οἶνον, _____.
7) μετὰ _____ σήμερον ἔπεμψας δοῦλον περὶ τὸν οἶκον.
8) περὶ τὸν κῆπον ἐν _____ ἐλέγετε;
9) σήμερον ἔβλεψε καλὰ ἀρνία περὶ Μαρίᾱν _____.

e. Notice carefully the following English words related to new Greek words in this lesson.

1) *acou*stic: related to *hearing*.
2) *George*: a man's name meaning *farmer*.
3) *peri*meter: the distance *around* a geometric figure.
4) *meta*physics: the next treatise *after* physics in Aristotle's works.

f. Read the Greek aloud and then translate:

1) καὶ ἔλεγεν, Ὅς (He who) ἔχει ὦτα (ears) ἀκούειν ἀκουέτω.
2) Ἐγώ εἰμι ἡ ἄμπελος (vine) ἡ ἀληθινή (true), καὶ ὁ πατήρ μου (my Father) ὁ γεωργός ἐστιν.

The sources of these excerpts are listed on page 244.

# Lesson 10

## 102. RESCUED: ONE LAMB, NO LAZARUS

Ἰάκωβος, ὁ γεωργὸς ὁ κακός, μακάριος ἦν ὅτι Λάζαρον τὸν ἐλεύθερον καὶ τὸ Μαρίας ἀρνίον εἶχεν.

Ἰάκωβος: "χρείαν δείπνου καλοῦ, δοῦλοι, ἔξω. ἐπιθυμίαν τοῦ μικροῦ ἀρνίου νῦν ἔχω. ἐν ἀληθείᾳ ἔξω καλὸν δεῖπνον, Λάζαρε." 5

Λάζαρος: "κακὲ Ἰάκωβε, πῶς ἰσχύεις ἔχειν ἐπιθυμίαν ἐσθίειν τὸ Μαρίας ἀρνίον τὸ μικρὸν ὅτε ἔχεις πλοῦτον ἐν ἀληθείᾳ; ἔχεις οὐ χρείαν τοῦ Μαρίας ἀρνίου."

Ἰάκωβος: "πῶς ἰσχύεις λέγειν τὴν ἀλήθειαν παρρησίᾳ; δοῦλος λέγειν παρρησίᾳ οὐκ ἰσχύει, καὶ δοῦλος κακὸς λέγειν 10 τὴν ἀλήθειαν οὐκ ἰσχύει. δοῦλε Λάζαρε, μὴ λέγε περὶ τοῦ πλούτου Ἰακώβου."

Λάζαρος: "κακέ, μετὰ μικρὸν χρόνον ἀπολύσουσι Λάζαρον καὶ τὸ Μαρίας ἀρνίον οἱ ἄνθρωποι τῆς κώμης. βλέψεις μετὰ μικρὸν χρόνον, Ἰάκωβε κακέ." 15

Ἰάκωβος: "μὴ λέγε, κακέ."

Λάζαρος: "ἐν ἀληθείᾳ σήμερον Φίλιππος καὶ Πέτρος, ἐλεύθεροι, τοὺς ἰδίους δούλους μετὰ τῶν ἐλευθέρων τῆς κώμης πέμψουσιν εἰς τὸν τοῦ κακοῦ γεωργοῦ οἶκον."

Ἰάκωβος: "πῶς ἰσχύεις λέγειν περὶ τῆς ἀληθείας; ἡ γὰρ 20 ἀλήθεια Λάζαρον, τὸν κακὸν δοῦλον, οὐκ ἀπολύσει."

Λάζαρος: "πῶς ἰσχύσεις ἔχειν ἐλεύθερον;"

Ἰάκωβος: "ἔξω τὸν δοῦλον τὸν ἴδιον ἐν σπηλαίῳ σὺν τῷ ἰδίῳ πλούτῳ. οὐ βλέψεις τὸν πλοῦτον ἐν τῇ τοῦ σπηλαίου σκοτίᾳ. πῶς βλέψεις τὸν πλοῦτον τοῦ σπηλαίου ἐν τῇ σκοτίᾳ; 25 οἱ τῆς κώμης ἐλεύθεροι οὐ βλέψουσι Λάζαρον καὶ οὐ πέμψουσι τὸν πλοῦτον Ἰακώβου εἰς τὴν κώμην."

μετὰ μικρὸν χρόνον ἔπεμψαν Φίλιππος καὶ Πέτρος τοὺς δούλους τοὺς ἰδίους σὺν τοῖς τῆς κώμης ἀνθρώποις εἰς τὸν Ἰακώβου οἶκον. ἀλλὰ οὐκ ἐν τῷ οἴκῳ ἦν Λάζαρος. ἴσχυσαν 30 τὸ ἀρνίον πάλιν Μαρίᾳ φέρειν, ἀλλὰ οὐ Λάζαρον τὸν ἐλεύθερον βλέψαι.

## 103. VOCABULARY

ἀλήθειᾰ, -ᾱς, ἡ:  truth, truthfulness
ἔχω, ἕξω (aor. later):  I have, hold
Ἰάκωβος, -ου, ὁ:  James
κακός, -ή, -όν:  bad, evil, wicked, dangerous
καλός, -ή, -όν:  fair, beautiful, good, excellent, noble
κώμη, -ης, ἡ:  village, town
πλοῦτος, -ου, ὁ:  wealth, riches
πῶς:  how?
σπήλαιον, -ου, τό:  cave

## 104. MORE PARADIGMS OF FIRST DECLENSION NOUNS

In number 72 the forms of καρδίᾱ and δωρεά were presented. These paradigms set the pattern for all first declension nouns ending in -εᾱ, -ιᾱ or -ρᾱ.

In this lesson three other patterns are being used: nouns ending in -η, in -ᾰ, and in -εᾰ, -ιᾱ, or -ρᾰ.

a. A noun in -η.

| | |
|---|---|
| κώμη | κῶμαι |
| κώμης | κωμῶν |
| κώμῃ | κώμαις |
| κώμην | κώμᾱς |

b. A noun in -ᾰ. (number 179)

| | |
|---|---|
| γλῶσσᾰ | γλῶσσαι |
| γλώσσης | γλωσσῶν |
| γλώσσῃ | γλώσσαις |
| γλῶσσᾰν | γλόσσᾱς |

Notice that the plural endings are the same as those shown in number 72.

c. A noun in -εᾰ, -ιᾰ, or -ρᾰ.

| | |
|---|---|
| ἀλήθειᾰ | ἀλήθειαι |
| ἀληθείᾱς | ἀληθειῶν |
| ἀληθείᾳ | ἀληθείαις |
| ἀλήθειᾰν | ἀληθείᾱς |

## 105. SUMMARY OF FIRST DECLENSION ENDINGS STUDIED THUS FAR

Since the plural of these first declension nouns are all the same, our special attention must be directed to the differences in the singular.

| Singular | | | | Plural |
|---|---|---|---|---|
| after ε, ι, ρ | | not after ε, ι, ρ | | |
| -ᾱ | -ᾰ | -η | -ᾰ | -αι |
| -ᾱς | -ᾱς | -ης | -ης | -ων |
| -ᾳ | -ᾳ | -ῃ | -ῃ | -αις |
| -ᾱν | -ᾰν | -ην | -ᾰν | -ᾱς |

## 106. MORE PARADIGMS OF FIRST AND SECOND DECLENSION ADJECTIVES

In number 74 δίκαιος was presented as an example of a first and second declension adjective whose feminine nominative singular ends in -εᾱ, -ιᾱ or -ρᾱ. Another kind of first and second declension has a feminine nominative singular that ends in -η. These two patterns include nearly all the adjectives of the first and second declensions.

| Singular | | | Plural | | |
|---|---|---|---|---|---|
| καλός | καλή | καλόν | καλοί | καλαί | καλά |
| καλοῦ | καλῆς | καλοῦ | καλῶν | καλῶν | καλῶν |
| καλῷ | καλῇ | καλῷ | καλοῖς | καλαῖς | καλοῖς |
| καλόν | καλήν | καλόν | καλούς | καλάς | καλά |
| καλέ | καλή | καλόν | | | |

## 107. POSITION OF ADJECTIVES

a. Attributive (see number 79).

   1) Preceding its substantive. The adjective stands between the modified noun and its definite article. The position emphasizes the adjective.

     *ὁ κακὸς γεωργός.*
     the *wicked* farmer.

   2) Following its substantive. The adjective stands after the modified noun and a repeated definite article. This position emphasizes the substantive.

     *ὁ γεωργὸς ὁ κακός.*
     the farmer, the *wicked* (one).

b. Predicate. The adjective stands in neither of the positions described in *a* but modifies a noun that has a definite article.

     *ὁ γεωργός κακός.* (or) *κακὸς ὁ γεωργός.*
     The farmer (is) *wicked.*

Notice (1) the absence of the verb in the first two examples, a common occurrence in Greek, and (2) the fact that these predicate adjectives are also predicate nominatives (see number 88).

c. Ambiguous. When a noun does not have a definite article, it is frequently impossible to know for sure whether an adjective is attributive or predicate.

     *γεωργὸς κακός* may mean
     a farmer (is) *wicked.*    (or)    a farmer (I mean) a *wicked* (one).

## 108. MODIFYING GENITIVES USED AS ADJECTIVES

A genitive of a noun may sometimes serve as the equivalent of an adjective.

τὸ *Μαρίας* ἀρνίον.
*Mary's* lamb.

εἰς τὸν *τοῦ γεωργοῦ* οἶκον.
into *the farmer's* house.

Μαρίας and τοῦ γεωργοῦ are used as adjectives in attributive position.

## 109. ADJECTIVES USED AS SUBSTANTIVES

In number 102 we have several instances of adjectives used without any expressed nouns for them to modify. Take as an example . . . τοὺς ἰδίους δούλους μετὰ τῶν ἐλευθέρων πέμψουσιν . . . , ". . . they will send their own slaves with the *free* (men). . . ." The context helps us to understand with ἐλευθέρων the noun ἀνθρώπων, but the adjective itself here serves as a substantive. Suppose we had αἱ ἐλεύθεραι. This we should translate "the free women" unless the context pointed to some other feminine plural Greek noun to be understood. Likewise τὰ ἐλεύθερα would usually mean "the free things."

## 110. EXERCISES

a. Translate number 102.

b. Write in Greek:
  1) wicked hearts.
  2) the wicked hearts.
  3) the hearts, I mean the wicked ones.
  4) the cups (were) small.
  5) out of the small cups.
  6) into the cups, I mean the small ones.
  7) for the brothers, the free ones.
  8) within the beautiful house.
  9) (Oh) happy farmer!
  10) around her own wealth.
  11) See the village, I mean the happy one.

c. Give the forms of καλός, μακάριος, and δίκαιος that will agree with each of the following:
  1) τῆς ἀληθείας        7) δωρεάν
  2) κώμῃ                8) σπηλαίων
  3) γεωργοῖς            9) Ἰάκωβε

| | |
|---|---|
| 4) τᾱς χρείᾱς | 10) σκοτίᾳ |
| 5) ἀγγέλους | 11) κώμην |
| 6) καρδίᾱ | 12) κώμη |

d. Associate the following English words with new Greek words used in this lesson.

1) *Alethea*: a woman's name meaning *"truth."*
2) *caco*phony: an *unpleasant (bad)* sound.
3) *pluto*crat: one who has power because of his *wealth*.
4) *spelae*an: related to *caves*.

e. Read the Greek aloud and then translate:

1) λέγει αὐτῷ (to him) ὁ Ἰησοῦς (Jesus), Ἐγώ εἰμι ἡ ὁδὸς (way) καὶ ἡ ἀλήθεια καὶ ἡ ζωή (life). . . .
2) . . . μὴ μιμοῦ (do not imitate) τὸ κακὸν ἀλλὰ τὸ ἀγαθόν (good).
3) . . . Οὐκ ἔστιν (It is) καλὸν λαβεῖν (to take) τὸν ἄρτον τῶν τέκνων καὶ βαλεῖν (to throw) τοῖς κυναρίοις (to the dogs) . . . .
4) βλέπετε οὖν (therefore) πῶς ἀκούετε . . . .

The sources of these excerpts are listed on page 244.

# Lesson 11

## 111. AN OLD SINNER SCARED TO DIE

Λάζαρον εἰς τὸ σπήλαιον Ἰάκωβος ἤγαγεν καὶ ἦλθεν εἰς τὸν ἴδιον οἶκον πάλιν.

"ἐνέγκατε νῦν ὀψάριον καὶ ἄρτον, δοῦλοι. χρείαν γάρ ἔσχον φαγεῖν," εἶπεν Ἰάκωβος.

τότε ἤνεγκαν ὀψάριον καὶ ἄρτον Ἰακώβῳ. 5

"εἴπατε ὅτι τὸ Μαρίας ἀρνίον ἠγάγετε πάλιν εἰς τὸν κῆπον Φιλίππου;" εἶπεν Ἰάκωβος.

"οὐκ ἠγάγομεν, Ἰάκωβε, ἀλλὰ οἱ ἐλεύθεροι τῆς κώμης καὶ οἱ Φιλίππου δοῦλοι τὸ ἀρνίον ἐκ τοῦ οἴκου ἤγαγον," εἶπαν οἱ δοῦλοι. 10

"οὐκέτι τὸ ἀρνίον ἔχω, ἀλλὰ ἔξω πάντοτε Λάζαρον," εἶπεν ὁ κακὸς γεωργός. "νῦν σὺν Ἰακώβῳ φαγέτωσαν καὶ πιέτωσαν οἱ δοῦλοι."

"λαβέτω τὸ ποτήριον οἴνου καλοῦ ὁ μακάριος γεωργός," εἶπαν οἱ δοῦλοι. 15

ἔπιε καὶ ἔπιον. ἔπινε καὶ ἔπινον. ὅτε ἔπινε, πυρετὸς Ἰάκωβον ἔλαβεν. κακὸς ἦν ὁ πυρετός.

μετὰ μικρὸν χρόνον ὁ κακὸς γεωργὸς ἀπέθνησκεν. τότε ἐμνημόνευσεν ὅτι ἦν κακὸς ἄνθρωπος καὶ ὅτι οὐκ ἦν ἕτοιμος ἀποθανεῖν. οὐκέτι ἦν μακάριος. 20

"ἄγαγε νῦν πάλιν ἐκ τοῦ σπηλαίου Λάζαρον," εἶπε δούλῳ. "ἐλπίζω ὅτι θεραπεύσει τὸν κακὸν γεωργόν."

ἐν τῷ σπηλαίῳ εἶπεν ὁ δοῦλος Λαζάρῳ, "ἐλθὲ νῦν πάλιν εἰς τὸν οἶκον Ἰακώβου."

ἦλθεν εἰς τὸν οἶκον μετὰ μικρὸν χρόνον Λάζαρος. 25

"κακὸν πυρετὸν ἔχω, ναί, κακὸν πυρετόν. χρείαν Λαζάρου ἔχω. θεράπευσον τὸν γεωργὸν τὸν κακὸν καὶ ἰσχύσεις ἀγαγεῖν πάλιν εἰς τὸν ἴδιον οἶκον," εἶπε Ἰάκωβος.

"ὅτι πυρετοὺς θεραπεῦσαι ἰσχύω ἤκουσας; ἤκουσας τὴν ἀλήθειαν," εἶπε Λάζαρος. 30

"πῶς ἰσχύσω ἀποθανεῖν; κακὸς ἀποθανεῖν οὐκ ἔχει ἐπιθυμίαν. νῦν, Λάζαρε, θεράπευσον τὸν γεωργὸν τὸν κακόν. οὐκέτι ἀκούσεις, 'σήμερον κακὸς ἦν Ἰάκωβος,'" εἶπε ὁ γεωργός.

"ἐλπίζω ὅτι λέγεις τὴν ἀλήθειαν," εἶπε Λάζαρος.   35
ἐθεράπευσε τὸν πυρετόν, καὶ ὁ γεωργὸς Λάζαρον ἀπέλυσε
καὶ ἔπεμψε δωρεὰς καλὰς ἐκ τοῦ ἰδίου πλούτου εἰς τὸν οἶκον
Λαζάρου.

## 112. VOCABULARY

ἄγω, ἄξω, ἤγαγον: I lead, bring, go
ἀποθνῄσκω, (fut. later), ἀπέθανον: I die
ἐσθίω, (fut. later), ἔφαγον: I eat
ἕτοιμος, -η, -ον: prepared, ready
ἔχω, ἕξω, ἔσχον: I hold, have, possess
ἦλθον, (pres. and fut. later): I came; ἐλθέ: Come!
λαμβάνω, (fut. later), ἔλαβον: I take, receive, seize
λέγω, (fut. later), εἶπον: I say, speak, declare, tell, ask, answer
πίνω, (fut. later), ἔπιον: I drink
φέρω, οἴσω, ἤνεγκα (cf. number 115 εἶπα): I carry, bring, endure

## 113. TENSE: SECOND AORIST INDICATIVE ACTIVE

Such forms as ἦλθεν, εἶπεν, φαγεῖν, and ἠγάγομεν used in this
lesson, are in the second aorist. In meaning this aorist is just like the
aorist using -σα, which is generally called the *first aorist*. Few verbs
have both first and second aorist forms. In formation, however, the
second aorist differs from the first aorist and is quite similar to the
imperfect. Both second aorist and imperfect have (1) augment, (2) the
thematic vowel ο/ε, and (3) the endings -ν, -ς, -, -μεν, -τε, -ν, known
as the secondary active endings. The imperfect can usually be distinguished from the second aorist by its stem. Compare the following
examples of the two tenses.

| Present | Imperfect | Second Aorist |
|---|---|---|
| ἄγω | ἦγον | ἤγαγον |
| ἀποθνῄσκω | ἀπέθνῃσκον | ἀπέθανον |
| ἐσθίω | ἤσθιον | ἔφαγον |
| ἔχω | εἶχον (=I was having) | ἔσχον (=I acquired) |
| λαμβάνω | ἐλάμβανον | ἔλαβον |
| λέγω | ἔλεγον | εἶπον |
| πίνω | ἔπινον | ἔπιον |

The differences in the stem are due to several causes.

a. Different roots are used in ἤσθιον and ἔφαγον, and in ἔλεγον
and εἶπον. Compare in English *I was going* with *I went*.

b. *Suffixes used in the present system, to which the imperfect
belongs*, account for the following differences.

58

| Imperfect | Suffix | Second Aorist |
|---|---|---|
| ἀπέθνῃσκον | -σκ- | ἀπέθανον |
| | (-θνη- is a changed form of -θαν-.) | |
| ἐλάμβανον | -αν- | ἔλαβον |
| | (A -μ- also crept into the present system stem.) | |
| ἔπινον | -ν- | ἔπιον |

c. The second aorist of ἄγω reduplicates (doubles) its root, that is, ἀγ- becomes ἀγαγ-.

d. εἶχον is developed from ἔ-σεχ-ον by the loss of the intervocalic σ and the contraction of ε+ε to ει, and ἔσχον uses the stem -σχ-.

## 114. PARADIGMS OF THE SECOND AORIST ACTIVE

a. Indicative

| | | | |
|---|---|---|---|
| ἤγαγον | ἦλθον | ἔσχον | ἔλαβον |
| ἤγαγες | ἦλθες | ἔσχες | ἔλαβες |
| ἤγαγε | ἦλθε | ἔσχε | ἔλαβε |
| ἠγάγομεν | ἤλθομεν | ἔσχομεν | ἐλάβομεν |
| ἠγάγετε | ἤλθετε | ἔσχετε | ἐλάβετε |
| ἤγαγον | ἦλθον | ἔσχον | ἔλαβον |

b. Imperative.

| | | | |
|---|---|---|---|
| ἄγαγε | ἐλθέ (Note Accent) | σχές | λάβε |
| ἀγαγέτω | ἐλθέτω | σχέτω | λαβέτω |
| ἀγάγετε | ἔλθετε | σχέτε | λάβετε |
| ἀγαγέτωσαν | ἐλθέτωσαν | σχέτωσαν | λαβέτωσαν |

c. Infinitive: Notice the accents.

| | | | |
|---|---|---|---|
| ἀγαγεῖν | ἐλθεῖν | σχεῖν | λαβεῖν |

## 115. VARIATIONS WITH *A* FOR *O* OR *E*

The endings of the first aorist and the perfect tenses had an influence on the second aorist, which resulted in the appearance of α for ο or ε in scattered instances. This substitution was not consistently made, but be ready to meet such forms as would give us a paradigm like the following one if they were collected.

a. Indicative

| | |
|---|---|
| εἶπα | εἴπαμεν |
| εἶπας | εἴπατε |
| εἶπε | εἶπαν |

b. Imperative

εἶπον and εἰπέ     εἴπατε
εἰπάτω           εἰπάτωσαν

c. Infinitive

εἰπεῖν

Notice that the substitution of α does not occur in the italicized forms.

## 116. EXERCISES

a. Read number 111 silently in Greek, trying to get the meaning as you go along.

b. Read the speeches in number 111 aloud, trying to group the words that naturally go together and to emphasize the places that call for emphasis.

c. Locate the following verb forms by giving whenever possible (1) tense, (2) mood, (3) voice, (4) person, (5) number, and (6) first principal part.

| | |
|---|---|
| 1) ἔπεμψεν | 10) εἰπέ |
| 2) ἔχει | 11) ἠνέγκατε |
| 3) θεραπεῦσαι | 12) σχεῖν |
| 4) ἦν | 13) οἴσετε |
| 5) ἰσχύσουσιν | 14) εἶπαν |
| 6) σχές | 15) λαμβενέτωσαν |
| 7) λάβετε | 16) ἐλθεῖν |
| 8) ἀγαγεῖν | 17) ἔσχες |
| 9) εἴχετε | |

d. Translate orally, omitting words in parentheses.

1) I was eating the fish.
2) I did eat the fish.
3) You were not drinking your own wine, Peter.
4) You did not drink your own wine, Peter.
5) She was ready to go into the house.
6) She did go into the house.
7) We brought the lamb (just once).
8) We brought the lamb (every evening).
9) Let them keep on speaking.
10) Let them speak (just once).
11) She was ready to keep on speaking.
12) We were ready to speak (just once).
13) The gift came from the man, the (one) ready to die.

e. Associate ἔφαγον with "sarcophagus" (flesh-eating): a limestone coffin used by the Greeks for the rapid disintegration of a corpse.

f. Read the Greek aloud and then translate:

1) Ἐφάγομεν ἐνώπιόν (before) σου (you) καὶ ἐπίομεν....
2) τί (What) δὲ (but) ἔχεις ὃ (which) οὐκ ἔλαβες;
3) οὐκ ἴσχυσα ἐλθεῖν σήμερον.

The sources of these excerpts are listed on page 244.

# Lesson 12

## 117. VOCABULARY IN LESSONS 7-11.

Review thoroughly.

| NOUNS | VERBS | ADJECTIVES |
|-------|-------|------------|
| ἄγγελος | ἄγω | δίκαιος |
| ἀλήθεια | ἀκούω | ἐλεύθερος |
| γεωργός | ἀποθνῄσκω | ἕτοιμος |
| δωρεά | εἶπον | ἴδιος |
| ἐπιθυμίᾱ | ἐλπίζω | κακός |
| Ἰάκωβος | ἔξω | καλός |
| καρδίᾱ | ἔφαγον | μακάριος |
| κώμη | ἔχω | μικρός |
| Μαρίᾱ | ἦλθον | |
| παρρησίᾱ | ἤμην | ADVERBS |
| πλοῦτος | ἤνεγκα | ναί |
| σκοτίᾱ | λαμβάνω | νῦν |
| σπήλαιον | μνημονεύω | ὁμοῦ |
| χρείᾱ | οἴσω | οὐκέτι |
| χρόνος | | πάλιν |
| | PREPOSITIONS | πάντοτε |
| CONJUNCTIONS | | παρρησίᾳ |
| | μετά | πῶς |
| ἀλλά | περί | σήμερον |
| ὅτε | σύν | τότε |

## 118. ADJECTIVE EXERCISE

Choosing from the forms listed, complete the following sentences with adjectives that are suitable in form and meaning:

| | | |
|---|---|---|
| δίκαιοι | ἰδίᾱς | καλῶν |
| ἐλευθέρᾱν | ἴδιον | μακάριοι |
| ἐλεύθερος | κακὸν | μικρῷ |
| ἕτοιμα | καλὰς | μικρῶν |

a. ὁ _____ γεωργὸς τὸν _____ πλοῦτον ἐν τῷ _____ σπηλαίῳ ἕξει.

62

b. τῶν ἀρνίων τῶν _____ μνημονεύσομεν;

c. ἕτοιμοι περὶ τὴν _____ κώμην ἐνεγκεῖν τὰς δωρεὰς τὰς_____ ἦσαν οἱ _____ ἄγγελοι.

d. πίνετε, _____ ἀδελφοί.

# 119. POSITIONING ADJECTIVES

Arrange the following Greek words, or as many of them as you need, so as to put the adjective (1) in attributive position and (2) in predicate position: καρδίᾱ, ἦν, ἡ, μακαρίᾱ, ἡ.

# 120. DISTINCTION OF TENSES

a. After reviewing the distinct meanings of the imperfect (number 84) and aorist (number 93) tenses, translate the italicized verbs.

1) While *we were looking* at the _____ lambs,
   Mary *heard* the messenger. _____

2) Philip *began to eat*, but the _____ slave *kept on speaking*. _____

3) He *did* not *die repeatedly*! _____

4) Lazarus, where *were you carrying* _____ the lamb?

b. After reviewing the distinct implications of the present and aorist imperatives (number 96), translate the italicized verbs.

1) *Carry* the cups to Mark every _____ day, my slaves.

2) Lazarus, *start treating* the little _____ child.

3) *Stop looking at me*, Mary. _____

4) *Get possession of* (a form of _____ ἔχω) the wealth, noble messengers.

# 121. ACCENTS IN PARTS OF SPEECH OTHER THAN FINITE VERBS, ADJECTIVES, AND NOUNS

To be learned by observation.

# 122. EXERCISES ON ACCENTS AND BREATHINGS

a. Résumé of material on accents and breathings.

1) Breathings: number 6.
2) Kinds of accents: number 7.
3) Syllables and accents: numbers 7, 35, 36, 37.
4) Recessive accent: number 38.
5) Persistent accent: number 49.

b. Table of accents permitted on the last three syllables of Greek words.

### IF THE ACCENT FALLS ON THE

| | ANTEPENULT | PENULT | | ULTIMA | |
|---|---|---|---|---|---|
| | | Short | Long | | |
| When a word has a *short* ultima | Acute ἄνθρωπος | Acute λόγος | Circumflex δοῦλος | Acute or Grave καλὸς ἀδελφός | |
| When a word has a *long* ultima | (No accent ever does!) | Acute λόγων | Acute δούλων | Acute or Circum- flex or Grave | ἀδελφούς ἀδελφῶν καλοὺς ἀδελφούς |

c. The following words are the only ones thus far studied which have the rough breathing:

| | |
|---|---|
| αἱ | ὁ |
| ἕξω (plus other future forms of ἔχω) | οἱ |
| ἕτοιμος | ὁμοῦ |
| ἡ | ὅτε |
| | ὅτι |

If you are familiar with this list, it will be easy to put smooth breathings everywhere else when a word begins with a vowel in the following exercises.

d. Applying the principle of recessive accent, put accents and breathings on the following finite verbs:

1) λαμβανετε
2) ηγαγον
3) εχουσῖ
4) αποθνῃσκει
5) εμνημονευσᾶν
6) ησᾶν
7) ισχυεις
8) απελυσᾶς
9) πεμψομεν
10) εβλεψεν

e. After being sure you know where the accent falls in the nominative singular of each of the following adjectives, put the right accents and breathings on the right syllables.

1) κακου
2) δικαιοι
3) ιδιᾳ
4) ελευθεραις
5) μικρα τεκνα
6) μακαριᾱ Μαριᾱ

64

f. After being sure you know where the accent falls in the nominative singular of each of the following nouns, put the right accents and breathings on the right syllables.

1) κωμην
2) αρτῳ
3) Φιλιππου
4) οινους
5) αγγελων

6) δωρεων
7) Λαζαρῳ
8) χρονους
9) αδελφοις
10) σπηλαιοις

g. Putting into action all your information on accents, arrange breathings and accents properly in the following sentences:

1) μνημονευετε των τεκνων εν τῳ σπηλαιῳ;
2) οι γεωργοι ελαβον τον πλουτον περι την κωμην.

# Lesson 13

## 123. OFF TO A NEW LAND

ὁ κύριος τῷ Αβραμ εἶπεν, "ἐλθὲ ἐκ τῆς γῆς σοῦ καὶ ἐκ τοῦ οἴκου σοῦ."

τότε ἐν τῇ Μεσοποταμίᾳ ἦν ὁ Αβραμ. ἀλλὰ οἱ ἄνθρωποι ἐν τῇ Μεσοποταμίᾳ ἦσαν κακοί, οὐ δίκαιοι, οὐχ ἔτοιμοι δουλεύειν τῷ κυρίῳ.                                              5

ἦλθον οὖν ἐκ τῆς γῆς τῆς Μεσοποταμίᾱς ὁ Αβραμ καὶ ἡ Σαρα καὶ ὁ Λώτ.

ὅτε ὁ Αβραμ ἐκ τῆς ἰδίᾱς γῆς ἦλθεν, τάχα εἶπαν ὁμοῦ ὁ Αβραμ καὶ ἡ Σαρα.

Σαρα: "Αβραμ, ἀδελφέ ἐμοῦ, εἶπεν ἄγγελος τοῦ κυρίου      10
σοί;"

Αβραμ: "οὐχί. ἐγὼ ἤκουσα τοῦ κυρίου ἡμῶν ἐν τῇ σκοτίᾳ. εἶπεν ἐμοί, 'ἐγὼ ὁ κύριος ἄξω ὑμᾶς ἐκ τῆς γῆς ὑμῶν καὶ ἐκ τοῦ οἴκου ὑμῶν, καὶ βλέψετε ὑμεῖς γῆν μακαρίᾱν, καὶ ἕξετε τὴν γῆν, σὺ καὶ ὁ οἶκος σοῦ. σὺ γὰρ ἦς δίκαιος. ἐγὼ γὰρ ἔβλεψα       15
σέ.'"

Σαρα: "πάντοτε οὖν κακοὶ ἦσαν οἱ ἄνθρωποι περὶ ἡμᾶς;"

Αβραμ: "ναί. ἡμεῖς, σὺ καὶ ἐγὼ καὶ Λώτ, ἐδουλεύομεν τῷ κυρίῳ, ἀλλὰ οἱ ἄνθρωποι τῆς Μεσοποταμίᾱς οὐκ ἐδούλευον τῷ κυρίῳ σὺν ἡμῖν. πολλάκις οὖν ἔπεμπον ἐμὲ ἐκ τῶν ἰδίων οἴκων      20
ὅτι ἐγὼ ἐδούλευον τῷ κυρίῳ. ὑμῖν, σοὶ καὶ τῷ Λώτ, κακὰ εἶπαν οἱ κακοὶ τῆς γῆς ὅτι ὑμεῖς, σὺ καὶ Λώτ, ἐδουλεύετε τῷ κυρίῳ;"

Σαρα: "ναί, πολλάκις ἔλεγον κακὰ ἡμῖν, ἐμοὶ καὶ τῷ Λώτ."

Αβραμ: "μακάριος οὖν ἤμην ἐγὼ ὅτι ἐμοὶ εἶπεν ὁ κύριος, 'ἐγὼ ἄξω ὑμᾶς ἐκ τῆς γῆς ὑμῶν, καὶ τὴν ἰδίᾱν γῆν τὴν μακαρίᾱν       25
βλέψετε ὑμεῖς.'"

Σαρα: "πῶς οὖν ἄξει ἡμᾶς ὁ κύριος ἡμῶν;"

Αβραμ: "βλέψομεν ἡμεῖς. τάχα οἱ κακοὶ τῆς Μεσοποταμίᾱς οὐ βλέψουσιν, ἀλλὰ ἡμεῖς βλέψομεν."

## 124. VOCABULARY

Αβραμ (indecl.), ὁ:  Abram
γῆ, γῆς, ἡ:  earth, land, country, ground

66

ἐγώ:  I
ἐμέ (acc. of ἐγώ):  me
ἐμοῦ (gen. of ἐγώ)
ἐμοί (dat. of ἐγώ)
ἡμᾶς (acc. of ἡμεῖς):  us
ἡμεῖς:  we
ἡμῖν (dat. of ἡμεῖς)
ἡμῶν (gen. of ἡμεῖς)
κύριος, -ου, ὁ:  Lord, lord, master
Λώτ (indecl.), ὁ:  Lot
Μεσοποταμίᾱ, -ᾶς, ἡ:  Mesopotamia
οὖν:  consequently, therefore, then, so, accordingly
οὐχ (form of οὐ used before a word with a rough breathing):  not
οὐχί (emphatic form of οὐ):  not at all, no, no indeed
πολλάκις:  often, many times
Σαρα, -ας, -α, -αν, ἡ:  Sarai
σέ (acc. of σύ)
σοῦ (gen. of σύ)
σοί (dat. of σύ)
σύ:  you (sing.), thou
τάχα:  perhaps, possibly, probably
ὑμᾶς (acc. of ὑμεῖς)
ὑμεῖς:  you (pl.)
ὑμῖν (dat. of ὑμεῖς)
ὑμῶν (gen. of ὑμεῖς)

## 125. DECLENSION OF γῆ

Since it is a contract noun from the form γέα, γῆ has a circumflex
accent throughout its declension.

γῆ                    (No plural is in use in the New Testament.)
γῆς
γῆ
γῆν

## 126. PERSONAL PRONOUNS

### First Person

| Singular | | Plural | |
|---|---|---|---|
| ἐγώ | (I) | ἡμεῖς | (we) |
| ἐμοῦ | (of me) | ἡμῶν | (of us) |
| ἐμοί | (for me) | ἡμῖν | (for us) |
| ἐμέ | (me) | ἡμᾶς | (us) |

## Second Person

| | | | |
|---|---|---|---|
| σύ | (you) | ὑμεῖς | (you) |
| σοῦ | (of you) | ὑμῶν | (of you) |
| σοί | (for you) | ὑμῖν | (for you) |
| σέ | (you) | ὑμᾶς | (you) |

## 127. DEFINITE ARTICLE WITH A PROPER NOUN

The definite article is sometimes used with a proper noun, but only rarely can such definite articles be translated.

οὐ δουλεύει τῷ Φιλίππῳ.
He is not a slave *to Philip*.

## 128. EXERCISES

a. As you translate number 123, bear in mind (1) that the definite article before proper nouns usually does not influence the translation, and (2) that more personal pronouns are used in this passage than are absolutely necessary.

b. Supply the Greek personal pronouns needed to complete the following sentences. The rest of the sentence in each instance should help you to recognize whether the second person is singular or plural.

1) πέμπετε οὖν τάχα τὸν πλοῦτον _____ (your) εἰς τὸν οἶκον _____ (my).

2) χαῖρε, 'Ιάκωβε. λέγει οὐχ ὁ ἀδελφός _____ (your) παρρησίᾳ σήμερον, ἀλλὰ ὁ ἄγγελος _____ (our) λέγει.

3) οἴσομεν τάχα _____ (our) ἄρτους.

4) οὐχί. οὐ δουλεύετε πολλάκις _____ (me).

5) οὐχί. οὐκ ἰσχύσομεν φαγεῖν _____ (you), τὰ τέκνα _____ (my).

6) πολλάκις _____ (to us) δωρεὰς ἔπεμπον.

7) ἐμνημόνευσε _____ (us) ὁ Πέτρος, οὐχ ἡ Μαρίᾱ.

8) βλέψουσι _____ (you), Μᾶρκε.

9) εἴπομεν _____ (to you), ἀδελφοί, ὅτι ἔφερε τὴν δωρεὰν, _____ (your) Νικόδημος.

10) βλέπετε _____ (me), ἄγγελοι, _____ (I) ἰσχύω ὀψάριον φαγεῖν.

c. Write in Greek, remembering that personal pronouns used as subjects often add emphasis to the personal idea in the inflectional endings of the verb. The italics in the following sentences are intended to add emphasis.

1) Are *you* speaking to me, Philip?
2) No. *I* am not speaking to you, but Mary is hoping to speak to you.
3) Yes. I am speaking to *you*, not to Mary.
4) Mary, did they carry *your* little lamb away from the garden?
5) Yes, Mark, and they have *our* fish, too.

d. Add to the predicate of each of the following sentences personal pronouns agreeing with the subject in person but differing from it in number, for example, ἀπολύομεν τὸν δοῦλον ἐμοῦ.

1) οὐκ ἔξω τοὺς καρποὺς ―――.
2) οὐχ ἔξεις τοὺς καρποὺς ―――.
3) οὐχ ἔξομεν τοὺς καρποὺς ―――.
4) οὐχ ἔξετε τοὺς καρποὺς ―――.
5) ἔπεμπον ἐγὼ τὸν ἄγγελον ―――.
6) ἐπέμπετε τὸν ἄγγελον ―――.
7) ἔπεμπες τὸν ἄγγελον ―――.
8) θεραπεύσω ―――.
9) θεραπεύσεις ―――.
10) θεραπεύσετε ―――.

e. Associate the following English words with the new Greek words in this lesson.

1) *Cyril*: a man's name meaning "*lordly.*"
2) *ego*tism: excessive use of the pronoun "*I.*"
3) *geo*graphy: a description of the *earth.*

f. Read the Greek aloud and then translate:

1) ῾Υμεῖς ἐστε (are) τὸ ἅλας (salt) τῆς γῆς . . . .
2) τοῦ κυρίου γὰρ ἡ γῆ καὶ τὸ πλήρωμα αὐτῆς (everything that is in it).
3) . . . ᾿Εγώ εἰμι τὸ φῶς (light) τοῦ κόσμου . . . .

The sources of these excerpts are listed on page 244.

# Lesson 14

---

## 129. HALF-SISTER: HALF-TRUTH

ἐπεὶ εἰς τὴν γῆν τὴν μακαρίαν ἦλθεν ὁ Αβραμ σὺν τῇ
Σαρα καὶ τῷ Λώτ, ἐν ταύτῃ τῇ γῇ χρείᾱν ἄρτου ἔσχον. εἰς τὴν
Αἴγυπτον οὖν ἤγαγον ὁ Αβραμ καὶ ἡ Σαρα ἡ γυνὴ καὶ Λώτ.

ἐπεὶ οὖν ὁ Αβραμ εἰς τὴν Αἴγυπτον ἦλθε, τῇ Σαρα εἶπεν
οὗτος, "ἐπεὶ βλέψουσι σὲ οἱ Αἰγύπτιοι, οὗτοι τάχα φονεύσουσιν     5
ἐμὲ καὶ οἴσουσι σὲ εἰς τὸν οἶκον τοῦ Φαραώ, σὲ τὴν καλὴν
Σαραν. ἐγὼ γὰρ τούτους τοὺς Αἰγυπτίους φονεῦσαι οὐκ
ἰσχύσω, ἀλλὰ οὗτοι οἱ Αἰγύπτιοι ἐμὲ φονεῦσαι ἰσχύσουσι.
εἰπὲ οὖν τότε τούτοις τοῖς Αἰγυπτίοις, 'βλέπετε τὴν ἀδελφὴν
τούτου τοῦ Αβραμ.'"     10

ὅτι γὰρ ἡ Σαρα ἦν ἀδελφὴ τοῦ Αβραμ, τοῦτο ἦν ἡ
ἀλήθεια, ἀλλὰ ἦν καὶ ἡ γυνὴ τοῦ Αβραμ.

ἐν τῇ Αἰγύπτῳ οὖν ἡ Σαρα ἡ γύνὴ καὶ ἡ ἀδελφὴ τοῦ
Αβραμ εἶπε ταῦτα τοῖς Αἰγυπτίοις, καὶ οὗτοι τὸν Αβραμ οὐκ
ἐφόνευσαν, ἀλλὰ τὴν ἀδελφὴν τούτου ἤγαγον εἰς τὸν οἶκον     15
τοῦ Φαραώ. τότε τούτῳ, τῆς Σαρας τῷ ἀδελφῷ, δωρεὰς καλὰς
ἔπεμψεν ὁ Φαραώ.

μετὰ τοῦτο ἔλαβεν ὁ Φαραώ ἀπὸ τοῦ κυρίου κακά. ἐπεὶ
οὖν ἤκουσε ὁ Φαραώ ὅτι αὕτη ἦν ἡ γυνὴ τοῦ Αβραμ, τούτῳ
εἶπεν ὁ Φαραώ, "οὐ παρρησίᾳ ἐμοὶ εἶπες περὶ ταύτης. σὺ γὰρ     20
εἶπες καὶ αὕτη εἶπεν, 'βλέπεις τὴν ἀδελφὴν τοῦ Αβραμ.' Λάβε
οὖν ταύτην καὶ ἀγάγετε ἐκ τῆς γῆς καὶ σὲ οὐ φονεύσω."

ἐπεὶ ὁ Φαραώ ταῦτα εἶπε τούτῳ καὶ ταύτῃ, ἐκ τῆς
Αἰγύπτου ἤγαγον Αβραμ καὶ Σαρα, ἡ γυνή, καὶ Λώτ.

## 130. VOCABULARY

ἀδελφή, -ῆς, ἡ: sister
Αἰγύπτιος, -ᾱ, -ον: Egyptian
Αἴγυπτος, -ου, ἡ: Egypt
γυνή (not a first declension noun, other forms to be given
    later): woman, wife
ἐπεί: after, when, since, because
οὗτος, αὕτη, τοῦτο: this
Φαραώ (indecl.), ὁ: Pharaoh
φονεύω, φονεύσω, ἐφόνευσα: I kill, murder

# 131. THE DEMONSTRATIVE οὗτος

a. Its use. Such words as ταύτῃ, τούτους, and οὗτοι are inflectional forms of the demonstrative οὗτος, αὕτη, τοῦτο: *this*, which can be used either as a pronoun by itself or as an adjective.

Adjectival use.

Pronominal use.

ἐν ταύτῃ τῇ γῇ.
in *this* land.

τῇ Σαρα εἶπεν *οὗτος.*
*This* (man) (or) *He* said to Sarai.

Notice that the Greek demonstrative adjective is in predicate position (number 107*b*). It either precedes or follows the combination of definite article and noun; it is not placed between them. No vocative is used.

b. Its declension.

| Masculine | Feminine | Neuter |
|-----------|----------|--------|
| οὗτος | αὕτη | τοῦτο |
| τούτου | ταύτης | τούτου |
| τούτῳ | ταύτῃ | τούτῳ |
| τοῦτον | ταύτην | τοῦτο |
| οὗτοι | αὗται | ταῦτα |
| τούτων | τούτων | τούτων |
| τούτοις | ταύταις | τούτοις |
| τούτους | ταύτᾱς | ταῦτα |

# 132. EXERCISES

a. Translate number 129.

b. Translate orally.

1) Kill this Egyptian.
2) These sisters.
3) These caves.
4) In this fish.
5) Concerning this land.
6) For these children.
7) Of these lambs.
8) Take this cup.
9) Out of this cup.
10) We shall not kill these Egyptians.
11) About these needs.
12) In these truths.
13) Away from these farmers.
14) With these sisters.
15) For these lords.

c. Match the adjectives in list 2 with the nouns in list 1.

List 1

1) τοῖς ἀνθρώποις
2) τὰ ἀρνία
3) τοὺς ἄρτους
4) τὸ δεῖπνον

List 2

α) τούτῳ
β) ταύτην
γ) τοῦτο
δ) ταύταις

| | |
|---|---|
| 5) τῷ δούλῳ | ε) αὕτη |
| 6) τὴν ἐπιθυμίᾶν | ζ) τούτους |
| 7) ταῖς καρδίαις | η) ταῦτα |
| 8) ἡ παρρησίᾱ | θ) ταύτης |
| 9) τῇ σκοτίᾳ | ι) ταύτῃ |
| 10) τῆς ἀληθείᾶς | κ) τούτοις |

d. Notice carefully the following English words related to new Greek words in this lesson.

1) *Egypto*logy: scientific study of ancient *Egypt*.
2) *gyn*archy: rule by *women*.
3) *gyneco*logist: a medical doctor who specializes in the treatment of *women*.
4) *phono*mania: an insane desire to *murder*.

e. Read the Greek aloud and then translate:

1) ... λέγουσιν αὐτῷ (to him), 'Ιδοὺ (See!) ἡ μήτηρ (mother) σου καὶ οἱ ἀδελφοί σου καὶ αἱ ἀδελφαί σου ἔξω (outside) ζητοῦσίν (are looking for) σε.
2) ... ἐφονεύσατε τὸν δίκαιον ....

The sources of these excerpts are listed on page 245.

# Lesson 15

## 133. A CHOICE AND A PROMISE

πάλιν εἰς τὴν γῆν τῆς ἐπαγγελίᾱς τοῦ κυρίου ἤγαγον τὰ πρόβατα αὐτῶν καὶ τοὺς καμήλους αὐτῶν οἱ ἄνθρωποι Αβραμ καὶ Λώτ. ἀλλὰ οὐχ ὁμοῦ ἐν τῷ αὐτῷ τόπῳ ἴσχυον ἐσθίειν καὶ πίνειν οἱ κάμηλοι καὶ τὰ πρόβατα. μικρὸς γὰρ ἦν ὁ τόπος.

εἶπεν οὖν ὁ Αβραμ τῷ Λώτ, "οὐκ ἰσχύσομεν ἔχειν τὸν 5 πλοῦτον ἡμῶν ἐν τῷ αὐτῷ τόπῳ. βλέπε περὶ ἡμᾶς. βλέπε ἐκείνην τὴν γῆν, τὴν γῆν τοῦ Ἰορδάνου, καί ταύτην τὴν γῆν περὶ ἡμᾶς. σὺ λάβε ἐκείνην καὶ ταύτην ἔξω ἐγώ, ἢ λάβε ταύτην καὶ ἐκείνην ἔξω."

τότε ἔβλεψεν ὁ Λώτ τὴν γῆν Ἰορδάνου, γῆν καλήν. 10 καὶ αὐτὸς ἔλαβεν αὐτήν. εἰς οὖν ἐκείνην τὴν γῆν ἤγαγεν ὁ Λώτ τοὺς ἰδίους καμήλους καὶ τὰ ἴδια πρόβατα ἀπὸ τοῦ Αβραμ.

μετὰ τοῦτο τῷ Αβραμ αὐτὸς ὁ κύριος εἶπεν, "σὺ ἕξεις ταύτην τὴν γῆν, σὺ καὶ τὰ τέκνα σου." αὕτη ἦν ἡ ἐπαγγελίᾱ τοῦ κυρίου τῷ Αβραμ. 15

## 134. VOCABULARY

αὐτός, αὐτή, αὐτό:  self, even, very, same, he, she, it
ἐκεῖνος, ἐκείνη, ἐκεῖνο:  that
ἐπαγγελίᾱ, -ᾱς, ἡ:  promise
ἤ:  or, than
Ἰορδάνης, -ου, ὁ:  Jordan
κάμηλος, -ου, ὁ or ἡ:  camel
πρόβατον, -ου, τό:  sheep
τόπος, -ου, ὁ:  place, spot, locality

## 135. MASCULINE NOUNS OF THE FIRST DECLENSION

The nouns of the first declension studied thus far are feminine and end in -ᾱ, -ᾰ, or -η. In this lesson a first declension masculine noun ending in -ης has been used. The endings differ from the patterns already presented only in the first and second inflectional forms of the singular.

73

| | |
|---|---|
| ’Ιορδάνης | No plural is in use for this noun. The plural |
| ’Ιορδάνου | endings, however, for this type of first |
| ’Ιορδάνῃ | declension noun are the same as for the |
| ’Ιορδάνην | other types. |

## 136. THE DEMONSTRATIVE ἐκεῖνος

As οὗτος is used to point out persons or things near at hand, so ἐκεῖνος is used to point out what is more remote.

| | | |
|---|---|---|
| ἐκεῖνος | ἐκείνη | ἐκεῖνο |
| ἐκείνου | ἐκείνης | ἐκείνου |
| ἐκείνῳ | ἐκείνῃ | ἐκείνῳ |
| ἐκεῖνον | ἐκείνην | ἐκεῖνο |
| ἐκεῖνοι | ἐκεῖναι | ἐκεῖνα |
| ἐκείνων | ἐκείνων | ἐκείνων |
| ἐκείνοις | ἐκείναις | ἐκείνοις |
| ἐκείνους | ἐκείνᾱς | ἐκεῖνα |

No vocative is used.

## 137. THE INTENSIVE αὐτός: ITS DECLENSION

The declension of αὐτός is like that of ἐκεῖνος except for the accent.

| | | |
|---|---|---|
| αὐτός | αὐτή | αὐτό |
| αὐτοῦ | αὐτῆς | αὐτοῦ |
| αὐτῷ | αὐτῇ | αὐτῷ |
| αὐτόν | αὐτήν | αὐτό |
| αὐτοί | αὐταί | αὐτά |
| αὐτῶν | αὐτῶν | αὐτῶν |
| αὐτοῖς | αὐταῖς | αὐτοῖς |
| αὐτούς | αὐτάς | αὐτά |

No vocative is used.

## 138. THE INTENSIVE αὐτός: ITS USES

There are three uses for αὐτός.

a. To emphasize the noun or pronoun with which it agrees.

Αβραμ *αὐτὸς* εἶχε δούλους.
Abram *himself* had slaves.

ὁ ἄνθρωπος *αὐτός* (or) *αὐτὸς* ὁ ἄνθρωπος.
The man *himself* (or) the *very* man.

Notice that either meaning fits either order and that αὐτός meaning *self* cannot come between a noun and its definite article.

74

b. To identify a noun or pronoun with something already mentioned.

ἐν τῷ αὐτῷ τόπῳ (or) ἐν τῷ τόπῳ τῷ αὐτῷ.
in the *same* place.

αὐτός meaning *same* must be in the attributive position (number 107a).

c. To serve as a personal pronoun.

ἡ γῆ ἦν καλή, καὶ αὐτὴν ἔλαβεν Λώτ.
The land was beautiful, and Lot took *it*.

# 139. EXERCISES

a. Translate number 133.

b. Write in Greek.

  1) This promise.
  2) That promise.
  3) The same promise.
  4) The promise itself.
  5) His promise.
  6) Her promise.
  7) Its promise.
  8) These camels or those sheep.
  9) The same sheep.
  10) In that place or in this place.
  11) In the Jordan itself.
  12) Into the same Jordan.
  13) These (things) or those (things).
  14) The camels themselves or the sheep themselves.
  15) That promise or the same gift.

c. Translate orally.

  1) ἡ αὐτὴ γυνὴ ἦν ἀδελφὴ αὐτή.
  2) τὰ πρόβατα ἐκεῖνα καὶ οἱ κάμηλοι οὗτοι ἦσαν τούτῳ ἢ ἐκείνῳ;
  3) ἐκ τοῦ Ἰορδάνου αὐτοῦ.
  4) εἰς ἐκεῖνον τὸν Ἰορδάνην.
  5) ἤμεθα ἐν τῇ αὐτῇ σκοτίᾳ.
  6) ἦτε σὺν τῷ Ἰακώβῳ αὐτῷ;
  7) ἐκεῖνοι οἱ γεωργοὶ ἦσαν ἕτοιμοι τούτοις τοῖς καμήλοις.
  8) ἤγαγον ἐκείνους περὶ τὴν αὐτὴν κώμην.
  9) βλέπετε τούτους τοὺς ἐλευθέρους;

10) οὐχί. ἀλλὰ ἐγὼ βλέπω τοὺς δούλους ἐκείνους.

11) ὁ 'Ιορδάνης ἦν ὁ τόπος;

12) οὐκ ἦν ὁ 'Ιορδάνης ἀλλὰ ἡ Αἴγυπτος.

13) ὁ 'Ιορδάνης οὐκ ἦν τῷ Λὼτ ἢ τῷ Αβραμ.

d. Associate the following English words with new Greek words in this lesson.

1) *auto*mobile:  a vehicle that moves *itself*.

2) *camel*: the English word *camel* is derived from Greek through Latin.

3) *topo*graphy:  map making (a drawing of a *place*).

e. Read the Greek aloud and then translate:

1) Μετὰ ταῦτα ἦλθεν ὁ 'Ιησοῦς (Jesus)  καὶ οἱ μαθηταὶ (disciples) αὐτοῦ εἰς τὴν 'Ιουδαίαν (Judean) γῆν . . . .

2) . . . 'Απόλυσον τοὺς ἀνθρώπους ἐκείνους.

3) . . . ὑμῖν γὰρ ἐστιν (is) ἡ ἐπαγγελίᾱ καὶ τοῖς τέκνοις ὑμῶν . . . .

4) ἦτε γὰρ ὡς (like) πρόβατα πλανώμενοι (going astray). (The last word agrees with the subject of ἦτε, not with πρόβατα.)

5) Ἤγαγεν δὲ (and) αὐτὸν εἰς 'Ιερουσαλήμ . . . .

The sources of these excerpts are listed on page 245.

76

# Lesson 16

## 140. A GLIMPSE AT LOT'S FUTURE

"μενῶ ἐν τοῖς Σοδόμοις," ἐρεῖ Λὼτ τάχα ὅτε ἕξει τόπον τοῖς καμήλοις αὐτοῦ καὶ τοῖς προβάτοις αὐτοῦ ἐν τῇ γῇ τοῦ Ἰορδάνου.

"ἀποστελῶ ἄγγελον εἰς τὰ Σόδομα καὶ ἐρῶ, 'μενοῦμεν ἐν τῇ αὐτῇ γῇ σὺν ὑμῖν.'"                                               5

ἀποστελεῖ δὲ τάχα ὑπηρέτην ὁ Λὼτ πρὸς τοὺς ἀνθρώπους τῶν Σοδόμων ἐπεὶ ἄξει τὰ πρόβατα καὶ τοὺς καμήλους ἀπὸ τοῦ Αβραμ εἰς τὴν γῆν τοῦ Ἰορδάνου.

οἱ δὲ ἄνθρωποι τῶν Σοδόμων οἱ κακοὶ οὐκ ἀποκτενοῦσι Λὼτ καὶ τοὺς ὑπηρέτας αὐτοῦ. μενοῦσι οὖν Λὼτ καὶ ἡ γυνὴ    10
αὐτοῦ ἐν τοῖς κακοῖς τῶν Σοδόμων καὶ βλέψουσι τὰ κακὰ τοῦ τόπου ἐκείνου.

ὅτε οἱ ἐχθροὶ τῶν Σοδόμων οἴσουσι τοὺς ἀνθρώπους τῶν Σοδόμων καὶ τὸν πλοῦτον αὐτῶν ἀπὸ τῆς γῆς τοῦ Ἰορδάνου, τότε ἐροῦσι τάχα ἐκεῖνοι τῷ Λώτ, "οὐ μενεῖτε ἐν τούτῳ τῷ τόπῳ,    15
σὺ καὶ ἡ γυνή σου καὶ ὁ πλοῦτος σου. ὑπηρέτην δὲ οὐκ ἀποστελεῖς πρὸς Αβραμ. οὐχί. ἀλλὰ ἡμεῖς σὲ καὶ τούτους τοὺς ἀνθρώπους οἴσομεν εἰς γῆν μακράν."

ὑπηρέτην δὲ Λὼτ ἀποστελεῖ πρὸς Αβραμ περὶ τῶν ἐχθρῶν τούτων. καὶ Αβραμ οὐ μενεῖ ἐν τῷ ἰδίῳ τόπῳ ὅτε ἀκούσει.    20
αὐτὸς δὲ ὁ Αβραμ οἴσει πάλιν τὸν Λὼτ καὶ τὸν πλοῦτον ἀπὸ τῶν ἐχθρῶν ἐν ἐκείνῃ τῇ μακρᾷ γῇ.

## 141. VOCABULARY

ἀποκτείνω, ἀποκτενῶ, ἀπέκτεινα:  I kill
ἀποστέλλω, ἀποστελῶ, ἀπέστειλα:  I send away, send forth
δ᾽:  δέ with vowel elided
δέ:  but, and, now (not temporal and never first in its clause)
ἐλπίζω, ἐλπιῶ, ἤλπισα (final stem consonant dropped before -σ- of
     tense suffix):  I hope, hope for
ἐχθρός, -οῦ, ὁ:  enemy
λέγω, ἐρῶ, εἶπον:  I say, speak, declare, tell, ask, answer
μακρός, -ά, -όν:  long, far distant
μένω, μενῶ, ἔμεινα:  I stay, remain, wait for, continue

77

πρός: (with dat.) near; (with acc.) to, towards, with

Σόδομα, -ων, τά: Sodom (a place name with plural form but singular meaning)

ὑπηρέτης, -ου, ὁ: assistant, servant, attendant

## 142. FUTURE OF LIQUID AND NASAL VERBS

In this lesson future forms of ἀποκτείνω, ἀποστέλλω, λέγω (ἐρῶ), and μένω have been used. The future stems of these verbs are called liquid (when ending in λ or ρ) and nasal (when ending in μ or ν). These futures differ from those previously observed in having no -σ- in the tense suffix and in having circumflex accents.

### Indicative

| | |
|---|---|
| μενῶ | μενοῦμεν |
| μενεῖς | μενεῖτε |
| μενεῖ | μενοῦσι |

These forms seem to be descended from the following, which are *not* in use.

### Indicative

| | |
|---|---|
| μενέσω | μενέσομεν |
| μενέσεις | μενέσετε |
| μενέσει | μενέσουσι |

The -σ- disappeared and the vowels on each side of the -σ- combined to produce the endings presented in the paradigms above. Although not having a liquid or nasal stem, ἐλπίζω has as its future active indicative ἐλπιῶ, ἐλπιεῖς, etc.

## 143. PRESENT OF LIQUID AND NASAL VERBS

In most of the verbs used before this lesson the future has been built upon the present stem by adding -σο/ε (or to state the same fact in other words) by inserting a -σ- between the present stem and the present endings, for example:

| Present | Future |
|---|---|
| πιστεύ-ω | πιστεύ-σ-ω |

In the regular pattern of liquid and nasal verbs the verb stem, for example, ἀποστελ-, was changed by the addition of -ίω, -ίεις, etc. to form the present. The -ἴ- was assimilated to a -λ-.

| | |
|---|---|
| (ἀποστελἴω) | ἀποστέλλω |
| (ἀποστελἴεις) | ἀποστέλλεις |

In μένω the nasal pattern for the present tense is not followed.

# 144. AORIST OF LIQUID AND NASAL VERBS

The first or sigmatic aorist was presented in numbers 93-97 and the second aorist in numbers 113-115. In number 140 verbs with liquid and nasal stems have been used in the future. These same verbs usually have peculiarities in the aorist, where the stem differs from that of the future, and where no -σ- appears in the tense suffix.

### Indicative

| | |
|---|---|
| ἔμεινα | ἐμείναμεν |
| ἔμεινας | ἐμείνατε |
| ἔμεινε | ἔμειναν |

### Imperative

| | |
|---|---|
| μεῖνον | μείνατε |
| μεινάτω | μεινάτωσαν |

### Infinitive

μεῖναι

These forms seem to be descended from the following, which are *not* in use.

### Indicative

| | |
|---|---|
| ἔμενσα | ἐμένσαμεν |
| ἔμενσας | ἐμένσατε |
| ἔμενσε | ἔμενσαν |

### Imperative

| | |
|---|---|
| μένσον | μένσατε |
| μενσάτω | μενσάτωσαν |

### Infinitive

μένσαι

It is supposed that -μεν- became -μειν- to make up for the loss of the -σ-. The aorist stems of ἀποκτείνω and ἀποστέλλω exhibit the same relationship with their future stems:

| Future | Aorist |
|---|---|
| ἀποκτενῶ | ἀπέκτεινα |
| (ἀποκτενέσω) | (ἀπέκτενσα) |
| ἀποστελῶ | ἀπέστειλα |
| (ἀποστελέσω) | (ἀπέστελσα) |

79

## 145. EXERCISES

a. Translate number 140.

b. Change every future to an aorist in number 140 unless the result does not make good sense.

c. Write in Greek.

1) You (sing.) are speaking (πρός) the attendant.
2) You (sing.) will speak to (πρός) the attendant.
3) You (sing.) did speak to (πρός) the attendant.
4) We do not kill the enemy.
5) We shall not kill the enemy.
6) We did not kill the enemy.
7) They remain in a far distant land.
8) They will remain in a far distant land.
9) They did remain in a far distant land.
10) She sends forth an assistant to (πρός) a far distant village.
11) She will send forth an assistant to (πρός) a far distant village.
12) She sent (once) forth an assistant to (πρός) a far distant village.

d. Translate into English.

1) ἐλπιοῦμεν ἀποκτεῖναι τοὺς ἐχθρούς.
2) οὐκ ἐλπιεῖτε, ἐχθροί, ἀποστεῖλαι ἡμᾶς πρὸς τοὺς ὑπηρέτας.
3) μὴ μεινάτωσαν πρὸς τοῖς Σοδόμοις.
4) ἄνθρωποι τῶν Σοδόμων, ἐλπιεῖτε ἀποκτεῖναι ἡμᾶς;
5) ἐχθρέ, ἐλπιεῖς μεῖναι ἐν τῷ αὐτῷ οἴκῳ σὺν ἡμῖν;
6) ὁ ὑπηρέτης ἀποστειλάτω τὸν ἐχθρὸν πρὸς μακρὰν γῆν.
7) ἀπόκτεινον ἡμᾶς, ἐχθρέ· ἐλπιοῦμεν δὲ ὅτι ὁ κύριος μενεῖ σὺν ἡμῖν. (Note: The raised period is the Greek semicolon.)
8) ἐλπιεῖτε μεῖναι ἐν τούτῳ τῷ τόπῳ;
9) δοῦλε, ἀποστελεῖς ἀρνίον πρὸς τὸν ἀδελφὸν ἐμοῦ;
10) πῶς ἀπέστειλας τὸ ἀρνίον;
11) ἀπόκτεινον τὸ ἀρνίον.
12) μὴ ἀποκτεινάτω τὸ ἀρνίον ὁ ἐχθρός.
13) μὴ ἀποκτεινάτωσαν ἀρνία οἱ ὑπηρέται.
14) ἀποστείλατε αὐτὰ ἀπὸ τῶν Σοδόμων.
15) ἔμεινας σὺ ἐν τῷ τόπῳ ἐκείνῳ· ἡμεῖς δὲ ἀπεστείλαμεν τοὺς ἀγγέλους ἀπὸ σοῦ.
16) ἐμείνατε· ἐλπίζομεν δὲ ὅτι οὐκ ἐμείνατε χρόνον μακρόν.
17) ἀπόστειλον ὑπηρέτην πρὸς ἐμέ.
18) μείνατε ἐν τῇ ἀληθείᾳ.

19) ἐμείνατε ἐν τῇ ἀληθείᾳ.

20) ἀποκετείνατε τοὺς κακοὺς ἐχθρούς, τοὺς δὲ καλοὺς ὑπηρέτᾱς ἀποστείλατε πρὸς τὸν Αβραμ.

21) Αβραμ, ἀπόστειλον ἐμὲ εἰς τὰ Σόδομα.

22) Αβραμ καὶ Λωτ μεινάτωσαν πρὸς τούτῳ τῷ τόπῳ.

23) Λὼτ μεινάτω, Αβραμ δὲ καὶ Σαρα ἀποστειλάτωσαν ἄγγελον.

24) ὁ ὑπηρέτης τῶν Σοδόμων μεινάτω πρὸς τοῖς Σοδόμοις.

e. Associate the following English words with new Greek words in this lesson.

1) *apostle*: one whom Jesus *sent forth* to preach.
2) *macron*: a mark over a vowel to indicate that its pronunciation is *long*.

f. Read the Greek aloud and then translate:

1) Κύριε, τοὺς προφήτας (prophets) σου ἀπέκτειναν . . . .
2) καθὼς (just as) ἐμὲ ἀπέστειλας εἰς τὸν κόσμον, κἀγὼ (I also) ἀπέστειλα αὐτοὺς εἰς τὸν κόσμον . . . .
3) ἡμεῖς δὲ ἡλπίζομεν ὅτι αὐτὸς ὁ μέλλων (the one who was about) λυτροῦσθαι (liberate) Ἰσραήλ . . . .
4) ἐγὼ δὲ λέγω ὑμῖν, ἀγαπᾶτε (love) τοὺς ἐχθροὺς ὑμῶν . . . .
5) καὶ ὑμεῖς τὸ χρῖσμα (anointing) ὃ (which) ἐλάβετε ἀπ᾽ αὐτοῦ μένει ἐν ὑμῖν . . . .
6) καὶ αἱ ἀδελφαὶ αὐτοῦ οὐχὶ πᾶσαι (all) πρὸς ἡμᾶς εἰσιν (are);
7) . . . εἶχον δὲ καὶ Ἰωάννην (John) ὑπηρέτην.
8) . . . ἐγὼ ἐν Ἀλεξανδρέᾳ (i.e. Ἀλεξανδρείᾳ) μένω.

The sources of these excerpts are listed on page 245.

# Lesson 17

## 146. ABRAM TO THE RESCUE

ὅτε ἔμενε Λὼτ ἐν τοῖς Σοδόμοις, ἐχθροὶ ἦλθον καὶ ἔλαβον αὐτόν. ἄγγελος δὲ πρὸς Αβραμ ἦλθε καὶ εἶπεν, "οἱ τῶν Σοδόμων ἐχθροὶ ἐληλύθᾱσι καὶ εἰλήφᾱσι πρὸς γῆν μακρὰν τὸν Λὼτ καὶ ἄλλους."

ἐπεὶ δὲ ἤκουσεν Αβραμ τοῦτο, ἔλαβε τοὺς ἰδίους ἀνθρώ- 5 πους καὶ ἐδίωξαν τοὺς ἐχθρούς. ἐν τῇ σκοτίᾳ Αβραμ αὐτὸς καὶ οἱ ἴδιοι ἀπέλυσαν Λὼτ καὶ τοὺς ἄλλους. πάλιν δὲ πρὸς τὰ Σόδομα ἦλθεν Αβραμ. οὐ γὰρ ἐδίωξαν αὐτὸν οἱ ἐχθροὶ τῶν Σοδόμων.

ἦλθε δὲ ὁ βασιλεὺς τῶν Σοδόμων πρὸς Αβραμ ὅτε οὗτος 10 ἦλθε πάλιν σὺν τῷ Λὼτ καὶ τοῖς ἄλλοις. ἄλλος δὲ βασιλεὺς ἤνεγκεν ἄρτους καὶ οἶνον τῷ Αβραμ. οὗτος ὁ βασιλεὺς ἦν ὑπηρέτης τοῦ κυρίου. οὗτος οὖν καλὰ τῷ Αβραμ εἶπε καὶ ἔλαβε δωρεὰς καλὰς ἀπὸ τοῦ Αβραμ.

τότε δὲ εἶπεν ὁ βασιλεὺς Σοδόμων πρὸς Αβραμ, "μενέτω- 15 σαν οἱ ἄνθρωποι ἐμοῦ σὺν ἐμοί, τὰ δὲ ἄλλα ἕξεις. εἴληφας γὰρ ἐκεῖνα ἀπὸ τῶν ἐχθρῶν. ἕξεις οὖν ἐκεῖνα."

πρὸς δὲ αὐτὸν εἶπεν Αβραμ, "εἴρηκα τῷ κυρίῳ, 'οὐχ ἕξω ἐκεῖνα. οὐχί. ὁ βασιλεὺς τῶν Σοδόμων οὐκ ἐρεῖ, "Αβραμ ἔχει τὸν πλοῦτον ἐμοῦ."' ἀπέλυσα τοὺς ἀνθρώπους σοῦ καὶ σοὶ 20 αὐτοὺς ἤγαγον. λάβε αὐτοὺς καὶ ἐκεῖνα. μεμενήκᾱσι σὺν σοὶ καὶ μενοῦσι."

## 147. VOCABULARY

ἄλλος, -η, -ο: other, another; οἱ ἄλλοι: the rest, the others
βασιλεύς (nom. sing.; other forms to be given later), ὁ: king
διώκω, διώξω, ἐδίωξα: I pursue, run after, put to flight, persecute
εἴληφας (perf. ind. act. 2nd s. of λαμβάνω): you have taken
εἰλήφᾱσιν (perf. ind. act. 3rd pl. of λαμβάνω): they have taken
εἴρηκα (perf. ind. act. 1st s. of λέγω): I have said
ἐληλύθᾱσι (perf. ind. act. 3rd pl. of the same verb as ἦλθον): they
   have come

82

## 148. FIRST PERFECT ACTIVE

In number 146 εἴρηκα, *I have said* is a first perfect. This tense indicates an action completed in the past and leaving behind its completion a more or less lasting result. Here Abram is represented as saying, "I made this statement and it still stands."

### Indicative

| | |
|---|---|
| εἴρηκα | εἰρήκαμεν |
| εἴρηκας | εἰρήκατε |
| εἴρηκε | εἰρήκᾱσι |

### Infinitive

εἰρηκέναι

The first perfect is made up of (1) reduplication (εἰ-), (2) the verb stem, (3) the tense suffix -κα (-κε inf. and third sing.), (4) the primary active endings (-μι, -ς, -σι, -μεν, -τε, -νσι). Notice that -μι and -σι do not appear in the first and third sing., and that -νσι is modified to -σι with the preceding -α- lengthened to compensate for the loss of the ν. The active infinitive ending is -ναι.

Another and more common type of reduplication appears in μεμενήκᾱσι. Its conjugation is like that of πιστεύω, our pattern for -ω verbs.

### Indicative

| | |
|---|---|
| πεπίστευκα | πεπιστεύκαμεν |
| πεπίστευκας | πεπιστεύκατε |
| πεπίστευκε | πεπιστεύκᾱσι |

### Infinitive

πεπιστευκέναι

The initial π in the simple verb stems is repeated with ε before the verb stem -πιστευ- to form the reduplication.

## 149. SECOND PERFECT ACTIVE

In number 146 ἐληλύθᾱσιν *they have come*, and εἰλήφᾱσι, *they have taken*, are second perfects.

### Indicative

| | |
|---|---|
| εἴληφα | εἰλήφαμεν |
| εἴληφας | εἰλήφατε |
| εἴληφε | εἰλήφᾱσι |

Infinitive

εἰληφέναι

Another type of reduplication appears in ἐληλύθᾱσι.

Indicative

| | |
|---|---|
| ἐλήλυθα | ἐληλύθαμεν |
| ἐλήλυθας | ἐληλύθατε |
| ἐλήλυθε | ἐληλύθᾱσι |

Infinitive

ἐληλυθέναι

In this verb -ἐλ- is the reduplication; -ηλυθ- is the verb stem (-η-being a lengthened form of -ε-); -α- or -ε- after -θ- is the tense suffix; and -ναι the active infinitive ending.

**150.** SUMMARY OF TYPES OF REDUPLICATION USED IN THIS LESSON

    a. A prefix made up of the initial consonant of the verb plus ε (πεπίστευκα).

    b. A prefix which earlier in the history of the language probably was the initial consonant of the verb stem plus ε (εἴληφα from σέσληφα, or εἴρηκα from ϜεϜρηκα, wewreka).

    c. A prefix made up of the first two letters of the verb stem (ἐλήλυθα from stem ἐλυθ-).

**151.** EXERCISES

    a. Translate number 146.

    b. Drill on the following list of principal parts in order to add the perfect tense to the present, future, and aorist tenses, most of which you already know from number 101. Some, but not all, of the blank spaces in this list will be filled by information appearing in later lessons.

| Present | Future | Aorist | Perfect |
|---|---|---|---|
| ἄγω | ἄξω | ἤγαγον | — |
| ἀκούω | ἀκούσω | ἤκουσα | ἀκήκοα |
| ἀποθνῄσκω | — | ἀπέθανον | |
| ἀπολύω | ἀπολύσω | ἀπέλυσα | — |
| ἀποστέλλω | ἀποστελῶ | ἀπέστειλα | ἀπέσταλκα |
| βλέπω | βλέψω | ἔβλεψα | — |

| δικω | διξω | ἐδίωξα | — |
| δουλεύω | δουλεύσω | ἐδούλευσα | δεδούλευκα |
| εἰμί | — | — | — |
| ἐλπίζω | ἐλπιῶ | ἤλπισα | ἤλπικα |
| ἐσθίω | — | ἔφαγον | — |
| — | — | ἦλθον | ἐλήλυθα |
| ἔχω | ἕξω | ἔσχον | ἔσχηκα |
| θεραπεύω | θεραπεύσω | ἐθεράπευσα | — |
| ἰσχύω | ἰσχύσω | ἴσχυσα | — |
| λαμβάνω | — | ἔλαβον | εἴληφα |
| λέγω | ἐρῶ | εἶπον | εἴρηκα |
| μένω | μενῶ | ἔμεινα | μεμένηκα |
| μνημονεύω | — | ἐμνημόνευσα | — |
| πέμπω | πέμψω | ἔπεμψα | πέπομφα |
| πίνω | — | ἔπιον | πέπωκα |
| πιστεύω | πιστεύσω | ἐπίστευσα | πεπίστευκα |
| φέρω | οἴσω | ἤνεγκα | — |
| φονεύω | φονεύσω | ἐφόνευσα | — |

c. Translate into English.

1) πέπωκας οἶνον, κακὲ ἐχθρέ;
2) μεμενήκᾱσιν ἐν τῷ οἴκῳ.
3) ἀπέσταλκε τὸ τέκνον ὁ βασιλεύς;
4) ἀκηκοέναι.
5) οὐκ πεπόμφαμεν.
6) τὸν ἄγγελον ἀπεστάλκατε;
7) ἤλπικα σχεῖν ἄρτον.
8) ὁ Λὼτ τῷ Αβραμ οὐ δεδούλευκε.
9) ἐλήλυθε εἰς τὰ Σόδομα.
10) ἐσχήκατε τοὺς ἄλλους ὑπηρέτᾱς.
11) πῶς εἴληφας τοὺς ἐχθρούς;
12) ὑμῖν εἰρήκαμεν;

d. Translate into Greek orally.

1) We have hoped.
2) The king has served as a slave of the Lord.
3) You, Peter, have sent forth the slave.

4) They have spoken.

5) I have not hoped to see you.

e. Associate the following English words with new Greek words in this lesson.

1) *allo*path:   one who practices medicine based on the theory that remedies producing in a well person symptoms *different* from those found in the sick person will heal the disease whose symptoms have been produced.

2) *basil*ic:   *kingly*.

f. Read the Greek aloud and then translate:

1) πάλιν ἀπέστειλεν ἄλλους δούλους . . . .

2) . . . Σὺ λέγεις ὅτι βασιλεύς εἰμι.

3) . . . ἤκουσεν φωνὴν (voice) λέγουσαν (saying) αὐτῷ, Σαοὺλ (Saul) Σαούλ, τί (why) με δικεις;

The sources of these excerpts are listed on page 245.

# Lesson 18

---

## 152. NEW VOCABULARY IN LESSONS 13-17

| NOUNS | PRONOUNS | ADJECTIVES |
|---|---|---|
| Αβραμ | αὐτός | Αἰγύπτιος |
| ἀδελφή | ἐγ | ἄλλος |
| Αἴγυπτος | ἐκεῖνος | μακρός |
| βασιλεύς | ἡμεῖς | |
| γῆ | οὗτος | ADVERBS |
| γυνή | σύ | |
| ἐπαγγελίᾱ | ὑμεῖς | οὐχ |
| ἐχθρός | | οὐχί |
| 'Ιορδάνης | | πολλάκις |
| κάμηλος | VERBS | τάχα |
| κύριος | | |
| Λτ | ἀποκτείνω | CONJUNCTIONS |
| Μεσοποταμίᾱ | ἀποστέλλω | |
| πρόβατον | δικω | δέ |
| Σαρα | ἐλπιῶ | ἐπεί |
| Σόδομα | ἐρῶ | ἤ |
| τόπος | ἤλπισα | οὖν |
| ὑπηρέτης | μένω | |
| Φαρα | φονεύω | PREPOSITION |
| | | πρός |

## 153. TABLE OF VERB ENDINGS

(Full inflections are given in the appendix, number 397 forward.)

| | | | | Indicative | | | | | |
|---|---|---|---|---|---|---|---|---|---|
| Pres. | Fut. (usual) | Fut. (liq. & nasal) | Aor. (1st) | Aor. (liq. & nasal) | Perf. (2nd) | Perf. (1st) | Aor. (2nd) | Imperf |
| -ω | -σω | -ῶ | -σα | -α | -α | -κα | -ον | -ον |
| -εις | -σεις | -εῖς | -σας | -ας | -ας | -κας | -ες | -ες |
| -ει | -σει | -εῖ | -σε(ν) | -ε(ν) | -ε | -κε | -ε(ν) | -ε(ν) |
| -ομεν | -σομεν | -οῦμεν | -σαμεν | -αμεν | -αμεν | -καμεν | -ομεν | -ομεν |
| -ετε | -σετε | -εῖτε | -σατε | -ατε | -ατε | -κατε | -ετε | -ετε |
| -ουσι(ν) | -σουσι(ν) | -οῦσι(ν) | -σαν | -αν | -ᾱσι | -κᾱσι | -ον | -ον |

87

| Imperative | | | | | | | | |
|---|---|---|---|---|---|---|---|---|
| -ε | None | None | -σον | -ον | None | None | -ε | None |
| -έτω | | | -σάτω | -άτω | | | -έτω | |
| -ετε | | | -σατε | -ατε | | | -έτωσαν | |
| -έτωσαν | | | -σάτωσαν | -άτωσαν | | | -έτωσαν | |
| Infinitive | | | | | | | | |
| -ειν | Rare -σειν | Rare -εῖν | -σαι | -αι | -έναι | -κέναι | -εῖν | None |

Tenses using augment: imperfect and aorist.

Tense using reduplication: perfect. (Note aorist of ἄγω.)

Tenses showing change of stem from the present in addition to augment and to the endings given above: liquid and nasal future and aorist, and second aorist.

## 154. LOCATION DRILL

Locate the following verb forms by studying their (1) endings, (2) stems, and (3) augments. A location consists of a correct indication of (1) tense, (2) mood, (3) voice, (4) person, (5) number, (6) first principal part.

Example: ἤγαγον (1) second aorist, (2) indicative, (3) active, (4){first, (5){singular, (6) ἄγω.
{third {plural

ἤγαγ |ον
first sing. act. or third pl. act.
second aor. indic. ἄγω

1) ἀποστελεῖτε
2) ἔσχομεν
3) ἄμειναν
4) ἐμένομεν
5) ἀπολυέτω
6) ἤσθιεν
7) ἐσθίειν
8) φαγεῖν
9) βλέψει
10) ἠκούσαμεν
11) ἐλπισάτωσαν
12) λάβε
13) εἰπεῖν
14) ἐροῦμεν
15) ἕξεις
16) ἀπολῦσαι
17) θεράπευσον
18) εἴχετε
19) σχεῖν
20) ἦμεν
21) εἰρήκᾱσι

## 155. TABLE OF NOUN ENDINGS

(Also see number 366 forward.)

### A or First Declension

#### Singular

| After ε, ι, or ρ | | Not after ε, ι, or ρ | | |
|---|---|---|---|---|
| -ᾱ | -ᾰ | -η | -ᾰ | -ης |
| -ᾱς | -ᾱς | -ης | -ης | -ου |

88

| -ᾳ | -ᾳ | | -η | -η | -η |
| -ᾱν | -ᾱν | | -ην | -ᾰν | -ην |

Plural

| -αι | (The middle column |
| -ων | above will be used in |
| -αις | number 179.) |
| -ᾱς | |

## O or Second Declension

| Singular | | | Plural | |
|---|---|---|---|---|
| Masc. | Neut. | | Masc. | Neut. |
| -ος | -ον | | -οι | -ᾰ |
| -ου | -ου | | -ων | -ων |
| -ῳ | -ῳ | | -οις | -οις |
| -ον | -ον | | -ους | -ᾰ |
| -ε | | | | |

## 156. TABLE OF ADJECTIVE ENDINGS: COMBINATION OF *A* AND *O* DECLENSIONS

(Also see number 366 and number 367.)

Singular

| Masc. | Fem. | | Neut. |
|---|---|---|---|
| | After ε, ι, or ρ | Not after ε, ι, or ρ | |
| -ος | -ᾱ | -η | -ον |
| -ου | -ᾱς | -ης | -ου |
| -ῳ | -ᾳ | -ῃ | -ῳ |
| -ον | -ᾱν | -ην | -ον |
| -ε | -ᾱ | -η | -ον |

Plural

| Masc. | Fem. | Neut. |
|---|---|---|
| -οι | -αι | -ᾰ |
| -ων | -ων | -ων |
| -οις | -αις | -οις |
| -ους | -ᾱ | -ᾰ |

# 157. LOCATION DRILL

Give the number, gender, and possible case of the following nouns and adjectives.

a. Nouns
1) δεῖπνα
2) ἀδελφῇ
3) πλοῦτοι
4) ἐπαγγελίαις
5) κυρίους

b. Adjectives.
1) μακαρίων
2) ἐλεύθερε
3) μακρῷ
4) μικρόν
5) Αἰγύπτιαι

# Lesson 19

## 158. ABRAM BELIEVES GOD

ἐπεὶ ὁ Λὼτ ἐμεμενήκει ἐν τοῖς Σοδόμοις τοῖς κακοῖς καὶ
ἐπεὶ ὁ Αβραμ ἀπέλυσε τὸν Λὼτ ἀπὸ τῶν ἐχθρῶν Σοδόμων καὶ
ἐπεὶ ἐληλύθει πρὸς Αβραμ ὁ βασιλεὺς τῶν Σοδόμων καὶ ἐπεὶ ὁ
ἄλλος βασιλεὺς εἰλήφει τὰς δωρεὰς τοῦ Αβραμ καὶ ἐπεὶ ὁ
Αβραμ οὐκ εἰλήφει τὰς δωρεὰς τῶν Σοδόμων, ὁ θεὸς εἶπε τῷ          5
Αβραμ, "μὴ ἔχε φόβον. ἕξεις τὴν ἐπιθυμίαν τῆς καρδίας σοῦ."
εἶπε δὲ Αβραμ, "ἀλλά, κύριε, ἐγὼ οὐκ ἔχω τέκνον, οὗτος ὁ
ὑπηρέτης ἕξει τὸν οἶκον ἐμοῦ."
εἶπε δὲ ὁ θεός, "ἕξεις υἱόν, τὸ ἴδιον τέκνον."
ἐπεὶ τὴν ἐπαγγελίαν τέκνου εἰλήφει, Αβραμ τῷ θεῷ          10
ἐπίστευεν.

## 159. VOCABULARY

θεός, -οῦ, ὁ:  God, god, deity
πιστεύω, πιστεύσω, ἐπίστευσα, πεπίστευκα:  I believe, trust (with
dative of person or thing believed to be telling the truth)
υἱός, -οῦ, ὁ:  son
φόβος, -ου, ὁ:  fear

## 160. FIRST PLUPERFECT ACTIVE

In number 158 ἐμεμενήκει, *he had remained*, is a first pluperfect. The
pluperfect has the idea of the perfect but locates it in a past context.
The pluperfect indicates an action completed in a relatively remote
past and leaving behind its completion a more or less lasting result in
a less remote past. In ἐμεμενήκει Lot is represented as having taken
up his residence in Sodom and continued it at a time earlier than that
of this conversation with God.

The pluperfect of πιστεύω follows:

### Indicative

| | |
|---|---|
| (ἐ)πεπιστεύκειν | (ἐ)πεπιστεύκειμεν |
| (ἐ)πεπιστεύκεις | (ἐ)πεπιστεύκειτε |
| (ἐ)πεπιστεύκει | (ἐ)πεπιστεύκεισαν |

The pluperfect has no form outside the indicative.

The first pluperfect is made up of (1) augment (often not used in Hellenistic Greek), (2) reduplication (identical with that used in the perfect), (3) verb stem, (4) tense suffix (-κει-), and (5) secondary active ending (-ν, -ς, —, -μεν, -τε, -σαν).

## 161. SECOND PLUPERFECT ACTIVE

In number 158 εἰλήφει, *he had received*, is a second pluperfect. The only difference between the first and second pluperfects is in the tense suffix where no κ appears in the second pluperfect.

Indicative

| | |
|---|---|
| εἰλήφειν | εἰλήφειμεν |
| εἰλήφεις | εἰλήφειτε |
| εἰλήφει | εἰλήφεισαν |

## 162. LIST OF SECOND PERFECTS AND PLUPERFECTS

| Present | Perfect | Pluperfect |
|---|---|---|
| ἀκούω | ἀκήκοα | ἠκηκόειν |
| — | ἐλήλυθα | ἠληλύθειν |
| λαμβάνω | εἴληφα | εἰλήφειν |
| πέμπω | πέπομφα | ἐπεπόμφειν |

## 163. EXERCISES

a. Translate number 158.

b. Translate into Greek.

1) We had heard about the fear of Abram.
2) She had received a son.
3) Fear had remained in the village.
4) They had sent a messenger concerning their fear.
5) I had not served because you had fear.
6) Had you (sing.) believed God?
7) Abram's son's sons have believed the promise.

c. Form the corresponding pluperfects.

1) πέπωκα
2) ἐληλύθᾱσι
3) πέπομφας
4) δεδούλευκε
5) ἠλπίκαμεν
6) πεπιστεύκατε
7) εἰλήφᾱσι
8) πεπώκατε
9) ἀκηκόαμεν
10) ἠλπίκατε
11) ἀπέσταλκας

92

d. Review the kinds of action presented by tense.

| Kind of action | Symbol | Tense |
|---|---|---|
| Progression | a line (――――) | present and imperfect |
| Occurrence | a point (.) | aorist |
| Completion+result | line-point-line (――――.――――) | perfect and pluperfect |

e. Associate the following English words with new Greek words in this lesson.

1) Anglo*phobe*: one who has a *fear* or dislike of things English.
2) *phobia*: an unreasonable *fear*.
3) hydro*phobia*: *fear* of water.
4) *the*ology: a systematic study of *God*.

f. Read the Greek aloud and translate:

1) ᾿Εν ἀρχῇ (In the beginning) ἦν ὁ λόγος (word), καὶ ὁ λόγος ἦν πρὸς τὸν θεόν, καὶ θεὸς ἦν ὁ λόγος.
2) φόβος οὐκ ἔστιν (is) ἐν τῇ ἀγάπῃ (love) . . . .
3) ὄμνυμι (I swear) Καίσαρα Αὐτοκράτορα (by Caesar Imperator) θεοῦ υἱόν . . . .

The sources of these excerpts are listed on page 245.

# Lesson 20

## 164. WHAT DO YOU KNOW ABOUT ABRAM?

α. τίς ἦν Αβραμ;
   υἱός ἀνθρώπου τινὸς ἐν τῇ Μεσοποταμίᾳ ἦν Αβραμ.
β. ἐν τίνι γῇ ἦν Αβραμ ὅτε ἦν τέκνον;
   ἐν γῇ τινι, Μεσοποταμίᾳ, ἔμενεν οὗτος ὅτε ἦν τέκνον.
γ. τίς ἦν Σαρα;                                                    5
   ἡ γυνὴ ἦν αὕτη τοῦ Αβραμ.
δ. τί ἦλθεν Αβραμ ἐκ τῆς ἰδίας γῆς;
   εἰρήκει ὁ θεὸς αὐτῷ ἐλθεῖν ἐκ τῆς ἰδίας γῆς, τῆς Μεσο-
   ποταμίας, καὶ εἰς ἄλλην τινὰ γῆν.
ε. εἰς τίνα γῆν ἦλθον Αβραμ καὶ Σαρα;                              10
   εἰς γῆν τινα μακρὰν ἦλθον.
ζ. μετὰ τίνος ἦλθον εἰς ταύτην τὴν γῆν;
   μετὰ τοῦ Λωτ ἦλθον.
η. τί οὐκ ὁμοῦ ἔμειναν Λωτ καὶ Αβραμ;
   ἐν τῷ αὐτῷ τόπῳ μένειν οὐκ ἴσχυον οἱ δοῦλοι αὐτῶν καὶ οἱ   15
   κάμηλοι καὶ τὰ πρόβατα.
θ. τίνι θεῷ ἐπεπιστεύκει Αβραμ;
   τῷ θεῷ τῆς ἀληθείας ἐπεπιστεύκει Αβραμ, ἀλλὰ οἱ ἄνθρωποι ἐν τῇ Μεσοποταμίᾳ οὐκ ἐπεπιστεύκεισαν τῇ ἀληθείᾳ
   περὶ τοῦ θεοῦ.                                                 20

## 165. VOCABULARY

τίς, τί:  who? which? what? (τί may mean "why?")
τὶς, τὶ:  (masc. and fem.) one, anyone, someone, a certain; (neut.)
          anything, something

## 166. INTERROGATIVE PRONOUN AND ADJECTIVE

| Masc. & Fem. | Neuter |
|---|---|
| Singular | |
| τίς | τί |
| τίνος | τίνος |
| τίνι | τίνι |
| τίνα | τί |

94

| | |
|---|---|
| τίνες | τίνα |
| τίνων | τίνων |
| τίσι | τίσι |
| τίνας | τίνα |

The interrogative pronoun and adjective always has an acute accent.

Used as a pronoun τίς in any of its forms serves as a substantive.

τίς ἦν Ἀβραμ;
*Who* was Abram?

Used as an adjective τίς in any of its forms modifies a noun.

τίς γυνὴ ἦν ἡ Μαρίᾱ;
*Which* woman was Mary?

## 167. INDEFINITE PRONOUN AND ADJECTIVE

| Masc. & Fem. | Neuter |
|---|---|
| **Singular** | |
| τὶς | τὶ |
| τινός | τινός |
| τινί | τινί |
| τινά | τὶ |
| **Plural** | |
| τινές | τινά |
| τινῶν | τινῶν |
| τισί | τισί |
| τινάς | τινά |

The indefinite pronoun and adjective is enclitic in all its forms and subject to the restrictions of that class of words, as will be explained in number 169. Except for its accent the indefinite τὶς is declined just like the interrogative τίς.

Used as a pronoun, τὶς in any of its forms serves as a substantive.

ἦν τις ἐν τῇ κώμῃ.
*Someone* was in the village.

Used as an adjective, τὶς in any of its forms modifies a noun.

ἦν ὑπηρέτης τις ἐν κώμῃ τινί.
There was *a certain* attendant in *a certain* village.

## 168. PROCLITICS

Certain Greek words such as αἱ, εἰς, ἐκ, ἐν, ἡ, ὁ, οἱ, οὐ, οὐκ, and οὐχ have no accents of their own and are each pronounced with the word immediately following.

ὁ δοῦλος οὐκ ἦν ἡ ἀδελφή.
*The* slave was *not the* sister.

These words are called *proclitics*. (Cf. προκλίνειν, to lean forward.)

## 169. ENCLITICS

Certain Greek words, such as the forms of the indefinite τὶς in most instances do not retain their own accent, but are each pronounced with the word immediately preceding.

ἀδελφή τις ἦν.
There was *a certain* sister.

These words are called *enclitics*. (Cf. ἐγκλίνειν, to lean on.)

   a. The accent of the enclitic is retained in the following situations:

      1) If it contains two syllables and follows a word with an acute on the penult.

         κώμῃ τινί, for *a certain* village

      2) If it contains two syllables and follows a proclitic.

         ἐν τινὶ κώμῃ, in *a certain* village

      3) When it is emphasized, as at the beginning of a sentence.

         τὶς ἦν ἐν τῇ κώμῃ, *someone* was in the village

   b. The accent of the enclitic is placed as an acute on the ultima of the preceding word in the following situations:

      1) When the preceding word is proclitic (except in the situation described above).

         εἴς τι σπήλαιον, into *a certain* cave

      2) When the preceding word is accented on the antepenult.

         ἀλήθειά τις, *a certain* truth

      3) When the preceding word is accented with a circumflex on the penult.

         κῶμαί τινες, *certain* villages

   c. In the remaining instances the accent of the enclitic is lost altogether:

      1) When it consists of one syllable and follows a word accented with an acute on the penult.

         τόπος τις, *a certain* place.

      2) When it follows a word accented on the ultima. (If the

96

accent of the preceding word is an acute, it remains an acute before the enclitic contrary to the general principle.)

ἀδελφή τις, *a certain* sister
ἀδελφᾶς τινας, *certain* sisters
ἀδελφῆς τινος, of *a certain* sister

## 170. EXERCISES

a. Translate number 164.

b. Put correct accents and breathings on the following words.

1) ανθρωποι τινες ησαν υιοι.
2) τις θεραπευσει κακην κωμην;
3) τινι επεμψατε τον γεωργον;
4) ακουσομεν τον αγγελον τινος.
5) τι βλεπομεν τον τοπον;

c. Ask a question in Greek beginning with each of the following words.

1) τίς            5) τινά
2) τίνος        6) τινῶν
3) τίνι          7) τισί
4) τίνα         8) τὶ

d. The following table indicates shift, loss, or preservation of accent on enclitics.

| Description of word preceding enclitic | Effect on accent of | |
|---|---|---|
| | monosyllabic enclitic | dissyllabic enclitic |
| Acute on antepenult | Shifted | Shifted |
| Circumflex on penult | Shifted | Shifted |
| Acute on penult | Lost | Kept |
| Acute or circumflex on ultima | Lost | Lost |
| Proclitic | Shifted | Kept |
| Enclitic | Lost | Lost |
| No word | Kept | Kept |

e. Translate into English.

1) τίνων τὴν δωρεὰν ἀπεστάλκειν;
2) τίσι δωρεὰς πέμψομεν;
3) τίνας δωρεὰς ἐλπιεῖτε λαβεῖν;

4) τίνα βλέπετε ἐν τῷ σπηλαίῳ;

5) τίνες οἴσουσί τινα εἰς τὸ σπήλαιον;

6) τίνων ἡ χρείᾱ ἦν μικρᾱ;

7) ἐν τίσι κώμαις ἠσθίομεν;

8) τίνας ἀδελφᾱς εἴληφας;

9) τίνες ἦσαν αἱ ἀδελφαὶ ἐν τῇ Μεσοποταμίᾳ;

10) τίνας τόπους ἐλπίζουσι βλέψαι;

f. Translate the English in parentheses by one Greek word.

1) ἀπεστάλκειν τὴν δωρεᾱν (belonging to certain men).

2) πέμψομεν δωρεᾱς (to certain women).

3) δωρεᾱς (some) ἐλπιεῖτε λαβεῖν.

4) βλέπετέ (certain things) ἐν τῷ σπηλαίῳ;

5) τίνα οἴσουσί (some people) εἰς τὸ σπήλαιον;

6) ἡ χρείᾱ (of some persons) μικρᾱ ἦν.

7) ἠσθίομεν ἔν (certain) κώμαις.

8) πέπομφάς (certain) αδελφᾱς.

9) ἠσάν (certain) ἀδελφαὶ ἐν τῇ Μεσοποταμίᾳ.

10) ἐλπίζουσι βλέψαι τόπους (certain).

11) ἐφάγετε πρόβατά (some).

12) ἤγαγον τέκνα (certain) εἰς τὸν οἶκον.

g. Read the Greek aloud and then translate:

εἶπεν δέ, Τίς εἶ (are you), κύριε; ὁ δέ (and he said), Ἐγώ εἰμι Ἰησοῦς ὃν (whom) σὺ διώκεις . . . .

The sources of these excerpts are listed on page 245.

# Lesson 21

## 171. JOSEPH'S FUTURE IN EGYPT

ὅτε Ἰωσὴφ ἔρχεται εἰς τὴν γῆν Αἰγύπτου, γενήσεται
δοῦλος Αἰγυπτίου τινὸς ἀλλὰ οὐ μενεῖ ἐν τῷ οἴκῳ τούτου. μετὰ
δὲ τοῦτο ἐλεύσεται Ἰωσὴφ πρὸς τὸν Φαραὼ καὶ γενήσεται
ὑπηρέτης αὐτοῦ. τότε Ἰωσὴφ καὶ ἄλλοι δοῦλοι τοῦ Φαραὼ
συνάξουσι σῖτον ἑπτὰ ἔτη. ὅτε δὲ μετὰ ταῦτα τὰ ἑπτὰ ἔτη ἔσται     5
οὐκέτι σῖτος τοῖς γεωργοῖς τῆς γῆς Αἰγύπτου, τότε ἐλεύσονται
οἱ Αἰγύπτιοι πρὸς Ἰωσὴφ καὶ λήμψονται σῖτον.

ἐλεύσονται δέ τινες ἐκ ἄλλων τόπων καὶ οὗτοι σῖτον λήμψονται. τότε ἐροῦσι, "νῦν φαγόμεθα. νῦν οὐκ ἀποθανούμεθα."

καὶ οἱ ἀδελφοὶ τοῦ Ἰωσὴφ ἐλεύσονται ὅτι ἕξουσι χρείαν     10
σίτου. ἐπιγνώσεται οὖν ἐκείνους οὗτος. ἀλλὰ ἐκεῖνοι τὸν
ἀδελφὸν Ἰωσήφ, τὸν ὑπηρέτην τοῦ Φαραώ, οὐκ ἐπιγνώσονται.

ὅτε ἐκεῖνοι οἴσουσιν ἐκ τῆς Αἰγύπτου τὸν σῖτον πρὸς τὰ
τέκνα εἰς τὴν ἄλλην γῆν, τότε ὁ Ἰωσήφ, ὁ ὑπηρέτης τοῦ
Φαραώ, λήμψεταί τινα τῶν ἀδελφῶν καὶ ἕξει αὐτόν. καὶ τότε     15
ἐροῦσιν οἱ ἀδελφοί, "τοῦτο γίνεται ὅτι ἐπέμψαμεν Ἰωσὴφ
δοῦλον εἰς τὴν Αἴγυπτον."

οἱ ἄλλοι οὖν ἄξουσιν ἐκ τῆς Αἰγύπτου εἰς τὴν ἄλλην γῆν.

## 172. VOCABULARY

ἀποθνῄσκω, ἀποθανοῦμαι, ἀπέθανον: I die
γίνομαι, γενήσομαι, (aor. later), γέγονα: I come into being, am
    born, am made, am ordained, become, come to pass, happen
ἐπιγινώσκω, ἐπιγνώσομαι, (aor. later), ἐπέγνωκα: I observe, per-
    ceive, recognize, know
ἑπτά (indecl.): seven
ἑπτὰ ἔτη (neut. nom. or acc. pl.): seven years, for seven years
ἔρχομαι, ἐλεύσομαι, ἦλθον, ἐλήλυθα: I come
ἐσθίω, φάγομαι, ἔφαγον: I eat
ἔσομαι: I shall be
ἔτη (neut. nom. or acc. pl.): years
Ἰωσήφ (indecl.), ὁ: Joseph
λαμβάνω, λήμψομαι, ἔλαβον, εἴληφα: I take, receive, seize
σῖτος, -ου, ὁ: wheat, corn, grain, food
συνάγω, συνάξω, συνήγαγον, —: I gather, bring together

# 173. MIDDLE VOICE: ITS MEANING

a. *In defective verbs.* A Greek verb that has all the forms that theoretically belong to it has three voices—active, middle, and passive. In all the lessons before this one verbs have been in the active voice. With the story in number 171 middle forms have been introduced. Later, passive forms will be used. Now some Greek verbs have in use only a part of the forms that are theoretically possible. A verb may, for instance, use a middle future like λήμψομαι in λαμβάνω without ever using a corresponding active form. λαμβάνω, then, is said to be *defective* in the future tense. But *the meaning of the future of λαμβάνω is not influenced at all by the use of middle forms.* λήμψομαι means "I shall take." Besides the future of λαμβάνω this lesson introduces several other examples of defective verbs. We find γίνομαι and ἔρχομαι defective in their present and future. We also find ἀποθνήσκω, εἰμί, ἐπιγινώσκω, and ἐσθίω defective in the future. Further notice will be taken of ἀποθνήσκω and ἐσθίω.

b. *In complete verbs.* When a Greek verb is not defective, the middle forms convey meanings different from those conveyed by active forms. The action of the verb is presented by the middle as being performed by the subject and as taking effect on the subject or on something more or less closely related to the subject. At any rate, the subject is shown to be more involved in the action of the verb than is the subject of an active form. *None of this kind of middle was used in number 171, but it will appear in the exercises.*

βλεπόμεθα, we see *ourselves.*

πέμψεται τὸν ἄγγελον, he will send *his own* messenger (or)
he will send the messenger *for himself.*

# 174. MIDDLE VOICE: ITS FORMS

a. Present Middle Indicative: πιστεύω.

| | |
|---|---|
| πιστεύομαι | πιστευόμεθα |
| πιστεύῃ | πιστεύεσθε |
| πιστεύεται | πιστεύονται |

To the verb stem πιστευ- are added (1) the tense suffix, which is here the variable vowel -ο/ε-, and (2) the primary middle personal endings.

Those primary middle personal endings are:

| | |
|---|---|
| -μαι | -μεθα |
| -σαι | -σθε |
| -ται | -νται |

The second singular -σαι appears unchanged only in the perfect (to be given later). Elsewhere (except numbers 176, 402, 403) the -σ- has been lost, resulting in the contracted ending -ῃ.

b. Present Middle Infinitive of πιστεύω: πιστεύεσθαι. This form is composed of the verb stem plus the tense suffix plus the middle infinitive ending.

c. Future Middle Indicative: πιστεύω.

| | |
|---|---|
| πιστεύσομαι | πιστευσόμεθα |
| πιστεύσῃ | πιστεύσεσθε |
| πιστεύσεται | πιστεύσονται |

To the verb stem πιστευ- are added (1) the tense suffix -σο/ε- and (2) the primary middle personal endings. πιστεύσῃ represents a shortening of πιστεύσεσαι by the loss of the second -σ- and by the contraction of -ε- and -αι.

d. Future Middle Indicative: εἰμί.

| | |
|---|---|
| ἔσομαι | ἐσόμεθα |
| ἔσῃ | ἔσεσθε |
| ἔσται | ἔσονται |

The third singular form ἔσται has lost the -ε- before the -τ-.

## 175. MIDDLE OF LIQUID AND NASAL FUTURES

Indicative

| | |
|---|---|
| ἀποθανοῦμαι | ἀποθανούμεθα |
| ἀποθανῇ | ἀποθανεῖσθε |
| ἀποθανεῖται | ἀποθανοῦνται |

These forms represent shortenings of the following, which are *not* in use:

| | |
|---|---|
| ἀποθανέσομαι | ἀποθανεσόμεθα |
| ἀποθανέσεσαι | ἀποθανέσεσθε |
| ἀποθανέσεται | ἀποθανέσονται |

101

The -σ- in the tense suffix (and in the second singular both -σ-'s) drops out and the vowels thus brought together are contracted.

$$\epsilon+o=ou \qquad\qquad \epsilon+\epsilon=\epsilon\iota \qquad\qquad \epsilon+\alpha\iota=\eta$$

## 176. FUTURE OF ἐσθίω AND πίνω

| | | | |
|---|---|---|---|
| φάγομαι | φαγόμεθα | πίομαι | πιόμεθα |
| φάγεσαι | φάγεσθε | πίεσαι | πίεσθε |
| φάγεται | φάγονται | πίεται | πίονται |

These forms have no sign of the future tense, and yet they are future.

## 177. EXERCISES

a. Translate number 171.

b. Translate the following expressions, which contain verbs with middle meanings.

1) πιστεύσεσθε;
2) οὐ φονευόμεθα.
3) διώκονται περὶ τὸν οἶκον.
4) ἀκούῃ, τέκνον;
5) οἱ κάμηλοι ἀπολύονται.
6) βλέπεσθε, ὑπηρέται.
7) ἐσθίεσθε τὸν σῖτον, ἄνθρωποι.
8) ἰσχύσουσι πέμπεσθαι τὰ τέκνα.
9) θεραπεύσομαι.
10) πῶς φέρεσθε;

c. Translate into Greek, distinguishing between what should be expressed by an active and what by a defective middle.

1) I am coming.
2) Will you be eating, Philip?
3) Can you eat yourselves, slaves?
4) We shall become noble.
5) How will you become noble?
6) Perhaps noble slaves will become free men.
7) We shall come into the garden.
8) Will you die? No, you will not die, Mark.
9) Mary, you will recognize Lazarus.
10) He will be in the Jordan.
11) Mary will not die.
12) Mary and Mark will not die.
13) Mary and Mark, you will not die.

d. Translate the following middles, some of which are defective.

1) λημψόμεθα σῖτον;

2) τίς ἐπιγνώσεται τὰ τέκνα μετὰ ἑπτὰ ἔτη;

3) φάγεσαι ἄρτον ἑπτὰ ἔτη.

4) ἐλεύσεσθε ἐκ τῆς γῆς ἐκείνης καὶ εἰς ταύτην.

5) ἔρχῃ εἰς τοῦτον τὸν οἶκον;

6) γενήσομαι βασιλεύς;

7) οὐκ ἀποθανούμεθα μετὰ ἑπτὰ ἔτη.

8) γίνεταί τις δοῦλος;

9) συνάξῃ κακοὺς εἰς τὴν Αἴγυπτον.

10) οἱ κακοὶ ὑπηρέται συνάγονται.

11) ἰσχύσετε συνάγεσθαι;

12) γέγονα καλός, ἀλλὰ ἀποθανοῦμαι.

13) μετὰ ἑπτὰ ἔτη ἐπιγνώσῃ τὸν ἀδελφὸν σοῦ.

14) φάγεσθε σῖτον· ἐγὼ δὲ ἀρνίον φάγομαι.

15) πῶς ἀποθανοῦνται οἱ Αἰγύπτιοι;

e. Conjugate, making necessary changes.

1) ἐλεύσομαι εἰς τὴν
γῆν ταύτην;

2) ἐπιγνώσομαι τοῦτον
τὸν τόπον.

3) ἔρχομαι πρὸς τὸν
κύριον.

4) ἀποθανοῦμαι ἐν
ἐκείνῳ τῷ οἴκῳ.

5) ἔσομαι ὑπηρέτης.

6) φάγομαι καλὸν ἄρτον.

7) οὐ πίομαι σῖτον.

f. Give one correct possible location for each ending.

1) -ῇ
2) -εῖται
3) -εσαι
4) -οῃ
5) -εται

6) -σεται
7) -ομαι
8) -σομαι
9) -σόμεθα
10) -ούμεθα

11) -οῦμαι
12) -όμεθα
13) -εῖσθε
14) -οῦνται

g. Associate the following English words with Greek words in the vocabulary of this lesson.

1) *genesis*: *a coming into being*.
2) *hepta*gon: a *seven*-sided geometric figure.
3) bacterio*phage*: something that *eats* bacteria.
4) *ete*sian winds: winds that blow each *year* at a certain season.
5) *sito*phobia: fear or dislike of *food*.

h. Read the Greek aloud and then translate:

1) Εἶπεν οὖν πάλιν αὐτοῖς, ᾿Εγὼ ὑπάγω (go away) καὶ ζητήσετέ (you will look for) με (me) καὶ ἐν τῇ ἁμαρτίᾳ (sin) ὑμῶν ἀποθανεῖσθε . . . .

103

2) Καὶ ὁ λόγος (word) σὰρξ (flesh) ἐγένετο . . . .

3) Ὅτε δὲ ἡμέρᾱ (day) ἐγένετο, τὴν γῆν οὐκ ἐπεγίνω-
σκον . . . .

4) . . . καὶ συνάξει τὸν σῖτον αὐτοῦ εἰς τὴν ἀποθήκην
(barn) . . . .

5) . . . ἀποθνήσκομεν ὅτι οὐ βλέπομέν σε καθ' ἡμέρᾱν (every
day).

The sources of these excerpts are listed on page 245.

# Lesson 22

## 178. I NEED TO LEARN EGYPTIAN

ὁ Αἰγύπτιος διδάσκαλος: "τίς εἶ σὺ ἐκεῖ ἐν τοῖς μαθηταῖς ἐμοῦ;"

ὁ μαθητὴς Ἰωσήφ: "δοῦλος ἐγώ εἰμι ἐν τῷ οἴκῳ Αἰγυπτίου ἐλευθέρου. δοῦλός εἰμι σήμερον, ἀλλ' αὔριον ἐλεύθερος γίνεσθαι ἐλπίζω." 5

ὁ διδάσκαλος: "τί εἶ συ ὧδε ἐν τοῖς μαθηταῖς τούτοις;

ὁ μαθητής: "τὴν γλῶσσαν τὴν Αἰγυπτίᾱν μανθάνειν θέλω λίαν. ὅτε ἐλεύθερος ἔσομαι, λέγειν ὑμῖν Αἰγυπτίοις ἐν ταῖς συναγωγαῖς ὑμῶν χρείᾱν ἕξω. ἀλλ' ὅτε ἤμην μικρὸν τέκνον, τὴν Αἰγυπτίᾱν γλῶσσαν οὐκ ἔμαθον. διὰ τοῦτο, διδάσκαλε, ὧδέ 10 εἰμι."

ὁ διδάσκαλος: "οὐ θέλεις οὖν γλῶσσαν ἄλλην μαθεῖν."

ὁ μαθητής: "οὐχί. τίς ἡμῶν ἐν τῇ Αἰγύπτῳ ἄλλην γλῶσσαν λέγειν χρείᾱν ἔχει; οὗτοι οἱ ἄλλοι μαθηταί σου γλῶσσαν τῆς Αἰγύπτου μαθεῖν οὐ θελήσουσι;" 15

ὁ διδάσκαλος: "ἐχθὲς ἦν ἐν ἡμῖν μαθητής τις καὶ ἄλλην γλῶσσαν μανθάνειν ἤθελε. ἀλλ' ἐκεῖνος νῦν ποῦ ἐστιν; οὐ βλέπω ἐκεῖνον ὧδε. μαθηταί μου, ποῦ ἐστιν ἐκεῖνος ὁ μικρὸς μαθητής;"

οἱ ἄλλοι μαθηταί: "ἡμεῖς σοι, διδάσκαλε καλέ, λέγειν οὐ 20 δυνατοί ἐσμεν. οὐ σήμερον ἐβλέψαμεν αὐτὸν ἡμεῖς. οὐ διὰ τοῦ κήπου ἡμῶν ἦλθε σήμερον. τάχα ἐν ἄλλῳ τόπῳ ἐστίν."

ὁ διδάσκαλος: "ναί, τάχα. τέκνον μικρὸν ἦν. δοῦλε καλὲ Ἰωσήφ, μετὰ ἐμοῦ οὖν σὺ θέλεις τὴν Αἰγυπτίᾱν γλῶσσαν μανθάνειν· καλόν ἐστιν. διὰ τὴν χρείᾱν σου δυνατὸς διδάσκειν 25 σε ἐγὼ ἔσομαι. διὰ δὲ τὸ αὐτὸ δυνατὸς μανθάνειν ἀπ' ἐμοῦ σὺ ἔσῃ. μένε μετὰ ἡμῶν ὧδε."

## 179. VOCABULARY

ἀλλ': ἀλλά with the final vowel elided

αὔριον: tomorrow, on the next day

γλῶσσα, -ης, ἡ: tongue, language (number 104)

διά: (with gen.) through, by; (with acc.) because of, on account of

διὰ τὸ αὐτό: for the same reason

διδάσκαλος, -ου, ὁ:  teacher

διδάσκω, διδάξω, ἐδίδαξα, — :  I teach (frequently used with a double accusative, one of the person taught and one of the subject matter taught)

δυνατός, -ή, -όν:  able, capable, strong, powerful, possible

εἰμί, ἔσομαι — , — :  I am

ἐκεῖ:  there

ἐχθές:  yesterday

θέλω, θελήσω, ἠθέλησα:  I will, am willing, wish, desire, want (imperfect ἤθελον)

λίαν:  exceedingly, very, very much

μαθητής, -οῦ, ὁ:  disciple, student, pupil

μανθάνω, — , ἔμαθον, μεμάθηκα:  I learn

ποῦ:  where?

συναγωγή, -ῆς, ἡ:  assembly, synagogue

ὧδε:  here

## 180. PERSONAL PRONOUNS

In addition to the personal pronouns presented in number 126, notice below the unaccented, slightly less emphatic, enclitic forms for the first and second persons, and the words used for the third person.

First Person

| Singular | | Plural | |
|---|---|---|---|
| ἐγώ | (I) | ἡμεῖς | (we) |
| ἐμοῦ, μου | (of me) | ἡμῶν | (of us) |
| ἐμοί, μοι | (for me) | ἡμῖν | (for us) |
| ἐμέ, με | (me) | ἡμᾶς | (us) |

Second Person

| σύ | (you) | ὑμεῖς | (you) |
|---|---|---|---|
| σοῦ, σου | (of you) | ὑμῶν | (of you) |
| σοί, σοι | (for you) | ὑμῖν | (for you) |
| σέ, σε | (you) | ὑμᾶς | (you) |

Third Person

The demonstratives οὗτος and ἐκεῖνος, and αὐτός may be used as personal pronouns in all their forms.

## 181. CONJUGATION OF εἰμί: I AM

Present Indicative

| | |
|---|---|
| εἰμί | ἐσμέν |
| εἶ | ἐστέ |
| ἐστί(ν) | εἰσί(ν) |

106

All these forms except the second singular, εἶ, are enclitic.

### Present Imperative

| | |
|---|---|
| ἴσθι | ἔστε |
| ἔστω | ἔστωσαν |

### Present Infinitive: εἶναι

### Imperfect Indicative

| | |
|---|---|
| ἤμην | ἦμεν or ἤμεθα |
| ἦς | ἦτε |
| ἦν | ἦσαν |

The forms ἤμην and ἤμεθα are middle without influencing the meaning.

### Future Indicative

| | |
|---|---|
| ἔσομαι | ἐσόμεθα |
| ἔσῃ | ἔσεσθε |
| ἔσται | ἔσονται |

This verb is defective in the future.

This verb is a -μι verb (so designated from the ending in the form εἰμί). Other verbs of this type will be met, but this is the one most frequently used. The pecularities of -μι verbs appear in the present, imperfect, and aorist. But εἰμί has no tenses except the present, imperfect, and future.

## 182. CASE: ACCUSATIVE OF DOUBLE DIRECT OBJECT

In the sentence διδάσκομεν ὑμᾶς τὴν Αἰγυπτίαν γλῶσσαν, "we teach you the Egyptian language," both ὑμᾶς and γλῶσσαν are accusative direct objects of διδάσκομεν. The one represents the persons, the other the subject matter directly affected by the action of the verb. This construction is used with other verbs besides διδάσκω.

## 183. EXERCISES

a. Translate number 178.

b. Conjugate the verbs in the following patterns, changing everything that needs to be changed for each new form.
For example:    σὺ ἴσθι δυνατός
            οὗτος ἔστω δυνατός
            ὑμεῖς ἔστε δυνατοί
            οὗτοι ἔστωσαν δυνατοί

1) ὁ διδάσκαλός εἰμι σήμερον.
2) ἐγὼ οὐκ ἔσομαι ἄγγελος αὔριον.
3) δοῦλος ἐκεῖ ἤμην ἐγὼ ἐχθές.

107

4) ὧδε διὰ τὸ αὐτό εἰμι.

5) ἴσθι μαθητὴς καλός.

6) Πέτρε, ἴσθι ὧδε αὔριον.

c. Translate into Greek.

1) Be a good child, Mary

2) Yes, let Mary be good.

3) Be good children, Mary and Sarai.

4) Yes, let Mary and Sarai be good.

5) Do you want to be good, my child?

6) I do not want to be good today, but I shall want to be good tomorrow.

7) Mary and Sarai wanted to be good yesterday.

8) Where is Lazarus?

9) I am here to learn.

10) Where are Peter and Philip?

11) They are not here for the same reason.

12) Peter and Philip, where are you?

13) Peter is in the synagogue.

14) Philip was there yesterday, but he was not happy.

15) Let them be in the same synagogue tomorrow.

d. Associate the following English words with new Greek words in this lesson.

1) *glossa*l: related to the *tongue*.

2) *didac*tic: related to *teaching*.

3) *dyna*mo: a machine capable of producing electrical *power*.

4) *math*ematics: a science made up of things *learned* and therefore known about exact quantitative relationships.

5) *gloss*ectomy: a surgical removal of the *tongue*.

6) chresto*math*y: a collection of passages useful for *learning* a language.

7) *synago*gue: a place where Jews *gather together* for worship.

e. Read the Greek aloud and then translate:

1) Ἰησοῦς Χριστὸς ἐχθὲς καὶ σήμερον ὁ αὐτός, καὶ εἰς τοὺς αἰῶνας (forever).

2) ὑμεῖς φωνεῖτέ με Ὁ διδάσκαλος καὶ Ὁ κύριος καὶ καλῶς (correctly) λέγετε, εἰμὶ γάρ.

3) καὶ ἀποστέλλουσιν αὐτῷ τοὺς μαθητὰς αὐτων μετὰ τῶν Ἡρῳδιανῶν (Herodians) λέγοντες (saying), Διδάσκαλε, οἴδαμεν (we know) ὅτι ἀληθὴς (truthful) εἶ καὶ τὴν ὁδὸν (way) τοῦ θεοῦ ἐν ἀληθείᾳ διδάσκεις . . . .

108

4) τότε οὖν εἶπεν αὐτοῖς ὁ Ἰησοῦς (Jesus) παρρησίᾳ, Λάζαρος ἀπέθανεν, καὶ χαίρω δι᾽ ὑμᾶς, ἵνα (in order that) πιστεύσητε (you may believe), ὅτι οὐκ ἤμην ἐκεῖ· ἀλλὰ ἄγωμεν (let us go) πρὸς αὐτόν.

5) ... ἵνα (in order that) πάλιν σε διδάξωμεν (we may teach) εἰ (if) οὖν σοι δοκ[εῖ] (it seems good to you) ἀκοῦσαι ....

6) γινώσκειν σε θέλω ὅτει (=ὅτι) εἰς γῆν ἐλήλυθα τῇ ϛ τοῦ Ἐπείθ μηνός (on the 6th of the month Epeith).

7) οὐ θέλω δὲ ὑμᾶς ἀγνοεῖν (to be ignorant), ἀδελφοί ....

8) πυνθανομένη (learning) μανθάνειν σε Αἰγύπτια γράμματα (letters) συνεχάρην (I congratulated) σοι καὶ ἐμαυτῆι (=ἐμαυτῇ).

The sources of these excerpts are listed on pages 245-46.

109

# Lesson 23

## 184. RELUCTANTLY JACOB LETS BENJAMIN GO TO EGYPT

ἐπεὶ εἶχε Ἰακὼβ πάλιν χρείᾱν σίτου, εἶπε τοῖς υἱοῖς, "ἀπερχέσθωσαν οἱ υἱοί μου εἰς τὴν Αἴγυπτον πάλιν. ἐνεγκέτωσαν σῖτον καὶ φαγόμεθα καὶ οὐκ ἀποθανούμεθα."

οἱ δὲ υἱοὶ ἐμνημόνευσαν τοῦ κυρίου τῆς Αἰγύπτου καὶ εἶπον τῷ Ἰακώβ, "ἡμεῖς οὐκ ἐσόμεθα δυνατοὶ βλέψαι τὸν 5 κύριον τῆς Αἰγύπτου. ἐρχέσθω οὖν ὁ Βενιαμίν, ὁ νεώτερος υἱός σου, σὺν ἡμῖν. ὁ γὰρ κύριος ἐκείνης τῆς γῆς ἡμῖν εἴρηκε, 'ἔρχεσθε μετὰ τοῦ ἀδελφοῦ ὑμῶν τοῦ νεωτέρου, ἢ οὐ βλέψετε ὑμεῖς ἐμέ.'"

τότε οὖν ἐμνημόνευεν Ἰακὼβ ὅτι πάλαι ἡ γυνὴ Ῥαχὴλ 10 ἔσχε υἱούς, Ἰωσὴφ καὶ βενιαμίν, τὸν νεώτερον. ἀλλὰ πάλαι Ῥαχὴλ ἀπέθανε καὶ ὁ Ἰωσὴφ ἀπεληλύθει, καὶ πάλαι ὁ Ἰακὼβ εἰρήκει, "ἀπέθανε Ἰωσήφ, καὶ αὐτὸν οὐ βλέψω πάλιν."

εἶπεν δὲ Ἰακὼβ πρὸς τοὺς υἱούς, "οὐκ ἀπελεύσεται Βενιαμίν, ὁ νεώτερος υἱὸς τῆς Ῥαχήλ." 15

ἀλλ' εἶπεν ὁ Ἰούδας πρὸς Ἰακώβ, "ἐγὼ ἄξω αὐτὸν πρὸς σε πάλιν."

ὅτι οὖν εἶπε τοῦτο ὁ Ἰούδας καὶ ὅτι ἦν οὐ μικρὰ χρείᾱ σίτου, εἶπεν Ἰακώβ, "ἀπερχέσθω Βενιαμὶν μετὰ τῶν ἄλλων υἱῶν." 20

ἡ δὲ καρδίᾱ τοῦ Ἰακὼβ οὐκ ἦν μακαρίᾱ ὅτε ἀπῆλθεν ὁ υἱὸς ὁ νεώτερος τῆς Ῥαχήλ.

## 185. VOCABULARY

ἀπέρχομαι, ἀπελεύσομαι, ἀπῆλθον, ἀπελήλυθα:  I go away, depart, depart from

Βενιαμίν (indecl.), ὁ:  Benjamin

Ἰακώβ (indecl.), ὁ:  Jacob

Ἰούδας, -α, (-ᾳ, -αν, α), ὁ:  Judah, Judas

νεώτερος, -ᾱ, -ον:  newer, young, younger, (in Hellenistic usage) youngest

πάλαι:  long ago, of old, in past time

Ῥαχήλ (indecl.), ἡ:  Rachel

110

## 186. PRESENT MIDDLE IMPERATIVE

### a. In defective verbs.

ἔρχου: come
ἐρχέσθω: let him come
ἔρχεσθε: come
ἐρχέσθωσαν: let them come

These forms, although middle in spelling, are active in meaning since ἔρχομαι is a defective verb.

### b. In complete verbs.

πιστεύου: believe yourself
πιστευέσθω: let him believe himself
πιστεύεσθε: believe yourselves
πιστευέσθωσαν: let them believe themselves

These forms carry distinct middle meanings.

## 187. EXERCISES

### a. Translate number 184 into English.

### b. Translate into Greek.

1) Go away, Benjamin, son of Rachel.
2) Let Judah come again.
3) Judah and Benjamin, stop departing.
4) Rachel went away long ago to another land.
5) Let Rachel serve herself.
6) Serve yourselves, sons of Judah.
7) Long ago Jacob said, "Go away to Egypt, Judah."
8) Do not go away, Rachel.
9) Let the Egyptians go away.
10) Become a strong man.

### c. Locate by giving (1) tense, (2) mood, (3) voice, (4) person, (5) number, and (6) first principal part.

1) συνάγεσθε
2) ἐρχέσθωσαν
3) ἀπέρχου
4) γινέσθωσαν
5) λήμψεσθε
6) ἀποστέλλεσθε
7) ἀποκτεινέσθωσαν
8) φάγεται
9) ἐλεύσῃ
10) ἐπιγινωσκέσθω

### d. Associate the following English words with the new Greek words presented recently.

1) *Jacob*ite: a supporter in England of James II (in Latin, *Jacobus*, derived from Greek).

2) *paleo*: a prefix used in technical scientific terms to mean "related to the distant past, *long ago*."

e. Read the Greek aloud and then translate:

. . . οἱ γὰρ μαθηταὶ αὐτοῦ ἀπεληλύθεισαν εἰς τὴν πόλιν (city) . . . .

The sources of these excerpts are listed on page 246.

# Lesson 24

## 188. TABLE OF SOME RELATED GROUPS OF VERB ENDINGS

(Full inflections are given in the appendix, number 397 forward.)

| Indicative Active | | | | Indicative Middle | | |
|---|---|---|---|---|---|---|
| Perf. (1st) | Perf. (2nd) | Plperf. (1st) | Plperf. (2nd) | Pres. | Future (usual) | Future (liq. & nasal) |
| -κα | -α | -κειν | -ειν | -ομαι | -σομαι | -οῦμαι |
| -κας | -ας | -κεις | -εις | -ῃ | -σῃ | -ῇ |
| -κε | -ε | -κει | -ει | -εται | -σεται | -εῖται |
| -καμεν | -αμεν | -κειμεν | -ειμεν | -όμεθα | -σόμεθα | -ούμεθα |
| -κατε | -ατε | -κειτε | -ειτε | -εσθε | -σεσθε | -εῖσθε |
| -κᾱσι | -ᾱσι | -κεισαν | -εισαν | -ονται | -σονται | -σοῦνται |
| **Infinitive Active** | | | | **Infinitive Middle** | | |
| -κέναι | -έναι | None | None | -εσθαι | Rare -σεσθαι | Rare -εῖσθαι |
| **Imperative Active** | | | | **Imperative Middle** | | |
| None | None | None | None | -ου -έσθω -εσθε -έσθωσαν | None | None |

## 189. LOCATION DRILL

Locate the following verb forms by giving (1) tense, (2) mood, (3) voice, (4) person, (5) number, and (6) first principal part.

a. ἀποθανοῦνται
b. ἔστε
c. ἐστέ
d. φάγεται
e. ἔρχῃ
f. ἐλεύσεσθε
g. ἔσται
h. ἀπελήλυθας

i. πιστευσόμεθα
j. ἴσθι
k. εἰρήκειτε
l. δουλεύσουσι
m. λεγέτω
n. ἐσθίειν
o. ἀπέστειλαν
p. ἔσθιε

## 190. VOCABULARY

Review thoroughly the vocabulary introduced since lesson 18.

| NOUNS | VERBS | ADVERBS |
|---|---|---|
| Βενιαμίν | ἀπέρχομαι | αὔριον |
| γλῶσσα | ἀποθανοῦμαι | διὰ τὸ αὐτό |
| διδάσκαλος | γίνομαι | ἐκεῖ |
| ἔτη | διδάσκω | ἐχθές |
| θεός | ἐπιγινώσκω | λίαν |
| Ἰακώβ | ἔρχομαι | πάλαι |
| Ἰούδας | ἔσομαι | ποῦ |
| Ἰωσήφ | θέλω | ὧδε |
| μαθητής | λήμψομαι | |
| Ῥαχηλ | μανθάνω | **PREPOSITION** |
| σῖτος | πιστεύω | |
| συναγωγή | συνάγω | διά |
| υἱός | | |
| φόβος | **PRONOUNS** | **ADJECTIVES** |
| | | |
| **CONJUNCTION** | τίς | δυνατός |
| | τὶς | ἑπτά |
| ἀλλ' | | νεώτερος |

## 191. INTERROGATIVES AND INDEFINITES

Use the form of τίς or τὶς suitable for each of the following situations.

a. (Who) διδάξει ἡμᾶς τὴν γλῶσσαν ταύτην;
b. ἐμάθετε γλῶσσαν (a certain).
c. υἱός (of someone) οὐκ ἔστι δίκαιος.
d. (To whom) ἀποστελεῖς τοῦτον τὸν ἄγγελον;
e. ἀπὸ (what) κώμης ἀπήλθομεν;
f. τεθεράπευκε ὁ νεώτερος υἱός (anybody) ἐν ἐκείνῳ τῷ οἴκῳ;

## 192. PROCLITICS AND ENCLITICS

By reference to number 168 and number 169 and vocabulary lists accent the following groups of words.

a. τις εστιν ουτος;
b. τινος ην εκεινη η αδελφη;
c. λεγετε τινι φαγειν τουτο το οψαριον.
d. βλεπομεν το αρνιον τινος εν τω κηπω.
e. ὁ δουλος τεθεραπευκε τινα τεκνα.

114

# Lesson 25

## 193. BENJAMIN FRAMED

ὅτε πάλιν εἰς τὴν Αἴγυπτον ἤρχοντο οἱ υἱοὶ τοῦ Ἰακώβ, ὁ Ἰωσὴφ ἔβλεψεν αὐτούς, τοὺς ἄλλους καὶ τὸν ἴδιον ἀδελφόν, Βενιαμίν.

ἐνετείλατο οὖν τῷ ἰδίῳ ὑπηρέτῃ, "ἐρχέσθωσαν εἰς τὸν οἶκον μου οὗτοι, μετ' ἐμοῦ γὰρ φάγονται ἄρτον σήμερον." 5

ἐσχήκει δὲ ὁ Ἰωσὴφ τῶν ἰδίων ἀδελφῶν τινα ὅτε οἱ ἄλλοι πρὸς Ἰακὼβ ἀπήρχοντο καὶ ἔμενον ἐκεῖ καὶ ἦγον Βενιαμὶν εἰς τὴν Αἴγυπτον. ναί, υἱός τις τοῦ Ἰακὼβ ἐμεμενήκει ἐν τῇ Αἰγύπτῳ μετὰ τοῦ Ἰωσήφ. τοῦτον τὸν ἀδελφὸν ἤγαγε πρὸς τοὺς ἄλλους ὁ Ἰωσὴφ καὶ εἶπεν αὐτοῖς ὅτε ἔβλεπε τὸν 10 Βενιαμίν, "οὗτός ἐστιν ὁ ἀδελφὸς ὑμῶν ὁ νεώτερος;"

καὶ εἶπον, "ναί."

ἐπεὶ οὖν ἔφαγον ἄρτον ὁμοῦ, ἐνετείλατο τῷ ἰδίῳ ὑπηρέτῃ ὁ Ἰωσήφ, "σχέτωσαν σῖτον οὗτοι. τὸ δὲ ἀργύριον ἑκάστου εἰς τὸν σῖτον βάλε. καὶ εἰς τὸν σῖτον τοῦ νεωτέρου βάλε τὸ 15 ἀργύριον αὐτοῦ καὶ τὸ ἀργυρίου ποτήριον ἐμοῦ." ταῦτα δὲ ἔβαλεν ὁ ὑπηρέτης ποῦ ἐνετείλατο ὁ Ἰωσήφ.

αὔριον οὖν ἐκ τῆς γῆς Αἰγύπτου οἱ ἀδελφοὶ ἀπήρχοντο. τότε δ᾽ ὁ Ἰωσὴφ τῷ ἰδίῳ ὑπηρέτῃ εἶπεν, "ἐντέλλομαί σοι διῶξαι τοὺς ἀνθρώπους τούτους. καὶ ἐρεῖς αὐτοῖς, 'τί ἐλάβεσθε 20 τὸ ἀργυρίου ποτήριον τοῦ κυρίου ἐμοῦ; ἐγένεσθε κακοί.'"

ἐδίωξεν οὖν ὁ ὑπηρέτης τοὺς υἱοὺς τοῦ Ἰακώβ, καὶ εἶπεν αὐτοῖς, "τί ἐλάβεσθε τὸ ἀργυρίου ποτήριον;"

οὗτοι δὲ ἔλεγον, "οὐχί. οὐκ ἐλαβόμεθα ἐκεῖνο τὸ ποτήριον. βλέπε τὸν σῖτον ἑκάστου ἡμῶν. οὐ βλέψεις αὐτὸ ἐν τῷ σίτῳ 25 τινὸς ἡμῶν."

"βλέψω," εἶπεν ὁ Αἰγύπτιος, "ἐν τῷ σίτῳ ἑκάστου ὑμῶν."

"τὸ ποτήριόν τις ἕξει; οὗτος ἀποθανέτω, καὶ οἱ ἄλλοι ἀδελφοὶ ἔστωσαν δοῦλοι τοῦ κυρίου σοῦ." ταῦτα ἔλεγον πολλάκις, οὐ γὰρ ἐπίστευον ὅτι τὸ ποτήριον ἐν τῷ σίτῳ αὐτῶν 30 ἦν.

ἔβλεψεν οὖν ὁ ὑπηρέτης τὸν σῖτον ἑκάστου. καὶ τὸ ποτήριον ἦν ἐν τῷ σίτῳ τοῦ νεωτέρου, τοῦ Βενιαμίν. μετὰ τοῦτο οἱ ἀδελφοὶ ἀπῆλθον πάλιν πρὸς τὸν Ἰωσήφ.

## 194. VOCABULARY

ἀργύριον, -ου, τό:  silver, money
βάλλω, βαλῶ, ἔβαλον, βέβληκα:  I throw, cast, put
ἕκαστος, -η, -ον:  each, every
ἐντέλλομαι, ἐντελοῦμαι, ἐνετειλάμην:  I order, command, give
    orders (with dat. of person and an infinitive)
μετ᾿:  μετά with final vowel elided

## 195. MORE MIDDLE FORMS

Imperfect Middle Indicative of πιστεύω

| | |
|---|---|
| ἐπιστευόμην | ἐπιστευόμεθα |
| ἐπιστεύου | ἐπιστεύεσθε |
| ἐπιστεύετο | ἐπιστεύοντο |

First Aorist Middle Indicative of πιστεύω

| | |
|---|---|
| ἐπιστευσάμην | ἐπιστευσάμεθα |
| ἐπιστεύσω | ἐπιστεύσασθε |
| ἐπιστεύσατο | ἐπιστεύσαντο |

Second Aorist Middle Indicative of γίνομαι

| | |
|---|---|
| ἐγενόμην | ἐγενόμεθα |
| ἐγένου | ἐγένεσθε |
| ἐγένετο | ἐγένοντο |

Liquid Aorist Middle Indicative of ἐντέλλομαι

| | |
|---|---|
| ἐνετειλάμην | ἐνετειλάμεθα |
| ἐνετείλω | ἐνετείλασθε |
| ἐνετείλατο | ἐνετείλαντο |

## 196. SECONDARY MIDDLE ENDINGS

In all the paradigms just presented the secondary middle endings have
been used.

| | |
|---|---|
| -μην | -μεθα |
| -σο | -σθε |
| -το | -ντο |

The second singular -σο appears unchanged only in the pluperfect (to
be given later). Elsewhere the -σ- has been lost and a contraction of
vowels has occurred.

| | Assumed earlier form | Form in actual use |
|---|---|---|
| Imperfect | ἐπιστεύεσο | ἐπιστεύου |
| 1st Aorist | ἐπιστεύσασο | ἐπιστεύσω |
| 2nd Aorist | ἐγένεσο | ἐγένου |
| Liquid Aorist | ἐνετείλασο | ἐνετείλω |

116

# 197. EXERCISES

a. Translate number 193.

b. Locate.

1) ἐγίνετο
2) ἐνετείλω
3) ἐβάλου
4) ἀπεστελλόμην
5) ἐροῦμεν
6) ἀπελύσω
7) ἐθεραπεύσασθε
8) πιστεύεσθαι

9) βεβλήκατε
10) βαλοῦνται
11) φάγεσθε
12) βαλοῦσι
13) ἐνετείλαντο
14) ἐθεραπεύσαντο
15) ἐβάλοντο

c. Write a synopsis of ἀπολύω (1) in the third person singular and (2) in the second person singular. A synopsis is a set of forms representing the behavior of a verb throughout its conjugation. Instead of a full inflection, one form is taken as a sample from each set of six (as in the indicative) or of four (as in the imperative). The following is a synopsis of ἀκούω in the third plural present and imperfect.

|  | Active | Middle |
|---|---|---|
| Present Indicative: | ἀκούουσι | ἀκούονται |
| Present Imperative: | ἀκουέτωσαν | ἀκουέσθωσαν |
| Imperfect Indicative: | ἤκουον | ἠκούοντο |

Do this for all tenses, moods, and voices which you have had.

d. Read the Greek aloud and then translate:

1) ἕκαστον γὰρ δένδρον (tree) ἐκ τοῦ ἰδίου καρποῦ γινώσκεται (is known). . . .
2) . . . γέγραπται (it is written) γὰρ ὅτι Τοῖς ἀγγέλοις αὐτοῦ ἐντελεῖται περὶ σοῦ . . . .
3) οἷς (whom) καὶ ἐντετάλμεθα ἀσπάσεσθαι (to greet) ὑμᾶς παρ᾽ (from) ἡμῶν φιλοφρόνως (affectionately).

The sources of these excerpts are listed on page 246.

# Lesson 26

## 198. "I AM YOUR BROTHER"

πάλιν ἀπῆλθε ὁ Ἰούδας σὺν τοῖς ἑαυτοῦ ἀδελφοῖς πρὸς
Ἰωσήφ. εἶπε δὲ αὐτοῖς Ἰωσήφ, "τί τοῦτο τὸ ποτήριον ἑαυτοῖς
ἐλάβετε;"

εἶπε δὲ Ἰούδας, "τί ἐρῶ τῷ κυρίῳ ἐμαυτοῦ; ὁ δὲ θεός
ἔβλεψεν ὅτι κακοί εἰσιν οἱ δοῦλοί σου. δοῦλοι σοῦ γὰρ      5
γενησόμεθα, ἡμεῖς καὶ Βενιαμίν."

εἶπε δὲ οὕτως Ἰωσήφ, "οὐ γενήσεσθε ὑμεῖς δοῦλοι ἐμοῦ,
ἀλλ' οὗτος ὁ ἄνθρωπος. ἀντὶ ὑμῶν, ἔξω τοῦτον. οὗτος ἔσται
δοῦλος ἐμοῦ. ὑμεῖς δὲ ἐλεύθεροι ἔσεσθε."

τότε δὲ αὐτῷ Ἰούδας οὕτως εἶπεν, "ὁ κύριος ἐμοῦ ἀκουσάτω      10
τοῦ δούλου ἑαυτοῦ. πάλαι εἴπομεν οὕτως τῷ ἑαυτῶν κυρίῳ.
ἔχομεν πατέρα πρεσβύτερον, καὶ οὗτος ἔχει ἄλλον υἱόν
νεώτερον. πάλαι εἶχε καὶ ἄλλον υἱόν, οὗτος δὲ ἀπέθανεν.' εἶπες
δὲ ἡμῖν, 'ὁ νεώτερος υἱός ἐλθέτω σὺν ὑμῖν πρὸς ἐμέ.' καὶ εἴπομεν
τῷ κυρίῳ ἑαυτῶν, 'ὁ πατὴρ ὁ πρεσβύτερος οὐκ ἔσται δυνατὸς      15
ἀποστεῖλαι τὸν ἑαυτοῦ υἱὸν τὸν νεώτερον. ὅτε γὰρ ὁ πατὴρ
ἀποστελεῖ τοῦτον, ὁ πατὴρ ὁ πρεσβύτερος ἀποθανεῖται.' νῦν δὲ
ἐληλύθαμεν μετὰ τοῦ νεωτέρου υἱοῦ, τοῦ ἀδελφοῦ ἑαυτῶν, ὅτι
ἐνετείλω ἡμῖν. ἀλλ' ὅτε ἀπελευσόμεθα πάλιν πρὸς τὸν πατέρα
ἑαυτῶν καὶ οὗτος οὐ βλέψει τὸν νεώτερον μεθ' ἡμῶν, ὁ πατὴρ      20
ἡμῶν ἀποθανεῖται. νῦν οὖν μενῶ ἐγὼ ἀντὶ τοῦ νεωτέρου
Βενιαμὶν τοῦ ἀδελφοῦ ἐμοῦ. ἐκεῖνος δε ἀπερχέσθω πάλιν πρὸς
τὸν πατέρα ἀντὶ ἐμοῦ. πῶς γὰρ βλέψω τὸν πατέρα ὅτε οὐκ ἄξω
πάλιν Βενιαμίν;"

τότε οὖν εἶπεν ὁ Ἰωσήφ πρὸς τοὺς ἑαυτοῦ ἀδελφούς, "ἐγώ      25
εἰμι Ἰωσήφ. ἐπιγινώσκετε ἐμέ; ἔστε μακάριοι, ἐμέ γὰρ ἀπέστειλεν ὁ θεός εἰς ταύτην τὴν γῆν. χρείᾳ σίτου ἔσται μακρά.
νῦν οὖν οὐχ ὑμεῖς με ἀπεστάλκατε ὧδε, ἀλλ' ὁ θεός. καὶ διὰ
τὸν θεὸν ἐγενόμην ὁ κύριος τῆς γῆς Αἰγύπτου. μὴ μένετε οὖν
ἀλλ' ἀπέρχεσθε πρὸς τὸν πατέρα ἡμῶν τὸν πρεσβύτερον καὶ      30
λέγετε αὐτῷ, 'οὕτως λέγει ὁ υἱός σοῦ Ἰωσήφ, "διὰ τὸν θεὸν
ἐγενόμην ὁ κύριος τῆς γῆς Αἰγύπτου. ἐλθέ, σὺ γὰρ ἔσῃ πρὸς

ἐμοί, σὺ καὶ οἱ υἱοὶ σεαυτοῦ καὶ οἱ υἱοὶ τῶν υἱῶν σεαυτοῦ καὶ τὰ πρόβατά σου.'' "

## 199. VOCABULARY

ἀντί: (with gen.) instead of, in place of, in exchange for, in return for, against

ἑαυτοῦ, -ῆς, -οῦ: of himself, herself, itself; (pl.) of ourselves, yourselves, themselves

ἐμαυτοῦ, -ῆς: of myself

μεθ' ἡμῶν: μετὰ ἡμῶν: with us (Before a following vowel the α in μετά is elided. When this following vowel is rough, the -τ- may be changed to -θ.)

οὕτως: thus, so, in this way

πατέρα (acc. sing.): father

πατήρ (nom. sing.): father

πρεσβύτερος, -ᾱ, -ον: elder, elderly, old

σεαυτοῦ, -ῆς: of yourself

## 200. REFLEXIVE PRONOUNS: THEIR USE

A reflexive pronoun refers to the subject of the clause in which it stands.

| | | |
|---|---|---|
| βλέπω {ἐμαυτόν / ἐμαυτήν} | (=βλέπομαι) | I see myself. |
| βλέπεις {σεαυτόν / σεαυτήν} | (=βλέπῃ) | You see yourself. |
| βλέπει ἑαυτόν | (=βλέπεται) | He sees himself. |
| βλέπει ἑαυτήν | (=βλέπεται) | She sees herself. |
| βλέπει ἑαυτό | (=βλέπεται) | It sees itself. |
| βλέπομεν {ἑαυτούς / ἑαυτάς} | (=βλεπόμεθα) | We see ourselves. |
| βλέπετε {ἑαυτούς / ἑαυτάς} | (=βλέπεσθε) | You see yourselves. |
| βλέπουσι {ἑαυτούς / ἑαυτάς / ἑαυτά} | (=βλέπονται) | They see themselves. |
| ἀκούω {ἐμαυτοῦ / ἐμαυτῆς} | (=ἀκούομαι) | I hear myself. |
| πιστεύεις {σεαυτῷ / σεαυτῇ} | (=πιστευῃ) | You believe yourself. |

119

# 201. REFLEXIVE PRONOUNS: THEIR FORMS

a. First Person

| | Masc. | Fem. | Masc. | Fem. | Neut. |
|---|---|---|---|---|---|
| | Singular | | Plural | | |
| N | — | — | — | — | — |
| G | ἐμαυτοῦ | ἐμαυτῆς | ἑαυτῶν | ἑαυτῶν | ἑαυτῶν |
| D | ἐμαυτῷ | ἐμαυτῇ | ἑαυτοῖς | ἑαυταῖς | ἑαυτοῖς |
| A | ἐμαυτόν | ἐμαυτήν | ἑαυτούς | ἑαυτάς | ἑαυτά |

b. Second Person

| | Masc. | Fem. | Masc | Fem. | Neut. |
|---|---|---|---|---|---|
| | Singular | | Plural | | |
| N | — | — | — | — | — |
| G | σεαυτοῦ | σεαυτῆς | ἑαυτῶν | ἑαυτῶν | ἑαυτῶν |
| D | σεαυτῷ | σευτῇ | ἑαυτοῖς | ἑαυταῖς | ἑαυτοῖς |
| A | σεαυτόν | σεαυτήν | ἑαυτούς | ἑαυτάς | ἑαυτά |

c. Third Person

| | Masc. | Fem. | Neut. | Masc. | Fem. | Neut. |
|---|---|---|---|---|---|---|
| | Singular | | | Plural | | |
| N | — | — | — | — | — | — |
| G | ἑαυτοῦ | ἑαυτῆς | ἑαυτοῦ | ἑαυτῶν | ἑαυτῶν | ἑαυτῶν |
| D | ἑαυτῷ | ἑαυτῇ | ἑαυτῷ | ἑαυτοῖς | ἑαυταῖς | ἑαυτοῖς |
| A | ἑαυτόν | ἑαυτήν | ἑαυτό | ἑαυτούς | ἑαυτάς | ἑαυτά |

Note: These reflexive pronouns are combinations of αὐτός and the personal pronoun stems ἐμ- (found in ἐμοῦ, ἐμοί, and ἐμέ), σε- (found in σέ, the accusative of σύ), and ἑ (found in ἕ, a third singular accusative pronoun not used in the New Testament.)

# 202. EXERCISES

a. Translate number 198.

b. Translate orally into Greek in two ways (1) by an active form and a reflexive pronoun, and (2) by a middle form alone.

1) I teach myself.
2) We taught ourselves.
3) They will teach themselves.
4) She believes herself (dat.).
5) You hear yourself (gen.).
6) We heard ourselves (gen.).

120

c. Using the expressions with βλέπω in number 200 as patterns, conjugate the following.

1) θεραπεύσω ἐμαυτήν ἀντὶ τοῦ μαθητοῦ.
2) ἐδούλευον ἐμαυτῷ ἀντὶ ἐκείνου.
3) ἀκήκοα ἐμαυτῆς ἀντὶ αὐτῆς.
4) ἐρῶ ἐμαυτῇ ἀντὶ τοῦ διδασκάλου.

d. Read the Greek aloud and then translate:

1) ἃ (the things which) οὖν ἐγὼ λαλῶ (I speak), καθὼς (as) εἴρηκέν μοι ὁ πατήρ, οὕτως λαλῶ.
2) ἀκούσας (having heard) δὲ περὶ τοῦ ᾽Ιησοῦ ἀπέστειλεν πρὸς αὐτὸν πρεσβυτέρους τῶν ᾽Ιουδαίων (Jews), ἐρωτῶν (asking) αὐτὸν ὅπως ἐλθὼν διασώσῃ (that he come and heal) τὸν δοῦλον αὐτοῦ.

The sources of these excerpts are listed on page 246.

# Lesson 27

**203. "UNTO YOU IS BORN . . ."**

πάλαι ἀπέστειλεν ὁ θεὸς τὸν ἑαυτοῦ υἱὸν γενέσθαι τέκνον ἐν ἀνθρώποις. ἐν Βηθλέεμ οὖν οὗτος ὁ υἱὸς ἐγένετο τὸ τέκνον τῆς Μαρίας.

εἰρήκει γὰρ ὁ θεὸς τῇ Μαρίᾳ, "γενοῦ ἡ μήτηρ τοῦ υἱοῦ ἐμοῦ." καὶ εἰρήκει ἡ Μαρίᾱ, "τοῦτο γενέσθω." ἡ δὲ Μαρίᾱ ἡ    5
μήτηρ τοῦ κυρίου ἡμῶν ἐγένετο.

μετὰ ταῦτα ἄγγελοί τινες ἦλθαν πρὸς ἀνθρώπους τινὰς μετὰ τῶν προβάτων ἐν τῇ γῇ Βηθλέεμ. εἶπαν δὲ τοῖς ἀνθρώποις περὶ τοῦ μικροῦ τέκνου ἐν Βηθλέεμ.

οἱ δὲ ἄγγελοι ἐνετείλαντο αὐτοῖς, "μακάριοι γένεσθε διὰ    10
τοῦτο τὸ τέκνον. οἱ ἄνθρωποι τῆς Βηθλέεμ μακάριοι γενέσθωσαν καὶ δεξάσθωσαν τὸ τέκνον. ἕκαστος ἐν Βηθλέεμ δεξάσθω αὐτό."

διὰ τοὺς ἀγγέλους ὁ φόβος τοὺς ἀνθρώπους ἔλαβεν, ἀλλὰ μετὰ μικρὸν χρόνον ἀπῆλθαν ἀπὸ τῶν ἑαυτῶν προβάτων εἰς    15
τὴν Βηθλέεμ. ἐκεῖ δὲ ἔβλεψαν τὸ τέκνον Μαρίας, τὸν υἱὸν τοῦ θεοῦ. ἐγένοντο λίαν μακάριοι.

μετὰ ταῦτα ἦλθον ἄλλοι ἀπὸ γῆς τινος μακρᾶς εἰς Ἱεροσόλυμα. οὗτοι καὶ ἤθελον βλέπειν τὸ αὐτὸ τέκνον ἐν Βηθλέεμ ὅτι περὶ αὐτοῦ ἠκηκόεισαν ἐν τῇ ἑαυτῶν γῇ. ἔφερον    20
οὖν δωρεὰς καλὰς ἐκ τοῦ ἑαυτῶν πλούτου. ἐκ Ἱεροσολύμων εἰς Βηθλέεμ ἦλθον, ἐκεῖ δὲ ἔβλεψαν τὸ μικρὸν τέκνον τῆς Μαρίας οὗτοι.

τότε δὲ εἶπαν τάχα, "δέξαι, Μαρίᾱ, ταύτᾱς τὰς δωρεάς. ἐγένου ἡ μήτηρ τούτου τοῦ τέκνου. αὗται γενέσθωσαν ὁ    25
πλοῦτος τοῦ τέκνου. σὺ καὶ Ἰωσήφ, δέξασθε ταύτᾱς."

ἀλλά τις βασιλεὺς ἠκηκόει ὅτι τὸ μικρὸν τέκνον ἔσται ἄλλος βασιλεύς. ἐκεῖνος οὖν ἤθελεν τοῦτο ἀποκτεῖναι.

ἐνετείλατο οὖν ὁ θεὸς τῷ Ἰωσήφ, "ἀπέρχου ἀπὸ τῆς Βηθλέεμ εἰς τὴν γῆν Αἰγύπτου, καὶ ἀπερχέσθωσαν μετὰ σοῦ ἡ    30
μήτηρ καὶ τὸ τέκνον. μένε δὲ ἐκεῖ μετὰ τῆς Μαρίας καὶ τοῦ τέκνου. ὅτε οὗτος ὁ κακὸς βασιλεὺς ἀποθανεῖται, ἐντελοῦμαί σοι ἐλθεῖν πάλιν εἰς ταύτην τὴν γῆν."

τὸ τέκνον οὖν ὁ κακὸς βασιλεὺς οὐκ ἀπέκτεινεν.

## 204. VOCABULARY

Βηθλέεμ (indecl.), ἡ: Bethlehem
δέχομαι, — , ἐδεξάμην: I receive, accept, welcome
Ἱεροσόλυμα, -ων, τά: Jerusalem
μήτηρ (nom. sing.), ἡ: mother

## 205. AORIST MIDDLE IMPERATIVES

a. First Aorist.

| | |
|---|---|
| πίστευσαι | πιστεύσασθε |
| πιστευσάσθω | πιστευσάσθωσαν |

b. Second Aorist.

| | |
|---|---|
| γενοῦ | γένεσθε |
| γενέσθω | γενέσθωσαν |

c. Liquid Aorist.

| | |
|---|---|
| ἔντειλαι | ἐντείλασθε |
| ἐντειλάσθω | ἐντειλάσθωσαν |

## 206. AORIST MIDDLE INFINITIVES

a. First Aorist: πιστεύσασθαι
b. Second Aorist: γενέσθαι.
c. Liquid Aorist: ἐντείλασθαι.

## 207. EXERCISES

a. Translate number 203.

b. Use aorist imperatives to translate the following italicized expressions.

  1) *Start welcoming* Mary, shepherds.
  2) *Start healing yourself,* doctor.
  3) *Command* little Joseph *once for all* to be quiet, Peter.
  4) *Let* the men *command* the children to go home.

c. Use present imperatives to translate the following italicized expressions.

  1) *Keep on welcoming* the strangers, my friends.
  2) *Let the mother* always *go away* after class.
  3) *Let them send themselves forth* every week.
  4) Disciples, *teach yourselves* by reading carefully whenever your instructor is absent.

d. Translate.

  1) καλοὶ γενέσθωσαν ὁ βασιλεὺς καὶ οἱ ἄλλοι ἐν τοῖς Ἱεροσολύμοις.

123

2) οἱ κακοὶ τῶν Ἱεροσολύμων δεξάσθωσαν τὸν υἱὸν τοῦ θεοῦ.

3) ἄγγελε, ἔντειλαι τοῖς δούλοις ἐκείνοις δεξάσθαι τὰς δωρεὰς ταυτᾶς.

4) υἱέ, γενοῦ ἄνθρωπος καὶ ἴσθι πάντοτε ὁ υἱός μου.

5) ὁ πατὴρ καὶ ἡ μήτηρ θελέτωσαν δεξάσθαι τὰ τέκνα.

6) ἐντείλασθε τοῖς καμήλοις μεῖναι ὧδε.

7) ὁ βασιλεὺς γενέσθω μαθητὴς τοῦ διδασκάλου ἐν Ἱεροσολύμοις.

8) βλεψάσθω ἡ μήτηρ.

9) γενέσθε μακάριοι ὅτε ἀκούσετε τῶν ἀγγέλων.

10) Πέτρε, θέλεις γενέσθαι καλός;

11) δέξαι τὰ τέκνα ταῦτα, Φίλιππε.

12) γενοῦ καλὸς ὑπηρέτης, υἱέ.

13) ἔρχου νῦν, δοῦλε.

14) ἐντειλάσθω ἡ μήτηρ τοῖς τέκνοις φαγεῖν.

e. Read the Greek aloud and then translate.

1) . . . ἀλλὰ ὡς (as) ἄγγελον θεοῦ ἐδέξασθέ με, ὡς Χριστὸν Ἰησοῦν.

2) οὐχ οὗτός ἐστιν ὁ τοῦ τέκτονος (of the carpenter) υἱός; οὐχ ἡ μήτηρ αὐτοῦ λέγεται (is called) Μαριάμ . . . ;

3) δέξε παρ' (from) αὐτοῦ τὰς (δραχμὰς) (drachmas) ρ̄ (100).

The sources of these excerpts are listed on page 246.

# Lesson 28

## 208. MOSES, A MAN WITH A PAST

ὁ Μωϋσῆς ἦν πρὸ Φαραὼ καὶ ἕτοιμος ἦν εἰπεῖν, "ὁ θεὸς ἐντέλλεται τῷ Ἰσραὴλ ἀπελθεῖν ἐκ ταύτης τῆς γῆς." τί οὖν ἦν Μωϋσῆς ἐκεῖ; τί ἐγεγένητο τούτῳ πρὸ ἐκείνου τοῦ χρόνου; πάλαι ἀπέκτεινε Μωϋσῆς Αἰγύπτιόν τινα καὶ ἐδεδίωκτο ὑπὸ τῶν δούλων τοῦ Φαραώ. ἀλλὰ Μωϋσῆς ἀπηληλύθει ἐκ τῆς 5 Αἰγύπτου εἰς γῆν μακράν. ἐκεῖ ἔβλεψε ἑπτὰ ἀδελφὰς μετὰ τῶν προβάτων αὐτῶν. τούτων δὲ τῶν ἑπτὰ ἀδελφῶν ὁ πατὴρ ἐδέδεκτο Μωϋσῆν. τῶν ἀδελφῶν τις ἐγεγένητο ἡ γυνὴ τοῦ Μωϋσέως.

ὅτε δὲ μετὰ μακρὰ ἔτη Μωϋσῆς ἀπέσταλτο ὑπὸ τοῦ θεοῦ 10 πάλιν εἰς τὴν Αἴγυπτον, ἐπέπειστο καὶ ὁ ἀδελφὸς αὐτοῦ ἐδέδεκτο αὐτόν, καὶ ὁμοῦ οὗτοι ἠληλύθεισαν πάλιν εἰς τὴν Αἴγυπτον.

τότε οἱ υἱοὶ τοῦ Ἰσραὴλ συνηγμένοι ἦσαν πρὸ τοῦ Μωϋσέως, καὶ αἱ ἐπαγγελίαι τοῦ θεοῦ εἰρημέναι ἦσαν τούτοις. 15

νῦν οὖν Μωϋσῆς καὶ οἱ ἴδιος ἀδελφὸς ἦσαν ἕτοιμοι λέγειν πρὸ τοῦ Φαραώ, "ἀπόλυσον τὸν λαὸν ἐκ τῆς γῆς σου. ἡμεῖς πρὸς σὲ ἀπεστάλμεθα ὑπὸ τοῦ θεοῦ τοῦ Ἰσραήλ. ὁ γὰρ λαὸς τοῦ Ἰσραὴλ ἀπέσταλται ἐκ τῆς γῆς."

## 209. VOCABULARY

γράφω, γράψω, ἔγραψα, γέγραφα, γέγραμμαι: I write
Ἰσραήλ (indecl.), ὁ: Israel
λαός, -οῦ, ὁ: people
Μωϋσῆς, Μωϋσέως, Μωϋσεῖ, Μωϋσῆν, ὁ: Moses
πείθω, πείσω, ἔπεισα, πέποιθα, πέπεισμαι: I persuade; (mid.) I believe, obey (dat. of dir. obj. with mid.)
πρό: (with gen.) before, in front of, earlier than, preferable to, in lieu of
ὑπό: (with gen.) by, under; (with acc.) under

## 210. LIST OF PERFECT AND PLUPERFECT MIDDLE OR PASSIVE INDICATIVES USED IN NUMBER 208

ἀπεστάλμεθα (ἀποστέλλω): we have been sent
ἀπέσταλται (ἀποστέλλω): it has been sent

ἀπέσταλτο (ἀποστέλλω):   he had been sent
ἐγεγένητο (γίνομαι):   she had become, it had happened
ἐδέδεκτο (δέχομαι):   he had welcomed
ἐδεδίωκτο (διώκω):   he had been pursued closely
εἰρημέναι ἦσαν (λέγω):   they had been declared
ἐπέπειστο (πείθω):   he had obeyed
συνηγμένοι ἦσαν (συνάγω):   they had been gathered together

## 211. PASSIVE VOICE: ITS MEANING

a. *In defective verbs.* In number 173 it has been explained that some verbs have middle forms with active meanings. There are also Greek verbs having passive forms with active meanings. This will be clearer when the future and aorist passive have been introduced.

b. *In complete verbs.* When a Greek verb is not defective, the passive forms have meanings different from the meanings of active and middle forms. The action of a passive form is presented as taking effect on the subject but as being performed usually by some agent other than the subject.

## 212. IDENTITY OF SOME MIDDLE AND PASSIVE FORMS

The middle forms of the present, imperfect, perfect, and pluperfect tenses are identical with the passive forms of these tenses. The following examples illustrate both the forms and meanings of the three voices.

*Present*
| | | |
|---|---|---|
| Active | βλέπω | I see |
| Middle | βλέπομαι | I see myself |
| Passive | βλέπομαι | I am seen |

*Imperfect*
| | | |
|---|---|---|
| Active | ἐθεράπευε | he was healing |
| Middle | ἐθεραπεύετο | he was healing himself |
| Passive | ἐθεραπεύετο | he was being healed |

*Perfect*
| | | |
|---|---|---|
| Active | εἰλήφαμεν | we have taken |
| Middle | εἰλήμμεθα | we have taken for ourselves |
| Passive | εἰλήμμεθα | we have been taken |

*Pluperfect*
| | | |
|---|---|---|
| Active | ἐπεγνώκειτε | you had recognized |
| Middle | ἐπέγνωσθε | you had recognized yourselves |

| Passive | ἐπέγνωσθε | you had been recognized |

## 213. PRESENT MIDDLE AND PASSIVE INDICATIVE AND INFINITIVE OF OMEGA VERBS

a. Indicative of πιστεύω.

| | |
|---|---|
| πεπίστευμαι | πεπιστεύμεθα |
| πεπίστευσαι | πεπίστευσθε |
| πεπίστευται | πεπίστευνται |

To the verb stem -πιστευ- is prefixed the reduplication πε-. No tense suffix is used here. Directly to the reduplicated verb stem are added the primary middle endings. Of course, in other verbs other forms of reduplication may be used as in ἀπέσταλμαι, the perfect middle of ἀποστέλλω.

b. Infinitive of πιστεύω: πεπιστεῦσθαι.

This form is composed of reduplication plus the verb stem plus the middle infinitive ending. Notice the accent.

## 214. PLUPERFECT MIDDLE AND PASSIVE INDICATIVE OF OMEGA VERBS

| | |
|---|---|
| (ἐ)πεπιστεύμην | (ἐ)πεπιστεύμεθα |
| (ἐ)πεπίστευσο | (ἐ)πεπίστευσθε |
| (ἐ)πεπίστευτο | (ἐ)πεπίστευντο |

The initial ἐ-, the augment, may be omitted in the pluperfect in Hellenistic Greek.

## 215. PERFECT MIDDLE AND PASSIVE SYSTEM OF VERBS WITH STEMS ENDING IN A MUTE OR LIQUID

The perfect middle and passive system includes the perfect and pluperfect tenses. The personal endings used in these tenses can be added without complication to stems terminating in a vowel, for example: πεπίστευ-ται, ἐπεπιστεύ-μεθα.

But verbs whose stems end with a consonant deviate from the pattern of πιστεύω. Certain changes in spelling occur where the personal endings touch the stem of the verb. Some combinations of consonants were more pleasing to the ancient Greeks or were easier for them to pronounce than others. The less agreeable combinations were often modified to make more acceptable sounds. Notice the various spellings of the prefix *in* in the following English words: *in*ability, *im*possible, *il*logical, *ir*regular. In the third plural we find not merely a modification but an outright substitution.

In the paradigms that follow, the unacceptable regular formation is placed in parentheses after the form in use.

a. Paradigms of γράφω to illustrate the formation of verbs whose stems end in π, β, or φ.

1) Perfect Indicative Middle and Passive.

| | |
|---|---|
| γέγραμμαι | (γέγραφμαι) |
| γέγραψαι | (γέγραφσαι) |
| γέγραπται | (γέγραφται) |
| γεγράμμεθα | (γεγράφμεθα) |
| γέγραφθε | (γέγραφσθε) |
| γεγραμμένοι εἰσί | (γέγραφνται) |

2) Perfect Infinitive Middle and Passive.

| | |
|---|---|
| γεγράφθαι | (γεγράφσθαι) |

3) Pluperfect Indicative Middle and Passive.

| | |
|---|---|
| ἐγεγράμμην | (ἐγεγράφμην) |
| ἐγέγραψο | (ἐγέγραφσο) |
| ἐγέγραπτο | (ἐγέγραφτο) |
| ἐγεγράμμεθα | (ἐγεγράφμεθα) |
| ἐγέγραφθε | (ἐγέγραφσθε) |
| γεγραμμένοι ἦσαν | (ἐγέγραφντο) |

b. Paradigms of διώκω to illustrate the formation of verbs whose stems end in κ, γ, or χ.

1) Perfect Indicative Middle and Passive.

| | |
|---|---|
| δεδίωγμαι | (δεδίωκμαι) |
| δεδίωξαι | (δεδίωκσαι) |
| δεδίωκται | (same form) |
| δεδιώγμεθα | (δεδιώκμεθα) |
| δεδίωχθε | (δεδίωκσθε) |
| δεδιωγμένοι εἰσί | (δεδίωκνται) |

2) Perfect Infinitive Middle and Passive.

| | |
|---|---|
| δεδιῶχθαι | (δεδιῶκσθαι) |

3) Pluperfect Indicative Middle and Passive.

| | |
|---|---|
| ἐδεδιώγμην | (ἐδεδιώκμην) |
| ἐδεδίωξο | (ἐδεδίωκσο) |
| ἐδεδίωκτο | (same form) |
| ἐδεδιώγμεθα | (ἐδεδιώκμεθα) |
| ἐδεδίωχθε | (ἐδεδίωκσθε) |
| δεδιωγμένοι ἦσαν | (ἐδεδίωκντο) |

c. Paradigms of πείθω to illustrate the formation of verbs whose stems end in τ, δ, or θ.

   1) Perfect Indicative Middle or Passive.

   | | |
   |---|---|
   | πέπεισμαι | (πέπειθμαι) |
   | πέπεισαι | (πέπειθσαι) |
   | πέπεισται | (πέπειθται) |
   | πεπείσμεθα | (πεπείθμεθα) |
   | πέπεισθε | (πέπειθσθε) |
   | πεπεισμένοι εἰσί | (πέπειθνται) |

   2) Perfect Infinitive Middle and Passive.

   | | |
   |---|---|
   | πεπεῖσθαι | (πεπεῖθσθαι) |

   3) Pluperfect Indicative Middle and Passive.

   | | |
   |---|---|
   | ἐπεπείσμην | (ἐπεπείθμην) |
   | ἐπέπεισο | (ἐπέπειθσο) |
   | ἐπέπειστο | (ἐπέπειθτο) |
   | ἐπεπείσμεθα | (ἐπεπείθμεθα) |
   | ἐπέπεισθε | (ἐπέπειθσθε) |
   | πεπεισμένοι ἦσαν | (ἐπέπειθντο) |

d. Paradigms of ἐντέλλομαι to illustrate the formation of verbs whose stems end in λ, μ, ν, or ρ.

   1) Perfect Indicative Middle and Passive.

   | | |
   |---|---|
   | ἐντέταλμαι | |
   | ἐντέταλσαι | (same forms) |
   | ἐντέταλται | |
   | ἐντετάλμεθα | |
   | ἐντέταλθε | (ἐντέταλσθε) |
   | ἐντεταλμένοι εἰσί | (ἐντέταλνται) |

   2) Perfect Infinitive Middle and Passive.

   | | |
   |---|---|
   | ἐντετάλθαι | (ἐντετάλσθαι) |

   3) Pluperfect Indicative Middle and Passive: (No forms in the New Testament).

# 216. AUGMENT IN THE PLUPERFECT

The pluperfect occur either with or without augment in the Greek of the New Testament period (number 160). The paradigms just presented have uniformly included augment. Exercises, however, will give both augmented and unaugmented forms.

## 217. SUMMARY OF CONSONANT CHANGES ILLUSTRATED IN NUMBER 215.

| Final stem consonant | Initial terminal consonant | Result of change |
|---|---|---|
| π β φ | μ σ + vowel σ + θ τ | μμ ψ + vowel φθ πτ |
| κ γ χ | μ σ + vowel σ + θ τ | γμ ξ + vowel χθ κτ |
| τ δ θ | μ σ + vowel σ + θ τ | σμ σ + vowel σθ στ |

## 218. PERIPHRASTIC THIRD PLURAL IN THE PERFECT AND PLUPERFECT INDICATIVE MIDDLE AND PASSIVE

Forms like δεδιωγμένοι ἦσαν and πεπεισμένοι εἰσί are made up of perfect middle or passive participles and the third plural indicative of εἰμί in the present for the perfect and in the imperfect for the pluperfect. The participle agrees with the subject and therefore has different endings to modify nouns of different gender. These combinations are called *periphrastics*.

*αἱ ἀδελφαι δεδιωγμέναι εἰσί.*
The sisters have been closely pursued, (or)
The sisters have closely pursued each other.

*οἱ δοῦλοι πεπεισμένοι ἦσαν.*
The slaves had been persuaded, (or)
The slaves had persuaded one another.

Notice that the participle can *never* have augment *at any time.* (number 95)

## 219. GENITIVE OF AGENT

The genitive case is used with the prepositions ἀπό, ἐκ, παρά, and ὑπό to indicate the person by whom an action is performed. This construction is used with the passive voice.

*διωκόμεθα ὑπὸ τοῦ ἐχθροῦ.*
We are being pursued *by the enemy.*

## 220. LIST OF VERBS WITH PERFECT MIDDLE AND PASSIVE SYSTEMS

| Present Active | Perfect Middle and Passive |
|---|---|
| ἀπολύω | ἀπολέλυμαι |
| ἀποστέλλω | ἀπέσταλμαι |
| βάλλω | βέβλημαι |
| γίνομαι | γεγένημαι |
| γράφω | γέγραμμαι |
| δέχομαι | δέδεγμαι |
| διώκω | δεδίωγμαι |
| ἐντέλλομαι | ἐντέταλμαι |
| θεραπεύω | τεθεράπευμαι |
| λαμβάνω | εἴλημμαι |
| λέγω | εἴρημαι |
| πείθω | πέπεισμαι |
| πιστεύω | πεπίστευμαι |
| συνάγω | συνῆγμαι |

## 221. EXERCISES

a. Translate number 208.

b. Locate by giving (1) tense, (2) mood, (3) voice, (4) person, (5) number, and (6) first principal part.

1) ἀπολέλυνται
2) βεβλημένοι ἦσαν
3) δεδίωχθε
4) πεπίστευσαι
5) πέπειστο
6) δεδέγμην
7) ἐνετείλω
8) εἰρημένοι εἰσί
9) ἠγάγετε
10) πεπεισμέναι ἦσαν
11) ἐπεπίστευντο

c. Translate in two ways if possible to show the ambiguity of tense and voice.

1) ἐδεδέγμεθα
2) εἰρημένοι ἦσαν
3) πέπεισο
4) συνῆκται
5) ἀπελέλυντο
6) πεπίστευνται
7) ἐτεθεράπευντο
8) ἀπολέλυνται
9) ἐπεπίστευντο
10) τεθεράπευνται

d. Translate.

1) ἑπτὰ ἔτη ἐν Αἰγύπτῳ Μωϋσῆς μεμενήκει καὶ ἑπτὰ ἔτη ἐν γῇ τινι μακρᾷ.

2) οὐκ ἦν Μωϋσῆς ἕτοιμος λέγειν τῷ λαῷ τοῦ ᾽Ισραήλ.

3) ὅτε ἐκ τῆς μακρᾶς γῆς εἰς τὴν Αἴγυπτον λέγειν πρὸ τοῦ

Φαραὼ Μωϋσῆς ἐληλύθει, οὐκ ἦν ἕτοιμος ὁ Φαραὼ ἐντειλάσθαι τῷ λαῷ ἀπέρχεσθαι ἐκ τῆς γῆς.

4) ὁ λαὸς ἀπέσταλται ὑπὸ τοῦ θεοῦ.

5) πρὸ τούτου τοῦ λαοῦ ἀπέσταλτο ἐκεῖνος ὑπὸ ἀγγέλου;

e. Associate the following words with new Greek words presented in this lesson.

   1) *lay*: related to the *people* as distinguished from the clergy.

   2) *pro*logue: a statement made *before* the main part of a play or poem.

   3) *hypo*dermic: related to what is *under* the skin.

f. Read the Greek aloud and then translate.

   1) ἔλεγον οὖν τῷ Πιλάτῳ (Pilate) οἱ ἀρχιερεῖς (the chief priests) τῶν Ἰουδαίων (Jews), Μὴ γράφε, Ὁ βασιλεὺς τῶν Ἰουδαίων, ἀλλ' ὅτι ἐκεῖνος εἶπεν, Βασιλεύς εἰμι τῶν Ἰουδαίων. ἀπεκρίθη ὁ Πιλᾶτος, Ὃ γέγραφα, γέγραφα.

   2) . . . τέξεται (she will bear) δὲ υἱὸν καὶ καλέσεις τὸ ὄνομα αὐτοῦ (you will name him) Ἰησοῦν, αὐτὸς γὰρ σώσει (will save) τὸν λαὸν αὐτοῦ ἀπὸ τῶν ἁμαρτιῶν (sins) αὐτῶν.

The sources of these excerpts are listed on page 246.

# Lesson 29

## 222. A PROPHETIC MEMORIAL

ὁ Μωϋσῆς ἐπέμφθη ὑπὸ τοῦ θεοῦ ἐντέλλεσθαι τῷ Φαραώ, "οἱ υἱοὶ τοῦ Ἰσραὴλ ἐκ τῆς γῆς Αἰγύπτου ὑπὸ σοῦ ἀπεσταλή- σονται."

ἀλλὰ οὗτοι οὐκ ἀπεστάλησαν. ὁ γὰρ βασιλεὺς εἶχεν αὐτοὺς καὶ οὐκ ἀπελύθησαν. διὰ τοῦτο ἐγενήθησαν πληγαὶ ἐπὶ    5
τοὺς Αἰγυπτίους καὶ ἐπὶ τὴν γῆν αὐτῶν καὶ ἐπὶ τὸν Φαραὼ αὐτόν.

πρὸ τῆς ἐσχάτης πληγῆς τῷ Φαραὼ ἐρρέθη ὑπὸ τοῦ Μωϋσέως, "ἐν ταύτῃ τῇ ἐσχάτῃ πληγῇ ὁ πρῶτος υἱὸς σοῦ ἀποκτανθήσεται." ὁ δὲ Φαραὼ τῷ θεῷ οὐκ ἐπείσθη καὶ ὁ    10
πρῶτος υἱὸς αὐτοῦ ἀπεκτάνθη ἐν τῇ ἐσχάτῃ πληγῇ καὶ οἱ ἄλλοι υἱοὶ πρῶτοι ἐν τοῖς Αἰγυπτίοις καὶ ἀπεκτάνθησαν ὑπό τινος ἀγγέλου τοῦ κυρίου. μετὰ ταῦτα ὁ Ἰσραὴλ ἐβλήθη ἐκ τῆς Αἰγύπτου ὑπὸ τῶν Αἰγυπτίων.

πρὸ δὲ ταύτης τῆς ἐσχάτης πληγῆς ὁ λαὸς τοῦ Ἰσραὴλ    15
ἐδιδάχθη τὴν ἑορτὴν τοῦ πάσχα. ἐν τῇ ἑορτῇ ταύτῃ ἀρνίον καλὸν ἐτύθη καὶ τὸ αἷμα τοῦ ἀρνίου ἐβλήθη ἐπὶ τὴν θύραν τοῦ οἴκου. διὰ τὰ αἷμα τοῦτο ὁ ἄγγελος τοῦ κυρίου οὐκ ἀπέκτεινε τοὺς πρώτους υἱοὺς ἐν τῷ λαῷ τοῦ Ἰσραήλ. ἀλλὰ οὐκ ἦν αἷμα ἐπὶ ταῖς θύραις τῶν Αἰγυπτίων. τὸ ἀρνίον τοῦ πάσχα οὐκ    20
ἐτύθη ὑπ' αὐτῶν καὶ οὐκ ἴσχυον χαρῆναι. ἀλλ' ὅτι οἱ πρῶτοι υἱοὶ τοῦ λαοῦ Ἰσραὴλ οὐκ ἀπεκτάνθησαν, ὁ λαὸς ἐχάρη.

αὕτη ἦν ἡ πρώτη ἑορτὴ τοῦ πάσχα. ὁ δὲ κύριος τῷ λαῷ ἐνετείλατο μνημονεύειν ταύτης τῆς ἑορτῆς καὶ τοῦ καλοῦ ἀρνίου. διὰ τῆς ἑορτῆς τοῦ πάσχα καὶ διὰ τοῦ ἀρνίου ὁ λαὸς    25
ἐδιδάχθη περὶ τοῦ ἀρνίου τοῦ θεοῦ, τοῦ κυρίου ἡμῶν Ἰησοῦ. μετὰ δὲ χρόνον λίαν μακρὸν οὗτος ἐτύθη, καὶ διὰ τὸ αἷμα αὐτοῦ ἡμεῖς, οἱ δοῦλοι αὐτοῦ, χαίρομεν. οὐκέτι θύομεν ἀρνία ἐν τῇ ἑορτῇ πάσχα. οὐκέτι βάλλομεν τὸ αἷμα ἐπὶ τὰς θύρᾱς τῶν οἴκων ἡμῶν. χαίρομεν καὶ χαρησόμεθα ὅτι Ἰησοῦς, τὸ    30
ἀρνίον ἡμῶν, ἐτύθη καὶ ὅτι ὁ θεὸς βλέπει τὸ αἷμα τούτου τοῦ ἐσχάτου πάσχα οὐκ ἐπὶ ταῖς θύραις τῶν οἴκων ἡμῶν ἀλλ' ἐπὶ ταῖς καρδίαις ἡμῶν.

## 223. VOCABULARY

αἷμα (nom. and acc. sing.), τό: blood
ἑορτή, -ῆς, ἡ: festival, feast
ἐπί: (with gen.) on, over, upon; (with dat.) on, at, upon, concerning; (with acc.) on, over, to, against
ἔσχατος, -η, -ον: last
θύρᾱ, -ᾱς, ἡ: door
θύω, — , ἔθυσα, — , τέθυμαι, ἐτύθην: I sacrifice, kill, slay, offer
'Ιησοῦς, -οῦ (gen., dat.), -οῦν, -οῦ, ὁ: Jesus, Joshua
πάσχα (indecl.), τό: Passover, paschal lamb
πληγή, -ῆς, ἡ: plague, calamity, blow
πρῶτος, -η, -ον: first, chief, principal
χαίρω, — , — , — , — , ἐχάρην: I rejoice, am glad

## 224. LIST OF AORIST AND FUTURE PASSIVES USED IN NUMBER 222

ἀπεκτάνθη (ἀποκτείνω): he was killed
ἀπεκτάνθησαν (ἀποκτείνω): they were killed
ἀπελύθησαν (ἀπολύω): they were released
ἀπεστάλησαν (ἀποστέλλω): they were sent away
ἀποκτανθήσεται (ἀποκτείνω): he will be killed
ἀποσταλήσονται (ἀποστέλλω): they shall be sent forth
ἐβλήθη (βάλλω): it was put
ἐγενήθησαν (γίνομαι): they were brought (upon)
ἐδιδάχθη (διδάσκω): it was taught
ἐπείσθη (πείθω): he obeyed
ἐπέμφθη (πέμπω): he was sent
ἐρρέθη (λέγω): it was said
ἐτύθη (θύω): it was slain
ἐχάρη (χαίρω): it rejoiced
χαρῆναι (χαίρω): to rejoice
χαρησόμεθα (χαίρω): we shall rejoice

## 225. TENSES WITH DISTINCT PASSIVE FORMS

Unlike the present, imperfect, perfect, and pluperfect (see number 212), whose middle and passive forms have the same spelling, the aorist and future tenses have passives that differ from their middle forms.

## 226. FIRST PASSIVE SYSTEM: AORIST

Indicative

| | |
|---|---|
| ἐπιστεύθην | ἐπιστεύθημεν |
| ἐπιστεύθης | ἐπιστεύθητε |
| ἐπιστεύθη | ἐπιστεύθησαν |

### Imperative

| | |
|---|---|
| πιστεύθητι | πιστεύθητε |
| πιστευθήτω | πιστευθήτωσαν |

### Infinitive

πιστευθῆναι

To the unreduplicated perfect middle and passive stem are added -θη- and the personal or infinitive endings.

## 227. SECOND PASSIVE SYSTEM: AORIST

### Indicative

| | |
|---|---|
| ἀπεστάλην | ἀπεστάλημεν |
| ἀπεστάλης | ἀπεστάλητε |
| ἀπεστάλη | ἀπεστάλησαν |

### Imperative

| | |
|---|---|
| ἀποστάληθι | ἀποστάλητε |
| ἀποσταλήτω | ἀποσταλήτωσαν |

### Infinitive

ἀποσταλῆναι

To the unreduplicated perfect middle and passive stem is added -η- and the personal or infinitive endings. The indicative forms have augment. Notice that the second singular imperative has the personal ending -θι instead of the -τι in the first aorist passive.

## 228. FIRST PASSIVE SYSTEM: FUTURE

### Indicative

| | |
|---|---|
| πιστευθήσομαι | πιστευθησόμεθα |
| πιστευθήσῃ | πιστευθήσεσθε |
| πιστευθήσεται | πιστευθήσονται |

### Infinitive

πιστευθήσεσθαι

To the unreduplicated perfect middle and passive stem are added -θη- then -σο/ε- and finally the primary middle personal endings. The ending -σῃ is a shortened form of -σεσαι.

## 229. SECOND PASSIVE SYSTEM: FUTURE

| Indicative | | Infinitive |
|---|---|---|
| ἀποσταλήσομαι | ἀποσταλησόμεθα | ἀποσταλήσεσθαι |
| ἀποσταλήσῃ | ἀποσταλήσεσθε | |
| ἀποσταλήσεται | ἀποσταλήσονται | |

Instead of -θη- the second future passive uses -η-. Otherwise, this formation is the same as the first future passive.

230. **AORIST AND FUTURE PASSIVES IN VERBS WHOSE STEMS END WITH A MUTE**

a. Verbs whose stems end with π, β, or φ use φ before -θη.

| | |
|---|---|
| ἐπέμφθην | (πεμπ-) |
| ἐλήμφθην | (λημβ-) |

(γράφω has second aorist and future passives: ἐγράφην & γραφήσεται.)

b. Verbs whose stems end with κ, γ, or χ use χ before -θη-.

| | |
|---|---|
| ἐδιώχθην | (διωκ-) |
| ἤχθην | (ἀγ-) |

c. Verbs whose stems end with τ, δ, or θ use σ before -θη-.

| | |
|---|---|
| ἐπείσθην | (πειθ-) |

231. **REFERENCE LIST FOR AORIST AND FUTURE PASSIVES**

| Present Active | Aorist Passive | Future Passive |
|---|---|---|
| ἄγω | ἤχθην | ἀχθήσομαι |
| ἀκούω | ἠκούσθην | ἀκουσθήσομαι |
| ἀποκτείνω | ἀπεκτάνθην | ἀποκτανθήσομαι |
| ἀπολύω | ἀπελύθην | ἀπολυθήσομαι |
| ἀποστέλλω | ἀπεστάλην | ἀποσταλήσομαι |
| βάλλω | ἐβλήθην | βληθήσομαι |
| γίνομαι | ἐγενήθην | γενηθήσομαι |
| γράφω | ἐγράφην | γραφήσομαι |
| διδάσκω | ἐδιδάχθην | διδαχθήσομαι |
| διώκω | ἐδιώχθην | διωχθήσομαι |
| ἐπιγινώσκω | ἐπεγνώσθην | ἐπιγνωσθήσομαι |
| θεραπεύω | ἐθεραπεύθην | θεραπευθήσομαι |
| θύω | ἐτύθην | τυθήσομαι |
| λαμβάνω | ἐλήμφθην | λημφθήσομαι |
| λέγω | ἐρρέθην | ῥεθήσομαι |
| πείθω | ἐπείσθην | πεισθήσομαι |
| πέμπω | ἐπέμφθην | πεμφθήσομαι |
| πιστεύω | ἐπιστεύθην | πιστευθήσομαι |
| φέρω | ἠνέχθην | ἐνεχθήσομαι |
| χαίρω | ἐχάρην | χαρήσομαι |

## 232. EXERCISES

a. Translate number 222.

b. Locate.

| | |
|---|---|
| 1) ἐνεχθῆναι | 6) διδαχθησόμεθα |
| 2) λημφθήσεσθε | 7) ἀκουσθήτωσαν |
| 3) ῥεθήσεται | 8) ἀχθήσονται |
| 4) ἀποστάληθι | 9) ἐπέμφθης |
| 5) ἐδιώχθησαν | 10) χάρηθι |

c. Translate into Greek.

1) We shall be healed because of the paschal lamb.
2) You (pl.) will be persuaded.
3) Joshua was recognized.
4) It will be made.
5) They were written upon the door.
6) You (sing.) will be thrown out of the doors.
7) I was released from the door.
8) We shall be killed.
9) Joshua wil be glad because of the paschal lamb.
10) It was said at the festival.

d. Classify each of the following forms as (1) a primary tense (present, future, or perfect), (2) a secondary tense (imperfect, aorist, or pluperfect), or (3) an ambiguous form if out of context.

| | |
|---|---|
| 1) ἀπεστάλμεθα | 6) συνήγμεθα |
| 2) εἴρητο | 7) εἰχόμην |
| 3) ἀπολέλυνται | 8) διώξονται |
| 4) ἀπελύσω | 9) ἠρχόμην |
| 5) πέπεισθε | 10) ἀπεληλύθει |

e. Associate the following English words with new Greek words used in this lesson.

1) *anem*ia: a deficiency in the *blood*.
2) *eschat*ology: teachings concerning the *last* events in Biblical revelation.
3) hemi*pleg*ia: a *stroke* that causes paralysis in half the body.

f. Read the Greek aloud and then translate:

1) . . . τοῦτο γάρ ἐστιν τὸ αἷμά μου . . . .
2) . . . ἐλθέτω ἡ βασιλεία (kingdom) σου, γενηθήτω τὸ θέλημά (will) σου, ὡς (as) ἐν οὐρανῷ (heaven) καὶ ἐπὶ γῆς.

3) Πολλοὶ (Many) δὲ ἔσονται πρῶτοι ἔσχατοι καὶ ἔσχατοι πρῶτοι.

4) καὶ ἐγένετο φωνὴ (voice) πρὸς αὐτόν, Ἀναστάς (Stand up), Πέτρε, θῦσον καὶ φάγε.

5) ἀπὸ τῶν τριῶν (three) πληγῶν τούτων ἀπεκτάνθησαν τὸ τρίτον (third) τῶν ἀνθρώπων . . . .

6) ἐχάρησαν οὖν οἱ μαθηταὶ ἰδόντες (when they saw) τὸν κύριον.

7) Ἐγὼ Ἰησοῦς ἔπεμψα τὸν ἄγγελόν μου μαρτυρῆσαι (to witness) ὑμῖν ταῦτα ἐπὶ ταῖς ἐκκλησίαις (for the churches).

8) Ἰάκωβος θεοῦ καὶ κυρίου Ἰησοῦ Χριστοῦ (Christ) δοῦλος ταῖς δώδεκα (twelve) φυλαῖς (tribes) ταῖς ἐν τῇ διασπορᾷ (dispersion) χαίρειν.

9) Ἀντιμένης (Antimenes) Ζήνωνι (to Zenon) χαίρειν. (Found in a letter written on a papyrus sheet during the third century B.C.)

The sources of these excerpts are listed on page 246.

138

# Lesson 30

## 233. PHARAOH'S FIASCO

ἐπεὶ ἀπέστειλε Φαραὼ τὸν λαὸν ἐκ τῆς γῆς Αἰγύπτου, ὁ θεὸς ἦγε αὐτοὺς τὴν ἡμέρᾱν ἐν στύλῳ νεφέλης, τὴν δὲ νύκτα ἐν στύλῳ πυρός. ἔμενε δὲ ὁ στύλος τῆς νεφέλης ἡμέρᾱς, καὶ ὁ στύλος τοῦ πυρὸς νυκτὸς πρὸ τοῦ λαοῦ παντός.

εἶπε κύριος πρὸς Μωϋσῆν, "ἐρεῖ Φαραὼ τῷ λαῷ αὐτοῦ, 5 'ἄγειν πάλιν τοὺς υἱοὺς Ἰσραὴλ δυνατοί ἐσμεν.' ἐγὼ δὲ σκληρυνῶ τὴν καρδίᾱν Φαραὼ κατὰ αὐτῶν, καὶ διώξει αὐτούς. ἐπιγνώσονται δὲ πάντες οἱ Αἰγύπτιοι ὅτι ἐγώ εἰμι κύριος."

ἐσκλήρυνε οὖν κύριος τὴν καρδίᾱν τοῦ Φαραώ, καὶ ἐδίω- ξεν τοὺς υἱοὺς Ἰσραήλ. ἐπεὶ οἱ υἱοὶ Ἰσραὴλ ἀπήρχοντο ἐκ 10 τῆς Αἰγύπτου ἐν χειρὶ ὑψηλῇ, ἐδίωξαν οἱ Αἰγύπτιοι αὐτοὺς κατὰ τὴν θάλασσαν.

ἐγένετο δὲ ὁ φόβος ἐπὶ τοὺς υἱοὺς Ἰσραὴλ ὅτε ἔβλεψαν τοὺς Αἰγυπτίους. τότε εἶπε κύριος πρὸς Μωϋσῆν, ἀπελθέτωσαν οἱ υἱοὶ Ἰσραὴλ εἰς μέσον τῆς θαλάσσης κατὰ τὸ ξηρόν. 15 καὶ ἐγὼ σκληρυνῶ τὴν καρδίᾱν τοῦ Φαραὼ καὶ τῶν Αἰγυπτίων πάντων, καὶ διώξουσιν ὑμᾶς. τότε ἐπιγνώσονται πάντες οἱ Αἰγύπτιοι ὅτι ἐγώ εἰμι κύριος."

πᾶσαν τὴν νύκτα ἡ θάλασσα ἐγίνετο ξηρά. ὅτε ἀπῆλθον οἱ υἱοὶ Ἰσραὴλ εἰς μέσον τῆς θαλάσσης κατὰ τὸ ξηρόν, 20 ἐδίωξαν αὐτοὺς οἱ Αἰγύπτιοι εἰς τὴν θάλασσαν κατὰ τὸ ξηρόν.

εἶπε δὲ κύριος, "ἐλθέτω τὸ ὕδωρ πάλιν εἰς τὸν ἑαυτοῦ τόπον, καὶ ἀποκτεινάτω τοὺς Αἰγυπτίους."

ἀπέκτεινε οὖν τὸ ὕδωρ τοὺς Αἰγυπτίους πάντας, καὶ ἀπέθανον ἐν τῇ θαλάσσῃ. διὰ τοῦτο ἐχάρησαν λίαν οἱ υἱοὶ 25 Ἰσραὴλ ὅτι ἐληλύθεισαν διὰ τῆς θαλάσσης κατὰ τὸ ξηρὸν ἐν μέσῳ τῶν ὑδάτων.

## 234. VOCABULARY

εἰς μέσον: into the middle
ἐν χειρὶ ὑψηλῇ: with a high hand
ἡμέρᾱ, -ᾱς, ἡ: day
θάλασσα, -ης, ἡ: sea, lake

κατά (καθ' before a vowel with a rough breathing): (with gen.)
    down upon, against, down from; (with acc.) down along,
    through, toward, by, according to
κατὰ τὸ ξηρόν:  by dry land
μέσος, -η, -ον:  middle, in the middle of
νεφέλη, -ης, ἡ:  cloud
νύξ, νυκτός, ἡ:  night
ξηρός, -ά, -όν:  dry
πᾶς, πᾶσα, πᾶν:  all, every
πῦρ, πυρός, τό:  fire
σκληρύνω, σκληρυνῶ, ἐσκλήρυνα, — , — , ἐσκληρύνθην:  I
    harden, make stubborn
στύλος, -ου, ὁ:  pillar
ὕδωρ, ὕδατος, τό:  water
ὑψηλός, -ή, -όν:  high, lofty, proud, haughty
χείρ, χειρός, ἡ:  hand

## 235. THIRD DECLENSION NOUNS

The nouns νύξ, πῦρ, ὕδωρ, and χείρ belong to the third declension.
Their stems end in consonants and may nearly always be discovered
by omitting the -ος from the second inflectional form in the singular.
A fifth inflection form (vocative) will be given in the declensions only
when this form is distinct from the first. (See number 366 and number
367 for first and second declensions.)

| (ἡ) | νύξ | νύκτες |
|---|---|---|
| | νυκτός | νυκτῶν |
| | νυκτί | νυξί |
| | νύκτα | νύκτας |

| (ἡ) | χείρ | χεῖρες |
|---|---|---|
| | χειρός | χειρῶν |
| | χειρί | χερσί |
| | χεῖρα | χεῖρας |

| (τό) | πῦρ | |
|---|---|---|
| | πυρός | |
| | πυρί | No plural in N.T. |
| | πῦρ | |

| (τό) | ὕδωρ | ὕδατα |
|---|---|---|
| | ὕδατος | ὑδάτων |
| | ὕδατι | ὕδασι |
| | ὕδωρ | ὕδατα |

πῦρ and ὕδωρ are neuter and have the same form for both first and
fourth inflectional forms.

Stems of one syllable accent the ultima in the second and third inflectional forms, e.g., νυκτός, χερσί, and πυρί, but ὕδατος.

## 236. THIRD DECLENSION ADJECTIVES

All the adjectives used before this lesson have belonged to the first and second declensions. In number 233 forms of πᾶς, πᾶσα, πᾶν have been introduced. This adjective has its feminine forms in the first declension, but its masculine and neuter forms in the third declension. (See number 380 for first and second declension adjectives.)

| Masculine | Feminine | Neuter |
|---|---|---|
| πᾶς | πᾶσα | πᾶν |
| παντός | πάσης | παντός |
| παντί | πάσῃ | παντί |
| πάντα | πᾶσαν | πᾶν |
| πάντες | πᾶσαι | πάντα |
| πάντων | πασῶν | πάντων |
| πᾶσι | πάσαις | πᾶσι |
| πάντας | πάσᾱς | πάντα |

## 237. ACCUSATIVE OF EXTENT OF TIME

The accusative may in a fitting context indicate a period of time throughout which some action occurs or some situation continues.

ὁ θεὸς ἦγε αὐτοὺς *τὴν ἡμέρᾱν*.
God was leading them *throughout the day (all day long)*.

## 238. GENITIVE OF TIME

The genitive may in a fitting context indicate a period of time within the limits of which some action occurs or some situation exists. This construction does not, however, carry the idea of duration as the accusative does.

*νυκτὸς* οὐκ ἀπῆλθεν ὁ στύλος τοῦ πυρός.
The pillar of fire did not go away *at night (within the limits of the night)*.

## 239. GENITIVE OF MATERIAL OR CONTENT

In the phrase ἐν στύλῳ *νεφέλης* and ἐν στύλῳ *πυρός* the italicized words tell us the materials from which the pillars were made. For that reason this construction is known as the genitive of material or content.

## 240. EXERCISES

a. Translate number 233.

b. Select an adjective in column 2 to agree with every noun in column 1.

Column 1

Column 2

| | | |
|---|---|---|
| 1) νυκτί | α) ὑψηλούς | 1. ( ) |
| 2) ἡμέραι | β) μέσου | 2. ( ) |
| 3) νεφέλᾱς | γ) κακῆς | 3. ( ) |
| 4) χεῖρας | δ) ὑψηλήν | 4. ( ) |
| 5) λαός | ε) πάσῃ | 5. ( ) |
| 6) πυρός | ζ) πρεσβύτεροι | 6. ( ) |
| 7) ὑδάτων | η) ὑψηλαῖς | 7. ( ) |
| 8) νεφέλαις | θ) ἰδίᾱς | 8. ( ) |
| 9) καρδίαις | ι) πρῶτος | 9. ( ) |
| 10) νεφελῶν | κ) ὑψηλαί | 10. ( ) |
| 11) στύλῳ | λ) τούτων | 11. ( ) |
| 12) νεφέλῃ | μ) μέσαις | 12. ( ) |
| | ν) ὑψηλῷ | |
| | ξ) πάντας | |
| | ο) ξηρᾷ | |
| | π) καλαί | |
| | ρ) πάσᾱς | |
| | ς) ἄλλων | |

c. Translate the sentences and give the case usage of the italicized words.

1) μὴ σκληρύνου τὴν κακὴν καρδίᾱν τὴν *νύκτα* *πᾶσαν*.
2) σκληρυνεῖ ὁ κύριος τὰς ὑψηλὰς καρδίᾱς τῶν κακῶν *νυκτί*.
3) ὁ 'Ιωσὴφ ἔμενεν ἐν τῇ Αἰγύπτῳ ἑπτὰ ἔτη.
4) ταύτης τῆς *ἡμερᾱς* φάγεται ἄρτον καὶ πίεται ὕδωρ.
5) οὐκ ἔβλεψας ἡμᾶς ἐκείνης τῆς *νυκτός*.
6) *νυκτὸς* ἡμᾶς ἐπιγνώσονται;
7) ἐπεγνώσθητε τῆς *νυκτός*;
8) ἐλθέ, Αἰγύπτιε, εἰς τὴν θάλασσαν, εἰς *μέσον* τῶν ὑδάτων, καὶ ἀπόθανε ταύτῃ τῇ *νυκτί*.

d. Associate each of the following English words with Greek words introduced in this lesson.

1) *nephel*ometer: a device for measuring the *cloudiness* of a liquid.
2) *nyct*alopia: *night* blindness, an inability to see well except in strong light.
3) *Pan*demonium: where *all* demons dwell, John Milton's capital of Hell.

4) *scler*oderma: a disease in which the skin is *hardened*.

5) Simeon *Sty*lites:   Simeon who lived at the top of a *pillar*.

6) *hydro*electric:   related to the production of electricity by the use of *water*.

7) *chir*ography:   *hand*writing.

e. Read the Greek aloud and then translate:

1) λέγει αὐτοῖς, Ἔρχεσθε καὶ ὄψεσθε (you will see). ἦλθαν οὖν καὶ εἶδαν (they saw) ποῦ μένει, καὶ παρ' αὐτῷ ἔμειναν τὴν ἡμέραν ἐκείνην . . . .

2) . . . καὶ εἶπαν, Δέσποτα (Lord), σὺ ὁ ποιήσας (who have made) τὸν οὐρανὸν (heaven) καὶ τὴν γῆν καὶ τὴν θάλασσαν καὶ πάντα τά (that are) ἐν αὐτοῖς . . . .

3) Τί οὖν ἐροῦμεν πρὸς ταῦτα; εἰ ὁ θεὸς ὑπέρ (for) ἡμῶν, τίς καθ' ἡμῶν;

4) γράψω τῇ ἰδίᾳ μου χειρί.

The sources of these excerpts are listed on page 246.

# Lesson 31

## 241. EAT A MAN!

ἡμέρᾳ τινὶ πάλαι διὰ τὸν Ἰησοῦν ἔφαγον ἄρτους καὶ
ὀψάρια πεντακισχίλιοι. μετὰ τὸ δεῖπνον ἐκεῖνο πάντας ἀπέστειλεν ὁ διδάσκαλος. ἤθελε γὰρ προσεύχεσθαι τῷ θεῷ μόνος
ἐκείνῃ τῇ νυκτί. μαρκὸν χρόνον προσηύξατο καὶ τότε πέραν
τῆς θαλάσσης ἀπῆλθεν. αὔριον δὲ ὁ ὄχλος ἔβλεψεν Ἰησοῦν 5
διδάσκοντα ἐν συναγωγῇ ἐν Καφαρναούμ.
"πῶς ἦλθες ὧδε;" εἶπεν τις τοῦ ὄχλου.
ἀπεκρίθη δὲ ὁ Ἰησοῦς, "ὅτι ἐφάγετε τὸν ἄρτον τὸν
μένοντα χρόνον μικρόν, ἐληλύθατε πρός ἐμὲ σήμερον. θέλετε
τὸν ἄρτον τὸν αἰώνιον;" 10
τότε οὖν ἀπεκρίθη τις ἄλλος τοῦ ὄχλου, "θέλομεν σχεῖν
τοῦτον τὸν αἰώνιον ἄρτον."
ἀπεκρίθη οὖν ὁ Ἰησοῦς, "ὁ αἰώνιος ἄρτος ἐστὶν ὁ
καταβαίνων ἐκ τοῦ οὐρανοῦ. οὗτός ἐστιν ὁ ἄρτος ὁ ἀληθινός.
οὗτος ὁ ἄρτος οἴσει τὴν ζωὴν τὴν αἰώνιον τῷ ἐσθίοντι αὐτόν. 15
καὶ ἐγώ εἰμι ὁ ἄρτος ὁ καταβαίνων ἐκ τοῦ οὐρανοῦ. ὁ δὲ
ἐσθίων ἐμὲ ἔχει τὴν ζωὴν τὴν μένουσαν."
ἀπεκρίθη δὲ ὁ ὄχλος, "πῶς ἰσχύσομεν ἐσθίειν σέ;"
ἀπεκρίθη οὖν ὁ Ἰησοῦς, "ὁ πιστεύων εἰς ἐμὲ ἐσθίει τοῦτον
τὸν ἄρτον τὸν ἀληθινόν, καὶ ὁ πιστεύων εἰς ἐμὲ ἕξει τὴν ζωὴν 20
τὴν ἀληθινήν."
οὕτως εἶπεν ὁ Ἰησοῦς πρὸς τὸν ὄχλον ἐν συναγωγῇ ἐν
Καφαρναούμ. τότε οὖν ἐπίστευσάν τινες αὐτῶν, ἄλλοι δὲ
ἀπῆλθον ὅτι αἱ καρδίαι ἐσκληρύνθησαν.

## 242. VOCABULARY

αἰώνιος, -ᾱ (but distinct fem. endings are rarely used, -ος, -ου, etc.,
    being usually found in forms agreeing with fem. nouns),
    -ον: eternal, everlasting
ἀληθινός, -ή, -όν: true, genuine (as opposed to spurious), real
ἀποκρίνομαι, — , ἀπεκρινάμην (rare), — , ἀπεκρίθην (frequent): I
    answer
ζωή, -ῆς, ἡ: life

καταβαίνω, καταβήσομαι, κατέβην (conjugation to be given in number 257), καταβέβηκα, — , — : I go down, come down, descend

Καφαρναούμ (indecl.), ἡ: Capernaum

μόνος, -η, -ον: alone, only

οὐρανός, -οῦ, ὁ: heaven

ὄχλος, -ου, ὁ: crowd, multitude, throng

πεντακισχίλιοι, -αι, -α: five thousand

πέραν: (with gen.) beyond, across, on the other side of

προσεύχομαι, προσεύξομαι, προσηυξάμην, — , — : I pray

## 243. THE PARTICIPLE: ITS FUNCTION

In number 241 participles have been used several times.

ὁ ὄχλος ἔβλεψεν ᾽Ιησοῦν *διδάσκοντα* ἐν συναγωγῇ ἐν Καφαρναούμ.
The crowd saw Jesus *teaching* in a synagogue in Capernaum.

ἐφάγετε τὸν ἄρτον τὸν *μένοντα* χρόνον μικρόν.
You ate the bread *which was lasting* a little time, (literally) *the lasting* a little time.

ὁ αἰώνιος ἄρτος ἐστὶν ὁ *καταβαίνων* ἐκ τοῦ οὐρανοῦ.
The lasting bread is *that which comes down* out of heaven, (literally) *the* (bread) *coming down* out of heaven.

οὗτος ὁ ἄρτος οἴσει τὴν ζωὴν τῷ *ἐσθίοντι* αὐτόν.
This bread will bring life *to the one who eats* it, (literally) *to the* (man) *eating* it.

A participle functions both as an adjective and as a verb. As an *adjective*, it modifies a noun or pronoun. In the following example μενῶν stands in attributive position (number 107).

ὁ ἄρτος ὁ *μενῶν* . . .
The bread *which will last* . . . , (literally) the bread *the being about to last.*

As a *verb*, a participle of a transitive verb, for example, can have a direct object, an indirect object, and adverbial modifiers.

. . . τῷ ἐσθίοντι *τοῦτον τὸν ἄρτον.*
. . . to the one who eats *this bread.* (direct object)

ὁ καταβαίνων *ἐκ τοῦ οὐρανοῦ* . . .
He who comes down *out of heaven* . . . (adverbial phrase)

Like other adjectives (see number 109) a participle may serve as a *noun.*

ὁ πιστεύων εἰς ἐμὲ ἕξει τὴν ζωὴν τὴν αἰώνιον.
He who believes, (literally) the believing (man), in me will have everlasting life.

Other functions of the participle will be explained later.

## 244. PRESENT ACTIVE PARTICIPLE

| Masculine | Feminine | Neuter |
|---|---|---|
| πιστεύων | πιστεύουσα | πιστεῦον |
| πιστεύοντος | πιστευούσης | πιστεύοντος |
| πιστεύοντι | πιστευούσῃ | πιστεύοντι |
| πιστεύοντα | πιστεύουσαν | πιστεῦον |
| | | |
| πιστεύοντες | πιστεύουσαι | πιστεύοντα |
| πιστευόντων | πιστευουσῶν | πιστευόντων |
| πιστεύουσι | πιστευούσαις | πιστεύουσι |
| πιστεύοντας | πιστεύσᾱς | πιστεύοντα |

The masculine and neuter forms belong to the third declension whereas the feminine forms belong to the first. The forms πιστεύουσι (masc. and neut.) represent a change from πιστεύοντσι (cf. ὤν number 297).

## 245. FUTURE ACTIVE PARTICIPLE

The future active participle of most verbs studied thus far differs from the present active participle as the future active indicative differs from the present active indicative.

| πιστεύω | πιστεύσω | πιστεύων | πιστεύσων |
|---|---|---|---|
| I believe | I shall believe | believing | being about to believe |
| μένω | μενῶ | μένων | μενῶν |
| I remain | I shall remain | remaining | being about to remain |
| διδάσκω | διδάξω | διδάσκων | διδάξων |
| I teach | I shall teach | teaching | being about to teach |

Future Active Participle of πιστεύω

| πιστεύσων | πιστεύσουσα | πιστεῦσον |
|---|---|---|
| πιστεύσοντος | πιστευσούσης | πιστεύσοντος |
| πιστεύσοντι | πιστευσούσῃ | πιστεύσοντι |
| πιστεύσοντα | πιστεύσουσαν | πιστεῦσον |
| | | |
| πιστεύσοντες | πιστεύσουσαι | πιστεύσοντα |
| πιστευσόντων | πιστευσουσῶν | πιστευσόντων |
| πιστεύσουσι | πιστευσούσαις | πιστεύσουσι |
| πιστεύσοντας | πιστευσούσᾱς | πιστεύσοντα |

### Future Active Participle of μένω

| | | |
|---|---|---|
| μενῶν | μενοῦσα | μενοῦν |
| μενοῦντος | μενούσης | μενοῦντος |
| μενοῦντι | μενούσῃ | μενοῦντι |
| μενοῦντα | μενοῦσαν | μενοῦν |
| μενοῦντες | μενοῦσαι | μενοῦντα |
| μενούντων | μενουσῶν | μενούντων |
| μενοῦσι | μενούσαις | μενοῦσι |
| μενοῦντας | μενού σᾶς | μενοῦντα |

Liquid verbs and other nasal verbs besides μένω have future active participles like μενῶν.

## 246. EXERCISES

a. Translate number 241.

b. After studying the examples in number 243, translate the following expressions.

1) ὁ διδάσκαλος ὁ διδάσκων τὰ τέκνα ἔσται μόνος ἐν Καφαρναούμ.
2) ὁ ἀδελφὸς τοῦ ἀληθινοῦ ἀγγέλου τοῦ σκληροῦντος τὴν καρδίαν αὐτοῦ. . . .
3) ἐροῦμεν ταῖς ἀδελφαῖς ταῖς ἐπιγινωσκούσαις τὴν ἀλήθειαν.
4) συνηγάγετε τοὺς γεωργοὺς τοὺς θύοντας τὰ ἀρνία.
5) ὁ καταβαίνων ἐκ τῶν νεφελῶν ἦν ὁ μόνος βασιλεύς.
6) ἐν τῷ ἄρτῳ τῷ καταβαίνοντι ἐκ τοῦ οὐρανοῦ ζωή ἐστιν.
7) ἡ ζωὴ ἡ μενοῦσα ἔσται τοῖς ἐσθίουσι τὸν ἀλήθινον ἄρτον.
8) ὁ μόνος ἐν Καφαρναοὺμ ἦν ὁ διδάξων πέραν τῆς θαλάσσης.
9) οἱ ἐσθίοντες ἦσαν πεντακισχίλιοι, αὐτῶν δὲ μόνον οἱ πιστεύοντες προσηύξαντο.
10) ἡ μενοῦσα πέραν τῆς κώμης ἐν Καφαρναοὺμ προσεύξεται τῷ θεῷ ἐν τῷ οὐρανῷ περὶ τῶν πεντακισχιλίων.
11) πέραν τῆς θαλάσσης ἤγαγεν ὁ ὄχλος τῶν πεντακισχιλίων τὸν διδάσκαλον τὸν μένοντα ἐν τῇ συναγωγῇ ἐν Καφαρναούμ.

c. Translate the English in parentheses so as to fit the Greek that is given. Use participles for all the verbal ideas.

1) (A hardening) θεός.
2) θεὸς (hardening hearts).
3) ὁ θεὸς (who hardens hearts).
4) μήτηρ (who is about to teach).

147

5) μήτηρ (who will teach).
6) τέκνου (remaining).
7) τέκνου (who remains).
8) τέκνῳ (who will remain in heaven).
9) τέκνοις (who will remain in heaven).
10) ἀπὸ πεντακισχιλίων μητρῶν (who eat).
11) πεντακισχιλίοις τέκνοις (who will believe).
12) ἐν πεντακισχιλίοις ἀνθρώποις (who will teach).

d. Read the Greek aloud and then translate:

1) ὁ πιστεύων εἰς τὸν υἱὸν ἔχει ζωὴν αἰώνιον· ὁ δὲ ἀπειθῶν (but the one who disobeys) τῷ υἱῷ οὐκ ὄψεται (will not see) ζωήν, ἀλλ᾽ ἡ ὀργὴ (wrath) τοῦ θεοῦ μένει ἐπ᾽ αὐτόν.
2) . . . καὶ ἐσμὲν ἐν τῷ ἀληθινῷ, ἐν τῷ υἱῷ αὐτοῦ Ἰησοῦ Χριστῷ. οὗτός ἐστιν ὁ ἀληθινὸς θεὸς καὶ ζωὴ αἰώνιος.
3) ἀπεκρίθη Ἰησοῦς καὶ εἶπεν αὐτῷ, Σὺ εἶ ὁ διδάσκαλος τοῦ Ἰσραὴλ καὶ ταῦτα οὐ γινώσκεις (do you not know);

The sources of these excerpts are listed on page 246.

# Lesson 32

## 247. CALEB AND JOSHUA

μακρὸν χρόνον ἐν τῇ ἐρήμῳ Μωϋσῆς ἦγε τοὺς υἱοὺς Ἰσραήλ. οὗτοι γὰρ οἱ ἐλθόντες διὰ τῆς θαλάσσης κατὰ τὸ ξηρὸν ἔμειναν ἐν τῇ ἐρήμῳ ἔτη καὶ ἐκεῖ τὸν νόμον ἔλαβον.

ὁ θεὸς ὁ γράψας τοῦτον τὸν νόμον ἐπὶ δύσι λίθοις εἶπε τῷ Μωϋσεῖ διδάσκειν τὸν λαὸν τὸν νόμον. ἀλλ' οὗτος ὁ λαὸς ὁ   5
εἰπὼν ὅτι πείσονται τῷ νόμῳ τοῦ θεοῦ οὐκ ἴσχυον. διὰ τοῦτο ἀπέθανον ἐκεῖ ἐν τῇ ἐρήμῳ. μόνοι οὖν δύο τῶν ἐλθόντων ἐκ τῆς Αἰγύπτου, Ἰησοῦς καὶ Χαλεβ, εἰς τὴν γῆν τῆς Χανάαν ἦλθον. ἐπιγινώσκομεν οὖν τὰ ὀνόματα τῶν δύο εἰπόντων καλὰ περὶ τοῦ θεοῦ καὶ περὶ τῆς Χανάαν. Χαλεβ καὶ Ἰησοῦς, ταῦτά   10
ἐστι τὰ δύο ὀνόματα τῶν ἐλθόντων εἰς τὴν Χανάαν καὶ μεινάντων ἐκεῖ κατὰ τὴν ἐπαγγελίᾱν τοῦ θεοῦ. τόπους ἑαυτοῖς ἐν τῇ γῇ Χανάαν ἔλαβον Χαλεβ καὶ Ἰησοῦς, δύο οἱ πιστεύ-σαντες τῷ κυρίῳ τῷ σωτῆρι ἑαυτῶν. τά οὖν ὀνόματα τούτων δύο μεμένηκεν. ἐπιγνώσῃ δὲ σὺ ὅτι Ἰησοῦς ἐστι καὶ τὸ ὄνομα   15
τοῦ κυρίου ἡμῶν. τοῦτο τὸ ὄνομα ἡμῖν λέγει ὅτι σωτήρ ἐστιν ὁ κύριος.

## 248. VOCABULARY

δύο (nom., gen., acc.), δυσί (dat.):  two
ἔρημος, -ου, ἡ:  desert, wilderness
λίθος, -ου, ὁ:  stone
νόμος, -ου, ὁ:  law
ὄνομα, -ατος, τό:  name
σωτήρ, -τῆρος, ὁ:  savior, deliverer, preserver
Χαλεβ (indecl.), ὁ:  Caleb
Χανάαν (indecl.), ἡ:  Canaan

## 249. MORE THIRD DECLENSION NOUNS: ὁ σωτήρ AND τὸ ὄνομα

| | | | |
|---|---|---|---|
| σωτήρ | σωτῆρες | ὄνομα | ὀνόματα |
| σωτῆρος | σωτήρων | ὀνόματος | ὀνομάτων |
| σωτῆρι | σωτῆρσι | ὀνόματι | ὀνόμασι |
| σωτῆρα | σωτῆρας | ὄνομα | ὀνόματα |

αἷμα, given in number 223, is declined like ὄνομα.

## 250. AORIST ACTIVE PARTICIPLE

(Notice that *no augment* is used.)

### First Aorist

| | | |
|---|---|---|
| πιστεύσᾱς | πιστεύσᾱσα | πιστεῦσαν |
| πιστεύσαντος | πιστευσάσης | πιστεύσαντος |
| πιστεύσαντι | πιστευσάσῃ | πιστεύσαντι |
| πιστεύσαντα | πιστεύσᾱσαν | πιστεῦσαν |
| ειστεύσαντες | πιστεύσᾱσαι | πιστεύσαντα |
| πιστευσάντων | πιστευσᾱσῶν | πιστευσάντων |
| πιστεύσᾱσι | πιστευσάσαις | πιστεύσᾱσι |
| πιστεύσαντας | πιστευσάσᾱς | πιστεύσαντα |

### Second Aorist

| | | |
|---|---|---|
| ελθών | ἐλθοῦσα | ἐλθόν |
| ἐλθόντος | ἐλθούσης | ἐλθόντος |
| ἐλθόντι | ἐλθούσῃ | ἐλθόντι |
| ἐλθόντα | ἐλθοῦσαν | ἐλθόν |
| ἐλθόντες | ἐλθοῦσαι | ἐλθόντα |
| ἐλθόντων | ἐλθουσῶν | ἐλθόντων |
| ἐλθοῦσι | ἐλθούσαις | ἐλθοῦσι |
| ἐλθόντας | ἐλθούσᾱς | ἐλθόντα |

Notice the accent in the second aorist active participle.

### Liquid and Nasal Aorist

| | | |
|---|---|---|
| μείνᾱς | μείνᾱσα | μεῖναν |
| μαίναντος | μεινάσης | μείναντος |
| μείναντι | μεινάσῃ | μείναντι |
| μείναντα | μείνᾱσαν | μεῖναν |
| μείναντες | μείνᾱσαι | μείναντα |
| μεινάντων | μεινᾱσῶν | μεινάντων |
| μείνᾱσι | μεινάσαις | μείνᾱσι |
| μείναντας | μεινάσᾱς | μείναντα |

The endings for liquid and nasal aorist active participles are the same as those for the first aorist minus the -σ-.

## 251. SIGNIFICANCE OF TENSE IN PARTICIPLES

a. *Kind of action.* Tense implies kind of action in participles as in finite forms of verbs.

The present participle indicates linear action.

ὁ λέγων ἐσθίει.
The man who *is speaking* is eating.

The aorist participle indicates punctiliar action.

ὁ εἰπὼν ἐσθίει.
The man who *spoke* is eating.

The perfect participle, which will be introduced later, indicates completed action.

b. *Relative time.* Besides kind of action the tense of a participle indicates time relative to that of the context.

1) Time *previous* to that of the context, when expressed by a participle, is usually indicated by the aorist or perfect.

ὁ εἰπὼν ἐσθίει.
The man who *has spoken* is eating.

ὁ εἰπὼν φάγεται.
The man who *will have spoken* will eat.

ὁ εἰπὼν ἔφαγε.
The man who *had spoken* ate.

2) Time *coincident* with that of the context, when expressed by a participle, is usually indicated by the present but frequently also by the aorist accompanying an aorist indicative

ὁ λέγων ἐσθίει.
The man who *is speaking* is eating.

ὁ λέγων ἤσθιε.
The man who *was speaking* was eating.

ὁ λέγων φάγεται.
The man who *will be speaking* will be eating.

ὁ εἰπὼν ἔφαγεν.
The man who *spoke* ate.

This last example by itself is ambiguous and may be translated, "The man who had spoken ate." A wider context than we have here is needed to establish εἰπών as expressing either previous or coincident time.

3) Time *subsequent* to that of the context, when expressed by a participle, is indicated by the future or the present.

ὁ ἐρῶν ἐσθίει.
The man who *will speak* is eating.

ὁ ἐρῶν αὔριον φάγεται σήμερον.
The man who *will speak* tomorrow will eat today.

ὁ ἐρῶν σήμερον ἔφαγεν ἐχθές.
The man who *was to speak* today ate yesterday.

## 252. COLLECTIVE NOUN IN SINGULAR AS SUBJECT OF A PLURAL VERB

In the sentence ὁ λαὸς πείθεσθαι τῷ νόμῳ οὐκ ἴσχυον, *the people were not able to obey the law*, the subject λαός is singular in form whereas the verb ἴσχυον with which it is used is plural. The reason for this plural verb lies in the fact that the subject λαός is a collective noun comprehending in its meaning many individuals. The plural verb shows that the individuals in the group were unable to obey the law. The construction is not infrequently used.

## 253. NEUTER NOUN IN PLURAL AS SUBJECT OF A SINGULAR VERB

In the sentence τὰ οὖν ὀνόματα τούτων δύο μεμένηκεν, *the names, therefore, of these two have remained*, we have an illustration of a frequent occurrence in the New Testament. Often a neuter plural subject has a singular verb.

## 254. EXERCISES

a. Translate number 247.

b. Give the appropriate form of μείνας, ἐλθών, ἐρῶν, and ἀκούσας to agree with each of the following nouns.

| | |
|---|---|
| 1) λίθῳ | 9) λίθους |
| 2) τὴν Χανάαν | 10) προβάτοις |
| 3) σωτῆρα | 11) ἡ γυνή |
| 4) τοῦ Χαλεβ | 12) προβάτου |
| 5) νόμων | 13) Μαρίᾳ |
| 6) λίθου | 14) νεφέλᾱς |
| 7) ὑπηρέται | 15) ἐρήμῳ |
| 8) τέκνα | 16) λίθοις |

c. Translate.

1) ἐγὼ ὁ βλέπων σε ὧδε ἐν τῇ ἐρήμῳ εἰμὶ Χαλεβ.
2) σὺ ὁ βλέψων ἐμὲ μενεῖς ἐν τῷ οἴκῳ.
3) ἡμεῖς οἱ βλέψαντες Χαλεβ ἦμεν μακάριοι.

d. Translate.

1) The thing that persuaded me was a stone.
2) The woman who taught the children . . .
3) The man who will want to throw stones is Caleb.

e. By combining each item in column 1 with each item in column 2, form nine sentences and translate them.

Column 1          Column 2

1) ὁ λαμβάνων τὸν σωτῆρα 1) βλέπει τὴν ἀλήθειαν ἐν αὐτῷ.
2) ὁ ἕξων τὸν σωτῆρα     2) βλέψει τὴν ἀλήθειαν ἐν αὐτῷ.
3) ὁ σχὼν τὸν σωτῆρα     3) ἔβλεψε τὴν ἀλήθειαν ἐν αὐτῷ.

f. Associate the following English words with the new Greek words in this lesson.

    1) *litho*graphy: printing by the use of *stone*.
    2) astro*nomy*: the *laws* of the stars, the body of knowledge about the stars.
    3) *onomato*poeia: making a *name* to imitate a sound.
    4) *soter*iology: that division of theology which deals with Jesus Christ as *Savior*.

g. Read the Greek aloud and then translate:

    1) ἀπεκρίθη οὖν αὐτῷ ὁ ὄχλος, Ἡμεῖς ἠκούσαμεν ἐκ τοῦ νόμου ὅτι ὁ Χριστὸς μένει εἰς τὸν αἰῶνα (forever), καὶ πῶς λέγεις σὺ ὅτι δεῖ ὑψωθῆναι (must be lifted up) τὸν υἱὸν τοῦ ἀνθρώπου; τίς ἐστιν οὗτος ὁ υἱὸς τοῦ ἀνθρώπου;

    2) οἱ πατέρες (fathers) ἡμῶν τὸ μάννα (manna) ἔφαγον ἐν τῇ ἐρήμῳ, καθώς (just as) ἐστιν γεγραμμένον, Ἄρτον ἐκ τοῦ οὐρανοῦ ἔδωκεν (he gave) αὐτοῖς φαγεῖν.

    3) ἐγὼ ἐλήλυθα ἐν τῷ ὀνόματι τοῦ πατρός (Father) μου καὶ οὐ λαμβάνετέ με· ἐὰν (if) ἄλλος ἔλθῃ (comes) ἐν τῷ ὀνόματι τῷ ἰδίῳ, ἐκεῖνον λήμψεσθε.

    4) υἱὸς τὸν εἴδιον (i.e., ἴδιον) πατέραν (i.e., πατέρα) φονεύσας καὶ τοὺς νόμους φοβηθείς (because he feared) ἔφυγεν (fled) εἰς ἐρημίαν (desert).

The sources of these excerpts are listed on page 246.

# Lesson 33

## 255. STIRRING WORDS FROM AN OLD SOLDIER

ἀγαγὼν τοὺς υἱοὺς Ἰσραὴλ πέραν τοῦ Ἰορδάνου εἰς τὴν
Χανάαν καὶ σχὼν τὴν γῆν Χανάαν, ὁ Ἰησοῦς δοῦλος κυρίου
συνήγαγε πάντας τοὺς υἱούς τοῦ Ἰσραήλ.

καὶ πρὸς τὸν λαὸν εἶπεν Ἰησοῦς, "ταῦτα λέγει κύριος ὁ
θεός, Ἰσραήλ, 'πάλαι ἐν γῇ μακρᾷ οἱ πατέρες ὑμῶν οὐκ      5
ἐλάτρευσαν ἐμοί. καὶ εἰληφὼς τὸν πατέρα ὑμῶν τὸν Αβραμ ἐκ
τῆς γῆς ἐκείνης, ἤγαγον αὐτὸν εἰς ταύτην τὴν γῆν. ἀλλὰ τότε
ταύτην τὴν γῆν αὐτῷ οὐκ ἔδωκα. υἱὸν δὲ αὐτῷ ἔδωκα, καὶ τῷ
υἱῷ τούτῳ ἔδωκα τὸν Ἰακὼβ καὶ τὸν ἀδελφόν. καὶ Ἰακὼβ καὶ
οἱ υἱοὶ αὐτοῦ κατέβησαν εἰς Αἴγυπτον, καὶ ἐγένοντο ἐκεῖ      10
ἔθνος. ἀλλ' ἐγένοντο δοῦλοι τῶν Αἰγυπτίων. καὶ ἐπεὶ ἐγένοντο
αἱ πληγαὶ ἐν τῇ Αἰγύπτῳ, ἤγαγον τοὺς πατέρας ὑμῶν ἐκ τῆς
γῆς. καὶ ὑμεῖς ἐβλέψατε τὰς τοῦ κυρίου πληγὰς ἐν τῇ γῇ
Αἰγύπτῳ, καὶ ἦτε ἐν τῇ ἐρήμῳ χρόνον μακρόν.'

"ἐγὼ ἤγαγον ὑμᾶς διὰ τοῦ Ἰορδάνου, καὶ ἔδωκε ταύτην      15
τὴν γῆν κύριος ὑμῖν. καὶ νῦν λατρεύσατε τῷ κυρίῳ. μὴ δὲ
θέλοντες λατρεύειν κυρίῳ, τίνι λατρεύσετε; τοῖς θεοῖς τῶν
πατέρων ὑμῶν, τοῖς ἐν τῇ μακρᾷ γῇ ἐκείνῃ λατρεύσετε; ἢ τοῖς
θεοῖς τῶν ἐχθρῶν ἐν ταύτῃ τῇ γῇ λατρεύσετε; ἐγὼ δὲ καὶ ὁ
οἰκός μου λατρεύσομεν κυρίῳ."      20

καὶ ὁ λαὸς εἶπε, "κύριος ὁ θεὸς ἡμῶν αὐτὸς θεός ἐστιν.
αὐτὸς ἤγαγεν ἡμᾶς καὶ τοὺς πατέρας ἡμῶν ἐξ Αἰγύπτου,
ἔβαλεν ἐκ τῆς γῆς ἡμῶν κύριος πάντα τὰ ἔθνη τὰ μεμενηκότα
ὧδε, καὶ ἔδωκε ἡμῖν τὴν γῆν. ἡμεῖς καὶ λατρεύσομεν κυρίῳ,
οὗτος γὰρ θεὸς ἡμῶν ἐστι."      25

## 256. VOCABULARY

ἔδωκα (aor. indic. act. first sing. δίδωμι: I give): I gave, have given
ἔδωκε (third sing. of ἔδωκα): he gave, has given
ἔθνος, -ους, τό: nation, people; (pl.) nations, Gentiles
λατρεύω, λατρεύσω, ἐλάτρευσα, — , — , — : I serve, worship (with
    dat. dir. obj.)

154

## 257. MI AORIST: καταβαίνω AND ἐπιγινώσκω

The aorist actives of καταβαίνω and ἐπιγινώσκω are classified with those of verbs whose first principal part ends in -μι. These verbs will be studied later.

### καταβαίνω

#### Indicative

| | |
|---|---|
| κατέβην | κατέβημεν |
| κατέβης | κατέβητε |
| κατέβη | κατέβησαν |

#### Imperative

| | |
|---|---|
| κατάβηθι | κατάβατε |
| καταβάτω | καταβάτωσαν |

#### Infinitive

καταβῆναι

#### Participle

| | | |
|---|---|---|
| καταβάς | καταβᾶσα | καταβάν |
| καταβάντος | καταβάσης | καταβάντος |
| καταβάντι | καταβάσῃ | καταβάντι |
| etc. | etc. | etc. |

### ἐπιγινώσκω

#### Indicative

| | |
|---|---|
| ἐπέγνων | ἐπέγνωμεν |
| ἐπέγνως | ἐπέγνωτε |
| ἐπέγνω | ἐπέγνωσαν |

#### Imperative

| | |
|---|---|
| ἐπίγνωθι | ἐπιγνῶτε |
| ἐπιγνώτω | ἐπιγνώτωσαν |

#### Infinitive

ἐπιγνῶναι

#### Participle

| | | |
|---|---|---|
| ἐπιγνούς | ἐπιγνοῦσα | ἐπιγνόν |
| ἐπιγνόντος | ἐπιγνούσης | ἐπιγνόντος |
| ἐπιγνόντι | ἐπιγνούσῃ | ἐπιγνόντι |
| etc. | etc. | etc. |

## 258. OTHER THIRD DECLENSION NOUNS: ὁ πατήρ AND τὸ ἔθνος

| | | | |
|---|---|---|---|
| πατήρ | πατέρες | ἔθνος | ἔθνη |
| πατρός | πατέρων | ἔθνους | ἐθνῶν |
| πατρί | πατράσι | ἔθνει | ἔθνεσι |
| πατέρα | πατέρας | ἔθνος | ἔθνη |
| πάτερ | | | |

ἔτος introduced in number 171 by the form ἔτη is declined like ἔθνος.

Notice the three grades of the last stem vowel in πατήρ, πατέρα, and πατρός: -η-, -ε-, and no vowel at all. We have a distinct vocative in the singular of this noun.

## 259. PERFECT ACTIVE PARTICIPLES

### First Perfect: πιστεύω

| | | |
|---|---|---|
| πεπιστευκώς | πεπιστευκυῖα | πεπιστευκός |
| πεπιστευκότος | πεπιστευκυίᾱς | πεπιστευκότος |
| πεπιστευκότι | πεπιστευκυίᾳ | πεπιστευκότι |
| πεπιστευκότα | πεπιστευκυῖαν | πεπιστευκός |
| πεπιστευκότες | πεπιστευκυῖαι | πεπιστευκότα |
| πεπιστευκότων | πεπιστευκυιῶν | πεπιστευκότων |
| πεπιστευκόσι | πεπιστευκυίαις | πεπιστευκόσι |
| πεπιστευκότας | πεπιστευκυίᾱς | πεπιστευκότα |

### Second Perfect: λαμβάνω

| | | |
|---|---|---|
| εἰληφώς | εἰληφυῖα | εἰληφός |
| εἰληφότος | εἰληφυίᾱς | εἰληφότος |
| εἰληφότι | εἰληφυίᾳ | εἰληφότι |
| εἰληφότα | εἰληφυῖαν | εἰληφός |
| εἰληφότες | εἰληφυῖαι | εἰληφότα |
| εἰληφότων | εἰληφυιῶν | εἰληφότων |
| εἰληφόσι | εἰληφυίαις | εἰληφόσι |
| εἰληφότας | εἰληφυίᾱς | εἰληφότα |

## 260. RÉSUMÉ OF ADJECTIVAL AND SUBSTANTIVAL EMPHASES OF PARTICIPLES

We have met in the last lessons participles used with an emphasis on the adjectival or substantival function.

ὁ λέγων ἄνθρωπος ἐσθίει.
The *speaking* man is eating.

ὁ εἰρηκὼς ἄνθρωπος ἐσθίει.
The *having-spoken* man is eating.

ὁ λέγων ἐσθίει.
The one who *speaks* is eating.

ὁ εἰρηκὼς ἐσθίει.
The one who *has spoken* is eating.

In the first two sentences λέγων and εἰρηκώς are used as adjectives modifying ἄνθρωπος; in the second two sentences λέγων and εἰρηκώς are used as substantives or nouns. The participles in both ὁ λέγων ἄνθρωπος and ὁ ἄνθρωπος ὁ λέγων are in attributive position.

## 261. ADVERBIAL EMPHASIS

Participles may be used in predicate position as well as in attributive position. Since no article is used with ἄνθρωπος in the following example, εἰρηκώς may be considered either attributive or predicate.

εἰρηκὼς ἄνθρωπος ἐσθίει. (attributive use assumed)
A having-spoken man is eating, (or) a man who has spoken is eating.

Understood this way, εἰρηκώς has an adjectival emphasis, but another interpretation is possible when an adverbial emphasis is understood.

εἰρηκὼς ἄνθρωπος ἐσθίει. (predicate use assumed)
Having spoken, a man eats.

But this ambiguity of interpretation immediately disappears when a definite article is used with ἄνθρωπος. Now εἰρηκώς is inevitably in predicate position.

εἰρηκὼς ὁ ἄνθρωπος ἐσθίει.
Having spoken, the man eats.

This may mean any one of several things, but in all of them the participle has an adverbial emphasis.

After he has spoken, the man eats. (He performs one action after the other.)

Although he has spoken, the man eats. (In spite of his having threatened not to eat, he eats anyway.)

Because he has spoken, the man eats. (He earns his living by public speaking.)

If he has spoken, the man eats. (His livelihood is dependent on his speaking.)

All of these various interpretations are merely deductions from imagined contexts, which are not given here. Still εἰρηκώς by itself means having spoken, and *this is all the Greek says*. The rest of the ideas suggested are legitimately expressed in a translation when the contexts justify them, not otherwise.

A participle with adverbial emphasis may be used in a context implying the following ideas listed in the order of the probable frequency of their occurrence: time, cause, attendant circumstance, condition, concession, manner, means, and purpose. These ideas applied to λέγων ὁ ἄνθρωπος ἐσθίει yield the following phrasings for λέγων.

a. Time:  While he speaks . . .
(εἰπών would mean "After he has spoken . . ."

b. Cause:  Because he speaks . . .

c. Attendant circumstance:  The man speaks and (eats).

d. Condition:  If he speaks . . .

e. Concession:  Although he speaks . . .

f. Manner:  In speaking . . .
By way of speaking . . .
(Such an interpretation is nonsense here.)

g. Means:  By means of speaking . . .

h. Purpose:  In order to speak . . . (a rather infrequent use)

## 262. EXERCISES

a. Translate number 255.

b. Translate literally and then more freely, using devices listed in number 261 for each indicated emphasis.

1) (Time) δουλεύουσα ἐν τῷ οἴκῳ ἤκουσε τοῦ πρεσβυτέρου.
2) (Time) δουλεύσασα ἐν τῷ οἴκῳ ἤκουσε τοῦ πρεσβυτέρου.
3) (Cause) τεθεραπευκότες ἐλάβετε δωρεὰς ἐκ τῶν ἐθνῶν.
4) (Attendant circumstance) ἐλθὼν εἰς τὸν οἶκον ὁ δοῦλος ἤνεγκε τὸ δεῖπνον τῷ κυρίῳ.
5) (Condition) μεμενηκυῖαι ἐν τῇ ἀληθείᾳ ἐπιγνώσονται τὸν θεόν.
6) (Manner) ἐλπίζων, μνημονεύει τῆς ἐπαγγελίας.
7) (Means) διδάσκοντες τὴν ἀλήθειαν ἐλπίζομεν πείθειν τὰ ἔθνη.
8) (Purpose) ὁ ὄχλος ἀπῆλθε πέραν τῆς θαλάσσης βλέψων τὸν διδάσκαλον.

c. Translate the following sentences. Notice that the sentence patterns are simple and that the Greek participles are usually more compact than the English needed to convey the meaning of the participles.

1) τίσι δωρεὰς οἴσετε πέραν τῆς θαλάσσης;
2) τίσι δύο δωρεὰς μενούσᾱς (pres.) οἴσετε;
3) τίσι τὰς δωρεὰς τὰς μενούσᾱς (fut.) πάντοτε οἴσετε;
4) τίσι τὰς δωρεὰς τὰς μεμενηκυίᾱς ὧδε χρόνον μακρὸν οἴσετε;
5) τίσι ἔχουσι τὸ ἀργύριον οἴσετε δωρεάς;
6) τίσι σχοῦσι τὸ ἀργύριον οἴσεις δωρεάς;
7) τίσι ἐσχηκυίαις τὸ ἀργύριον οἴσεις τὰς δωρεὰς τὰς μεινάσᾱς ἐν τούτῳ τῷ οἴκῳ;
8) τινῶν τὰ τέκνα βλέπομεν;
9) τὰ τέκνα τινῶν ἀνθρώπων ἐπιγνόντων τὴν ἀλήθειαν βλέπομεν;
10) τινῶν τὰ τέκνα τὰ σκληρύνοντα τὰς καρδίᾱς βλέπομεν;
11) τινῶν τὰ τέκνα βλέπομεν καταβαίνοντες ἐκ τῶν Ἱεροσολύμων;
12) τινῶν ἀνθρώπων ἐπιγνόντων τὴν ἀλήθειαν βλέπομεν τὰ σκληρύνοντα τὰς καρδίᾱς τέκνα καταβαίνοντες ἐκ τῶν Ἱεροσολύμων;

d. Make the perfect active participle of each of the verbs in column 2 agree with each of the nouns in column 1.

| Column 1 | Column 2 |
|---|---|
| 1) τοῦ ἔθνους | λέγω |
| 2) ἡ ἡμέρᾱ | πείθω |
| 3) τῷ ὀνόματι | μένω |
| 4) τὴν θάλασσαν | ἔρχομαι |
| 5) τὸν σωτῆρα | λαμβάνω |
| 6) τὰς νεφέλᾱς | θεραπεύω |
| 7) τῇ ζωῇ | |
| 8) αἱ νύκτες | |
| 9) ταῖς χερσί | |
| 10) τῷ πυρί | |
| 11) τὰ ὕδατα | |
| 12) τῶν στύλων | |
| 13) τῇ πληγῇ | |
| 14) τῷ ξηρῷ | |

e. Associate the following English words with new Greek words in this lesson.

1) *ethno*logy: study of *racial* divisions of mankind.
2) ido*latry*: *worship* of an image.

f. Read the Greek aloud and then translate:

1) . . . καὶ ἠγόρασας (you purchased) τῷ θεῷ ἐν τῷ αἵματί σου ἐκ πάσης φυλῆς (tribe) καὶ γλώσσης καὶ λαοῦ καὶ ἔθνους,

καὶ ἐποίησας (you made) αὐτοὺς τῷ θεῷ ἡμῶν βασιλείαν (a kingdom) καὶ ἱερεῖς (priests), καὶ βασιλεύσουσιν (they will reign) ἐπὶ τῆς γῆς.

2) ... καὶ ὁ θρόνος (throne) τοῦ θεοῦ καὶ τοῦ ἀρνίου ἐν αὐτῇ ἔσται, καὶ οἱ δοῦλοι αὐτοῦ λατρεύσουσιν αὐτῷ ...

The sources of these excerpts are listed on page 247.

# Lesson 34

### 263. A NEW GENERATION THAT KNEW NOT THE LORD

καὶ ἐδούλευσεν ὁ λαὸς τῷ κυρίῳ πάσᾱς τὰς ἡμέρᾱς Ἰησοῦ
τοῦ δούλου κυρίου καὶ πάσᾱς τὰς ἡμέρᾱς τῶν πρεσβυτέρων
τῶν ἐπιγνόντων πᾶν τὸ ἔργον κυρίου καὶ πῶς ἐσεσώκει τὸν
Ἰσραήλ.

ἐπεὶ δ᾽ ἀπέθανεν Ἰησοῦς ὁ δοῦλος κυρίου καὶ ἀπέθανε 5
πᾶσα ἡ γενεὰ ἐκείνη, οὐκέτι ἐμνημόνευεν ὁ λαὸς τῶν ἔργων
τοῦ κυρίου. καὶ ἐγένοντο οἱ υἱοὶ Ἰσραήλ κακοί, καὶ ἐλάτρευσαν
τοῖς θεοῖς τῶν ἐθνῶν. καὶ ἐγκατέλιπον τὸν κύριον τὸν θεὸν
τῶν πατέρων αὐτῶν τὸν ἀγαγόντα αὐτοὺς ἐκ γῆς Αἰγύπτου, καὶ
ἐδίωξαν τοὺς θεοὺς τῶν ἐθνῶν. 10

ὀργιζόμενος οὖν τοῖς ἔργοις τοῦ Ἰσραήλ, οὐκ ἔσωσεν ὁ
θεὸς αὐτοὺς ἐκ τῶν ἐχθρῶν αὐτῶν. προσευξαμένοις δὲ τῷ θεῷ
διὰ τοὺς ἐχθροὺς αὐτῶν τοῖς υἱοῖς Ἰσραήλ οὐκέτι ὠργίζετο
ἀλλ᾽ ἔδωκεν ὁ θεὸς σωτῆρα κριτὴν σώσοντα Ἰσραήλ ἐκ τῶν
χειρῶν τῶν ἐχθρῶν αὐτῶν, καὶ ἦν κύριος μετὰ τοῦ κριτοῦ. 15
σωζόμενοι οὖν ἦσαν πάσᾱς τὰς ἡμέρᾱς τοῦ κριτοῦ.

ὅτε δ᾽ ἀπέθανεν ὁ κριτής, πάλιν ἐγκατέλειπον τὸν κύριον
τὸν θεὸν τῶν πατέρων αὐτῶν δεώξοντες τοὺς θεοὺς τῶν ἐθνῶν
καὶ λατρεύσοντες αὐτοῖς. πάλιν ὀργιζόμενος τοῖς κακοῖς ἔργοις
οὐκ ἔσωσεν ὁ θεὸς ἐκ τῶν ἐχθρῶν αὐτῶν. 20

### 264. VOCABULARY

γενεά, -ᾶς, ἡ: generation
ἐγκαταλείπω, ἐγκαταλείψω, ἐγκατέλιπον, — , — , ἐγκατελείφθην:
    I abandon, forsake, desert, leave behind
ἔργον, -ου, τό: work, task, deed, action
κριτής, -οῦ, ὁ: judge
ὀργίζομαι, — , — , — , ὠργίσθην: I am provoked to anger, am
    angry (with dat. of person)
σῴζω, σώσω, ἔσωσα, σέσωκα, σέσωσμαι, ἐσώθην: I save, preserve,
    rescue, keep safe

## 265. MIDDLE PARTICIPLES

(Forms ending in -μενος, -μένη, -μενον.)

a. Tenses having middle participles distinct in form from the corresponding passive.

1) Future.

| | | |
|---|---|---|
| πιστευσόμενος | πιστευσομένη | πιστευσόμενον |
| πιστευσομένου | πιστευσομένης | πιστευσομένου |
| etc. | etc. | etc. |

The endings of all middle participles are like those of καλός, καλή, καλόν given in number 106, but the accents are like those of δίκαιος in number 74, except for the perfect in *b.2)* below.

| | | |
|---|---|---|
| ἀποστελούμενος | ἀποστελουμένη | ἀποστελούμενον |

Liquid and nasal stems differ from πιστεύω only in having -ου- instead of -σο-.

2) Aorist.

| | | |
|---|---|---|
| πιστευσάμενος | πιστευσαμένη | πιστευσάμενον |
| πιστευσαμένου | πιστευσαμένης | πιστευσαμένου |
| etc. | etc. | etc. |

Notice again that the aorist participle has *no augment.*

| | | |
|---|---|---|
| ἐντειλάμενος | ἐντειλαμένη | ἐντειλάμενον |

Liquid and nasal stems differ from πιστεύω only in having -α- instead of -σα-.

| | | |
|---|---|---|
| γενόμενος | γενομένη | γενόμενον |

The second aorist middle participle differs from the present (γινόμενος) only in the stem.

b. Tenses having middle participles identical in form with the corresponding passive.

1) Present.

| | | |
|---|---|---|
| πιστευόμενος | πιστευομένη | πιστευόμενον |
| πιστευομένου | πιστευομένης | πιστευομένου |
| etc. | etc. | etc. |

2) Perfect.

| | | |
|---|---|---|
| πεπιστευμένος | πεπιστευμένη | πεπιστευμένον |
| πεπιστευμένου | πεπιστευμένης | πεπιστευμένου |
| etc. | etc. | etc. |

162

The accent *always falls on the penult* in the perfect middle and passive participle.

## 266. A COMPARISION OF THE INDICATIVE AND THE PARTICIPLE IN THE MIDDLE

| Present | πιστεύομαι | I trust myself (middle) |
| | | I am trusted (passive) |
| | πιστευόμενος | trusting oneself (middle) |
| | | being trusted (passive) |
| Future | πιστεύσομαι | I shall trust myself |
| | πιστευσόμενος | being about to trust oneself |
| Aorist | ἐπιστευσάμην | I trusted myself |
| | πιστευσάμενος | having trusted oneself |
| Perfect | πεπίστευμαι | I have trusted myself (middle) |
| | | I have been trusted (passive) |
| | πεπιστευμένος | having trusted myself (middle) |
| | | having been trusted (passive) |

## 267. THE SUPPLEMENTARY PARTICIPLE

a. In periphrastic verbs. In addition to the uses of the participle summarized or explained in lesson 33 we have in number 263 an example of a supplementary use.

*ἦσαν σῳζόμενοι πάσας τὰς ἡμέρας τοῦ κριτοῦ.*
*They were being preserved* all the days of the judge.

The thought could have been expressed by an imperfect passive thus: ἐσῴζοντο. This single word and the longer form, which is called a periphrastic imperfect passive, were both in use at the time the New Testament was written.

The term *supplementary* carries the idea that the participle furnishes what is otherwise lacking in the meaning expressed by the verb.

b. With some verbs indicating sense perception, often equivalent to indirect discourse.

ὁ λαὸς ἤκουσε τοῦ διδασκάλου *λέγοντος* περὶ τῶν ἑαυτοῦ ἔργων.
The people heard the prophet *speaking* about his own deeds.

ὁ μαθητὴς ἀκούει τοὺς ἀνθρώπους *πιστεύσαντας* εἰς Ἰησοῦν.
The disciple hears that the men *believed* on Jesus, (literally) the men *having believed* on Jesus.

It will be observed that ἀκούω is both a verb of sense perception and one capable of introducing indirect discourse.

## 268. EXERCISES

a. Translate number 263.

b. Translate.

1) αὕτη ἡ γενεὰ τῶν υἱῶν τοῦ Ἰσραὴλ ὑπὸ διδασκάλου πειθομένη ἦν ἐγκαταλιπεῖν τὸν ἀληθινὸν θεόν.

2) οὗτος εἴληπται λέγων ταύτῃ τῇ γενεᾷ ὅτι οἱ θεοὶ τῶν ἐθνῶν εἰσι καλοί.

3) ὁ λέγων ταῦτα πείθεται τῷ ἀληθινῷ θεῷ.

4) οὐχί. τῷ ἑαυτῶν κριτῇ τῷ κακῷ ἐπίστευσαν ἐκεῖναι αἱ γενεαί.

5) ἀποκτείνων τὸν ἐχθρὸν ὁ λαὸς χαρήσεται.

c. Locate the following participles by giving (1) tense, (2) voice, (3) gender, (4) number, (5) case, and (6) first principal part.

1) ἀπερχόμενοι        6) γενομένᾱς
2) ἐγκαταλιποῦσι      7) καταβησομένη
3) λατρεύουσι         8) ἄγον
4) ἐγκαταλειψόντων   9) προσευξαμένῳ
5) ὀργιζομένους      10) καταβάντα

d. Select the participles which correctly and most suitably complete the following sentences.

1) ἀκούσομεν ταύτης ⸻.

a) διδάσκοντος
b) διδάσκων
c) διδαξομένη
d) διδασκούσης
e) διδασκομένων

2) ἡ ⸻ τὸ ἑαυτῆς ὄνομα ἀπῆλθεν ἐχθές.

a) γραφομένης
b) γράψᾱσα
c) γράφουσαν
d) γεγραμμένη
e) γράψων

3) ἐβλέψατε τὰ τέκνα ⸻.

a) φαγομένη
b) φαγόν
c) ἐσθίον
d) ἐσθίουσα
e) ἐσθίοντα

164

4) _____ οὐκ ἦν δυνατὸς θεραπεῦσαι τὸν πατέρα.

   a) ἐληλυθώς
   b) ἦλθον
   c) ἐλθόν
   d) ἐρχομένων
   e) ἐλευσομένου

e. Associate the following English words with new Greek words in this lesson.

   1) *genea*logy: a record of *generations*, a family tree.
   2) *erg*: a unit for measuring energy or *work*.
   3) *crit*ic: one given to expressing *judgment*.

f. Read the Greek aloud and then translate.

   1) Τίνι οὖν ὁμοιώσω (shall I compare) τοὺς ἀνθρώπους τῆς γενεᾶς ταύτης, καὶ τίνι εἰσὶν ὅμοιοι (like);
   2) . . . Θεέ μου θεέ μου, ἵνα τί (why) με ἐγκατέλιπες;
   3) ἀπεκρίθη ὁ Ἰησοῦς καὶ εἶπεν αὐτοῖς, Τοῦτό ἐστιν τὸ ἔργον τοῦ θεοῦ, ἵνα πιστεύητε (that you believe) εἰς ὃν (on him whom) ἀπέστειλεν ἐκεῖνος.

The sources of these excerpts are listed on page 247.

## 269. REVIEW

Review thoroughly the vocabulary introduced since lesson 24.

# Lesson 35

## 270. TERROR AT NIGHT

καὶ πάλιν ἐγένετο ὁ λαὸς Ἰσραὴλ κακὸς καὶ ἔδωκεν αὐτοὺς κύριος εἰς χεῖρα Μαδιὰμ ἑπτὰ ἔτη. καὶ προσεύξαντο οἱ υἱοὶ Ἰσραὴλ πρὸς κύριον διὰ Μαδιάμ.

ἐκείνων ἀκουσθέντων, ἔδωκε κύριος κριτὴν Γεδεών. τριακοσίων ἀνδρῶν συναχθέντων κατὰ Μαδιάμ, εἶπε κύριος πρὸς 5
Γεδεών, "ἐν τοῖς τριακοσίοις ἀνδράσι τούτοις σώσω ὑμᾶς, καὶ δώσω τὴν Μαδιὰμ εἰς χεῖρα σοῦ."

καὶ εἶπε Γεδεὼν πρὸς τοὺς τριακοσίους ἄνδρας, "ἔδωκε κύριος εἰς χεῖρα ἡμῶν τὴν παρεμβολὴν Μαδιάμ." καὶ ἔδωκε Γεδεὼν ἑκάστῳ τῶν τριακοσίων ἀνδρῶν κερατίνην καὶ λαμπάδα. 10
καὶ εἶπε πρὸς αὐτούς, "ἐγὼ ἀπελεύσομαι πρὸς τῇ παρεμβολῇ. καὶ σαλπίσω ἐν τῇ κερατίνῃ ἐγώ, καὶ πάντες ὑμεῖς μετ᾽ ἐμοῦ σαλπίσετε ἐν ταῖς κερατίναις περὶ πᾶσαν τὴν παρεμβολήν, καὶ ἐρεῖτε, 'τῷ κυρίῳ καὶ τῷ Γεδεών.'"

καὶ ἀπῆλθον Γεδεὼν καὶ οἱ τριακόσιοι ἄνδρες περὶ τὴν 15
παρεμβολὴν νυκτός. Γεδεὼν δὲ ἐσάλπισεν ἐν τῇ κερατίνῃ, καὶ ἐσάλπισαν πάντες οἱ τριακόσιοι ἄνδρες ἐν ταῖς κερατίναις καὶ ἔλαβον ἐν χερσὶν αὐτῶν τὰς λαμπάδας, καὶ τὰς κερατίνᾱς σαλπίσαντες εἶπον, "τῷ κυρίῳ καὶ τῷ Γεδεών." καὶ πᾶσα ἡ παρεμβολὴ ἔφυγε. καὶ ἐδίωξαν οἱ υἱοὶ Ἰσραὴλ Μαδιὰμ τὸν 20
φεύγοντα. καὶ ἔφυγον οἱ ἐχθροί. ἠκηκόει δὲ Ἰσραὴλ σωθησόμενος ἐν χειρὶ τοῦ Γεδεών, καὶ οὕτως ἐγένετο.

## 271. VOCABULARY

ἀνήρ, ἀνδρός, ὁ: man, husband
Γεδεών (indecl.), ὁ: Gideon
δώσω (fut. indic. act. first sing. δίδωμι: I give): I shall give, will give
  (see number 324)
κερατίνη, -ης, ἡ: trumpet, horn
λαμπάς, λαμπάδος, ἡ: torch, lamp
Μαδιάμ (indecl.), ὁ: Midian
παρεμβολή, -ῆς, ἡ: camp, army

σαλπίζω, σαλπίσω, ἐσάλπισα, — , — , — :  I sound a trumpet, blow
   a trumpet
σχολή, -ῆς, ἡ:  school
τριακόσιοι, -αι, -α:  three hundred
φεύγω, φεύξομαι, ἔφυγον, — , — , — :  I flee from, flee away, take
   flight

## 272. DECLENSIONS OF ὁ ἀνήρ  AND ἡ λαμπάς

| | | | |
|---|---|---|---|
| ἀνήρ | ἄνδρες | λαμπάς | λαμπάδες |
| ἀνδρός | ἀνδρῶν | λαμπάδος | λαμπάδων |
| ἀνδρί | ἀνδράσι | λαμπάδι | λαμπάσι |
| ἄνδρα | ἄνδρας | λαμπάδα | λαμπάδας |
| ἄνερ | | | |

The -δ- in ἀνδρός and similar forms seems to have been substituted
for an -ε- to facilitate pronunciation.

## 273. AORIST PASSIVE PARTICIPLE

### First Passive

| | | |
|---|---|---|
| πιστευθείς | πιστευθεῖσα | πιστευθέν |
| πιστευθέντος | πιστευθείσης | πιστευθέντος |
| πιστευθέντι | πιστευθείσῃ | πιστευθέντι |
| πιστευθέντα | πιστευθεῖσαν | πιστευθέν |
| πιστευθέντες | πιστευθεῖσαι | πιστευθέντα |
| πιστευθέντων | πιστευθεισῶν | πιστευθέντων |
| πιστευθεῖσι | πιστευθείσαις | πιστευθεῖσι |
| πιστευθέντας | πιστευθείσᾱς | πιστευθέντα |

### Second Passive

| | | |
|---|---|---|
| ἀποσταλείς | ἀποσταλεῖσα | ἀποσταλέν |
| ἀποσταλέντος | ἀποσταλείσης | ἀποσταλέντος |
| ἀποσταλέντι | ἀποσταλείσῃ | ἀποσταλέντι |
| ἀποσταλέντα | ἀποσταλεῖσαν | ἀποσταλέν |
| ἀποσταλέντες | ἀποσταλεῖσαι | ἀποσταλέντα |
| ἀποσταλέντων | ἀποσταλεισῶν | ἀποσταλέντων |
| ἀποσταλεῖσι | ἀποσταλείσαις | ἀποσταλεῖσι |
| ἀποσταλέντας | ἀποσταλείσᾱς | ἀποσταλέντα |

It is evident that both first and second aorist passive participles may
be formed from the aorist passive indicative first singular by dropping
the augment and the ending -ην, and by adding the participial
endings -είς, -εῖσα, -έν.

167

## 274. FUTURE PASSIVE PARTICIPLE

### First Passive

πιστευθησόμενος πιστευθησομένη πιστευθησόμενον
  etc.          etc.          etc.

### Second Passive

ἀποσταλησόμενος ἀποσταλησομένη ἀποσταλησόμενον
  etc.          etc.          etc.

## 275. GENITIVE ABSOLUTE

In number 270 two phrases occur which cannot be explained by any constructions given before this lesson.

ἐκείνων ἀκουσθέντων, ἔδωκε κύριος κριτὴν Γεδεών.
*Those having been heard* (or) *because they were heard*, the Lord gave a judge Gideon.

τριακοσίων ἀνδρῶν συναχθέντων κατὰ Μαδιάμ, εἶπε κύριος πρὸς Γεδεών . . . .
*Three hundred men having been gathered together* against Midian (or) *after three hundred men had been gathered together* against Midian, the Lord said to Gideon . . . .

These groups of italicized words are called *genitive absolutes*.

The participles have adverbial emphasis, and the noun and the pronoun with which they agree have by themselves no grammatical construction in the rest of the sentence. Genitive absolutes are generally best translated as adverbial clauses since the group of words in absolute construction is the equivalent of a big adverb.

## 276. EXERCISES

a. Translate number 270.

b. Bearing in mind that the participle in a genitive absolute may ɒe translated in as many different ways as any other adverbial participle (see number 261), translate the following sentences as appropriately as possible.

    1) τῆς πραεμβολῆς διωκομένης ὑπὸ τοῦ Γεδεών, ἔφευγον πάντες οἱ ἐχθροί

    2) πάντων φυγόντων διὰ τὰς κερατίνας, Γεδεὼν ἐχάρη.

    3) τοῦ κριτοῦ ἀποθανόντος, ἐγκατέλιπεν᾽ Ἰσραὴλ τὸν ἀληθινὸν θεόν.

    4) κυρίου ἐγκαταλειφθέντος ὑπὸ τοῦ λαοῦ, ἦλθεν Μαδιὰμ εἰς τὴν γῆν.

5) τούτων τῶν ἀνδρῶν λατρευσόντων κακοῖς ὀργισθήσεται ὁ θεὸς ἡμῶν.

c. Make the aorist passive participle of each of the verbs in column 2 agree with each of the nouns in column 1.

Column 1

1) τοῦ λίθου
2) τὸν λίθον
3) οἱ ἄνδρες
4) τοὺς ἄνδρας
5) τῇ λαμπάδι
6) τὰς λαμπάδας
7) ἡ παρεμβολή
8) ταῖς παρεμβολαῖς
9) τοῖς ἔργοις
10) τὰ ἔργα
11) τὸ ἔργον
12) τῶν ἔργων
13) τῇ γενεᾷ
14) τὴν γενεάν

Column 2

γράφω
ἐπιγινώσκω
ἀποστέλλω
διδάσκω

d. Select the translation most appropriate for each Greek sentence.

1) πιόντες ὕδωρ οὐκ ἐφάγομεν ἄρτον.

α) By having drunk water, we do not eat bread.
β) If we have drunk water, we do not eat bread.
γ) Although we had drunk water, we did not eat bread.
δ) Because we drank water, we shall not eat bread.
ε) In order that we have drunk water, we have not eaten bread.

2) μανθάνουσι τὴν ἀλήθειαν ὑμῖν δουλεύσω ἐν ταύτῃ τῇ σχολῇ.

α) If you have learned the truth, I serve you in this school.
β) While you are learning the truth, I will serve you in this school.
γ) Because you will learn the truth, I serve you in this school.
δ) I served you in this school in order to learn the truth.
ε) I serve although you have learned the truth in this school.

3) ἐλεύσεται εἰς τὴν σχολὴν διδάξων ὑμᾶς τὴν παρρησίαν.

α) He will proceed into the school in order that he may teach you boldness.
β) He will proceed into the school although he was teaching you boldness.

γ) He will proceed into the school when it is about to teach you boldness.

δ) He will proceed into the school if it is about to teach you boldness.

ε) He will proceed into the school after he has taught you boldness.

e. Select the Greek most suitable for translating all the italicized English.

1) The elder brought fish into the village *because he was wishing* to eat them.

α) θελήσων
β) ἠθέλων
γ) θέλων
δ) ἐθελήσᾱς
ε) θέλει

2) *After we have cast* the slave out of the land, we shall rejoice.

α) βεβληκότες
β) βάλλοντες
γ) βαλοῦντες
δ) βεβλήκαμεν
ε) βληθησόμεθα

3) We used to see him *although he used to pursue* his enemies only at night.

α) διώξοντα
β) διώξαντα
γ) ἐδίωκεν
δ) ἐδίωξεν
ε) διώκοντα

4) You believed us at any particular time *if we were speaking* the truth.

α) λέγοντες
β) λεγόντων
γ) λέγουσι
δ) λέγοντας
ε) εἰπόντες

5) Remember us at the moment *when we shall be sending* our sons across the sea.

α) πέμψαντας
β) πεμψάντων

γ) πέμψοντας
δ) πεμπόντων
ε) πέμποντας

f. Read the Greek aloud and then translate:

1) καὶ νῦν πέμψον ἄνδρας εἰς Ἰόππην (Joppa) καὶ μετάπεμψαι (summon) Σίμωνά τινα ὃς (who) ἐπικαλεῖται (is also called) Πέτρος . . . .

2) ἐγώ εἰμι ὁ ἄρτος ὁ ζῶν (living) ὁ ἐκ τοῦ οὐρανοῦ καταβάς · ἐάν (if) τις φάγῃ (eats) ἐκ τούτου τοῦ ἄρτου ζήσει (will live) εἰς τὸν αἰῶνα (forever) · καὶ ὁ ἄρτος δὲ ὃ (which) ἐγὼ δώσω ἡ σάρξ (flesh) μού ἐστιν ὑπὲρ (for the sake of) τῆς τοῦ κόσμου ζωῆς.

The sources of these excerpts are listed on page 247.

# Lesson 36

**277.** A VOICE IN THE NIGHT

καὶ τὸ τέκνον Σαμουὴλ ἦν ὑπηρέτης τοῦ κυρίου μετὰ Ηλι
τοῦ ἱερέως. ἐν νυκτί τινι Ηλι ἐκάθευδεν ἐν τῷ ἑαυτοῦ τόπῳ, καὶ
Σαμουὴλ ἐκάθευδεν ἐν ἄλλῳ τόπῳ. καὶ ἐκάλεσε κύριος,
"Σαμουήλ, Σαμουήλ." καὶ εἶπεν, "ἰδοὺ ἐγώ." καὶ ἔδραμε πρὸς
Ηλι, καὶ εἶπεν, "ἰδοὺ ἐγώ, ὅτι κέκληκας." καὶ εἶπεν, "οὐ     5
κέκληκά σε, ἀνάστρεφε, κάθευδε." καὶ ἀνέστρεψε καὶ ἐκάθευδε.
   καὶ πάλιν ἐκάλεσε κύριος, "Σαμουήλ, Σαμουήλ." καὶ
ἔδραμε πρὸς Ηλι, καὶ εἶπεν, "ἰδοὺ ἐγώ, ὅτι κέκληκάς με." καὶ
εἶπεν, "οὐ κέκληκά σε. ἀνάστρεφε, κάθευδε."
   καὶ Σαμουὴλ οὔπω ἐγνώκει τὸν θεόν, καὶ οὔπω ἠκηκόει τὸ   10
ῥῆμα τοῦ κυρίου. καὶ πάλιν ἐκάλεσε κύριος Σαμουήλ. καὶ
πάλιν ἔδραμε πρὸς Ηλι, καὶ εἶπεν, "ἰδοὺ ἐγώ, ὅτι κέκληκάς με."
καὶ ἐπέγνω Ηλι ὅτι κύριος κέκληκε Σαμουήλ. καὶ εἶπεν,
"ἀνάστρεφε, κάθευδε, τέκνον. καὶ ὅτε καλέσει σε, ἐρεῖς, 'λέγε,
ὅτι ἀκούει ὁ δοῦλός σου.'"                                        15
   καὶ ἀπῆλθε Σαμουήλ. καὶ ἐκάθευδεν ἐν τῷ ἑαυτοῦ τόπῳ.
καὶ ἦλθε κύριος καὶ ἐκάλεσε αὐτὸν πάλιν. καὶ εἶπε Σαμουήλ,
"λέγε, ὅτι ἀκούει ὁ δοῦλός σου." καὶ εἶπε κύριος πρὸς Σαμουήλ,
"ἰδοὺ γενήσεται τὰ ῥήματά μου ἐν ᾽Ισραήλ, τῷ γὰρ οἴκῳ Ηλι
κακὰ γενήσεται."                                                  20
   καὶ αὔριον διὰ τὸν φόβον Σαμουὴλ οὐκ ἤθελεν εἰπεῖν τῷ
ἱερεῖ τὰ κακὰ τὰ γενησόμενα τῷ οἴκῳ αὐτοῦ. ἀλλ᾽ εἶπεν Ηλι
πρὸς Σαμουήλ, "τί ἐστι τὸ ῥῆμα τὸ ῥηθὲν πρὸς σέ;" καὶ εἶπε
Σαμουὴλ πάντα τὰ ῥήματα τοῦ κυρίου. πᾶς οὖν ἔγνω ὅτι
Σαμουὴλ ἔσται προφήτης.                                           25

**278.** VOCABULARY

ἀναστρέφω, — , ἀνέστρεψα, — , — , ἀνεστράφην: I overturn,
   return, (pass.) sojourn, dwell
γινώσκω, γνώσομαι, ἔγνων, ἔγνωκα, ἔγνωσμαι, ἐγνώσθην: I come
   to know, perceive, understand
Ηλι (indecl.), ὁ: Eli
ἰδού: behold, see, look
ἰδοὺ ἐγώ: Here am I

172

ἱερεύς, -έως, ὁ: priest

καθεύδω (only pres. and imperf. tenses in the New Testament): I sleep

καλέω (the paradigm of the pres. to be given in number 327), καλέσω, ἐκάλεσα, κέκληκα, κέκλημαι, ἐκλήθην: I call, invite

οὔπω: not yet

προφήτης, -ου, ὁ: prophet

ῥηθέν (aor. pass. part. neut. nom. sing. λέγω: I speak. See numbers 415, 273. The part. has the stem ῥηθε- instead of ῥεθη- found in the indic.): spoken

ῥῆμα, -ατος, τό: word, statement, thing, matter

Σαμουήλ (indecl.), ὁ: Samuel

τρέχω, — , ἔδραμον, — , — , — : I run

## 279. DECLENSION OF ἱερεύς

| (ὁ) ἱερεύς | ἱερεῖς |
|---|---|
| ἱερέως | ἱερέων |
| ἱερεῖ | ἱερεῦσι |
| ἱερέα | ἱερεῖς |
| ἱερεῦ | |

βασιλεύς also follows this pattern.

At an earlier period of the language these stems ended in -ηυ- before consonants and -ηF- before vowels. F is digramma, a letter lost from the Greek alphabet, equivalent to our "w." With the disappearance of F a transfer of quantity occurred, for example βασιληFος became βασιλέως.

## 280. INDIRECT DISCOURSE

The words of a speaker may be quoted exactly as they were first uttered. This kind of quotation is *direct discourse.*

εἶπε Πέτρος, "ἀνέστρεψα."
Peter said, "I returned."

A speaker's words may also be quoted with appropriate alterations in person and tense to suit the introductory expression in such a way as to give the sense of what was said without presuming to furnish the accuracy of a verbatim quotation. This kind of quotation is *indirect discourse.*

Peter said that he had returned.

Greek has three ways of expressing indirect discourse: (1) with a participle, (2) with an infinitive, and (3) with a clause introduced by a conjunction like ὅτι. Very few verbs are followed by all three kinds of indirect discourse.

a. *With a participle.* The following verbs already used in these lessons may introduce participial indirect discourse: ἀκούω βλέπω, γινώσκω. This type is infrequent in the New Testament.

ἤκουσε Πέτρος ἡμᾶς ἀναστρέφοντας.
Indirect: Peter heard that we were returning.
Direct: Peter heard (us say), "We are returning."

The tense of the participle in indirect discourse is that of the verb in the original quotation. The accusative ἡμᾶς is the direct object of ἤκουσε.

b. *With an infinitive.* The following verbs already used in these lessons may introduce the infinitive type of indirect discourse: ἀκούω, ἀποκρίνομαι, λέγω, πείθω, πιστεύω. This type is also infrequent in the New Testament.

ἤκουσε Πέτρος ἡμᾶς ἀναστρέφειν.
Indirect: Peter heard that we were returning.
Direct: Peter heard (us say), "We are returning."

Here again the tense of the original quotation is that of the indirect statement. *Notice carefully* that the agent performing the action of the infinitive is put in the *accusative of general reference.*

c. *With a ὅτι clause.* The following verbs already studied may introduce indirect discourse in a ὅτι clause: ἀκούω, βλέπω, γινώσκω, διδάσκω, ἐλπίζω, λέγω, πείθω, πιστεύω. This is the usual type in the New Testament.

ἤκουσε Πέτρος ὅτι ἀναστρέφομεν.
Indirect: Peter heard that we were returning.
Direct: Peter heard (us say), "We are returning."

Here as in the other two types the tense of the original statement is that of the indirect statement. Since a finite verb is used in the ὅτι clause, no pronoun is necessary to express the subject of the dependent verb in this particular instance.

Let us study an instance of this type of indirect discourse in number 277. καὶ ἐπέγνω Ἠλι ὅτι κύριος κέκληκε τὸ τέκνον, *and Eli recognized that the Lord had called the child.*

Although κέκληκε is a perfect, it is here translated as a pluperfect, ". . . the Lord had called. . . ." This is due to English sequence of tenses. Suppose we change the Greek sentence thus, καὶ ἐπιγινώσκει Ἠλι ὅτι κύριος κέκληκε τὸ τέκνον. The ὅτι clause has not been changed, but notice the translation: *And Eli recognizes that the Lord has called the child.* This illustrates the fact that normal translations of tenses in indirect discourse are used after the tenses that are translated as English presents and futures. The changes necessary after tenses translated as English past tenses are shown in the tabulation below.

## 281. TRANSLATIONS OF GREEK TENSES IN INDIRECT DISCOURSE AFTER TENSES TRANSLATED AS ENGLISH PASTS

| Greek Tense in indirect discourse | English Translation |
|---|---|
| Present | |
| ἔγνω ὅτι ἔρχεσθε. | He understood that *you were coming.* |
| Future | |
| ἔγνω ὅτι ἐλεύσεσθε. | He understood that *you would come.* |
| Perfect | |
| ἔγνω ὅτι ἐληλύθατε. | He understood that *you had come.* |
| Imperfect | |
| ἔγνω ὅτι ἤρχεσθε. | He understood that *you had been coming.* |
| Aorist | |
| ἔγνω ὅτι ἤλθετε. | He understood that *you had come.* |
| Pluperfect | |
| ἔγνω ὅτι ἐληλύθειτε. | He understood that *you had come.* |

## 282. EXERCISES

a. Translate number 277.

b. In translating the following sentences, be careful to use the appropriate English in the subordinate clause.

1) ἔγνωμεν αὐτὸν ἐσόμενον προφήτην.

2) ὁ προφήτης οὐκ ἐπίστευσε τὸν θεὸν εἰπεῖν διὰ κερατίνης αὐτῷ τῆς νυκτός.

3) ἐλπίζει ὅτι οὗτος οὐκ ἐρεῖ πάλιν τῷ προφήτῃ.

4) ἤκουσεν Ηλι ὁ ἱερεὺς τοῦ τέκνου δουλεύοντος τὴν νύκτα.

5) ἤκουσε Σαμουὴλ ὁ προφήτης τὸν κύριον ὀργισθῆναι τοῖς κακοῖς ἔργοις τῶν υἱῶν τοῦ ἱερέως.

6) οὔπω ἠκηκόει τὰ ῥήματα τοῦ ἱερέως.

7) γέγονε Σαμουὴλ ἀνήρ; οὔπω.

8) εἴπομεν ὅτι Σαμουὴλ τρέχει πρὸς τὸν ἱερέα.

9) δράματε νῦν, τέκνον.

10) ὠργίσθητε ἐμοί;

c. Change the indirect discourse in *b. 1* and *b. 8* into a direct form which could have been the original statement, for example:

εἶπε Πέτρος τὸν δοῦλον ἀπελθεῖν.

"ὃ δοῦλος ἀπῆλθε."

d. Associate the following English words with new Greek words in this lesson.

1) *anastrophe*: a rhetorical *turning upside down* of the usual order of words in a sentence.
2) *hier*atic: related to *priests*.
3) *rhema*tic: related to the formation of *words*.
4) *drom*edary: a *running* camel.

e. Read the Greek aloud and then translate:

1) καὶ λέγει αὐτοῖς, Ἰδοὺ ὁ ἄνθρωπος.
2) ὁ δὲ (But he) εἶπεν, Μὴ κλαίετε (stop weeping), οὐ γὰρ ἀπέθανεν ἀλλὰ καθεύδει.
3) Καὶ τῇ ἡμέρᾳ τῇ τρίτῃ (third) γάμος (a wedding celebration) ἐγένετο ἐν Κανὰ τῆς Γαλιλαίας, καὶ ἦν ἡ μήτηρ τοῦ Ἰησοῦ ἐκεῖ. ἐκλήθη δὲ καὶ ὁ Ἰησοῦς καὶ οἱ μαθηταὶ αὐτοῦ εἰς τὸν γάμον.
4) τὴν τοῦ βασιλέως ἑορτὴν ἐπιτελείτωσαν (let them celebrate).

The sources of these excerpts are listed on page 247.

176

# Lesson 37

## 283. ISRAEL ASKS FOR A KING

πολλάκις εἶχεν Ἰσραὴλ κριτὰς οἳ ἔσῳζον ἐν πολέμῳ τὸν λαὸν ἀπὸ τῶν ἐχθρῶν. ἀποθανόντος δὲ ἑκάστου τῶν κριτῶν, πάλιν ἐγκατέλειπεν ὁ λαὸς τὸν θεὸν οὗ ὁ κριτὴς αὐτοὺς σεσώκει. διὰ δὲ τὰ κακὰ ἔργα ὁ θεὸς ἔδωκε τὸν ἴδιον λαὸν διὰ πολέμου εἰςτὰς χεῖρας τῶν ἐχθρῶν. ἀλλ' οἱ υἱοὶ Ἰσραήλ, ὧν αἱ   5
καρδίαι οὐκ ἐπείθοντο τῇ ἀληθείᾳ, ἔλεγον πολλάκις ἀλλήλοις, "ὅτι οὐκ ἔκει ἡ γῆ ἡμῶν βασιλέα, διὰ τοῦτο ἀπέκτειναν ἡμᾶς οἱ ἐχθροὶ ἡμῶν. δεῖ οὖν τὴν γῆν ἡμῶν σχεῖν βασιλέα. σὺν δὲ αὐτῷ δεῖ ἡμᾶς ἄγειν εἰς πόλεμον ὑπὲρ ἀλλήλων."

ἀκούσας οὖν ταῦτα τὰ ῥήματα ὁ Σαμουήλ, ὃς ἦν νῦν   10
πρεσβύτερος, προσηύξατο πρὸς κύριον. κακὰ γὰρ ἦν ταῦτα ἐν τοῖς ὠσὶ τοῦ προφήτου. καὶ εἶπε κύριος πρὸς Σαμουήλ, "ἄκουε τῆς φωνῆς τοῦ λαοῦ. ἀπὸ τῆς ἡμέρας ἐν ᾗ ἐγὼ ἤγαγον τὸν λαὸν ἐμοῦ ἐξ Αἰγύπτου πολλάκις ἐγκατέλιπόν με. οὕτως ἐγκαταλείπουσί σε. ἀλλὰ εἰπὲ αὐτοῖς ἃ γενήσεται ἐν πολέμῳ   15
ὅτε ἕξουσι βασιλέα." καὶ εἶπε Σαμουὴλ πᾶν τὸ ῥῆμα τοῦ κυρίου πρὸς τὸν λαόν.

"ὁ βασιλεὺς λήμψεται ὑμῶν τοὺς υἱοὺς καὶ δουλεύσουσι αὐτῷ καὶ λήμψεται ὑμῶν τὴν γῆν καὶ τὰ πρόβατα. καὶ οὐκ ἀκούσει κύριος ὑμῶν ἐν ταῖς ἡμέραις ἐκείναις ὅτι ὑμεῖς ἐλάβ-   20
εσθε ἑαυτοῖς βασιλέα."

τότε εἶπεν ὁ λαός, "οὐχί, ἀλλὰ δεῖ ἡμᾶς σχεῖν βασιλέα. πάντων τῶν ἄλλων ἐθνῶν ἐχόντων βασιλεῖς, δεῖ καὶ ἡμᾶς σχεῖν βασιλέα."

καὶ ἤκουσε Σαμουὴλ πάντα τὰ ῥήματα τοῦ λαοῦ, καὶ   25
εἶπεν αὐτὰ εἰς τὰ ὦτα κυρίου.

καὶ εἶπε κύριος πρὸς Σαμουήλ, "ἄκουε τῆς φωνῆς αὐτῶν, ὅτι δεῖ σχεῖν αὐτοῖς βασιλέα."

## 284. VOCABULARY

ἀλλήλων, ἀλλήλοις, ἀλλήλους:  one another, each other (see number 372)

δεῖ (pres. indic. third sing. δέω):  it is necessary (followed by an infinitive with an acc. of general reference), one must, one ought

ὅς, ἥ, ὅ:  who, which, that, what
οὖς, ὠτός, τό:  ear
πόλεμος, -ου, ὁ:  war, battle
ὑπέρ:  (with gen.) for, on behalf of, for the sake of, about; (with acc.) over, beyond (In the New Testament always figurative. See Gingrich and Danker under ὑπέρ.)
φωνή, -ῆς, ἡ:  voice, sound

## 285. ANOTHER THIRD DECLENSION NOUN

| (τό) οὖς | ὦτα |
|---|---|
| ὠτός | ὤτων |
| ὠτί | ὠσί |
| οὖς | ὦτα |

## 286. PARADIGM OF ὅς, ἥ, ὅ

| ὅς | ἥ | ὅ | οἵ | αἵ | ἅ |
|---|---|---|---|---|---|
| οὗ | ἧς | οὗ | ὧν | ὧν | ὧν |
| ᾧ | ᾗ | ᾧ | οἷς | αἷς | οἷς |
| ὅν | ἥν | ὅ | οὕς | ἅς | ἅ |

## 287. RELATIVE PRONOUNS

a. *Their function.* Relative pronouns connect clauses. The relative clause is usually adjectival but may be substantival.

   1) Adjectival clause.

   ... κριτὰς οἳ ἔσῳζον ... τὸν λαόν ...
   ... judges *who used to save* ... *the people* ...

   2) Substantival clause.

   εἰπὲ αὐτοῖς ἃ γενήσεται.
   Tell them *what will happen.*

b. *Their agreement.* A relative pronoun usually agrees in gender and number with its antecedent but has a case conforming to the construction of its own clause. Not infrequently, however, the relative pronoun is attracted into the case of its antecedent when that antecedent has a second or third inflectional form.

   1) Usual agreement.

   περὶ τοῦ λαοῦ ὅν ἔσῳζον ...
   Concerning the people *whom* they saved ...

   2) Attraction of relative pronoun to the case of its antecedent.

   περὶ τοῦ λαοῦ οὗ ἔσῳζον ...
   Concerning the people *whom* they saved

## 288. DEFINITE RELATIVE CLAUSES

Relative clauses which make specific reference are called definite relative clauses. This kind only has been used in this lesson.

## 289. THE RECIPROCAL PRONOUN

ἀλλήλων, *of one another*, *of each other*, has no nominative function, and in the New Testament no feminine or neuter forms. The only forms occurring are masculine:

ἤσθιον τοὺς ἄρτους ἀλλήλων.
They used to eat *one another's* loaves.

πιστεύομεν ἀλλήλοις.
We believe *one another*.

## 290. EXERCISES

a. Translate number 283.

b. Translate the words in parentheses in each of the following sentences.

1) οὔπω ἔδωκα βασιλέα ἐμοῦ τῷ λαῷ (who) ἐγκατέλιπέ με.
2) ἤκουσε Σαμουὴλ πάντα τὰ ῥήματα (which) εἴρητο ὑπὸ τῶν υἱῶν Ἰσραήλ.
3) οὗτός ἐστιν ὁ βασιλεὺς (to whom) οὔπω ἔδωκα τοῦτο τὸ ἔθνος.
4) οὔπω ἐπιγινώσκεις τὸν Ἰσραὴλ (whose, of whom) οἱ υἱοί ἐσμεν;
5) ἐχθὲς ἔβλεψας τὸν προφήτην (whom) βλέψομεν αὔριον.
6) οὔπω δεῖ βλέπειν τὸν ἄνδρα εἰς τὰ ὦτα (of whom) εἰρήκαμεν.
7) ὑπὲρ ἑαυτῶν ἀκούσομεν τῆς φωνῆς τοῦ βασιλέως (whose) ἐσμεν.

c. Translate into Greek.

1) On behalf of the Lord, Samuel spoke.
2) Instead of the voices of the people the prophet heard the voice of God.
3) Do stones speak with the voices of men?
4) No, but some men who have voices throw stones.
5) Priests who do not have ears cannot hear.
6) Bread was not brought into being for the sake of our Lord.
7) She carries a beautiful stone in her hand.

d. Associate the following English words with new Greek words in this lesson.

1) *allelo*morph: two distinctly different characteristics observed in a family line as alternating with *one another*.
2) *polemics*: practice of controversy (*war* of words).
3) *phonology*: description of *sounds*.
4) *otitis*: inflammation of the *ear*.

e. Read the Greek aloud and then translate:

1) πῶς δύνασθε (can) ὑμεῖς πιστεῦσαι, δόξαν (honor) παρὰ (from) ἀλλήλων λαμβάνοντες καὶ τὴν δόξαν τὴν παρὰ τοῦ μόνου θεοῦ οὐ ζητεῖτε (seek);

2) καὶ καθὼς (just as) Μωϋσῆς ὕψωσεν (lifted up) τὸν ὄφιν (snake) ἐν τῇ ἐρήμῳ, οὕτως ὑψωθῆναι (to be lifted up) δεῖ τὸν υἱὸν τοῦ ἀνθρώπου, ἵνα (in order that) πᾶς ὁ πιστεύων ἐν αὐτῷ ἔχῃ (may have) ζωὴν αἰώνιον.

3) εἶπεν δὲ πρὸς αὐτούς, Τίνες οἱ λόγοι (words) οὗτοι οὓς ἀντιβάλλετε (you are exchanging) πρὸς ἀλλήλους περιπατοῦντες (as you are walking along);

4) ὑμῶν δὲ μακάριοι οἱ ὀφθαλμοὶ (eyes) ὅτι βλέπουσιν, καὶ τὰ ὦτα ὑμῶν ὅτι ἀκούουσιν.

5) ἀμὴν (Truly) ἀμὴν λέγω ὑμῖν ὅτι ἔρχεται ὥρα (a time) καὶ νῦν ἐστιν ὅτε νεκροὶ (dead) ἀκούσουσιν τῆς φωνῆς τοῦ υἱοῦ τοῦ θεοῦ καὶ οἱ ἀκούσαντες ζήσουσιν (will live).

The sources of these excerpts are listed on page 247.

# Lesson 38

## 291. SAMUEL FINDS THE HIDDEN KING

τοῦ ἔθνους ἐκλεξαμένου βασιλέα ἀντὶ κριτοῦ, εἶπε Σαμουὴλ
πρὸς αὐτούς, "οὕτως εἶπε κύριος ὁ θεὸς Ἰσραήλ, λέγων, 'ἐγὼ
ἤγαγον τοὺς υἱοὺς Ἰσραὴλ ἐξ Αἰγύπτου. καὶ ὑμεῖς σήμερον
θέλετε ἄνδρα βασιλέα ὑμῶν ἀντὶ ἐμοῦ ὃς αὐτός εἰμι ὁ σωτὴρ
ὑμῶν ἐκ πάντων τῶν κακῶν ὑμῶν καὶ τῶν θλίψεων ὑμῶν. καὶ    5
εἴπετε, "οὐχί, ἀλλὰ βασιλέα σχεῖν θέλομεν."'"
    καὶ ἐξελέξατο ὁ κύριος Σαοὺλ γενέσθαι βασιλέα τοῦ
ἔθνους. ὁ δὲ Σαοὺλ οὐχ εὑρίσκετο ἐν τῷ λαῷ τῷ συναχθέντι
πρὸς Σαμουὴλ ὅτι ὁ Σαοὺλ ἐν τοῖς σκεύεσι ἦν. καὶ προσηύξατο Σαμουὴλ γνωσόμενος ποῦ ἐστι Σαούλ. καὶ εἶπεν ὁ κύριος,  10
"ἰδοὺ αὐτὸς εὑρεθήσεται ἐν τοῖς σκεύεσι." καὶ Σαμουὴλ ἔδραμε
ἐπὶ τὰ σκεύη καὶ ἔλαβε Σαοὺλ ἐκ τῶν σκευῶν.
    καὶ εἶπεν Σαμουὴλ πρὸς πάντα τὸν λαόν, "βλέπετε Σαοὺλ
τὸν ἄνδρα ὃν ἐκλέλεκται ἑαυτῷ κύριος;"
    καὶ ἔγνωσαν πᾶς ὁ λαός, καὶ ἐχάρησαν. καὶ εἶπε Σαμουὴλ  15
πρὸς τὸν λαὸν τοὺς νόμους τοῦ βασιλέως. καὶ ἀπέστειλε
Σαμουὴλ πάντα τὸν λαόν, καὶ ἀπῆλθεν ἕκαστος εἰς τὸν ἑαυτοῦ
τόπον.

## 292. VOCABULARY

ἐκλέγομαι, — , ἐξελεξάμην, ἐκλέλεγμαι, — : I choose
εὑρίσκω, εὑρήσω, εὗρον, εὕρηκα, — , εὑρέθην: I find, discover
    (followed by participial indirect discourse)
θλῖψις, -εως, ἡ: affliction, distress
Σαούλ (indecl.), ὁ: Saul
σκεῦος, -ους, τό: vessel, utensil, implement; (plural) baggage, gear,
    goods

## 293. THIRD DECLENSION NOUNS WITH STEMS ENDING IN -ει AND -ι

| (ἡ) θλῖψις | θλίψεις |
| θλίψεως | θλίψεων |
| θλίψει | θλίψεσι |
| θλῖψιν | θλίψεις |

This pattern will be found in several other nouns to be presented later, so it is worth knowing. It may be simpler to learn the forms than to try to explain them all. At any rate, the stem endings -ει and -ι may be regarded as two grades of a vowel system. θλίψι- appears in the singular first and fourth inflectional forms: θλίψις and θλίψιν. θλίψει- is supposed to have lost its final -ι- before the vowels of the inflectional endings -ος, -ι, -ες, -ων. The forms θλίψεις (fourth plural) and θλίψεσι are assumed to have followed the analogy of θλίψεις (first plural from θλίψε-ες). This leaves still unexplained the accents of θλίψεως and θλίψεων. At an earlier period in the history of the language θλίψεως is thought to have been θλίψηος. With such a spelling the accent would be normal. When a transfer of quantity resulted in θλίψεως, the accent did not shift from the antepenult to the penult. θλίψεων is considered analogous in formation to θλίψεως.

## 294. EXERCISES

a. Translate number 291.

b. Review indirect discourse by translating the following sentences.

1) ἐχθὲς ὁ λαὸς ἤκουσαν τοῦ ἐσχάτου κριτοῦ εἰπόντος, "ἰδοὺ ἐξελεξάμην βασιλέα ὑμῖν."

2) εἰρήκει ὁ θεὸς ὅτι αὐτός ἐστιν ὁ ἔσχατος βασιλεὺς τούτου τοῦ ἔθνους.

3) γινώσκομεν τὸ ἔθνος νῦν ἔχειν βασιλέα.

4) ἠκούσαμεν τὸν Σαοὺλ ἐν τοῖς σκεύεσιν εὑρεθέντα.

c. Translate the italicized words (1) with adjectival participles and (2) with relative clauses.

1) I see the king *who has been found.*
2) We found a prophet *who was choosing.*
3) God has given a leader to the nation *that had chosen* a king.
4) The father of the child *who is coming* into our house died last night.

d. Review of genitive absolutes. Translate the genitive absolutes (1) literally and (2) more freely and in better English.

1) τῶν τέκνων εὑρηκότων ἀλλήλους ἐν τοῖς σκεύεσι οἱ ἄνδρες ἐχάρησαν.

2) τοῦ ἀνδρὸς τούτου ἀναστρεφομένου ὧδε, χαρησόμεθα.

3) φευξομένων τῶν τριακοσίων, εἶπον οἱ ἐχθροί, "ὧδέ ἐστιν ὁ βασιλεὺς ἡμῶν.

4) τῶν καλῶν ἱερέων μεινάντων ἐν τῷ σπηλαίῳ ἐκείνῳ, ὁ ἱερεὺς ὁ κακὸς ὠργίσθη.

e. Review of relative pronouns. Translate the English words in parentheses so as to fit their contexts.

1) δεῖ καθεύδειν ἐν τοῖς σκεύεσι τὸν (priest who fled).
2) εὑρίσκονται οἱ (judges to whom he gave) τὴν γῆν.
3) ἐβλέψαμεν τὸν (priest whose son) ἐν τῷ πολέμῳ ἀπεκτάνθη.
4) ἀκούσετε τῆς (voice which saved) τριακόσια τέκνα.

f. Review of participle usage. In the following paragraph tell which participles are adjectival and which are adverbial in emphasis, and translate appropriately.

*ἐλθόντες* οἱ ἄνδρες τοῦ Μαδιὰμ εἰς τὴν γῆν 'Ισραὴλ ἔλαβον πάντα τὸν σῖτον. *προσευξαμένων* τῷ θεῷ τῶν υἱῶν 'Ισραήλ, Γεδεὼν ἀπεστάλη *γενησόμενος* ὁ κριτὴς τοῦ λαοῦ. ἔδωκεν δὲ ὁ θεὸς τούτῳ τριακοσίους ἄνδρας τοὺς *σαλπίζοντας. σαλπισάντων* τῶν τριακοσίων νυκτός, οἱ ἐχθροὶ *σχόντες* φόβον καὶ *ἐγκαταλιπόντες* τὴν παρεμβολὴν ἔφυγον.

g. Read the Greek aloud and then translate:

1) ἀπεκρίθη αὐτοῖς ὁ 'Ιησοῦς, Οὐκ ἐγὼ ὑμᾶς τοὺς δώδεκα (twelve) ἐξελεξάμην, καὶ ἐξ ὑμῶν εἷς (one) διάβολός (a devil) ἐστιν;
2) εὑρίσκει Φίλιππος τὸν Ναθαναήλ (Nathanael) καὶ λέγει αὐτῷ, "Ον (Him of whom) ἔγραψεν Μωυσῆς ἐν τῷ νόμῳ καὶ οἱ προφῆται εὑρήκαμεν, 'Ιησοῦν υἱὸν τοῦ 'Ιωσὴφ τὸν ἀπὸ Ναζαρέτ (Nazareth).
3) ... ἐν τῷ κόσμῳ θλῖψιν ἔχετε, ἀλλὰ θαρσεῖτε (be courageous), ἐγὼ νενίκηκα (I have conquered) τὸν κόσμον.

The sources of these excerpts are listed on page 247.

# Lesson 39

## 295. WHEN THE VOICE OF THE PEOPLE WAS NOT THE VOICE OF GOD

ὢν καλὸς ἐν ταῖς πρώταις ἡμέραις τῆς βασιλείᾱς, Σαοὺλ οὐκ ἐπείθετο τῷ θεῷ πάντοτε. εἰρήκει γὰρ κύριος τῷ βασιλεῖ καταλῦσαι τὴν βασιλείᾱν τοῦ Ἀμαληκ, πάντας τοὺς ἄνδρας τοῦ Ἀμαληκ, πάσᾱς τὰς γυναῖκας καὶ πάντα τὰ τέκνα καὶ πάντα τοῦ Ἀμαληκ. 5

ἀλλ' οὐκ ἐπείσατο Σαοὺλ πᾶσιν ἃ εἰρήκει ὁ θεός, ἔπεισε γὰρ ὁ λαὸς τὸν βασιλέα σῶσαι τὸν ἡγεμόνα τοῦ Ἀμαληκ καὶ πρόβατά τινα καλά. εἶπον γὰρ, "ἀποκτείνωμεν τοῦτον τὸν ἡγεμόνα καὶ ταῦτα τὰ καλὰ πρόβατα; οὐχί. σώσωμεν τὰ πρόβατα ταῦτα γενησόμενα θυσίᾱς κυρίῳ τῷ θεῷ ἡμῶν." 10

Σαοὺλ οὖν ἐπείσατο τῷ ῥήματι τοῦ λαοῦ. διὰ τοῦτο ὠργίσθη ὁ θεὸς τῷ βασιλεῖ τοῦ Ἰσραὴλ καὶ εἶπε τῷ Σαμουήλ, "εἰπὲ τῷ Σαούλ, 'οὐχ ἕξει ὁ υἱός σου ταύτην τὴν βασιλείᾱν μετά σε. ἀλλ' ἡ βασιλείᾱ σου δοθήσεται ἄλλῳ ὄντι κρείσσονι σοῦ.'" 15

ἤθελε γὰρ κύριος διδάξαι Σαοὺλ ὅτι ἡ ὑπακοὴ κρείσσων ἐστὶ θυσίᾱς οὔσης λίαν καλῆς. ἐπείσθη οὖν Σαμουὴλ κυρίῳ καὶ εἶπε ταῦτα τὰ ῥήματα τῷ βασιλεῖ. μετὰ ταῦτα ἀπέκτεινε ὁ προφήτης αὐτὸς τὸν ἡγεμόνα τῆς βασιλείᾱς τοῦ Ἀμαληκ, καὶ ἀπῆλθε πρὸς τὸν ἑαυτοῦ οἶκον. 20

## 296. VOCABULARY

Ἀμαληκ (indecl.), ὁ: Amalek
βασιλείᾱ, -ᾱς, ἡ: kingdom, royal power, dominion, rule, reign
γυνή, γυναικός, ἡ: woman, wife
δοθήσεται (fut. indic. pass. third sing. δίδωμι: I give): it shall be given
ἡγεμών, -όνος, ὁ: leader, governor, chief
θυσίᾱ, -ᾱς, ἡ: sacrifice
καταλύω, καταλύσω, κατέλυσα, — , — , κατελύθην: I destroy, overthrow
κρείσσων, κρεῖσσον: better
ὑπακοή, -ῆς, ἡ: obedience

184

## 297. PRESENT PARTICIPLE OF εἰμί (See number 244)

| | | |
|---|---|---|
| ὤν (=being) | οὖσα | ὄν |
| ὄντος | οὔσης | ὄντος |
| ὄντι | οὔσῃ | ὄντι |
| ὄντα | οὖσαν | ὄν |
| | | |
| ὄντες | οὖσαι | ὄντα |
| ὄντων | οὐσῶν | ὄντων |
| οὖσι | οὔσαις | οὖσι |
| ὄντας | οὔσᾱς | ὄντα |

## 298. PARADIGM OF ἡ γυνή

| | |
|---|---|
| γυνή | γυναῖκες |
| γυναικός | γυναικῶν |
| γυναικί | γυναιξί |
| γυναῖκα | γυναῖκας |
| γύναι | |

You will notice that this noun like several others of the third declension is formed on two stems.

## 299. PARADIGM OF κρείσσων

| Masculine and Feminine | Neuter |
|---|---|
| κρείσσων | κρεῖσσον |
| κρείσσονος | κρείσσονος |
| κρείσσονι | κρείσσονι |
| κρείσσονα | κρεῖσσον |
|    or | |
| κρείσσω (κρείσσοσα) | |
| | |
| κρείσσονες | κρείσσονα |
|    or |    or |
| κρείσσους (κρείσσοσες) | κρείσσω (κρείσσοσα) |
| κρεισσόνων | κρεισσόνων |
| κρείσσοσι | κρείσσοσι |
| κρείσσονας | κρείσσονα |
|    or |    or |
| κρείσσους (κρείσσοσες) | κρείσσω (κρείσσοσα) |

The forms in parentheses are not used. They are intended merely to explain the origin of the forms after which they are placed.

## 300. GENITIVE WITH A COMPARATIVE

A comparison may be expressed by a comparative adjective followed by a genitive noun or pronoun.

ἡ ὑπακοή ἐστι κρείσσων θυσίας.
Obedience is better than *sacrifice*.

## 301. SUBJUNCTIVE MOOD

Two verbs in this lesson, ἀποκτείνωμεν and σώσωμεν, neither make statements or ask questions as do indicative forms. These two new forms belong to the subjunctive mood, which carries with it an idea of uncertainty or of some emotional coloring.

## 302. DELIBERATIVE QUESTION

When the people ask Saul, "Shall we kill this leader?" they are represented as saying ἀποκτείνωμεν τοῦτον τὸν ἡγεμόνα; This question is on the surface an appeal for counsel as to what is to be done. But the rest of the story shows that the people already had their minds made up that they should not kill the leader of the Amalekites. This question then is rhetorical, asked to produce an effect, not to gain information. The future is used in English. The subjunctive can be used also in questions of sincere appeal for information.

εἰς τίνα τόπον ἀπέλθωμεν;   εἰς τίνα τόπον ἀπέλθωσιν;
To what place shall we go?   To what place will they go?

The implication is that the questioner is not sure whether there is an answer or not. But suppose we ask a similar question of a guide who knows the way and in whom we have complete confidence. In such a situation an indicative form will be used.

εἰς τίνα τόπον ἀπελευσόμεθα;   εἰς τίνα τόπον ἀπελεύσονται;
To what place shall we go?   To what place will they go?

The indicative reveals our assumption that an answer is to be had.

## 303. HORTATORY SUBJUNCTIVE

The people try to influence Saul by saying

σώσωμεν τὰ πρόβατα ταῦτα γενησόμενα θυσίας.
Let us save these sheep in order that they may become sacrifices.

The first person plural is used, and the translation begins "Let us ..."

## 304. PARADIGMS OF THE SUBJUNCTIVE: πιστεύω, ἔρχομαι, γίνομαι ἀποστέλλω

In the forms to be given two points should be observed: (1) *no augment* is used in the aorist subjunctive; and (2) the forms are made up of the tense stem plus the variable vowel -ω/η- plus the personal endings. The tenses chiefly used are the present and the aorist. No future subjunctive exists. *No one* translation fits all constructions.

| Present Active of πιστεύω | | Present Middle and Passive of πιστεύω | |
|---|---|---|---|
| πιστεύω | πιστεύωμεν | πιστεύωμαι | πιστευώμεθα |
| πιστεύῃς | πιστεύητε | πιστεύῃ | πιστεύησθε |
| πιστεύῃ | πιστεύωσι | πιστεύηται | πιστεύωνται |

| First Aorist Active of πιστεύω | | Second Aorist Active of ἔρχομαι | |
|---|---|---|---|
| πιστεύσω | πιστεύσωμεν | ἔλθω | ἔλθωμεν |
| πιστεύσῃς | πιστεύσητε | ἔλθῃς | ἔλθητε |
| πιστεύσῃ | πιστεύσωσι | ἔλθῃ | ἔλθωσι |

| First Aorist Middle of πιστεύω | | Second Aorist Middle of γίνομαι | |
|---|---|---|---|
| πιστεύσωμαι | πιστευσώμεθα | γένωμαι | γενώμεθα |
| πιστεύσῃ | πιστεύσησθε | γένῃ | γένησθε |
| πιστεύσηται | πιστεύσωνται | γένηται | γένωνται |

| Aorist First Passive of πιστεύω | | Aorist Second Passive of ἀποστέλλω | |
|---|---|---|---|
| πιστευθῶ | πιστευθῶμεν | ἀποσταλῶ | ἀποσταλῶμεν |
| πιστευθῇς | πιστευθῆτε | ἀποσταλῇς | ἀποσταλῆτε |
| πιστευθῇ | πιστευθῶσι | ἀποσταλῇ | ἀποσταλῶσι |

Note the peculiar accent in the aorist passive.

Liquid and nasal aorists use the same endings as the second aorist, for example, ἀποστείλω and μείνω.

The distinction between the present and the aorist subjunctive is in kind of action, not in time of action. The present represents progressive or repeated action whereas the aorist represents action as an occurrence.

305. EXERCISES

a. Translate number 295.

b. In translating the following, distinguish carefully between indicative and subjunctive forms.

1) πιστεύσωμεν ταύτῃ τῇ γυναικί;
2) πιστεύσομεν ταύτῃ τῇ γυναικί;
3) πιστεύσωμεν ταύτῃ τῇ γυναικί.
4) πιστεύωμεν ἐκείνῳ τῷ ἡγεμόνι τοῦ ᾽Αμαληκ.
5) πιστεύωμεν ἐκείνῳ τῷ ἡγεμόνι τοῦ ᾽Αμαληκ;
6) πιστεύομεν ἐκείνῳ τῷ ἡγεμόνι τοῦ ᾽Αμαληκ;

c. Say in Greek.

1) Let us be healing the child (pres. subj.).
2) Let the child be healed (an occurrence not a process: aorist imperative).

3) What shall I destroy? (uncertainty implied: aor. subj.).
4) What shall I destroy? (a definite answer assumed as available: fut. indic.).
5) Let us save the sacrifice.
6) Is obedience better than sacrifice?
7) Sacrifice will not be better than obedience.
8) God remembered the prophet's obedience.

d. Locate.

| | |
|---|---|
| 1) καταλύητε | 6) ἀγάγωμεν |
| 2) λαμβάνωσι | 7) φεύγῃ |
| 3) καταλυθῇς | 8) μείνῃς |
| 4) δεχώμεθα | 9) φάγητε |
| 5) σώσηται | 10) πεμφθῇ |

e. Translate the italicized portions of the following sentences by genitive absolutes:

1) *While the priest was returning*, the king sounded the trumpet.
2) *After the chief had destroyed the torch*, the woman ran into the house.
3) *Although his ear had been destroyed*, the prophet was hoping to hear.
4) *If the women flee*, we shall be able to sleep.
5) *Because voices were heard in the baggage*, the king was found there.

f. Read the Greek aloud and then translate:

1) ἀπεκρίθη ᾽Ιησοῦς, ῾Η βασιλεία (kingdom) ἡ ἐμὴ (my) οὐκ ἔστιν ἐκ τοῦ κόσμου τούτου....

2) θέλω δὲ ὑμᾶς εἰδέναι (to know) ὅτι παντὸς ἀνδρὸς ἡ κεφαλὴ (head) ὁ Χριστός ἐστιν, κεφαλὴ δὲ γυναικὸς ὁ ἀνήρ, κεφαλὴ δὲ τοῦ Χριστοῦ ὁ θεός.

3) ἀποκριθεὶς δὲ ὁ ἡγεμὼν εἶπεν αὐτοῖς, Τίνα θέλετε ἀπὸ τῶν δύο ἀπολύσω ὑμῖν; οἱ δὲ (and they) εἶπαν, Τὸν Βαραββᾶν (Barabbas).

4) καλῶς (well) ποιήσεις (you will do), ἀδελφέ, (ἐ)ὰν (if) εἰσέρχῃ (you come in) ἐνεγκὼν μετὰ σεαυτοῦ τὴν γυναῖκά μου, ἔγραψα (γ)ὰρ αὐτῇ σὺν σοὶ εἰσελθεῖν.

5) ἐβεβαίωσεν (he confirmed) δὲ τὴν ἐπαγγελίαν παραστή(σ)ας (by offering)... τοῖς ἐντεμενίοις (who had statues within the temple precinct) θεοῖς τὴν θυσίαν.

The sources of these excerpts are listed on page 247.

g. Review all the new words introduced in the vocabularies of Lessons 35-39.

# Lesson 40

## 306. SAUL'S SUCCESSOR CHOSEN

καὶ εἶπε κύριος πρὸς Σαμουήλ, "οὐκ ἔσται Σαοὺλ πάντοτε βασιλεὺς ἐπὶ Ἰσραήλ. λάβε τὸ κέρας σου ἐλαίου, καὶ ἀποστελῶ σε πρὸς Ἰεσσαὶ ἐν Βηθλέεμ, ὅτι εὕρηκα ἐν τοῖς υἱοῖς αὐτοῦ βασιλέα."

καὶ εἶπε Σαμουήλ, "πῶς ἔλθω; ὅτι ἀκούσει Σαούλ, καὶ 5 ἀποκτενεῖ με."

καὶ εἶπε κύριος, "ἐρεῖς, ΄θῦσαι τῷ κυρίῳ ἥκω. ΄καὶ καλέσεις τὸν Ἰεσσαὶ εἰς τὴν θυσίαν, καὶ γνώσῃ ἃ ἐρεῖς."

καὶ ἐπείσατο Σαμουὴλ πᾶσιν ἃ εἰρήκει αὐτῷ κύριος. καὶ λαβὼν τὸ κέρας ἐλαίου ἀπῆλθεν εἰς Βηθλέεμ, καὶ οἱ πρεσ- 10 βύτεροι τῆς Βηθλέεμ εἶπον, "τί ἥκεις;"

καὶ εἶπεν, "θῦσαι τῷ κυρίῳ ἥκω, ἁγιάσθητε καὶ φάγεσθε μετ' ἐμοῦ σήμερον." καὶ ἡγίασε τὸν Ἰεσσαὶ καὶ τοὺς υἱοὺς αὐτοῦ, καὶ ἐκάλεσεν αὐτοὺς εἰς τὴν θυσίαν.

καὶ ὅτε ἔβλεψε τὸ πρόσωπον τοῦ πρώτου υἱοῦ, εἶπεν, "ὁ 15 χριστὸς κυρίου ἐστὶν ὧδε."

ἀλλ' εἶπε κύριος πρὸς Σαμουήλ, "μὴ βλέψῃς τὸ πρόσωπον αὐτοῦ. οὗτος γὰρ οὐ μὴ γένηται ὁ χριστός, ὅτι βλέπει τὸ πρόσωπον ἄνθρωπος, ἀλλὰ ὁ θεός βλέπει τὴν καρδίαν."

καὶ ἤγαγεν Ἰεσσαὶ ἑπτὰ υἱοὺς ἵνα βλέψῃ αὐτοὺς Σαμουήλ. 20 καὶ εἶπε Σαμουήλ, "οὐ μὴ χρίσω τινὰ ἐν τούτοις. ἔχεις ἄλλον υἱόν;"

καὶ εἶπεν Ἰεσσαί, "ἰδοὺ ὁ μικρὸς Δαυὶδ μετὰ τῶν προβάτων ἐστί."

καὶ εἶπε Σαμουὴλ πρὸς Ἰεσσαί, "ἀπόστειλον ἵνα Δαυὶδ ᾖ 25 μεθ' ἡμῶν."

καὶ ἀπέστειλε καὶ ἤγαγεν Δαυίδ. καὶ εἶπε κύριος πρὸς Σαμουήλ, "χρίσον τὸν Δαυὶδ ὅτι τοῦτον ἐξελεξάμην."

καὶ ἔλαβε Σαμουὴλ τὸ κέρας τοῦ ἐλαίου καὶ ἔχρισεν Δαυὶδ ἐν μέσῳ τῶν ἀδελφῶν αὐτοῦ. 30

## 307. VOCABULARY

ἁγιάζω, — , ἡγίασα, — , ἡγίασμαι, ἡγιάσθην:  I dedicate, set apart for God, sanctify, purify

Δαυίδ (indecl.), ὁ:  David

189

ἔλαιον, -ου, τό: olive oil
ἥκω, ἥξω, ἧξα, — , — , — : I have come, am present
'Ιεσσαί (indecl.), ὁ: Jesse
ἵνα: that, in order that
κέρας, -ατος, τό: horn
οὐ μή: no, (a strong negative) by no means, not at all
πρόσωπον, -ου, τό: face
χριστός, -οῦ, ὁ: anointed, Christ
χρίω, — , ἔχρισα, — , — , ἐχρίσθην: I anoint

## 308. PRESENT SUBJUNCTIVE OF εἰμί

| | |
|---|---|
| ὦ | ὦμεν |
| ᾖς | ἦτε |
| ᾖ | ὦσι |

## 309. NEGATIVES USED WITH THE SUBJUNCTIVE

The negative adverb μή is usually found alone with subjunctive forms. Less frequently οὐ μή is used.

## 310. SUBJUNCTIVE IN STRONG DENIALS

The aorist subjunctive with the negative οὐ μή expresses a rather strong denial of a future possibility.

*οὐ μὴ γένηται ὁ χριστὸς τοῦ 'Ισραήλ.*
*He shall by no means become* the anointed of Israel.

## 311. SUBJUNCTIVE IN PROHIBITIONS

The aorist subjunctive with the negative μή expresses a negative command or prohibition.

*μὴ βλέψῃς τὸ πρόσωπον αὐτοῦ.*
*Do not look at* his face.

## 312. SUBJUNCTIVE IN PURPOSE CLAUSES

Purpose is often expressed by the subjunctive in clauses introduced by ἵνα.

*λάβε αὐτὸν ἵνα ᾖ μεθ' ἡμῶν.*
Take him *in order that he may be* with us.

## 313. EXERCISES

a. Translate number 306.

b. Complete the following sentences in the ways indicated.

1) ἐλθὲ εἰς τὴν Βηθλέεμ ἵνα μεθ' ἡμῶν....

...you may be.
...you may eat (once).

... you may eat (regularly).
... you may be purified.

2) οὐ μὴ ... he will choose ... τοῦτο τὸ πρόσωπον.
    he will anoint with olive oil
    he will dedicate
    he will look at

3) μὴ ... start to destroy yourself ..., Σαούλ.
    start to choose
    start to dedicate yourself
    start to anoint yourself with olive oil

c. Put suitable negatives with all the verbs in the following sentences.

1) Σαμουὴλ _____ ἥκει ἵνα _____ χρίσῃ ἐλαίῳ πάντας υἱοὺς τοῦ Ἰεσσαί.

2) _____ ἥξῃ πρὸς Βηθλέεμ πάλιν μετὰ τοῦ κέρατος τοῦ ἐλαίου.

3) _____ ἁγιάσησθε κέρατι ἐλαίου, ἀδελφοὶ Δαυίδ, ἵνα ἦτε καλοί.

4) _____ ὦμεν κακοὶ ἵνα ἥκῃ πρὸς ἡμᾶς μετὰ τοῦ κέρατος τοῦ ἐλαίου ἵνα ἁγιάσῃ Δαυίδ.

5) κρεῖσσόν τι τούτου _____ εἴπωμεν.

6) _____ ἐλευσόμεθα ὧδε πάλιν μετὰ τῶν κεράτων.

7) _____ ἔλθωμεν ὧδε πάλιν.

8) _____ ἐλευσόμεθα ὧδε πάλιν;

9) _____ ἔλθωμεν ὧδε πάλιν.

10) _____ ἁγιάζωμεν μόνον τὸ κέρας ἀλλὰ καὶ τὸ ἔλαιον.

11) _____ βλέψητε τὰ πρόσωπα τῶν ἀδελφῶν.

d. Remember by way of review that usually

1) οὐ and its compounds are used with the indicative.
2) μή and its compounds are used with other parts of a Greek verb.

e. Associate these words with your new vocabulary.

1) *cerat*oid: shaped like a *horn*.
2) *Christ*: God's *Anointed*.

f. Put the following sentences into forms using indirect discourse as explained in number 280.

1) ὁ ἀνὴρ ὁ ἔχων ὦτα ἤκουσε, "σαλπίζουσι οἱ τριακόσιοι."
2) ἀπεκρίθημεν, "ἡμεῖς φευξόμεθα."
3) βλέψετε (ταύτην τὴν ἀλήθειαν) "πάντες οἱ ἄνθρωποι ἀπο-θανοῦνται."

191

4) ἔγνωμεν, "ἡ ὑπακοὴ κρείσσων τοῦ ἀργυρίου ἐστίν."

5) ἐρῶ, "ἡ βασιλείᾱ αὕτη καταλυθήσεται."

g. Translate the English carefully.

1) εὑρήσουσι τὸν ἄνδρα (whose son) σαλπίζει ἐν τοῖς ὠσὶν τοῦ ἱερέως;

2) ποῦ καθεύδει ἡ γυνὴ (to whom) τὰ σκεύη ἐπέμψαμεν;

3) ἀνήρ τις ἦν (than whom) κρείσσων ἦς;

4) (on behalf of whom) ἐδράμομεν πρὸς τὸν ἡγεμόνα;

5) τοῦτό ἐστι τὸ τέκνον (on behalf of whom) ἐδράμομεν πρὸς τὸν ἡγεμόνα.

h. Translate carefully.

| | |
|---|---|
| 1) φεύγωσι; | 7) φεύγωμεν; |
| 2) φεύγουσι; | 8) φύγωμεν; |
| 3) φευγέτωσαν. | 9) ἐφύγομεν. |
| 4) φεύγωμεν. | 10) ἐφύγομεν; |
| 5) φευξόμεθα. | 11) φύγωμεν. |
| 6) φυγέτωσαν. | |

i. Read the Greek aloud and then translate:

1) ... Πάτερ ἡμῶν ὁ ἐν τοῖς οὐρανοῖς, ἁγιασθήτω τὸ ὄνομά σου ....

2) αἱ γὰρ μωραὶ (foolish maidens) λαβοῦσαι τὰς λαμπάδας αὐτῶν οὐκ ἔλαβον μεθ' ἑαυτῶν ἔλαιον· αἱ δὲ φρόνιμοι (sensible maidens) ἔλαβον ἔλαιον ἐν τοῖς ἀγγείοις (containers) μετὰ τῶν λαμπάδων ἑαυτῶν.

3) Πᾶν ὃ δίδωσίν (gives) μοι ὁ πατὴρ πρὸς ἐμὲ ἥξει, καὶ τὸν ἐρχόμενον πρὸς ἐμὲ οὐ μὴ ἐκβάλω ἔξω (I will cast out) ....

4) Οὕτως γὰρ ἠγάπησεν (loved) ὁ θεὸς τὸν κόσμον, ὥστε (that) τὸν υἱὸν τὸν μονογενῆ (only) ἔδωκεν, ἵνα πᾶς ὁ πιστεύων εἰς αὐτὸν μὴ ἀπόληται (may perish) ἀλλ' ἔχῃ ζωὴν αἰώνιον.

The sources of these excerpts are listed on page 247.

# Lesson 41

---

314. A VOLUNTEER ANSWERS A CHALLENGE

καὶ συνήγαγον οἱ ἀλλόφυλοι τὰς παρεμβολὰς αὐτῶν εἰς
πόλεμον, καὶ Σαοὺλ καὶ οἱ ἄνδρες Ἰσραὴλ συνήχθησαν. καὶ
ἦλθεν ἀνὴρ δυνατὸς ἐκ τῶν παρεμβολῶν τῶν ἀλλοφύλων,
μέγας καὶ φοβερός. Γολιαθ ἦν ὄνομα αὐτοῦ. καὶ ἤρχετο Γολιαθ
καὶ ὠνείδιζε τὴν παρεμβολὴν τοῦ Ἰσραὴλ λέγων, "τί ἔρχεσθε       5
κατὰ ἡμῶν; οὐκ ἐγώ εἰμι Γολιαθ ὁ ἀλλόφυλος, καὶ ὑμεῖς οἱ
δοῦλοι τοῦ Σαούλ; ἐκλέξασθε ἑαυτοῖς ἕνα ἄνδρα μάχεσθαι
πρός με. καὶ ἐὰν δυνηθῇ οὗτος ὁ εἷς μόνος πατάξαι με, ἡμεῖς
ἐσόμεθα ὑμῖν δοῦλοι. ἐὰν δὲ ἐγὼ δυνηθῶ πατάξαι αὐτόν, ὑμεῖς
ἔσεσθε ἡμῖν δοῦλοι καὶ δουλεύσετε ἡμῖν. ἰδοὺ ἐγὼ ὠνείδισα      10
τὴν παρεμβολὴν Ἰσραὴλ σήμερον. πέμψον μοι ἄνδρα ἕνα, καὶ
μαχώμεθα μόνοι πρὸς ἀλλήλους." οὕτως ὠνείδιζε Γολιαθ τὸν
Ἰσραήλ.

καὶ τὰ ῥήματα τοῦ Γολιαθ τοῦ ἀλλοφύλου ἦν οὕτως
φοβερὰ ὥστε ἔσχον μέγαν φόβον Σαοὺλ καὶ πᾶς ὁ Ἰσραήλ.     15

καὶ εἶπε Σαοὺλ πρὸς Δαυίδ, "οὐ μὴ δυνήσῃ πορευθῆναι
πρὸς τὸν ἀλλόφυλον ἵνα μάχῃ πρὸς αὐτόν. ὅτι τέκνον εἶ σύ,
αὐτὸς δὲ ἀνὴρ μαχόμενος πᾶσαν τὴν ζωήν."

καὶ εἶπε Δαυίδ πρὸς Σαούλ, "καὶ λέοντα καὶ ἄρκον ἐπάταξε
ὁ δοῦλος σου, καὶ ἀποθανεῖται ὁ ἀλλόφυλος οὗτος. οὐχὶ       20
πορεύσομαι καὶ πατάξω αὐτόν; τίς ἐστιν οὗτος ὃς ὠνείδισε τὴν
παρεμβολὴν τοῦ θεοῦ ἡμῶν;"

καὶ εἶπε Σαοὺλ πρὸς Δαυίδ, "πορεύου καὶ ἔσται κύριος
μετά σου."

315. VOCABULARY

ἀλλόφυλος, -ου, ὁ:  foreigner, Gentile, Philistine
ἄν:  (No individual translation, used in apodosis of type 2 conditions
    and elsewhere)
ἄρκος, -ου, ὁ or ἡ:  bear
Γολιαθ (indecl.), ὁ:  Goliath
δύναμαι, δυνήσομαι, — , — , ἠδυνήθην:  I am able, have power, can
ἐάν:  if
εἰ:  if (introducing a cond. clause); whether (introducing an ind.
    quest.); that (following a verb of emotion)

εἰ μή:  if not, unless
εἷς, μία, ἕν:  one
λέων, λέοντος, ὁ:  lion
μάχομαι (present system only):  I fight
μέγας, μεγάλη, μέγα:  great, large, tall, big
ὀνειδίζω, — , ὠνείδισα, — , — , — :  I reproach, upbraid, revile
πατάσσω, πατάξω, ἐπάταξα, — , — , — :  I strike, smite, kill
πορεύομαι, πορεύσομαι, — , πεπόρευμαι, ἐπορεύθην:  I go on my
    way, proceed, travel
φοβερός, -ά, -όν:  fearful, terrifying, causing fear
ὥστε:  so that

## 316. CONDITIONAL SENTENCES

A conditional sentence is one whose reality or probability depends on a supposed situation.

If it rains, the grass grows.
If it rains, we shall have no picnic.

In these sentences, "the grass grows" and "we shall have no picnic" are not made as absolute statements. Their reality or probability depends on the weather, that is, on the subordinate clauses "If it rains." The subordinate clause is called the *protasis*, and the independent clause the *apodosis*.

## 317. TYPES OF CONDITIONAL SENTENCES

Greek of the New Testament period used chiefly three types of conditional sentences.

a. Type 1, in which the protasis is *assumed to be true.*

εἰ οὐ πατάξει με, ἡμεῖς οὐκ ἐσόμεθα ὑμῖν δοῦλοι.
If he does not smite me (and we assume that he will not), we shall not be slaves to you.

The indicative is used in both clauses. The protasis is introduced by εἰ.

b. Type 2, in which the protasis is *assumed to be false.*

εἰ μὴ ἐπάταξέ με, ἡμεῖς οὐκ ἂν ἐγενόμεθα ὑμῖν δοῦλοι.
If he had not smitten me (but he did), we would not have become slaves to you (but we have).

εἰ μὴ ἐπάτασσέ με, ἡμεῖς οὐκ ἂν ἐγινόμεθα ὑμῖν δοῦλοι.
If he were not smiting me (but he is), we would not be becoming slaves to you (but we are so becoming).

The aorist indicates a past contrary to fact situation; the imperfect indicates a present contrary to fact situation. In this type

194

of conditional sentence the Greek word ἄν has no individual translation, but in the context (εἰ plus a secondary tense of the indicative in the protasis, and ἄν plus a secondary tense of the indicative in the apodasis) it is a signal of a contrary to fact condition.

c. Type 3, in which the protasis is *assumed to be neither true nor false, but is left in doubt.*

ἐὰν μὴ πατάξῃ με, ἡμεῖς οὐκ ἐσόμεθα ὑμῖν δοῦλοι.
If he does not smite me (and we make no predictions about whether he will or not), we shall not be slaves to you.

The protasis is introduced by ἐάν and uses the subjunctive. The apodosis may use any form that expresses futurity, the time to which type 3 refers.

d. Mixed Conditions, in which a protasis of one type is used with an apodosis of another type. The most frequently used combination is a type 3 protasis with a type 1 apodosis, often called the "present general condition."

ἐὰν πατάξῃ με, ἡμεῖς γινόμεθα ὑμῖν δοῦλοι.
If (ever) he smites me, we (always) become slaves to you.

## 318. RESULT CLAUSES WITH ὥστε

A result of some action or situation may be expressed by ὥστε followed by either an indicative or an infinitive.

τὰ ῥήματα τοῦ ἀλλοφύλου ἦν οὕτως φοβερὰ ὥστε ἔσχον μέγαν φόβον Σαοὺλ καὶ πᾶς ὁ Ἰσραὴλ (ὥστε σχεῖν μέγαν φόβον Σαοὺλ καὶ πάντα τὸν Ἰσραήλ).

If an infinitive is used, one must substitute an accusative of general reference for the nominative subject with the indicative.

## 319. οὐ AND μή INTRODUCING QUESTIONS

a. A question introduced by οὐ, οὐκ, οὐχ, or οὐχί implies that the questioner expects an affirmative answer.

οὐχ ὑμεῖς ἐμὲ πατάξετε;
You will smite me, won't you?

b. A question introduced by μή implies that the questioner expects a negative answer.

μὴ ὑμεῖς ἐμὲ πατάξετε;
You will not smite me, will you?

c. A question introduced by neither οὐ nor μή implies nothing about the answer expected.

ὑμεῖς ἐμὲ πατάξετε;
Will you smite me?

## 320. PARADIGM OF εἷς

| εἷς | μία | ἕν |
|------|------|------|
| ἑνός | μιᾶς | ἑνός |
| ἑνί | μιᾷ | ἑνί |
| ἕνα | μίαν | ἕν |

The meaning of the word excludes a plural.

## 321. PARADIGM OF μέγας

With the exception of the four italicized forms in the paradigm below, μέγας is an adjective of the first and second declensions.

| *μέγας* | μεγάλη | *μέγα* |
|------|------|------|
| μεγάλου | μεγάλης | μεγάλου |
| μεγάλῳ | μεγάλῃ | μεγάλῳ |
| *μέγαν* | μεγάλην | *μέγα* |
| μεγάλοι | μεγάλαι | μεγάλα |
| μεγάλων | μεγάλων | μεγάλων |
| μεγάλοις | μεγάλαις | μεγάλοις |
| μεγάλους | μεγάλᾱς | μεγάλα |

## 322. EXERCISES

a. Translate number 314.

b. (1) Identify the type of each of the following conditional sentences, (2) tell the implications of each, and (3) translate.

1) εἰ συνάγουσιν οἱ αλλόφυλοι τὰς παρεμβολὰς εἰς πόλεμον, Σαοὺλ καὶ οἱ ἄνδρες αὐτοῦ συνάγονται, ἀλλὰ οὐ μάχονται.

2) εἰ συνῆγον οἱ ἀλλόφυλοι τὰς παρεμβολὰς εἰς πόλεμον, Σαοὺλ καὶ οἱ ἄνδρες αὐτοῦ ἂν συνήγοντο, ἀλλὰ οὐκ ἂν ἐμάχοντο.

3) εἰ συνήγαγον οἱ ἀλλόφυλοι τὰς παρεμβολὰς εἰς πόλεμον, Σαοὺλ καὶ οἱ ἄνδρες αὐτοῦ ἂν συνηγάγοντο.

4) ἐὰν συνάγωσιν οἱ ἀλλόφυλοι τὰς παρεμβολὰς εἰς πόλεμον, Σαοὺλ καὶ οἱ ἄνδρες αὐτοῦ συνάξονται.

c. Tell into which type of conditional sentence each of the following should be translated.

1) If you were a good teacher, you would improve with practice.
2) If you had been a good teacher, you would have improved with practice.
3) If you are made a good teacher, you will improve with practice.

4) If you are a good teacher (as I see clearly you are), you are improving with practice.

d. Translate.

1) Γολιὰθ ἦν οὕτως μέγας καὶ φοβερὸς ὥστε οὐκ εὗρεν ἕνα ἄνδρα ὃς δυνήσεται μάχεσθαι ὑπὲρ τοῦ Ἰσραήλ.

2) οὐκ εἶχε φόβον τοῦ Γολιὰθ ὁ Δαυὶδ ὥστε δυνηθῆναι μάχεσθαι ἐπὶ τὸν μέγαν ἀλλόφυλον.

3) ὠνείδισεν οὕτως ὁ ἀλλόφυλος τὴν παρεμβολὴν τοῦ Ἰσραὴλ ὥστε Δαυὶδ ἠθέλησεν ἀποκτεῖναι τοῦτον τὸν φοβερὸν ἐχθρόν.

4) εἰ φόβον ἄρκου ἢ λέοντος οὐκ εἶχε ὁ Δαυίδ, οὐ δεῖ σχεῖν φόβον τοῦ Γολιάθ.

5) ἄρκοι καὶ λέοντες δύνανται γενέσθαι οὕτως φοβεροὶ ὥστε ἐπὶ αὐτοὺς οὐ μάχονται ἄνδρες.

6) εἰ ἄρκον ἢ λέοντα φοβερὸν ἀπεκτείναμεν, οὐκ ἂν ἔσχομεν φόβον τοῦ Γολιάθ.

7) ἐὰν ἡμᾶς εὕρωσιν σήμερον οἱ ἄρκοι τῆς γῆς ταύτης καὶ οἱ λέοντες, πῶς φύγωμεν;

8) εἰ κέρας ἐλαίου εὕρομεν, τὰ ἑαυτῶν πρόσωπα ἂν ἐχρίσαμεν.

e. Associate the following words with your new vocabulary.

1) *allophyl*ian: non-Indo-European or non-Semitic, i.e., *foreign*.
2) *arc*tic: located under the polar constellation of the Bear.
3) *dyna*sty: a series of rulers (*powerful* people) in the same family.
4) *Leo*, *Leon*, *Leon*ard, *Leon*idas: given names derived entirely or in part from the Greek word for *lion*.
5) logo*machy*: a *fight* about words.

f. Read the Greek aloud and then translate:

1) εἰ γὰρ ἐπιστεύετε Μωϋσεῖ, ἐπιστεύετε ἂν ἐμοί, περὶ γὰρ ἐμοῦ ἐκεῖνος ἔγραψεν.

2) οὗτος ἦλθεν πρὸς αὐτὸν νυκτὸς καὶ εἶπεν αὐτῷ, ʿΡαββί, (Rabbi), οἴδαμεν (we know) ὅτι ἀπὸ θεοῦ ἐλήλυθας διδά-σκαλος· οὐδεὶς (no one) γὰρ δύναται ταῦτα τὰ σημεῖα (signs, miracles) ποιεῖν (perform) ἃ σὺ ποιεῖς, ἐὰν μὴ ᾖ ὁ θεὸς μετʼ αὐτοῦ.

3) λέγει Νικόδημος πρὸς αὐτούς, ὁ ἐλθὼν πρὸς αὐτὸν πρότερον (previously), εἷς ὢν ἐξ αὐτῶν, Μὴ ὁ νόμος ἡμῶν κρίνει (condemn) τὸν ἄνθρωπον ἐὰν μὴ ἀκούσῃ πρῶτον (first) παρʼ (from) αὐτοῦ καὶ γνῷ τί ποιεῖ (he does);

The sources of these excerpts are listed on page 247.

# Lesson 42

## 323. ONE LITTLE STONE

καὶ Δαυὶδ ὁ υἱὸς τοῦ Ἰεσσαὶ ἐν τῇ χειρὶ αὐτοῦ ἔλαβε τὴν ῥάβδον αὐτοῦ. καὶ ἐξελέξατο ἑαυτῷ μικροὺς λίθους τινάς. λαβὼν δὲ τὴν σφενδόνην αὐτοῦ ἐπορεύθη πρὸς τὸν ἀλλόφυλον ὃς τὸ ὄνομα τοῦ θεοῦ ἐβλασφήμει.

βλέψας δὲ ὁ Γολιὰθ τὸν Δαυίδ, ὠνείδισεν αὐτὸν ὅτι Δαυὶδ    5
ἦν τέκνον ἔχον πρόσωπον καλόν. καὶ ἐλάλει ὁ ἀλλόφυλος πρὸς Δαυίδ, "τί λαμβάνεις ῥάβδον καὶ λίθους τινὰς ἐρχόμενος ἐπ᾽ ἐμέ; ἔρχου πρὸς ἐμέ, καὶ δώσω σε τοῖς πετεινοῖς τοῦ οὐρανοῦ καὶ τοῖς θηρίοις τῆς γῆς."

καὶ ἐλάλησε ὁ υἱὸς τοῦ Ἰεσσαὶ πρὸς τὸν ἀλλόφυλον, "σὺ    10
ἥκεις πρός με ἐν ῥομφαίᾳ ἀλλὰ ἐγὼ ἥκω πρός σε ἐν ὀνόματι κυρίου θεοῦ τῆς παρεμβολῆς Ἰσραήλ, ἐν τῷ ὀνόματι ὃ βλασφημεῖς σήμερον. καὶ δώσει σε κύριος σήμερον εἰς τὴν χεῖρά μου καὶ ἀποκτενῶ σε. καὶ ἀποκόψω τὴν κεφαλήν σου καὶ δώσω τὸ σῶμά σου καὶ τὰ σώματα τῶν ἀλλοφύλων σήμερον    15
τοῖς πετεινοῖς τοῦ οὐρανοῦ καὶ τοῖς θηρίοις τῆς γῆς. λέοντα καὶ ἄρκον ἀπέκτεινα καὶ ἀποκτενῶ σε. καὶ γνώσεται πᾶσα ἡ γῆ ὅτι ἐστὶ θεὸς ἐν Ἰσραήλ. γνώσεται δὲ πᾶσα ἡ παρεμβολὴ αὕτη ὅτι οὐκ ἐν ῥομφαίᾳ σῴζει κύριος, ὅτι τοῦ κυρίου ἐστὶν ὁ πόλεμος, καὶ δώσει κύριος ὑμᾶς εἰς χεῖρας ἡμῶν."    20

ἐπορεύθη δὲ ὁ ἀλλόφυλος πρὸς Δαυίδ. ἔλαβεν οὖν ὁ υἱὸς τοῦ Ἰεσσαι λίθον μικρὸν ἕνα καὶ ἔβαλεν αὐτὸν τῇ σφενδόνῃ καὶ ὁ μέγας ἔπεσεν ἐπὶ πρόσωπον αὐτοῦ ἐπὶ τὴν γῆν. καὶ ἔδραμε Δαυὶδ καὶ ἔλαβε τὴν ῥομφαίαν τοῦ ἀλλοφύλου καὶ ἐν ταύτῃ τῇ ῥομφαίᾳ ἡ κεφαλὴ τοῦ ἐχθροῦ ἀπεκόπη.    25

ὅτε δὲ ἔβλεψαν οἱ ἀλλόφυλοι ὅτι ἡ κεφαλὴ τοῦ δυνατοῦ ἀπεκόπη ὑπὸ τοῦ Δαυίδ, ἔφυγον.

## 324. VOCABULARY

ἀποκόπτω, ἀποκόψω, ἀπέκοψα, — , — , ἀπεκόπην: I cut off
βλασφημέω, — , ἐβλασφήμησα, — , — , ἐβλασφημήθην: I revile,
    rail at, blaspheme, slander, speak evil of God
δώσω, -εις, -ει, etc. (fut. indic. act. of δίδωμι, which is to be given
    later): I shall give, you will give, etc.

θηρίον, -ου, τό:  wild beast

κεφαλή, -ῆς, ἡ:  head

λαλέω, λαλήσω, ἐλάλησα, λελάληκα, λελάλημαι, ἐλαλήθην:  I utter, speak, say

πετεινόν, -οῦ, τό:  bird

πίπτω, πεσοῦμαι, ἔπεσον and ἔπεσα, πέπτωκα, — , — :  I fall

ῥάβδος, -ου, ἡ:  staff, rod

ῥομφαία, -ᾱς, ἡ:  sword

σφενδόνη, -ης, ἡ:  sling

σῶμα, σώματος, τό:  body, dead body, living body, person

## 325. CONTRACT VERBS

a. Nature of contract verbs. Some verbs have stems ending in a vowel that regularly contracts with the thematic or variable vowel following it. There are three verb stems of this kind: those ending in α, those ending in ε, and those ending in ο. The peculiarities of these verbs occur only in the present and imperfect tenses. In this lesson the verb forms βλασφημεῖς, ἐβλασφήμει, and ἐλάλει represent verbs whose stems end in ε. Before the contractions took place, βλασφημεῖς was βλασφημέεις, ἐβλασφήμει was ἐβλασφήμεε, and ἐλάλει was ἐλάλεε. In this lesson only the -εω paradigms will be presented. The -αω paradigms will be given in a later lesson, but the -οω forms will be reserved for the appendix, since no present or imperfect forms appear in 1 John, which we will be reading.

b. Accent of contract verbs. The accent of contract verbs depends upon the accent in the uncontracted form.

1) If the first of the uncontracted parts is accented, the contracted syllable is circumflexed; for example, βλασφημέεις becomes βλασφημεῖς.

2) If the second of the two uncontracted parts is accented, the contracted syllable receives an acute accent; for example, βλασφημεόμεθα becomes βλασφημούμεθα.

3) If the accent falls on neither of the uncontracted parts, the same accent remains where it is; for example, ἐλάλεε becomes ἐλάλει.

## 326. LIST OF FORMULAS FOR CONTRACT VERBS IN -ΕΩ

| | |
|---|---|
| ε+ε=ει | ε+ο=ου |
| ε+ει=ει | ε+ου=ου |
| ε+η=η | ε+ω=ω |
| ε+ῃ=ῃ | |

## 327. PARADIGMS OF λαλέω

### PRESENT

Active                 Middle and Passive

#### Indicative

| | | | |
|---|---|---|---|
| λαλῶ | λαλοῦμεν | λαλοῦμαι | λαλούμεθα |
| λαλεῖς | λαλεῖτε | λαλῇ | λαλεῖσθε |
| λαλεῖ | λαλοῦσι | λαλεῖται | λαλοῦνται |

#### Subjunctive

| | | | |
|---|---|---|---|
| λαλῶ | λαλῶμεν | λαλῶμαι | λαλώμεθα |
| λαλῇς | λαλῆτε | λαλῇ | λαλῆσθε |
| λαλῇ | λαλῶσι | λαλῆται | λαλῶνται |

#### Imperative

| | | | |
|---|---|---|---|
| λάλει | λαλεῖτε | λαλοῦ | λαλεῖσθε |
| λαλείτω | λαλείτωσαν | λαλείσθω | λαλείσθωσαν |

#### Infinitive

λαλεῖν               λαλεῖσθαι

#### Participle

λαλῶν λαλοῦσα λαλοῦν      λαλούμενος, -η, -ον

### IMPERFECT INDICATIVE

| | | | |
|---|---|---|---|
| ἐλάλουν | ἐλαλοῦμεν | ἐλαλούμην | ἐλαλούμεθα |
| ἐλάλεις | ἐλαλεῖτε | ἐλαλοῦ | ἐλαλεῖσθε |
| ἐλάλει | ἐλάλουν | ἐλαλεῖτο | ἐλαλοῦντο |

## 328. EXERCISES

a. Translate number 323.

b. Locate by (1) tense, (2) mood, (3) voice, (4) person, (5) number, and (6) first principal part.

1) ἐλελάλητο
2) βλασφημείσθωσαν
3) ἀποκόψῃ (3 places)
4) ἐλάλει
5) ἐλαλεῖτε
6) βλασφημείτω
7) δώσεις
8) λαλεῖν
9) βλασφημοῦ
10) λαλήθητι
11) ἀποκοπῆναι

16) λάλει
17) λαλεῖ
18) λαλείτω
19) λαλῇ (3 places)
20) λαλῶμεν
21) πεσεῖν
22) πεσεῖσθε
23) ἐπέσομεν
24) πεσούμεθα
25) πίπτομεν
26) χρισάτω

200

12) λαλῆται
13) λάλησον
14) λαλεῖσθε
15) λαλήσει

27) χρίσον
28) ὀνείδισαι
29) ὀνειδισάσης
30) ὀνείδιζε

c. Translate.

1) ἐλελάλητο ὑπὸ τοῦ ἀλλοφύλου τὸ ῥῆμα.
2) βλασφημείσθωσαν αἱ ῥομφαῖαι τοῦ ἡγεμόνος, ἀλλὰ μὴ βλασφημείτωσαν οἱ ἀλλόφυλοι τὸ ὄνομα τοῦ βασιλέως ἡμῶν.
3) εὑρήκατε τὸν ἀλλόφυλον εἶναι μικρόν;
4) ἤθελέ τινα δυνησόμενον μάχεσθαι ῥομφαίᾳ ὑπὲρ τοῦ Ἰσραήλ.
5) οὐ μὴ λαλήσητε ὅτι βληθήσονται ἡ κεφαλὴ καὶ τὸ σῶμα τοῦ βασιλέως ἡμῶν τοῖς θηρίοις καὶ τοῖς πετείνοις.
6) "τῇ ἐμῇ σφενδόνῃ καὶ τῇ ἐμῇ ῥάβδῳ," ἐλάλησε Δαυίδ, "ἀποκτεῖναι δύναμαι θηρία, λέοντας καὶ ἄρκους, καὶ βαλεῖν τὰ σώματα τοῖς πετείνοις."
7) δεῖ ἔχειν σφενδόνην καὶ ῥάβδον ἐάν τις ἔχῃ πρόβατα.
8) οἱ λέοντες καὶ οἱ ἄρκοι καὶ ἄλλα θηρία καὶ τὰ πετεῖνα φάγονται πρόβατον ἀποκτανθὲν ἐν τῇ ἐρήμῳ.
9) διὰ ταῦτα Δαυὶδ εἶχε πάντοτε σφενδόνην καὶ ῥάβδον.
10) ἐὰν τὴν κεφαλὴν τοῦ φοβεροῦ Γολιαθ ἀποκόψῃ ὁ Δαυίδ, ἀποθανεῖται τὸ σῶμα τοῦ Γολιαθ.
11) οὐκ ἂν ἔσχε τὴν βασιλείᾶν ὁ Δαυὶδ εἰ μὴ τὸν φοβερὸν Γολιαθ ἀπέκτεινεν.

d. Associate the following words with the new vocabulary.

1) *apocope*: a *cutting off* of the last part of a word.
2) *blasphemy*: *reviling* something sacred.
3) *therio*morphic: formed like an *animal*.
4) *rhabdo*mantist: one who divines by *rods*.

e. Read the Greek aloud and then translate:

1) ... καὶ εἶπεν αὐτῷ, Ταῦτά σοι πάντα δώσω ἐὰν πεσὼν προσκυνήσῃς (you worship) μοι.
2) Λέγω δὲ ὑμῖν τοῖς φίλοις (friends) μου, μὴ φοβηθῆτε (do not be afraid) ἀπὸ τῶν ἀποκτεινόντων τὸ σῶμα καὶ μετὰ ταῦτα μὴ ἐχόντων περισσότερόν (more) τι ποιῆσαι (to do).

The sources of these excerpts are listed on page 247.

# Lesson 43

**329.** READING: 1 John 1:1-6

**330.** NEW VOCABULARY NEEDED FOR THIS PASSAGE

ἀγγελίᾱ, -ᾱς, ἡ:   message, command

ἀπαγγέλλω, ἀπαγγελῶ, ἀπήγγειλα, — , — , ἀπηγγέλην:   I announce, report

ἀρχή, -ῆς, ἡ:   beginning, rule, sovereignty

ἡμέτερος, -ᾱ, -ον:   our

θεάομαι, — , ἐθεασάμην, τεθέαμαι, ἐθεάθην:   I behold, look upon, contemplate, view

κοινωνίᾱ, -ᾱς, ἡ:   fellowship, joint participation

λόγος, -ου, ὁ:   word, statement, speech, teaching

μαρτυρέω, μαρτυρήσω, ἐμαρτύρησα, μεμαρτύρηκα, μεμαρτύρημαι, ἐμαρτυρήθην:   I am witness, bear witness, testify

ὁράω, ὄψομαι, εἶδον, ἑώρακα, — , ὤφθην:   I see

ὅστις, ἥτις, ὅ τι:   whoever, whatever, who, what

οὐδείς, οὐδεμίᾱ, οὐδέν:   nobody, nothing, no, none

ὀφθαλμός, -οῦ, ὁ:   eye

περιπατέω, περιπατήσω, περιεπάτησα, περιπεπάτηκα, — , — :   I walk, live, conduct my life

πληρόω, πληρώσω, ἐπλήρωσα, πεπλήρωκα, πεπλήρωμαι, ἐπληρώθην:   I make full, fill, complete

ποιέω, ποιήσω, ἐποίησα, πεποίηκα, πεποίημαι, ἐποιήθην:   I make, do

σκότος, -ους, τό:   darkness

φανερόω, φανερώσω, ἐφανέρωσα, πεφανέρωκα, — , ἐφανερώθην:   I make visible, known, clear, manifest

φῶς, φωτός, τὸ:   light

χαρά, ᾶς, ἡ:   joy

ψεύδομαι, ψεύσομαι, ἐψευσάμην, — , — , — :   I lie, deceive by lies

ψηλαφάω, — , ἐψηλάφησα, — , — , — :   I handle, touch, feel

**331.** FORMS OF ὅστις

In the New Testament only the following forms of ὅστις are used. In 1 John 1:2 we find the form ἥτις.

Singular

| | | | |
|---|---|---|---|
| Nominative | ὅστις | ἥτις | ὅ τι |
| Genitive | ὅτου | | |
| Accusative | | | ὅ τι |

Plural

| | | | |
|---|---|---|---|
| Nominative | οἵτινες | αἵτινες | ἅ τινα |

## 332. PARADIGM OF οὐδείς

| | | |
|---|---|---|
| οὐδείς | οὐδεμία | οὐδέν |
| οὐδενός | οὐδεμιᾶς | οὐδενός |
| οὐδενί | οὐδεμιᾷ | οὐδενί |
| οὐδένα | οὐδεμίαν | οὐδέν |

## 333. EXERCISES

a. Translate 1 John 1:1-6.

b. Try to answer the following questions:

1) What does each ἵνα clause tell us?
2) What difference would it make if we had ῞Ος ... ὅν ... ὅν ... ὅν ... in verse one instead of ῞Ο ... ὅ ... ὅ ... ὅ ... ?
3) If in verse 6 λέγωμεν were substituted for εἴπωμεν, how would that change alter the meaning?
4) What would be lost if we dropped οὐδεμία at the end of verse 5?

c. Locate by (1) tense, (2) mood, (3) voice, (4) person, (5) number, and (6) first principal part.

1) ἐθεάσω
2) ἐθεῶ
3) πληροῖς
4) πληροῦν
5) φανεροῦ
6) φανέρου
7) ἐφανέρου
8) ἐφανεροῦ
9) ἐμαρτυροῦντο

d. Associate the following words with the new vocabulary.

1) *martyr*: one who *testifies* to his faith by his death.
2) olig*archy*: *rule* by a few.
3) *Peripate*tics: a group of ancient philosophers who met in a covered *walking* place called a *peripatos*.
4) *photo*phobia: an aversion to *light*.
5) *pseudo*nym: a *false* name.
6) *scoto*phobia: an abnormal fear of *darkness*.
7) *thea*ter: a place where dramas may be *viewed*.

# Lesson 44

**334.** READING: 1 John 1:7-10.

**335.** NEW VOCABULARY NEEDED FOR THIS PASSAGE

ἀδικίᾱ, -ᾱς, ἡ:  unrighteousness, iniquity, injustice

ἁμαρτάνω, ἁμαρτήσω, ἡμάρτησα and ἥμαρτον, ἡμάρτηκα, —,
— :  I sin

ἁμαρτίᾱ, -ᾱς, ἡ:  sin

ἀναγγέλλω, ἀναγγελῶ, ἀνήγγειλα, —, —, ἀνηγγέλην:  I report,
announce, declare

ἀφίημι, ἀφήσω, ἀφῆκα, —, ἀφεῖμαι, ἀφέθην:  I send away, let go,
forgive, allow, remit (ἀφῇ in 1 John 1:9 is third sing. aor. subj.
act., and ἀφέωνται in 1 John 2:12 is third pl. perf. indic. pass.)

δίδωμι, δώσω, ἔδωκα, δέδωκα, δέδομαι, ἐδόθην:  I give

καθαρίζω, καθαριῶ, ἐκαθάρισα, —, κεκαθάρισμαι, ἐκαθαρίσθην:  I
make clean, cleanse

ὁμολογέω, ὁμολογήσω, ὡμολόγησα, —, —, — :  I agree, confess,
acknowledge

πιστός, -ή, -όν:  trusty, faithful, reliable

πλανάω, πλανήσω, ἐπλάνησα, —, πεπλάνημαι, ἐπλανήθην:  I lead
astray, deceive (πλανῶμεν in 1 John 1:8 is first pl. pres. indic.
act.)

τίθημι, θήσω, ἔθηκα, τέθεικα, τέθειμαι, ἐτέθην:  I put, place, lay
down (θεῖναι in 1 John 3:16 is aor. inf. act.)

ψεύστης, -ου, ὁ:  liar

ὡς:  as

**336.** RESULT CLAUSE WITH ἵνα

In 1 John 1:9 we have a ἵνα clause that seems to express result rather
than purpose.

... πιστός ἐστιν καὶ δίκαιος, *ἵνα ἀφῇ ἡμῖν τὰς ἁμαρτίᾱς καὶ καθαρίσῃ
ἡμᾶς ἀπὸ πάσης ἀδικίᾱς.*
... He is faithful and righteous, *so that he forgives us our sins and
cleanses us from all unrighteousness.*

God's faithfulness and righteousness result in the forgiveness of
the sins of those who confess them to Him. He has always been

faithful to His promises and righteous in His character. He is not faithful and righteous just in order to forgive us.

## 337. MI VERBS

Some verbs, called -μι verbs from the ending of the first principal part, are formed without the variable or thematic vowel except in the subjunctive. Consequently, the personal endings are added directly to the stem of the tense. These verbs have peculiar inflections only in the present, the imperfect, and the second aorist.

The stems of these verbs end in α (ἵστημι), ε (τίθημι), ο (δίδωμι), and υ (δείκνυμι). First John does not have examples of ἵστημι and δείκνυμι, which are given in the Greek-English Vocabulary at the end of the book. For the paradigms of these verbs see number 403 and number 404 in the appendix.

## 338. EXERCISES

a. Translate 1 John 1:7-10.

b. Answer the following questions.

1) What are the personal endings of -μι verbs in the present indicative active? Middle and passive?
2) How does the final stem vowel of -μι verbs change from the singular to the plural in the present and imperfect indicative active?
3) What should be noticed about the second singular in the present and imperfect indicative middle and passive?
4) What distinguishes the present from the aorist subjunctive in some -μι verbs?
5) What are the endings of -μι verbs in the imperfect indicative active? Middle and passive?

c. Associate the following words with the new vocabulary.

1) *cathar*tic: related to what *cleanses.*
2) *deic*tic: pertaining to that which *shows* or points out.
3) *homolog*ous: *agreeing* or parallel in structure.
4) *stat*ic: related to what is at rest or *standing* still.
5) *U*topia: Sir Thomas More's description of a perfect community which existed in *no* place.

205

# Lesson 45

**339.** READING: 1 John 2:1-8

**340.** NEW VOCABULARY NEEDED FOR THIS PASSAGE

ἀγαπητός, -ή, -όν: beloved

ἀληθής, -ές: true (to fact; actual as opposed to apparent), truthful. (For the paradigm see number 381.)

ἀληθῶς: truly, certainly, surely

ἐντολή, -ῆς, ἡ: order, command

ἤδη: now already, now at length

ἱλασμός, -οῦ, ὁ: means of appeasing, propitiation, expiation

καθώς: as, just as

καινός, -ή, -όν: new, unused, unknown, strange, remarkable

μόνον (adv.): only

ὅλος, -η, -ον: whole, complete, entire

ὀφείλω, — , — , — , — , — : I owe, ought

παλαιός, -ά, -όν: old, ancient

παράγω, — , — , — , — , — : I pass away, disappear, go by (The middle or passive form in 1 John 2:8 has the same meaning as the active.)

παράκλητος, -ου, ὁ: advocate, helper, intercessor

τεκνίον, -ου, τό: little child

τελειόω, — , ἐτελείωσα, τετελείωκα, τετελείωμαι, ἐτελειώθην: I finish, complete, accomplish

τηρέω, τηρήσω, ἐτήρησα, τετήρηκα, τετήρημαι, ἐτηρήθην: I take care of, guard, observe, give heed to, keep

φαίνω, φανοῦμαι, ἔφανα, — , — , ἐφάνην: I give light, shine; come to light, appear

**341.** INDEFINITE RELATIVE CLAUSES

In 1 John 2:5 we find the clause ὃς δ᾽ ἂν τηρῇ αὐτοῦ τὸν λόγον..., *but whoever keeps his word*... The antecedent of ὅς is not expressed. This indefiniteness is accentuated by the use of ἄν and the subjunctive. Indefinite relative clauses of this kind are parallel in construction and idea to the protasis of third type conditional sentences.

ἐὰν δέ τις τηρῇ αὐτοῦ τὸν λόγον
but *if anyone* keeps his word

ὃς δ' ἂν τηρῇ αὐτοῦ τὸν λόγον
but *whoever* keeps his word

**342. EXERCISES**

Exegesis is drawing the correct meaning from the text. This process includes a careful consideration of (1) the meaning of the roots of the words, (2) the meaning of the forms of the words, and (3) the meaning of the context. Since beginning the study of Greek, you have learned numerous items of vocabulary and scores of inflectional endings. Now we have started reading the Greek New Testament together, and our keen desire is to see more in the Greek than we have seen in even the best English translations that we have read. The way to do this is to put together in our thinking the meanings of (1) roots, (2) forms, and (3) context. Naturally skill in exegesis develops with practice. To begin to accomplish this purpse we shall work on fairly simple problems.

  a. Try to answer the following questions.

      1) Does John teach the possibility of sinless perfection for a Christian here on earth in 1 John 2:1?

         a) Check the vocabulary meaning of ἁμαρτάνω.

         b) Identify the tense of ἁμάρτητε and ἁμάρτῃ.

         c) Read the context, especially 1 John 1:8, for limitations on John's meaning.

         d) Now write out in one or two clear sentences what you think John means by his first statement in 1 John 2:1.

      2) How secure is the basis of the assurance John offers in 1 John 2:3?

         a) What is the assurance?

         b) On what is the continuation of the assurance dependent?

         c) What does John assume in ἐὰν . . . τηρῶμεν?

         d) State John's idea clearly in your own words.

  b. Associate the following words with the new vocabulary.

      1) *holo*caust: a *whole* burnt offering.

      2) *miso*gynist: one who *hates* women.

      3) *phenomenon*: an event that can be observed from what *appears*.

      4) *tele*ost: a fish belonging to a group that has *complete* or true bones.

      5) *typhlo*logy: the systematic study of *blind*ness.

# Lesson 46

**343.** READING: 1 John 2:9-17

**344.** NEW VOCABULARY NEEDED FOR THIS PASSAGE

ἀγαπάω, ἀγαπήσω, ἠγάπησα, ἠγάπηκα, ἠγάπημαι, ἠγαπήθην: I love

ἀγάπη, -ης, ἡ: love

αἰών, αἰῶνος, ὁ: eternity, universe, present age

ἀλαζονείᾱ, -ᾱς, ἡ: boastfulness, vain display

ἄρτι: now, just now, just at this moment

βίος, -ου, ὁ: life, period of life, means of living, course of life

εἰς τὸν αἰῶνα: forever

ἕως: (prep. with gen.) until, as far as; (conj.) until

θέλημα, -ατος, τό: will, choice, the action purposed, the act of willing

ἰσχυρός, -ά, -όν: powerful, mighty, strong

μηδέ: and not, but not, nor, not even

μισέω, μισήσω, ἐμίσησα, μεμίσηκα, μεμίσημαι, — : I hate

νεανίσκος, -ου, ὁ: young man, youth, lad

νικάω, νικήσω, ἐνίκησα, νενίκηκα, — , ἐνικήθην: I conquer, win the victory over

ὁ ἀπ' ἀρχῆς: he who has been from the beginning

οἶδα: I know (see number 404 for other forms.)

παιδίον, -ου, τό: young child, little one

πονηρός, -ά, -όν: bad, evil, wicked

σάρξ, σαρκός, ἡ: flesh

σκάνδαλον, -ον, τό: stumbling block, cause of sin, snare

τυφλόω, — , ἐτύφλωσα, τετύφλωκα, — , — : I make blind, blind

ὑπάγω, — , — , — , — , — : I go away, depart

**345.** LIST OF FORMULAS FOR CONTRACT VERBS IN -αω

| | |
|---|---|
| α+ε=ᾱ | α+η=ᾳ |
| α+ει (=ε+ε)=ᾱ | α+ο=ω |
| α+ει (=ε+ι)=ᾳ | α+ου=ω |
| α+η=ᾱ | α+ω=ω |

# 346. PARADIGMS OF ἀγαπάω

## PRESENT

Active                                    Middle and Passive

### Indicative

| | | | |
|---|---|---|---|
| ἀγαπῶ | ἀγαπῶμεν | ἀγαπῶμαι | ἀγαπώμεθα |
| ἀγαπᾷς | ἀγαπᾶτε | ἀγαπᾷ | ἀγαπᾶσθε |
| ἀγαπᾷ | ἀγαπῶσι | ἀγαπᾶται | ἀγαπῶνται |

### Subjunctive

| | | | |
|---|---|---|---|
| ἀγαπῶ | ἀγαπῶμεν | ἀγαπῶμαι | ἀγαπώμεθα |
| ἀγαπᾷς | ἀγαπᾶτε | ἀγαπᾷ | ἀγαπᾶσθε |
| ἀγαπᾷ | ἀγαπῶσι | ἀγαπᾶται | ἀγαπῶνται |

### Imperative

| | | | |
|---|---|---|---|
| ἀγάπα | ἀγαπᾶτε | ἀγαπῶ | ἀγαπᾶσθε |
| ἀγαπάτω | ἀγαπάτωσαν | ἀγαπάσθω | ἀγαπάσθωσαν |

### Infinitive

ἀγαπᾶν                                    ἀγαπᾶσθαι

(This represents an original
ἀγαπάεεν which became ἀγαπᾶεν
and later ἀγαπᾶν.)

### Participle

ἀγαπῶν  ἀγαπῶσα  ἀγαπῶν        ἀγαπώμενος, -η, -ον

## IMPERFECT INDICATIVE

| | | | |
|---|---|---|---|
| ἠγάπων | ἠγαπῶμεν | ἠγαπώμην | ἠγαπώμεθα |
| ἠγάπας | ἠγαπᾶτε | ἠγαπῶ | ἠγαπᾶσθε |
| ἠγάπα | ἠγάπων | ἠγαπᾶτο | ἠγαπῶντο |

# 347. SUBJECTIVE AND OBJECTIVE GENITIVES

In number 77 we have three examples of objective genitives. Each of these genitives modifies a noun that implies the action of a verb. One example, χρείαν δωρεῶν, *need of gifts* implies that someone needs gifts.

In a similar example, ἡ χρεία Φιλίππου, *the need of Philip*, the implied meaning could be (1) *Someone needs Philip*, or (2) *Philip needs someone* or *something*.

The second interpretation takes Φιλίππου as a *subjective genitive*, a genitive furnishing the idea of the subject of the implied verb.

209

In 1 John 2:15-17 we have several examples of genitives that are either subjective or objective.

In verse 15 does ἡ ἀγάπη τοῦ πατρός imply *love for the Father* (i.e., Someone loves the Father)? With this understanding τοῦ πατρός is taken as an objective genitive. Or does this expression imply *the Father's love* (i.e., The Father loves someone)? Such an understanding assumes that τοῦ πατρός is a subjective genitive. Within the context of the New Testament both ideas are possible. In this verse, however, the Father and the world stand in contrast with each other. In the command "Do not love the world" and the conditional clause "If one loves the world," the object of the two verbs is made prominent by repetition. If ἡ ἀγάπη τοῦ πατρός is taken to imply a parallel but contrasting object of love, we may reach the conclusion "If a man loves the world, he does not love the Father." Such a conclusion fits the context. If, however, τοῦ πατρός is understood as giving us the subject of the implied verb love, the conclusion reached is "If a man loves the world, the Father does not love him."

## 348. PROBLEMS TO STUDY

    a. Classify τῆς σαρκός and τῶν ὀφθαλμῶν in verse 16 and αὐτοῦ and τοῦ θεοῦ in verse 17 as either subjective or objective genitives. Give reasons for your decision.

    b. What kind of conditional sentence occurs in verse 15? What does it imply? See number 317*d*.

210

# Lesson 47

---

**349.** READING: 1 John 2:18—3:3

**350.** NEW VOCABULARY NEEDED FOR THIS PASSAGE

ἅγιος, -ᾱ, -ον: holy

ἁγνίζω, — , ἥγνισα, ἥγνικα, ἥγνισμαι, ἡγνίσθην: I purify

ἁγνός, -ή, -όν: pure, clean

αἰσχύνομαι, — , — , — , — , ᾐσχύνθην: I am ashamed, am put to shame

ἀντίχριστος, -ου, ὁ: Antichrist, one who tries to take the place of the Messiah and who withstands Him

ἀρνέομαι, ἀρνήσομαι, ἠρνησάμην, — , ἥρνημαι, — : I deny, say "No," refuse to acknowledge, disown

γεννάω, γεννήσω, ἐγέννησα, γεγέννηκα, γεγέννημαι, ἐγεννήθην: I beget, become the father of, bear

δικαιοσύνη, -ης, ἡ: righteousness

εἰδῆτε: second pl. second perf. subj. act. οἶδα (See number 405.)

ἐλπίς, ἐλπίδος, ἡ: hope

ἐξέρχομαι, ἐξελεύσομαι, ἐξῆλθον, ἐξελήλυθα, — , — : I come out, go out

ἐπαγγέλλομαι, — , ἐπηγγειλάμην, — , ἐπήγγελμαι, — : I promise

ὅθεν: whence, wherefore

ὅμοιος, -ᾱ, -ον: like, resembling, similar to, of the same kind as

οὐδέ: and not, also not, nor, not even

παρουσίᾱ, -ᾱς, ἡ: presence, coming, arrival

πολύς, πολλή, πολύ: (sing.) much, (pl.) many

ποταπός, -ή, -όν: what?, of what sort?, what kind of?

χρῖσμα, -ατος, τό: anointing

ψεῦδος, -ους, τό: lie, falsehood (See number 258.)

ὥρᾱ, -ᾱς, ἡ: hour, season

**351.** PARADIGM OF πολύς

With the exception of the four italicized forms in the paradigm below, πολύς is an adjective of the first and second declensions.

| | | |
|---|---|---|
| πολύς | πολλή | πολύ |
| πολλοῦ | πολλῆς | πολλοῦ |
| πολλῷ | πολλῇ | πολλῷ |
| πολύν | πολλήν | πολύ |
| | | |
| πολλοί | πολλαί | πολλά |
| πολλῶν | πολλῶν | πολλῶν |
| πολλοῖς | πολλαῖς | πολλοῖς |
| πολλούς | πολλάς | πολλά |

## 352. NOTES ON 1 John 2:18-21

a. ἀλλ' ἵνα (v. 19). This is an ellipsis, an omission of what must be supplied to complete the meaning. From the beginning of the verse supply ἐξῆλθαν between ἀλλ' and ἵνα.

b. πᾶν ... οὐκ (v. 21). *No.* When these two words occur in the same clause, be alert to two possible translations, (1) *not all* or *not every*, and (2) *no.*

## 353. SUBSTANTIVE CLAUSES WITH ἵνα

In 1 John 2:27 we have a ἵνα clause which is used as a substantive (i.e., a noun).

...καὶ οὐ χρείαν ἔχετε ἵνα τις διδάσκῃ ὑμᾶς...
...and you have no need *that any one teach you*...

The ἵνα clause stands as an appositive to χρείαν.

## 354. POINTS TO STUDY

a. Was John uncertain about the Lord's return? See ἐάν in 1 John 2:28. (F. Wilbur Gingrich and F. W. Danker, et al, eds. and trans., *A Greek-English Lexicon of the New Testament and Other Early Christian Literature*, 2d rev. and augmented ed. [Chicago: U. of Chicago, 1979], p. 211, under ἐάν 1.*d*: "At times the m[eani]ng of ἐάν approaches closely that of ὅταν *whenever*, or of *when* ... 1 J[ohn] 2:28 ... ; J[ohn] 12:32; 14:3; H[e]brews 3:7...").

b. Can you give a plausible explanation of John's use of σχῶμεν and αἰσχυνθῶμεν in 2:28 instead of ἔχωμεν and αἰσχυνώμεθα?

# Lesson 48

## 355. READING: 1 John 3:4-18

## 356. NEW VOCABULARY NEEDED FOR THIS PASSAGE

αἴρω, ἀρῶ, ἦρα, ἦρκα, ἦρμαι, ἤρθην:  I take up, lift up, raise, carry, take away, remove

ἀνθρωποκτόνος, -ου, ὁ:  murderer

ἀνομίᾱ, -ᾱς, ἡ:  lawlessness, transgression, iniquity

διάβολος, -ου, ὁ:  devil, accuser

θάνατος, -ου, ὁ:  death

θαυμάζω, θαυμάσομαι, ἐθαύμασα, — , — , ἐθαυμάσθην:  I wonder, wonder at

θεωρέω, θεωρήσω, ἐθεώρησα, — , — , — :  I look at, behold, gaze at, see

Κάϊν (indecl.), ὁ:  Cain

κλείω, κλείσω, ἔκλεισα, — , κέκλεισμαι, ἐκλείσθην:  I shut

λύω, — , ἔλυσα, — , λέλυμαι, ἐλύθην:  I loose, destroy

μεταβαίνω, μεταβήσομαι, μετέβην, μεταβέβηκα, — , — :  I pass over (from one place to another), depart

μηδείς, μηδεμία, μηδέν:  no one, no, nothing

σπέρμα, -ατος, τό:  seed, offspring, posterity, children

σπλάγχνον, -ου, τό:  heart, affections

σφάζω, σφάξω, ἔσφαξα, — , ἔσφαγμαι, ἐσφάγην:  I slay, slaughter

φανερός, -ά, -όν:  visible, manifest

χάριν:  (prep. with gen.) for, on account of, for the sake of

ψυχή, -ῆς, ἡ:  soul, life

## 357. PRESENT PROGRESSIVE

In 1 John 3:8, . . . ὅτι ἀπ᾽ ἀρχῆς ὁ διάβολος ἁμαρτάνει the verb indicates an action begun in the past and still going on in the present. The clause can be translated: . . . *because the devil has been sinning from the beginning.*

## 358. PROBLEMS AND QUESTIONS

a. In 3:4 which noun is the subject in ἡ ἁμαρτία ἐστιν ἡ ἀνομία?

b. Explain in 3:6 ἁμαρτάνει and ἁμαρτάνων. Is there a man, a woman, or a child who does not sin (Rom. 3:23)? Is "does not

213

sin" the only possible translation of οὐχ ἁμαρτάνει? Is it the best one here?

c. In 3:9 comment on the tense of ποιεί and ἁμαρτάνειν.
d. In 3:13 what does the tense of θαυμάζετε imply?
e. Bauer-Gingrich-Danker refer to θαυμάζω as a verb of emotion. How does this influence the translation of εἰ?
f. In 3:14 does μεταβεβήκαμεν indicate a probable return ἐκ τῆς ζωῆς εἰς τὸν θάνατον?
g. In 3:16 what is the duration of the obligation stated in ὀφείλομεν?

# Lesson 49

---

**359.** READING: 1 John 3:19-4:21

**360.** NEW VOCABULARY NEEDED FOR THIS PASSAGE

αἰτέω, αἰτήσω, ἤτησα, ἤτηκα, — , — : I ask

ἀρεστός, -ή, -όν: pleasing, agreeable

δοκιμάζω, δοκιμάσω, ἐδοκίμασα, — , δεδοκίμασμαι, — : I test, prove, approve

ἔμπροσθεν: (with gen.) in front of, before

ἐνώπιον: (with gen.) before, in the presence of, in the sight of

ἔξω: outside

ζῶ (ζάω), ζήσω, ἔζησα, — , — , — : I live, am alive

καταγινώσκω, — , — , — , κατέγνωσμαι, — : I blame, condemn

κόλασις, -εως, ἡ: correction, punishment, penalty

κρίσις, -εως, ἡ: decision, judgment, right, justice

μείζων, μεῖζον (comparative of μέγας): greater

μονογενής, -ές: only of its kind, unique

πλάνη, -ης, ἡ: error, going astray

πνεῦμα, -ατος, τό: spirit

πώποτε: ever yet

τέλειος, -ᾱ, -ον: mature, complete, perfect

φοβέομαι, — , — , — , — , ἐφοβήθην: I fear, am afraid of

ψευδοπροφήτης, -ου, ὁ: false prophet

**361.** PROBLEMS

Comment on each of the following words in its context.

a. v. 1   πιστεύετε
b. v. 1   δοκιμάζετε
c. v. 2   ἐληλυθότα
d. v. 4   νενικήκατε
e. v. 12  τετελειωμένη . . . ἐστίν
f. v. 16  ἐγνώκαμεν
g. v. 16  πεπιστεύκαμεν

# Lesson 50

**362.** READING: 1 John 5:1-21

**363.** VOCABULARY

αἴτημα, -ατος, τό:  request, what is asked for

ἅπτω, — , ἧψα, — , — , — :  I fasten to, set on fire; (mid.) I cling to, fasten myself to, lay hold of, assail

βαρύς, -εῖα, -ύ:  heavy, burdensome

διάνοια, -ᾱς, ἡ:  understanding, mind

εἴδωλον, -ου, τό:  idol, image of a false god, false god

ἐρωτάω, ἐρωτήσω, ἠρώτησα, — , — , — :  I ask a question, make a request

κεῖμαι, — , — , — , — :  I lie, am located

μαρτυρίᾱ, -ᾱς, ἡ:  witness, testimony, evidence

νίκη, -ης, ἡ:  victory

ὅταν:  when, whenever

πίστις, -εως, ἡ:  faith

τρεῖς, τρία:  three

φυλάσσω, φυλάξω, ἐφύλαξα, πεφύλαχα, — , ἐφυλάχθην:  I guard, keep, watch, protect

**364.** PARADIGM OF βαρύς

| βαρύς | βαρεῖα | βαρύ |
|-------|--------|------|
| βαρέος | βαρείᾱς | βαρέος |
| βαρεῖ | βαρείᾳ | βαρεῖ |
| βαρύν | βαρεῖαν | βαρύ |
| βαρεῖς | βαρεῖαι | βαρέα |
| βαρέων | βαρειῶν | βαρέων |
| βαρέσι | βαρείαις | βαρέσι |
| βαρεῖς | βαρείᾱς | βαρέα |

**365.** PROBLEMS

a. Classify and explain the meaning of every subordinate clause in verses 15 and 16.

b. Clauses introduced by ἵνα may be classified as follows:

216

1) Purpose clauses, giving the aim or goal which one has in performing some action.
2) Substantive clauses, clauses serving as nouns.
3) Subfinal clauses, clauses expressing both purpose and content, a combination of purpose and substantive.
4) Result clauses, giving the result of some action.

Classify each of the ἵνα clauses in 1 John 5 in one of these four groups.

# APPENDIX

## Nouns

## 366. FIRST OR *A* DECLENSION NOUNS

### a. Stems ending in ε, ι, or ρ.

| | | | |
|---|---|---|---|
| καρδίᾱ | καρδίαι | ἀλήθεια | ἀλήθειαι |
| καρδίᾱς | καρδιῶν | ἀληθείᾱς | ἀληθειῶν |
| καρδίᾳ | καρδίαις | ἀληθείᾳ | ἀληθείαις |
| καρδίᾱν | καρδίᾱς | ἀλήθειαν | ἀληθείᾱς |

### b. Stems not ending in ε, ι, or ρ.

| | | | | | | | |
|---|---|---|---|---|---|---|---|
| κώμη | κῶμαι | θάλασσα | θάλασσαι | προφήτης | προφῆται | γῆ | No |
| κώμης | κωμῶν | θαλάσσης | θαλασσῶν | προφήτου | προφητῶν | γῆς | |
| κώμῃ | κώμαις | θαλάσσῃ | θαλάσσαις | προφήτῃ | προφήταις | γῇ | Plural |
| κώμην | κώμᾱς | θάλασσαν | θαλάσσᾱς | προφήτην | προφήτᾱς | γῆν | |
| | | | | προφῆτα | | | |

## 367. SECOND OR *O* DECLENSION NOUNS

| | | | |
|---|---|---|---|
| ἄνθρωπος | ἄνθρωποι | ποτήριον | ποτήρια |
| ἀνθρώπου | ἀνθρώπων | ποτηρίου | ποτηρίων |
| ἀνθρώπῳ | ἀνθρώποις | ποτηρίῳ | ποτηρίοις |
| ἄνθρωπον | ἀνθρώπους | ποτήριον | ποτήρια |
| ἄνθρωπε | | | |

## 368. THIRD OR CONSONANT DECLENSION NOUNS

### a. Stems ending in a palatal mute (κ, γ, χ).

| | | | |
|---|---|---|---|
| ἡ σάρξ | σάρκες | ἡ γυνή | γυναῖκες |
| σαρκός | σαρκῶν | γυναικός | γυναικῶν |
| σαρκί | σαρξί | γυναικί | γυναιξί |
| σάρκα | σάρκας | γυναῖκα | γυναῖκας |
| | | γύναι | |

### b. Stems ending in a linguo-dental (τ, δ, θ).

| | | | | | |
|---|---|---|---|---|---|
| ὁ λέων | λέοντες | τὸ ὄνομα | ὀνόματα | τὸ ὕδωρ | ὕδατα |
| λέοντος | λεόντων | ὀνόματος | ὀνομάτων | ὕδατος | ὑδάτων |
| λέοντι | λέουσι | ὀνόματι | ὀνόμασι | ὕδατι | ὕδασι |
| λέοντα | λέοντας | ὄνομα | ὀνόματα | ὕδωρ | ὕδατα |

| | | | | | |
|---|---|---|---|---|---|
| ἡ ἐλπίς | ἐλπίδες | ἡ λαμπάς | λαμπάδες | ἡ νύξ | νύκτες |
| ἐλπίδος | ἐλπίδων | λαμπάδος | λαμπάδων | νυκτός | νυκτῶν |
| ἐλπίδι | ἐλπίσι | λαμπάδι | λαμπάσι | νυκτί | νυξί |
| ἐλπίδα | ἐλπίδας | λαμπάδα | λαμπάδας | νύκτα | νύκτας |

c. Stems ending in a liquid (λ, ρ).

| ὁ πατήρ | πατέρες | ἡ μήτηρ | μητέρες | ὁ ἀνήρ | ἄνδρες | ὁ σωτήρ | σωτῆρες |
|---------|---------|---------|---------|--------|--------|---------|---------|
| πατρός | πατέρων | μητρός | μητέρων | ἀνδρός | ἀνδρῶν | | σωτῆρος σωτήρων |
| πατρί | πατράσι | μητρί | μητράσι | ἀνδρί | ἀνδράσι | σωτῆρι | σωτῆρσι |
| πατέρα | πατέρας | μητέρα | μητέρας | ἄνδρα | ἄνδρας | σωτῆρα | σωτῆρας |
| πάτερ | | | | ἄνερ | | | |

d. Stems ending in a nasal (μ, ν).

| ὁ αἰών | αἰῶνες | ὁ ἡγεμών | ἡγεμόνες |
|--------|--------|----------|----------|
| αἰῶνος | αἰώνων | ἡγεμόνος | ἡγεμόνων |
| αἰῶνι | αἰῶσι | ἡγεμόνι | ἡγεμόσι |
| αἰῶνα | αἰῶνας | ἡγεμόνα | ἡγεμόνας |

e. Stems ending in -ος/-ες.

| τὸ ἔθνος | ἔθνη |
|----------|------|
| ἔθνους | ἐθνῶν |
| ἔθνει | ἔθνεσι |
| ἔθνος | ἔθνη |

f. Stems ending in -ει/-ι.

| ἡ θλῖψις | θλίψεις | ὁ ἱερεύς | ἱερεῖς |
|----------|---------|----------|--------|
| θλίψεως | θλίψεων | ἱερέως | ἱερέων |
| θλίψει | θλίψεσι | ἱερεῖ | ἱερεῦσι |
| θλῖψιν | θλίψεις | ἱερέα | ἱερεῖς |
| | | ἱερεῦ | |

PRONOUNS

# 369. PERSONAL PRONOUNS

| ἐγώ | σύ | αὐτός | αὐτή | αὐτό |
|-----|-----|-------|------|------|
| ἐμοῦ, μου | σοῦ, σου | αὐτοῦ | αὐτῆς | αὐτοῦ |
| ἐμοί, μοι | σοί, σοι | αὐτῷ | αὐτῇ | αὐτῷ |
| ἐμέ, με | σέ, σε | αὐτόν | αὐτήν | αὐτό |
| ἡμεῖς | ὑμεῖς | αὐτοί | αὐταί | αὐτά |
| ἡμῶν | ὑμῶν | αὐτῶν | αὐτῶν | αὐτῶν |
| ἡμῖν | ὑμῖν | αὐτοῖς | αὐταῖς | αὐτοῖς |
| ἡμᾶς | ὑμᾶς | αὐτούς | αὐτάς | αὐτά |

# 370. REFLEXIVE PRONOUNS

| ἐμαυτοῦ | ἐμαυτῆς | σεαυτοῦ | σεαυτῆς | ἑαυτοῦ | ἑαυτῆς | ἑαυτοῦ |
|---------|---------|---------|---------|--------|--------|--------|
| ἐμαυτῷ | ἐμαυτῇ | σεαυτῷ | σεαυτῇ | ἑαυτῷ | ἑαυτῇ | ἑαυτῷ |
| ἐμαυτόν | ἐμαυτήν | σεαυτόν | σεαυτήν | ἑαυτόν | ἑαυτήν | ἑαυτό |
| ἑαυτῶν | ἑαυτῶν | ἑαυτῶν | ἑαυτῶν | ἑαυτῶν | ἑαυτῶν | ἑαυτῶν |
| ἑαυτοῖς | ἑαυταῖς | ἑαυτοῖς | ἑαυταῖς | ἑαυτοῖς | ἑαυταῖς | ἑαυτοῖς |
| ἑαυτούς | ἑαυτάς | ἑαυτούς | ἑαυτάς | ἑαυτούς | ἑαυτάς | ἑαυτά |

## 371. INTENSIVE PRONOUN

| | | | | | |
|---|---|---|---|---|---|
| αὐτός | αὐτή | αὐτό | αὐτοί | αὐταί | αὐτά |
| αὐτοῦ | αὐτῆς | αὐτοῦ | αὐτῶν | αὐτῶν | αὐτῶν |
| αὐτῷ | αὐτῇ | αὐτῷ | αὐτοῖς | αὐταῖς | αὐτοῖς |
| αὐτόν | αὐτήν | αὐτό | αὐτούς | αὐτάς | αὐτά |

## 372. RECIPROCAL PRONOUN (In the New Testament only masculine forms are used.)

| | | |
|---|---|---|
| ἀλλήλων | ἀλλήλων | ἀλλήλων |
| ἀλλήλοις | ἀλλήλαις | ἀλλήλοις |
| ἀλλήλους | ἀλλήλᾱς | ἄλληλα |

## 373. DEMONSTRATIVE PRONOUNS

| | | | | | |
|---|---|---|---|---|---|
| οὗτος | αὕτη | τοῦτο | ἐκεῖνος | ἐκείνη | ἐκεῖνο |
| τούτου | ταύτης | τούτου | ἐκείνου | ἐκείνης | ἐκείνου |
| τούτῳ | ταύτῃ | τούτῳ | ἐκείνῳ | ἐκείνῃ | ἐκείνῳ |
| τοῦτον | ταύτην | τοῦτο | ἐκεῖνον | ἐκείνην | ἐκεῖνο |
| οὗτοι | αὗται | ταῦτα | ἐκεῖνοι | ἐκεῖναι | ἐκεῖνα |
| τούτων | τούτων | τούτων | ἐκείνων | ἐκείνων | ἐκείνων |
| τούτοις | ταύταις | τούτοις | ἐκείνοις | ἐκείναις | ἐκείνοις |
| τούτους | ταύτᾱς | ταῦτα | ἐκείνους | ἐκείνᾱς | ἐκεῖνα |

## 374. RELATIVE PRONOUN

| | | | | | |
|---|---|---|---|---|---|
| ὅς | ἥ | ὅ | οἵ | αἵ | ἅ |
| οὗ | ἧς | οὗ | ὧν | ὧν | ὧν |
| ᾧ | ᾗ | ᾧ | οἷς | αἷς | οἷς |
| ὅν | ἥν | ὅ | οὕς | ἅς | ἅ |

## 375. GENERAL OR INDEFINITE RELATIVE PRONOUN

| | | | | | |
|---|---|---|---|---|---|
| ὅστις | ἥτις | ὅ τι | οἵτινες | αἵτινες | ἅτινα |
| ὅτου | — | — | — | — | — |
| — | — | — | — | — | — |
| — | — | ὅ τι | — | — | — |

## 376. INTERROGATIVE PRONOUN (AND ADJECTIVE)

| | |
|---|---|
| τίς | τί |
| τίνος | τίνος |
| τίνι | τίνι |
| τίνα | τί |
| τίνες | τίνα |
| τίνων | τίνων |
| τίσι | τίσι |
| τίνας | τίνα |

# 377. INDEFINITE PRONOUN (AND ADJECTIVE)

τὶς     τὶ
τινός    τινός
τινί     τινί
τινά    τὶ

τινές    τινά
τινῶν   τινῶν
τισί     τισί
τινάς    τινά

# 378. NEGATIVE PRONOUNS

| μηδείς | μηδεμία | μηδέν | οὐδείς | οὐδεμία | οὐδέν |
|--------|---------|-------|--------|---------|-------|
| μηδενός | μηδεμιᾶς | μηδενός | οὐδενός | οὐδεμιᾶς | οὐδενός |
| μηδενί | μηδεμιᾷ | μηδενί | οὐδενί | οὐδεμιᾷ | οὐδενί |
| μηδένα | μηδεμίαν | μηδέν | οὐδένα | οὐδεμίαν | οὐδέν |

### ADJECTIVES

# 379. DEFINITE ARTICLE

| ὁ | ἡ | τό | οἱ | αἱ | τά |
|---|---|----|----|----|----|
| τοῦ | τῆς | τοῦ | τῶν | τῶν | τῶν |
| τῷ | τῇ | τῷ | τοῖς | ταῖς | τοῖς |
| τόν | τήν | τό | τούς | τάς | τά |

# 380. FIRST AND SECOND DECLENSION

## a. Two terminations

| αἰώνιος | αἰώνιον | αἰώνιοι | αἰώνια |
|---------|---------|---------|--------|
| αἰωνίου | αἰωνίου | αἰωνίων | αἰωνίων |
| αἰωνίῳ | αἰωνίῳ | αἰωνίοις | αἰωνίοις |
| αἰώνιον | αἰώνιον | αἰωνίους | αἰώνια |

## b. Three Terminations. (including middle participles, πιστευόμενος, -η, -ον)

| καλός | καλή | καλόν | δίκαιος | δικαίᾱ | δίκαιον |
|-------|------|-------|---------|--------|---------|
| καλοῦ | καλῆς | καλοῦ | δικαίου | δικαίᾱς | δικαίου |
| καλῷ | καλῇ | καλῷ | δικαίῳ | δικαίᾳ | δικαίῳ |
| καλόν | καλήν | καλόν | δίκαιον | δικαίᾱν | δίκαιον |
| καλέ | | | δίκαιε | | |

| καλοί | καλαί | καλά | δίκαιοι | δίκαιαι | δίκαια |
|-------|-------|------|---------|---------|--------|
| καλῶν | καλῶν | καλῶν | δικαίων | δικαίων | δικαίων |
| καλοῖς | καλαῖς | καλοῖς | δικαίοις | δικαίαις | δικαίοις |
| καλούς | καλάς | καλά | δικαίους | δικαίᾱς | δίκαια |

## 381. THIRD DECLENSION

| | | | |
|---|---|---|---|
| ἀληθής | ἀληθές | κρείσσων | κρεῖσσον |
| ἀληθοῦς | ἀληθοῦς | κρείσσονος | κρείσσονος |
| ἀληθεῖ | ἀληθεῖ | κρείσσονι | κρείσσονι |
| ἀληθῆ | ἀληθές | κρείσσονα (κρείσσω) | κρεῖσσον |
| ἀληθές | | | |

| | | | |
|---|---|---|---|
| ἀληθεῖς | ἀληθῆ | κρείσσονες (κρείσσους) | κρείσσονα (κρείσσω) |
| ἀληθῶν | ἀληθῶν | κρεισσόνων | κρεισσόνων |
| ἀληθέσι | ἀληθέσι | κρείσσοσι | κρείσσοσι |
| ἀληθεῖς | ἀληθῆ | κρείσσονας (κρείσσους) | κρείσσονα (κρείσσω) |

## 382. FIRST AND THIRD DECLENSION

| | | | | | |
|---|---|---|---|---|---|
| βαρύς | βαρεῖα | βαρύ | πᾶς | πᾶσα | πᾶν |
| βαρέος | βαρείᾱς | βαρέος | παντός | πάσης | παντός |
| βαρεῖ | βαρείᾳ | βαρεῖ | παντί | πάσῃ | παντί |
| βαρύν | βαρεῖαν | βαρύ | πάντα | πᾶσαν | πᾶν |
| βαρεῖς | βαρεῖαι | βαρέα | πάντες | πᾶσαι | πάντα |
| βαρέων | βαρειῶν | βαρέων | πάντων | πασῶν | πάντων |
| βαρέσι | βαρείαις | βαρέσι | πᾶσι | πάσαις | πᾶσι |
| βαρεῖς | βαρείᾱς | βαρέα | πάντας | πάσᾱς | πάντα |

## 383. IRREGULAR ADJECTIVE

| | | | | | |
|---|---|---|---|---|---|
| μέγας | μεγάλη | μέγα | μεγάλοι | μεγάλαι | μεγάλα |
| μεγάλου | μεγάλης | μεγάλου | μεγάλων | μεγάλων | μεγάλων |
| μεγάλῳ | μεγάλῃ | μεγάλῳ | μεγάλοις | μεγάλαις | μεγάλοις |
| μέγαν | μεγάλην | μέγα | μεγάλους | μεγάλᾱς | μεγάλα |

## 384. DECLENSION OF THE FIRST FOUR CARDINAL NUMBERS

| | | | | | | | |
|---|---|---|---|---|---|---|---|
| εἷς | μία | ἕν | δύο | τρεῖς | τρία | τέσσαρες | τέσσαρα |
| ἑνός | μιᾶς | ἑνός | δύο | τριῶν | τριῶν | τεσσάρων | τεσσάρων |
| ἑνί | μιᾷ | ἑνί | δυσί | τρισί | τρισί | τέσσαρσι | τέσσαρσι |
| ἕνα | μίαν | ἕν | δύο | τρεῖς | τρία | τέσσαρας | τέσσαρα |

## 385.

| CARDINALS | ORDINALS |
|---|---|
| 1. εἷς, μία, ἕν | πρῶτος |
| 2. δύο | δεύτερος |
| 3. τρεῖς, τρία | τρίτος |
| 4. τέσσαρες, τέσσαρα | τέταρτος |
| 5. πέντε | πέμπτος |
| 6. ἕξ | ἕκτος |
| 7. ἑπτά | ἕβδομος |

|  |  |
|---|---|
| 8. ὀκτώ | ὄγδοος |
| 9. ἐννέα | ἔνατος |
| 10. δέκα | δέκατος |
| 11. ἕνδεκα | ἑνδέκατος |
| 12. δώδεκα and δεκαδύο | δωδέκατος |
| 14. δεκατέσσαρες | τεσσαρεσκαιδέκατος |
| 15. δεκαπέντε | πεντεκαιδέκατος |
| 16. δεκαέξ | |
| 18. δεκαοκτώ and δέκα καὶ ὀκτώ | |
| 19. δεκαεννέα | |
| 20. εἴκοσι | |
| 30. τριάκοντα | |
| 40. τεσσαράκοντα | |
| 50. πεντήκοντα | |
| 60. ἑξήκοντα | |
| 90. ἐνενήκοντα | |
| 100. ἑκατόν | |
| 200. διακόσιοι, -αι, -α | |
| 300. τριακόσιοι, -αι, α | |
| 1,000. χίλιοι, -αι, -α | |
| 10,000. μύριοι, -αι, -α | |

## 386. PRESENT PARTICIPLE OF εἰμί

(The second aorist active participle of βάλλω: βαλών, βαλοῦσα, βαλόν, is like this paradigm.)

| | | |
|---|---|---|
| ὤν | οὖσα | ὄν |
| ὄντος | οὔσης | ὄντος |
| ὄντι | οὔσῃ | ὄντι |
| ὄντα | οὖσαν | ὄν |
| | | |
| ὄντες | οὖσαι | ὄντα |
| ὄντων | οὐσῶν | ὄντων |
| οὖσι | οὔσαις | οὖσι |
| ὄντας | οὔσᾱς | ὄντα |

## 387. PRESENT ACTIVE PARTICIPLE OF πιστεύω

| | | |
|---|---|---|
| πιστεύων | πιστεύουσα | πιστεῦον |
| πιστεύοντος | πιστευούσης | πιστεύοντος |
| πιστεύοντι | πιστευούσῃ | πιστεύοντι |
| πιστεύοντα | πιστεύουσαν | πιστεῦον |
| | | |
| πιστεύοντες | πιστεύουσαι | πιστεύοντα |
| πιστευόντων | πιστευουσῶν | πιστευόντων |
| πιστεύουσι | πιστευούσαις | πιστεύουσι |
| πιστεύοντας | πιστευούσᾱς | πιστεύοντα |

## 388. FUTURE ACTIVE PARTICIPLE OF πιστεύω

| | | |
|---|---|---|
| πιστεύσων | πιστεύσουσα | πιστεῦσον |
| πιστεύσοντος | πιστευσούσης | πιστεύσοντος |
| πιστεύσοντι | πιστευσούσῃ | πιστεύσοντι |
| πιστεύσοντα | πιστεύσουσαν | πιστεῦσον |
| πιστεύσοντες | πιστεύσουσαι | πιστεύσοντα |
| πιστευσόντων | πιστευσουσῶν | πιστευσόντων |
| πιστεύσουσι | πιστευσούσαις | πιστεύσουσι |
| πιστεύσοντας | πιστευσούσᾱς | πιστεύσοντα |

## 389. FUTURE ACTIVE PARTICIPLE OF μένω

| | | |
|---|---|---|
| μενῶν | μενοῦσα | μενοῦν |
| μενοῦντος | μενούσης | μενοῦντος |
| μενοῦντι | μενούσῃ | μενοῦντι |
| μενοῦντα | μενοῦσαν | μενοῦν |
| μενοῦντες | μενοῦσαι | μενοῦντα |
| μενούντων | μενουσῶν | μενούντων |
| μενοῦσι | μενούσαις | μενοῦσι |
| μενοῦντας | μενούσᾱς | μενοῦντα |

## 390. AORIST ACTIVE PARTICIPLE OF πιστεύω

| | | |
|---|---|---|
| πιστεύσᾱς | πιστεύσᾱσα | πιστεῦσαν |
| πιστεύσαντος | πιστευσάσης | πιστεύσαντος |
| πιστεύσαντι | πιστευσάσῃ | πιστεύσαντι |
| πιστεύσαντα | πιστεύσᾱσαν | πιστεῦσαν |
| πιστεύσαντες | πιστεύσᾱσαι | πιστεύσαντα |
| πιστευσάντων | πιστευσᾱσῶν | πιστευσάντων |
| πιστεύσᾱσι | πιστευσάσαις | πιστεύσᾱσι |
| πιστεύσαντας | πιστευσάσᾱς | πιστεύσαντα |

## 391. PERFECT ACTIVE PARTICIPLE OF πιστεύω

| | | |
|---|---|---|
| πεπιστευκώς | πεπιστευκυῖα | πεπιστευκός |
| πεπιστευκότος | πεπιστευκυίᾱς | πεπιστευκότος |
| πεπιστευκότι | πεπιστευκυίᾳ | πεπιστευκότι |
| πεπιστευκότα | πεπιστευκυῖαν | πεπιστευκός |
| πεπιστευκότες | πεπιστευκυῖαι | πεπιστευκότα |
| πεπιστευκότων | πεπιστευκυιῶν | πεπιστευκότων |
| πεπιστευκόσι | πεπιστευκυίαις | πεπιστευκόσι |
| πεπιστευκότας | πεπιστευκυίᾱς | πεπιστευκότα |

## 392. AORIST PASSIVE PARTICIPLE OF πιστεύω

| | | |
|---|---|---|
| πιστευθείς | πιστευθεῖσα | πιστευθέν |
| πιστευθέντος | πιστευθείσης | πιστευθέντος |
| πιστευθέντι | πιστευθείσῃ | πιστευθέντι |
| πιστευθέντα | πιστευθεῖσαν | πιστευθέν |
| | | |
| πιστευθέντες | πιστευθεῖσαι | πιστευθέντα |
| πιστευθέντων | πιστευθεισῶν | πιστευθέντων |
| πιστευθεῖσι | πιστευθείσαις | πιστευθεῖσι |
| πιστευθέντος | πιστευθείσᾱς | πιστευθέντα |

## 393. PRESENT ACTIVE PARTICIPLE OF δίδωμι

| | | |
|---|---|---|
| διδούς | διδοῦσα | διδόν |
| διδόντος | διδούσης | διδόντος |
| διδόντι | διδούσῃ | διδόντι |
| διδόντα | διδοῦσαν | διδόν |
| | | |
| διδόντες | διδοῦσαι | διδόντα |
| διδόντων | διδουσῶν | διδόντων |
| διδοῦσι | διδούσαις | διδοῦσι |
| διδόντας | διδούσᾱς | διδόντα |

## 394. PRESENT ACTIVE PARTICIPLE OF ποιέω

| | | |
|---|---|---|
| ποιῶν | ποιοῦσα | ποιοῦν |
| ποιοῦντος | ποιούσης | ποιοῦντος |
| ποιοῦντι | ποιούσῃ | ποιοῦντι |
| ποιοῦντα | ποιοῦσαν | ποιοῦν |
| | | |
| ποιοῦντες | ποιοῦσαι | ποιοῦντα |
| ποιούντων | ποιουσῶν | ποιούντων |
| ποιοῦσι | ποιούσαις | ποιοῦσι |
| ποιοῦντας | ποιούσᾱς | ποιοῦντα |

## 395. PRESENT ACTIVE PARTICIPLE OF ἀγαπάω

| | | |
|---|---|---|
| ἀγαπῶν | ἀγαπῶσα | ἀγαπῶν |
| ἀγαπῶντος | ἀγαπώσης | ἀγαπῶντος |
| ἀγαπῶντι | ἀγαπώσῃ | ἀγαπῶντι |
| ἀγαπῶντα | ἀγαπῶσαν | ἀγαπῶν |
| | | |
| ἀγαπῶντες | ἀγαπῶσαι | ἀγαπῶντα |
| ἀγαπώντων | ἀγαπωσῶν | ἀγαπώντων |
| ἀγαπῶσι | ἀγαπώσαις | ἀγαπῶσι |
| ἀγαπῶντας | ἀγαπώσᾱς | ἀγαπῶντα |

## 396. PERSONAL ENDINGS OF VERBS AND VERB ANALYSIS OF THE INDICATIVE

| | | Active | Middle and Passive |
|---|---|---|---|
| **Primary** | | Ω Verbs<br>Present & Future with variable vowel<br><br>-ω<br>-εις<br>-ει<br>-ομεν<br>-ετε<br>-ουσι<br>———————<br>Perfect without variable vowel<br><br>—<br>-ς<br>—<br>-μεν<br>-τε<br>-ᾱσι (-νσι) | Present, Future, and Perfect Indicative, and Present and Aorist Subjunctive<br><br>-μαι<br>-σαι (often contracted)<br>-ται<br>-μεθα<br>-σθε<br>-νται |
| | | MI Verbs<br>-μι<br>-ς<br>-σι<br>-μεν<br>-τε<br>-ᾱσι (-νσι) | |
| **Secondary** | | Imperfect, Aorist, Pluperfect, and Aorist Passive<br><br>-ν<br>-ς<br>— | Imperfect, Aorist, and Pluperfect except Aorist Passive<br><br>-μην<br>-σο (often contracted)<br>-το |

|  | -μεν | -μεθα |
|---|---|---|
|  | -τε | -σθε |
|  | -ν & -σαν | -ντο |
| Imperative | —, -ς, & -θι | -σο |
|  | -τω | -σθω |
|  | -τε | -σθε |
|  | -τωσαν | -σθωσαν |

## 397. PARADIGMS OF πιστεύω

### PRESENT

| | Active | | Middle & Passive | |
|---|---|---|---|---|
| Ind. | πιστεύω | πιστεύομεν | πιστεύομαι | πιστευόμεθα |
| | πιστεύεις | πιστεύετε | πιστεύῃ | πιστεύεσθε |
| | πιστεύει | πιστεύουσι | πιστεύεται | πιστεύονται |
| Sub. | πιστεύω | πιστεύωμεν | πιστεύωμαι | πιστευώμεθα |
| | πιστεύῃς | πιστεύητε | πιστεύῃ | πιστεύησθε |
| | πιστεύῃ | πιστεύωσι | πιστεύηται | πιστεύωνται |
| Opt. | πιστεύοιμι | πιστεύοιμεν | πιστευοίμην | πιστευοίμεθα |
| | πιστεύοις | πιστεύοιτε | πιστεύοιο | πιστεύοισθε |
| | πιστεύοι | πιστεύοιεν | πιστεύοιτο | πιστεύοιντο |
| Impv. | πίστευε | πιστεύετε | πιστεύου | πιστεύεσθε |
| | πιστευέτω | πιστευέτωσαν | πιστευέσθω | πιστευέσθωσαν |
| Inf. | πιστεύειν | | πιστεύεσθαι | |
| Part. | πιστεύων, -ουσα, -ον | | πιστευόμενος, -η, -ον | |

### IMPERFECT

| | | | | |
|---|---|---|---|---|
| Ind. | ἐπίστευον | ἐπιστεύομεν | ἐπιστευόμην | ἐπιστευόμεθα |
| | ἐπίστευες | ἐπιστεύετε | ἐπιστεύου | ἐπιστεύεσθε |
| | ἐπίστευε | ἐπίστευον | ἐπιστεύετο | ἐπιστεύοντο |

### FUTURE

| | Active | Middle | Passive |
|---|---|---|---|
| Ind. | πιστεύσω | πιστεύσομαι | πιστευθήσομαι |
| | πιστεύσεις | πιστεύσῃ | πιστευθήσῃ |
| | πιστεύσει | πιστεύσεται | πιστευθήσεται |
| | πιστεύσομεν | πιστευσόμεθα | πιστευθησόμεθα |
| | πιστεύσετε | πιστεύσεσθε | πιστευθήσεσθε |
| | πιστεύσουσι | πιστεύσονται | πιστευθήσονται |

227

| Opt. | πιστεύσοιμι | πιστευσοίμην | πιστευθησοίμην |
| | πιστεύσοις | πιστεύσοιο | πιστευθήσοιο |
| | πιστεύσοι | πιστεύσοιτο | πιστευθήσοιτο |
| | πιστεύσοιμεν | πιστευσοίμεθα | πιστευθησοίμεθα |
| | πιστεύσοιτε | πιστεύσοισθε | πιστευθήσοισθε |
| | πιστεύσοιεν | πιστεύσοιντο | πιστευθήσοιντο |
| Inf. | πιστεύσειν | πιστεύσεσθαι | πιστευθήσεσθαι |
| Part. M. | πιστεύσων | πιστευσόμενος | πιστευθησόμενος |
| F. | πιστεύσουσα | πιστευσομένη | πιστευθησομένη |
| N. | πιστεῦσον | πιστευσόμενον | πιστευθησόμενον |

## AORIST

| | Active | Middle | Passive |
|---|---|---|---|
| Ind. | ἐπίστευσα | ἐπιστευσάμην | ἐπιστεύθην |
| | ἐπίστευσας | ἐπιστεύσω | ἐπιστεύθης |
| | ἐπίστευσε | ἐπιστεύσατο | ἐπιστεύθη |
| | ἐπιστεύσαμεν | ἐπιστευσάμεθα | ἐπιστεύθημεν |
| | ἐπιστεύσατε | ἐπιστεύσασθε | ἐπιστεύθητε |
| | ἐπίστευσαν | ἐπιστεύσαντο | ἐπιστεύθησαν |
| Subj. | πιστεύσω | πιστεύσωμαι | πιστευθῶ |
| | πιστεύσῃς | πιστεύσῃ | πιστευθῇς |
| | πιστεύσῃ | πιστεύσηται | πιστευθῇ |
| | πιστεύσωμεν | πιστευσώμεθα | πιστευθῶμεν |
| | πιστεύσητε | πιστεύσησθε | πιστευθῆτε |
| | πιστεύσωσι | πιστεύσωνται | πιστευθῶσι |
| Opt. | πιστεύσαιμι | πιστευσαίμην | πιστευθείην |
| | πιστεύσαις | πιστεύσαιο | πιστευθείης |
| | πιστεύσαι | πιστεύσαιτο | πιστευθείη |
| | πιστεύσαιμεν | πιστευσαίμεθα | πιστευθείημεν |
| | πιστεύσαιτε | πιστεύσαισθε | πιστευθείητε |
| | πιστεύσαιεν & | πιστεύσαιντο | πιστευθείησαν |
| | πιστεύσειαν | | |
| Impv. | πίστευσον | πίστευσαι | πιστεύθητι |
| | πιστευσάτω | πιστευσάσθω | πιστευθήτω |
| | πιστεύσατε | πιστεύσασθε | πιστεύθητε |
| | πιστευσάτωσαν | πιστευσάσθωσαν | πιστευθήτωσαν |
| Inf. | πιστεῦσαι | πιστευσάσθαι | πιστευθῆναι |
| Part. | πιστεύσᾱς, -ᾱσα, | πιστευσάμενος, | πιστευθείς, |
| | -αν | -η, -ον | -εῖσα, -έν |

## PERFECT

| Ind. | πεπίστευκα | | πεπίστευμαι |
|------|-----------|--|------------|
| | πεπίστευκας | | πεπίστευσαι |
| | πεπίστευκε | | πεπίστευται |
| | πεπιστεύκαμεν | | πεπιστεύμεθα |
| | πεπιστεύκατε | | πεπίστευσθε |
| | πεπιστεύκᾱσι | | πεπίστευνται |

| Subj. | πεπιστευκώς ὦ | | πεπιστευμένος ὦ |
|-------|--------------|--|----------------|
| | ᾖς | | ᾖς |
| | ᾖ | | ᾖ |
| | πεπιστευκότες ὦμεν | | πεπιστευμένοι ὦμεν |
| | ἦτε | | ἦτε |
| | ὦσι | | ὦσι |

Impv. None        πεπίστευσο πεπίστευσθε
πεπιστεύσθω πεπιστεύσθωσαν

Inf. πεπιστευκέναι      πεπιστεῦσθαι

Part. πεπιστευκώς, -υῖα, -ός      πεπιστευμένος, -η, -ον

## PLUPERFECT

| Ind. | (ἐ)πεπιστεύκειν | (ἐ)πεπιστεύμην |
|------|----------------|----------------|
| | (ἐ)πεπιστεύκεις | (ἐ)πεπίστευσο |
| | (ἐ)πεπιστεύκει | (ἐ)πεπίστευτο |
| | (ἐ)πεπιστεύκειμεν | (ἐ)πεπιστεύμεθα |
| | (ἐ)πεπιστεύκειτε | (ἐ)πεπίστευσθε |
| | (ἐ)πεπιστεύκεισαν | (ἐ)πεπίστευντο |

## 398. SECOND AORIST OF βάλλω

| | Active | | Middle | |
|------|--------|--------|--------|--------|
| Ind. | ἔβαλον | ἐβάλομεν | ἐβαλόμην | ἐβαλόμεθα |
| | ἔβαλες | ἐβάλετε | ἐβάλου | ἐβάλεσθε |
| | ἔβαλε | ἔβαλον | ἐβάλετο | ἐβάλοντο |
| Subj. | βάλω | βάλωμεν | βάλωμαι | βαλώμεθα |
| | βάλῃς | βάλητε | βάλῃ | βάλησθε |
| | βάλῃ | βάλωσι | βάληται | βάλωνται |
| Opt. | βάλοιμι | βάλοιμεν | βαλοίμην | βαλοίμεθα |
| | βάλοις | βάλοιτε | βάλοιο | βάλοισθε |
| | βάλοι | βάλοιεν | βάλοιτο | βάλοιντο |
| Impv. | βάλε | βάλετε | βάλου | βάλεσθε |
| | βαλέτω | βαλέτωσαν | βαλέσθω | βαλέσθωσαν |

Inf.  βαλεῖν                              βαλέσθαι

Part.  βαλών, -οῦσα, -όν                   βαλόμενος, -η, -ον

# 399. FUTURE AND AORIST OF LIQUID AND NASAL VERBS

## FUTURE OF ἀποστέλλω

| | Active | | Middle | |
|---|---|---|---|---|
| Ind. | ἀποστελῶ | ἀποστελοῦμεν | ἀποστελοῦμαι | ἀποστελούμεθα |
| | ἀποστελεῖς | ἀποστελεῖτε | ἀποστελῇ | ἀποστελεῖσθε |
| | ἀποστελεῖ | ἀποστελοῦσι | ἀποστελεῖται | ἀποστελοῦνται |
| Inf. | ἀποστελεῖν | | ἀποστελεῖσθαι | |
| Part. | ἀποστελῶν, -οῦσα, -οῦν | | ἀποστελούμενος, -η, -ον | |

## PASSIVE

| Ind. | ἀποσταλήσομαι | ἀποσταλησόμεθα |
|---|---|---|
| | ἀποσταλήσῃ | ἀποσταλήσεσθε |
| | ἀποσταλήσεται | ἀποσταλήσονται |
| Inf. | ἀποσταλήσεσθαι | |
| Part. | ἀποσταλησόμενος, -μένη, -μενον | |

## AORIST OF ἀποστέλλω

### Active

| Ind. | ἀπέστειλα | ἀπεστείλαμεν |
|---|---|---|
| | ἀπέστειλας | ἀπεστείλατε |
| | ἀπέστειλε | ἀπέστειλαν |
| Subj. | ἀποστείλω | ἀποστείλωμεν |
| | ἀποστείλῃς | ἀποστείλητε |
| | ἀποστείλῃ | ἀποστείλωσι |
| Imper. | ἀπόστειλον | ἀποστείλατε |
| | ἀποστειλάτω | ἀποστειλάτωσαν |
| Inf. | ἀποστεῖλαι | |
| Part. | ἀπόστείλᾱς, -ᾱσα, -αν | |

### Middle

| Ind. | ἀπεστειλάμην | ἀπεστειλάμεθα |
|---|---|---|
| | ἀπεστείλω | ἀπεστείλασθε |
| | ἀπεστείλατο | ἀπεστείλαντο |
| Subj. | ἀποστείλωμαι | ἀποστειλώμεθα |
| | ἀποστείλῃ | ἀποστείλησθε |
| | ἀποστείληται | ἀποστείλωνται |

| | | |
|---|---|---|
| Impv. | ἀπόστειλαι | ἀποστείλασθε |
| | ἀποστειλάσθω | ἀποστειλάσθωσαν |
| Inf. | ἀποστείλασθαι | |
| Part. | ἀποστειλάμενος, -η, -ον | |

Passive

| | | |
|---|---|---|
| Ind. | ἀπεστάλην | ἀπεστάλημεν |
| | ἀπεστάλης | ἀπεστάλητε |
| | ἀπεστάλη | ἀπεστάλησαν |
| Subj. | ἀποσταλῶ | ἀποσταλῶμεν |
| | ἀποσταλῇς | ἀποσταλῆτε |
| | ἀποσταλῇ | ἀποσταλῶσι |
| Impv. | ἀποστάληθι | ἀποστάλητε |
| | ἀποσταλήτω | ἀποσταλήτωσαν |
| Inf. | ἀποσταλῆναι | |
| Part. | ἀποσταλείς, -εῖσα, -έν | |

## 400. PERFECT AND PLUPERFECT MIDDLE AND PASSIVE OF MUTE VERBS

PERFECT

| | (γράφω) | (ἄγω) | |
|---|---|---|---|
| Ind. | γέγραμμαι | ἦγμαι | |
| | γέγραψαι | ἦξαι | |
| | γέγραπται | ἦκται | |
| | γεγράμμεθα | ἤγμεθα | |
| | γέγραφθε | ἦχθε | |
| | γεγραμμένοι εἰσί | ἠγμένοι εἰσί | |
| Subj. | γεγραμμένος ᾦ | ἠγμένος | |
| | ᾖς | | ᾖς |
| | ᾖ | | ᾖ |
| | γεγραμμένοι ὦμεν | ἠγμένοι ὦμεν | |
| | ἦτε | | ἦτε |
| | ὦσι | | ὦσι |

No optative or imperative are in use in the New testament.

| | | |
|---|---|---|
| Inf. | γεγράφθαι | ἦχθαι |
| Part. | γεγραμμένος, -η, -ον | ἠγμένος, -η, -ον |
| | (πείθω) | (ἀποστέλλω) |

231

| Ind. | πέπεισμαι | ἀπέσταλμαι |
|---|---|---|
| | πέπεισαι | ἀπέστασαι |
| | πέπεισται | ἀπέσταλται |
| | πεπείσμεθα | ἀπεστάλμεθα |
| | πέπεισθε | ἀπέσταλθε |
| | πεπεισμένοι εἰσί | ἀπεσταλμένοι εἰσί |
| Subj. | πεπεισμένος ὦ | ἀπεσταλμένος ὦ |
| | ᾖς | ᾖς |
| | ᾖ | ᾖ |
| | πεπεισμένοι ὦμεν | ἀπεσταλμένοι ὦμεν |
| | ἦτε | ἦτε |
| | ὦσι | ὦσι |

No optative or imperative are in use in the New Testament.

| Inf. | πεπεῖσθαι | ἀπεστάλθαι |
|---|---|---|
| Part. | πεπεισμένος, -η, -ον | ἀπεσταλμένος, -η, -ον |

## PLUPERFECT

| Ind. | (ἐ)γεγράμμην | ἤγμην |
|---|---|---|
| | (ἐ)γέγραψο | ἤξο |
| | (ἐ)γέγραπτο | ἤκτο |
| | (ἐ)γεγράμμεθα | ἤγμεθα |
| | (ἐ)γέγραφθε | ἤχθε |
| | γεγραμμένοι ἦσαν | ἠγμένοι ἦσαν |
| Ind. | (ἐ)πεπείσμην | ἀπεστάλμην |
| | (ἐ)πέπεισο | ἀπέστασο |
| | (ἐ)πέπειστο | ἀπέσταλτο |
| | (ἐ)πεπείσμεθα | ἀπεστάλμεθα |
| | (ἐ)πέπεισθε | ἀπέσταλθε |
| | πεπεισμένοι ἦσαν | ἀπεσταλμένοι ἦσαν |

## 401. TABLE OF CONTRACTIONS
### Vowels in Suffixes

| | ε | ει (=ε+ε) | ει (=ε+ι) | η | ῃ | ο | ου | ω |
|---|---|---|---|---|---|---|---|---|
| Final Stem Vowels α | α | α (inf.) | ᾳ | α | ᾳ | ω | ω | ω |
| ε | ει | ει (inf.) | ει | η | ῃ | ου | ου | ω |
| ο | ου | ου (inf.) | οι | ω | οι/ῳ | ου | ου | ω |

## 402. CONTRACT VERBS

| | ἀγαπάω | | λαλέω | | πληρόω | |
|---|---|---|---|---|---|---|

### PRESENT ACTIVE

| Ind. | ἀγαπῶ | ἀγαπῶμεν | λαλῶ | λαλοῦμεν | πληρῶ | πληροῦμεν |
|---|---|---|---|---|---|---|
| | ἀγαπᾷς | ἀγαπᾶτε | λαλεῖς | λαλεῖτε | πληροῖς | πληροῦτε |
| | ἀγαπᾷ | ἀγαπῶσι | λαλεῖ | λαλοῦσι | πληροῖ | πληροῦσι |

232

| Subj. | ἀγαπῶ | ἀγαπῶμεν | λαλῶ | λαλῶμεν | πληρῶ | πληρῶμεν |
|---|---|---|---|---|---|---|
| | ἀγαπᾷς | ἀγαπᾶτε | λαλῇς | λαλῆτε | πληροῖς | πληρῶτε |
| | ἀγαπᾷ | ἀγαπῶσι | λαλῇ | λαλῶσι | πληροῖ | πληρῶσι |

No optative of contract verbs is used in the New Testament.

| Impv. | ἀγάπα | ἀγαπᾶτε | λάλει | λαλεῖτε | πλήρου | πληροῦτε |
|---|---|---|---|---|---|---|
| | ἀγαπάτω | ἀγαπάτωσαν | λαλείτω | λαλείτωσαν | πληρούτω | πληρούτωσαν |

| Inf. | ἀγαπᾶν | | λαλεῖν | | πληροῦν | |
|---|---|---|---|---|---|---|

Part. ἀγαπῶν, -ῶσα, -ῶν     λαλῶν, -οῦσα, -οῦν     πληρῶν, -οῦσα, -οῦν

## IMPERFECT ACTIVE

| Ind. | ἠγάπων | ἠγαπῶμεν | ἐλάλουν | ἐλαλοῦμεν | ἐπλήρουν | ἐπληροῦμεν |
|---|---|---|---|---|---|---|
| | ἠγάπᾱς | ἠγαπᾶτε | ἐλάλεις | ἐλαλεῖτε | ἐπλήρους | ἐπληροῦτε |
| | ἠγάπᾱ | ἠγάπων | ἐλάλει | ἐλάλουν | ἐπλήρου | ἐπλήρουν |

## PRESENT MIDDLE

| Ind. | ἀγαπῶμαι | ἀγαπώμεθα | λαλοῦμαι | λαλούμεθα | πληροῦμαι | πληρούμεθα |
|---|---|---|---|---|---|---|
| | ἀγαπᾷ | ἀγαπᾶσθε | λαλῇ | λαλεῖσθε | πληροῖ | πληροῦσθε |
| | ἀγαπᾶται | ἀγαπῶνται | λαλεῖται | λαλοῦνται | πληροῦται | πληροῦνται |

| Subj. | ἀγαπῶμαι | ἀγαπώμεθα | λαλῶμαι | λαλώμεθα | πληρῶμαι | πληρώμεθα |
|---|---|---|---|---|---|---|
| | ἀγαπᾷ | ἀγαπᾶσθε | λαλῇ | λαλῆσθε | πληροῖ | πληρῶσθε |
| | ἀγαπᾶται | ἀγαπῶνται | λαλῆται | λαλῶνται | πληρῶται | πληρῶνται |

No optative of contract verbs is used in the New Testament.

| Impv. | ἀγαπῶ | ἀγαπᾶσθε | λαλοῦ | λαλεῖσθε | πληροῦ | πληροῦσθε |
|---|---|---|---|---|---|---|
| | ἀγαπάσθω | ἀγαπάσθωσαν | λαλείσθω | λαλείσθωσαν | πληρούσθω | πληρούσθωσαν |

| Inf. | ἀγαπᾶσθαι | | λαλεῖσθαι | | πληροῦσθαι | |
|---|---|---|---|---|---|---|

Part. ἀγαπώμενος, -η, -ον     λαλούμενος, -η, -ον     πληρούμενος, -η, -ον

## IMPERFECT MIDDLE

| Ind. | ἠγαπώμην | ἠγαπώμεθα | ἐλαλούμην | ἐλαλούμεθα | ἐπληρούμην | ἐπληρούμεθα |
|---|---|---|---|---|---|---|
| | ἠγαπῶ | ἠγαπᾶσθε | ἐλαλοῦ | ἐλαλεῖσθε | ἐπληροῦ | ἐπληροῦσθε |
| | ἠγαπᾶτο | ἠγαπῶντο | ἐλαλεῖτο | ἐλαλοῦντο | ἐπληροῦτο | ἐπληροῦντο |

# 403. COMPARATIVE PARADIGMS OF FOUR MI VERBS
## PRESENT ACTIVE

| Ind. | ἵστημι | τίθημι | δίδωμι | δείκνῡμι |
|---|---|---|---|---|
| | ἵστης | τίθης | δίδως | δείκνῡς |
| | ἵστησι | τίθησι | δίδωσι | δείκνῡσι |
| | ἵσταμεν | τίθεμεν | δίδομεν | δείκνυμεν |
| | ἵστατε | τίθετε | δίδοτε | δείκνυτε |
| | ἱστᾶσι | τιθέᾱσι | διδόᾱσι | δεικνύᾱσι |
| Subj. | ἱστῶ | τιθῶ | διδῶ | δεικνύω |
| | ἱστῇς | τιθῇς | διδῷς (διδοῖς) | δεικνύῃς |
| | ἱστῇ | τιθῇ | διδῷ (διδοῖ) | δεικνύῃ |

|  | ἱστῶμεν | τιθῶμεν | διδῶμεν | δεικνύωμεν |
|  | ἱστῆτε | τιθῆτε | διδῶτε | δεικνύητε |
|  | ἱστῶσι | τιθῶσι | διδῶσι | δεικνύωσι |
| Opt. | None in N.T | None in N T | None in N T | None in N.T |
| Impv. | ἵστη | τίθει | δίδου | δείκνυ |
|  | ἱστάτω | τιθέτω | διδότω | δεικνύτω |
|  | ἵστατε | τίθετε | δίδοτε | δείκνυτε |
|  | ἱστάτωσαν | τιθέτωσαν | διδότωσαν | δεικνύτωσαν |
| Inf. | ἱστάναι | τιθέναι | διδόναι | δεικνύναι |
| Part. | ἱστάς, -ᾶσα, -άν | τιθείς, -εῖσα, -έν | διδούς, -οῦσα, -όν | δεικνύς, -ῦσα, ύν |

## IMPERFECT ACTIVE

| Ind. | ἵστην | ἐτίθην | ἐδίδουν | ἐδείκνῦν |
|  | ἵστης | ἐτίθεις | ἐδίδους | ἐδείκνῦς |
|  | ἵστη | ἐτίθει | ἐδίδου | ἐδείκνῦ |
|  | ἵσταμεν | ἐτίθεμεν | ἐδίδομεν | ἐδείκνυμεν |
|  | ἵστατε | ἐτίθετε | ἐδίδοτε | ἐδείκνυτε |
|  | ἵστασαν | ἐτίθεσαν | ἐδίδοσαν | ἐδείκνυσαν |

## PRESENT MIDDLE

| Ind. | ἵσταμαι | τίθεμαι | δίδομαι | δείκνυμαι |
|  | ἵστασαι | τίθεσαι | δίδοσαι | δείκνυσαι |
|  | ἵσταται | τίθεται | δίδοται | δείκνυται |
|  | ἱστάμεθα | τιθέμεθα | διδόμεθα | δεικνύμεθα |
|  | ἵστασθε | τίθεσθε | δίδοσθε | δείκνυσθε |
|  | ἵστανται | τίθενται | δίδονται | δείκνυνται |
| Subj. | ἱστῶμαι | τιθῶμαι | διδῶμαι | δεικνύωμαι |
|  | ἱστῇ | τιθῇ | διδῷ | δεικνύη |
|  | ἱστῆται | τιθῆται | διδῶται | δεικνύηται |
|  | ἱστώμεθα | τιθώμεθα | διδώμεθα | δεικνυώμεθα |
|  | ἱστῆσθε | τιθῆσθε | διδῶσθε | δεικνύησθε |
|  | ἱστῶνται | τιθῶνται | διδῶνται | δεικνύωνται |
| Opt. | None in N.T. | None in N.T. | None in N.T. | None in N.T. |
| Impv. | ἵστασο | τίθεσο | δίδοσο | δείκνυσο |
|  | ἱστάσθω | τιθέσθω | διδόσθω | δεικνύσθω |
|  | ἵστασθε | τίθεσθε | δίδοσθε | δείκνυσθε |
|  | ἱστάσθωσαν | τιθέσθωσαν | διδόσθωσαν | δεικνύσθωσαν |
| Inf. | ἵστασθαι | τίθεσθαι | δίδοσθαι | δείκνυσθαι |

| Part. | ἱστάμενος, | τιθέμενος, -η, | διδόμενος, | δεικνύμενος |
|---|---|---|---|---|
| | -η, -ον | -ον | -η, -ον | -η, -ον |

## IMPERFECT MIDDLE

| Ind. | ἱστάμην | ἐτιθέμην | ἐδιδόμην | ἐδεικνύμην |
|---|---|---|---|---|
| | ἵστασο | ἐτίθεσο | ἐδίδοσο | ἐδείκνυσο |
| | ἵστατο | ἐτίθετο | ἐδίδοτο | ἐδείκνυτο |
| | ἱστάμεθα | ἐτιθέμεθα | ἐδιδόμεθα | ἐδεικνύμεθα |
| | ἵστασθε | ἐτίθεσθε | ἐδίδοσθε | ἐδείκνυσθε |
| | ἵσταντο | ἐτίθεντο | ἐδίδοντο | ἐδείκνυντο |

## AORIST ACTIVE

| | -μι Aor. | "κ" Aor. | "κ" Aor. | 1st Aor. |
|---|---|---|---|---|
| Ind. | ἔστην | ἔθηκα | ἔδωκα | ἔδειξα |
| | ἔστης | ἔθηκας | ἔδωκας | ἔδειξας |
| | ἔστη | ἔθηκε | ἔδωκε | ἔδειξε |
| | ἔστημεν | ἐθήκαμεν | ἐδώκαμεν | ἐδείξαμεν |
| | ἔστητε | ἐθήκατε | ἐδώκατε | ἐδείξατε |
| | ἔστησαν | ἔθηκαν | ἔδωκαν | ἔδειξαν |
| Subj. | στῶ | θῶ | δῶ | δείξω |
| | στῇς | θῇς | δῷς (δοῖς) | δείξῃς |
| | στῇ | θῇ | δῷ (δοῖ, δώῃ) | δείξῃ |
| | στῶμεν | θῶμεν | δῶμεν | δείξωμεν |
| | στῆτε | θῆτε | δῶτε | δείξητε |
| | στῶσι | θῶσι | δῶσι | δείξωσι |
| Opt. | None in N.T. | None in N.T. | Only 3rd S. — in N.T. δῴη — — | δείξαιμι δείξαις δείξαι δείξαιμεν δείξαιτε δείξαιεν (δείξειαν) |
| Impv. | στῆθι | θές | δός | δεῖξον |
| | στήτω | θέτω | δότω | δειξάτω |
| | στῆτε | θέτε | δότε | δείξατε |
| | στήτωσαν | θέτωσαν | δότωσαν | δειξάτωσαν |
| Inf. | στῆναι | θεῖναι | δοῦναι | δεῖξαι |
| Part. | στάς, -ᾶσα, -άν | θείς, -εῖσα, -έν | δούς, -οῦσα, -όν | δείξᾱς, -ᾶσα, -αν |

## MI AORIST MIDDLE

| Ind. | None | ἐθέμην | ἐδόμην | None |
|------|------|--------|--------|------|
| | | ἔθου | ἔδου | |
| | | ἔθετο | ἔδοτο | |
| | | ἐθέμεθα | ἐδόμεθα | |
| | | ἔθεσθε | ἔδοσθε | |
| | | ἔθεντο | ἔδοντο | |

| Subj. | θῶμαι | δῶμαι |
|-------|-------|-------|
| | θῇ | δῷ |
| | θῆται | δῶται |
| | θώμεθα | δώμεθα |
| | θῆσθε | δῶσθε |
| | θῶνται | δῶνται |

| Impv. | θοῦ | δοῦ |
|-------|-----|-----|
| | θέσθω | δόσθω |
| | θέσθε | δόσθε |
| | θέσθωσαν | δόσθωσαν |

| Inf. | θέσθαι | δόσθαι |
|------|--------|--------|

| Part. | θέμενος, -η, -ον δόμενος, -η, -ον |
|-------|-----------------------------------|

# 404. PARADIGMS OF ἀφίημι

## PRESENT

| | Active | | Middle | |
|------|--------|--------|--------|--------|
| Ind. | ἀφίημι | ἀφίεμεν(ἀφίομεν) | ἀφίεμαι | ἀφιέμεθα |
| | ἀφεῖς | ἀφίετε | ἀφίεσαι | ἀφίεσθε |
| | ἀφίησι | ἀφίουσι | ἀφίεται | ἀφίενται |
| | | | | (ἀφίονται) |

| Subj. | ἀφιῶ | ἀφιῶμεν |
|-------|------|---------|
| | ἀφιῇς | ἀφιῆτε |
| | ἀφιῇ | ἀφιῶσι |

| Impv. | ἀφίει | ἀφίετε |
|-------|-------|--------|
| | ἀφιέτω | ἀφιέτωσαν |

| Inf. | ἀφιέναι |
|------|---------|

| Part. | ἀφιείς, -εῖσα, -έν |
|-------|--------------------|

## IMPERFECT

| Ind. | ἤφιον | ἠφίομεν |
|------|-------|---------|
| | ἤφιες | ἠφίετε |
| | ἤφιε | ἤφιον |

## AORIST

Ind. ἀφῆκα    ἀφήκαμεν
      ἀφῆκας    ἀφήκατε
      ἀφῆκε    ἀφῆκαν

Subj. ἀφῶ    ἀφῶμεν
      ἀφῇς    ἀφῆτε
      ἀφῇ    ἀφῶσι

Opt. ἀφείην    ἀφείημεν
      ἀφείης    ἀφείητε
      ἀφείη    ἀφείησαν

Impv. ἄφες    ἄφετε
      ἀφέτω    ἀφέτωσαν

Inf. ἀφεῖναι

Part. ἀφείς, -εῖσα, -έν

## 405. PARADIGMS OF οἶδα

| | 2ND PERFECT | | 2ND PLUPERFECT | |
|---|---|---|---|---|
| Ind. | οἶδα | οἴδαμεν | ᾔδειν | ᾔδειμεν |
| | οἶδας | οἴδατε | ᾔδεις | ᾔδειτε |
| | οἶδε | οἴδᾱσι (ἴσᾱσι) | ᾔδει | ᾔδεισαν |
| Subj. | εἰδῶ | εἰδῶμεν | | |
| | εἰδῇς | εἰδῆτε | | |
| | εἰδῇ | εἰδῶσι | | |
| Impv. | ἴσθι | ἴστε | | |
| | ἴστω | ἴστωσαν | | |

Inf. εἰδέναι

Part. εἰδώς, -υῖα, -ός

### FUTURE INDICATIVE ACTIVE

εἰδήσω    εἰδήσομεν
εἰδήσεις    εἰδήσετε
εἰδήσει    εἰδήσουσι

## 406. PARADIGMS OF εἰμί

| | PRESENT | | IMPERFECT | |
|---|---|---|---|---|
| Ind. | εἰμί | ἐσμέν | ἤμην | ἤμεν and ἤμεθα |
| | εἶ | ἐστέ | ἦς and ἦσθα | ἦτε |
| | ἐστί(ν) | εἰσί(ν) | ἦν | ἦσαν |

| Subj. | ὦ | ὦμεν | **FUTURE** | |
|---|---|---|---|---|
| | ᾖς | ἦτε | ἔσομαι | ἐσόμεθα |
| | ᾖ | ὦσι | ἔσῃ | ἔσεσθε |
| Opt. | Only third s. in N.T | | ἔσται | ἔσονται |
| | — | — | | |
| | εἴη | — | | |
| Impv. | ἴσθι | ἔστε | | |
| | ἔστω and | ἔστωσαν | | |
| | ἤτω | | | |
| Inf. | εἶναι | | ἔσεσθαι | |
| Part. | ὤν, οὖσα, ὄν | | ἐσόμενος, -η, -ον | |

## 407. INFREQUENT USE OF THE OPTATIVE IN THE NEW TESTAMENT

Because the optative mood is not frequently used in the New Testament it has not been introduced in these lessons. But for reference some forms have been made available in the paradigms just given since verb forms in this mood appear in the writings of Luke and Paul.

## 408. OPTATIVE OF WISH

The optative may be used to express a wish. The negative is μή.

*μὴ γένοιτο, may it not happen.* (Rom 3:4, 6 and elsewhere)

μηκέτι εἰς τὸν αἰῶνα ἐκ σοῦ μηδεὶς καρπὸν φάγοι.
*May no one eat fruit of you any more forever.* (Mark 11:14)

οὗτος διδάσκοι τὴν ἀλήθειαν πάντοτε.
*May he always teach the truth.*

## 409. POTENTIAL OPTATIVE

A mild or unemphatic future statement may be made by use of the optative with ἄν. The negative is οὐ.

*ἔλθοιεν ἄν τῇ τρίτῃ ἡμέρᾳ.*
*They may (might) go on the third day.*

αὕτη οὐκ ἄν δέχοιτο τὸν προφήτην.
*This woman would not welcome the prophet.*

## 410. TYPE FOUR CONDITION (Less Vivid Future Condition)

The subordinate clause of the type 3 (more vivid future) condition expresses a contingency, the realization of which is somewhat doubtful. In type 4 the realization of the conditional clause is presented as even more doubtful than in type 3. The protasis uses εἰ and the optative, the apodosis ἄν and the optative.

*εἰ ὁ ἄγγελος φαίνοιτο, αὐτὸν ἂν δεξαίμεθα.*
*If the messenger should appear we would receive him*

*εἰ μὴ εὕροιτε τὴν οἰκίαν ἑτοίμην, οὐκ ἂν εἰσέλθοιτε.*
*If you should not find the house ready you would not enter..*

Although no complete type 4 conditional sentence occurs in the New Testament, the protasis is used in mixed conditions. The apodosis occurring alone is equal to the potential optative.

## 411. GENERAL OBSERVATIONS ABOUT ACCENT

a. Final -αι and -οι are considered short in determining accent.
b. An acute accent on the ultima becomes a grave when another word, not an enclitic, follows without intervening punctuation

## 412. EXAMPLES OF RECESSIVE ACCENT

a. In finite verbs of three or more syllables.

   1) Having a short ultima: *acute on antepenult.* ἀπολύσομεν, ἤγαγον
   2) Having a long ultima: *acute on penult.* ἀπολύει, ἀποθνῄσκω

b. In finite verbs of two syllables.

   1) Having a short ultima and a long penult: *circumflex on penult.* εἶχε
   2) Having a short ultima and a short penult: *acute on penult.* ἔχε
   3) Having a long ultima and a long penult: *acute on penult.* χαίρω
   4) Having a long ultima and a short penult: *acute on penult.* λέγει

c. In finite verbs of one syllable.

   1) Long: *circumflex.* ἦν
   2) Short: *acute* or *grave.* σχές, σχὲς τόπον.

## 413. EXAMPLES OF PERSISTENT ACCENT

a. In adjectives.

   1) Accented on the ultima in masculine nominative singular (see number 106).

      a) Acute on the first and fourth (plus vocative) inflectional forms both singular and plural.

239

b) Circumflex on second and third inflectional forms both singular and plural.

2) Accented on the antepenult in masculine nominative singular (see number 74).

   a) Acute used throughout the paradigm.
   b) Antepenult accented when ultima is short.
   c) Penult accented when ultima is long.

b. In nouns.

   1) Accented on the antepenult in nominative singular.

      a) In the second declension.

         (1) Nouns in -ος like masculine column of δίκαιος (see number 74).
         (2) Neuter like neuter column of δίκαιος (see number 74).

      b) In the first declension (see number 104).

         (1) On the antepenult when ultima is short: *acute*.
         (2) On the penult when ultima is long: *acute* (EXCEPT in second inflectional form plural where ultima is circumflexed).

   2) Accented on the penult in nominative singular.

      a) In the second declension (see number 48).

         (1) With the acute on the penult in nominative singular: *acute on the penult throughout the paradigm.*
         (2) With the circumflex on the penult in nominative singular: *circumflex made acute when ultima becomes long.*

      b) In the first declension: acute on penult in nominative singular (see numbers 72, 104).

         (1) Acute retained when ultima is long except for (3) below.
         (2) Circumflex used on penult in nominative plural when the penult is long.
         (3) Circumflex used on ultima is second inflectional form of plural.

   3) Accented on the ultima in nominative singular.

      a) Nouns in -ος like masculine column of καλός.
      b) Neuter nouns like neuter column of καλός.
      c) Feminine nouns like feminine column of καλός.

## 414. ACCENTS IN PARTS OF SPEECH OTHER THAN FINITE VERBS, ADJECTIVES, and NOUNS

To be learned by observation.

A REFERENCE LIST OF THE PRINCIPAL PARTS USED IN THIS BOOK

## 415. 
The forms in the following list are based on the entries in F. Wilbur Gingrich and Frederick W. Danker, et al, eds. and trans., *A Greek-English Lexicon of the New Testament and Other Early Christian Literature*, 2d rev. and augmented ed. (Chicago: U. of Chicago, 1979). If a form representing a tense system is given by Gingrich and Danker, the principal part of that tense system is assumed to exist. If, however, no such representative form is given in the lexicon, as a rule, no principal part for that tense system is included in the following list. The omission is indicated by a dash (—).

| Present Act. & Mid. | Future Act. & Mid. | Aorist Act. & Mid. | Perfect Active | Perfect Mid. & Pass. | Aorist Passive |
|---|---|---|---|---|---|
| ἀγαπάω | ἀγαπήσω | ἠγάπησα | ἠγάπηκα | ἠγάπημαι | ἠγαπήθην |
| ἁγνίζω | — | ἥγνισα | ἥγνικα | ἥγνισμαι | ἡγνίσθην |
| ἄγω | ἄξω | ἤγαγον | — | — | ἤχθην |
| αἴρω | ἀρῶ | ἦρα | ἦρκα | ἦρμαι | ἤρθην |
| αἰσχύνομαι | — | — | — | — | ᾐσχύνθην |
| αἰτέω | αἰτήσω | ᾔτησα | ᾔτηκα | — | — |
| ἀκούω | ἀκούσω | ἤκουσα | ἀκήκοα | — | ἠκούσθην |
| ἁμαρτάνω | ἁμαρτήσω | ἡμάρτησα ἥμαρτον | ἡμάρτηκα | — | — |
| ἀναγγέλλω | ἀναγγελῶ | ἀνήγγειλα | — | — | ἀνηγγέλην |
| ἀναστρέφω | — | ἀνέστρεψα | — | — | ἀνεστράφην |
| ἀπαγγέλλω | ἀπαγγελῶ | ἀπήγγειλα | — | — | ἀπηγγέλην |
| ἀπέρχομαι | ἀπελεύσομαι | ἀπῆλθον | ἀπελήλυθα | — | — |
| ἀποθνῄσκω | ἀποθανοῦμαι | ἀπέθανον | — | — | — |
| ἀποκόπτω | ἀποκόψω | ἀπέκοψα | — | — | ἀπεκόπην |
| ἀποκρίνομαι | — | ἀπεκρινάμην | — | — | ἀπεκρίθην |
| ἀποκτείνω | ἀποκτενῶ | ἀπέκτεινα | — | — | ἀπεκτάνθην |
| ἀπολύω | ἀπολύσω | ἀπέλυσα | — | ἀπολέλυμαι | ἀπελύθην |
| ἀποστέλλω | ἀποστελῶ | ἀπέστειλα | ἀπέσταλκα | ἀπέσταλμαι | ἀπεστάλην |
| ἅπτω | — | ἧψα | — | — | — |
| ἀρνέομαι | ἀρνήσομαι | ἠρνησάμην | — | ἤρνημαι | — |
| ἀφίημι | ἀφήσω | ἀφῆκα | — | ἀφεῖμαι | ἀφέθην |
| βάλλω | βαλῶ | ἔβαλον | βέβληκα | βέβλημαι | ἐβλήθην |
| βλασφημέω | — | ἐβλασφήμησα | — | — | ἐβλασφημήθην |
| βλέπω | βλέψω | ἔβλεψα | — | — | — |
| γεννάω | γεννήσω | ἐγέννησα | γεγέννηκα | γεγέννημαι | ἐγεννήθην |
| γίνομαι | γενήσομαι | ἐγενόμην | γέγονα | γεγένημαι | ἐγενήθην |
| γινώσκω | γνώσομαι | ἔγνων | ἔγνωκα | ἔγνωσμαι | ἐγνώσθην |
| γράφω | γράψω | ἔγραψα | γέγραφα | γέγραμμαι | ἐγράφην |
| δεῖ | — | — | — | — | — |

| | | | | | |
|---|---|---|---|---|---|
| δείκνυμ· | δειξω | ἔδειξα | δέδειχα | — | ἐδείχθην |
| δεικνύ· | | | | | |
| δέχομα | – | ἐδεξάμην | — | δέδεγμαι | ἐδέχθην |
| διδάσκ· | διδάξω | ἐδίδαξα | | — | ἐδιδάχθην |
| δίδωμ· | δώσω | ἔδ ωκα | δέδωκα | δέδομαι | ἐδόθην |
| διώκω | διώξω | ἐδίωξα | — | δεδίωγμαι | ἐδιώχθην |
| δοκιμάζω | δοκιμάσω | ἐδοκίμασα | — | δεδοκίμασμαι | — |
| δουλεύω | δουλεύσω | ἐδούλευσα | δεδούλευκα | — | — |
| δύναμαι | δυνήσομαι | — | — | — | ἠδυνήθην |
| ἐγκαταλείπ· | ἐγκαταλείψω | ἐγκατέλιπον | — | ἐγκαταλέλειμμαι | ἐγκατελείφθην |
| εἰμί | ἔσομαι | -̃- | — | — | — |
| ἐκλέγομαι | — | ἐξελεξάμην | — | ἐκλέλεγμαι | — |
| ἐλπίζω | ἐλπιῶ | ἤλπισα | ἤλπικα | | |
| ἐντέλλομαι | ἐντελοῦμαι | ἐνετειλάμην | — | ἐντέταλμαι | |
| ἐξέρχομαι | ἐξελεύσομαι | ἐξῆλθον | ἐξελήλυθα | | |
| ἐπαγγέλλομαι | — | ἐπηγγειλάμην | — | ἐπήγγελμαι | |
| ἐπιγινώσκω | ἐπιγνώσομαι | ἐπέγνων | ἐπέγνωκα | — | ἐπεγνώσθην |
| ἔρχομαι | ἐλεύσομαι | ἦλθον | ἐλήλυθα | — | — |
| ἐρωτάω | ἐρωτήσω | ἠρώτησα | | — | — |
| ἐσθίω | φάγομαι | ἔφαγον | — | — | — |
| εὑρίσκω | εὑρήσω | εὗρον | εὕρηκα | — | εὑρέθην |
| ἔχω | ἔξω | ἔσχον | ἔσχηκα | — | — |
| ζῶ (ζάω) | ζήσω | ἔζησα | — | — | — |
| ἥκω | ἥξω | ἧξα | — | — | — |
| θαυμάζω | θαυμάσομαι | ἐθαύμασα | — | — | ἐθαυμάσθην |
| θεάομαι | — | ἐθεασάμην | — | τεθέαμαι | ἐθεάθην |
| θέλω | θελήσω | ἠθέλησα | — | — | — |
| θεραπεύω | θεραπεύσω | ἐθεράπευσα | — | τεθεράπευμαι | ἐθεραπεύθην |
| θεωρέω | θεωρήσω | ἐθεώρησα | — | — | — |
| θύω | — | ἔθυσα | — | τέθυμαι | ἐτύθην |
| ἵστημι | στήσω | ἔστησα ἔστην | ἔστηκα | — | ἐστάθην |
| ἰσχύω | ἰσχύσω | ἴσχυσα | — | — | — |
| καθαρίζω | καθαριῶ | ἐκαθάρισα | — | κεκαθάρισμαι | ἐκαθαρίσθην |
| καθεύδω | | | | | |
| καλέω | καλέσω | ἐκάλεσα | κέκληκα | κέκλημαι | ἐκλήθην |
| καταβαίνω | καταβήσομαι | κατέβην | καταβέβηκα | | |
| καταγινώσκω | — | — | | κατέγνωσμαι | — |
| καταλύω | καταλύσω | κατέλυσα | — | — | κατελύθην |
| κεῖμαι | — | — | — | — | — |
| κλείω | κλείσω | ἔκλεισα | — | κέκλεισμαι | ἐκλείσθην |
| λαλέω | λαλήσω | ἐλάλησα | λελάληκα | λελάλημαι | ἐλαλήθην |
| λαμβάνω | λήμψομαι | ἔλαβον | εἴληφα | εἴλημμαι | — |
| λατρεύω | λατρεύσω | ἐλάτρευσα | — | — | — |
| λέγω | ἐρῶ | εἶπον | εἴρηκα | εἴρημαι | ἐρρέθην |
| λύω | — | ἔλυσα | — | λέλυμαι | ἐλύθην |
| μανθάνω | — | ἔμαθον | μεμάθηκα | — | — |
| μαρτυρέω | μαρτυρήσω | ἐμαρτύρησα | μεμαρτύρηκα | μεμαρτύρημαι | ἐμαρτυρήθην |
| μάχομαι | — | — | — | — | — |

242

| | | | | | |
|---|---|---|---|---|---|
| μένω | μενῶ | ἔμεινα | μεμένηκα | — | — |
| μεταβαίνω | μεταβήσομαι | μετέβην | μεταβέβηκα | — | — |
| μισέω | μισήσω | ἐμίσησα | μεμίσηκα | μεμίσημαι | — |
| μνημονεύω | — | ἐμνημόνευσα | — | — | — |
| νικάω | νικήσω | ἐνίκησα | νενίκηκα | — | ἐνικήθην |
| οἶδα (Perfect with present meaning) | εἰδήσω | — | — | — | — |
| ὁμολογέω | ὁμολογήσω | ὡμολόγησα | — | — | — |
| ὀνειδίζω | — | ὠνείδισα | — | — | — |
| ὁράω | ὄψομαι | εἶδον | ἑώρακα | — | ὤφθην |
| ὀργίζομαι | — | — | — | — | ὠργίσθην |
| ὀφείλω | — | — | — | — | — |
| παράγω | — | — | — | — | — |
| πατάσσω | πατάξω | ἐπάταξα | — | — | — |
| πείθω | πείσω | ἔπεισα | πέποιθα | πέπεισμαι | ἐπείσθην |
| πέμπω | πέμψω | ἔπεμψα | πέπομφα | — | ἐπέμφθην |
| περιπατέω | περιπατήσω | περιεπάτησα | περιπεπάτηκα | — | — |
| πίνω | πίομαι | ἔπιον | πέπωκα | — | — |
| πίπτω | πεσοῦμαι | ἔπεσον ἔπεσα | πέπτωκα | — | — |
| πιστεύω | πιστεύσω | ἐπίστευσα | πεπίστευκα | πεπίστευμαι | ἐπιστεύθην |
| πλανάω | πλανήσω | ἐπλάνησα | — | πεπλάνημαι | ἐπλανήθην |
| πληρόω | πληρώσω | ἐπλήρωσα | πεπλήρωκα | πεπλήρωμαι | ἐπληρώθην |
| ποιέω | ποιήσω | ἐποίησα | πεποίηκα | πεποίημαι | ἐποιήθην |
| πορεύομαι | πορεύσομαι | — | — | πεπόρευμαι | ἐπορεύθην |
| προσεύχομαι | προσεύξομαι | προσηυξάμην | — | — | — |
| σαλπίζω | σαλπίσω | ἐσάλπισα | — | — | — |
| σκληρύνω | σκληρυνῶ | ἐσκλήρυνα | — | — | ἐσκληρύνθην |
| συνάγω | συνάξω | συνήγαγον συνῆξα | — | συνῆγμαι | συνήχθην |
| σφάζω | σφάξω | ἔσφαξα | — | ἔσφαγμαι | ἐσφάγην |
| σῴζω | σώσω | ἔσωσα | σέσωκα | σέσωσμαι | ἐσώθην |
| τελειόω | — | ἐτελείωσα | τετελείωκα | τετελείωμαι | ἐτελειώθην |
| τηρέω | τηρήσω | ἐτήρησα | τετήρηκα | τετήρημαι | ἐτηρήθην |
| τίθημι | θήσω | ἔθηκα | τέθεικα | τέθειμαι | ἐτέθην |
| τρέχω | — | ἔδραμον | — | — | — |
| τυφλόω | — | ἐτύφλωσα | τετύφλωκα | — | — |
| φαίνω | φανοῦμαι | ἔφανα | — | — | ἐφάνην |
| φανερόω | φανερώσω | ἐφανέρωσα | πεφανέρωκα | πεφανέρωμαι | ἐφανερώθην |
| φέρω | οἴσω | ἤνεγκα ἤνεγκον | — | — | ἠνέχθην |
| φεύγω | φεύξομαι | ἔφυγον | — | — | — |
| φοβέομαι | — | — | — | — | ἐφοβήθην |
| φονεύω | φονεύσω | ἐφόνευσα | — | — | ἐφονεύθην |
| φυλάσσω | φυλάξω | ἐφύλαξα | πεφύλαχα | — | ἐφυλάχθην |
| χαίρω | — | — | — | — | ἐχάρην |
| χρίω | — | ἔχρισα | — | — | ἐχρίσθην |
| ψεύδομαι | ψεύσομαι | ἐψευσάμην | — | — | — |
| ψηλαφάω | — | ἐψηλάφησα | — | — | — |

SOURCES OF ITEMS USED IN THE EXERCISES FOR READING ALOUD
AND TRANSLATION

SECTION   SOURCE

8. f    Rev. 1:8
25. g   1) Matt. 26:49
        2) John 21:20
        3) Matt. 5:23
39. f   1) Mark 7:5
        2) 1 Cor. 9:7
50. f   1) Mark 2:11
        2) John 2:3
        3) Mark 7:5
        4) 1 Cor. 11:28
64. e   1) John 6:9
        2) Luke 2:29
        3) Rom. 9:12
80. i   1) 1 Cor. 9:1
        2) 1 John 2:17
        3) W. Dittenberger, ed., *Sylloge Inscriptionum Graecarum*, 2d
        ed., Leipzig, 1888-1901, 376.31. In James Hope Moulton
        and George Milligan, *The Vocabulary of the Greek Testa-
        ment* (Grand Rapids: Eerdmans, 1949, hereafter referred to
        as *M-M*), p. 356, s.v. κόσμος.
90. g   1) Rom. 8:24
        2) John 7:33
        3) Luke 17:32
        4) John 21:2
        5) Phil. 4:4
101. f  1) Mark 4:9
        2) John 15:1
110. e  1) John 14:6
        2) 3 John 11
        3) Matt. 15:26
        4) Luke 8:18
116. f  1) Luke 13:26
        2) 1 Cor. 4:7
        3) B. P. Grenfell and A. S. Hunt, eds., *The Oxyrhynchus Papyri*
        X, 1345. In *M-M*, p. 308, s.v. ἰσχύω.
128. f  1) Matt. 5:13
        2) 1 Cor. 10:26
        3) John 8:12

244

132. e  1) Mark 3:32
       2) James 5:6
139. e  1) John 3:22
       2) Acts 16:35
       3) Acts 2:39
       4) 1 Pet. 2:25
       5) Luke 4:9
145. f  1) Rom. 11:3
       2) John 17:18
       3) Luke 24:21
       4) Matt. 5:44
       5) 1 John 2:27
       6) Matt. 13:56
       7) Acts 13:5
       8) B. P. Grenfell and A. S. Hunt, eds., *The Oxyrhynchus Papyri*
          IV, 744.5. In *M-M*, p. 397, s.v. μένω.
151. f  1) Matt. 21:36
       2) John 18:37
       3) Acts 9:4
163. f  1) John 1:1
       2) 1 John 4:18
       3) *Ägyptische Urkunden aus den königlichen Museen zu Berlin:*
          *Griechische Urkunden* II. 543.2. In *M-M*, p. 448, s.v.
          ὄμνυμι.
170. g  Acts 9:5
177. h  1) John 8:31
       2) John 1:14
       3) Acts 27:39
       4) Matt. 3:12
       5) O. Eger, E. Kornemann, and P. M. Meyer, eds., *Griechische*
          *Papyri zu Giessen*, I, Leipzig, 1910-12, 17.9. In *M-M*, p. 62,
          s.v. ἀποθνήσκω.
183. e  1) Heb. 13:8
       2) John 13:13
       3) Matt. 22:16
       4) John 11:14-15
       5) C. Wessely, ed., *Corpus Papyrorum Hermopolitanorum* I,
          Leipzig, 1905, 25.ii.5. In *M-M*, p. 159, s.v. διδάσκω.
       6) *Ägyptische Urkunden aus den königlichen Museen zu Berlin:*
          *Griechische Urkunden*, I, 27.4. In *M-M*, p. 127, s.v.
          γινώσκω.
       7) 1 Cor. 10:1

8) F. G. Kenyon, ed., *Greek Papyri in the British Museum* I, p. 48. In *M-M*, p. 387, s.v. μανθάνω.

187. e John 4:8

197. d 1) Luke 6:44
2) Matt. 4:6
3) B. P. Grenfell, ed., *An Alexandrian Erotic Fragment, and other Greek Papyri, chiefly Ptolemaic*, Oxford, 1896, 30.3. In *M-M*, p. 217, s.v. ἐντέλλομαι.

202. d 1) John 12:50
2) Luke 7:3

207. e 1) Gal. 4:14
2) Matt. 13:55
3) B. P. Grenfell, A. S. Hunt, and E. J. Goodspeed, eds., *The Tebtunis Papyri* II, London, 1902-1907, 422.11. In *M-M*, p. 143, s.v. δέχομαι.

221. f 1) John 19:21-22
2) Matt. 1:21

232. f 1) Matt. 26:28
2) Matt. 6:10
3) Matt. 19:30
4) Acts 10:13
5) Rev. 9:18
6) John 20:20
7) Rev. 22:16
8) James 1:1
9) C. C. Edgar, ed., *Zenon Papyri in the University of Michigan Collection*, no. 10 (Ann Arbor: U. of Michigan, 1931).

240. e 1) John 1:39
2) Acts 4:24
3) Rom. 8:31
4) B. P. Grenfell and A. S. Hunt, eds., *The Oxyrhynchus Papyri* III, 495.15. In *M-M*, p. 298, s.v. ἴδιος.

246. d 1) John 3:36
2) 1 John 5:20
3) John 3:10

254. g 1) John 12:34
2) John 6:31
3) John 5:43
4) B. P. Grenfell and A. S. Hunt, eds., *New Classical Fragments, and other Greek and Latin Papyri*, Oxford, 1897, 84.4, In *M-M*, p. 253, s.v. ἐρημία.

262. f  1) Rev. 5:9-10
         2) Rev. 22:3
268. f  1) Luke 7:31
         2) Matt. 27:46
         3) John 6:29
276. f  1) Acts 10:5
         2) John 6:51
282. e  1) John 19:5
         2) Luke 8:52
         3) John 2:1-2
         4) A. S. Hunt, ed., *The Oxyrhynchus Papyri* IX, 1185.29. In
            *M-M*, p. 226, s.v. ἑορτή.
290. e  1) John 5:24
         2) John 3:14-15
         3) Luke 24:17
         4) Matt. 13:16
         5) John 5:25
294. g  1) John 6:70
         2) John 1:45
         3) John 16:33
305. f  1) John 18:36
         2) 1 Cor. 11:3
         3) Matt. 27:21
         4) B. P. Grenfell, A. S. Hunt, and E. J. Goodspeed, eds., *The
            Tebtunis Papyri* II, London, 1902-1907, 418.8ff. In *M-M*,
            p. 188, s.v. εἰσέρχομαι.
         5) H. von Gaertringen, ed., *Die Inschriften von Priene*, Berlin,
            1906, 123.9. In *M-M*, p. 226, s.v. ἐπαγγελία.
313. i  1) Matt. 6:9
         2) Matt. 25:3-4
         3) John 6:37
         4) John 3:16
322. f  1) John 5:46
         2) John 3:2
         3) John 7:50-51
328. e  1) Matt. 4:9
         2) Luke 12:4

# ENGLISH-GREEK VOCABULARY
(For use in the English-Greek exercises)

## A

a, an: τὶς, τὶ, (often no word)
able, to be able: δυνατὸς εἶναι,
                    δύνασθαι, ἰσχύειν
Abram: Αβραμ
about, concerning: περί
again: πάλιν
all, once for all:  an implication of the aorist tense
am: εἰμί
am glad: χαίρω
am made: γίνομαι
among: ἐν
and: καί, δέ
anoint: χρίω
another: ἄλλος
anybody: τὶς
around: περί
ask: αἰτέω, ἐρωτάω, λέγω
at: ἐπί
attendant: ὑπηρέτης
away from: ἀπό

## B

baggage: σκεύη (plural of σκεῦος)
be, to be: γίνεσθαι, εἶναι
be a slave: δουλεύω
be brought into being, be made· γίνομαι
beautiful: καλός
because: ὅτι
because of: διά
become: γίνομαι
believe: πιστεύω
Benjamin: βενιαμίν
better· κρείσσων, κρεῖσσον
bread ἄρτος
bring, carry: ἄγω, φέρω
brother. ἀδελφός
but: ἀλλά, δέ

248

# C

Caleb: Χαλέβ
camel: κάμηλος
can, to be able: δυνατός, εἶναι, δύνασθαι, ἰσχυειν
carry: ἄγω, φέρω
cave: σπήλαιον
certain or someone: τὶς
chief: ἡγεμών
child: τέκνον
choose: ἐκλέγομαι
come: ἔρχομαι
command: verb ἐντέλλομαι, noun ἐντολή
concerning: περί
continually: an implication of the present and imperfect tenses
cup: ποτήριον
cure, heal: θεραπεύω

# D

dedicate: ἁγιάζω
depart: ἀπέρχομαι
depart from: ἀπέρχομαι
destroy: καταλύω, λύω
die: ἀποθνήσκω
dinner: δεῖπνον
door: θύρᾱ
drink: πίνω

# E

ear: οὖς
eat: ἐσθίω
Egypt: Αἴγυπτος
Egyptian: Αἰγύπτιος
enemy: ἐχθρός
excellent: καλός

# F

far distant: μακρός
farmer: γεωργός
fear: φόβος
fever: πυρετός
festival, feast: ἑορτή

find: εὑρίσκω
fish: ὀψάριον
flee: φεύγω
for: (often indicated by the dative case without a preposition)
for the sake of: ὑπέρ
for the same reason: διὰ τὸ αὐτό
free: ἐλεύθερος
from, away from: ἀπό
from, out of: ἐκ
fruit: καρπός

## G

garden: κῆπος
get possession of: ἔχω (aorist)
gift: δωρεά
give: δίδωμι
glad, be glad: χαίρω
go: ἄγω
go away: ἀπέρχομα
God: θεός
good: καλός
"Good-bye": χαῖρε, χαίρετε
"Good morning": χαῖρε, χαίρετε
"Greetings": χαῖρε, χαίρετε

## H

hand: χείρ
happy: μακάριος
harden: σκληρύνω
have: ἔχω
he: αὐτός, ἐκεῖνος, οὗτος, (often only the verb ending)
heal: θεραπεύω
hear: ἀκούω
heart: καρδίᾱ
heaven: οὐρανός
her: αὕτη, ἐκείνη (in oblique cases)
here: ὧδε
herself: αὐτή, ἑαυτῆς, ἑαυτῇ, ἑαυτήν
himself: ἑαυτοῦ, αὐτός
his: (gen. of possession of αὐτός, ἐκεῖνος, οὗτος)
hope: ἐλπίζω
house: οἶκος
how: πῶς

# I

I: ἐγώ (often only the verb ending)
"I mean": (implied by the attributive position of an adjective after its noun)
in, within: ἐν
instead of: ἀντί (with gen.)
into: εἰς
is: ἐστίν
it: αὐτό, ἐκεῖνο, τοῦτο, (often only the verb ending)
its: (gen. of possession of neuter of αὐτός, ἐκεῖνος, οὗτος)
itself: αὐτό, ἑαυτοῦ

# J

Jordan: 'Ιορδάνης
Joshua: 'Ιησοῦς
Judah: 'Ιούδας
judge: κριτής
just, righteous: δίκαιος

# K

kill: ἀποκτείνω, φονεύω
king: βασιλεύς

# L

lamb: ἀρνίον
land: γῆ
large: μέγας
last: ἔσχατος
Lazarus: Λάζαρος
leader: ἡγεμών
learn: μανθάνω
leave: ἀπέρχομαι
let: (in this book used as a part of the translation of a third person imperative verb)
let go: ἀπολύω
life: ζωή
lion: λέων
listen: ἀκούω
little lamb: αρνιον
long ago: πάλαι
look at: βλέπω
lord: κύριος
love: verb ἀγαπάω, noun ἀγάπη

# M

made, be made: γίνομαι
man: ἀνήρ, ἄνθρωπος
Mark: Μᾶρκος
Mary: Μαρίᾱ
messenger: ἄγγελος
mother: μήτηρ
my: ἐμός, ἐμοῦ
myself: ἐμαυτοῦ

# N

nation: ἔθνος
need: χρείᾱ
Nicodemus: Νικόδημος
night: νύξ
no: οὐ, μή, οὐχί
noble: καλός
not: οὐ, οὐκ, οὐχ, μή

# O

obedience: ὑπακοή
of: genitive case
Oh: (sometimes indicates a vocative)
on behalf of: ὑπέρ
once, once for all: an implication of the aorist tense
or: ἤ
our: ἡμῶν (gen. of possession), ἡμέτερος, -ᾱ, -ον
ourselves: ἑαυτῶν, αὐτοί
out of: ἐκ
over: ὑπέρ
own (one's, my, our, your, his, her, its, their): ἴδιος

# P

paschal lamb, passover: πάσχα
people: λαός, ὁ; ἔθνος, τό
perhaps: τάχα
persuade: πείθω
Peter: Πέτρος
Philip: Φίλιππος
place: τόπος
priest: ἱερεύς
promise: ἐπαγγελίᾱ
prophet: προφήτης
purify: ἁγιάζω, καθαρίζω

# R

Rachel: ʻΡαχήλ
ready: ἕτοιμος
reason, for the same: διὰ τὸ αὐτό
receive: λαμβάνω, δέχομαι
recognize: ἐπιγινώσκω
release: ἀπολύω
remain: μένω
remember: μνημονεύω
return: ἀναστρέψω

# S

sacrifice: θυσίᾱ
same: αὐτός
Samuel: Σαμουήλ
Sarai: Σαρα
save: σῴζω
say: λαλέω, λέγω
see: βλέπω, ὁράω
send: πέμπω
send forth: ἀποστέλλω
servant: ὑπηρέτης
serve as a slave: δουλεύω
she: αὐτή, αὕτη, ἐκείνη
sheep: προβατον
sister: ἀδελφή
slave: δοῦλος
small: μικρός
some: τὶς
someone: τὶς
son: υἱός
speak: λέγω, λαλέω
stay: μένω
stone: λίθος
strong: δυνατός

# T

take: λαμβάνω
teach: διδάσκω
teacher: διδάσκαλος
than: ἤ
that: ἐκεῖνος, ὅτι, ἵνα
the: ὁ, ἡ, τό
themselves: ἑαυτῶν, αὐτοί

there: ἐκεῖ

these: οὗτοι

they: αὐτοί, -αί, -ά; ἐκεῖνοι, -αι, -α; οὗτοι, αὗται, ταῦτα, (often only the verb ending)

thing: implication of the neuter, ῥῆμα

this: οὗτος

those: ἐκεῖνοι

throw: βάλλω

to: πρός

today: σήμερον

tomorrow: αὔριον

torch: λαμπάς

treat: θεραπεύω

truth: ἀλήθεια

## U & V

upon: ἐπί

very: λίαν

village: κώμη

voice: φώνη

## W

want: θέλω

war: πόλεμος

was: ἦν

we: ἡμεῖς, (often only the personal ending of a verb)

wealth: πλοῦτος

welcome: δέχομαι

"Welcome": χαῖρε, χαίρετε

what: (as an interrogative) τίς, τί; (as a relative) ὅ or ἅ

where: ποῦ

which: ὅς, ἥ, ὅ

who: ὅς, ἥ, ὅ (relative pronoun); τίς (interrogative)

why: τί

wicked: κακός

wine: οἶνος

with: σύν, μετά

within: ἐν

woman: γυνή

word: λόγος, ῥῆμα

write: γράφω

# Y

yes: ναί
yesterday: ἐχθές
you: σύ (sing.), ὑμεῖς (pl.), (often only the personal ending of a verb)
your: σοῦ, ὑμῶν (gen. of possession); ὑμέτερος, -ᾱ, -ον
yourself: σεαυτοῦ, ἑαυτῶν

# GREEK-ENGLISH VOCABULARY

(Numbered according to section)

## A

Αβραμ (indecl.), ὁ:   Abram (124)

ἀγαπάω, ἀγαπήσω, ἠγάπησα, ἠγάπηκα, ἠγάπημαι, ἠγαπήθην:   I love (344)

ἀγάπη, -ης, ἡ:   love (344)

ἀγαπητός, -ή, -όν:   beloved (340)

ἀγγελίᾱ, -ᾱς, ἡ:   message, command (330)

ἄγγελος, -ου, ὁ:   angel, messenger (82)

ἁγιάζω, — , ἡγίασα, — , ἡγίασμαι, ἡγιάσθην:   I dedicate, set apart for God, sanctify, purify (307)

ἅγιος, -ᾱ, -ον:   holy (350)

ἁγνίζω, — , ἥγνισα, ἥγνικα, ἥγνισμαι, ἡγνίσθην:   I purify (350)

ἁγνός, -ή, -όν:   pure, clean (350)

ἄγω, ἄξω, ἤγαγον, — , — , ἤχθην:   I lead, bring, go (112)

ἀδελφή, -ῆς, ἡ:   sister (130)

ἀδελφός, -οῦ, ὁ:   brother (10)

ἀδικίᾱ, -ᾱς, ἡ:   unrighteousness, iniquity, injustice (335)

Αἰγύπτιος, -ᾱ, -ον:   Egyptian (130)

Αἴγυπτος, -ου, ἡ:   Egypt (130)

αἷμα, -ατος, τό:   blood (223)

αἴρω, ἀρῶ, ἦρα, ἦρκα, ἦρμαι, ἤρθην:   I take up, lift up, raise, carry, take away, remove (356)

αἰσχύνομαι, — , — , — , — , ᾐσχύνθην:   I am ashamed, am put to shame (350)

αἰτέω, αἰτήσω, ᾔτησα, ᾔτηκα, — , — :   I ask (360)

αἴτημα, -ατος, τό:   request, what is asked for (363)

αἰών, αιῶνος, ὁ:   eternity, universe, present age (344)

αἰώνιος, -ᾱ, -ον (but distinct feminine endings are rarely used, -ος, -ου, etc. being usually found in forms agreeing with feminine nouns), eternal, everlasting (242)

ἀκούω, ἀκούσω, ἤκουσα, ἀκήκοα, — , ἠκούσθην:   I hear, listen (followed by acc. or gen. dir. obj.) (92)

ἀλαζονείᾱ, -ᾱς, ἡ:   boastfulness, vain display (344)

ἀλήθειᾰ, -ᾱς, ἡ:   truth, truthfulness (103)

ἀληθής, -ές:   true (to fact), actual (as opposed to apparent), truthful (340)

ἀληθινός, -ή, -όν:   true, genuine (as opposed to spurious), real (242)

ἀληθῶς:   truly, certainly, surely (340)

ἀλλά (ἀλλ'):   but (stronger than δέ) (71, 179)

ἀλλήλων, ἀλλήλοις, ἀλλήλους:   one another, each other (284)

ἄλλος, -η, -ο:  other, another; οἱ ἄλλοι: the rest, the others (147)
ἀλλόφυλος, -ου, ὁ:  foreigner, Gentile, Philistine (315)
᾿Αμαλήκ (indecl.), ὁ:  Amalek (296)
ἁμαρτάνω, ἁμαρτήσω, ἡμάρτησα and ἥμαρτον, ἡμάρτηκα, — , — :
    I sin (335)
ἁμαρτίᾱ, -ᾱς, ἡ:  sin (335)
ἄν:  (No individual translation, used in apodosis of Type II conditions and
    elsewhere) (315)
ἀναγγέλλω, ἀναγγελῶ, ἀνήγγειλα, — , — , ἀνηγγέλην:  I report, an-
    nounce, declare (335)
ἀναστρέφω, — , ἀνέστρεψα, — , — , ἀνεστράφην:  I overturn, return;
    (pass.) sojourn, dwell (278)
ἀνήρ, ἀνδρός, ὁ:  man, husband (271)
ἀνθρωποκτόνος, -ου, ὁ:  murderer (356)
ἄνθρωπος, -ου, ὁ:  man, human being (10)
ἀνομίᾱ, -ᾱς, ἡ:  lawlessness, transgression, iniquity (356)
ἀντί:  (with gen.) instead of, in place of, in exchange for, in return for,
    against (199)
ἀντίχριστος, -ου, ὁ:  Antichrist, one who tries to take the place of the
    Messiah and who withstands Him (350)
ἀπαγγέλλω, ἀπαγγελῶ, ἀπήγγειλα, — , — , ἀπηγγέλην:  I announce,
    report (330)
ἀπέρχομαι, ἀπελεύσομαι, ἀπῆλθον, ἀπελήλυθα, — , — :  I go away,
    depart from, depart (185)
ἀπό:  (with gen.) from, away from (41)
ἀποθνῄσκω, ἀποθανοῦμαι, ἀπέθανον, — , — , — :  I die (112, 172)
ἀποκόπτω, ἀποκόψω, ἀπέκοψα, — , — , ἀπεκόπην:  I cut off (324)
ἀποκρίνομαι, — , ἀπεκρινάμην (rare), — , — , ἀπεκρίθην (frequent):  I
    answer (242)
ἀποκτείνω, ἀποκτενῶ, ἀπέκτεινα, — , — , ἀπεκτάνθην:  I kill (141)
ἀπολύω, ἀπολύσω, ἀπέλυσα, — , ἀπολέλυμαι, ἀπελύθην:  I release, set
    free, let go (52)
ἀποστέλλω, ἀποστελῶ, ἀπέστειλα, ἀπέσταλκα, ἀπέσταλμαι, ἀπεστάλην:
    I send away, send forth (141)
ἅπτω, — , ἧψα, — , — , — :  I fasten to, set on fire; (mid.) I fasten myself
    to, cling to, lay hold of, assail (362)
ἀργύριον, -ου, τό:  silver, money (194)
ἀρεστός, -ή, -όν:  pleasing, agreeable (360)
ἄρκος, -ου, ὁ or ἡ:  bear (315)
ἀρνέομαι, ἀρνήσομαι, ἡρνησάμην, — , ἤρνημαι, — :  I deny, say "No,"
    refuse to acknowledge, disown (350)
ἀρνίον, -ου, τό:  lamb, little lamb (41)
ἄρτι:  now, just now, just at this moment (344)

257

ἄρτος, -ου, ὁ: bread, loaf of bread (27)
ἀρχή, -ῆς, ἡ: beginning, rule, sovereignty (330)
αὔριον: tomorrow, on the next day (179)
αὐτός, -ή, -ό: self, even, very, same, he, she, it (134)
ἀφίημι, ἀφήσω, ἀφῆκα, — , ἀφεῖμαι, ἀφέθην: I send away, let go,
forgive, allow, remit (ἀφῇ in 1 John 1:9 is third sing. aor. subj. act.
and ἀφέωνται in 1 John 2:12 is third pl. perf. indic. pass.) (335)

## B

βάλλω, βαλῶ, ἔβαλον, βέβληκα, βέβλημαι, ἐβλήθην: I throw, cast, put
(194)
βαρύς, -εῖα, -ύ: heavy, burdensome (363)
βασιλείᾱ, -ᾱς, ἡ: kingdom, royal power, dominion, rule, reign (296)
βασιλεύς, -έως, ὁ: king (147, 279)
Βενιαμίν (indecl.), ὁ: Benjamin (185)
Βηθλέεμ (indecl.), ἡ: Bethlehem (204)
βίος, -ου, ὁ: life, period of life, means of living, course of life (344)
βλασφημέω, — , ἐβλασφήμησα, — , — , ἐβλασφημήθην: I revile, rail at,
blaspheme, slander, speak evil (of God) (324)
βλέπω, βλέψω, ἔβλεψα, — , — , — : I see, look at, watch; (as imperative)
beware (10)

## Γ

γάρ: for, since; indeed, then (41)
Γεδεών (indecl.), ὁ: Gideon (271)
γενεά, -ᾱς, ἡ: generation (264)
γεννάω, γεννήσω, ἐγέννησα, γεγέννηκα, γεγέννημαι, ἐγεννήθην: I beget,
become the father of, bear (350)
γεωργός, -οῦ, ὁ: farmer, vinedresser (92)
γῆ, γῆς, ἡ: earth, land, country, ground (124)
γίνομαι, γενήσομαι, ἐγενόμην, γέγονα, γεγένημαι, ἐγενήθην: I come
into being, am born, am made, am ordained, become, come to pass,
happen (172)
γινώσκω, γνώσομαι, ἔγνων, ἔγνωκα, ἔγνωσμαι, ἐγνώσθην: I come to
know, perceive, understand (278)
γλῶσσα, -ης, ἡ: tongue, language (179)
Γολιαθ (indecl.), ὁ: Goliath (315)
γράφω, γράψω, ἔγραψα, γέγραφα, γέγραμμαι, ἐγράφην: I write (209)
γυνή, γυναικός, ἡ: woman, wife (296)

## Δ

Δαυίδ (indecl.), ὁ: David (307)
δέ (δ'): but, and, now (not temporal and never first in its clause) (141)

δεῖ (pres. indic. act. third sing. δέω): it is necessary (followed by an infinitive with an acc. of general reference), one must, one ought (284)

δείκνυμι (δεικνύω), δείξω, ἔδειξα, δέδειχα, — , ἐδείχθην: I show, exhibit (337)

δεῖπνον, -ου, τό: dinner, supper (41)

δέχομαι, — , ἐδεξάμην, — , δέδεγμαι, ἐδέχθην: I receive, accept, welcome (204)

διά: (with gen.) through, by; (with acc.) because of, on account of (179)

διὰ τὸ αὐτό: for the same reason (179)

διάβολος, -ου, ὁ: devil, accuser (356)

διάνοια, -ας, ἡ: understanding, mind (363)

διδάσκαλος, -ου, ὁ: teacher (179)

διδάσκω, διδάξω, ἐδίδαξα, — , — , ἐδιδάχθην: I teach (frequently used with a double accusative) (179)

δίδωμι, δώσω, ἔδωκα, δέδωκα, δέδομαι, ἐδόθην: I give (256, 271, 296, 324, 335)

δίκαιος, -ᾱ, -ον: righteous, just (71)

δικαιοσύνη, -ης, ἡ: righteousness (350)

διώκω, διώξω, ἐδίωξα, — , δεδίωγμαι, ἐδιώχθην: I pursue, run after, put to flight, persecute (147)

δοκιμάζω, δοκιμάσω, ἐδοκίμασα, — , δεδοκίμασμαι, — : I test, prove, approve (360)

δουλεύω, δουλεύσω, ἐδούλευσα, δεδούλευκα, — , — : I serve, serve as a slave, am a slave to, am subject to (dat. dir. obj.) (52)

δοῦλος, -ου, ὁ: slave, bondslave (41)

δύναμαι, δυνήσομαι, — , — , — , ἠδυνήθην: I am able, have power, can (315)

δυνατός, -ή, -όν: able, capable, strong, powerful, possible (179)

δύο (nom., gen., acc.) δυσί (dat.): two

δωρεά, -ᾶς, ἡ: gift (71)

## E

ἐάν: if (315)

ἑαυτοῦ, -ῆς, -οῦ: of himself, herself, itself; (pl.) of ourselves, yourselves, themselves (199)

ἐγκαταλείπω, ἐγκαταλείψω, ἐγκατέλιπον, — , ἐγκαταλέλειμμαι, ἐγκατελείφθην: I abandon, forsake, desert, leave behind (264)

ἐγώ, ἐμοῦ: I, of me (124)

ἔθνος, -ους, τό: nation, people; (pl.) nations, Gentiles (256)

εἰ: if (introducing a conditional clause); whether (introducing an indirect question); that (following a verb expressing emotion) (315)

εἰ μή: if not, unless

εἰδῆτε (second pl. second perf. subj. act. οἶδα) (350)

εἴδωλον, -ου, τό: idol, image of a false god, false god (363)

εἴληφα (first sing. second perf. indic. act. λαμβάνω) (149)

εἰμί, ἔσομαι, — , — , — , — : I am (82, 85, 86, 172, 179)

εἴρηκα (first sing. perf. indic. act. λέγω) (148)

εἰς: (with acc.) into, in, to, towards, for, among (41)

εἰς τὸν αἰῶνα: forever (344)

εἷς, μία, ἕν: one (315)

εἰς μέσον: into the middle (234)

ἐκ (ἐξ): (with gen.) from, out of, from within, of (i.e. belonging to) (41)

ἕκαστος, -η, -ον: each, every (194)

ἐκεῖ: there (179)

ἐκεῖνος, -η, -ον: that, he, she, it (134)

ἐκλέγομαι, — , ἐξελεξάμην, — , ἐκλέλεγμαι, — : I choose (292)

ἔλαιον, -ου, τό: olive oil (307)

ἐλεύθερος, -ᾱ, -ον: free (71)

ἐληλύθᾱσι (third pl. perf. indic. act. ἔρχομαι) (147)

ἐλπίζω, ἐλπιῶ, ἤλπισα, ἤλπικα, — , — : I hope, hope for (82, 141)

ἐλπίς, ἐλπίδος, ἡ: hope (350)

ἐμαυτοῦ, -ῆς: of myself (149)

ἔμπροσθεν: (with gen.) in front of, before (360)

ἐν: (with dat.) in, within, among, with, by means of, with the help of (41, 271)

ἐντέλλομαι, ἐντελοῦμαι, ἐνετειλάμην, — , ἐντέταλμαι, — : I command, order, give orders, (with dat. of person and an infinitive) (194)

ἐντολή, -ῆς, ἡ: order, command (340)

ἐνώπιον: (with gen.) before, in the presence of, in the sight of (360)

ἐξ (ἐκ): (with gen.) from, out of, from within, of (i.e. belonging to) (41)

ἐξέρχομαι, ἐξελεύσομαι, ἐξῆλθον, ἐξελήλυθα, — , — : I come out, go out (350)

ἔξω: outside (360)

ἑορτή, -ῆς, ἡ: festival, feast (223)

ἐπαγγελίᾱ, -ᾱς, ἡ: promise (134)

ἐπαγγέλλομαι, — , ἐπηγγειλάμην, — , ἐπήγγελμαι, — : I promise (350)

ἐπεί: after, when, since, because (130)

ἐπί: (with gen.) on, over, upon; (with dat.) on, at, upon, concerning; (with acc.) on, over, to, against (223)

ἐπιγινώσκω, ἐπιγνώσομαι, ἐπέγνων, ἐπέγνωκα, — , ἐπεγνώσθην: I observe, perceive, recognize, know (172)

ἐπιθυμίᾱ, -ᾱς, ἡ: longing, desire (71)

ἑπτά (indecl.): seven (172)

ἔργον, -ου, τό:   work, task, deed, action (264)
ἔρημος, -ου, ἡ:   desert, wilderness (248)
ἔρχομαι, ἐλεύσομαι, ἦλθον, ἐλήλυθα, — , — :   I come (112, 172)
ἐρωτάω, ἐρωτήσω, ἠρώτησα, — , — , — :   I ask a question, make a request (363)
ἐσθίω, φάγομαι, ἔφαγον, — , — , — :   I eat (27, 112, 172)
ἔσχατος, -η, -ον:   last (223)
ἕτοιμος, -η, -ον:   prepared, ready (112)
ἔτος, ἔτους, τό:   year (172, 258)
εὑρίσκω, εὑρήσω, εὗρον, εὕρηκα, — , εὑρέθην:   I find, discover (followed by participial indirect discourse) (292)
ἐχθές:   yesterday (179)
ἐχθρός, -οῦ, ὁ:   enemy (141)
ἔχω, ἕξω, ἔσχον, ἔσχηκα, — , — :   have, hold, possess (10, 103, 112)
ἕως:   (prep. with gen.) until, as far as; (conj.) until (344)

## Z

ζῶ (ζάω), ζήσω, ἔζησα, — , — , — :   I live, am alive (360)
ζωή, -ῆς, ἡ:   life (242)

## H

ἤ:   or, than (134)
ἡγεμών, -όνος, ὁ:   leader, governor, chief (296)
ἤδη:   now, already, now at length (340)
ἥκω, ἥξω, ἧξα, — , — , —    I have come, am present (307)
Ηλι (indecl.), ὁ:   Eli
ἡμεῖς, ἡμῶν:   we, of us (124)
ἡμέρᾱ, -ᾱς, ἡ:   day (234)
ἡμέτερος, -ᾱ, -ον:   our (330)

## Θ

θάλασσα, -ης, ἡ:   sea, lake (234)
θάνατος, -ου, ὁ:   death (356)
θαυμάζω, θαυμάσομαι, ἐθαύμασα, — , — , ἐθαυμάσθην:   I wonder, wonder at (356)
θεάομαι, — , ἐθεασάμην, — , τεθέαμαι, ἐθεάθην:   I behold, look upon, contemplate, view (330)
θέλημα, -ατος, τό:   will, choice, the action purposed, the act of willing (344)
θέλω, θελήσω, ἠθέλησα, — , — , — :   I will, am willing, wish, desire (179)
θεός, -οῦ, ὁ:   God, god, deity (159)

θεραπεύω, θεραπεύσω, ἐθεράπευσα, — , τεθεράπευμαι, ἐθεραπεύθην:  Ι
    treat, cure, heal (52)
θεωρέω, θεωρήσω, ἐθεώρησα, — , — , — :  I look at, behold, gaze at, see
    (356)
θηρίον, -ου, τό:  wild beast (324)
θλῖψις, -εως, ἡ:  affliction, distress (292)
θύρᾱ, -ᾱς, η:  door (223)
θυσίᾱ, -ᾱς, ἡ:  sacrifice (296)
θύω, — ἔθυσα, — τέθυμαι, ἐτύθην:  I sacrifice, kill, slay, offer (223)

# I

Ἰακώβ (indecl.), ὁ:  Jacob (185)
Ἰάκωβος, -ου, ὁ:  James (103)
ἴδιος, -ᾱ, -ον:  one's (my, our, your, his, her, its, their) own, belonging to
    one's self (71)
ἰδού:  behold, see, look (278)
ἱερεύς, -έως, ὁ:  priest (278)
Ἱεροσόλυμα, -ων, τό:  Jerusalem (204)
Ἰεσσαί (indecl.), ὁ:  Jesse (307)
Ἰησοῦς, -οῦ (gen., dat.), -οῦν, -οῦ, ὁ:  Jesus, Joshua (223)
ἱλασμός, -οῦ, ὁ:  means of appeasing, propitiation, expiation (340)
ἵνα:  that, in order that (307)
Ἰορδάνης, -ου, ὁ:  Jordan (134)
Ἰούδας, -α, (-ᾳ, -αν, -α), ὁ:  Judah, Judas (185)
Ἰσκαριώτης, -ου, ὁ:  Iscariot (344)
Ἰσραήλ (indecl.), ὁ:  Israel (209)
ἵστημι, στήσω, ἔστησα and ἔστην, ἔστηκα, — , ἐστάθην:  I cause to
    stand (transitive in pres., imperf., fut., first aor. act.); I stand, stand by
    (intransitive in -mi aor., perf., plup. act. and fut. mid. and fut. and aor.
    pass.) (337)
ἰσχυρός, -ᾱ́, -όν:  powerful, mighty, strong (344)
ἰσχύω, ἰσχύσω, ἴσχυσα, — , — , — :  I can, am able, prevail (52)
Ἰωσήφ (indecl.), ὁ:  Joseph (172)

# K

καθαρίζω, καθαριῶ, ἐκαθάρισα, — , κεκαθάρισμαι, ἐκαθαρίσθην:  I
    make clean, cleanse (335)
καθεύδω (only pres. and impf. tenses in New Testament); I sleep (278)
καθώς:  as, just as (340)
καί:  and, and so, and yet, and indeed; also, too, even, still (10)
καί . . . καί . . . .:  both . . . and . . . . (10)
Κάϊν (indecl.), ὁ:  Cain (356)

καινός, -ή, -όν:  new, unused, unknown, strange, remarkable (340)
κακός, -ή, -όν:  bad, evil, wicked, dangerous (52, 103)
καλέω (see number 327 for the paradigm of this kind of present tense),
     καλέσω, ἐκάλεσα, κέκληκα, κέκλημαι, ἐκλήθην:  I call, invite (278)
καλός, -ή, -όν:  beautiful, good, excellent, fair, noble (41, 52)
κάμηλος, -ου, ὁ or ἡ:  camel (134)
καρδίᾱ, -ᾱς, ἡ:  heart (71)
καρπός, -οῦ, ὁ:  fruit (27)
κατά (καθ' before a vowel with a rough breathing):  (with gen.) down
     upon, against, down from; (with acc.) down along, through, toward,
     by, according to (234)
καταβαίνω, καταβήσομαι, κατέβην, καταβέβηκα, — , — :  I go down,
     come down, descent (242)
καταγινώσκω, — , — , — , κατέγνωσμαι, — :  I blame, condemn (360)
καταλύω, καταλύσω, κατέλυσα, — , — , κατελύθην:  I destroy, overthrow
     (296)
Καφαρναούμ (indecl.), ἡ:  Capernaum (242)
κεῖμαι, — , — , — , — , — :  I lie, am located (363)
κέρας, -ατος, τό:  horn (307)
κερατίνη, -ης, ἡ:  trumpet, horn (271)
κεφαλή, -ῆς, ἡ:  head (324)
κῆπος, -ου, ὁ:  garden (41)
κλείω, κλείσω, ἔκλεισα, — , κέκλεισμαι, ἐκλείσθην:  I shut (356)
κοινωνίᾱ, -ᾱς, ἡ:  fellowship, joint participation (330)
κόλασις, -εως, ἡ:  correction, punishment, penalty (360)
κόσμος, -ου, ὁ:  universe, world, earth (71)
κρείσσων, κρεῖσσον:  better (296)
κρίσις, -εως, ἡ:  decision, judgment, right, justice (360)
κριτής, -οῦ, ὁ:  judge (264)
κύριος, -ου, ὁ:  Lord, lord, master (124)
κώμη, -ης, ἡ:  village, town (103)


Λ

Λάζαρος, -ου, ὁ:  Lazarus (52)
λαλέω, λαλήσω, ἐλάλησα, λελάληκα, λελάλημαι, ἐλαλήθην:  I utter,
     speak, say (324)
λαμβάνω, λήμψομαι, ἔλαβον, εἴληφα, εἴλημμαι, — :  I take receive, seize
     (112, 172)
λαμπάς, λαμπάδος, ἡ:  torch, lamp (271)
λαός, -οῦ, ὁ:  people (209)
λατρεύω, λατρεύσω, ἐλάτρυσα, — , — , — :  I serve, worship (with dat.
     dir. obj.) (256)

263

λέγω, ἐρῶ, εἶπον, εἴρηκα, εἴρημαι, ἐρρέθην: I say, speak, declare, tell, ask, answer (10, 112, 141)
λέων, λέοντος, ὁ: lion (315, 368)
λίαν: exceedingly, very, very much (179)
λίθος, -ου, ὁ: stone (248)
λόγος, -ου, ὁ: word, statement, speech, teaching (330)
λύω, — , ἔλυσα, — , λέλυμαι, ἐλύθην: I loose, destroy (356)
Λώτ (indecl.), ὁ: Lot (124)

## M

Μαδιάμ (indecl.), ὁ: Midian (271)
μαθητής, -οῦ, ὁ: disciple, student, pupil (179)
μακάριος, -ᾱ, -ον: happy, blessed (71)
μακρός, -ᾱ́, -όν: long, far distant (141)
μανθάνω, — , ἔμαθον, μεμάθηκα, — , — : I learn (179)
Μαρίᾱ, -ᾱς, ἡ: Mary (71)
Μᾶρκος, -ου, ὁ: Mark (10)
μαρτυρέω, μαρτυρήσω, ἐμαρτύρησα, μεμαρτύρηκα, μεμαρτύρημαι, ἐμαρτυρήθην: I am witness, bear witness, testify (330)
μαρτυρίᾱ, -ᾱς, ἡ: witness, testimony, evidence (363)
μάχομαι (present system only): I fight (315)
μέγας, μεγάλη, μέγα: great, large, tall, big (315)
μείζων, μεῖζον (comparative of μέγας): greater (360)
μένω, μενῶ, ἔμεινα, μεμένηκα, — , — : I stay, remain, wait for, continue (141)
Μεσοποταμίᾱ, -ᾱς, ἡ: Mesopotamia (124)
μέσος, -η, -ον: middle, in the middle of (234)
μετά (μεθ᾽ before a vowel with a rough breathing, μετ᾽ before a vowel with a smooth breathing): (with gen.) with; (with acc.) after (92)
μεταβαίνω, μεταβήσομαι, μετέβην, μεταβέβηκα, — , — : I pass over (from one place to another), depart (356)
μή: not (used with impv., inf., partic., subj.) (92)
μηδέ: and not, but not, nor, not even (344)
μηδείς, μηδεμία, μηδέν: no one, no, nothing (356)
μήτηρ, μητρός, ἡ: mother (204, 368)
μικρός, -ᾱ́, -όν: small, little, short (82)
μισέω, μισήσω, ἐμίσησα, μεμίσηκα, μεμίσημαι, — : I hate (344)
μνημονεύω, — , ἐμνημόνευσα, — , — , — : I remember, call to mind (82)
μονογενής, -ές: only of its kind, unique (360)
μόνον (adv.): only (340)
μόνος, -η, -ον: alone, only (242)
Μωϋσῆς, -έως, -εῖ, -ῆν, -ῆ, ὁ: Moses (209)

# N

ναί: yes (71)
νεανίσκος, -ου, ὁ: young man, youth, lad (344)
νεφέλη, -ης, ἡ: cloud (234)
νεώτερος, -ᾱ, -ον: young, newer, younger, (or in Hellenistic usage) youngest (185)
νικάω, νικήσω, ἐνίκησα, νενίκηκα, — , ἐνικήθην: I conquer, win the victory over (344)
νίκη, -ης, ἡ: victory (363)
Νικόδημος, -ου, ὁ: Nicodemus (10)
νόμος, -ου, ὁ: law (248)
νῦν: now (71)
νύξ, νυκτός, ἡ: night (234)

# Ξ

ξηρός, -ά, -όν: dry (234)

# O

ὁ, ἡ, τό: the (10, 41, 76)
ὅθεν: whence, wherefore (350)
οἶδα: I know (See number 404 for the other forms.) (344)
οἶκος, -ου, ὁ: house, family (41)
οἶνος, -ου, ὁ: wine (41)
ὅλος, -η, -ον: whole, complete, entire (340)
ὅμοιος, -ᾱ, -ον: like, resembling, similar to, of the same kind as (350)
ὁμολογέω, ὁμολογήσω, ὡμολόγησα, — , — , — : I agree, confess, acknowledge (335)
ὁμοῦ: together (82)
ὀνειδίζω, — , ὠνείδισα, — , — , — : I reproach, upbraid, revile (315)
ὄνομα, -ατος, τό: name (248)
ὁράω, ὄψομαι, εἶδον, ἑώρακα, — , ὤφθην: I see (330)
ὀργίζομαι, — , — , — , — , ὠργίσθην: I am provoked to anger, am angry (with dat.) (264)
ὅς, ἥ, ὅ: who, which, that, what (284)
ὅστις, ἥτις, ὅ τι: whoever, whatever, who, what (330)
ὅταν: when, whenever (363)
ὅτε: when, while (82)
ὅτι: because, that (52)
οὐ, οὐκ, οὐχ: not (27, 41, 124)
οὐ μή: no, (a strong negative) by no means, not at all (307)
οὐδέ: and not, also not, nor, not even (350)
οὐδείς, οὐδεμία, οὐδέν: nobody, nothing, no, none (330)
οὐκέτι: no longer, no more (71)

οὖν: consequently, therefore, so, accordingly, really (124)
οὔπω: not yet (278)
οὐρανός, -οῦ, ὁ: heaven (242)
οὖς, ὠτός, τό: ear (284)
οὗτος, αὕτη, τοῦτο: this (130)
οὕτως: thus, so, in this way (199)
οὐχί (emphatic form of οὐ): no, no indeed, not at all (124)
ὀφείλω, — , — , — , — , — : I owe, ought (340)
ὀφθαλμός, -οῦ, ὁ: eye (330)
ὄχλος, -ου, ὁ: crowd, multitude, throng (242)
ὀψάριον, -ου, τό: fish (41)

# Π

παιδίον, -ου, τό: young child, little one (344)
πάλαι: long ago, of old, in past time (185)
παλαιός, -ά, -όν: old, ancient (340)
πάλιν: again, back (82)
πάντοτε: always, at all times, at any time (71)
παρά (παρ'): (with gen.) from; (with dat.) beside, with; (with acc.) along (290)
παράγω, — , — , — , — , — : I pass away, disappear, go by (340)
παράκλητος, -ου, ὁ: advocate, helper, intercessor (340)
παρεμβολή, -ῆς, ἡ: camp, army (271)
παρουσίᾱ, -ᾱς, ἡ: presence, coming, arrival (350)
παρρησίᾱ, -ᾱς, ἡ: freedom (of speech), confidence, openness, boldness (71)
παρρησίᾳ (dative of παρρησίᾱ used as an adverb): frankly, freely, plainly (71)
πᾶς, πᾶσα, πᾶν: all, every (234)
πάσχα (indecl.), τό: Passover, paschal lamb (223)
πατάσσω, πατάξω, ἐπάταξα, — , — , — : I strike, smite, kill (315)
πατήρ, πατρός, ὁ: father (199)
πείθω, πείσω, ἔπεισα, πέποιθα, πέπεισμαι, ἐπείσθην: I persuade; (mid.) I believe, obey (dat. of dir. obj. with mid.) (209)
πέμπω, πέμψω, ἔπεμψα, πέπομφα, — , ἐπέμφθην: I send (41)
πεντακισχίλιοι, -αι, -α: five thousand (242)
πέντε: five (402)
πέραν: (with gen.) beyond, across, on the other side of (242)
περί: (with gen. in figurative sense) around, about, concerning; (with acc. in local sense) around, about (71, 92)
περιπατέω, περιπατήσω, περιεπάτησα, περιπεπάτηκα, — , — : I walk, live, conduct my life (330)

πετεινόν, -οῦ, τό: bird (324)

Πέτρος, -ου, ὁ: Peter (10)

πίνω, πίομαι, ἔπιον, πέπωκα, — , — : I drink (41, 112)

πίπτω, πεσοῦμαι, ἔπεσον and ἔπεσα, πέπτωκα, — , — : I fall (324)

πιστεύω, πιστεύσω, ἐπίστευσα, πεπίστευκα, πεπίστευμαι, ἐπιστεύθην: I believe, trust (with dat. dir. obj.) (27, 159)

πίστις, -εως, ἡ: faith (363)

πιστός, -ή, -όν: trusty, faithful, reliable (335)

πλανάω, πλανήσω, ἐπλάνησα, — , πεπλάνημαι, ἐπλανήθην: I lead astray, deceive (πλανῶμεν in 1 John 1:8 is first pl. pres. indic. act.) (335)

πλάνη, -ης, ἡ: going astray, error (360)

πληγή, -ῆς, ἡ: calamity, blow, plague, (223)

πληρόω, πληρώσω, ἐπλήρωσα, πεπλήρωκα, πεπλήρωμαι, ἐπληρώθην: I make full, fill, complete (330)

πλοῦτος, -ου, ὁ: wealth, riches (103)

πνεῦμα, -ατος, τό: spirit (360)

ποιέω, ποιήσω, ἐποίησα, πεποίηκα, πεποίημαι, ἐποιήθην: I make, do (330)

πόλεμος, -ου, ὁ: war, battle (284)

πολλάκις: often, many times (124)

πολύς, πολλή, πολύ: (sing.) much, (pl.) many (350)

πονηρός, -ά, -όν: bad, evil, wicked (344)

πορεύομαι, πορεύσομαι, — , — , πεπόρευμαι, ἐπορεύθην: I go on my way, proceed, travel (315)

ποταπός, -ή, -όν: what?, of what sort?, what kind of? (350)

ποτήριον, -ου, τό: cup (41)

ποῦ: where (179)

πρεσβύτερος, -ᾱ, -ον: elder, elderly, old (199)

πρό: (with gen.) before, in front of, earlier than, preferable to, in lieu of (209)

πρόβατον, -ου, τό: sheep (134)

πρός: (with dat.) near; (with acc.) to, towards, with (141)

προσεύχομαι, προσεύξομαι, προσηυξάμην, — , — , — : I pray (242)

πρόσωπον, -ου, τό: face (307)

προφήτης, -ου, ὁ: prophet (278)

πρῶτος, -η, -ον: first, chief, principal (223)

πῦρ, πυρός, τό: fire (234)

πυρετός, -οῦ, ὁ: fever (52)

πώποτε: ever yet (360)

πῶς: how? (103)

# P

ῥάβδος, -ου, ἡ:  staff, rod (324)
Ῥαχήλ (indecl.), ἡ:  Rachel (185)
ῥηθέν (neut. nom. sing. aor. partic. pass. λεγω):  spoken (278)
ῥῆμα, -ατος, τό:  word, statement, thing, matter (278)
ῥομφαίᾱ, -ᾱς, ἡ:  sword (324)

# Σ

σαλπίζω, σαλπίσω, ἐσάλπισα, — , — , — :  I sound a trumpet, blow a
     trumpet (271)
Σαμουήλ (indecl.), ὁ:  Samuel (278)
Σαούλ (indecl.), ὁ:  Saul (292)
Σαρα, -ας, -α, αν, ἡ:  Sarai (124)
σάρξ, σαρκός, ἡ:  flesh (344)
σεαυτοῦ, -ῆς:  of yourself (sing.) (199)
σήμερον:  today (92)
σῖτος, -ου, ὁ:  wheat, corn, grain, food (172)
σκάνδαλον, -ου, τό:  stumbling block, cause of sin, snare (344)
σκεῦος, -ους, τό:  vessel, utensil, implement; (plural) baggage, gear, goods
     (292)
σκληρύνω, σκληρυνῶ, ἐσκλήρυνα, — , — , ἐσκληρύνθην:  I harden,
     make stubborn (234)
σκοτίᾱ, -ᾱς, ἡ:  darkness, dark (92)
σκότος, -ους, τό:  darkness (330)
Σόδομα, -ων, τά:  Sodom (a place name with plural form but singular
     meaning) (141)
σπέρμα, -ατος, τό:  seed, offspring, posterity, children (356)
σπήλαιον, -ου, τό:  cave (103)
σπλάγχνον, -ου, τό:  heart, affections (356)
στύλος, -ου, ὁ:  pillar (234)
σύ, σοῦ:  you (sing.), of you (124)
σύν:  (with dat.) with (71)
συνάγω, συνάξω, συνήγαγον and συνῆξα, — , συνῆγμαι, συνήχθην:  I
     gather, bring together (172)
συναγωγή, -ῆς, ἡ:  assembly, synagogue (179)
σφάζω, σφάξω, ἔσφαξα, — , ἔσφαγμαι, ἐσφάγην:  I slay, slaughter (356)
σφενδόνη, -ης, ἡ:  sling (324)
σχολή, -ῆς, ἡ:  school (179)
σῴζω, σώσω, ἔσωσα, σέσωκα, σέσωσμαι, ἐσώθην:  I save, preserve,
     rescue, keep safe (264)
σῶμα, -ατος, τό:  body, dead body, living body, person (324)
σωτήρ, -ῆρος, ὁ:  savior, deliverer, preserver (248)

# T

τάχα: perhaps, possibly, probably (124)

τεκνίον, -ου, τό: little child (340)

τέκνον, -ου, τό: child (41)

τέλειος, -ᾱ, -ον: mature, complete, perfect (360)

τελειόω, — , ἐτελείωσα, τετελείωκα, τετελείωμαι, ἐτελειώθην: I finish, complete, accomplish (340)

τηρέω, τηρήσω, ἐτήρησα, τετήρηκα, τετήρημαι, ἐτηρήθην: I take care of, guard, observe, give heed to, keep (340)

τίθημι, θήσω, ἔθηκα, τέθεικα, τέθειμαι, ἐτέθην: I put, place, lay down (θεῖναι in 1 John 3:16 is an aor. inf. act.) (335)

τίς, τί: who?, which?, what?, (τί may mean why.) (165)

τὶς, τὶ: (masc. and fem.) one, anyone, someone, a certain; (neut.) anything, something (165)

τόπος, -ου, ὁ: place, spot, locality (134)

τότε: then, at that time (82)

τρεῖς, τρία: three (362)

τρέχω, — , ἔδραμον, — , — , — : I run (278)

τριακόσιοι, -αι, -α: three hundred (271)

τυφλόω, — , ἐτύφλωσα, τετύφλωκα, — , — : I make blind, blind (344)

# Y

ὕδωρ, ὕδατος, τό: water (234)

υἱός, -οῦ, ὁ: son (159)

ὑμεῖς, ὑμῶν: you (pl.), of you (124)

ὑπάγω, — , — , — , — , — : I go away, depart (344)

ὑπακοή, -ῆς, ἡ: obedience (296)

ὑπέρ: (with gen.) for, on behalf of, for the sake of, about; (with acc.) over, beyond (in a figurative sense) (284)

ὑπηρέτης, -ου, ὁ: assistant, servant, attendant (141)

ὑπό: (with gen.) by, under; (with acc.) under (209)

ὑπομιμνήσκω, ὑπομνήσω, ὑπέμνησα, — , — , ὑπεμνήσθην: I cause to remember, remind (344)

ὑψηλός, -ή, -όν: high, lofty, proud, haughty (234)

# Φ

φαίνω, φανοῦμαι and φανήσομαι, ἔφᾱνα, — , — , ἐφάνην: I give light, shine; (pass.) come to light, appear (340)

φανερός, -ά, -όν: visible, manifest (356)

φανερόω, φανερώσω, ἐφανέρωσα, πεφανέρωκα, πεφανέρωμαι, ἐφανερώθην: I make visible, known, clear, manifest (330)

Φαραώ (indecl.), ὁ: Pharaoh (130)

φέρω, οἴσω, ἤνεγκα and ἤνεγκον, — , — , ἠνέχθην: I carry, bring, endure (27, 112)

φεύγω, φεύξομαι, ἔφυγον, — , — , — : I flee from, flee away, take flight (271)

Φίλιππος, -ου, ὁ: Philip (10)

φοβέομαι, — , — , — , — , ἐφοβήθην: I fear, am afraid of (360)

φοβερός, -ά, -ον: fearful, terrifying, causing fear (315)

φόβος, -ου, ὁ: fear (159)

φονεύω, φονεύσω, ἐφόνευσα, — , — , ἐφονεύθην: I kill, murder (130)

φυλάσσω, φυλάξω, ἐφύλαξα, πεφύλαχα, — , ἐφυλάχθην: I guard, keep, watch, protect (363)

φωνή, -ῆς, ἡ: voice, sound (284)

φῶς, φωτός, τό: light (330)

## X

χαῖρε (addressed to one person), χαίρετε (addressed to two or more): greetings, hail, welcome, good morning, farewell, good-by; rejoice (10)

χαίρω, — , — , — , — , ἐχάρην: I rejoice, am glad (223)

Χαλέβ (indecl.), ὁ: Caleb (248)

Χανάαν (indecl.), ἡ: Canaan (248)

χαρά, -ᾶς, ἡ: joy (330)

χάριν: (prep. with gen.) for, on account of, for the sake of (356)

χείρ, χειρός, ἡ: hand (234)

χρεία, -ᾶς, ἡ: need, necessity (71)

χρῖσμα, -ατος, τό: anointing (350)

χριστός, -οῦ, ὁ: anointed, Christ (307)

χρίω, — , ἔχρισα, — , — , ἐχρίσθην: I anoint (307)

χρόνος, -ου, ὁ: time, a period of time, a while (82)

## Ψ

ψεύδομαι, ψεύσομαι, ἐψευσάμην, — , — , — : I lie, deceive by lies (330)

ψευδοπροφήτης, -ου, ὁ: false prophet (360)

ψεῦδος, -ους, τό: lie, falsehood (350)

ψεύστης, -ου, ὁ: liar (335)

ψηλαφάω, — , ἐψηλάφησα, — , — , — : I handle, touch, feel (330)

ψυχή, -ῆς, ἡ: soul, life (356)

## Ω

ὧδε: here (179)

ὥρα, -ᾶς, ἡ: hour, season (350)

ὡς: as (335)

ὥστε: so that (315)

# INDEX

## (Numbered according to section)

### A

272

273

## D

274

277

278

Q

281